A Guide to World Markets

T H E
WORLD'S EMERGING STOCK MARKETS

Structure,
Developments,
Regulations &
Opportunities

KEITH K. H. PARK & ANTOINE W. VAN AGTMAEL

EDITORS

IRWIN
Professional Publishing®
Chicago • London • Singapore

This publication is designed to provide accurate and authoritative information in regard to the subject matter covered. It is sold with the understanding that the publisher is not engaged in rendering legal, accounting, or other professional service.

ISBN 1-55738-240-9

Printed in the United States of America

BB

5 6 7 8 9 0

To people I met at the factory of Polycity Industrial, Ltd. in Dong Guang, China last April. You are the ones who have made it all happen.

Keith K.H. Park

To my parents

Antoine W. van Agtmael

Table of Contents

Preface

Nearly a decade ago, in the introduction to the first book on emerging markets, *Emerging Securities Markets* (Antoine W. van Agtmael, Euromoney Publications, London, January 1984), it was shown "why investment bankers, investors and development experts can no longer ignore emerging markets . . . viewed by many as too small and irrelevant to warrant much attention . . . The frontiers of international investment are beginning to push toward the major emerging markets. . . . This trend is likely to accelerate." Since then, investing in the emerging markets has gained much respectability from pension sponsors and fund managers. Markets such as Korea, Thailand, Mexico, and Chile are no longer viewed as illiquid and exotic but as markets of the future which are increasingly becoming an integral part of the mainstream of international investment. Today the key question for pension sponsors and fund managers is no longer whether and why to invest in the emerging stock markets but, rather, whether they fall short in their fiduciary duty if they fail to recognize the importance of investing a portion of their assets in these markets.

The 1980s were a decade of dramatic change and growth for the emerging stock markets. They had to endure the global economic recession of the early 1980s, and the emerging markets in Latin America had to overcome a major debt crisis. However, the major economic policy upheavals that embraced more open economies and actively pursued privatization and reliance on market forces brought about an unprecedented economic expansion. During this process, many rising emerging stock markets became widely recognized by local and international investors.

The emerging stock markets should not be viewed as a static universe but as a constantly evolving group of markets. After the tumultuous 1980s, the 1990s will perhaps be less dramatic but far from uneventful. As the economies of the emerging markets continue to grow at a much faster pace than the industrialized economies, the emerging markets' share of the global stock market capitalization will grow further from about 7% in 1991 to 15–20% by the end of this decade. Moreover, China, India, and Eastern Europe will become active (or, in the case of India, better organized) stock markets for their growing industries and vast populations and will be recognized as the newest frontiers of international investing.

The total investment in emerging markets by international investors, which was a mere US$500 million in 1984, impressively grew to US$25 billion in 1991, and is expected to reach over US$100 billion by the end of this decade. The top 100 companies from the emerging markets will become household names among international investors as they float their new securities in the United States, Europe, and Asia and emerge as significant participants in the global capital markets. In the 1990s, vastly expanded research, truly global brokerage activities, and a proliferation of specialized investment managers will make the major emerging markets more efficient and liquid. In the meantime, a new list of markets will offer barely imaginable opportunities.

This book consists of three major sections. First, the book discusses the opportunities and risks of investing in the emerging markets with a presentation of portfolio management and research techniques. In the second section, individual markets are examined with brief profiles of their major listed companies. The last section of the book compiles articles which discuss the important issues in deciding how to distribute a portfolio across the markets. Despite the investment opportunities, mastering the emerging markets can be an intimidating task. The editors hope this book provides readers with a wealth of factual information as well as the tools to put this knowledge to work.

Keith K. H. Park   *Antoine W. van Agtmael*
Los Angeles   *Washington, D.C.*

Acknowledgments

Putting *The World's Emerging Stock Markets* together was a task that took more than two years and involved coordination between many people throughout the world. Many thanks must be given to each of the contributing authors for taking time from their hectic schedules, and to Pamela van Giessen and Kevin Thornton of Probus Publishing, Linda Shin of Global Strategies Group, and Yvonne Wise of Emerging Markets Management for their assistance without which the book could never have been completed.

Keith K. H. Park

Managing an investment bank in Thailand opened my eyes to the potential (and volatility) of emerging markets. Working at the Capital Markets Department of the International Finance Corporation, the private sector arm of the World Bank, broadened my outlook. During the past five years as president of Emerging Markets Management, I had an opportunity to utilize all of this experience in managing emerging market portfolios. Everywhere I have had the privilege of working with bright and highly professional colleagues from whom I learned a great deal.

Local participants in many markets contributed chapters for this book. All of them have busy jobs and I am very grateful for the time and effort they devoted. I could not have co-edited this cook without the help of several of the members of my team at Emerging Markets Management. Felicia Morrow and Catherine Fry contributed chapters and assisted in turning "Spanglish" into English. Rob Ginis and Stephanie Atkins provided and checked data for many chapters of the book. My executive assistant, Yvonne Wise, coordinated the contacts with authors and the publisher, a difficult task which she handled with her usual efficiency. All of them should share in the credit for this book but only I can be held responsible for whatever errors remain.

I am blessed with a wonderful and understanding family who put up with the many evenings I wrote chapters or edited others. Thanks again, Emily, Jenny and Peter for coping with more absent-mindedness than you deserve.

Finally, this book is dedicated to my parents. They instilled in me the drive to persist and were tolerant of my habit of pursuing untrodden paths. Even years after my mother's death, I often miss her enthusiasm; I feel extremely lucky to have my father's continued encouragement.

Antoine W. van Agtmael

INTRODUCTION

1

ENHANCED EFFICIENCY OF GLOBAL PORTFOLIO DIVERSIFICATION THROUGH EMERGING MARKET INVESTING

Keith K. H. Park, Partner
Global Strategies Group
Los Angeles, United States

Introduction

As the world equity markets become further globalized in the 1990s, the ever-increasing outflow of investment into the international equity markets will continue. According to an estimate by Salomon Brothers, the worldwide investment in foreign shares increased from $300bn in 1985 to $1,600bn in 1989, and more than one transaction in every seven in the global equity markets has a foreign investor on the other side. Furthermore, according to the survey of Greenwich Associates, U.S. corporate pension fund managers plan to increase the international equity portion of their total assets to 9.5% by 1993 from the 1990 average of 5.6%, which is an almost 100% increase in just three years. Equity investing has truly become a global transaction. See Table 1-1 for the breakdown of global equity flows in 1989.

The phenomenal growth in international equity investing is fueled by the two distinctive benefits inherent in the investment: 1) the reduction of market risk; and 2) the enhancement of returns.[1] The analysis of risk and return has been the major building block of modern portfolio theory (MPT). An investment which generates superior returns and at the same time reduces the degree of risk intrinsic to the investment, will more than likely attract the attention of prudent pension sponsors. This has been the case for global equity investing.

Table 1-1   Gross Cross-Border Equity Flows, 1989
(U.S. Dollars in Billions)

	U.S.	Japan	U.K.	Continental Europe	Rest of World	Investor Total
			Market to			
Investor From:						
U.S.	–	84.16	83.38	50.35	57.58	275.47
Japan	60.77	–	5.25	8.22	101.99	176.23
U.K.	97.22	76.50	–	109.59	40.82	324.13
Continental Europe	107.08	66.48	28.57	148.98	17.01	368.12
Rest of World	151.77	205.72	24.09	26.12	46.41	454.12
Market Total	416.84	432.86	141.30	343.26	263.81	1,598.05

Source:Salomon Brothers, Inc.

However, the current trends in global equity investing elicit great concern because their long-term impact will be a displacement of the risk/return profile of the investment strategies currently in vogue. Given this concern, investing in the world's emerging equity markets provides a means to insure the efficient risk/return profile of global equity investment. This chapter examines: 1) the long-term impact of the current trends in global equity investing; 2) the significance and benefits of emerging market investing in the overall global equity investment programs of pension sponsors; and 3) the recent developments in the emerging equity markets.

Current Trends in Global Equity Investing

One major strategy for domestic and international investing increasingly adopted by institutional investors worldwide since the mid-1980s has been passive equity port-folio indexation. According to Birinyi Associates, at the end of 1989, 25.2% of the total U.S. ERISA (Employee Retirement Income Security Act) assets were indexed to major international equity indices such as S&P 500, FT-SE 100, Nikkei 225, or MSCI EAFE (Europe, Australia, Far East) Indices. According to Salomon Brothers, in 1985 only 1.03% of the total pension assets were indexed. In the U.K., according to Greenwich Associates, 8.8% of the total pension assets were indexed as of March 1990. The benchmark indices used for passive management are market capitaliza-tion-weighted, and their constituent shares are largely-capitalized, global blue-chip equities.

Furthermore, because the performance of active international fund managers is measured against benchmark market indices such as MSCI EAFE Index, even the construction of active portfolios has been looking more and more like benchmark market indices. This performance measurement methodology has been steering active managers away from taking risk by holding shares which do not belong to benchmark market indices.

As a result, investments by international fund managers have been mostly concentrated on some 1,000 largely-capitalized, major international shares, which are the constituent shares of S&P 500, Nikkei 225, FT-SE 100 and Eurotrack 100 Indices.[2] As Michael Howell of Salomon Brothers writes, "it is not difficult to envisage a future characterized by a 'thundering thousand' superleague of global stocks, to rival the 'nifty fifty' of popular growth stocks that dominated the U.S. market in the late 1960s."

Another new investment strategy which emerged in the mid-1980s and maintains its strong presence in the global investment scene in the 1990s is global tactical asset allocation (GTAA). The GTAA fund managers are not concerned with the prospect of individual shares; they base their investment decision instead on the assessment of broad economic conditions and expected currency movements of specific markets. They switch in and out of markets by trading baskets of shares or utilizing index derivatives. This strategy requires the liquidity of shares included in their buy/sell baskets and the availability of index derivatives for their buy/sell baskets. Consequently, the shares eligible for the inclusion in GTAA buy/sell baskets have been largely-capitalized, international blue-chip shares.

In addition to passive indexation and GTAA, international investment managers have been preferring largely-capitalized equities because of the following: 1) their liquidity; 2) the comfort of worldwide name recognition; 3) the efficiency and safety of an already-established international trading structure for the 'thundering thousand' superleague; and 4) the availability of index derivatives which can be used for managing the risk of holding these shares.

Long-Term Impact of Current Trends

The extensive concentration of investment in globally recognized, largely-capitalized, and highly liquid shares is bound to distort the fair valuation of these shares and will result in a periodic correction of their prices. For instance, in June of 1991 the share price of Rentokil, a U.K. pest-control company, jumped over 5% in one day despite no significant improvement in the company's earning prospect except that Rentokil became a constituent share of the FT-SE 100 (Financial Times-Stock Exchange) Index. Had the share of Rentokil been undervalued by 5% or was a 5% premium attached to the share for no substantive reason except that it had just joined the 'thundering thousand' superleague?

Global institutional investors have already seen the consequence of the blind subscription of largely-capitalized shares. At the end of 1989, according to all three major global equity indices (MSCI World, Financial Times-Actuaries World, and

Salomon-Russell Global Indices), the Japanese market accounted for more than 35% of the world's equity markets. As a result, the capitalization-weighted global portfolios had some 35% of their equity holdings in Japan. However, at the end of 1989, the price/earning ratios of Japanese equities were reaching a breathtaking height of 60. By the end of 1990, the Nikkei Stock Average (Nikkei 225) had fallen some 40% from the previous year end.

Many western institutional fund managers might claim that they did not inflate the valuation of Japanese equities in the second half of the 1980s, but that the speculative frenzy among Japanese investors was responsible for the irrational valuation of Japanese equities. However, this claim would not be consistent with their heavy weighting in Japanese equities in the second half of the previous decade. For instance, as shown in Table 1-1, U.S. and European investors poured $230bn into the Japanese market in 1989 alone. An overvaluation of largely-capitalized, global blue-chip equities will make it infeasible to achieve superior returns by investing in them.

International investment by U.S. pension sponsors, which was initiated in order to take advantage of market imperfection overseas, has been making global equity markets increasingly efficient. However, the extensive concentration in largely-capitalized, global blue-chip equities will reverse this process and bring back imperfection to market equilibrium. Moreover, a prudent institutional investor cannot claim to have achieved an optimal diversification of market risk by putting 35% of his or her eggs in one basket.

Also, as world economies and financial markets become more and more integrated, the correlations among the "thundering thousand" superleague shares have been rising (Table 1-2). These rising correlations among the major international equity markets will not contribute to reducing the volatility of portfolio.

One last remark to the current trends in global equity investing is that despite the high liquidity of the global superleague shares, institutional investors are locking themselves into an investment position the unwinding of which will become more and more difficult and costly. Some large U.S. pension sponsors each own 1% or even 2% of a largely-capitalized company. Moreover, all pension sponsors together own a sizeable stake of the company's total capitalization. For instance, pension sponsors own 75% of the outstanding shares of Chase Manhattan Bank.

The 1% shareholder of a large corporation usually finds the liquidation of its position quite expensive. Given this, it will be almost impossible for the 75% shareholder (that is, the pension fund community as a whole in the case of Chase Manhattan Bank) to unload its holding. In his 1991 article in Harvard Business Review, *Reckoning With the Pension Fund Revolution,* Peter Drucker estimated that pension funds would have to invest $100bn to $200bn in new resources each year in the 1990s. Pouring more and more pension contribution into a limited universe of equities will result in a poor liquidity and diversification of portfolio.

As the 1990s continue, global equity investment has reached a juncture where the assessment of the current investment strategies is necessary. Institutional investors need to broaden their universe of global equity investment in order to insure the adequate diversification of global equity investment programs and to achieve the superior returns from them. The second-tier, small-capitalization shares of established international equity markets should be screened, and the newly-emerging equity markets tapped.[3] Here, the rising importance of emerging market investment programs to pension sponsors and other institutional investors is apparent.

Diversification of Risk Offered by Emerging Market Investment

As the world economies become increasingly interdependent, the correlations among the major equity markets have been rising. Consequently, the effectiveness of diversification of portfolio via global equity investing has been somewhat reduced. However, the emerging equity markets still remain lowly correlated with the established equity markets of the world. As shown in Table 1-2, the average correlation coefficient of MSCI EAFE Index (which is a composite index for 20 established equity markets of Europe, Australia, and the Far East) with the United States, United Kingdom and Japan is close to 0.48.[4] The correlation of MSCI EAFE Index with IFC Composite Index (which is a composite index for the world's 21 emerging equity markets) is 0.27.[5] The correlation coefficients of MSCI EAFE Index with IFC Asia Index is 0.26, and with IFC Latin America Index, 0.20. Table 1-3 lists correlation coefficients among the constituent countries of IFC Composite Index.

Because of the low correlations between the emerging and established equity markets, the further diversification of a global portfolio (which presently invests only in the established markets) by including the emerging markets will enhance the effectiveness of risk reduction. For a detailed modern portfolio theory (MPT) discussion of correlation and risk reduction, see Appendix at the end of this chapter.

Table 1-2   Correlation Coefficients of Established and Emerging Markets

	EAFE*	USA	UK	JAPAN
EAFE	1.00	0.44	0.50	0.49
USA	0.44	1.00	0.82	0.24
UK	0.05	0.82	1.00	0.20
JAPAN	0.49	0.24	0.20	1.00
EAFE	1.00	0.44	0.50	0.49
IFCC**	0.26	0.36	0.41	0.32
IFCA**	0.20	0.35	0.40	0.37
IFCL**	0.26	0.30	0.25	0.17

*MSCI EAFE (Europe, Australia, Far East) Index
**IFC (International Finance Corporation) Composite, Asia and Latin America Indices

Source: International Finance Corp.

Enhancement of Returns Offered by Emerging Market Investment

The economies of the emerging markets are still in the early stage of modernization and industrialization and have been growing robustly—like teenagers who outgrow their pants every month. In Asia, countries such as Thailand, China, Indonesia, and Malaysia have emerged as new NICs (Newly Industrialized Countries), and are expected to repeat the impressive growth of Asia's four dragons (Taiwan, Korea, Hong Kong, and Singapore) in the 1980s. Latin American countries, such as Chile and Mexico, have been effective in reducing their external debts and controlling high inflation rates, setting the stage for achieving vigorous growth in the 1990s and beyond.

The earning growth rates of companies in the emerging markets have been higher than those of mature companies in the developed markets resulting in faster rising share prices for the emerging companies. For instance, a telephone company in Mexico has neither superior products nor better management than telephone companies in the developed markets. It will take more than a decade for that company to compete against its counterparts in the industrialized economies. However, as the Mexican economy expands robustly, the demand for telephone lines in Mexico are much higher than in the developed markets where most households have already equipped themselves with telephone lines. Consequently, the growth prospect for a Mexican telephone company is much brighter than its counterparts in the developed economies. This growth prospect has been influencing the movement of the emerging stock markets and will continue to do so. As shown in Figure 1-1, a number of the world's emerging equity markets significantly outperformed MSCI EAFE Index during the six-year period between 1984 and 1990.

Table 1-3

Table 1-3 Correlation Coefficients Among the Constituent Country of IFC Composite Index (Total Returns From December 1984 to December 1990)

	Arg	Bra	Chi	Col	Gre	Ind	Idn	Jor	Kor	Mal	Mex	Nig	Pak	Phi	Por	Tai	Tha	Tur	Ven	Zim
Argentina	1.00																			
Brazil	-0.21	1.00																		
Chile	-0.09	0.09	1.00																	
Columbia	-0.14	0.04	0.42	1.00																
Greece	0.10	0.01	0.14	0.33	1.00															
India	0.31	-0.03	-0.07	-0.08	-0.03	1.00														
Indonesia	-0.07	-0.16	0.42	0.23	0.20	-0.07	1.00													
Jordan	-0.13	-0.14	-0.01	0.12	0.16	-0.08	0.24	1.00												
Korea	-0.17	0.06	0.06	0.00	-0.27	-0.11	-0.16	-0.20	1.00											
Malaysi a	0.00	0.07	0.25	0.01	0.02	-0.03	0.37	0.03	0.19	1.00										
Mexico	0.11	-0.08	0.35	0.07	0.16	0.04	0.18	-0.07	0.22	0.45	1.00									
Nigeria	0.11	0.03	0.05	0.08	0.13	0.03	0.09	-0.10	0.03	-0.21	-0.14	1.00								
Pakistan	0.10	-0.04	0.06	0.18	-0.11	0.22	-0.03	0.07	0.12	-0.10	-.04	0.01	1.00							
Philippines	-0.15	0.11	0.23	0.11	0.05	-0.10	0.63	0.15	0.26	0.26	0.07	0.07	0.01	1.00						
Portugal	-0.01	0.09	0.21	0.33	0.42	-0.12	0.16	-0.02	0.05	0.22	0.39	-0.23	0.09	0.04	1.00					
Taiwan	-0.01	0.09	0.36	0.14	0.04	-0.14	0.19	0.09	-0.03	0.24	0.38	-0.23	0.02	0.02	0.39	1.00				
Thailand	0.15	0.07	0.29	0.15	0.28	-0.03	0.45	0.09	0.01	0.52	0.46	-0.10	0.14	0.23	0.02	-0.40	1.00			
Turkey	0.20	0.18	0.09	0.07	0.14	0.27	0.06	-0.11	-0.07	0.24	0.20	0.14	0.05	-0.04	0.17	0.09	0.18	1.00		
Venezeula	0.03	-0.31	-0.20	-0.14	-0.10	0.17	0.13	-0.05	-0.18	-0.13	-0.12	-0.01	0.06	-0.24	-0.08	-0.27	-0.25	-0.17	1.00	
Zimbabwe	-0.24	-0.06	0.00	0.20	0.05	0.12	0.05	0.12	-0.17	-0.11	-0.11	-0.02	0.17	-0.01	0.15	-0.08	-0.11	0.00	0.02	1.00

Note: Portugal starts January 1986, Turkey starts December 1986, and Indonesia starts December 1989.
Source: International Finance Corp.

Figure 1-1 Returns of Emerging Markets (in comparison with MSCI EAFE Index)

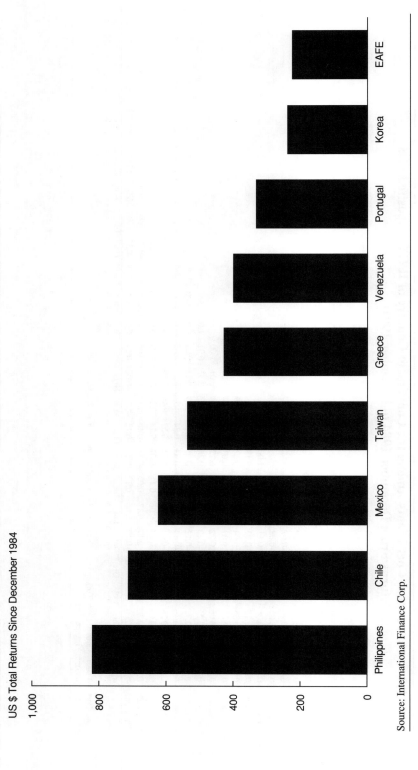

US $ Total Returns Since December 1984

Source: International Finance Corp.

How Large Are the Emerging Markets?

In 1990, the emerging markets accounted for a mere 5% of the total market capitalization of the world ($9,529bn). However, their growth has been quite impressive.
As Figure 1-2 shows, between 1981 and 1990, the total market capitalization of the
emerging markets grew 466% from $83bn to $470bn, whereas that of the developed
markets grew 262% from $2,502bn to $9,059bn. The emerging equity markets will
play an important role for their fast-growing economies as a locus for capital formation and will continue to expand at a vigorous pace.

Currently, the Asian markets account for a substantial portion of the total
market capitalization of the emerging markets. Figure 1-3 shows that in 1990, 72%
of the world's emerging markets were located in Asia and 17% in Latin America .

Conclusion

Since the new decade began, more and more pension sponsors and institutional
investors have been scouting for investment opportunities in the emerging markets.
Nonetheless, their participation in these markets has been in a limited scale. As
institutional fund managers expand their research coverage of these markets, a
greater inflow of investment into the emerging markets will occur. Also, as the

---

Figure 1-2   Composition of World Markets

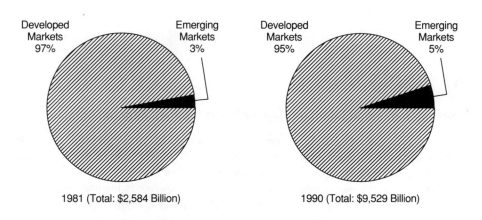

1981 (Total: $2,584 Billion)   1990 (Total: $9,529 Billion)

Source: International Finance Corp.

Figure 1-3   Composition of World Emerging Markets

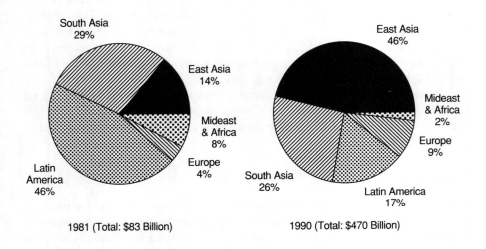

1981 (Total: $83 Billion)   1990 (Total: $470 Billion)

Source: International Finance Corp.

emerging markets become more receptive to capital inflow from industrialized countries, the participation in these markets by fund managers from the developed markets will be enhanced. Table 1-4 details the current status of market openings by the emerging markets.

APPENDIX

Definition of Risk by Modern Portfolio Theory

According to modern portfolio theory (MPT), risk entailed by an investment can be measured by the variance of its historical returns.[6] The definition of risk by means of variance, therefore, implicates the upside potential of return as well as the possibility of downside loss. In other words, variance defines risk as the unpredictability (or variability) of returns. For instance, assuming that the returns from an investment display a bell-shaped, normal distribution, its historical average return of 15% with standard deviation of 7% implicates that the average return of the investment will vary: (1) with 68% probability within one standard deviation, which is between 8% and 22%; and (2) with 95% probability within two standard deviations, which is between 1% and 29%.

Table 1-4   Current Status of Market Openings by Emerging Markets

Are listed stocks freely available to foreign investors?	Repatriation of: Income	Capital
Free entry		
Argentina	Free	Free
Brazil	Free	Free
Jordan	Free	Free
Malaysia	Free	Free
Pakistan	Free	Free
Portugal	Free	Free
Turkey	Free	Free
Relatively Free Entry		
Chile	Free	After 3 years
Columbia	Some restrictions	Free
Costa Rica	Some restrictions	Some restrictions
Greece	Some restrictions	Some restrictions
Indonesia	Some restrictions	Some restrictions
Jamaica	Some restrictions	Some restrictions
Kenya	Some restrictions	Some restrictions
Mexico	Free	Free
Sri Lanka	Some restrictions	Some restrictions
Taiwan, China	Free	Free
Thailand	Free	Free
Trinidad & Tobago	Relatively Free	Relatively Free
Venezuela	Some restrictions	Some restrictions
Special Classes of Shares		
Philippines	Free	Free
Zimbabwe	Restricted	Restricted
Special Funds Only		
India	Some restrictions	Some restrictions
Korea	Free	Free
Closed		
Bangladesh	Some restrictions	Some restrictions
Nigeria	Some restrictions	Some restrictions
Peru	Restricted	Restricted

Note:

Some industries in some countries are considered strategic and are not availabe to foreign/nonresident investors, and the level of foreign investment in other cases may be limited by national law or corporate policy to minority positions not to aggregate more than 49% of voting stock. The summaries above refer to new money investment by foreign institutions; other regulations may apply to capital invested through debt conversion schemes or other sources.

Key to Access:

Free Entry–No significant restrictions to purchasing stocks
Relatively Free Entry–Some registration procedures required to ensure repatriation rights
Special Classes–Foreigners restricted to certain classes of stocks, designated for foreign investors
Special Funds Only–Only approved foreign funds may buy stocks
Closed–Access prohibited or severely restricted (e.g., for nonresident nationals only)

Key to Repatriation:

Income–dividends, interest, and realized capital gains
Capital–Initial capital invested
Some Restrictions–Typically, requires some registration with or permission of Central Bank, Ministry of Finance or an Office of Exchange Controls that may restrict the timing of exchange release.
Free–Repatriation done routinely

Source: International Finance Corp.

Risk of a Globally Diversified Portfolio

Modern portfolio theory in the form of the capital asset pricing model (CAPM)[7] claims that the total risk entailed by investment in an individual stock consists of: (1) unsystematic or firm-specific risk; and (2) systematic or market risk.[8] According to the CAPM, firm-specific risk can be eliminated by proper diversification, but market risk cannot be. In other words, even if a fund manager successfully diversified his or her portfolio domestically, the portfolio would still be exposed to the unfavorable movement of the market as a whole.

However, if the market movement of an individual country is independent of those of the others, a fund manager can reduce the market risk of the portfolio by diversifying its exposure to a number of different equity markets around the globe. If a fund manager invests in two countries, the portfolio risk will be (assume that the portion invested in each country is so diversified as to eliminate the firm-specific risk; consequently, that each portion of the portfolio is only susceptible to the market risk of its own market[9])

$$W_1{}^2 S_1{}^2 + W_2{}^2 S_2{}^2 + 2W_1 W_2 r_{1,2} S_1 S_2$$

W_n = the fraction of the portfolio invested in country n $(W_1 + W_2 = 1)$

S_n = the standard deviation of the returns from the portion invested in country n, that is, the market risk of country n

$r_{n,m}$ = the correlation of the returns from the portions invested in country n and m

$r_{n,m} S_n S_m$ = the covariance of the returns from the portions invested in country n and m

This definition of portfolio risk is induced from the statistical definition that th variance of a sum is:

$$\text{var}(X + Y) = \text{var } X + \text{var } Y + 2\text{cov}(X, Y)$$

In case of a portfolio which invests in three countries, its variance will be:

$$W_1{}^2 S_1{}^2 + W_2{}^2 S_2{}^2 + W_3{}^2 S_3{}^2 + 2W_1 W_2 r_{1,2} S_1 S_2 + 2W_2 W_3 r_{2,3} S_2 S_3 + 2W_1 W$$

Following this reasoning, a portfolio which invests in n countries with an equal weighting will entail the following variance:

$$n(1/n)^2 S_{av}^2 + (n^2 - n)(1/n)^2 r_{av} S_{av}^2$$

$$= (1/n)S_{av}^2 + {}^{(1-1/n)^r} av^s av^s$$

$$= (1/n) \times \text{ average variance} + (1-1/n) \times \text{average covariance}$$

S_{av} = the average of the standard deviations of the returns from the portions invested in n countries; that is, the average market risk

r_{av} = the average correlation of the returns from the constituent countries of the portfolio

$rav^s av^2$ = the average covariance of the returns from the contitutent countries of the portfolio

This formula demonstrates that as n increases: (1) the first term, $(1/n)Sav^2$, will be substantially reduced and could almost become zero[10]; and (2) the second term, $(1-1/n)r_{av}S_{av}^2$, will approach $r_{av}S_{av}^2$. In other words, if a portfolio is diversified by making investments in a significant number of countries, the risk of the portfolio will be close to the average covariance of the returns from the constituent countries of the portfolio. Consequently, if the average correlation (r_{av}) of the market movements of the portfolio's constituent countries is zero (that is, completely independent of each other), the portfolio variance will be almost reduced to zero.[11]

In reality, however, the market movement of each country is not completely independent of the others. Actually, as the world equity markets become more and more integrated, the major equity markets have become more and more interdependent on the others. As Table 1-2 in Chapter 1 showed, the correlations among the major global equity markets have been rising. Nonetheless, empirical evidence presented in Table 1-3 in Chapter 1 showed that the correlations among the world's emerging equity markets are still significantly low enough to substantially reduce the variance of a globally diversified portfolio.

Definition of Correlation Coefficient

The previous mathematical maneuvering shows that if a fund manager invests in a significant number of countries, and if the market movement of each country is quite independent of the others (that is, the low correlations among the market movements), he or she will be able to substantially reduce the portfolio risk. In this section, the concept of correlation coefficient, which is used to measure the level of correlation, will be explained.

Correlation coefficient, which ranges from -1 to 1, measures the strength or degree of linear association between two variables. In other words, if the correlation coefficient between the equity market movements of Country A and B is 1, this means that the linear movement of one market is completely the same as that of the other. If the correlation coefficient is -1, the linear movement of one market is completely opposite to that of the other. Also, if the correlation coefficient is zero, the linear movement of one market has no association with that of the other.

Practitioners must be aware that correlation coefficient does not say anything about the nonlinear association between two variables. For instance, even if the correlation coefficient between two variables is zero, the two variables might still have a strong nonlinear association. Moreover, correlation coefficient explains only association, not causation. Even if the correlation coefficient between the equity market movements of Country A and B is quite strong, say, 1 or -1, this does not necessarily mean that the equity market of one country is causing the other to move in a certain direction.

One statistical measurement, conceptually quite different from correlation coefficient but often referred in conjunction with correlation coefficient, is the coefficient of determination of bivariate regression, R-squared. R-squared, which ranges from 0 to 1, measures the extent to which the variation in a dependent variable is explained by that of an independent variable. For instance, in case of a bivariate regression, $Y = a + bX$, if R-squared is 0.85, 85% of the variation of Y (dependent variable) can be explained by that of X (independent variable).

This definition of R-squared is quite different from that of correlation coefficient. However, if you look at how R-squared and correlation coefficient are calculated, R-squared is just the square of correlation coefficient.

$$\text{Correlation Coefficient} = \frac{COV_{ab}}{S_a S_b}$$

$$R - \text{squared} = \frac{(COV_{ab})^2}{VAR_a VAR_b}$$

a	$= \text{variable a}$
b	$= \text{variable b}$
COV	$= \text{covariance}$
VAR	$= \text{variance} = S^2$
S	$= \text{standard deviation}$

In other words, if the correlation coefficient of the equity markets of the United States and Mexico is 0.29, one could say: (1) either that the U.S. and Mexican markets have 0.29 linear association; or (2) that 8.41% of variation of the Mexican market can be explained by that of the U.S. market, and vice versa.

End Notes

[1]For a detailed discussion of the risk/return benefits of global equity investing, see Keith K. H. Park, "Reduction of Risk and Enhancement of Return through Global Equity Diversification," *The Global Equity Markets,* (Probus Publishing, 1991).

[2]Eurotrack 100 Index is a market capitalization-weighted, composite index for 11 major, continental European markets excluding the United Kingdom, which are Germany, France, the Netherlands, Switzerland, Italy, Spain, Belgium, Sweden, Ireland, Norway, and Denmark.

[3]This trend has already begun. Given the sizeable interest in small capitalization equities in the United States, the Chicago Mercantile Exchange and the American Stock Exchange will be launching stock index futures and options on second-tier U.S. equities, S&P MidCap 400, in 1992.

[4]The constituent countries of MSCI EAFE Index are Australia, Austria, Belgium, Canada, Denmark, Finland, France, Germany, Hong Kong, Italy, Japan, Netherlands, New Zealand, Norway, Singapore/Malaysia, Spain, Sweden, Switzerland, and the United Kingdom.

[5]The constituent countries of IFC Composite Index are Argentina, Brazil, Chile, Colombia, Greece, India, Indonesia, Jordan, Korea, Malaysia, Mexico, Nigeria, Pakistan, Philippines, Portugal, Taiwan, Thailand, Turkey, Venezuela, and Zimbabwe.

[6]Variance is defined as:

$$\text{Var} = \frac{1}{n-1} \sum_{i=1}^{n} \left(R_i - \overline{R} \right)^2$$

R_i = the return in time period i

$\overline{R}$ = the mean of the returns over n time periods

$$\overline{R} = \frac{1}{n} \sum_{i=1}^{n} R_i$$

[7]W.F. Sharpe, "Capital Asset Prices: A Theory of Market Equilibrium Under Conditions of Risk," *Journal of Finance,*, 19, (September, 1964), p. 425-442.
J. Lintner, "The Valuation of Risk Assets and the Selection of Risky Investments in Stock Portfolio and Capital Budgets," *Review of Economics and Statistics,* 47, (February, 1965), p. 13-47.

[8]

Portfolio Variance	= Portfolio Market Variance + Portfolio Firm – Specific Variance
Portfolio Market Variance	= Portfolio Beta × Market Variance
Portfolio Beta	= the weighted average of the betas of the constituent stocks of the portfolio
Market Variance	= Variance of Benchmark Index

[9]A good example of this type of portfolio invested in the emerging markets is one that is indexed to the broad market indices of the emerging markets. Currently, there are two emerging market equity indices available to achieve this type of diversification: Morgan Stanley Capital International Emerging Market Indices and the Emerging Market Indices of International Finance Corporation.

[10]Imagine that a fund manager invests in 15 different markets the average standard deviation of which is 20%. In this case, the first term, $(1/n)S_{av}^2$, will become 0.0027. If investing in the 20 different markets, the first term will be 0.002. Currently, Morgan Stanley Capital International Emerging Market Indices consist of 14 countries. In the case of the Emerging Market Indices of International Financial Corporation, the total number of constituent countries is 21.

[11]The authors would like to reiterate that here, as we assumed earlier, the portion invested in each country is effectively diversified so that its unsystematic risk is nonexistent. As a result, the portfolio is only exposed to the systematic risks (or, market risks) of the equity markets of its constituent countries. As stated earlier, we can create this type of equity portfolio through passive indexation which broadly replicates local markets.

2

INVESTING IN EMERGING MARKETS

Antoine W. van Agtmael
President, Emerging Markets Management
Washington, D.C., United States

A decade ago, when hardly any attention was paid to emerging markets by international investors, early proponents of investing in this last frontier of international investing offered a number of arguments.[1]

- Risk diversification.

- High economic growth.

- Expansion of investment orbit to select "winners".

- Emerging markets include some of the most competitive global producers.

- Still undiscovered by most international investors.

- Still little institutional ownership.

A decade after these arguments were first developed, many emerging markets are no longer "undiscovered" by leading international investors, although most other traditional reasons remain valid to a surprising degree. However, there has been a gradual evolution in the rationale for investing in emerging markets.

---

[1]First discussed at an International Finance Corporation/Salomon Brothers conference for institutional investors in 1981 by Antoine W. van Agtmael and later summarized in his *Emerging Securities Markets* (Euromoney Publications, London, 1984).

17

Risk Diversification

As discussed in Chapter 1, correlation coefficients among industrialized markets remain considerably higher than those between the industrialized markets and the emerging markets. Emerging markets continue to "push out the efficient frontier" in the parlance of modern portfolio theory even though markets such as Mexico, Singapore, Malaysia, and Thailand have become part of the global investment orbit for sophisticated international investors. Some better known emerging markets are more affected by global equity trends today than they were 10 or 15 years ago. This is evidenced by their correlation with the U.S. market (S & P) or the Morgan Stanley Capital International EAFE Index, which represents the industrialized markets of Europe, Australia, and the Far East (see Table 2-1). More anecdotal evidence of the closer links between *selected* emerging and industrialized markets was the behavior of markets such as Singapore, Mexico, and Thailand after the October Crash of 1987 in New York and after the invasion of Kuwait in August 1990.

Ties between *some* of the leading emerging markets and worldwide equity trends are increasing with the growing interdependence of the world economy and improved communications. However, quite a few other emerging markets show little sign (as yet) of following the mature markets in their ups and downs. For example, most of Latin America has followed a quite separate pattern in recent

---

**Table 2-1   Correlations Between Emerging Markets—
The U.S. Market and the EAFE Index**

Correlations with the S&P 500

	Five Years Ending 1980	Ten Years Ending 1988	Five Years Ending 1988	Five Years Ending 1990	Five Years Ending 1991
Mexico	0.22	0.16	0.26	0.46	0.54
Malaysia	–	–	0.16	0.66	0.71
Thailand	-0.36	0.20	0.27	0.43	0.54

Correlations with EAFE

	Five Years Ending 1980	Ten Years Ending 1988	Five Years Ending 1989	Five Years Ending 1990	Five Years Ending 1991
Mexico	–	–	0.08	0.20	0.29
Malaysia	–	–	0.20	0.37	0.57
Thailand	–	–	0.15	0.39	0.47

Source: IFC Emerging Markets Database

---

years, more influenced by domestic political and economic events than world trends. In Asia, major markets such as Korea, Taiwan, and India have also shown little tendency to be moved by either longer-term international equity trends or major crises such as the 1987 Crash or the Kuwait invasion.

Moreover, there are *economic* reasons to believe that correlation coefficients do not necessarily need to increase as the emerging markets become a better known part of the global investment orbit. While the Latin American markets (with their presently very low correlations with the U.S. market and with each other) may become more closely tied together as tariff barriers fall and a pattern of freer trade emerges, many Asian emerging markets are becoming less, rather than more, dependent on trade with the United States and Europe as domestic consumption, infrastructure spending, and regional trade have become more important (Figure 2-1 and Figure 2-2).

Higher Economic Growth

During the 1980s, the record of economic growth in the emerging markets has been mixed—strong in much of Asia, improving in the Indian subcontinent, and above average in the Mediterranean but declining in Latin America and stagnating in Africa (where there are few accessible stock markets). However, as a group, the countries with emerging markets have been leaders in economic growth not only in the developing world but also if compared with the mature economies or the world average. It is interesting to examine the sources of this above average growth on a regional basis in an effort to find out whether it is likely to continue in the future (Figure 2-3).

During the past decades, the traditional "tigers" of *emerging Asia* (Korea, Taiwan, Hong Kong, and Singapore) as well as more recent tigers (Thailand, Malaysia, Indonesia, and Guandong Province in China) have consistently shown the best record with growth at a rate well above that of the more mature economies of the OECD countries (see Table 2-2). While often protecting their domestic economies from too much international competition (on the basis of "infant industry" arguments), these countries have conquered an increasing share of world exports by becoming highly efficient and internationally competitive producers. For example, the aggregate nonoil exports of Guangdong, Thailand, Malaysia, and Indonesia increased from $32 billion to over $115 billion in 1986-1991, with annual growth rates of 20% to 40%.[2] Initially, hard-driving entrepreneurs in these countries used their comparative labor cost advantage in labor intensive industries such as textiles, agribusiness, footwear, toys, consumer electronics, and computer components as well as in services such as tourism and shipping. At the same time, they

[2]Alan Butler-Henderson, W.I. Carr, February 1992.

Figure 2-1   Correlations of Emerging Markets with the EAFE Index Five Years Ending December 1991

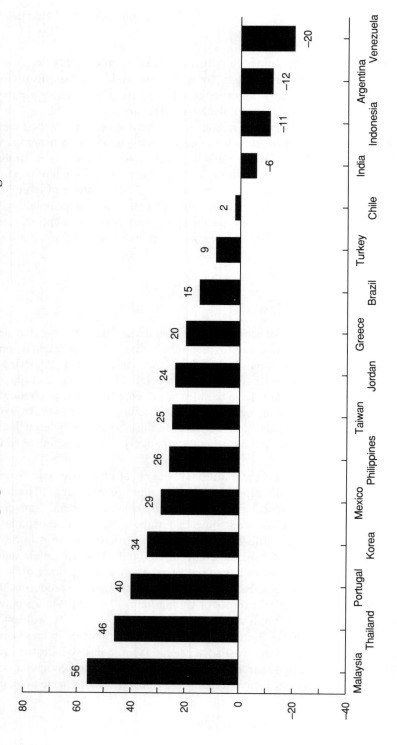

Source: IFC Emerging Markets Database

Figure 2-2   Correlations of Emerging Markets with the S&P 500 Five Years Ending December 1991

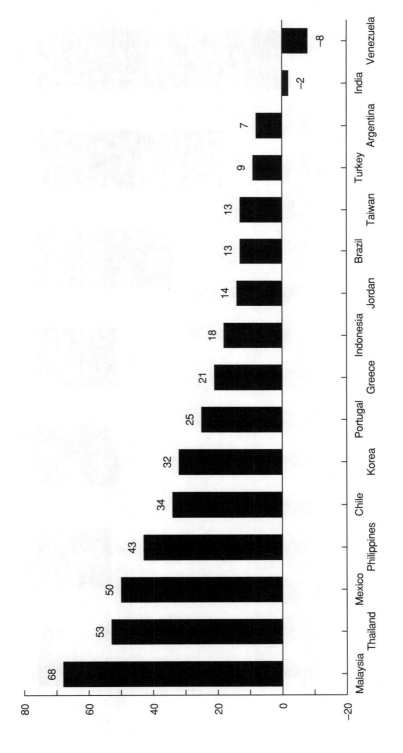

Source: IFC Emerging Markets Database

Figure 2-3   Real GDP Growth of Select Emerging Markets Annualized 1970–1991 (Estimate)

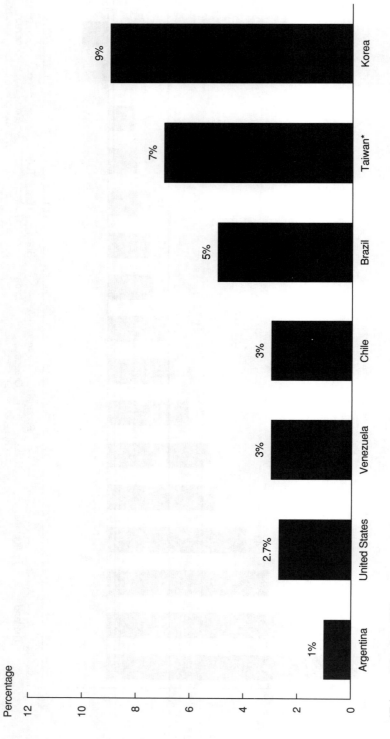

*Taiwanese data from 1991.

Table 2-2   Economic Growth of Asian Tigers—Growth of Selected Emerging Markets in Comparison with OECD Countries

Emerging Asia	Average Annual Growth GNP/Capita 1965-89
Korea	7.0%
Hong Kong	6.3%
Singapore	7.0%
Thailand	4.2%
China	5.7%
OECD Countries	
USA	1.6%
UK	2.0%
Japan	4.3%
OECD weighted average	2.5%

Source: World Development Report 1991, World Bank Publication

benefited from vast and eager labor pools, cheap land, free-enterprise oriented policies and only limited environmental regulation. Moreover, multinationals in these countries from Japan, the United States, and Europe frequently formed joint ventures with local entrepreneurs in order to regionally source components or gain access to local markets.

Because of their late start in industrialization, machinery tended to be modern and embodied the latest technology. Over time, emerging market companies carved out their own niches in world markets, improved productivity (at a rate which was often far higher than that in the more mature economies), upgraded quality, and established stable client relationships. As exporters who had to constantly beat their worldwide competitors and as suppliers of items which were subject to frequent fashion changes, entrepreneurs in the Asian tigers learned to be flexible and constantly change their product mix. This adaptability has proven to be a major asset as their labor cost advantage has eroded.

It is not widely recognized that emerging markets companies, while they may be losing some of their traditional advantages (such as low labor costs and lax environmental controls) are also beginning to shake off some of their comparative disadvantages. For example, emerging market producers have been handicapped traditionally by high cost of capital as a result of inefficient domestic financial markets, but local stock market booms have led to substantial new issue activity and a lower cost of equity while access to international bond and equity markets has improved. Traditional spending on research and development by emerging market companies has been low and the accelerating tempo of technological changes has left behind many smaller companies which did not spend enough on product innovation through research and development. However, others have adapted well. Industrial experience and massive enrollment of Asian students in American graduate schools has eroded the traditional lack of skilled engineers and managers. And finally, infrastructural bottlenecks (in transportation, telecommunications, and education) are slowly being addressed.

A new era of growth in emerging Asia has begun, based not on low-tech exports to mature markets but rather on intraregional trade, domestic consumer spending, massive infrastructure programs, and the gradual integration of emerging Asian producers in a worldwide sourcing chain of components for mulitnational car, plane, computer, etc. producers. Moreover, the rapid increase in income levels and wealth creation in emerging Asia itself, the economic transformation of southern China by Hong Kong and Taiwan, and the turnaround in economic policies in the Indian subcontinent as well as the countries of former Communist Indochina are major structural forces which should keep growth in emerging Asia well above world levels for at least another decade.

During the 1960s and 1970s, growth in *Latin America* was also high (see Table 2-3) but it gradually fossilized as a result of inefficient import substitution (rather than export orientation) and a high degree of government intervention, which sought a "soft" path to economic development by creating state monopolies, allowing private cartels, and creating uncompetitive labor legislation. Mexico and Venezuela initially benefited from the international oil crisis while other countries did not heed its warning. Overindebtedness at the national and corporate level created a massive debt crisis in the 1980s which led to a decade of stagnation and restructuring. Only in the late 1980s did a new crop of politicians and economists abandon the inward looking, state-oriented, and undisciplined policies of the past and, instead, embrace (or was forced to accept) monetary discipline, trade liberalization, deregulation, and a private sector focus. The turnaround began in Chile and, soon thereafter, in Mexico and was followed by Venezuela (in a more ambivalent fashion), Argentina (in the most radical break with its past), Peru, and Bolivia. Brazil, the largest country in Latin America, is only in the early stages of this process.

Table 2-3   Latin American Economic Growth

| | Average Annual GDP Growth Rate | |
	1965-1980	1980-1989
Argentina	3.4%	-0.3%
Brazil	9.0%	3.0%
Chile	1.9%	2.7%
Colombia	5.7%	3.5%
Mexico	6.5%	0.7%
Venezuela	3.7%	1.0%

Source: World Development Report 1991

The dramatic drop in inflation, privatization, and restoration of financial stability have led to a renaissance in economic growth in many Latin American countries which is beginning to stimulate corporate earnings, investment, and purchasing power. As a result, during the early 1990s the outlook for growth in most of Latin America became not only better than it has been for several decades but also much more solidly based. Moreover, the accelerating process of economic integration within Latin America (with the gradual impact of the Mercosur and Andean "common markets") and between North and South America (with the expanding network of free trade agreements) should have a further positive impact on economic growth.

By the end of the 20th century, the embryonic stock markets of *Eastern Europe* should come to life and may constitute as much as a quarter of the total market capitalization of emerging markets (Figure 2-4). As industries must be reconstructed from the ground up and entirely new sectors of economic activity are established, the need for private capital is evident, but it will take time before reasonably well-organized stock markets will be able to make a significant contribution. The return to growth—which is likely to take several years from the time of the disintegration of Communism and the introduction of new economic policies— is a necessary (but not sufficient) condition for the development of viable new issues and trading markets in equities. Other requirements, if Eastern Europe wants to avoid building just the facade of a capital market rather than a real one, are a legal framework for property rights, market prices, accounting standards, reasonable disclosure, and at least rudimentary protection of minority shareholders.

In conclusion, the sources of economic growth are changing in emerging Asia but remain strong. The turnaround in Latin America should stabilize at a new, higher level of growth over the next decade. Meanwhile, after several years of economic chaos, growth should be revitalized in Eastern Europe. Thus, the potential for significantly higher growth than can be expected in the more mature OECD economies remains a powerful engine for better stock market returns in these regions. Just as many emerging markets have been among the world's top performers during the past five and ten years, we may expect some of the same and several new markets to lead the performance tables during the next decade again. Active management will remain important because of high volatility in performance which has frequently dropped a top performing market in one year to the bottom of the list the next year.

Growth Has Led to Vastly Increased Market Capitalization

Little over a decade ago, emerging markets had a combined market capitalization of only $78 billion (December 1980, excluding Singapore), or less than 3% of all world markets (see Table 2-4). As of December 1991, their market capitalization had increased to $628 billion or more than 6% of world market capitalization (including the emerging markets) of $10,400 billion and 10% of the non-U.S.

Figure 2-4 Growth of Emerging Markets

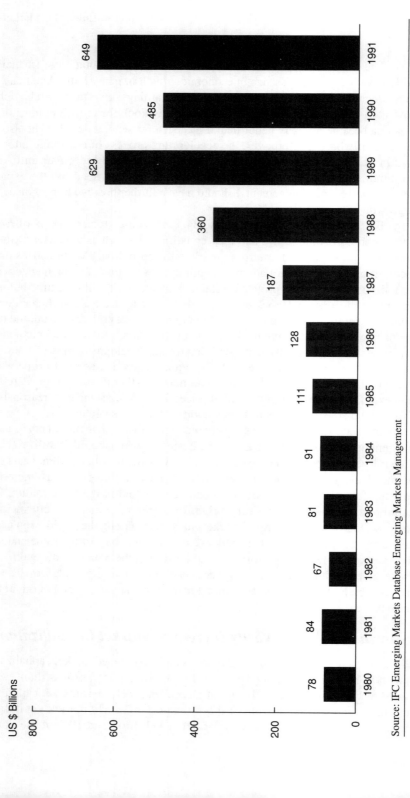

US $ Billions

Source: IFC Emerging Markets Database Emerging Markets Management

Table 2-4 Emerging Markets Statistics

Figures in US $ Billions Major Emerging Markets	Market Capitalization 1980	Market Capitalization 1991	Number of Listings 1980	Number of Listings 1991	Average Daily Trading US $M	GDP 1991 (E)	Market Capital. % of GDP	Stock Market Returns '84-'91	Stock Market Returns '75-'91	% World GDP 1991	% Emerging Markets Capital.	Percent World Market Capitalization Inc. U.S.	Percent World Market Capitalization Excl. U.S.
Latin America													
Argentina	3.9	18.5	278	174	33.2	85.4	21.7%	1917%	2460%	0.4%	2.8%	0.18%	0.27%
Brazil	9.2	42.8	426	570	58.9	350.0	12.2	78	194	1.7	6.4	0.41	0.63
Chile	9.4	28.0	265	221	9.2	26.7	104.8	2,832	14,185	0.1	4.2	0.27	0.41
Mexico	13.0	101.2	271	209	190.8	223.9	45.2	1,979	4,407	1.1	15.1	0.97	1.50
Venezuela	2.7	11.2	78	66	26.6	46.0	24.4	838	—	0.2	1.7	0.11	0.17
Total	38.1	201.7	1,318	1,240	318.8	732.0	27.6	562	4,709	3.5	30.1	1.93	2.99
Asia													
India	7.6	38.6	2,265	2,557	85.1	335.1	11.5%	241%	1936%	1.6%	5.8%	0.37%	0.57%
Indonesia	0.1	6.8	6	141	11.0	118.0	5.8	-40	—	0.6	1.0	0.07	0.10
Korea	3.8	96.4	352	686	312.1	255.6	37.7	408	2,499	1.2	14.4	0.92	1.43
Malaysia	12.4	58.6	182	321	27.9	48.3	121.4	94	—	0.2	8.7	0.56	0.87
Pakistan	1.2	7.3	242	542	4.1	42.0	17.4	462	—	0.2	1.1	0.07	0.11
Philippines	3.5	10.2	195	161	6.4	45.0	22.7	1,764	—	0.2	1.5	0.10	0.15
Singapore	24.4	49.6	261	172	52.9	40.2	123.5	78	—	0.2	7.4	0.48	0.73
Taiwan	6.1	124.9	102	221	701.1	151.1	82.6	611	1,380	0.7	18.6	1.20	1.85
Thailand	1.2	35.8	77	276	102.5	93.4	38.3	798	—	0.4	5.3	0.34	0.53
Total	60.2	428.3	3,682	5,077	1,303.2	1,129.1	37.9	244	2,137	5.4	63.8	4.10	6.34
South Europe/Middle East													
Greece	3.0	13.1	116	126	6.1	65.0	20.2%	678%	498%	0.3%	2.0%	0.13%	0.19%
Jordan	1.6	2.5	71	101	2.5	3.6	69.2	37	262	0.0	0.4	0.02	0.04
Portugal	0.2	9.6	25.0	180	15.8	60.9	15.8	757	—	0.3	1.4	0.09	0.14
Turkey	0.5	15.7	—	132	21.6	129.9	12.1	3,124	460	0.6	2.3	0.15	0.23
Total	5.3	40.9	212	539	46.0	259.5	15.8	N.A.	—	1.2	6.1	0.39	0.61
Total of Listed Markets	**103.6**	**670.9**	**5,212**	**6,856**	**1,668.0**	**2,120.5**	**31.6%**	**255%**	**3367%**	**10.2%**	**100.0%**	**6.42%**	**9.93%**
Total of all World Markets	651	10,443	—	—	—	20,849.7	50.1%	—	—	—	—	—	—

Sources: Research by Emerging Markets Management, based on IFC Emerging Market Database, IMF International Financial Statistics, and Official National Sources.

market capitalization. While emerging markets increased more than eight-fold during this period, the mature markets less than quadrupled in size from $2,700 billion to $10,400 billion. Liquidity in emerging markets skyrocketed even further during the past decade as evidenced by an increase in daily trading volume from $93 million in 1980 to $2.3 billion in 1991. Average daily trading volume regularly exceeds $100 million in at least seven emerging markets (Taiwan, Korea, Mexico, Thailand, Malaysia, Argentina, and Brazil). The number of listed stocks exceeded 6,800 at year-end 1991 (excluding multiple listings on Indian stock exchanges) although probably only 500-800 are actively traded. As a group, emerging markets are comparable in size to some of the world's largest individual markets outside the United States and Japan (Figure 2-5).

The fact that emerging markets have been growing (and are continuing to grow) at a much more rapid pace than the mature markets is not surprising based on the following factors:

1. Emerging markets generally are found in the most successful dynamic and developing countries which rely on the private sector as the main engine for growth. They represent a growing part of the world economy (Figure 2-5a). In 1960, these markets contributed less than 5% to the world economy—but by 1990 they contributed 10%. These countries have benefitted from the shift in industrial production from higher to lower labor cost countries. The increase in economic activity has, in turn, led to greater purchasing power and domestic consumer demand, as well as increased savings flows for stock market investment. This trend is likely to continue as growth in Latin America accelerates and Eastern Europe comes out of the deep economic depression which has accompanied the transition from a Communist to a market-oriented system.

2. As a result of a shift in emphasis in economic policy from debt to equity and from banking to securities markets in many countries, market capitalization in the emerging markets has grown to 32% of GNP in 1991, although it still remains well below the average for mature markets of 46%. Again, there is little reason to believe that this trend will not continue for the next decade(s) (Figure 2-5b).

3. New listings, rights issues, and (more recently) privatizations have added significantly to the *supply* of equity. Only in recent years has this trend gained momentum. We are likely witnessing just the beginning of a steady stream of privatizations, particularly in Latin American and Eastern Europe but perhaps also in the Indian subcontinent and China. Obviously, the high rate of economic expansion in emerging Asia has also led to the need for raising more capital (Figure 2-6).

Figure 2-5a Market Capitalization of Emerging Markets Versus Developed Markets As of December 1991

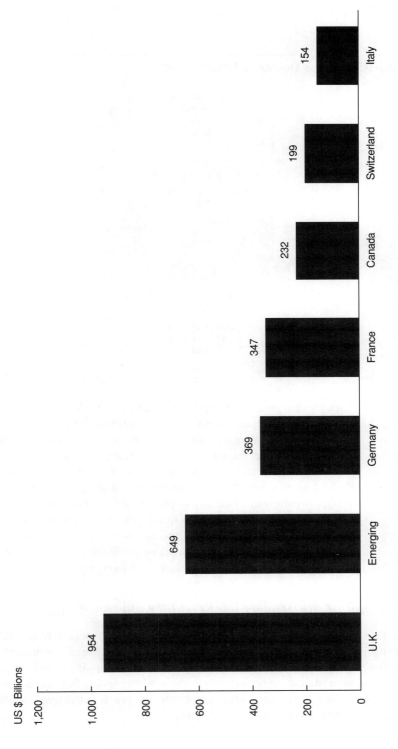

US $ Billions

Source: Morgan Stanley Capital International, International Finance Corporation

Figure 2-5b Gross Domestic Product, 1990

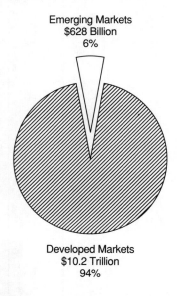

Emerging Markets
$628 Billion
6%

Developed Markets
$10.2 Trillion
94%

4. Stock market prices have moved up, often from depressed levels, as economic performance (and corporate earnings) in many countries improved, equity markets have become better organized, and international investors became active. As a result, these markets seem to have gone through a permanent "re-rating" based on their fundamentals. While stock prices will continue to fluctuate and significant run-ups are inevitably followed by technical corrections, market ratings (as measured by price/earnings multiples or price/book values) are not likely to return to the depressed levels of the past when economic policies discriminated against private enterprise, equity market returns in comparison with other investment instruments, and foreign portfolio investment.

Expansion of the "Investment Orbit" to Select Winners

It has become increasingly foolish for institutional and even individual investors to ignore the growing part of the world's market capitalization which is represented by emerging markets. This is not only because of the sheer size of this group of markets and their increasing importance to the world economy but also because of the recognition that many individual companies represent attractive investment prospects within their industry or in a global context.

Figure 2-6 IFC Total Return Indexes

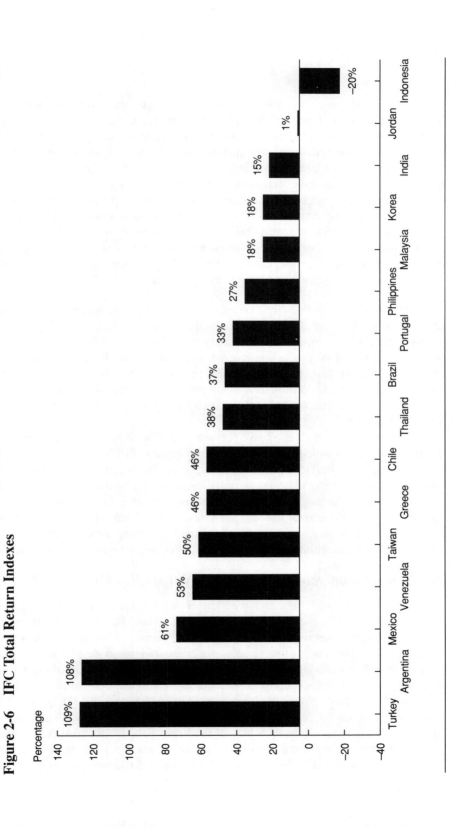

Much has been written about "sunset" and "sunrise" industries and the shift of industrial production from the United States, Europe, and Japan to the developing world. Textile, shoe, electronics, food canning, ship building, pulp and paper, printed circuits, ceramics, and shipping—often but not always labor-intensive by nature—are just a few examples of industries which were traditionally found in the mature economies but have increasingly "moved" to emerging markets. The most competitive companies in these and other industries are now frequently found in the newly industrializing economies. These industries, in turn, brought into existence other support industries to supply them with components or services. And finally, the growth in purchasing power in many emerging markets has led to a surge in demand for consumer goods, ranging from packaged food products to washing machines and color televisions, which are increasingly manufactured, or at least assembled, locally.

Obviously, this process is not static or irreversible. Well-managed companies in traditionally low-tech, labor-intensive industries have specialized on high value-added market niches, upgraded machinery, robotized so that little manual labor remains involved in the production process, and added design features which distinguish their products from the more common "commodities." Others may leave production to newly industrializing nations but capitalize on their brand names (such as Reebok, Nike, Benetton, or Panasonic) and effectively serve as the coordination and marketing centers.

It has become possible to make regional or global comparisons between companies within the same industry, despite the difficulties of different accounting conventions, because barriers to international trade keep falling while financial information on emerging market companies has become available and local research capabilities (often through international brokerage firms or investment managers) have expanded. This enables industry analysts to pick "global winners" among companies in emerging markets by focusing on the most competitive and productive companies—not just within their own countries or continents—but on a global basis.

No Longer Undiscovered But Still Not Widely Held

A number of "emerging" markets are no longer undiscovered. In rapid succession, Korea, Thailand, Indonesia, Mexico, Chile, Argentina, and Brazil each had their day in the sun among international investors. An avalanche of **country funds** (see Table 2-5) has made many of these countries household names despite the fact that they were looked upon not so long ago as small casinos which were of little relevance for their own economic development or as a responsible domain for portfolio investment. The first country fund was created in 1981 for Mexico but quickly fell into disfavor when oil prices dropped and the Mexican economy became over-indebted. It was not until the launching of the Korea Fund in 1984 that the wave of popularity of emerging market investing began. Since that time, more than 150 country funds for emerging markets have been launched resulting in a total market capitalization of more than $15 billion at year-end 1991, according to data collected by the Lipper Directory of Emerging Markets Funds. Most of these funds are for individual countries, but there are also a number of regional funds for emerging Asia and Latin America and several globally diversified emerging markets funds.

The wave of country funds only represents a portion of the flow of international money directed toward emerging markets in recent years. Following the success of the Korea Fund and recognizing the restrictions which (until January 1992 when the market became more open) hindered portfolio investment in Korea, a number of Korean companies issued **convertible debentures** which would be allowed to be converted at a premium into Korean stocks at a later time. Companies in Taiwan and Indonesia followed the Korean example (see Table 2-6). In recent years, offerings of **American Depository Receipts or International Depository Receipts** of emerging market companies have become increasingly important. In many cases, these issues are to the general public and become listed on the New York Stock Exchange or the London Stock Exchange. The most successful

---

Table 2-5   Country Funds (Numbers and investment Amounts by Market and Total)

December 1991

Category	Total Net Assets ($million)
Global	2,730.4
Number of Funds	13
Asian Region	2,653.6
Number of Funds	28
South Korea	1,041.4
Number of Funds	13
Taiwan	412.1
Number of Funds	2
Thailand	1,339.8
Number of Funds	15
Malaysia	471.5
Number of Funds	8
Indonesia	385.5
Number of Funds	13
Philippines	274.5
Number of Funds	5
India	995.8
Number of Funds	5
Europe/Mideast	2,238.2
Number of Funds	28
Latin America	3,272.3
Number of Funds	24
All Funds	15,815.0
Number of Funds	154

Source: Lipper Emerging Markets Fund Directory

example has been the sale of a portion of the Mexican government holdings in Telefonos de Mexico in a worldwide underwriting which raised over $1 billion and more than doubled in price within a year after its launching. This was followed by a number of other issuers from Mexico, Chile, Venezuela, Argentina, and Brazil, although many of these issues have been privately placed in the form of so-called 144a offerings which are restricted to qualified, institutional investors (see Table 2-7). An estimated total of $6 billion has been raised in convertible debentures and international equity offerings by emerging market companies. Buyers include not only specialized emerging market funds but also global portfolios and funds and, in the case of Mexico, even U.S. pension funds and growth stock managers.

Because of the difficulties involved in monitoring 20-30 emerging markets and the many, often relatively small companies in newly industrializing countries, institutional investors (such as pension funds, insurance companies, family trusts, endowments, and foundations with large international portfolios) have begun to invest in local emerging markets directly. This recent trend typically occurs with the help of specialized managers or funds. At present, there are numerous investment managers specializing in the Asia-Pacific region and a few who specialize in Latin America. There are also several with a specialization in diversified portfolios of emerging markets investments in Asia, Latin America, the Mediterranean, and Eastern Europe.

Good estimates of international investment in emerging markets are scarce and not fully reliable but tend to be around $25-30 billion, up from less than $0.5 billion in 1984. This would represent less than 5% of the market capitalization of emerging markets although it may be as high as 20%-30% in individual countries such as Thailand and Mexico. However, this amount represents only a tiny fraction of the trillions of U.S. dollars in assets of institutional investors in the United States, Japan, Europe, and Australia. If the continuous rise of investing internationally over the past decade, in absolute amounts as well as its share of total assets or equity investments, is a guide to what is likely to happen in emerging markets, we may be witnessing only the beginning of a trend which will last another few decades during which emerging market investing will continue to grow steadily from its small base. Recent market returns or disappointments may lead to changes from year to year, as this area will be trendy over time, but the secular trend is likely to be one of increasing globalization.

Emerging markets are not widely held and international involvement in emerging markets continues to grow. Moreover, it would be much too early to say that the "discovery" process is over for two reasons:

First, **new markets which are now only embryonic will "emerge."** As countries such as Korea, Thailand, and Mexico become firmly entrenched in the international investment orbit, there are numerous others which are only at the beginning of their equity market development and in many ways comparable to where better known countries were 10-15 years ago when they had few listings, a

Table 2-6 Convertible Debentures by Korean, Taiwanese, and Indonesian Companies

Name	(U.S. $ mn) Size	Conversion Terms	Premium*	Yield to Put*
YFY Paper	100	1999,2%	526.2	11.38
ACER	45	2001,4%	14.5	15.45
Microtek	29	2001,3.5%	31.3	13.35
Tung Ho Steel	40	2001,4%	16.9	7.40
Far E. Textile	50	2006,4%	20.8	6.64
Pacific Elec.				
W & C	65	2001,3.75%	2.6	9.61
	US $329 mn			

*28th December, 1991

Issue	Issue Amount	Issue Date	Coupon Rate	Maturity	Put Date	Put Price	Convertible Preferred or Ordinary
Anam Ind	SFR 50.0	Mar-91	6.00	1-Sep-96	31-Dec-93	110.50	P
Daewoo Heavy Ind	$40.0	May-86	3.00	31-Dec-01	31-Dec-91	119.00	O
Daewoo Telecom	$50.0	June-91	3.50	31-Dec-06	19-Jun-96	128.32	O
Dong a Pharm	$25.0	Oct-91	3.13	31-Dec-06	31-Oct-96	123.03	O
Dong Ah Const	$50.0	Feb-90	1.25	31-Dec-04	14-Feb-95	123.72	O
Goldstar	$30.0	Aug-87	1.75	31-Dec-02	11-Aug-92	117.99	P
Goldstar P	$70.0	Jun-91	3.25	24-June-06	24-June-96	126.18	O
Han Yan Chem	$56.0	Oct-91	3.25	31-Dec-06	4-Oct-96	125.00	P
Jindo	SFR 25.0	Mar-91	6.00	28-Feb-96	31-Dec-93	110.88	P
Kangwon Ind	$40.0	Oct-91	3.13	31-Aug-06	17-Oct-96	122.11	P
Kolon	$28.5	Mar-91	4.00	31-Dec-05	31-Dec-95	123.66	P
Miwon	$30.0	Jul-90	1.75	31-Dec-05	11-Jul-95	130.18	P
Saehan Media	$30.0	Oct-88	1.75	31-Dec-03	4-Oct-93	123.95	O
Samick Musical	$30.0	Mar-90	1.00	31-Dec-04	8-Mar-95	125.11	O
Samsung Elect	$20.0	Dec-85	5.00	31-Dec-00	31-Dec-90	117.00	O
Ssangyong Cement	$70.0	Nov-91	3.50	31-Dec-05	14-Nov-96	123.75	O
STC	$30.0	Jan-90	1.25	31-Dec-04	31-Dec-94	122.33	P
Sunkyong Ltd	SFR 65.0	May-91	4.75	16-May-96	30-Jun-94	111.25	P
Sunkyong Ind	$40.0	Sep-90	1.50	31-Dec-05	14-Sep-95	136.48	O
Tongyang Nylon	$30.0	Jul-91	3.25	31-Dec-05	10-Jul-96	127.80	O
Trigem	$30.0	Jun-91	3.50	31-Dec-05	4-Jun-96	120.06	O
Yukong	$20.0	Jul-96	3.00	31-Dec-01	31-Dec-92	122.00	O
	US $692.5 mn						
	SFR $140 mn						

Source: Warburg Securities

Table 2-7   ADRs and IDRs by Emerging Market Companies

ADRs

	$(000)
Mexico	
Femsa	87.5
Vitro	36.5
Telmex	1,900
Cemex	140
Cemex	50
Gigante	50
Empaques Ponderosa	32.7
Grupo Carso	214
Gigante	52
Telmex	463
Tamsa	41
Vitro	165
Grupo Situr	50.5
Grupo Televisa	747
Grupo Videovisa	45
Transportacion Martina Mexicana	32
Tamsa	30
AeroMexico	140
Cumulative ADRs of Under US$20 mn	15
Argentina	
Telefonica de Argentina	536
Total	4,827

---

market capitalization of $1 billion or less, and little market activity. This is especially true not only because of the change in economic policies in formerly Communist or socialist countries, but also because markets in regions such as Africa will develop one day after decades of stagnancy.
For example:

- Stock markets have been established in Shenzhen (near Hong Kong) and Shanghai in China which are likely to develop rapidly now that the Communist leadership has given its formal approval.

- Hungary, Poland, and Czechoslovakia have set up markets which, although still embryonic in nature, show long-term promise, anticipating when the period of economic turmoil turns into renewed growth and privatization takes hold. Even in Leningrad and several of the former Soviet republics efforts are made to create markets which are more than status symbols or facades of market development.

- Peru and Bolivia are beginning to get inflation under control, often a first sign of impending economic turnaround. Peru has also liberalized foreign investment regulations, although many other problems (such as the absence of international custodians and adequate research) remain.

- India, long virtually closed to foreign portfolio investment except for funds, announced in February 1992 that it will allow investment by foreign pension funds and foreign issues by its major corporations.

- Vietnam may also establish a stock market in order to aid the recent privatization process.

- In Africa, the Nigerian and Zimbabwe markets have been functioning for many years, but foreign investors have not been allowed to invest because of foreign exchange or other foreign investment impediments. These are not likely to remain in place forever. In other countries such as Morocco, Tunisia, and Ghana, more serious efforts are being made to establish or revive markets.

Second, many **second tier stocks** remain "undiscovered." As emerging markets become better researched, the "discovery" element of emerging market investing will shift from the larger stocks to less liquid, smaller stocks, as well as privatizations of state enterprises, such as telephone companies and utilities, which will require massive investments. Thus, there are—at least for a long time to come—many stocks which remain undiscovered by international investors and, as a result, are often mispriced by international standards. An example is the Korean stock market, which is large (with a size of over $100 billion, ranking among the three largest emerging markets) but was, until January 1992, virtually closed to international investors. As the opening of the market drew nearer, foreign and local brokers began to examine smaller companies in Korea and discovered that there were dozens of companies overlooked by local investors and trading on price/earnings multiples of 5-10x despite 20%-30% annual growth rates. Not surprisingly, immediately upon the opening of the market, there was a brief stampede into some of these companies.

In summary, it is likely that emerging markets are only at the very beginning of their development and that they will become increasingly integrated in the growing global portfolios of institutions and even individual investors.

Appendix: Introduction to the Directory of Emerging Market Funds*

The emerging market funds universe is now growing at an accelerated pace. New funds are being launched at an ever increasing rate as developing countries open their markets up to foreigners. A perfect example is the recent spate of "China Funds". In fact, the number of China Funds now exceeds the number of listed Chinese stocks that are available to foreigners. The following Directory of Emerging Market Funds contains some 400 funds with total net assets exceeding US $20 billion. A milestone in the industry was reached earlier this year, when the world's largest emerging market fund, Capital International's Emerging Markets Growth Fund, surpassed the US $1 billion mark in total net assets in January.

The Directory is quite comprehensive, because not only the more well known publicly traded open and closed end funds, but also private placements and even some venture capital funds have been included.

The information provided in the Directory includes the name of the fund, the name of its investment adviser(s), its size as at December 31, 1991 (unless indicated otherwise), whether the fund is open (O) or closed (C) end, the stock exchange on which it is listed (if applicable), the funds' currency and its inception date. Fund sizes have all been converted to U.S. dollars for comparative purposes. Those funds where the December 31, 1991 size was unavailable are indicated with a bracketed number preceding the size as follows: (1) size as at June 30, 1991; (2) size as at February 29, 1992; (3) size as at September 30, 1991; (4) size as at November 30, 1991; (5) size as at March 31, 1991; (6) size as at July 31, 1991. Funds which commenced operations after December 31, 1991, are listed as "new" in the Net Assets column. Under the "Stock Exchange" heading, "Not Listed" includes public open end funds, such as U.S. and Canadian mutual funds or U.K. Unit Trusts while "Private" funds are not available to the general public, and are also obviously unlisted. Information that was not available or not provided is marked "n.a."

Funds are grouped by geographic focus and are ranked based on their size as at December 31, 1991. To be included in the Directory, a fund must first meet the definition of an "emerging market fund". The definition of an emerging market used is the same as that used by the World Bank, namely those countries with a GDP of less than US $6,000 per person except that Taiwan and Korea are still considered by many international investors to be "emerging" even though their per capita GDPs exceed the US $6,000 level. Also, their stock markets have until recently been closed to direct foreign investment. This definition excludes the markets of Hong Kong, Singapore, Spain and Austria. Another criteria, is that a fund must generally have greater than 50% of its total net assets invested directly in emerging markets. This criteria eliminates such funds as the "emerging Europe" ones, which state their investment objective is to take advantage of future growth in Eastern Europe by investing in companies listed in major markets which do business in Eastern Europe. There seems little difference between one of these funds and a European fund, with a very similar portfolio, that does not call itself an "emerging market fund". The last rule is that a fund must have a majority of its net assets invested in equities. In other words, bond funds and money market funds are not

* by Ian Wilson

included. However, this rule does not eliminate newly launched emerging market funds just because they have high cash levels. Obviously, because funds are continuously changing their holdings, the percentage invested directly into emerging markets, sometimes fluctuates above and below the 50% level. For these funds, I have had to make a somewhat arbitrary decision on whether or not to include them.

In September 1992 the first annual *Wilson Directory of Emerging Market Funds* will be published which will contain more extensive information on each of the funds listed in the following Directory. Included will be each fund's top ten equity holdings, performance figures, fund contacts (managers, registrars, trustees, custodians, auditors, legal advisers, etc.), country allocation of assets and much more. It will also contain data and other information on many of the world's emerging stock markets; profiles and contact details of many of the major players in the industry; as well as complete contact details for all of the funds. This Directory may be ordered from

Wilson Emerging Market Funds Research, Inc., 223 Crean Crescent, Saskatoon, CANADA S7J3W9 (Tel: 306-975-5963 Fax: 306-955-1699)

The information contained in the Directory is copyrighted by Ian M. Wilson. All rights are reserved. No part of it may be reproduced, stored in a retrieval system, or transmitted, in any form or by any means, electronic, mechanical, photocopying, recording or otherwise, without the prior written permission of Ian M. Wilson. This information is based on data obtained from sources considered to be reliable, but is not guaranteed as to accuracy and does not purport to be complete. This information shall not be construed, implicitly, or explicitly, as containing any investment recommendations and it does not constitute an offer of or an invitation to purchase or sell any of the funds mentioned, nor should it be considered as investment advice.

DIRECTORY OF EMERGING MARKET FUNDS

Name of Fund	Investment Adviser(s)	Net Assets $US mill	T	Stock Exchange	Curr	Inception
GLOBAL FUNDS						
Emerging Markets Growth Fund, Inc.	Capital International, Inc.	985.8	C	Private	US $	May-86
Emerging Markets Investment Fund	Capital International, Inc.	371.0	C	Private	US $	Dec-87
Emerging Markets Investors Fund	Emerging Markets Investors Corporation	210.0	O	Private	US $	Apr-88
Templeton Emerging Markets Fund, Inc.	Templeton, Galbraith & Hansberger	198.6	C	New York	US $	Mar-87
Morgan Stanley Emerging Markets Fund	Morgan Stanley Asset Management	155.3	C	New York	US $	Nov-91
Emerging Markets Strategic Fund	Emerging Markets Management	151.5	O	Luxembourg	US $	Jul-88
Capital International Emerging Markets Fund	Capital International, Inc.	141.8	O	Luxembourg	US $	Apr-90
Templeton Emerging Markets Investment Trust	Templeton, Galbraith & Hansberger	135.9	C	London	UK $	Jun-89
Baring Chrysalis Fund	Baring International Asset Management	134.7	C	London	US $	Dec-90
New Frontiers Development Trust plc	Ivory & Sime	119.3	C	London	UK $	Dec-89
Fleming Emerging Markets Investment Trust plc	Fleming Investment Trust Mangaement	112.5	C	London	UK $	Jun-91
Merrill Lynch Developing Capital Markets Fund	Merrill Lynch Asset Management	109.7	O	Not Listed	US $	Sep-89
Genesis Emerging Markets Fund	Genesis Investment Management	99.5	C	London	US $	Jul-89
GT Emerging Markets Fund	GT Management	75.4	O	Hong Kong	US $	Jun-90
Commonwealth Equity Fund	Batterymarch Financial Management	69.3		Private	US $	Aug-90
Gartmore Frontiers Markets Trust	Gartmore Investment	55.5	O	Not Listed	UK $	Feb-87
Beta Global Emerging Markets Investment Trust	Beta Funds	42.4	C	London	UK $	Feb-90
Pictet & Cie Emerging Markets Fund	Pictet & Cie	29.5	O	Luxembourg	US $	Sep-91
Prosperity Emerging Markets Trust	Prosperity Investment Management Limited	24.3	O	Not Listed	UK $	Mar-87
Templeton Developing Markets Trust	Templeton, Galbraith & Hansberger	23.7	O	Not Listed	US $	Oct-91
Martin Currie Emerging Markets Fund	Martin Currie Investment Management	20.5	O	Not Listed	US $	Sep-91
Invesco MIM Pioneer Markets Fund	Invesco MIM	18.0	O	London	UK $	Jul-98
Templeton Emerging Markets Fund	Templeton, Galbraith & Hansberger	17.8	O	Not Listed	CD $	Sep-91
Gartmore CS Emerging Markets Fund	Gartmore Investment	(2) 11.1	O	London	UK $	Jun-87
Credit Lyonnais Funds Portfolio	Credit Lyonnais Asset Management	11.0	O	Hong Kong	US $	Nov-90
PFC Dynamic Markets Portfolio	Matheson PFC Limited	6.7	O	Not Listed	US $	Oct-90
Universal Emerging Markets Fund	BEA Associates	6.7	O	Not Listed	CD $	Sep-91
Templeton GS Emerging Markets Fund	Templeton, Galbraith & Hansberger	4.6	O	Luxembourg	US $	Nov-90
Invesco MIM PS Global Emerging Markets Fund	Invesco MIM	2.2	O	Luxembourg	US $	Jan-91
Emerging Markets Country Trust	City of London Unit Trust Managers	1.9	O	Not Listed	UK $	Sep-91
Multimanager Emerging Markets Fund	Multiadvisers Ltd.	n.a.	O	Not Listed	US $	Dec-90
Baring Global Emerging Markets Fund	Baring Global Fund Managers Limited	new	O	Dublin	US $	Feb-92
Connaught Venture Portfolio Limited	Connaught Investment Limited	new	O	Not Listed	US $	Feb-92
GT Global Emerging Markets Fund	GT Management	new	O	Not Listed	US $	May-92
Kleinwort Benson Emerging Markets Fund Ltd.	Kleinwort Benson International Fund Managers	new	C	Not Listed	UK $	Feb-92
Montgomery Emerging Markets Fund	Montgomery Asset Management	new	O	Not Listed	US $	Mar-92
Partner Emerging Markets Global Fund	Emerging Markets Management	new	O	Luxembourg	US $	Feb-92
Schroder Emerging Markets Fund	Schroder Investment Management	new	O	Not Listed	US $	May-92
Skandifond Equity Emerging Markets	Enskilda Asset Management	new	O	Luxembourg	US $	Mar-92
REGIONAL FUNDS - ASIA						
ASEAN Fund Limited	Wardley Investment Services	187.4	C	Singapore	US $	Oct-88
Asian Tigers Fund N.V.	Algemene Bank Nederland	179.3	O	Amsterdam	Dfl	Nov-88
GT ASEAN Fund	GT Management	137.2	O	Hong Kong	US $	Sep-80
GT Newly Industrialized Countries Fund	GT Management	135.4	O	Not Listed	US $	Sep-86
Thornton Asian Emerging Markets I.T. plc	Thornton Management	128.9	C	London	UK $	Jul-89
IS Himalayan Fund N.V.	Indosuez Asia Investment Services	118.1	C	London	US $	Jun-90
Asian Development Equity Fund B	Nomura Capital Mgmt./Morgan Grenfell	113.4	C	Luxembourg	US $	Jan-88
JF Asia Select Limited	Jardine Fleming Investment Management	108.3	C	London	US $	Dec-89
TR Pacific Investment Trust plc	Touche Remnant Investment Management	100.0	C	London	UK $	Nov-87
Asia Emerging Fund	Baring International Asset Management	99.6	O	Not Listed	US $	Nov-89
Asian Investment Fund	Morgan Grenfell Investment Management	97.3	O	Not Listed	UK $	Mar-81
Daehan Asia Trust	Daehan Investment Trust Co.	90.6		Hong Kong	US $	Jun-90
Korea Pacific Trust	Korea Investment Trust Co./Kleinwort Benson	90.6	C	Amsterdam	KWon	Jul-90
JF ASEAN Trust	Jardine Fleming Investment Management	90.3	O	Hong Kong	US $	Jul-83
Seoul Asia Index Trust	Citizens Investment Trust Management	80.8	O	Singapore	KWon	Jul-90
CS Tiger Fund	Credit Suisse	77.6	O	Not Listed	SFr	Nov-89
Abtrust Far East Emerging Economies Fund	Aberdeen Fund Managers	77.3	O	Not Listed	UK $	Apr-87
Malacca Fund (Cayman) Limited	Indosuez Asia Investment Services	76.1	C	London	US $	Jan-89
Midland Mandarin Trust	Midland Montagu Asset Management	70.1	O	Not Listed	UK $	Jun-88
Asian Development Equity Fund A	Templeton, Galbraith & Hansberger	67.1	C	Luxembourg	US $	Jan-88
EFM Dragon Trust plc	Edinburgh Fund Managers	64.7	C	London	UK $	Sep-87
Asian Convertibles & Income Fund	Wardley Services/Nikko Capital Mgmt.	61.3	O	Not Listed	US $	Jan-91
Gartmore Emerging Pacific Investment Trust plc	Gartmore Investment	60.5	C	London	UK $	Jan-90
Abtrust New Dawn Investment Trust plc	Aberdeen Fund Managers	58.0	C	London	UK $	May-89
New Asia Fund Limited	Aberdeen Fund Managers	51.4	C	Amsterdam	US $	Apr-90
JF Eastern Trust	Jardine Fleming Investment Management	50.2	O	Not Listed	US $	Jan-71
Asia Venture Fund Ltd.	Transpac Capital Limited	50.0	C	Private	US $	Jan-90
Providence Capitol Emerging Asia Trust	Providence Capitol Fund Managers	49.5	O	Not Listed	UK $	Oct-88
FFF Fleming Eastern Opportunities Fund	Fleming Fund Management	45.1	O	Not Listed	US $	Sep-89
Wardley South East Asia Trust	Wardley Investment Services	(1) 42.4	O	Not Listed	US $	Jun-74
Fidelity South East Asia Fund	Fidelity International	42.1	O	Not Listed	US $	Oct-84
Indosuez Asian Growth Fund	Indosuez Asia Investment Services	39.7	O	Not Listed	US $	Nov-84
Pacven Investment Ltd.	Walden Management	37.9	C	Private	S $	Apr-88

Name of Fund	Investment Adviser(s)	Net Assets $US mill	T	Stock Exchange	Curr	Inception
Asia-Pacific Ventures Ltd.	NIF Management Singapore Pte Ltd.	36.2	C	Private	US $	Jun-90
Perpetual Asian Smaller Markets Fund	Perpetual Investment Management Services	31.4	O	Not Listed	UK $	Feb-90
ASEAN Strategic Capital Fund	ASC Advisory Pte Ltd	29.5	C	Private	US $	Nov-89
James Capel Tiger Index Fund	James Capel Fund Managers	28.8	O	Not Listed	UK $	Oct-89
CEF New Asia Trust	CEF New Asia Management	25.0	C	Private	US $	Dec-88
Asian Emerging Markets Fund	Emerging Markets Management	22.8	O	Private	US $	Nov-89
Fidelity ASEAN Country Select Fund	Fidelity International	21.9	O	Not Listed	US $	Oct-90
Pacific Horizon Investment Trust plc	Tyndall Investment Management	21.2	C	London	UK $	Sep-89
Scimitar WSF Asian Smaller Markets Fund	Standard Chartered Equitor Asset Management	15.2	O	London	US $	Jun-87
Henderson Asian Enterprise Trust	Henderson Unit Trust Management	14.0	O	Not Listed	UK $	Sep-90
SHK Oriental Emerging Economies Fund	Sun Hung Kai Fund Management	(1) 11.9	O	Not Listed	HK $	Apr-89
Tyndall Global Fund Tiger Portfolio	Tyndall Investment Management	(3) 11.5	O	Luxembourg	UK $	Nov-90
Indosuez Oriental Ventures Trust	Indosuez Asia Investment Services	6.5	O	Not Listed	US $	Jun-85
GT Orient Fund	GT Management	6.2	O	Not Listed	UK $	Oct-91
Citiportfolios Emerging Asian Markets Equity	Citibank Investment Management	5.7	O	Luxembourg	US $	Aug-90
Kleinwort Benson SF Emerging Asia Fund	Kleinwort Benson Investment Management	4.4	O	Luxembourg	ECU	Feb-90
CMI GN Far East Emerging Economies Equity	James Capel Fund Managers	4.2	O	Luxembourg	US $	Apr-90
Touche Remnant WS Far East Fund	Touche Remnant Investment Management	(3) 4.2	O	Luxembourg	UK $	Nov-88
Cambridge Pacific Fund	Sagit Investment Management Ltd.	4.1	O	Not Listed	CD $	May-89
CIBC-CEF Emerging Pacific Markets Trust	CEF Investment Management	3.4	O	Not Listed	US $	Sep-88
Scimitar WSF Singapore Indo-Malaysia Equity	Standard Chartered Equitor Asset Mgt.	3.4	O	London	US $	May-90
Connaught Baraccuda Fund	Connaught Investments Limited	1.7	O	Not Listed	US $	Nov-87
Guinness Flight GS ASEAN Fund	Guinness Flight Fund Managers	1.4	O	Not Listed	UK $	Nov-90
Aetna ASEAN Development Trust	Aetna Investment Management	1.0	O	Not Listed	US $	Jun-90
CIBC-CEF Golden Buddha Trust	CEF Investment Management	0.7	O	Not Listed	US $	Dec-89
CIBC-CEF Indonesia-Philippine Trust	CEF Investment Management	0.7	O	Not Listed	US $	Dec-89
CIBC-CEF Thai-Philippine Trust	CEF Investment Management	0.7	O	Not Listed	US $	Dec-89
Gota Global Selection ASEAN Fund	Wardley Investment Services	n.a.	O	Luxembourg	US $	n.a.
Nomura Asian Infrastructure Fund SICAV	Nomura Capital Management	n.a.	O	Luxembourg	US $	Aug-90
Asia Pacific Growth Fund	Hambrecht & Quist	new	O	Private	US $	Pending
Merrill Lynch Dragon Fund, Inc.	Merrill Lynch Asset Management	new	O	Not Listed	US $	n.a.
Partner Emerging Markets Asia Fund	Emerging Markets Management	new	O	Luxembourg	US $	Feb-92
REGIONAL FUNDS - LATIN AMERICA						
Equity Fund of Latin America	Batterymarch Financial Management	325.3	C	Luxembourg	US $	Apr-89
New World Investment Fund	Capital International, Inc.	179.3	C	Private	US $	May-89
GT Latin America Growth Fund	GT Management	140.7	O	Not Listed	US $	Aug-91
Latin American Investment Trust plc	Latin American Securities Limited	133.1	C	London	US $	Jul-90
Baring Puma Fund	Baring International Asset Management	114.2	C	London	US $	Apr-91
Latin American Investment Fund, Inc.	BEA Associates	104.4	C	New York	US $	Aug-90
Latin American Equity Fund, Inc.	BEA Associates	92.8	C	New York	US $	Oct-91
Merrill Lynch Latin America Fund, Inc.	Merrill Lynch Asset Management	88.8	O	Not Listed	US $	Aug-91
South America Fund N.V.	BEA Associates	73.5	C	London	US $	Jul-91
Latin American Capital Fund	Fidelity International	48.4	C	Dublin	US $	Nov-91
Latin American Fund	Schroder Investment Management	48.0	O	Not Listed	US $	Dec-90
GT Latin America Fund	GT Management	41.8	C	Dublin	US $	Mar-91
Merrill Lynch Latin America Portfolio	Merrill Lynch Asset Management	28.1	O	Luxembourg	US $	Nov-91
Providence Capitol Latin American Companies	Providence Capitol Fund Managers	25.7	O	Not Listed	UK $	Sep-91
Genesis Condor Fund	Genesis Investment Management	22.0	C	Dublin	US $	Apr-91
Libra 2000 Fund	Citibank Investment Management	20.0	C	Dublin	US $	Sep-91
Latin American Emerging Markets Fund	Emerging Markets Management	17.7	O	Luxembourg	US $	Oct-90
Edinburgh Exempt Latin American Fund	Edinburgh Fund Managers	new	O	Not Listed	UK $	Jan-92
FFF Fleming Latin American Fund	Fleming Fund Management	new	O	Not Listed	US $	May-92
Latin American Discovery Fund, Inc.	Morgan Stanley Asset Management	new	C	New York	US $	
Latin American Investment Company SICAV	Latin American Securities Limited	new	O	Luxembourg	US $	May-92
Partner Emerging Markets Latin America Fund	Emerging Markets Management	new	O	Luxembourg	US $	Feb-92
REGIONAL FUNDS - EUROPE						
East Europe Development Fund Limited	Invesco MIM	40.2	C	Private	US $	Dec-90
Emerging Eastern Europe Limited	Tyndall Investment Management	15.0	C	Private	US $	Nov-89
Central & Eastern European Growth Fund	Salomon Brothers Inc.	new	C	Private	n.a.	n.a.
COUNTRY FUNDS - ASIA						
China						
China Assets (Holdings) Limited	China Assets Management	45.0	C	Hong Kong	US $	Apr-91
JF China Investment Company Limited	Jardine Fleming Investment Management	23.0	C	Private	US $	Mar-87
ChinaVest II N.V.	Orange Nassau	n.a.	C	Private	US $	n.a.
ChinaVest N.V.	Orange Nassau	n.a.	C	Private	US $	Jul-86
Barclays Asian Selection China Fund	Barclays de Zoete Wedd Investment Mgt.	new	O	Hong Kong	n.a.	n.a.
China Fund	CEF Investment Management	new	C	Hong Kong	US $	Apr-92
Credit Lyonnais Emerging China Equities	Credit Lyonnais Asset Management	new	C	Hong Kong	US $	May-92
GT Shenzhen & China Fund	GT Management	new		n.a.	n.a.	Mar-92
Jardine Fleming China Region Fund, Inc.	Jardine Fleming Investment Management	new	C	New York	US $	Pending
JF China Trust	Jardine Fleming Investment Management	new	O	Not Listed	US $	May-92
SHK China Fund	Shenyin Securities/China Merchants Bank Secs	new	O	Not Listed	US $	Jun-92
SHK Pearl River Delta Investment Company Ltd	Sun Hung Kai Fund Management	new	C	Private	HK $	Dec-91
Tyndall Global Fund China Portfolio	Tyndall Investment Management	new	O	Luxembourg	n.a.	n.a.
India						
India Fund	Unit Trust of India	440.5	C	London	UK $	Jun-86
India Magnum Fund N.V.	Morgan Stanley Asset Management	305.1	C	Amsterdam	US $	Oct-89

| India Growth Fund Inc. | Unit Trust of India | 83.3 | C | New York | US $ | Dec-88 |

Name of Fund	Investment Adviser(s)	Net Assets $US mill	T	Stock Exchange	Curr	Inception
Second India Fund Limited	ANZ Grindlays 3i Investment Services	9.8	C	Private	US $	Jul-90
India Investment Fund Limited	ANZ Grindlays 3i Investment Services	9.5	C	Private	US $	May-87
Gujarat Venture Capital Fund 1990 Ltd.	Gujarat Venture Finance Limited	9.4	C	Private	IRp	Nov-90
Credit Capital Venture Fund (India) Limited	Creditcapital Finance Corporation	4.2	O	Bombay	IRp	1986
Indus Venture Capital Fund I	Indus Venture Management Ltd.	n.a.	n.a.	n.a.	n.a.	
Information Technology Fund	Creditcapital Finance Corporation	n.a.	n.a.	n.a.	n.a.	
Unit Trust of India Venture Capital Fund	n.a.	n.a.	n.a.	n.a.	n.a.	n.a.
Indonesia						
Indonesia Development Fund Limited	Templeton, Galbraith & Hansberger	57.0	C	Singapore	US $	May-90
JF Indonesia Fund, Inc.	Jardine Fleming Investment Management	48.6	C	London	US $	Mar-89
Indonesia Fund, Inc.	BEA Associates	35.6	C	New York	US $	Mar-90
Jakarta Growth Fund	Nomura Investment Management	31.0	C	New York	US $	Apr-90
Indonesian Capital Fund Limited	Fidelity International	26.1	C	Amsterdam	US $	Nov-89
SHK Indonesia Fund Limited	Sun Hung Kai Fund Management	(1) 22.5	C	London	US $	Aug-90
Java Fund (Cayman) Limited	Wardley Investment Services	(1) 21.8	C	Singapore	US $	Feb-90
Nomura Jakarta Fund	Nomura Investment Management	19.3	O	Not Listed	US $	Sep-89
Jakarta Fund	Thornton Management	17.9	C	London	US $	Aug-89
Batavia Fund	Morgan Grenfell Investment Management	16.5	C	London	US $	Jun-90
EFM Java Trust plc	Edinburgh Fund Managers	14.5	C	London	UK $	May-90
Indonesia Equity Fund Limited	Daiwa International Capital Management	12.2	C	London	US $	Apr-90
Barclays Asian Selection Indonesia Fund	Barclays de Zoete Wedd Investment Mgt.	3.6	O	Hong Kong	US $	Nov-90
Credit Lyonnais Indonesian Growth Fund	Credit Lyonnais Asest Management	3.3	O	Hong Kong	US $	Apr-89
Connaught Indonesian Growth Fund	Connaught Investments Limited	1.8	O	Not Listed	US $	Jun-89
Thornton New Tiger Selections Fund-Indonesia	Thornton Management	1.1	O	Not Listed	US $	Mar-90
Templeton GS Indonesia Fund	Templeton, Galbraith & Hansberger	new	O	Luxembourg	US $	Jan-92
Korea						
Korea Fund, Inc.	Scudder, Stevens & Clark/Daewoo Cap Mgt	235.9	C	New York	US $	Aug-84
Korea-Europe Fund Limited	Schroder Investment Management	134.6	C	London	US $	Jun-87
Seoul International Trust	Korea Investment Trust Co.	103.2	O	Not Listed	KWon	Apr-85
Korea Asia Fund Limited	Wardley Invst Svcs/Korea Asia Fund Mgmt	(1) 100.2	C	London	US $	Apr-91
Korea International Trust	Korea Investment Trust Co.	99.6	O	Not Listed	KWon	Nov-81
Seoul Trust	Daehan Investment Trust Co.	(4) 93.6	O	Not Listed	KWon	Apr-85
Korea Growth Trust	Citizens Investment Trust Management	86.9	C	Hong Kong	KWon	Mar-85
Korea Trust	Daehan Investment Trust Co.	84.7	O	Not Listed	KWon	Nov-81
Drayton Korea Trust	Invesco MIM	43.0	C	London	UK $	Dec-91
Daehan Korea Trust	Daehan Investment Trust Co.	39.6	C	London	US $	May-90
Korea Liberalization Fund Limited	Tyndall Investment Mgtt/Lucky Inv Mgmt	38.6	C	London	US $	Feb-90
Korea Equity Trust	Korea Investment Trust Co.	38.2	O	Hong Kong	KWon	May-90
Korea 1990 Trust	Citizens Investment Trust Management	37.1	O	Hong Kong	KWon	Apr-90
Korea Development Investment Corporation	Korea Development Investment Corp.	(1) 33.4	C	Private	KWon	Dec-82
Baring Korea Fund Limited	Baring International Asset Management	26.1	O	Not Listed	US $	Oct-88
Schroder Korea Fund plc	Schroder Investment Management	21.7	C	London	US $	Dec-91
GT Korea Fund Limited	GT Management	21.4	O	Not Listed	US $	Oct-89
Korea Emerging Companies Trust	Daehan Investment Trust Co.	(4) 17.0	C	London	KWon	Mar-86
Korea Small Companies Trust	Korea Investment Trust Co.	14.2	O	Not Listed	US $	Dec-85
Bordier Korea Fund	Bordier Securities & Ssangyong Invt Mgmt.	9.9	O	Not Listed	US $	Jun-89
KODICO I Venture Capital Investment Ptship	Korea Development Investment Corp.	(1) 7.9	C	Private	KWon	Aug-88
Barclays Asian Selection Korea Fund	Barclays de Zoete Wedd Investment Mgt	7.4	O	Hong Kong	US $	Nov-90
KODICO II Venture Capital Investment Ptship	Korea Development Investment Corp.	(1) 5.8	C	Private	KWon	Mar-91
JF Korea Offshore Trust	Jardine Fleming Investment Management	2.2	0	Not Listed	US $	Dec-91
Regent Korea Fund	Regent Fund Mgmt./Daewoo Capital Mgt	1.3	O	Not Listed	CD $	Sep-91
Baring Eastern Venture Trust	Baring Venture Partners	n.a.	n.a.	n.a.	n.a.	
Korea Technology Development Corporation	Korea Technology Development Corp.	n.a.	n.a.	n.a.	n.a.	
First Korea Smaller Companies Fund	Regent Fund Management Limited	new	C	Not Listed	US $	Dec-91
GT Korean Securities	GT Management	new	O	Not Listed	UK $	Apr-92
Indosuez Korea Fund	Indosuez Asia Investment Services	new	O	Not Listed	US $	Jan-92
JF Korea Trust	Jardine Fleming Investment Management	new	O	Not Listed	US $	Dec-91
Korea Investment Fund	Orion Asset Management	new	C	New York	US $	Feb-92
Thornton Korea Fund	Thornton Management	new	O	Paris	US $	May-92
Malaysia						
Malaysia Fund, Inc.	Morgan Stanley Asset Management	98.3	C	New York	US $	Dec-87
Malaysian Emerging Companies Fund Limited	John Govett	78.1	C	London	US $	Dec-89
Malaysia Capital Fund Limited	Pierson Capital Management	77.2	C	London	US $	Feb-90
Malaysia Equity Fund Limited	Daiwa International Capital Management	67.5	C	London	US $	Dec-89
Malaysia Select Fund Limited	Crosby Asset Management	(5) 60.6	C	London	US $	Jan-90
JF Malaysia Trust	Jardine Fleming Investment Management	52.7	O	Not Listed	US $	Dec-89
Malaysia Growth Fund	Nikko Intl Cap Mgmt/Arab-Malaysian Trst	48.0	C	Not Listed	US $	Apr 89
Malaysian Smaller Companies Fund Limited	Credit Lyonnais Asset Management	38.5	C	London	US $	Nov-89
Aetna Malaysian Growth Fund	Aetna Investment Management	35.9	C	London	US $	May-90
Genesis Malaysia Maju Fund	Genesis Investment Management	23.9	C	London	US $	Feb-90
Fidelity Malaysia Country Select Fund	Fidelity International	9.7	O	Not Listed	US $	Oct-90
CIBC-CEF Malaysia Trust	CEF Investment Management	5.5	O	Not Listed	US $	Oct-89
Wardley GS Malaysia Fund	Wardley Investment Services	(6) 4.2	O	Luxembourg	US $	Feb-87
Barclays Asian Selection Malaysia Fund	Barclays de Zoete Wedd Investment Mgt	3.2	O	Hong Kong	US $	Nov-90
Connaught Malaysian Fund	Connaught Investments Limited	1.0	O	Not Listed	US $	May-90
Thornton New Tiger Selections Fund-Malaysia	Thornton Management	0.9	O	Not Listed	US $	Mar-90
Malaysian Ventures Berhad	Malaysian Ventures Management	n.a.	n.a.	n.a.	n.a.	n.a.
Malaysian Ventures Fund (Two) Sdn Bhd	Malaysian Ventures Management	n.a.	n.a.	n.a.	n.a.	n.a.

Pakistan

Name of Fund	Investment Adviser(s)	Net Assets $US mill	T	Stock Exchange	Curr	Inception
ICP State Enterprise Mutual Fund Series "A"	Investment Corporation of Pakistan	(1) 51.1	C	Karachi	PRs	n.a.
Pakistan Fund	Morgan Grenfell Investment Management	33.5	C	Hong Kong	US $	Jul-91
Pakistan Growth Fund	Credit Lyonnais Asset Management	29.7	O	Not Listed	US $	Nov-91
Nineteenth ICP Mutual Fund	Investment Corporation of Pakistan	(1) 2.8	C	Karachi	PRs	n.a.
Eighteenth ICP Mutual Fund	Investment Corporation of Pakistan	(1) 2.8	C	Karachi	PRs	n.a.
Twentieth ICP Mutual Fund	Investment Corporation of Pakistan	(1) 2.6	C	Karachi	PRs	n.a.
Ninth ICP Mutual Fund	Investment Corporation of Pakistan	(1) 2.5	C	Karachi	PRs	n.a.
Eighth ICP Mutual Fund	Investment Corporation of Pakistan	(1) 2.3	C	Karachi	PRs	n.a.
Eleventh ICP Mutual Fund	Investment Corporation of Pakistan	(1) 2.2	C	Karachi	PRs	n.a.
Second ICP Mutual Fund	Investment Corporation of Pakistan	(1) 2.2	C	Karachi	PRs	n.a.
Tenth ICP Mutual Fund	Investment Corporation of Pakistan	(1) 2.1	C	Karachi	PRs	n.a.
Third ICP Mutual Fund	Investment Corporation of Pakistan	(1) 2.0	C	Karachi	PRs	n.a.
Twelfth ICP Mutual Fund	Investment Corporation of Pakistan	(1) 1.9	C	Karachi	PRs	n.a.
Fourth ICP Mutual Fund	Investment Corporation of Pakistan	(1) 1.9	C	Karachi	PRs	n.a.
First Interfund Modaraba	Universal Management Services	1.6	C	Karachi	PRs	Jul-91
Thirteenth ICP Mutual Fund	Investment Corporation of Pakistan	(1) 1.6	C	Karachi	PRs	n.a.
Sixth ICP Mutual Fund	Investment Corporation of Pakistan	(1) 1.6	C	Karachi	PRs	n.a.
Seventeenth ICP Mutual Fund	Investment Corporation of Pakistan	(1) 1.5	C	Karachi	PRs	n.a.
Seventh ICP Mutual Fund	Investment Corporation of Pakistan	(1) 1.4	C	Karachi	PRs	n.a.
Fourteenth ICP Mutual Fund	Investment Corporation of Pakistan	(1) 1.2	C	Karachi	PRs	n.a.
Fifteenth ICP Mutual Fund	Investment Corporation of Pakistan	(1) 0.9	C	Karachi	PRs	n.a.
Fifth ICP Mutual Fund	Investment Corporation of Pakistan	(1) 0.8	C	Karachi	PRs	n.a.
Sixteenth ICP Mutual Fund	Investment Corporation of Pakistan	(1) 0.8	C	Karachi	PRs	n.a.
First ICP Mutual Fund	Investment Corporation of Pakistan	(1) 0.6	C	Karachi	PRs	n.a.
Credit Lyonnais Pakistan Special Situations Fund	Credit Lyonnais Asset Management	new	C	Not Listed	US $	Apr-92
Equity International Modaraba	B.R.R. Investments (Private) Limited	new	C	Karachi	PRs	n.a.
GT Karachi Fund	GT Management	new	O	Dublin	US $	Mar-92
Universal Management Fund	Universal Management Services	new	O	Not Listed	PRs	Jan-92
Philippines						
First Philippine Fund, Inc.	Clemente Capital	101.2	C	New York	US $	Nov-89
JF Philippine Fund, Inc.	Jardine Fleming Investment Management	60.5	C	London	US $	Nov-89
Manila Fund (Cayman) Limited	Indosuez Asia Investment Services	44.3	C	London	US $	Sep-89
Philippine Long Term Equity Fund Limited	ATSP Management	40.5	C	Not Listed	US $	May-87
First Philippine Investment Trust plc	Tyndall Investment Management	37.0	C	London	UK $	Dec-89
H & Q Philippine Ventures	Hambrecht & Quist	12.1	C	Private	US $	n.a.
JF Philippine Trust	Jardine Fleming Investment Management	5.9	O	Not Listed	US $	Jul-74
Barclays Asian Selection Philippines Fund	Barclays de Zoete Wedd Investment Mgt	0.9	O	Hong Kong	US $	Nov-90
Thornton Philippines Redevelopment Fund Ltd	Thornton Management	0.9	O	Not Listed	US $	May-86
Soviet Union						
Soviet Companies Fund	Batterymarch Financial Management	new	C	Private	US $	Pending
Taiwan						
China Success Securities Investment Trust	China Securities Investment Trust Corp.	259.6	C	Taiwan	NT $	Aug-90
Kwang Hua Growth Fund	Kwang Hua Securities	250.6	C	Taiwan	NT $	Jan-88
ROC Taiwan Fund	International Investment Trust Company	244.1	C	New York	US $	May-89
NITC Fuyuan Fund	National Investment Trust Company	225.0	C	Taiwan	NT $	Mar-88
China Growth Securities Investment Trust	China Securities Investment Trust Corp.	212.3	C	Taiwan	NT $	Apr-88
Citizens Securities Investment Trust Fund	International Investment Trust Company	203.1	O	Not Listed	NT $	n.a.
Kwang Hua Fortune Fund	Kwang Hua Securities	188.6	C	Taiwan	NT $	Aug-90
Taiwan Fund, Inc.	China Securities Investment/Fidelity Intl	167.4	C	New York	US $	Dec-86
Formosa Fund	Kwang Hua Securities	133.7	O	London	NT $	Oct-91
Taipei Fund	National Investment Trust Co./GT gtt	88.0	O	London	US $	May-86
Taiwan Tracker Fund Limited	Barclays de Zoete Wedd Investment Mgt	52.5	C	Hong Kong	US $	Nov-91
GT Taiwan Fund Limited	GT Management	51.1	O	Not Listed	US $	May-91
Invesco MIM Taiwan Growth Fund	Invesco MIM	50.0	O	Luxembourg	US $	Oct-91
Formosa Growth Fund Limited	Kwang Hua Securities	44.5	C	Hong Kong	NT $	Oct-91
HanTech Venture Capital Corp.	Hambrecht & Quist	35.7	C	Private	US $	n.a.
Thornton Taiwan Equity Growth Fund	Thornton Management	33.2	O	Hong Kong	US $	Aug-91
International Venture Capital Investment Corp	Walden Management	25.2	O	Private	NT $	Mar-88
HanMore Venture Capital Corp.	Hambrecht & Quist	22.4	C	Private	US $	n.a.
JF Taiwan Trust	Jardine Fleming Investment Management	9.0	O	Not Listed	US $	Feb-91
First Securities Investment Trust Fund	International Investment Trust Company	8.8	O	Not Listed	NT $	Jan-86
Thornton Taiwan Equity Income Fund	Thornton Management	6.4	O	Hong Kong	US $	Aug-91
JF Taipei Trust	Jardine Fleming Investment Management	2.2	O	Not Listed	US $	Sep-90
ROC Venture Co. Ltd.	China Venture Management	n.a.	C	Private	n.a.	n.a.
TaiwanVest N.V.	Orange Nassau	n.a.	C	Private	US $	Dec-87
New Taipei Fund	National Invt Trust Co./Daiwa Intl Cap Mgt	new	C	Hong Kong	US $	Jan-92
Thailand						
Thai Prime Fund Limited	Normura Capital Mgmt/Mutual Fund Company	236.5	C	London	US $	Dec-88
Ruam Pattana Two Fund	Mutual Fund Company	198.6	C	Thailand	ThB	Sep-90
Siam Fund (Cayman) Limited	Indosuez Asia Investment Services	179.1	C	London	US $	Jan-88
Bangkok Fund Limited	Bangkok First Investment & Trust	163.5	C	London	ThB	Jul-85
Thai Fund, Inc.	Morgan Stanley Asset Mgt/Mutual Fund Co	154.3	C	New York	US $	Feb-88
Thailand International Fund Limited	Fidelity Intl/Mutual Fund Company	139.3	C	London	US $	Dec-88
Thai-Euro Fund Limited	Lloyds Bank Fund Mgmt/Mutual Fund Co.	138.0	C	London	US $	Mar-88
JF Thailand Trust	Jardine Fleming Investment Management	84.4	O	Hong Kong	US $	Aug-89
Thailand Growth Fund	Nikko Intl Cap Mgmt/Mutual Fund Company	69.4	C	Not Listed	ThB	May-88
Ruam Pattana Fund	Mutual Fund Company	69.1	C	Thailand	ThB	Nov-87
Sinpinyo Five Fund	Mutual Fund Company	67.8	C	Thailand	ThB	Aug-87

Thai Capital Fund, Inc.	Daiwa Intl Capital Mgmt/Mutual Fund Co.	56.0	C	New York	US $	May-90
Thai Equity Trust	DBS Asset Management/Mutual Fund Co.	53.8	O	Not Listed	US $	Mar-90
Thai Asset Fund Limited	BKW Investment Advisers/Mutual Fund Co.	47.7	C	Hong Kong	US $	Oct-89
Thai-Asia Fund Limited	Scimitar Asset Management/Mutual Fund Co.	47.5	C	Hong Kong	US $	May-89
Thailand Fund	Morgan Stanley Asset Mgmt/Mutual Fund Co.	46.5	O	London	ThB	Dec-86

Name of Fund	Investment Adviser(s)	Net Assets $US mill	T	Stock Exchange	Curr	Inception
Thana Phum Fund	Mutual Fund Company	40.7	C	Thailand	ThB	Jul-89
Sub-Thawee Two Fund	Mutual Fund Company	34.1	C	Thailand	ThB	Jun-88
Thai Investment Fund Limited	Yamaichi Capital Mgmt/Asia Securities	30.3	C	London	US $	Apr-88
Siam Smaller Companies Fund Limited	Credit Lyonnais Asset Management	29.3	C	London	US $	Oct-89
Sinpinyo Four Fund	Mutual Fund Company	28.3	C	Thailand	ThB	Mar-87
Siam Selective Growth Trust plc	SEAMICO Asset Management	24.7	C	London	UK $	Mar-90
Siam Ventures N.V.	Hambrecht & Quist	19.0	C	Private	US $	n.a.
Abtrust New Thai Investment Trust plc	Aberdeen Fund Managers	18.8	C	London	UK $	Dec-89
Thai Development Capital Fund Limited	Crosby Asset Management	(1) 15.5	C	London	US $	Oct-90
Providence Capitol Thailand Trust	Providence Capitol Fund Managers	12.0	O	Not Listed	UK $	Sep-89
CIBC-CEF Thai Trust	CEF Investment Management	8.8	O	Not Listed	US $	Aug-89
Connaught Thailand Fund	Connaught Investments Limited	7.0	O	Not Listed	UK $	Apr-88
Commercial Union PPT Thailand Trust	Commercial Union Prestige Fund Mgt	6.6	O	Not Listed	UK $	n.a.
Barclays Asian Selection Thailand Fund	Barclays de Zoete Wedd Investment Mgt	6.4	O	Hong Kong	US $	Nov-90
Thornton New Tiger Selections Fund-Thailand	Thornton Management	3.0	O	Not Listed	US $	Mar-90
Fidelity Thailand Country Select Fund	Fidelity International	1.7	O	Not Listed	US $	Oct-90
Vietnam						
Vietnam Fund Limited	Lloyds Bank Fund Management	10.0	C	Dublin	US $	Oct-91
COUNTRY FUNDS - LATIN AMERICA						
Argentina						
Argentina Fund, Inc.	Scudder, Stevens & Clark	64.2	C	New York	US $	Oct-91
Argentinian Investment Company SICAV	Latin American Securities Limited	51.2	O	Luxembourg	US $	Feb-91
Argentine Investment Company	TCW Funds Banco Frances del Rio de la Plata	new	C	Dublin	US $	Jan-92
Brazil						
Brazil Fund, Inc.	Scudder, Stevens & Clark	166.7	C	New York	US $	Mar-88
Equity Fund of Brazil	Batterymarch Financial Management	105.3	C	Private	US $	Oct-87
Brazilian Investment Company SICAV	Latin American Securities Limited	56.7	O	Luxembourg	US $	Dec-87
Brazilian Investment Fund, Inc.	Morgan Stanley Asset Management	51.2	C	Private	US $	Jun-91
Brazilian Investment Trust plc	Latin American Securities Limited	new	C	London	US $	May-92
Chile						
GT Chile Growth Fund	GT Management	234.9	C	London	US $	Feb-90
Genesis Chile Fund	Genesis Investment Management	182.0	C	London	US $	Nov-89
Chile Fund, Inc.	BEA Associates	160.4	C	New York	US $	Sep-89
Five Arrows Chile Fund Limited	NM Rothschild Asset Management	159.3	C	London	US $	Feb-90
International Investment Company of Chile	Investment Management Company Chile	144.8	C	Private	ChP	Jun-89
Chile Investment Company, S.A.	Investment Management Company Chile	110.4	C	Private	ChP	Jun-88
Toronto Trust Mutual Fund	FCMI Financial Corporation	37.7	O	Not Listed	ChP	May-87
Colombia						
Colombian Investment Company SICAV	Latin American Securities Limited	new	O	Luxembourg	US $	May-92
Mexico						
Mexico Fund, Inc.	Impulsora del fondo Mexico	499.3	C	New York	US $	Jun-81
Accival	Acciones y Valores de Mexico	498.0	O	Mexico	Peso	May-80
Accipat	Acciones y Valores de Mexico	245.6	O	Mexico	Peso	Jul-87
Fonibur	n.a.	213.3	O	Mexico	Peso	Aug-87
Fondo Banamex	Banamex	183.1	O	Mexico	Peso	Nov-87
Acciar	n.a.	182.4	O	Mexico	Peso	Jun-87
Inbursa	n.a.	139.1	O	Mexico	Peso	Apr-81
Promer	Probursa	115.1	O	Mexico	Peso	Apr-87
Finlat6	Inverlat	112.1	O	Mexico	Peso	Dec-85
GBMV1	n.a.	106.7	O	Mexico	Peso	Jul-87
Mexico Equity & Income Fund, Inc.	Oppenheimer & Co./Acciones y Valores	95.0	C	New York	US $	Aug-90
Emerging Mexico Fund, Inc.	Santander Management Inc.	92.1	C	New York	US $	Oct-90
Profyt	n.a.	84.5	O	Mexico	Peso	Aug-88
Fobursa	n.a.	62.1	O	Mexico	Peso	Apr-80
Mexican Investment Company SICAV	Latin American Securities Limited	60.1	O	Luxembourg	US $	Nov-89
GBMV2	n.a.	58.8	O	Mexico	Peso	Oct-88
Valmer	n.a.	48.4	O	Mexico	Peso	Sep-87
Banafin	n.a.	46.6	O	Mexico	Peso	Sep-88
Abacof	n.a.	38.4	O	Mexico	Peso	Nov-87
ICapital	n.a.	37.5	O	Mexico	Peso	Jul-87
Mexican Horizons Investment Company Limited	John Govett	31.7	C	Dublin	US $	Jan-91
Finca	n.a.	30.8	O	Mexico	Peso	Jul-86
Fomex	n.a.	30.6	O	Mexico	Peso	Feb-80
Fimsa	n.a.	30.1	O	Mexico	Peso	May-64
Banacob	n.a.	26.2	O	Mexico	Peso	Aug-88
Finlat4	Inverlat	25.9	O	Mexico	Peso	Jun-87
Afinrv	n.a.	24.9	O	Mexico	Peso	Jul-87
Eficas	n.a.	24.8	O	Mexico	Peso	Jul-81
Primerv	n.a.	24.5	O	Mexico	Peso	Oct-80
COUNTRY FUNDS - EUROPE						
Cyprus						
Cytrustees	Cyprus Investment & Securities Corp.	3.8	C	Cyprus	Cy L	Jul-91

Czechoslovakia

Czechoslovakia Investment Corporation Inc.	Robert Fleming Management	new	C	London	US $	n.a.

Greece

Greek Progress Fund S.A.	Baring Investment Mgmt/Ergobank SA	71.5	C	Athens	Drach	Jun-90
Greece Fund Limited	Schroder Investment Management	46.3	C	London	US $	Sep-88

Name of Fund	Investment Adviser(s)	Net Assets $US mill	T	Stock Exchange	Curr	Inception
Hungary						
Hungarian Investment Company	John Govett	104.6	C	London	US $	Feb-90
Euroventures Hungary	Antra Kft.	n.a.	C	Not Listed	NLG	Jul-90
First Hungary Fund Limited	First Hungarian Investment Advisory	n.a.	C	Private	n.a.	Oct-89
Creditanstalt Hungary Investment Partners	CA Developmental Investment Partners	new	C	Private	US $	Pending
Poland						
Polish Private Equity Fund	CA Developmental Investment Partners	new	C	Private	n.a.	Pending
Portugal						
Capital Portugal Fund	Gestifundo SA/Baring Securities Ltd.	99.2	C	Lisbon	Esc	Oct-89
Portugal Fund, Inc.	BEA Associates	57.0	C	New York	US $	Nov-89
Oporto Growth Fund Ltd.	Shearson Lehman Global Asset Management	24.1	C	London	US $	May-88
Portuguese Investment Fund Limited	Morgan Stanley Asset Mgmt/Finantia Soc.	22.7	C	London	US $	May-90
Portugal Fund Limited	Lloyds Bank Fund Management	20.4	C	London	US $	Aug-87
Finantia Capital	Finantia-Sociedade de Investimentos	n.a.	C	Private	n.a.	n.a.
Sri Lanka						
Pyramid Unit Trust	C.K.N. Fund Management	new	O	Not Listed	SRp	Jan-92
Ceylon Guardian Investment Trust	n.a.	n.a.	n.a.	n.a.	n.a.	n.a.
Turkey						
Turkish Investment Fund, Inc.	Morgan Stanley Asset Management	52.7	C	New York	US $	Dec-89
Turkey Trust plc	Ivory & Sime	35.8	C	London	UK $	Aug-90
AFRICAN FUNDS						
Venture Capital Company of Zimbabwe	Venture Capital Company of Zimbabwe	14.7	C	Private	Z$	Jul-91
Mauritius Development Investment Trust	Mauritius Development Investment Trust Co.	(1) 10.5	C	Mauritius	MRs	Mar-67
Africa Growth Fund	Equator Investment Services Limited	9.0	C	Private	US $	Mar-89
Sechaba Investment Trust Company Ltd.	Sechaba Investment Trust Company Ltd.	n.a.	C	Botswana	n.a.	n.a.
Egyptian Tourism and Investment Company	Egyptian Finance Company	new	C	Cairo	El	n.a.
Private Enterprise Fund For Africa	Meridien	new	C	Private	n.a.	n.a.

TWO DECADES OF CHANGE IN EMERGING MARKETS

David Gill
Former Director,
Capital Markets Department,
International Finance Corporation
Director, a Number of Boards of Emerging Markets Funds
Washington, D.C., United States

In 20 years, the decades of the 1970s and 1980s, as well as the first years of the 1990s, probably will be looked upon as a period of giant leaps forward for technology and democracy, but a period of mixed blessings in terms of economic well-being for a large part of the world's population. Some countries were clear winners, but there were many losers and, within countries, the poor often ended up relatively poorer. How securities markets, and particularly equity markets in developing countries grew, or did not grow, may be seen as part of this story. The connection is that, as television and the fax machine facilitated mass communications and furthered democracy, computer-based analytical and data communications technology facilitated securities market and economic efficiency. The following statistics on emerging equity markets give an overview of what occurred.

At the start of 1970, 32 developing countries had securities markets or stock exchanges. The oldest was Argentina's, founded in 1854. However, only a few actually functioned. Six had some form of securities legislation and two, Argentina and the Philippines, had embryonic securities commissions. As of early 1992, over 50 developing countries had securities markets and 21 had securities commissions. During this period, the total equity market capitalization grew from less than US $50 billion equivalent to over US $600 billion and the number of listed companies increased from around 5,000 to over 10,000. Also, capital investment in these countries was bolstered by the increased flow of savings into new equity issues that these markets facilitated. While the statistics are sparse, it is believed that net new equity issues approximated nearly 3% of GDP annually during the period, some three times the OECD country average. Much of this is detailed on a country by country basis in the following chapters.

These figures are not meant to lay special claims with respect to the importance of emerging markets as they have grown and matured over the last 20 years, but rather to place their role in perspective in order to highlight the lessons that can be learned from successes and failures. To emphasize the positive, the development of broad-based equity markets has helped focus attention on the importance of sound economic development of efficient allocation of capital—access to capital by new entrants to the business community and on income distribution. The experiences of the 1970s and 1980s have shown that there is a correlation between those countries that experienced strong and relatively consistent economic growth and countries that have implemented successfully policies to strengthen their equity markets. Conversely, the last 20 years have also provided examples of countries, such as Brazil, whose growth rates have fallen after previous policies favoring equity markets were reversed; this is compared to other countries, such as South Korea, which were encouraging them during the same period. The main lesson is that the fundamental preconditions for an efficient equity market are the same as the legislative and policy structures and educational levels needed to produce an efficient economy overall. On the other hand, there are some who will say that the role of securities markets is of only marginal importance. History will decide. However, to move from conjecture to an assessment of the facts, there are a number of basic points about the development of emerging markets which are important to recognize before any serious review can be undertaken of what has happened, country by country, over the last 20 years.

Development of Emerging Markets

First, a great deal of the political thrust to establish new stock markets in the 1960s and early 1970s was a fad very much like earlier fads followed by new nation states wishing to acquire quickly the images of prestige which marked the older and stronger countries. At the beginning of this century it was important for a country to have a battleship. After World War II, as many old colonies became new nations, the priority was to have an airline—a national "flag carrier" linking it to the major foreign capitals. In the 1950s, this coincided with establishing central banks as the foundation for an independent domestic banking system. Then in the 1960s, stock exchanges came into fashion. This was even the case for those countries which first formed them around the time they were buying battleships, but let them languish in favor of politics and policies which promoted command economies.

Second, during the early early 1960s and 1970s, most of the world's economists and government financial officials were of the opinion that financial markets had no significant role in real economic development. They saw stock markets as, at best, a misuse of human resources, and, at worst, as gambling dens draining away financial resources from the real economy. It was not until the early 1970s that there was any meaningful academic literature on the subject and, thus, the beginnings of an understanding that financial markets in general and equity markets in particular, especially the primary equity markets, could play a positive role in economic development. Recognizing this was an important precondition for the support of policy makers who had to be convinced that there was a real reason to promote a strong equity market. This deserves special emphasis.

Perhaps the best examples of positive benefits from encouraging competitive real and financial markets are Hong Kong and Singapore, which are no longer developing countries, and Korea. In Korea, local businessmen, until the early 1980s, did not consider the equity market a viable source of new capital. They only listed their company's common stocks because of government pressure and the fiscal benefits they gained from so doing. One benefit was access to the local bond market which was a significant source of term finance. However, once equity market prices moved from the four to five times earnings range in the 1970s to the 15 times and more range, as they did in 1987, new equity issues became an important capital source. Equally important was the opening to foreigners of the new issue market for convertible bonds at the end of the 1980s. The volume of foreign issues alone in the most recent 12 month period was approximately one billion U.S. dollars, or about 1% of the total Korean equity market capitalization. Moving to Latin America, the best example of the connection between economic growth and strong securities markets was Chile during the 1980s debt problem. After the debt induced collapse of its banking system and the consequent government bailout of most of the banks and many other enterprises, policies were implemented to rebuild the system and give special impetus to the equity market. This involved removing tax dis-incentives, establishing a pension fund system and encouraging debt-equity conversions by both foreign and domestic creditors. The Chilean equity market capitalization grew from about US $2 billion in 1982 to US $28.7 billion in January 1992, while Chile's real GDP growth rate was well above the region's average and its inflation rate well below the average.

Of course, there are exceptions. Hard work, discipline, and good management, as demonstrated by Germany and some developing countries in the post-war period, can make up for some equity market deficiencies. High standards of education at the secondary and tertiary levels, available for all of the population, are essential for developing the academic, analytical, and technical skills needed to provide the infrastructure for an efficient market economy as well as a competitive equity market. However, concerning Germany, an important deficiency in the equity market is seen to be lack of access to equity financing for small businesses—

a consequence of its quite concentrated universal banking system and the bank's effective control of most of the leading nonbanking companies.

In contrast, Japan, starting in the early 1960s, helped by hard work and high educational standards, built a strong domestic securities market infrastructure and a robust equity market. Japan also led the way in encouraging foreign portfolio investment. The Japan Fund Inc., listed in New York in 1964, could be considered the first important post-war emerging market country fund. This led to an increasing flow of Japanese equity and quasi-equity issues in the euro-markets, reaching annual volumes of over US $30 billion during most of the years in the 1980s. Japan's superior economic performance, significantly helped by low cost domestic and foreign capital, even compared to Germany's, speaks for itself as to the benefits.

Third, it was, and is, people who actually made things happen. The national policies and infrastructures that brought about equity market development were usually the result of far-sighted, strong leaders who had the vision, understood the issues, and were prepared to face down the fainthearted and the downright opposed. One example is Octavio Gouvea de Bulhoes, Brazil's Finance Minister from 1964 to 1967, who initiated the policies that rebuilt the Brazilian securities market and produced Brazil's economic success story of the early 1970s. He laid the framework for an open market and the establishment of investment banks, pension funds, and mutual funds. Equally importantly, he provided tax incentives for savers to buy equities and for companies to go public as well as to establish fully funded pension funds. The result was that, in the 1970s, the volume of new equity issues through the primary equity market exceeded the equivalent of 3% of GNP, a high level by any standard. During this period, Brazil's new fixed capital investment reached about 25% of GDP, contributing to a real growth rate averaging over 8% annually. Also, the Brazilian equity market became the largest of the emerging markets.

Then there was South Korea's Finance Minister, Nam Duck Woo, who reformed the Korean equity market and made it a serious institution. He was responsible for establishing the most comprehensive set of policies and infrastructural mechanisms found prior to then in any emerging Asian market and matching Brazil's. Starting in the early 1970s, Korea became one of the largest emerging equity markets, surpassing Brazil's in the early 1980s when new Brazilian administrations began to reverse the equity market policies of the 1964-1978 period. Korea also developed the largest long-term corporate bond market in the developing world.

It is impossible to list all the key policymakers who played similar roles in other countries. However, it is important to remember the people who contributed to the legitimacy of the equity markets in other ways. One is Raymond Goldsmith of Yale University who wrote the first serious book on financial structure and the relationships between real growth and financial intermediation. One should also mention the earlier work of Alvin Shaw of Harvard and the subsequent work of Ronald McKinnon of Stanford, both of whom addressed the subject in broader macroeconomic terms. This was at a time when most professional economists still did not recognize the differences in the "quality" of money. Money was money to them, and it made little difference whether a development project was financed with 100% short-term, floating rate loans or 100% equity—a view held quite widely until the 1980s debt crisis. Then, there were the founders of the World Bank and the International Monetary Fund at Bretton Woods who included in the Articles of the IBRD a clause that stated that capital market development was an important objective to be pursued. However, it was not until the tenure of Robert McNamara as President of the World Bank that this was taken seriously. It was McNamara who caused the establishment in 1971 of a unit in The International Finance Corporation to be the focal point for capital market development work for The World Bank Group as a whole. This initiative, for the first time, focused the attention of The World Bank Group's member countries on securities markets, both domestic and international, as an important mechanism to mobilize domestic savings, attract foreign portfolio capital, and to allocate savings to its most productive uses through a competitive market system.

The foregoing says something about why and how some 40 new or revitalized securities markets "emerged" as serious financing mechanisms in the developing countries over the last 20 years.

Before delving into how this was done, it is instructive to first think back to the reasons behind promoting those other symbols of nationhood that were popular before stock markets became fashionable and then truly valuable. Clearly, the underlying theme was national prestige. Battleships reflected military might to defend the nation. Airlines connoted the impression of global reach and modern communications. Stock markets were something different. They were seen as a symbol of commercial sophistication. Fortunately, unlike the tendency to construct large, modern, and physically dominant central bank buildings as symbols of the importance and prestige of banking, stock markets were always understood to be more relevant as a financial mechanism. Thus, while the prestige of having a stock exchange building was important in many countries, most took the economic and social objectives more seriously and concentrated on the policies and the infrastructure. In this sense, and also for central banks and the banking system, the "why" was based on different motives. The importance of the banking system needs no explanation. As to equity markets, some policy makers saw them primarily as a means of broadening the ownership base of large family-owned enterprises and thus improving indirectly the distribution of income or "shareholder democracy" as it was called. Others saw them as an efficient way of increasing domestic savings and providing more reliable, and more risk reward-related, long-term finance for industry. In many countries, both of these objectives were pursued and attained to varying degrees.

Basic Steps to Build Efficient Securities Markets

This leads to the "hows"—what they did to get from where they were to where they wanted to be. It is useful now to summarize what policymakers then thought had to be done. By and large, all of the countries that achieved these objectives in the 1970s and 1980s followed much the same policy path in building the legal, fiscal, and institutional infrastructures. They addressed these issues in the following way. Thinking ahead, if the decision makers in the emerging democracies of Eastern Europe and Central/Northern Asia wish to build efficient securities markets to help forge strong market economies, these are still the basic steps they must take.

The first step for many countries was the legal structure for "investor protection." This is sometimes a misunderstood objective. Investor protection, as emphasized by the U.S. SEC was, for most countries, less important than broadening and deepening the securities market. As Delfim Netto, the Brazilian Finance Minister from 1967 to 1974 said, "policing" was not particularly relevant until there was a large enough market with sufficient wealthy players to police. Nevertheless, investor protection as the means to build the confidence of savers in the securities market, if not the first, is certainly a very close second issue to be considered. The fundamentals behind investor protection: full, accurate, comparable and timely company financial reporting and disclosure; fair securities issuance and trading practices; and the sanctity of contract law. All are all essential if securities markets are to achieve their key objectives.

The second step was the fiscal and principally the tax environment. There are still many countries, including the United States, where the tax system punishes savers who are risk takers and, simultaneously, rewards companies that finance through borrowing. Interest on debt is often tax free to savers and a tax deductible expense for borrowers while both dividend income and capital gains are taxable. The United States is one of the few developed countries that taxes dividend income twice—once at the corporate level as profits and again at the individual level as income. These policies lead to over- indebtedness. Income earned from securities, and especially from equities, should be taxed on the same basis as income from other debt instruments. If anything, taxes on income from equities should be lower than tax rates on income from debt instruments to encourage capital formation and saver acceptance of the real risks that go with equity investment. Further, financial institutions, such as insurance companies and pension funds, should be encouraged by conducive fiscal polities to invest some of their resources in securities and especially in equities. Mutual funds and pension funds should be exempt from all taxes. Corporate taxes should encourage balanced company capital structures. Finally, securities transactions should be exempt from stamp or transfer taxes to encourage liquidity.

A third step was to encourage owners of businesses to issue common stock through the market in order to broaden ownership of companies as well as to reduce dependence on debt. This could be considered another tax issue because tax policy was used as a tool to encourage family companies to go public. In reality, it has more to do with politics and broadening the private ownership base of enterprises than economic policy. Expanding enterprise ownership, along with increasing the number of people owning land and homes, was seen as a means of increasing social stability in the poorer countries. In recent years, this has been central to "privatization" programs. Many countries, previously skeptical about the practicalities, found that policies that increased the supply of equities seemed to produce a demand from savers that was never recognized before. Even the United Kingdom's privatization programs, which included privatizing government housing by transferring ownership to resident renters, was believed to have increased political support for market economies as the percentage of the adult population owning equities increased from around 5% to over 25%.

A final and rather all-encompassing step was bringing up-to-date laws relating to securities markets and widely publicizing the securities markets' important role. These were educational and confidence building activities. Finally, on the updating of laws, the starting point for any country is a contract law, a company law, a banking law, and a justice system which enforces the laws effectively. If these do not work, or are faulty, the first step must be establishing or fixing them and the system to make them work. The second step is enacting a securities law based on these building blocks to enforce investor protection and promote securities market development. Addressing these issues constructively ensured the growth of equity markets so long as there was a basic market economy and legal system in place. The establishment of a formal securities commission or similar organization was often a result, as well as a means, of furthering these objectives and addressing implementation of all of the infrastructure and fiscal steps raised by these issues. The number of securities acts or capital market laws enacted by countries to establish securities commissions in the 1970s and 1980s exceeded the number previously in existence. Many of the 50 or more new securities commissions (not just those in developing countries but also in major countries such as the United Kingdom and France) were given equity market developmental roles as a primary mandate.

Practical Issues to Consider

However, many developing countries still have a long way to go if they are to catch up with the major markets. This leads to considering some of the practical issues. In many countries, securities markets are still considered of secondary importance and a somewhat inferior type of financial activity compared to banking. Of course, the same could be said of the situation in many developed countries, notwithstanding the recent banking problems in some of them. While there is no question that the banking system is the central part of any national financial system, it is sometimes missed that securities markets are equally important, albeit in a different respect. While a country cannot get along without a financial payment and clearing system, it is equally true that, if it is to have a market economy, it cannot get along without an equity market either. Banks, when behaving prudently, do not provide 100% financing to businesses; they expect adequate equity bases to support their loans. Thus, financial systems, and there are still many of them, that favor the banking system at the expense of the equity market are often doing damage to banking as well as impeding efficient economic growth. The recent debt crises in Latin America and the United States demonstrate this. Further, the importance of an efficient and transparent mechanism for measuring economic performance and risks in the capital allocation process cannot be overstated. In command economies and in countries where the banking system is dominant, financial analysis and performance measurement of economic units is either not done effectively or the results are seen by only a few. Conversely, with an active equity market, such information has a high degree of accuracy, is highly visible, widely disbursed, and actively used. Thus, successes and failures of economic units become common knowledge, forcing both public and private sector managements to perform or face replacement.

Consequently, a primary issue for policy makers and securities commissions is to ensure that the securities markets, and especially the equity markets, are given equal status with the banking system to allow them to fulfill their key role of providing long-term debt and permanent equity finance, and to complement the banking system's more conventional short-term working capital financing. Only a few countries have independent securities commissions where the chairman is appointed by the head of government. In most countries the chairman, even if appointed by the head of government, reports to a second or third ranking official in the ministry of finance or another, often junior, ministry. By comparison, the governor of the central bank usually reports directly to the minister of finance, or is independent. While such reporting lines may be considered as symbolism, they carry with them bureaucratic realities which are translated into practical advantages or disadvantages when it comes to implementing policies that are seen as threats to vested interests. The end result is that banking interests generally are better served than those of the securities markets.

This leads to considering the implications of the current move in many countries towards permitting the integration of banking and securities market institutions under circumstances where the banks will become more dominant. While there are claims as to the efficiencies that integration can provide, there is growing evidence as to the weakening effect it has on equity market development and the risks of abuses resulting from concentration of financial power and conflicts of interest. The evidence of the past indicates that countries with universal banking systems have smaller and less efficient equity markets and greater concentration of economic power than those countries that followed the U.S. Glass Steagall approach requiring the separation of these functions. Whether the pressures, especially in the United States, now resulting in the growing dominance of the banking system started with the increasing power that banks gained when they became the principal recyclers of petro dollars in the 1970s or with the banks' superior lobbying power, or both, is not important. What is important is for all countries to ascertain whether reducing prudential constraints on banks and allowing them to enter the securities business will help the economy, as promised by the proponents, or simply result in further concentration of power and a renewed race towards the lowest common denominator of national financial regulation, leading ultimately to weaker banks and a weaker economy, as feared by the opponents.

Finally, there is the matter of the internationalization of securities markets, as a means of both increasing domestic market efficiency and attracting foreign, politically neutral, equity from the capital exporting countries to those countries with capital shortages. The economic benefits a country can gain from opening its securities markets to foreign investors and from making it possible for their domestic companies to tap foreign capital markets for long-term funds are clear. History shows that countries which have opened their equity markets to foreigners to obtain lower cost capital have tended to do better economically and financially than those that have not. Japan, Hong Kong, and Singapore and, more recently Thailand, Malaysia, Chile, and Mexico are the best examples. Lower cost capital made available from foreign markets for new investment and being able to utilize the accompanying financial technology clearly have already benefited these countries. There have been three conventional instruments: country funds, low interest rate convertible bonds or bonds with warrants, as favored by Japanese companies, and equity issues in the form of ADRs taking advantages of the higher prices foreign investors are prepared to pay for an issue listed in their own market.

It is recognized that some countries have done well despite their limiting quite severely the inward flow of foreign portfolio equity. Until quite recently, Taiwan and Korea were examples. Many developing countries feared foreign "hot money" and "creeping takeovers" and, thus, limited portfolio capital inflows to closed-end country funds. However, for capital importing countries, the effects of the resulting over-reliance on foreign borrowing have been, at least in this last decade, devastating. In the meantime, these fears have not proven to be serious problems in practice. This is largely because portfolio investors have long-term time horizons and are not interested in controlling companies.

More importantly, the pool of capital in the international capital markets that developing countries can tap is larger now than that in both the international banking market and the group of multinational companies that provide direct investment. The challenge now for the developing countries is to tap this large and rapidly growing international capital market to raise new capital for their leading companies. The 1980s was the decade of emerging market country funds. Over 100 were established, raising over US $4 billion new capital for equity investments in developing countries. While there will be more new country funds, the 1990s will be the decade of international equity issues directly by companies located in developing countries. In 1991, over US $6 billion has been raised by such issues and the estimate for 1992 is for an even higher amount. The demand from international investors is growing rapidly and could reach $100 billion annually within the next five years.

For emerging markets to become mature, the acid test will be their desire and ability to become part of the global market. Their desire or political will to do so remains a function of both governmental policy makers and of the controlling interests of the domestic companies to welcome and encourage foreign portfolio investors. Their ability to do so will be a function of their technical skills and their willingness to import foreign financial technology if they do not have it. Failure to move towards financial maturity will condemn those countries and their companies to longer periods of economic under-performance than necessary.

The last 20 years have seen many countries that have addressed these financial market challenges. Some have already reaped the benefits. The early examples have been listed. More recently, Argentina and Indonesia have begun to see the beginnings of the benefits. Importantly, the new surge toward democracy worldwide may set the framework for major financial market reforms in the largest but most economically lagging countries, like Russia and China. The development of emerging markets, helped by privatization of government enterprises, over the next 20 years is bound to make a fascinating story. In the meantime, there is much to learn from the past. The fact that over the last 20 years, the size of the emerging markets increased more than tenfold in U.S. dollar terms and from less than 2% to more than 5% of global equity market capitalization suggests that the rate of expansion in the next period will be even faster as education, technology, and the acceptance of market economies also will be increasing at a more rapid rate than in the past.

After all, the now developing countries' GDP growth rates remain higher than those of the "mature" countries. Logic suggests that their share of global market capitalization should eventually reach the same percentage as their share of global GDP, which is now some 15%, even if some of the countries will no longer be defined as "developing" and their markets as "emerging."

PORTFOLIO MANAGEMENT IN EMERGING MARKETS: COUNTRY ALLOCATION AND STOCK RESEARCH

Antoine W. van Agtmael, President
Emerging Markets Management
Washington, D. C., United States

Fundamentally, portfolio management in emerging markets is not really different from the process through which asset categories, countries, and stocks are selected in more mature markets. An international money manager with a "top-down" orientation who invests in emerging markets faces two distinct issues: (1) how to first select and then allocate between the various markets; and (2) how to pick individual stocks within each of the markets. A "bottom-up" manager researches markets on a global basis with the aim of finding the most attractive companies within particular industries. In both cases, the objective is to add value through stock selection. The first type of manager is likely to compare more closely valuations and prospects of stocks *within a particular market in their historical and comparative context.* In contrast, the selection criteria of the second type of manager focuses on *global comparative* valuations. "Bottom-up" managers may ignore the explicit country allocation decision entirely and simply focus on companies, but there are such big differences in returns between markets and for the same market from year to year that it seems wise to give explicit attention to this issue. In any case, experience around the world has clearly demonstrated that returns on individual stocks within a market, despite their differences, show a relatively high degree of correlation with overall market returns.

Factors that Determine Market Returns and Risk

To construct a systematic approach (or quantitative model) for managing emerging market portfolios, first analyze the factors that are likely to determine market returns and risk (volatility) and determine to what extent they are different from those that influence the major industrialized markets. Then focus on specific indicators and statistics that measure each of these factors and how they relate to each other. The major factors that make emerging markets move are:

1. Valuation
2. Earnings growth and momentum
3. Investment alternatives (or interest rates)
4. Market liquidity
5. Economic policies and trends
6. Political environment
7. Market sentiment and speculation

Valuation

As a market becomes more expensive in a historic and comparative context, downside risk increases and upside potential diminishes. Of course, the extent to which markets may be compared without looking at "apples and oranges" is always a question mark in view of the differences between accounting methods. Over time, markets have a tendency to return to their long-term trendline although it is not easy to figure out how stable the trendline of an individual market is, particularly if fundamental economic changes have taken place or a market is opened up to foreign investors. A market is not overvalued simply because the market index has recently had a strong run. This may reflect an adjustment for inflation, a rise from previously depressed levels, or an expectation of or reaction to economic recovery. Thus, valuation should be viewed in light of both past and anticipated earnings growth, growth potential, and some measure of "intrinsic" value.

Commonly used measures of valuation include the market's price/earnings multiple, P/E to growth, price/cash flow, dividend yield, price/book value, price/adjusted book value, and price/replacement cost in addition to the market index in real terms. Differences in accounting methods distort comparisons between markets unless a serious effort is made to adjust for these distortions, which is not an easy task. Accounting methods may even distort *historical* comparisons when inflation or exchange rates change rapidly and erratically or there are changes in accounting (which has happened frequently in Brazil and Argentina).

Earnings Growth and Momentum

Investors tend to react (often dramatically) to a change in the *pattern* of earnings growth, particularly if it is unexpected. Unsophisticated markets react more to market rumor while better researched markets tend to focus on revisions in earnings estimates by leading analysts. Markets with traditions of strong earnings growth and expectations that high growth will continue typically trade at higher valuations but are also more vulnerable to earnings disappointments. The *potential* for earnings growth over longer periods is determined by a country's economic growth pattern while shorter-term changes often reflect the stage of the economic cycle (recession, recovery, peaking, and adjustment to new economic realities).

Economic policies also play a vital part in earnings growth potential as well as short-term ups and downs of earnings. For example, a major infrastructure spending program is likely to boost economic growth for some years, but a tightening of monetary policy leads to higher interest rates, lower demand, and less growth. Privatization, deregulation, and trade liberalization (three major tenets of the new economic policies pursued all over Latin America) typically depress profit margins of existing companies in the short run but boost productivity and economic activity in the longer run. Currency policy also affects the bottom line of companies. Wage pressures and inflation generally hurt currency competitiveness and profit margins, unless offset by currency devaluation or rising productivity.

Investment Alternatives (or Interest Rates)

Investors constantly compare stock market returns (from price appreciation and dividend yield) with how much they can earn from keeping their money in local bank deposits (or other short-term money market instruments), bonds (at least in countries with a history of moderate inflation), gold, foreign currency deposits (whether this is officially allowed or not), or investing in land or real estate. High short-term interest rates, the fear of a major devaluation, and a boom in land or real estate prices tend to drain money away from the stock market. Economic policies which promote negative real interest rates may make the stock market more attractive in the short run but are only an "investment illusion" as they also lead to capital flight, devaluation, and market instability.

Market Liquidity

Liquidity in the market is influenced by structural factors such as the savings and investment rates, development of local pension funds, restrictions on stock market investment by insurance companies, and the existence of mutual funds. Regulatory barriers (and their disappearance) against foreign portfolio investment also have a major impact, as evidenced by the jump in market prices after liberalizations in Indonesia, Sri Lanka, Pakistan, Brazil, and Peru. In the short run, monetary policy (through its effect on interest rates, current account surpluses, and deficits), and new issue activity (or "cash calls") are important.

Economic Policies and Trends

High growth countries offer ample opportunities for earnings growth and expansion which are typically rewarded by investors by higher price/earnings multiples.

Economic policies may put a country on a high growth path, but they may also promote stagnancy or instability, both of which investors try to avoid. While difficult to quantify, changes in economic policy are of crucial importance. For example, the (ultimately ill-fated) shock therapies in Brazil and Argentina led to short-term market booms that quickly fizzled when it became evident that their structural impact was not taking hold. More structural reforms such as Chile's market-oriented policies, Mexico's turnaround, Argentina's tying of the Austral to the dollar, or the opening up of the Indian and Chinese economies are having a more lasting effect. A judgment needs to be made: Are the reforms for real or are they just cosmetic? Moreover, countries are subject to economic cycles (with certain lead and lag effects) that have an impact on markets in the short run. Monetary tightening often foreshadows higher interest rates and a slowdown in earnings, and early signs of a recovery are often greeted with enthusiasm by the stock market. A careful analysis of major macro-economic indicators over longer time periods gives the analyst insights into the direction and strength of market reactions to economic events.

Political Environment

It is virtually impossible to quantify or even make sense of the impact of coups, changes in leadership, elections, revolutions, assassinations, and other less dramatic political events on stock markets. More often than not, the reaction is different from anticipated, not in the least because *fear* of such events taking place was already largely discounted in stock prices. If a judgment needs to be made, the key question to ask is whether the political event is likely to lead to significant changes in economic policy (toward or away from needed economic reforms) or to prolonged periods of market uncertainty.

Market Sentiment and Speculation

The impact of market sentiment on short-term market moves cannot be denied but, more often than not, it is virtually random "noise" which is of more importance to traders than longer term investors. Those with a two-to five-year investment view are best advised to completely ignore this factor or use it to their advantage as a contrary indicator. What is quantifiable is the intensity of market activity. Is trading volume on a rising or declining trend? Is it well above or below longer-term average turnover in that market? A sagging in the momentum of market activity may presage the peak of a speculative flurry, whereas low points in market activity often offer attractive opportunities for bargain hunting.

The Use of Modern Investment Techniques

Common modern investment techniques may be applied successfully in emerging equity markets, although the collection and maintenance of a long-time series of consistent and comparable data is much more difficult because of the impact of different inflation rates, exchange rate fluctuations, and discrepancies in accounting methods. In fact, in the major markets the use of quantitative models and other modern investment methods is so widespread in managing broadly diversified equity portfolios that it has eroded their potential for adding value in these markets. Interestingly, their application has been virtually absent in non-traditional asset classes, such as emerging markets, despite the fact that their use offers even greater potential in view of strong existing inefficiencies in both *country allocation* and *stock selection*. The downplaying of their use is perhaps also due to a perceived lack of data and familiarity with these "border" areas of the investible universe, the dramatic changes in economic policies (which make it difficult to establish trendlines), differences in accounting methods, and the limited number of specialized practicioners in this recently discovered area.

The First Step: Country Allocation

Investment management in emerging markets may be approached in three distinct steps: (1) country allocation, (2) stock selection within individual markets and (3) detailed company analysis. Central to a disciplined, top-down investment process is the idea that the bulk of the returns from investing in an internationally diversified equity portfolio is attributable to the country allocation decision rather than the individual security selection decision. This proposition is acutely valid in the case of emerging equity markets where individual market volatility is typically a multiple of volatility of developed countries' equity markets and where sophisticated foreign portfolio investment has begun to play a meaningful role only recently (and remains restricted largely to emerging Asia), thus leaving largely undisturbed the inefficiencies of individual emerging markets.

An Emerging Market's Country Allocation Model [1]

A typical emerging market's country allocation model uses value-based derivations of expected equity market returns together with historical measures of volatility and correlations as the measured components of portfolio risk to systematically allocate between competing emerging markets. The model incorporates the technology of modern portfolio theory, a mean-variance optimizer, to provide portfolio construction guidance using notions of risk and return that are now a part of the common

[1]This section on the country allocation model by Michael A. Duffy, Managing Director, Emerging Markets Management.

machinery of investment management.[2] The application of these no longer exotic techniques to emerging markets requires a significant amount of data discovery and an accommodation to the comparatively short series of historical market data for many of the individual countries in our investment orbit. Despite these data difficulties and deficiencies, a relatively simple tactical asset allocation methodology may provide solid value, as individual emerging markets swing from the extremes of overvaluation and undervaluation with great volatility. In short, the model provides a *disciplined top-down investment process* enabling the manager or investor to profitably navigate in the rough seas of emerging markets.

An emerging market's country allocation model derives from the assumptions common to all mean variance optimizers, i.e., that market players trade off return and volatility in a consistent manner, that the co-movement of individual countries' equity markets and volatility characteristics are relatively stable over time, and that market returns can be modeled in some way. The country allocation ultimately suggested by the model is a theoretically efficient portfolio providing the highest return for a given level of volatility and a portfolio that provides an acceptable tradeoff of risk and return. This acceptable tradeoff of risk and return, or risk tolerance, has been defined in terms of the historical return/volatility combination available to an investor in an internationally diversified equity portfolio as embodied in the Morgan Stanley Capital International EAFE Index. This approach is graphically portrayed in Figure 4-1.

Each point on the efficient frontier represents a unique country allocation producing a portfolio of the highest achievable return for a given volatility level. This locus of points is determined by the expected returns in each country's equity market, the historical volatility of each country's market returns, and correlations between the returns of each country's markets. The optimal allocation is found in the portfolio identified by an equality between what markets offer in return/risk tradeoff (the efficient frontier) and what investors require in a return/risk tradeoff (i.e., the investor's required risk-return schedule). In order to achieve an acceptably broad diversification at all times, maximum country allocations are constrained to certain multiples of their market weight.

The individual markets that achieve the highest relative allocations are those with the most favorable combinations of high returns, low volatility, and a low correlation with other attractive markets. For each country's equity market, expected returns vary over time with the swings in valuation and earnings producing changes over time in the model's allocation recommendations. In this model, expected returns are derived assuming two fundamental drivers of expected equity market performance: the *valuation* level of the market (over/undervalued) in the context of the market's historical as well as comparative performance and the degree to which expected *earnings growth* is "abnormally" high or low. In determining expected

---

[2]In fact, Harry Markowitz, winner of the Nobel prize for economics, pioneered the mean variance optimizing approach to investment management.

Figure 4-1   Mean-Variance Asset Allocation Model

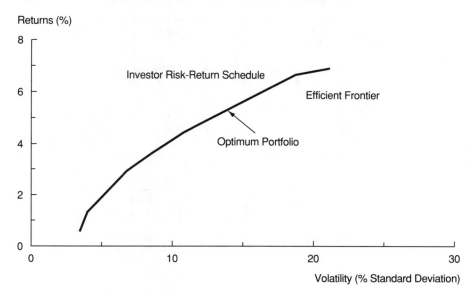

returns, investment managers using a country allocation model will differ on the weights they assign to growth versus valuation components.

Normalization of the fundamental valuation data proceeds from two principles: (1) a country's returns are determined primarily by domestic market considerations; and (2) accounting methods differ more significantly between markets than they differ between time periods in the same market. Thus, a market with a low P/E in relation to its own history appears more attractive than another market with a lower P/E but for which the P/E is unusually high in relation to its own history. A schematic description of the model is shown in Figure 4-2.

While the model's country mix recommendations are a key discipline in the investment process, the model should represent only the starting point for allocation considerations rather than final conclusions. It is the navigational instrument rather than the pilot. Investment managers (the "pilots") also have to make informed judgments in order to account for the myriad of factors that are not part of any formal model but are likely to affect returns and allocations. Other important factors which should be *systematically* examined include various macroeconomic variables that have a direct impact on medium-term economic prospects, currency competitiveness, financial market liquidity, and political risks which may limit favorable polit-

Figure 4-2   Asset Allocation Model

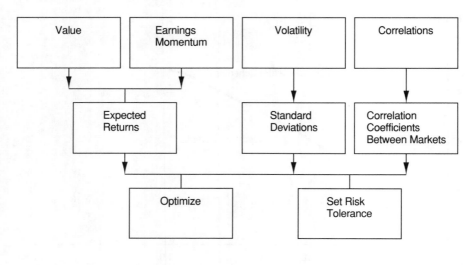

ical or economic developments, although political considerations are often subjective and imprecise.

Second Step: Stock Selection Within Each Market

Only after establishing a target allocation by country follows the second step of actual *stock selection within each market.* Stocks available for foreign investment are first screened for certain minimum market capitalization and liquidity requirements (which brings down the potential investment orbit considerably). Then a range (buy-hold-sell) for each of the stocks in the remaining orbit may be established in terms of their relative attractiveness within that market on the basis of fundamental characteristics of value and growth.

Before a stock "passes" as a potential candidate for the target portfolio, the *final step in this stock selection process is a thorough, bottom-up analysis* which includes a review of several years of financial data. These may be summarized in a computerized company data sheet to allow an easy, quantitative comparison of growth, valuation, and financial strength. Differences in accounting treatment, in particular the different methods of inflation accounting in Latin America, and the variety of required language skills suggest that this process is still far from the "cookie cutting" stage. Moreover, as is the case with the quantitative part of the country allocation, this purely quantitative part of the analysis provides a much-needed discipline but is not sufficient. Meetings with management and plant visits remain an essential part of the investment process in order to obtain a first-hand impression of important considerations such as international competitiveness, corporate culture, and hidden assets and liabilities.

The remainder of this chapter focuses on issues involved in researching emerging markets stocks, methods that may be used for screening stocks within a particular market or industry, aspects to focus on in a company analysis within an emerging market environment (which is often quite different from the more mature context of major international markets), ways of finding stocks with attractive long-term potential, and avoiding those which hide downside risk under cosmetic appeal.

Emerging markets tend to be less efficient than the major industrialized markets. In other words, new and other relevant information regarding a particular company or industry is less immediately reflected in relative prices. This is often viewed as a *risk* of emerging markets, but it should rather be seen as an opportunity for investors because it means that it is still possible to "discover" stocks that are undervalued.

Research Requirements

Availability of information published on an annual and quarterly basis by companies is a first requirement for any research effort. To the surprise of many newcomers to emerging markets, disclosure and reporting standards imposed by local securities market legislation are usually more than adequate to make informed judgments assuming a good knowledge of local language and accounting standards. Until recent years, the main comprehensive information available besides annual reports from the companies themselves was from stock exchanges or securities commissions. They often published a daily market index and an annual fact book as well as compiled historic databases on markets and individual listings, sometimes including summaries of data from balance sheet and income statements. However, the availability and quality of local research varies enormously. While each investor makes his or her own independent judgments, it often makes sense to "piggy back" internal research efforts on external research available from brokers and stock exchanges as a starting point.

Availability of Local Research

Traditionally, stock price movements in many emerging markets were driven more by market rumor than thorough analysis, despite the fact that much of the standard financial information required for fundamental company analysis was often available. More often than not, stock trading was short-term oriented and the main market participants were a rather small group of individuals and brokers together with occasional involvement by banks, insurance companies, and other institutional investors. As a result, local brokers in many emerging markets saw little demand for company reports from their customers until the mid 1980s and gave research little attention with sporadic exceptions. Research, if done at all by local brokers, was typically primitive by international standards, mostly descriptive and focusing only on limited historic data while rarely including independent earnings forecasts.

The advent of more active participation by international institutional investors in many markets has created a real demand for research for the first time. Brokers are now increasingly selected on the basis of the comprehensiveness and quality of their research product. Regional brokers were locked out of direct participation in markets because of limitations on stock exchange membership in many countries. They had no choice but to make a name for themselves by filling the vacuum left by local brokers. As international investors increasingly traded through the regional brokers, local brokers caught on to the need of more efforts in this area and began to create databases and research departments.

As a result, the availability of research in Asian emerging markets (except the Indian subcontinent), Mexico, Portugal and, more recently, Argentina has undergone a rapid and profound transformation during the past few years. Regional and local brokers have beefed up their efforts from virtually nothing to increasingly insightful analyses. Research on Latin America (with the exception of Mexico) still lags well behind while, in any case, inflation accounting and drastic currency fluctuations make it hard to compare company information with the rest of the world or even in a historic context. Research on Greece and Turkey is improving but is still behind that of most Asian markets. The absence of well-established accounting principles and the pervasive effect of price controls and government intervention still prohibit the development of research in Eastern Europe but this will undoubtedly change rapidly over the next decade.

The improvement in the availability of research from brokers and other sources does not mean that an investor would now be well advised to base his or her investment decisions on recent brokers reports without independent analysis. The main problems with relying too heavily on external research are that coverage of companies remains limited to those which are more actively traded, and broker interest seems to move in cycles from and to particular stocks and industries while earnings forecasts and buy recommendations are often influenced by the peer pressures of market consensus. Not infrequently, favorable reports are prepared in connection with new issues for which the broker is an underwriter or, worse, after the broker has "front run" the market by purchasing an inventory of the stock. These practices are prevalent particularly in countries with inadequate securities legislation or a weak securities commission. It is more useful to view data and analysis from external broker research as "raw material" for the investor's own research efforts. Unless the investor has no independent research capability (in which case he or she should probably not get involved in the market or use a specialized investment manager for this purpose), "buy" and "sell" recommendations from brokers are only a useful guide to figuring out market consensus and perhaps short-term trading opportunities but are less reliable for long-term investment purposes.

Stock selection within a market represents the second and third step of the *three-step process* of portfolio management. The same steps may be used for stock selection within an industry on a global basis or the emerging market orbit. After country allocation, the next step is a screening of all stocks (or those on which data are available) within the market or industry. This will facilitate the last step (and focus of the research efforts) by weeding out a number of stocks that are unlikely candidates for ultimate investment because of size, liquidity, volatility, financial strength, or other criteria that may be used. The final step zeroes in on the selected sample and subjects those companies to a more rigorous analysis. Obviously, screening stocks on the basis of a series of benchmarks requires vast amounts of historic data.

Screening the Market or Industry

It is virtually impossible to analyze all emerging markets stocks in detail. Over 9,200 stocks are listed in the 20 major emerging markets although some 6,000 of those are double listings on the various Indian exchanges. This leaves a more realistic number of 3,200 stocks as a potential research orbit. Electronic market monitoring services, such as Reuter, provide daily price quotes on some 2,000 stocks in over 20 emerging markets. Typically, between 100 and 700 stocks are listed in individual markets, but in most cases between 25 and 100 stocks dominate the market capitalization and constitute the bulk of the trading volume. The IFC Emerging Markets Data Base monitors over 800 of the most actively traded stocks with the aim of including at least 60% of the market capitalization in each country as part of its index. Morgan Stanley Capital International includes approximately 250 stocks in its Emerging Markets Global Index.

Usually, a diversified investment portfolio consists of 20-200 stocks. A portion of such a portfolio is likely to consist of the blue chips in various markets which can be found among those with the largest market capitalization and the greatest liquidity. However, unless the investor seeks to mimic the return of one of the emerging markets indices, he or she may want to include smaller and less discovered stocks with strong earnings potential or asset backing which requires screening of less commonly known stocks. The following simple screening criteria may be used effectively to narrow the research orbit without significant risk of missing out on attractive stocks:

1. *Size:* A minimum market capitalization, net worth, revenues, or profits may be used. Investors with a broadly diversified portfolio or those specializing in investing just in emerging markets or a particular country are likely to set a much lower limit than those who seek just a few stocks in the entire emerging market orbit. Those investors who try to

achieve an index-type return should keep in mind that several local market indices (particularly in Latin America) use a basket of the most actively traded stocks, irrespective of market capitalization.

2. *Liquidity:* A minimum trading volume for the past year (or two to five years) or number of days traded over a recent period may be used. An alternative is setting a minimum percentage of the total shares outstanding which is available for trading by others than the majority owners ("float"). The risk of setting this benchmark too high is that many stocks remain illiquid until they are "discovered" by brokers or investors resulting in a major price jump. Some of the most attractive investment opportunities are small, illiquid stocks but, of course, a well-diversified portfolio should not be too heavily invested in illiquid stocks because it is often more difficult to trade out of these stocks than to buy them.

3. *Financial strength:* Minimum net worth, debt/equity ratio, current ratio, working capital, debt service coverage, or other similar ratio are used as screens to avoid investing in potential bankruptcies. Caution should again be used because financial weakness is usually discounted in the stock price and temporary problems in this area may represent opportunities for a turnaround.

4. *Relative market valuation:* Recent price history or more fundamental valuation criteria such as price/earnings multiple, price/book value, price/cash flow, or dividend yield may be chosen as indicators of current and potential market performance. Having historic data helps in analyzing whether a stock trades at a relatively stable discount or premium to its market/industry or whether and why this range is subject to high volatility. When longer-term data are available, a range relative to the market (or industry) for each stock over a historic period may be calculated which serves as a useful guide in establishing buy/hold/sell points. Instead of relying on historical ranges, investors may develop their own system for formulating a relative valuation range based on such factors as quality of earnings, earnings growth, financial strength, international competitiveness, and adjusted asset value.

The Final Step: Detailed Company Analysis

Screening the universe of stocks within a market or industry narrows down the choice to a more manageable number. The final task is to analyze this target list of 300-800 portfolio candidates in much greater detail. The financial statements of a company and, if available, various brokers reports are a first input into this process. Local newspaper and magazine clippings as well as articles in trade journals and global industry or commodity reports issued by various brokerage houses are also indispensable. Such a desk analysis may already eliminate a further group of companies from consideration but in the final analysis, there is no substitute for visiting countries for discussions with the company's management, competitors, suppliers, customers, government officials, bankers, trade union representatives, and journalists. The research analyst acts very much like a detective, searching for missing clues and clearing up misleading or inaccurate information.

Researching emerging markets stocks is often more rewarding (and fun) than the same process in the United States and other industrialized countries where information is more abundant and investigative reporting better developed. In addition, securities legislation prevents the more blatant abuse of insider information and stock manipulation through the "planting" of stories by brokers and other interested parties. Management is sometimes more reluctant to disclose business secrets but is also often intrigued by the novelty of an interview and less restrained in discussing competitors or seemingly innocuous business aspects which may be the missing pieces of the puzzle the analyst is looking for. As always, good preparation is the key to a successful company interview. Few managers can resist their pride in their company's successes or a rebuttal of an allegation by a competitor, regulator, journalist, or trade union representative.

Issues to be analyzed from financial statements and through company visits are found in Figure 4-3. The objective is not just to understand the company and its environment but to find out whether there are special aspects, problems, or opportunities which the market consensus has not yet discounted in the price of the stock. Although broker research has improved in many emerging markets, they remain—in various degrees—less efficient and underresearched. Language barriers, accounting practices, and less available and transparent information present not only problems but also represent opportunities for diligent analysts to find "jewels in the rough."

Effort expended on projecting earnings in great detail without critically examining the assumptions on which growth, margins, prices, the market, and financial burden are based may be a waste of time.

In an emerging markets context, there are three main questions to focus on. Some are aspects which a securities analyst trained in the industrialized markets may overlook.

- Is the company internationally competitive and likely to remain so?

- What is the impact of deregulation and other macroeconomic changes?

- How will new economic alliances such as Free Trade Agreements affect the company?

Figure 4-3   Structure of a Company Report

Background

- When founded, when listed
- Major lines of business
- Market share
- Ranking within industry (e.g., largest of four companies...)
- Exports
- Major institutional owners (if any), part of a group? Percentage float ?
- Number of employees/shareholders
- Known as a major blue chip?

Major Factors

1. Valuation
   - How do P/E, P/Cash flow, dividend yield, P/sales, and P/BV compare with the market and industry?
   - Are P/E and P/BV cheap on historic basis?
   - Quality of earnings?
   - Is P/E, etc., attractive in view of growth prospects?
2. Earnings Growth and Potential
   - Cyclical or stable earnings?
   - Do market conditions/economy favor growth?
   - Is earnings growth accelerating? Why? Temporary or sustainable?
   - Earnings growth from operations or "extraordinary" items?
   - Sales growth or margin expansion? Why? Sustainable?
   - Is production process becoming more efficient? Why?
   - Is earnings growth real or accounting gimmick?
   - High inflation countries impact of monetary correction?
   - Is company expanding? Are capital expenditures adequate?
   - Does company invest in R&D?
3. Special Aspects (Unnoticed by market)
   - Turnaround situation (factors that inhibited profits in the past have disappeared or change in management).
   - Asset play (undervalued land, real estate, investments, cash).
   - Market unaware nature of company has changed?
4. Financial Condition
   - Healthy/stable operating margin, ROE, ROA?
   - Acceptable debt/equity, current ratio, interest coverage? Improving or deteriorating?
   - Adequate asset turnover?
   - Can capital expenditures be financed adequately?
   - Impact of changes in interest rates or inflation?
   - Changes in receivables/sales or inventories/sales?
5. Impact of Economic Reforms
   - Is existing monopoly/cartel being broken up?
   - Dependent on protection? Risk of losing protection or subsidies?
   - Is government slow on paying government contracts?
   - Competitive bidding where company was previously favored?
   - Import liberalization a threat?
   - Privatization offers opportunities for takeovers or causes additional competition?
6. Market/(International) Competitiveness
   - Is market changing? Growing? Declining?
   - Is company falling behind/gaining technologically?
   - What factors make the company/country internationally competitive (labor costs, technology, raw materials, energy, "piggy back" on well developed industry)?

Figure 4-3   (Continued)

- Who are its world class competitors in the same country? Abroad? What countries?
- Are producers in other countries becoming more competitive?
- Has inflation or overvaluation of currency changed international competitiveness?
- New competitors in market?
- Are existing competitors expanding or becoming more efficient?

7. Management

- Does management have a clear strategic vision? Does vision make sense?
- Is operating management experienced? Tight? Quality oriented? Motivating?
- Is the founder still the manager? How much is the family involved?
- Is there a level of professional managers? What is their reputation?
- Does management have a reputation for honesty in dealing with suppliers, key staff, employees?
- Is management dependent on close relations with government officials for its contracts?
- Is management known to "siphon off" revenues before distributing profits to minority shareholders?
- Are bathrooms in factory clean?
- How are labor relations? Have there been strikes or are any expected?
- What is reputation of company for employee training?
- Are the "best and brightest" attracted to working with the company?

8. Plant and Equipment

- Are plants modern? Well laid out? Do they offer economies of scale?
- Is machinery technologically up-to-date in comparison with world class competitors?
- What has been the experience with productivity levels and increases (in comparison with world-class competitors)?

9. Cost Structure

- Are prices of raw materials likely to fall/increase?
- Changes in use of energy (from oil to gas, coal, or bagasse, etc.)?
- How has cost of labor increased? And in future?
- Major changes in productivity?
- Does a planned expansion offer economies of scale? Or does financing raise interest costs too much in comparison with world class competitors?

10. Accounting Aspects

- Is the company audited by an internationally recognized firm?
- Do accounting standards used differ from those common in the country and industry?
- What is the impact of monetary correction on balance sheet and income statement? How does it influence the quality and sustainability of earnings in comparison with other companies in that country and industry?
- Is land and real estate "on the books" undervalued or overvalued because of inflation adjustments and in/decreases in market prices?
- Does the company have (listed or unlisted) subsidiaries? Are they consolidated or accounted for on an equity or dividend basis? Will there be changes in this accounting method and what will their impact be?
- Does the company have guarantees to or loans to/from affiliates?
- Are there unlisted affiliates in the group? Are there intercompany transactions through which profits could be siphoned off?

Figure 4-3   (Continued)

Additional Questions for Specialized Areas

Banking
- Is capital in accordance with B.I.S. requirements?
- Is spread between cost of funds and lending rate increasing?
- Does bank benefit from an environment of high interest rates or low interest rates?
- What is the loan/deposit ratio?
- Does the bank have many branches or is it dependent on interbank funding?
- How high is fee income? Growing?
- Does the bank have attractive real estate assets (branches, headquarters, collateral on defaulted loans?
- Is income from capital gains/losses on securities transactions important?
- What is the bank's customer mix? Does it have a clear strategy?
- To what extent are maturities of assets and liabilities matched (e.g., many long-term, fixed-rate loans with short-term deposits, mortgage loans?)
- Any major known bad debts? Bad debt experience rising or improving? Outlook?
- Bad debt provisions (as percentage of risk assets) adequate in view of experience? How does it compare with other banks?
- Any changes in bank regulation or entry of foreign competition?
- Are operations computerized? What areas are not computerized yet?
- Are computer systems integrated? Linked with international systems (e.g., SWIFT)?
- How many ATMs (automatic teller machines) in comparison with competitors?

Mining:
- How many years of reserves? Quality of reserves?
- Exploration programs? Making use of satellite photography?
- Any new land concessions expected?
- Are energy costs high in comparison with international levels?
- What are the trends in worldwide demand? Substitution products?
- Are major new mines coming on stream?
- Are production costs high by international standards?
- Transportation costs? Own railroad?

Conglomerates
- How are affiliates accounted for? Consolidates, equity, or dividend accounting?
- Are consolidated statements available?
- Are there hidden debts? Guarantees?
- Is the strategic mix of operations sensible? Are businesses related or unrelated? Vertically integrated? How is it changing? Why?
- Do new acquisitions make strategic sense? Does management have the experience to deal with new operations?

International Competitiveness

Many companies in emerging markets were established in a protected economic environment without much international competition and, within the domestic market, operated as an effective monopoly or member of a cartel. In recent years, countries are increasingly abandoning import substitution policies in favor of a more open, deregulated, competitive economic model. Under this new economic policy framework, companies survive and thrive only when they are not just able to beat domestic competition and imports but have a distinct competitive advantage on a wordwide basis. The analysis should focus on basic competitive advantages (or disadvantages) based on raw materials, labor, land, capital (a rarity outside the industrialized world), climate, location, access to cheap energy or industrial tradition, as well as management attitude. Those rare companies that are not protected from competition through some natural barrier (for example, electric utilities) or those that function in a unique, small local niche of the market (for example, certain national foods) must *think* as world class producers and have the size and cost structure to compete globally; otherwise they will not grow or will even wither away.

Impact of deregulation

The need to be internationally competitive has already been cited as one of the results of the modern economic reforms that many emerging markets are adopting. But the impact of such reforms is more pervasive. First, price controls and subsidies to producers and consumers are disappearing, thus leading to more realistic prices. Second, the need to obtain licenses for new projects (effectively creating cartels) and, more generally, industrial policy of many government bureaucracies favored major existing conglomerates (who overdiversified as a result into businesses where they had no competitive advantage) in the past and discriminated against local newcomers and foreign companies. Instead, foreign investment is more openly welcomed and competition is promoted. Third, public enterprises which often functioned as monopolies are being privatized and their work force subjected to the test of market productivity. As a result of all of these developments, local entrepreneurs need to spend less time seeking government favors and contracts but need to focus more on whether and how they are able to produce competitively at world market prices.

New Economic Alliances

New economic alliances are being formed in Asia, Latin America, and the Mediterranean area. In Asia, Japanese investment dominates new projects in many countries and the resulting subcontracting, licensing, and marketing ties are a key factor. In Greece, Portugal, and Turkey, the impact of membership (or not) in the Common Market are essential to understand a company's market opportunities. A more recent development is the establishment of Free Trade Agreements (partially in response to other economic alliances being formed) between the United States and Mexico; in the Caribbean, between Mexico and Chile; and in the South of Latin America between Brazil, Argentina, Uruquay, and Paraguay (Mercosur). While companies are only beginning to adjust to these new competitive realities and opportunities, the effects will be much more far reaching than many presently recognize. Management awareness, adaptability, and vision will be hard to measure but essential qualitative factors in a company's growth, risks, and prospects.

The ultimate objective of any "value-oriented" company analysis is to determine whether there is anything unnoticed by the market which makes the company special. As discussed earlier in this chapter, market return is usually the most important factor in individual share price movements but stock selection may add to long-term performance. In his book, *One up on Wall Street,* Peter Lynch classifies companies in the United States on the basis of several attributes which make a company particularly attractive as an investment (high growth, turnaround, asset play, depressed cyclical.....). Because emerging markets are under-researched and less efficient, it is even more possible than in the major markets to find stocks which are undiscovered by local investors or are out of favor making them cheaper than they should be. Analysts should look for six major factors which may lead to long-term outperformance:

1. ***Strong, sustainable but unrecognized growth potential:*** Small companies operating in a newly discovered market niche and large companies that are in a major growth sector fall into this category. Analysts must set aside their preconceived ideas and recognize that slow growth industries in the industrialized world may be on a fast growth track in emerging markets because of differences in infrastructure needs, changes in distribution systems, demographic trends, and competitive advantages. Examples include the following: (1) telephone companies which are mature in the United States, Europe, and Japan but growing at a phenomenal pace in many developing countries; (2) retailers that are increasingly replacing smaller outlets; or (3) pulp and paper companies which may be a dying industry in the major markets but benefit from fast growing eucalyptus trees in Brazil and Chile. Another important part of this analysis is to figure out whether a particular industry has or will achieve the critical mass and support industries to be competitive on a worldwide basis, or whether it is, in fact losing this advantage. For example, the footwear industry used to be concentrated in Korea and Taiwan but increasingly moved first to Thailand and then to Indonesia and China. Growth potential should not only be strong but also sustainable in the longer run. And finally, the attractiveness of a stock disappears as rapidly as its price earnings multiple climbs. Only when growth is not adequately recognized by the market does it make an interesting investment opportunity.

2. ***Illiquid or boring:*** While popular stocks and industries typically sell at high price/earnings multiples, sectors that do not attract this attention can be bought more cheaply and are often better values. Illiquid stocks with little past price movements and trading activity rarely attract a broker following and may languish despite a high return on investment, strong margins, and excellent financial condition. Such stocks are often considered "boring" because "nothing happens to the price." However, sometimes a major reason for the lack of float in a stock is that the owners are not willing to sell at what they consider to be undervalued prices but turn into active sellers of at least a portion of their holdings once a certain value is reached. It may take months to accumulate a reasonable position in such stocks without moving prices but for long-term investors who are not interested in immediate performance and are not concerned about locking themselves in for a longer period, such stocks may be among the most interesting around. Sooner or later, brokers or other investors will "discover" them and, then, the lack of liquidity is, in fact an advantage to existing shareholders because prices are pushed up quickly.

3. ***Hidden assets:*** Finding what Peter Lynch calls "asset plays" in emerging markets takes painstaking analysis, reading of footnotes, detailed knowledge of accounting quirks in various countries, and even visits to land and property registrars, but the results may be especially rewarding. There are three main types of hidden assets. The first type is based on local accounting standards in many emerging markets. Earnings of subsidiaries are not consolidated but only dividends (if they are declared at all) are included. Because so many major corporations in emerging markets are conglomerates, this may hide substantial profits (or losses). Second, book values for land, machinery, stock holdings, and other fixed assets are sometimes inadequately adjusted for inflation even when inflation accounting is used especially when they were purchased many years ago. Third, in depressed economic environments, land and real estate on the company's books may not at all reflect values in a more dynamic economic environment. Some companies have plants, distribution facilities, or other buildings in strategic locations and could move their production facilities. Agribusinesses or plantations often own potentially valuable land banks. Banks may own substantial properties from foreclosed developers.

4. ***Turnaround potential:*** Losses may suddenly turn into profits when price controls are removed, a new management takes over, assets are sold off, new activities started, debts restructured, or prices in a cyclical industry are rising again. Companies with a poor earnings history or shaky financials are rarely fashionable with investors. It is the challenge

of the analyst to find out whether the causes of past earnings or debt problems were temporary or due to poor management.

5. ***Building a brand name:*** Many companies in emerging markets are subcontractors of multinationals or other major marketing companies who earn a major share of the retail price because food and other consumer goods are sold at the best margins when there is a strong brand name. Few emerging markets companies have reached the stage at which their name and image are widely recognized, with the possible exception of some of the major Korean companies. Several Korean companies (Samsung, Gold Star, Hyundai) are now recognizing the importance of brand names, while a few others have even purchased international names. For example, Unicord in Thailand bought Bumble Bee, a major tuna brand, and Semitech bought the Singer Company for its well-recognized name in sewing machines and other consumer goods. Concha y Toro, a Chilean wine, and Corona beer from Mexico are examples of brands which are becoming widely recognized in the United States. Those companies which develop brand loyalty and strong international distribution capabilities have an opportunity to become the new, emerging blue chips of the future.

6. ***Undervalued privatizations:***   Many poorly managed state enterprises are being privatized in Latin America and Eastern Europe. They often (but obviously not always) represent potential turnaround situations. Spectacular examples have been the telephone companies in Mexico and Argentina, but there are many others. A careful analysis is required, however, because a state monopoly may lose its privileged status, debt levels may be high, and the new market environment more competitive, etc.

SECTION **II**

ASIA

KOREA*

Keith K. H. Park, Partner
Global Strategies Group
Los Angeles, United States

The Korean equity market, which had been a sleepy place unknown to international institutional investors during the first half of the 1980s, started attracting attention as it splendidly surged during the second half of the 1980s. Between the end of 1985 and the first quarter of 1989, Korean equities rose 514% in local currency terms. See Figure 5-1 for the performance of the Korean equity market since 1984 in comparison with IFC Composite Index and MSCI EAFE Index. As the 1990s began, the Korean equity market had grown to become the world's largest emerging market.

As of the end of 1990, the Korean equity market accounted for 23% of the market capitalization of IFC Composite Index and was larger than some of the major established equity markets, including Switzerland. Figure 5-2 details the Korean and regional market capitalizations of IFC Composite Index. In the beginning of 1992, the Korean market was liberalized to include foreign investment and, consequently, it is frequently studied by international institutional investors who look for the diversification of portfolio and enhancement of returns.

The rising current account surpluses of Korea, which were poured into its equity market, were largely responsible for the stellar performance of the Korean market during the second half of the 1980s. As the world economy came out of recession in the early 1980s and began its longest-run, peacetime economic expansion, the Korean economy, which heavily relies its growth on export, found strong international demand for its products. During the second half of the 1980s, Korea accumulated current account surpluses of US $33 billion, and its GNP expanded in

*The author would like to thank Ahn Suk Cho, Chief Representative of Hanshin Securities Company's New York office for his valuable suggestions.

**Figure 5-1   Korean Market Performance in Comparison
with Major Global Markets**

US $ Total Return Indices/December 1984 = 100

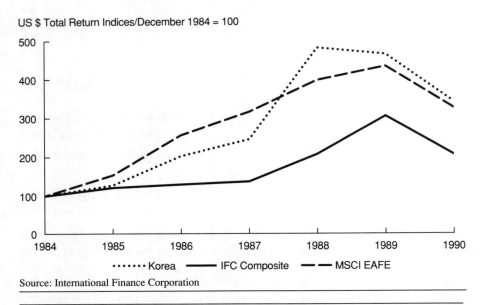

Source: International Finance Corporation

Figure 5-2   Composition of World Emerging Markets

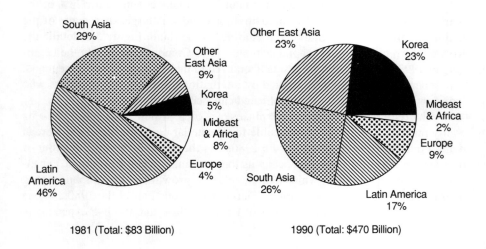

Source: International Finance Corporation

double digit rates — between 1985 and 1989 the average growth rate was 10%. See Figure 5-3 for the yearly current account balances of Korea and its real GNP growth rates since 1981.

Because foreign exchange control was strictly imposed in Korea, the trade surpluses of Korea could not be recycled into international capital markets. Given their limited investment choices, Koreans directed their newly-acquired wealth mainly to their equity and real estate markets. Subsequently, the Korean equity market saw its market capitalization grow by 1800% between the end of 1985 and that of 1989— from US $7.4 bn of 1985 to US $140.5 bn in 1989. Also, the apartment prices in Seoul shot up so high that in 1990 they exceeded those in New York.

This growth has brought about a significant change in Korean corporate financing. Korean companies, which heavily relied on bank loans, looked to the equity market as a more efficient and cheaper source of their corporate financing. Top-rated Korean firms were paying bank loan interest over 15%. Consequently, the number of listed companies on the Korea Stock Exchange (KSE) increased from 342 in 1985 to 687 in 1990. See Figure 5-4 for the change in the number of listed companies on the KSE and the Korean market performance since 1981.

Moreover, the Korean government saw equity financing as a means to wean Korean conglomerates from their heavy reliance on high-cost bank loan financing, and by doing so they sought to increase the competitiveness of Korean firms.

**Figure 5-3   Current Account Balances and
GNP Growth Rates of Korea**

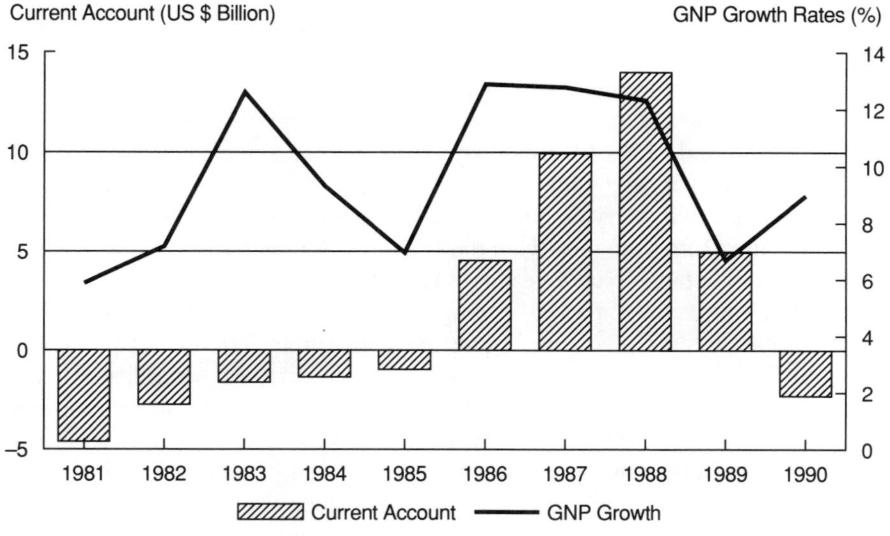

Source: Ssangyong Research Institute

**Figure 5-4   Number of Listed Companies on the KSE
                and Market Performance**

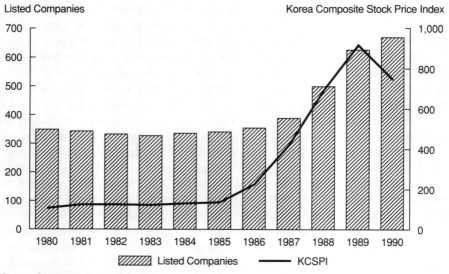

Source: Ssangyong Research Institute

Consequently, the average debt-equity ratios of Korean firms fell from as high as 500% in the mid-1980s to the current 220%. The government projected the Korea Stock Exchange as an integral part of the domestic capital markets. Also, it attempted to achieve an equitable redistribution of newly acquired wealth from export by pressuring family-controlled conglomerates to go public. These conglomerates, called chaebols in Korea, have been producing more than 90% of Korean GNP. At the end of 1985, only 2% of Korean population owned stocks, but at the end of 1989, this ratio dramatically jumped to 45%.

While this gravity-defying bull market was going in full throttle, international institutional investors were mostly on the sidelines. A direct access to the Korean equity market by international investors was not possible. The Korean Ministry of Finance (MoF) limited the market opening to the floatation of indirect investment vehicles, such as close-end country funds and convertible Eurobonds. The Korea Fund— the first exchange-traded, close-end country ever created —was listed on the New York Stock Exchange in August 1984 and was trading at a steep premium during most of the second half of the 1980s because of its novelty, offering an access to the closed, stellar-performing Korean market. Given its popularity, the Korea Europe Fund was subsequently listed on the London Stock Exchange in March 1987.

In addition to the exchange-traded country funds, there was a flurry of issuance of convertible Eurobonds by Korean corporations, which also offered international investors indirect access to the Korean equity market. They were also bought by international investors at significant premiums, given the superb performance of the Korean market and the accessibility to the market they offered. During this bullmarket, the xenophobic Korean Ministry of Finance was slow to respond to international demand for market liberalization. However, the outlook for the Korean market started changing quickly after the first quarter of 1989. The market began heading south, and the MoF had a change of heart in order to prop up the market by attracting international investors via the 1992 market liberalization.

Market Performance Since 1989

After the Korea Composite Stock Price Index (KCSPI) broke through the 1,000 level in early April 1989 from its rebased level of 100 on January 4, 1980, the bull market began running out of steam. In 1989, the Korean market ended the year with a gain of mere 0.28% and saw its total market capitalization shrink by almost 25% in 1990. When Korean equities rose tenfold from 1980 to early 1989, their average price/earning ratio was approaching 30. Given any standard at that time — except Japanese equities whose P/E ratios were well over 50 — Korean equities were overvalued. However, in early 1989 the future earning prospect for Korean firms was rosier than ever before, and Korea was perceived by many in the West to become another Japan, Inc. in no time.

Because equities are not valued by present earnings but by future earning potential, the valuation of Korean equities might have not been far off from the efficient equilibrium of the market in early 1989. However, after the first quarter of 1989, the fundamentals of the Korean economies began changing dramatically. Labor cost and the Korean Won rose so substantially that goods manufactured in Korea began losing their global competitiveness significantly. The Korean labor, which was once well-disciplined and docile under the dictatorial regimes of President Park and President Chun, began demanding their rights and higher wages. Rowdy labor strikes ensued and Korean export machines lay idle many times in 1989. By the end of 1989, labor costs had risen more than 60% since 1987.

Furthermore, the Korean government was accused by the United States (which had been running a significant amount of trade deficits with Korea throughout the 1980s) of manipulating its currency to remain artificially undervalued. By the end of 1989, the Korean Won appreciated some 25% vis-a-vis U.S. dollar from 1985. These two unfavorable factors, combined with rising inflation and import, brought about major setbacks to the Korean economy. In 1989, the economy grew at a half rate of the previous three years. In 1990, the Korean economic problems seemed incurable and the equity market fell 23.5%. As it nears the 1992 market liberalization, the Korean equity market seems to be stabilizing. As of October 1991, the market was down 0.02% from the previous year-end and many of its equities seem to be undervalued. The market liberalization in 1992 will offer internationally savvy institutional investors buying opportunities.

History

Public subscriptions and bond flotations occurred in Korea as far back as the 1880s. However, it was not until 1911 that the first organized exchange was established by the Japanese. During this period of colonization, Japanese firms dominated listings on the stock exchange in Korea, and Japanese brokers carried out most of the trading. However, this market disintegrated after the Japanese defeat in World War II in 1945.

In 1956, the stock exchange in Korea was revived under the name of the Daehan Stock Exchange (DSE) which was renamed later as the Korea Stock Exchange (KSE). From its inception, the Korean equity market faced insurmountable obstacles. For instance, the entrenched system of family business ownership reduced the utility of the market as a place for capital formation.

Furthermore, the securities regulations at that time did not adequately differentiate equity issuance from loan financing and required publicly-listed firms to pay dividends that were equal to time deposit rates. Dividends were sometimes as high as 20% to 25%.

The formation of a modernized equity market began in the early 1970s. Given the 1970 market crash and the active curb market (private, unregulated money market), few companies used the equity market for corporate financing. In order to nurture a developed market, the government introduced the August 3 Emergency Decree and the Going Public Encouragement Act in 1972. The former act was aimed at eliminating the unregulated curb market, while the latter enabled the Ministry of Finance to force Korean firms to issue common shares. The latter act also required designated corporations to give employees preference to subscribe up to 10% of new shares floated to the public.

As a result, there was a surge in public offerings. Between 1972 and 1976, the number of new public flotations increased from 6 to 56. Meanwhile, the number of listed companies on the KSE rose to 274 from 66. Furthermore, in 1974 the first investment trust company, Korea Investment Trust Co., was established.

In 1977, the Securities Exchange Commission and its enforcement arm, the Securities Supervisory Board, were formed. With the exception of the major market corrections in 1980 and 1982, the Korean equity market continued to expand steadily. As discussed in the beginning of this chapter, the growth has been quite dramatic since 1985. In December 1988, the government announced a detailed schedule for market liberalization steps to be implemented between 1989 and 1992. Since then, the 1992 market liberalization has continued to influence the market movement and investor sentiment.

Market Structure

The Korea Stock Exchange (KSE) was established under the ownership of securities firms in 1956, and since the extinction of an exchange in Pusan in 1978 it has been the only exchange in Korea. In 1963, the KSE became a government-controlled special corporation. However, since 1988 the ownership of the KSE has been reverted to 25 member securities firms.

The shares listed on the KSE are categorized by four groups: First, Second, Administrative Sections, and Supervised Issues. In general, the First Section is the marketplace for the shares of larger companies and the Second Section for those of smaller and newly-listed companies. If shares traded on the Second Section satisfy the reassignment rules of the First Section within three years of their listing, they will be traded in the First Section. Conversely, if a share traded on the First Section does not meet the requirement of the First Section assignment any more, it will be moved to the Second Section. As of June 30, 1991, 490 companies were listed on the First Section, accounting for 91% of the total market capitalization of the KSE. There were 197 companies listed on the Second Section.

The Administrative Section consists of companies that face severe financial difficulties or have fallen within the exchange's delisting criteria. As of June 30, 1991, there were 25 companies traded on this section. These shares are normally low priced and are often targets of speculative trading. They are subject to tighter daily price fluctuation limits.

Shares are categorized as Supervised Issues when unusual trading patterns emerge for them, implying that they may be the subject of speculative manipulation. The status of Supervised Issues usually lasts a few weeks in order to cool off over-heated share price movements. Supervised shares stay in their usual listing section but are subject to even tighter price fluctuation limit than the shares on the Administrative Section.

Market Index

The Korea Composite Stock Price Index (KCSPI) is a market capitalization-weighted index and consists of all companies listed on the KSE. As a result, larger capitalization shares exert more influence on the change of the index. The KCSPI was rebased to 100 on January 4, 1980 and is recalculated every ten minutes during exchange trading hours. The KSE also calculates 34 industry subindices and three additional indices based upon the size of the constituent shares' capital base. Table 5-1 lists 25 largest constituent shares of the KCSPI, and Table 5-2 lists the industrial sector weightings of the KCSPI.

Table 5-1   Largest Companies of KCSPI (as of December 31, 1991)

Rank	Company Name	Market Capital (Won bn)	Percent of Total Market Capital
1	Korea Electric Power Co. (KEPCO)	9,855	12.5
2	Pohang Iron & Steel (POSCO)	2,120	2.7
3	Hanil Bank	1,637	2.1
4	Korea First Bank	1,599	2.0
5	Cho Hung Bank	1,586	2.0
6	The Commercial Bank of Korea	1,560	2.0
7	Bank of Seoul	1,560	2.0
8	Shinhan Bank	1,386	1.8
9	Samsung Electronics	1,318	1.7
10	Daewoo	1,303	1.6
11	Goldstar	1,093	1.4
12	Hyundai Motor	1,076	1.4
13	Daewoo Securities	1,064	1.3
14	Yu Kong	1,057	1.3
15	Lucky Securities	995	1.3
16	Lucky	988	1.2
17	Dongsuh Securities	949	1.2
18	Daishin Securities	928	1.2
19	Hyundai Engineering & Const.	875	1.1
20	Kia Motors	864	1.1
21	Daewoo Heavy Ind.	862	1.1
22	Daewoo Electronics	821	1.0
23	Korean Air	703	0.9
24	Ssangyong Investment & Securities	656	0.8
25	Korea Long-Term Credit Bank	581	0.7
TOTAL MARKET CAPITALIZATION OF LARGEST 25		37,418	47.4
TOTAL MARKET CAPITALIZATION OF THE KSE		79,020	100.0

Source: The Korea Stock Exchange and Hanshin Securities Co.

Turnover and Liquidity

It has been estimated that only 25% of the total market capitalization is investable because the majority of Korean corporations are tightly held by family members. The average daily trading value was 0.34% of the total market capitalization in 1990. This has been a significant improvement in liquidity from a 0.016% in 1980. Table 5-3 details the trading value of 25 most actively traded shares on the KSE in 1990, and Figure 5-5 shows daily average trading volumes and values since 1980.

Table 5-2   Industrial Sector Composition of the KCSPI (as of December 31, 1990)

Industry	Market Capital (US$ bn)	Percent of Total Market Capitalization
Fisheries	0.37	0.33
Mining	0.18	0.16
Food & Beverages	1.62	1.46
Textiles & Apparel	3.11	2.82
Wood (& Products)	0.53	0.48
Paper (& Products)	1.16	1.05
Chemicals	7.31	6.63
Rubber	0.92	0.84
Pharmaceuticals	1.10	1.00
Plastic	0.31	0.28
Nonmetallic Minerals	2.54	2.30
Iron & Steel	5.49	5.38
Nonferrous Metals	1.12	1.01
Fabricated Metals	0.97	0.88
Machinery	2.49	2.26
Electronics	9.73	8.82
Transport Equipment	4.77	4.32
Other Manufacturing	0.19	0.17
Utilities	13.76	12.47
Construction	6.83	6.19
Wholesale & Retail Trade	6.28	5.69
Transport & Storage	1.46	1.32
Telecommunication	0.23	0.21
Banks	18.75	17.00
Short-Term Finance	3.37	3.06
Other Financial Institutions	0.63	0.57
Securities	13.39	12.14
Insurance	1.25	1.13
Recreational Service	0.10	0.01
TOTAL MARKET CAPITALIZATION	110.30	100.00

Source: The Korea Stock Exchange and Hanshin Securities Co.

Types of Shares

In addition to common shares, preferred shares are traded on the KSE. They do not offer voting right but carry higher dividends. In the event of company liquidation, preferred shares rank ahead of common shares. The dividends of preferred shares, as a fraction of par, are usually 100 basis points higher than common share dividends.

**Table 5-3   Twenty-Five Most Actively Traded Shares
on the KSE in 1990**

Rank	Company Name	Trading Value (Won bn)	Percent of Total Market Turnover
1	Daewoo Group	1,823	3.4
2	Bank of Seoul	1,488	2.8
3	The Commercial Bank of Korea	1,463	2.7
4	Goldstar	1,286	2.4
5	Dongsuh Securities	1,204	2.3
6	Daewoo Electronics	1,145	2.1
7	Cho Hung Bank	1,134	2.1
8	Hyundai Engineering & Const.	1,059	2.0
9	Lucky Securities	1,002	1.9
10	Daewoo Heavy Industry	995	1.9
11	Korea First Bank	870	1.6
12	Daeshin Securities	854	1.6
13	Daewoo Securities	835	1.6
14	Hanil Bank	801	1.5
15	Saeil Heavy Ind. (Tong II)	644	1.2
16	The Kwang Ju Bank	607	1.1
17	The Dae Gu Bank	595	1.1
18	Lucky	510	1.0
19	Chung Buk Bank	485	0.9
20	Samsung Electronics	483	0.9
21	Coryo Securities	464	0.9
22	Ssangyong Invest. & Securities	447	0.8
23	Daewoo Telecommunication	435	0.8
24	Yu Kong	423	0.8
25	Kyung Ki Bank	406	0.8
TOTAL MARKET TURNOVER OF 25 MOST ACTIVELY TRADED COMPANIES		21,458	40.1
TOTAL MARKET TURNOVER OF THE KSE		53,455	100.0

Source: The Korea Stock Exchange and Hanshin Securities Co.

OTC (Over the Counter) Market

The Korean OTC market was established in April 1987 by the government to provide small companies with an access to equity financing. However, since the inception trading activity in this market has been slow, and wide spreads between bid and offer prices are quite common. Nevertheless, the liquidity and size of the OTC market has been improving steadily. The number of listed shares increased from 47 in 1989 to 66 in 1990. Shares traded on the OTC market are not subject to daily price fluctuation limits.

Figure 5-5   Trading Volume and Value (Trading Volume Since 1986)

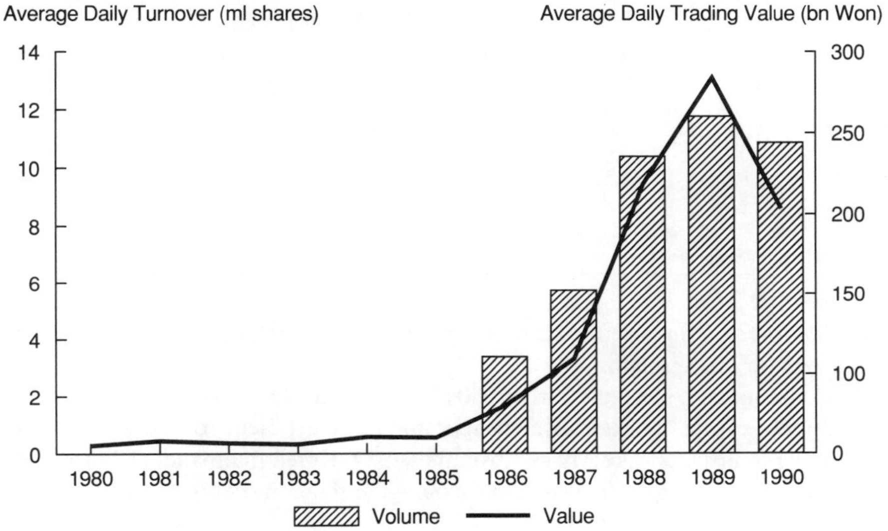

Average Daily Turnover (ml shares)   Average Daily Trading Value (bn Won)

Source: Ssangyong Research Institute

Investors

Trading by individual investors accounts for a substantial portion of daily market activity on the Korean Stock Exchange. Table 5-4 shows the share ownership composition by investor categories. As shown, individual investors held 55% of the outstanding shares in the Korean market at the end of 1989. The share ownership by individual investors peaked in 1988, and its significance vis-a-vis institutional share holdings is expected to fall as Korean institutional investors are becoming larger and more sophisticated.

The government, which used to be the biggest investor during the infancy of the Korean market, has seen its direct share holding decrease substantially. However, because it has a strong say in the market participation by brokerage firms, commercial banks and other institutional investors, it still wields significant influence on the market.

Internationalization

In addition to the high cost of the domestic bank loans, there has traditionally been a severe shortage of capital in Korea because, except for the second half of the 1980s, the Korean economy has never generated a significant amount of trade surpluses. As

Table 5-4   Proportional Share Holdings by Investor Categories (%)

Year	Government	Banks	Brokers	Other Institutions	Individuals	Foreigners
1965	56.4	8.6	6.7	7.3	20.8	0.2
1975	13.9	8.1	6.3	17.7	52.9	1.0
1985	0.4	7.1	7.4	30.0	52.5	2.6
1986	0.2	7.0	6.7	30.6	52.4	3.0
1987	0.1	5.6	2.6	26.0	62.3	3.3
1988	1.4	6.5	3.1	23.3	63.0	2.7
1989	11.8	3.2	5.1	23.2	54.6	2.1

Source: Hanshin Securities Co.

a result, Korean firms used to have no choice but to substantially rely on foreign bank loans for their growth.

Consequently, since the early 1980s Korean firms have been trying to tap the international capital markets as a cheaper and more efficient source of corporate financing. For instance, as early as November 1981, Korea International Trust — an investment trust — was established to encourage foreign investors to indirectly participate in the Korean equity market.

Until 1985, the majority of foreign investment in the Korean equity market had been established through investment trusts managed by three Korean investment trust companies — Korea Investment Trust Co. (KITC), Daehan Investment Trust Co. (DITC), and Citizens Investment Trust Management Co. (CITMC). Table 5-5 details the investment trusts managed by the above three companies for foreign investors.

Table 5-5   Korean Investment Trusts for Foreign Investors

Name	Value (in US $)	Inception Date	Manager	Type*	Premium 11/26/91
Korea Int's Trust	25m	11/81	KITC	O	-2.85%
Korea Trust	25m	11/81	DITC	O	-2.26%
Korea Growth Trust	30m	3/85	CITMC	C	-2.09%
Seoul Int'l Trust	30m	4/85	KITC	O	-3.11%
Seoul Trust	30m	4/85	DITC	O	-2.29%
Korea Small Companies Trust	2m	12/85	KITC	C	n/a
Korea Emerging Companies Trust	3m	3/86	DITC	O	n/a
Korea 1990 Trust	50m	4/90	CITMC	C	-3.35%
Korea Equity Trust	n/a	5/90	KITC	O	-3.12%
Daehan Korea Trust	n/a	5/90	DITC	O	-2.74%
Daehan Asia Trust	100m	6/90	DITC	C	-18.97%
Seoul Asia Index Trust	n/a	7/90	CITMC	O	-15.08%
Korea Pacific Trust	n/a	7/90	KITC	O	-17.48%

*"O" for open-ended and "C" for close-ended.
Source: Hanshin Securities Co. and Dongsuh Securities Co.

Most of the funds are traded in the form of International Depository Receipts. Most of the investment trusts are open-end funds. However,they are actually closed-end funds because the managers do not have freedom to issue new units without the approval of the Korean Ministry of Finance. The managers have to wait until the pre-existing units are redeemed before issuing new units. Because the Korean government currently determines the amount of foreign investment entering into the Korean equity market, the funds will not truly become open-ended until the liberalization of the market, which is scheduled to occur in the beginning of 1992.

The most well-known vehicles for indirect foreign investment in the Korean equity market are two exchange-listed, closed-end country funds: the Korea Fund traded on the New York Stock Exchange and the Korea Europe Fund on the London Stock Exchange (LSE). In July 1990, the Korea Asia Fund was listed on the LSE and the Hong Kong Stock Exchange. Table 5-6 contains information on these close-end funds. The Korea Fund is not allowed to hold more than 5% of the total outstanding shares of a listed company; the Korea Europe Fund is not allowed to hold more than 3%. Both funds may not invest more than 5% of their net asset value in one share or more than 25% of their NAV in one industrial sector.

In December 1985, the Korean corporations whose operation had become more international began raising capital abroad and repatriating it by issuing convertible bonds in the Eurobond market. Table 5-7 lists Korean corporate convertible, warrant bonds, and depositary receipts offered to foreign investors.

Liberalization Outline

At the end of 1988, the Korean government announced a detailed plan for the liberalization of its capital markets. However, after the announcement of the plan, the implementation of the liberalization had to be delayed immediately due to a rapid increase in money supply in the Korean economy. As trade surpluses accumulated, excessive liquidity began to exert a severe upward pressure on inflation.

Table 5-6   Offshore Korean Close-End Funds for Foreign Investors

Name	Value (in U.S. $)	Inception Date	Manager	Premium (Percent) 11/26/91
Korea Fund	100m	8/84	Scudder	19.44
Korea Europe Fund	60m	3/87	Korea Schroder Fund Management	11.99
Korea Asia Fund	n/a	7/90	Korea Asia Fund Management	6.77

Source: Hanshin Securities Co.

Table 5-7   Korean Convertible and Warrant Eurobonds and Depositary Receipts

Name	Amount (in U.S. $)	Issuance Date	Coupon Rate	Conversion Begins	Premium 11/26/91
Samsung Electronics (CB)	20m	12/19/85	5%	10/19/87	12.56%
Daewoo Heavy Industries (CB)	40m	5/23/86	3%	11/23/87	8.32%
Yukong (CB)	20m	7/15/86	2%	1/15/88	78.11%
Goldstar (CB)	30m	8/11/87	1.75%	2/11/89	102.70%
Saehan Media (CB)	30m	10/04/88	1.75%	4/04/90	103.93%
Sammi Steel (BW)	50m	11/08/89	1.25%	3/08/91	313.15%
STC (CB)	30m	1/03/90	1.25%	7/03/91	299.00%
Dong Ah Construction	50m	2/14/90	1.25%	8/14/91	191.02%
Hyundai Motor (BW)	70m	2/23/90	1.00%	8/23/91	130.13%
Samic (BW)	n/a	3/08/90	n/a	n/a	299.61%
Miwon (CB)	n/a	7/11/90	n/a	n/a	110.96%
Sunkyong Ind. (CB)	n/a	9/14/90	n/a	n/a	76.89%
Samsung Co. (DR)	40m	12/18/90	-	-	8.77%
Jindo Co. (CB)	SFR 25m	2/28/91	6.00%	8/28/92	33.33%
Samsung Elec. (DR)	100m	3/09/91	-	-	10.58%
Anam Ind. (CB)	SFR 45m	3/11/91	6.00%	9/11/92	23.35%
Kolon (CB)	28.5m	3/14/91	4.00%	9/14/91	11.40%
Sunkyong (CB)	65m	5/16/91	4.75%	2/16/92	12.61%
Sam Bo (CB)	30m	6/04/91	3.5%	3/04/92	n/a
Daewoo Telecom (CB)	50m	6/18/92	3.5%	3/18/92	26.32%

Source: Hanshin Securities Co. and Dongsuh Securities Co.

Consequently, the government tried to limit the inflow of foreign capital by delaying the market opening.

However, the Korean equity market did not show any sign of recovery in 1991 after it began heading south in the second quarter of 1989. The Korean government seems to be much inclined to invite foreign capital in order to prop up its sagging equity market. The liberalization is scheduled to happen in the beginning of 1992.

According to the liberalization outline announced by the Korean government, Korean industries will be categorized by '*Limited*' and '*Non-Limited*.' Foreign investors will be permitted to invest up to 10% of the market capitalization of companies in *Non-Limited* industries and up to 8% of the market capitalization of companies in *Limited* industries such as public utilities, defense, shipping, transportation, finance, and communication. Furthermore, a 3% limit is imposed for the maximum amount of investment in one company by any one foreign investor. Also, foreign investors will not be permitted to purchase the shares of POSCO (Pohang Iron & Steel) and KEPCO (Korea Electric Power Company).

Equities held by the investment trusts listed in Table 5-5 and those converted from the Euro convertible bonds listed in Table 5-7 will not be counted in calculating foreign investment limit. According to the liberalization outline, foreign investors need to acquire an investment identification card.

At the end of 1990, the foreign ownership of Korean equities via indirect investment accounted for almost 2% ($2.2 billion) of the total Korean equity market capitalization. Figure 5-6 shows how orders from overseas foreign investors will be directed and executed on the KSE.

Dealing Procedures

All transactions of listed equities must be done on the Korean Stock Exchange. The KSE does not have market makers or specialists and instead runs a continuous auction system. The auction principles are based on priorities of price, time, customer orders (over member firm's orders for their own account), and order size. All bids and offers submitted prior to a certain point in time are treated as simultaneous orders. In auction, the mid-price level is set so that all bids above and all offers below that price can be filled.

A computerized on-line system for matching orders was first installed in February 1983. Since then, as much as 94% of all trading was carried out through the Stock Market Automated System (SMATS) in 1990.

Board lots are generally ten shares. Small orders are handled byoff-floor brokers. All orders must be placed within daily price limits listed in Table 5-8. Figure 5-7 shows transaction flow on the Korean Stock Exchange.

Margin Trading and Short-Selling

Margin trading is allowed on shares of all First Section companies with paid-in capital of over Won 1bn, except securities company shares and supervised issues. Margin trading is estimated to account for 7% of turnover in eligible shares and 6% of total market turnover on the KSE. Margin trading is limited to 20% of an eligible company's shares. Presently, 40% of margin requirement is imposed by the Ministry of Finance.

Short-selling is also allowed by the KSE. However, it is a much less common practice than margin trading, accounting for perhaps 0.12% of turnover of eligible shares and 0.09% of total market turnover on the KSE. The same shares that are eligible for margin trading are eligible for short-selling. The settlement period is within 150 days, with a loan limit of 50% of a broker's net worth and Won 20m per customer. Short-selling is limited to 10% of an eligible company's shares.

Settlement and Clearance

Figure 5-8 and Figure 5-9 show the procedures for trade settlement and clearance in Korea.

Figure 5-6   Flow of Transaction Orders from Overseas

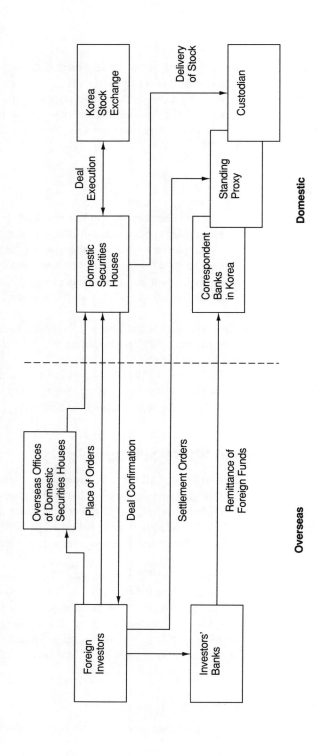

Source: Ssangyong Investment and Securities Company

Table 5-8   Daily Price Limits

	Previous Day's Closing Price	Daily Price Limit
First & Second Section	Less than 3,000	100
	3,000 - 4,999	200
	5,000 - 6,999	300
	7,000 - 9,999	400
	10,000 - 14,999	600
	15,000 - 19,999	800
	20,000 - 29,999	1,000
	30,000 - 39,999	1,300
	40,000 - 49,999	1,600
	50,000 - 69,999	2,000
	70,000 - 99,999	2,500
	100,000 - 149,999	3,000
	150,000 or more	4,000
Supervised Issues	same price range as above	50% of above limits
Administrative Section	Less than 500	10
	500 - 999	20
	1,000 - 1,999	30
	2,000 - 2,999	40
	3,000 - 4,999	50
	5,000 or more	100

Source: Hanshin Securities Co.

Figure 5-7   Transaction Flow on the KSE

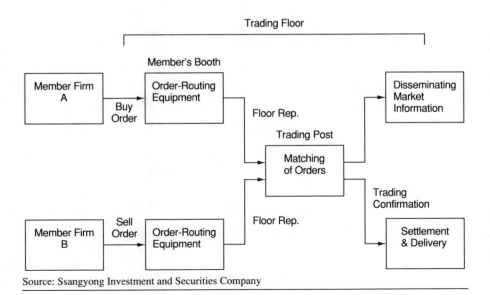

Source: Ssangyong Investment and Securities Company

Figure 5-8   Settlement and Clearance for Book-Entry

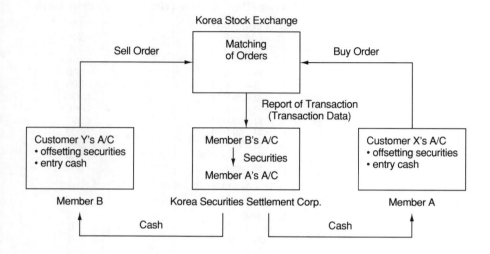

Source: Ssangyong Investment and Securities Company

Figure 5-9   Settlement Clearance for Physical Delivery

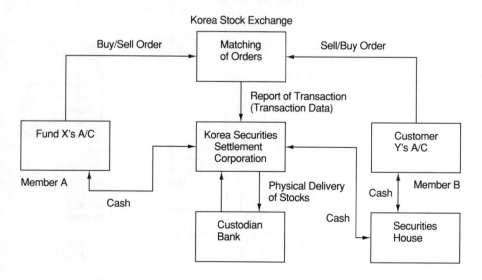

Source: Ssangyong Investment and Securities Company

Trading Commissions and Transaction Tax

Since 1989 when trading commissions were deregulated, trading commissions and transaction tax are negotiable within a band of 0.2%-0.4%. Despite the deregulation, most brokers charge the same standard commission rates as Table 5-9 shows. Besides trading commissions, transaction tax of 0.2% is levied on sellers. If transacted share price is below par, no transaction tax is levied.

Taxation

Table 5-10 lists countries with which Korea has established tax treaties. Foreign investors' returns from investing in the Korean equity market will be taxed according to these treaties, and the tax rates are detailed in Table 5-10.

Market Regulations

The Korean equity market is regulated by the Ministry of Finance. Under the auspice of the Finance Ministry, the Securities Exchange Commission acts as a central regulatory agency and entrusts the Securities Supervisory Board with executive authority. All members of the KSE are also governed by the rules of the Korea Securities Dealers Association, a self-regulatory trade organization.

The Securities and Exchange Law contains clauses enacted to protect investors. Although regulations are modeled after U.S. securities regulations, enforcement is not as strict as in the United States. For instance, in order to prevent insider trading, the SEC prohibits all employees of securities firms and investment trust companies from investing in the equity market. However, it is a common practice that they invest in the market through street name accounts or accounts in the name of friends.

Figure 5-10 shows the organizational structure of the Korean market regulatory bodies.

Table 5-9   Standard Commission Rates

Transaction Value	Rate For Board Lot (10 shares)	Rate For Odd Lot (Less than 10 shares)
Below 200m Won	0.4%	0.4%
200m - 500m Won	0.3% + Won 200,000	0.4%
Above 500m Won	0.2% + Won 700,000	0.4%

Source: Hanshin Securities Co.

Table 5-10   Taxation Rates for Foreign Investors

Country	Interest (%)	Dividend (%)	Capital Gains
Australia	15	15	Normal rate (3)
Austria	10	10 or 15 (3)	0 or Normal rate (4)
Bangladesh	10	10	0
Belgium	15	15	0
Canada	16 1/8 (1)	16 1/8 (1)	0 or Normal rate (4)
Denmark	15	15	0
Finland	10	10 or 15 (3)	0
France	15	10 or 15 (3)	0 or Normal rate (4)
India	10 or 15 (2)	15 or 20 (3)	0
Japan	12	12	Normal rate
Luxemburg	10	10 or 20 (3)	0
Malaysia	15	10 or 15 (3)	0
Netherlands	10 or 15 (2)	10 or 15 (3)	0
New Zealand	10	15	0
Norway	15	15	0
Pakistan	12.5	10 or 12.5 (3) 0	0 or Normal rate (4)
Philippines	10 or 15 (2)	10 or 15 (3)	0
Singapore	10	10 or 15 (3)	Normal rate
Sri Lanka	10	10 or 15 (3)	0
Sweden	10 or 15 (2)	10 or 15 (3)	0
Switzerland	10	10 or 15 (3)	0
Thailand	10 3/4 (1)	10 3/4 or 21 1/2 (1, 3)	Normal rate
Turkey	10 or 15 (2)	15 or 20	0
United Kingdom	10 or 15 (2)	10 or 15	0
United States of America	12.9 or Normal Rate (1, 5)	10 3/4, 16 1/8 or Normal Rate (1, 3, 5)	0 or Normal rate (5)
West Germany	10 or 15 (2)	10 or 15 (3)	Normal rate

Note:

(1) The tax treaties with Canada, the United States of America, and Thailand do not exempt resident's tax and, thus, the tax rate above has been increased.

(2) Rates vary depending on the term of the loan or debenture in the main.

(3) Rates vary depending on whether the dividend paying company is owned over a particular percentage by the dividend receiving company (the range of share ownership is from over 10% to 25%: Austria 10%, Finland 25%, France 25%, India 20%, Luxemburg 25%, Malaysia 25%, Netherlands 25%, Pakistan 20%, Philippines 25%, Singapore 25%, Sri Lanka 25%, Sweden 25%, Switzerland 25%, Thailand 25%, U.S.A. 10%, and West Germany 21%).

(4) No capital gains tax is payable unless the shares sold are of a corporation in which the seller owns 25% or more of the shares.

(5) Normal rates will apply if the company receiving the interest, dividends, or capital gains is owned 25% or more (directly or indirectly) by individuals who are not residents of the United States of America and by reason of special measures the tax imposed on such company by the United States of America with respect to such interest, dividends, or capital gain is substantially less than the tax generally imposed by the United States of America on corporate profits.

Source: Hanshin Securities Co.

Figure 5-10 Organizational Structure of the Korean Market Regulatory Bodies

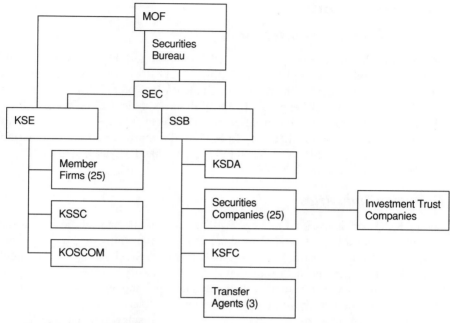

- **MOF (Ministry of Finance):**
  - Establishment and execution of the basic policies for the securities market
  - Supervision of the business of SEC, SSB and KSE
  - permission of establishment and operation of securities related companies
- **SEC (Securities and Exchange Commision):**
  - major regulatory body under MOF
  - decision making on major issues related to both new stocks and trading markets
- **SSB (Securities Supervisory Board):**
  - executive body of SEC
  - implementation of decision made by SEC and supervision of securities houses
- **KSE (Korea Stock Exchange):**
  - only exchange in Korea
  - supervision of the member firms and maintenance of a fair and orderly market
- **KSSC (Korea Securities Settlement Corporation):**
  - wholly owned subsidiary of KSE
  - settlement of securities transaction underbook-entry clearing system
- **KOSCOM (Korea Securities Computer Corporation):**
  - subsidiary of KSE
  - computer center for securities trading and market information
- **KSFC (Korea Securities Finance Corporation):**
  - only institution specializing in securities financing
- **KSDA (Korea Securities Dealers Association):**
  - 25 KSE's member firms
  - coordination and conflicts—mediation among members
- **Transfer Agents:**
  - agents for ownership transfer (Bank of Seoul, The National Citizen's Bank, KSSC)

Source: The Korea Stock Exchange

Company Profiles*

Daewood Heavy Industry Ltd.

Machinery   Daewood Heavy Industry (DHI) is the largest machinery manufacturer in Korea producing diesel engines, rolling stocks, forklifts and machine tools. DHI's main projects are: construction equipment (26% of 1991 sales), industrial vehicles (18%), and diesel engines (16%). With its technological superiority, it is a play on the booming government infrastructure project. The combination of rationalization of costs and localization of parts should improve SHI's profit margin. Major shareholders are: Bank of Seoul (14.5%), Daehan Kyoyuk Insurance (2.8%), and Daewood Foundation (2.7%).

Kangwon Industries

Steel   Kangwon Industries, Ltd. began with the coal briquet industry in 1962 and is currently the third largest local electric arc furnace (mini-mill) steel manufacturer with a 17.5% market share, following Inchon Iron & Steel (20%) and Dongkuk Steel Mill (26%). It has an 18% market share of domestic reinforcing bar market and 21% of the steel shape market. It is the flagship company of the 23rd largest local business group, Kangwon Industries group, which has 14 member companies. Steel operation production accounted for 78% of total sales, steel casting for 8%, machinery for 6%, and others for 8%. A new product, H-beams, will come on stream in 1994. About 14% of revenues came from exports. The construction sector takes around 70% of sales. Currently, it has an annual capacity of 1.1 mln tons which will increase to 3.2mln by 2000. It has 2,400 employees, mostly at its main plant in Pohang.

KIA Motors

Auto   Kia Motors (KM) was established in 1944 as a manufacturer of bicycles and is currently the second largest local producer of passenger cars (with a market share of 34%) after Hyundai Motors (50%). KM is the leading company in manufacturing compact size commercial vehicles (with a market share of 49%). KM is a conglomerate with 7 affiliates involved in motors and related businesses. Its affiliates include Asia Motors (37%), Kia Machine Tools (81%), Kia Steel (57%), Kia Service (33%), Kia Precision Works (46%), Seohae Industrial (53%), Kia Economic Research Institute (50%), Ashin Venture Capital Financial Co. (60%), and KM (51%). Major products are passenger cars (42%), trucks and special purpose vehicles (35%), minivans (16%) and auto parts (8%). Export ratio was about 13% in 1990. It has branches in Tokyo, HK, North America and Europe. With a 10% ownership from Ford, 8% from Mazda and 2% from C. Itoh, total foreign ownership has exceeded the 10% limit. Around 35% of shares are owned by institutional investors.

---

* Company profiles are provided by the editors.

Kolon

Manufacturing   Kolon Industries is one of the largest synthetic producers in Korea and ranks third among three local producers of nylon fibre. The company is attempting to diversify from its textile fibers into higher value-added polymerchemicals, including video tape, engineering plastics and industrial fibers (cord and carpet). The Kolon group, of which Kolon Industries is the "flagship", includes manufacturing operations in the areas of chemicals, pharmaceuticals, machine tools, and fabric dyes as well as presences in local auto and garment retailing, and construction.

Korea Europe Fund

Country Fund   The Korea Europe Fund is listed in London and is the second largest of the three existing funds for investment in Korea. It has the largest exposure to electronics of all the Funds, with the second and third largest exposure in the construction and banking industries. It is managed by Korea Schroder Fund Management.

Samsung Electronics

Electronics   Samsung Electronics (SE) was established in 1969 to develop an electronics export industry, went public in 1875, and was merged with Samsung Semiconductors and Telecommunications Company in 1988. It is the largest operating entity of the Samsung Group, with about 30% of sales and 50% of earnings. The Samsung Group is Korea's largest and most broadly diversified conglomerate with sales of US$19 billion (1988), 11% of Korea's GNP. SE has four major divisions. Home electronics (TV's, VCR's, microwave ovens) continues to be the largest division (57% of sales and 30% of revenues), but a strategic shift is underway to focus increasingly on semi-conductors (22% and 48%), telecommunications (15% and 20%) and computers (6% and 2%). SE holds stakes in other companies of the Samsung Group including Samsung Hewlett Packard (45%) and Samsung Petrochemicals (50%).

SE has 11 offshore manufacturing operations (3% of production), as well as its own distribution companies in 8 countries. SE is 21% owned by the Chairman and related companies.

Seoul International Trust

Mutual Fund   Seoul International Trust has a market capitalization of over U.S. $100 million and is the third largest of the 11 Korean trusts. It was listed in April 1985, and is managed by the Korean Investment (Trust) Company.

6

TAIWAN*
Sam Chang, Vice President
Salomon Brothers Taiwan Limited
Taipei, Taiwan

General Background on Taiwan, Republic of China

Taiwan is located about 100 miles southeast off the China mainland. With a total area of about 13,900 square miles, the island is approximately the size of the Netherlands. One-fourth of the land is arable and the rest is predominantly mountainous. With a population of nearly 20.5 million people, Taiwan's population density at 566 persons per square kilometer is among the highest in the world.

Political Environment

The government of Republic of China (ROC) asserts sovereignty over all of China as does the government of People's Republic of China (PRC). Neither recognizes the legitimacy of the other government. The PRC has consistently refused to renounce the possibility of using force to gain control of Taiwan. In the international community, although only 29 countries maintain formal diplomatic relations with the ROC, it has active trade and financial relations with more than 160 countries and territories.

Although election of local officials began in the 1950s, democratization has accelerated since July 1987 when martial law and ban on political parties were lifted. Travel to mainland China was allowed beginning in November 1987. The ruling Nationalist Party-Kuomingtang (KMT), continues to dominate all levels of government and legislatures. It achieved a landslide victory in the November 1991 election for National Assembly members and won 75% of the seats. The vociferous

---

*This article reflects only the author's views and does not necessarily reflect that of Salomon Brothers.

opposition Democratic Progressive Party (DPP) gains much media attention through disruptive tactics in the legislatures. However, DPP's ability to achieve limited political gains are often more attributable to factional infighting within the KMT than to DDP's appeal to the electorate.

Economy

Real GNP grew at the average annual rate of 7.9% through the 1980s. The rapid growth was mainly export driven, and large sustained trade surplus since 1985 led to fast accumulation of foreign exchange reserve, which totaled about US $82.4 billion at the end of 1991, the highest in the world followed by Japan (Table 6-1 and Table 6-2).

The rapid accumulation of foreign exchange reserves was inevitably accompanied by fast growth in the money supply and appreciation of the NT dollar against the currencies of its major trading partners. The NT$ rose from about US $1 to NT

Table 6-1   Basic Economic Indicators

GNP (1991)	US $180 billion
GNP per capita	US $8815
CPI change (1991 average)	3.6%
Prime rate (year end 1991)	8.35%
Exchange rate (year end 1991)	US $1 - NT $25.75
MIB growth (1991)	5.9%
Exports (1991)	US $76.2 billion
Imports (1991)	US $62.9 billion
Surplus (1991)	US $13.3 billion
Foreign exchange reserve (year end 1991)	US $82.4 billion
Population (Oct., 1990)	20.5 million
Unemployment (Oct., 1990)	1.6%

Sources: Department of Statistics, Ministry of Economic Affairs; The Central Bank of China.

Table 6-2

	Real GNP Grown	Trade Surplus (US$ billion)	Foreign Exchange Reserve (US$ billion)	Mlb Growth
1984	10.5%	$8.5	$15.7	9.3%
1985	5.1%	$10.6	$22.6	12.2%
1986	11.6%	$15.6	$46.3	51.4%
1987	11.9%	$18.7	$76.8	37.8%
1988	7.5%	$10.9	$74.0	24.4%
1989	7.3%	$14.0	$73.2	6.1%
1990	5.0%	$12.5	$72.4	−6.6%
1991 (est)	7.2%	$13.3	$82.4	12.0%

Source: Domestic & Foreign Express Report of Economic Statistics Indicators

$40 in 1985 to US $1 to NT $25.75 at the end of 1991. With limited investment alternatives, the excess liquidity quickly pushed up real estate and stock prices.

In addition to facing the appreciating currency and slower growth in the international economy, Taiwan's manufacturers also saw domestic investment environment become increasingly unfavorable with higher land cost, labor shortage, and more stringent environment regulations. Political democratization also meant more juggling for power, less consensus, and slower progress in legislative reform and government actions to provide effective assistance. In 1990, industrial production dropped 1.2% for the first time since the energy crisis of 1982, and GNP growth slowed down to 5.3%. In 1991, however, GNP growth recovered to 7.2%, significantly aided by fast expansion of trade with China (Table 6-3).

In January 1991, the ROC government announced a Six-Year National Development Plan under which about US $300 billion are to be spent for construction of large public works and infrastructure projects. GNP growth is likely to remain at a healthy pace as Taiwan's domestic demand takes on even greater importance (Table 6-4).

Table 6-3   Trade with China

	Export to China (US $ million)	Growth Rate
1982	194	−42.1%
1983	157	−2.8%
1984	425	170.7%
1985	987	131.4%
1986	811	− 17.8%
1987	1227	51.2%
1988	2242	82.8%
1989	2896	29.2%
1990	3278	13.2%
1991	4667	42.4%

Source: United World Chinese Commercial Bank

Table 6-4   Domestic and External Demand of the GNP

	Domestic	External
1986	78.3%	19.3%
1987	80.9%	17.1%
1988	86.8%	10.8%
1989	90.1%	7.7%
1990	92.3%	5.3%
1991 (est.)	92.8%	4.9%

Source: Executive Yuan General Accounting Office

Brief History of the Stock Market

The origin of the securities market in Taiwan stemmed from the 1953 Land Reform. To compensate the land owners who were required to distribute their land to the tillers under the "Land-to-the-Tiller" program, the government issued land bonds and shares of four large government-owned enterprises.[1] Gradually, sporadic markets and brokerage companies for trading in these stocks and bonds were formed.

The Securities and Exchange Commission (SEC) was established on September 1, 1960 to supervise and control all aspects of securities market operations. The Taiwan Stock Exchange (TSE) began operations on February 9, 1962. The TSE is a corporation owned by government-controlled private banks and enterprises. The TSE is independent of the brokerage firms that transact business through it, each of which pays a user's fee. All transactions in listed shares must be made through the TSE except a few, very limited exemptions.

By the end of 1962, shares of 18 corporations were listed on the TSE with a total market capitalization of NT $6.9 billion (about US $170 million). During the remainder of the 1960s, the TSE grew at a slow pace mainly due to an unwillingness on the part of Taiwan businesses offering their shares to the public and lack of experience among issuers and investors. During the early 1980s, the ROC government more actively encouraged new listings on the TSE, and the number of listed companies grew from 102 in 1980 to 221 by the end of 1991.

Value and Performance of the TSE

On December 28, 1991, the aggregate market value of shares listed on the TSE was NT $3,184 billion (US $124 billion) — see Figure 6-1 for the market capitalization by thousand; this equaled two-thirds of the GNP. In 1991, the average daily trading volume was 615 million shares, and average daily trading value was NT $33.9 billion (US $1.3 billion). Performance of the TSE has in recent years been characterized by extreme price volatility as shown in Table 6-5 and Figure 6-2. Since 1987, the market has gone through three major cycles of boom and bust. The most pronounced cycle reached its peak on February 10, 1990 when the TSE closed at 12,495. It was soon followed by a precipitous drop of 80% to 2,560 on October 1, 1990.

The volatility of Taiwan's stock market seemed to bear little relationship to the underlying economy. This may be attributed to the following three main factors: (1) excess money resulting from trade surpluses; (2) structural issues such as the limited supply of shares, the predominance of individual investors, and the daily price fluctuation limit; and (3) the absence of capital gains tax.

---

[1] The four companies were Taiwan Cement Co., Ltd., Taiwan Paper Co., Ltd., Agriculture and Forestry Co., Ltd., and Industrial and Mining Co., Ltd.

Figure 6-1   Market Capitalization by Industry (Percentage)

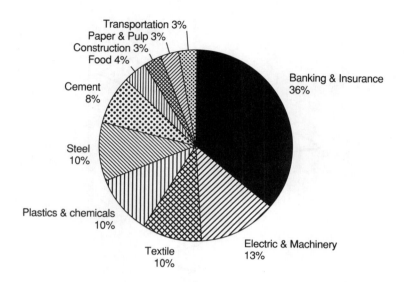

Table 6-5   TSE Index (1966=100)

Year	Number of Listed Companies (Year-End)	Trading Value (In billions of NTS)	High	Index Low	Close	Turnover Ratio
1982	113	133.9	546	421	444	
1983	119	363.8	766	435	762	
1984	123	324.5	969	764	838	95.4%
1985	127	195.2	841	636	835	68.1%
1986	130	675.7	1039	840	1039	162.1%
1987	141	2,668.6	4673	1063	2340	267.5%
1988	163	7,868.0	8790	2341	5119	332.6%
1989	181	25,408.0	10773	4873	9624	590.1%
1990	199	19,031.3	12495	2560	4530	506.4%
1991	221	9,682.7	6305	3316	4601	316.2%

Source: TSE

Figure 6-2   TSE Index—Monthly Close

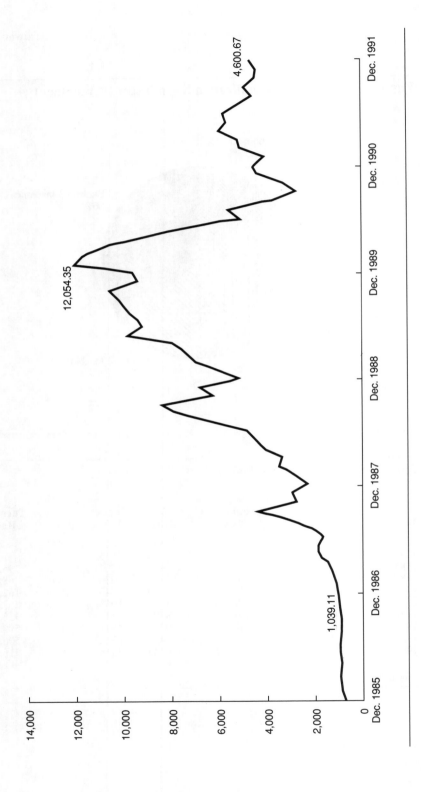

Limited Supply of Shares

Since 1985, 94 shares have been listed (Table 6-6). Nevertheless, the supply of shares is still relatively small. In addition, most listed companies are still largely owned and tightly controlled by the founding families or, in the case of financial institutions, by the government. Float is often 40% or less of the outstanding shares. The limited float along with excess liquidity leads to misleading "market" valuation. The most glaring example is perhaps government-owned Taiwan Machinery, which at its peak valuation in 1991 had a "market" capitalization of US $3.9 billion but only US $0.1 million in trading volume.

Investors

The Taiwan stock market is dominated by individuals who account for half of the capital contributed but more than 95% of turnover by volume (Table 6-7). The pre-

Table 6-6   Number of Listed Companies and Market Value

	1985	1986	1987	1988	1989	1990	1991
Listed Companies							
1st Category	65	67	80	104	125	145	166
2nd Category	62	63	61	59	56	54	55
Total	127	130	141	163	181	199	221
Market Value							
(NT $ billion)							
1st Category	$370	$471	$1,307	$2,829	$5,354	$2,414	$2,924
2nd Category	$46	$78	$79	$554	$820	$268	$260
Total	$416	$548	$1,386	$3,383	$6,174	$2,682	$3,184

Source: Taiwan Stock Exchange

Table 6-7   Share Ownership by Investor Type

	1985	1986	1987	1988	1989	1990
Domestic Individuals	40.53%	41.09%	40.27%	43.52%	46.72%	51.11%
Government Agencies	25.96%	25.99%	27.11%	25.94%	21.56%	18.01%
Domestic Financial Institutions	9.43%	8.54%	7.50%	5.78%	4.74%	4.68%
Domestic Trust Funds	0.39%	0.10%	0.32%	0.48%	0.75%	0.96%
Corporations	11.21%	11.68%	11.85%	11.73%	13.09%	14.06%
Other Juridical Persons	3.71%	3.50%	3.32%	3.08%	3.52%	2.68%
Foreign Financial Institutions	0.11%	0.13%	0.08%	0.08%	0.06%	0.05%
Foreign Juridical Persons	2.64%	3.09%	3.68%	4.62%	5.28%	4.83%
Foreign Trust Funds	0.24%	0.59%	0.77%	0.46%	0.42%	0.19%
Foreign Individuals	5.77%	5.29%	5.10%	4.31%	3.86%	3.43%

Source: Taiwan Stock Exchange

dominance of unsophisticated individual investors has helped fuel the volatility of the market. With increased participation of mutual fund management companies and foreign institutions, plus the fact that many individual investors have lost money in the market, turnover rate is likely to be reduced in the future.

7% Price Fluctuation Limit

In its desire to limit market volatility, the government has imposed a 7% daily limit on price change from the previous day's close. The restriction has led to several predictable results: reduction in liquidity, increase in trading risk, and easier price manipulation. Since trading is restricted to a narrow price range each day, it is often not possible to buy when prices are heading up and to sell when prices are going down. Small float plus this 7% price limit then enable manipulators to bid up an individual stock to its daily ceiling quickly. At the closing seconds of the trading session, such players often load the market with large bid orders to reinforce the illusion that many bids for the stock are unfulfilled. Unsophisticated investors, following tips and rumors, then chase after such shares, often unsuccessfully for several days, until they finally are able to buy it when the majors are ready to unload. Similar tactics can drive prices down.[2]

The 7% limit does the most damage when stock prices are going down. An investor, regardless of sophistication or size, is always threatened with the risk that he or she may not be able to convert his or her stock holding to cash, even if he or she is willing to take a loss. The need or desire for liquidity can then aggravate the pressure to sell when prices go down.

The daily percentage limit also creates a misleading impression among the unsophisticated investors that one may (with luck or following the right tip) earn 7% profit per day (compared to the yearly bank deposit interest of 5%), and that when the market turns sour, the government should take steps to protect the investors against losses since the government has set a limit to protect the investors. The SEC has announced that limitations on price fluctuations will be relaxed with a plan to abolish eventually all share price fluctuation controls.

Commissions and Transaction Tax

Since July 3, 1990, the commission rate for brokers has been 0.1425% of the transaction price. A securities transaction tax, currently levied at the rate of 0.6% of the transaction price, is payable by the seller. There is no capital gains tax.

Tax on Dividends

For resident individuals, combined cash dividends and interest income are exempt from taxes up to a household maximum of NT $360,000 per year. Stock dividends

[2] Insider trading and market manipulation are illegal, but enforcement has been less than satisfactory.

valued at par value are exempt from taxes up to NT $120,000 per year. Stock dividends representing a distribution of capital surplus or an asset revaluation surplus are not subject to income tax. Stock dividends representing a distribution of earnings are subject to income tax which is payable on receipt or, in certain cases, on disposal of the stock dividends. For domestic corporations, 80% of dividend income is exempt from taxes, and the corporate income tax rate is 25%.

Withholding tax applicable to cash dividends for a nonresident investor is 35%, but such rate may be reduced to 20% if an FIA has been obtained from the Investment Commission of the Ministry of Economic Affairs or if the investor is a Qualified Foreign Institutional Investor. Stock dividends that are paid to nonresident investors are subject to withholding tax as above, applying the appropriate tax rate to the par value of the dividend stock. However, shareholders of "productive enterprises" (which for practical purposes apply to most industrial firms) may defer payment of income tax on stock dividends until the date of disposal of the shares received as a stock dividend.

Operations

Trading

Trading sessions are held from 9:00 a.m. to 12:00 noon Monday through Friday and 9:00 a.m. to 11:00 a.m. on Saturday. The minimum unit of trading is 1,000 shares. Daily price movements of stocks are not allowed to be up or down more than 7% from the closing price of the preceding day. Trading is carried out by the Computer-Assisted Trading System of the Exchange. Only brokers and traders are allowed to trade on the exchange. The broker or trader enters the number and price of a share to be bought or sold through his terminal into the main computer of the exchange. The trading clerks at the exchange will then match the order according to price and time priority. When a transaction is consummated, the broker or dealer will immediately receive the trade report via the printer installed in his or her office. The broker will then confirm the trade with his or her customer.

Brokers and Traders

Prior to the revision of the Securities Exchange Law in January 1988, there were only 28 brokers and 10 traders. Revision of the law lifted the ban on licensing of new firms. By the end of 1991, there were a total of 45 integrated securities firms (which are licensed as brokers and dealers as well as underwriters) and 282 brokers. A brokerage license permits the firm to trade for its customers only. A licensed dealer may transact in securities for his own account. Brokers and dealers may not accept deposits or extend loans nor borrow or lend securities. Some brokerage houses are formed by major investors (including owners of listed companies) and often focus trades of favored stocks through their own brokerage firms. It is interesting to observe that new brokerage companies are still being organized and there are three brokerage companies for every two listed companies. In any given month during the second half of 1991, two-thirds of the brokerage firms were losing money.

Table 6-8 lists the top brokers in 1991. Table 6-9 lists the top three underwriters for 1991.

Margin Trading

Margin trading is limited to six month's duration and positions have to be liquidated prior to dividend payout day and/or date of the annual stockholder meeting. Prior to 1991, Fu-Hwa Securities Finance Co., Ltd., a quasigovernment company, was the only company licensed to provide securities finance. Since January of 1991, 22 of the 45 integrated securities firms have started margin loan business and have taken about 16% of the margin trade by December 1991. Margin trading has varied between 15%-30% of the total market volume during 1991.

Table 6-8   Top Ten Brokers in 1991

Company	Market share
Jih-Sun Securities	1.691%
Kuo Hua Securities	1.441%
Ting Kong Securities	1.313%
Fu Bon Securities	1.253%
Yuan Ta Securities	1.212%
Fu Gui Securities	0.974%
Asia Securities	0.944%
Shin Kuang Securities	0.889%
Hung Fu Securities	0.886%
Yung Li Securities	0.876%

Table 6-9   Top Three Underwriters in 1991

	IPO's Lead-Managed
Grand Cathay Securities	6
Taiwan International Securities	5
Taiwan Securities	3

Disclosure Requirements

Listed companies are required to submit a prospectus in the standard format prescribed by the SEC that includes information on company history, organization, business scope and facilities available, capital structure and share distribution, record of corporate bond issues, plans and business prospects, audited financial statements, etc. A prospectus must be submitted on initial public offering and when capital stock is increased, but it does not need to be renewed on a regular basis.

Listed companies must publish monthly reports that include the sales figure of the preceding month and financial statements on a quarterly basis. The semi-annual and annual financial statements shall be fully audited and certified. Following the annual meeting of shareholders, a listed company must file the resolution, operating reports, and financial statements with the exchange. In addition, a listed company is required to report to the exchange and make public immediately any event that might affect significantly its shareholders' interest or securities prices. All reports filed by the listed companies are kept by the exchange for reference by the general public.

Foreign Investment and Exchange Controls

Historically, foreign investment in the securities markets of Taiwan has been restricted. In 1982, the Ministry of Finance set the policy of gradually introducing foreign participation into local securities market in three phases:

- Phase I: Allow indirect investment through investment trust funds established in the ROC.

- Phase II: Allow direct investment by foreign institutions.

- Phase III: Free access to foreign capital.

The implementation of Phase I was started August of 1983 when International Investment Trust Company Limited was established, and in October of 1983 Taiwan (ROC) fund raised US $41 million in Europe and Japan for investment in the Taiwan stock market. Later on, three other fund management companies were licensed, and Formosa Fund, Taipei Fund, and Taiwan Fund were issued.

Phase II began on January 1, 1991. Eligible foreign institutional investors may now invest directly in ROC securities if they have applied for and received SEC approval (each a "Qualified Foreign Institutional Investor" or QFII). QFIIs include:

(a) banks that rank among the top 500 banks in the noncommunist world and hold securities assets of at least US $300 million;

(b) insurance companies that have existed for more ten years and hold securities assets of at least US $500 million; and

(c) fund management institutions that have existed for more than five years and manage assets of at least US $500 million.

Eligible institutions who wish to invest directly in Taiwan securities are required to apply for and receive a permit from the SEC to be a QFII. Each QFII may invest between a minimum of US $5 million and a maximum of US $50 million and are required to remit the full amount into the ROC within three months of receiving an investment permit. Total foreign investment by all QFII is limited to a maximum of US $2.5 billion.

Outward remittance is permitted three months after the capital is remitted to ROC. Earnings may be remitted outward only at the end of the QFII's fiscal year rather than after completion of a one-year period. QFIIs are also required to submit to the Central Bank of China and the SEC a monthly report of trading activities and status of assets under custody.

Each foreign institution is limited to hold a maximum of 5% of any listed company, and total foreign holding in any listed company may not exceed 10% of the total shares outstanding.

As of the end of 1991, 23 foreign institutions have applied for a total investment amount of US $1.16 billion. Eighteen companies had been approved to invest a total of US $711 million. The rest are either in process or disapproved. Only two applications have been rejected, mainly because the institutions had obtained investment permit in the earlier approval tranches. The Central Bank apparently does not like to see one institution submitting multiple applications. It is estimated that approximately US $550 million of the approved funds have been remitted into ROC.

In addition to buying stocks and beneficiary certificates (mutual funds or unit trusts), the funds are presently allowed to be invested in government bonds, treasury notes, corporate bonds, and short-term money market instruments.

Exchange Control

The Central Bank of China keeps a tight control of foreign exchange in Taiwan. The NT dollar is not traded in international markets and is not freely traded in Taiwan. Although foreign exchange control has been liberalized significantly since July 15, 1987, and any resident ROC national may remit up to US $3 million per year inward or outward, the Central Bank keeps close watch on the remittance of QFII funds and encourages the foreign institutions to remit funds in small tranches in order to avoid disturbance of the exchange rate.

Outlook for Foreign Investors

Fundamental outlook for Taiwan remains very attractive as one of the fastest-growing economies in the world. Near-term domestic demand from the Six-Year National Development Plan should provide a strong cushion to mitigate effects of any slower international economic growth. The inevitable bankruptcy of communist ideology and fast growth along the coastal regions of mainland China will provide a significant push for the Taiwanese economy in the coming decades.

While the financial system in Taiwan has been a bottleneck, the government has followed and implemented a clear policy of liberalization and internationalization, albeit with occasional back stepping such as the Central Bank's temporary halt of inward remittance of QFII funds in February of 1992. The stock market is becoming less volatile. The monthly average index close for the period of August through December of 1991 was 4779, 469, 4541, 4449, and 4439, while the trough for the period was only 20% off the peak. The supply of shares will also increase rapidly as the government accelerates the privatization of national enterprises. Foreign institutions that decide to participate in the local stock market may also find it rewarding to invest funds in local government bonds that provide yields higher than what Taiwan might otherwise pay in international capital markets.

Foreigners that cannot invest as QFII in Taiwan may invest indirectly through the funds managed by the QFIIs or funds managed by the four local fund management companies, or purchase selected issues of Euro-convertible bonds or Global Depositary Receipts of Taiwan companies as a growing number of them begin to tap international capital markets.

Publications Issued by the Taiwan Stock Exchange

Some of the publications issued by the Taiwan Stock Exchange include the following:

1. The Status of Securities on the Taiwan Stock Exchange (monthly)

2. Stock Exchange Monthly Review

3. Taiwan Stock Exchange Statistical Data (monthly)

4. An Introduction to The Taiwan Stock Exchange (annual)

5. Taiwan Stock Exchange Trading Volume, Value, and Stock Price Index (annual)

7. Taiwan Stock Exchange Annual Report

The address for the Taiwan Stock Exchange is as follows:
Taiwan Stock Exchange
7-10 Fl. 85 Yen Ping S. Rd.
Taipei, Taiwan

Republic of China
Telephone: (02) 311-4020
Fax: (02) 391-5591

Some of the publications issued by the Securities and Exchange Commission include the following:

1. SEC Statistics (annual)

2. Annual Report of Securities Management in R.O.C.

3. Securities Management (bimonthly)

The address for the Securities and Exchange Commission is as follows:
Securities and Exchange Commission
Ministry of Finance
12th Fl., 3 Nan-Hai Road
Taipei, Taiwan
Republic of China
Telephone: (02) 341-3101

Company Profiles*

Asia Cement Corporation

Cement   Asia Cement Corp. (ACC) will become Taiwan's largest cement producer (from second largest currently) after its third plant comes on stream in June 1992. It has been listed since 1960 and is the second largest company on the Taiwan Stock Exchange excluding banking stocks. ACC was established by Mr. Y. S. Hsu and is a leading member of the Far East Group, which includes four listed companies (Far Eastern Textile, Far Eastern Department Store, U-Ming Marine and Oriental Union Chemical) and about 60 unlisted affiliates. ACC operates two cement and clinker production plants in Hsinchu (northern Taiwan) and Hualien (eastern coast), one grinding plant in Keelung, and four ready-mixed cement factories in northern Taiwan. ACC is currently operating at full capacity. A third cement plant is scheduled to open in Huyalien in 1992. Exports accounted for 14% of total sales in 1989, of which 74% went to Japan, 17% to Hong Kong, and the rest to the United States. Major shareholders are the Hsu family (30%), Far Eastern Textile (27%), Sing Kong Life Insurance (6%) and Hsu Yuen Chi Medical Foundation (5%).

*Company profiles are provided by the editors.

Compeq

Electronics   Compeq is the largest printed circuit board (PCB) manufacturer in Taiwan with a local market share of around 13% (300 PCB producers in Taiwan). In global terms, it is the 10th-largest company specializing in PCB manufacturing. It was incorporated in 1973 to produce single- and double-sided PCBs. In 1982, Compeq became an authorized supplier to IBM and thus opened up the U.S. market. Since then, it has begun the production of technically more sophisticated multilayered PCBs. In 1987, it became an authorized supplier to Fujitsu. Therefore, Compeq entered the Japanese market. In 1990, it became an authorized supplier to Siemens and hopes this will be the springboard to the European market. The products are used in PC peripherals (42%), PC mainboards (25%), workstations (10%), mainframe computers (7%), large disk drives (7%), minicomputers (4%), and telecommunications equipment (2%). Compeq has two factories in Taoyuan with 1,240 employees and a new factory in Utah. Approximately 25% of profits in 1990 were from a 40% owned joint venture with National (Japan) to produce laminate and prepreg. About 50% of the shares are owned by the board. Mr. C. Wu, President of Compeq, owns 10% of the company. Two other major shareholders, Chen and Chang families, are also responsible for key management positions.

Chuan Yuan Steel

Steel   Chuan Yuan Steel (CYS) was established in 1965. In terms of revenues, it is the largest private listed steel company in TSE. It is a steel plate processing company and its products include hot-rolled and cold-rolled steel plate, structural steel, special steel, silicon steel, container steel, and parts. Sales break down as follows: steel plate (50%), container parts (24%), special steel (15%), casting steel (6%), and others (5%). CYS sources about 80% of raw material from China Steel and the rest from import. Over 95% of the products are sold domestically.

Evergreen Marine Corporation Taiwan

Transportation   Evergreen Marine Corporation Taiwan (EMC) is the largest container shipper in the world. It operates six regular container lines: eastbound round-the-world (rtw); westbound rtw; Taiwan, Hong Kong, U.S. west coast; Japan pacific Northwest; Far East/Mediterranean; western Mediterranean, U.S. east coast. In addition to mother vessels plying between the world's major ports, EMC also maintains a feeder network of container ships to nearby ports in each region. Combined with its inland transportation network, this gives Evergreen a total intermodal transportation system. EMC owns 34 vessels, with the 19th largest less than 7 years old, and with 15-20 more vessels through its 40% owned listed subsidiary Uniglory. It also has five other major subsidiaries in shipping-related businesses. Operations are fully computerized (EMC is the largest client of IBM in Taiwan), and its ships are some of the most efficient and operationally advanced in the world. EMC, along with others of the Evergreen group, have taken a 30% stake in EVA Airlines, Taiwan's first private airline with 2 planes and 24 ordered. EMC is owned 29% by a Panamanian holding company and is controlled by its founder, Chang Yung-fa.

International Bills Finance

Finance   International Bills Finance (IBF) was established in 1976 by a group of government-controlled banks at the request of the Ministry of Finance and is the largest of the three bills finance companies in Taiwan. Bills finance companies underwrite, trade, and guarantee short-term bills, which include treasury bills, negotiable certificates of deposit (NCD), bank acceptances (BA), commercial paper (CP), and bonds maturing within one year. Trading gains on short-term NCDs and bills contributed to 61% of total revenues in 1990 (a 217% increase over 1989), handling charges 18% (72%), and interest income 21% (118%). The Taiwan money market is an oligopoly dominated by these three companies, with all having approximately an equal market share, while only IBF and Chung Hsin Bills Finance are listed. The major shareholders are Taiwan Sugar (9%), Taiwan Cooperative Bank (7%), Taipei City Bank (7%).

Microtek International

Electronics   Microtek International (MI) is one of the leading high-tech companies in the Hsinchu Science-based Industrial Park, about 80 km southwest of Taipei, where a number of higher academic institutions of science and technology are located. It was established in 1980 to produce MICE (microprocessor in-circuit emulator, a facility used to develop microcomputers) and image scanners. MICE is used in the design and testing of integrated circuits. The three main product lines are scanner systems (46%), MICE (37%), EPROM (externally programmable read only memory) programmer systems (8%), and laser printers. MICE and EPROM programmers are popular in the European market, while scanners are mostly sold in the United States. Around 85% of products are exported (38% to the United States, 34% to Europe, and 28% to Asia). Microtek is owned 32% by Vicky Wong and 7% by Benny Hsu. Foreign ownership of Microtek amounts to 34% and is composed of 50% institutional and 50% individual investors.

Microelectronics Technology Incorporated

Telecommunications   Microelectronic Technology Inc. (MTI) is Taiwan's only large producer of sophisticated telecommunications products using the latest microwave integrated circuit technology. It was established in 1982 in Hsinchu Science-based Industrial Park by a group of experts trained in Silicon Valley. MTI concentrates on two main areas: satellite communications systems (SCS) and digital microwave radio transceivers (DMRT), which accounted for about 37% and 63% of operating profits respectively. Major product lines in satellite communication systems are direct broadcasting satellites, marine satellite systems (MARISAT), portable satellite communication systems (one of the lightest products was the portable satellite phone system used by CNN during the Gulf war) and very small satellite terminals. Satellite communication systems are expected to rise to 45% of operating profits in 1991. Exports accounted for over 80% of the total sales in 1990. Hewlett Packard and Dynateck Development Corp. (USA) are the major shareholders, owning 23% and 17% respectively.

President Enterprises

Food/Retail Trade   President Enterprises is the largest food company in Taiwan. It was founded in Tainan in 1967 by Kao Chin-Yen and was listed in 1987. It began as a flour manufacturer and later expanded into feed and grain, processed food, beverages, retailing, electronics, securities brokering, and service industries. President is part of the Tainan group, which includes Tainan Spinning and Universal Cement, one of the largest conglomerates in Taiwan. In terms of total assets, President was ranked 14th among the business groups in Taiwan. In terms of turnover, it was ranked ninth, which corresponds to a Fortune 500 ranking of 450. President has a wide range of products in the food business. About 17% of the sales in 1990 were from canned foods, 15% from dairy products, 15% from nonfood merchandise, 13% from feedmeal, 12% from noodles, 9% from oils and fats, 5% from bread and 14% from other operations.

Taiwan (ROC) Fund

Country Fund   The Taiwan (ROC) Fund is one of four Taiwan funds and one of two listed on the New York Stock Exchange. It has a conservative management and traditionally trades at a premium to NAV.

Teco

Electric and Electronic Products   Teco was established in 1956 as the first electric motor producer in Taiwan and is now one of Taiwan's leading electric and electronic appliance companies. Teco is a conglomerate with 11 affiliates in related businesses, such as Great Teco Trading (75%), Teco Information (70%), Tecom (50%), Teco Industrial (25%), and United Microelectronic (20%), etc. These subsidiaries provided about 30% of pre-tax income. In 1990, household appliances accounted for 43% of sales, industrial machinery for 37%, and the electronics division (Teco Information) 20%. Motors and air-conditioners are the main products, which contributed 49% and 37% to net profits respectively. Teco operates four factories in Northern Taiwan and has about 3,000 employees. Currently, Teco has several branch offices in Australia, Singapore, and the USA. Exports accounted for 19% of total sales in 1990. Major export markets were the USA, Australia, and Singapore.

Thanalux

Textiles and Clothing   Thanalux (TNL) was founded in 1975 and listed in 1984 to manufacture shirts for the domestic market under the Arrow trademarks and is one of the manufacturing arms of the Saha Pathanpibul group. It currently manufactures a broad range of middle- to up-market garments and leather products produced under established French and U.S. names such as Arrow, Guy Laroche, Absorba, Ellesse, and others. Sales breakdown by product lines are shirts (41%), leather products (20%), children's wear (17%), and ladies' garments, sportswear, and other (22%). Domestic marketing is handled exclusively through International Cosmetics (ICC), another member of the Saha Pathana Group, whose strength allows TNL products to command prime display sites in department stores. TNL has 2,500 employees, comprising 90% production workers and 10% administrative staff. Labor accounts for 16% of production costs, raw materials 72%. Over 90% of raw materials are sourced in the domestic market.

Tung Ho Steel

Steel   Tung Ho Steel (THS) is the largest electric steel producer in Taiwan. Major products are billets and steel bars (95% of sales), all sold domestically. A new product, H-beams used in large building construction, will come on stream in 1993 and when in full operation will account for 50% of total sales. THS concentrates on the higher-end market and commands 10% of the local steel bars market. It is the market leader in local high-tension steel bars with a 50% market share. Current annual capacity is 528,000 tons. Around 60% of the scrap steel is sourced from the local market. Imports mainly come from South Africa (32% of imports), the United States (26%), and the Netherlands (25%). The major shareholder is the Ho family, which owns 36% of THS.

Yuen Foong Yu Paper

Paper and Pulp   Yuen Foong Yu Paper (YFY) was established in 1950 by the Ho family and is the only fully-integrated paper producer in Taiwan. YFY is one of the largest members of the Yuen Foong Yu Group, a major conglomerate in Taiwan involved in paper, computer, chemical production, and financial services. It is now the largest manufacturer of printing and writing paper, with a 44% market share and ranking as the 24th largest industrial corporation in Taiwan in 1990. Four major product lines are printing and writing paper (57% of sales), kraft and paper board (27%), converting paper (13%), and tissue (4%). Domestic sales decreased to 75% in 1990 from 85% in 1989 due to increased capacity. About 50% of the exports went to South East Asia, 25% to China, and 25% to Japan. YFY was the first company in Taiwan to issue an overseas convertible bond. In 1988, YFY merged with another family paper company, Yuen Foon Yuan, and issued preferred stocks to convert

Yuen Foon Yuan shares into YFY paper. YFY is owned by the Ho family (16%) and various directors of the company (18%).

1. The four companies were Taiwan Cement Co., Ltd., Taiwan Paper Co., Ltd., Agriculture and Forestry Co., Ltd., and Industrial and Mining Co., Ltd.

2. Insider trading and market manipulation are illegal, but enforcement has been less than satisfactory.

3. Capital gains tax on sale of listed stocks was suspended in 1976 in order to encourage companies to go public. It was reimposed at the beginning of 1989 but with a loophole: exemptions applied to gains of each individual whose value of stock sales totaled less than NT $10 million a year. Under pressure from investors and legislative members (many of whom are affiliated with brokerage firms), the government rescinded the tax in one year.

THAILAND: FROM MINI-MARKET
TO LEADING EMERGING MARKET

Antoine W. van Agtmael
President, Emerging Markets Management
Washington, D. C., United States

Over the past decade, the Securities Exchange of Thailand (SET) has developed from a mini-market into one of the world's major emerging markets, with market capitalization growing from $1 billion to $36 billion, annual trading volume from $100 million to $30 billion, and the number of listed companies more than tripling from 80 to 276 between December 1981 and December 1991.

Fueling this rapid market growth were strong economic and industrial growth, sound and stable economic policies, high savings and investment rates, growing local wealth, attractive stock market returns, a generally stable political climate, and—in recent years—a heavy influx of foreign portfolio investment, including a number of country funds.

While research has improved tremendously, the SET has steadily modernized its operations and the brokers have significantly upgraded their facilities, Thailand's regulatory structure, despite improvements, remains antiquated and has not fully adapted to the needs of a much more sophisticated marketplace.

Market Size and Trading Activity

As of December 1991, the market capitalization of the SET reached Baht 897 billion ($36 billion). The Thai market represents 5% of the emerging markets. Market capitalization equals approximately 38% of GNP which is relatively high among developing countries. Not only has the size of the market increased dramatically from only $1 billion in 1981 and below $2 billion in 1985, but liquidity and market depth have also improved significantly over the years. Daily average trading volume was about $125 million during 1991. The turnover in the market (trading volume/average market capitalization) of 102% in 1991 was exceeded only by the 167% and 112% in the two boom years of 1978 and 1987 but was much higher than the 10%-20% level during the early 1980s when trading volume amounted to only $100-300 million annually. The number of companies listed has risen steadily over the years from 21 in 1975, 77 in 1980, and 100 in 1985. Foreign investors were virtually absent until the mid-1980s but have more recently played an important although not dominant part. Foreign board trading amounted to a daily average of $30 million or about 20% of the total trading volume. A historical perspective on key market statistics is presented in Table 7-1.

History

The SET, a combination of both marketplace and regulatory agency, was established in April 1975. It followed the enactment in 1974 of more comprehensive securities legislation based on a study by Professor Sidney Robbins, a former official of the U.S. Securities and Exchange Commission. Robbins recommended a major overhaul of the existing, more informal stock market established in earlier years by a group of local brokers in favor of a central, more regulated institution.

It took the SET several years to overcome the speculative image of earlier activities, unfamiliarity of the general public with stocks, and reluctance of company founders to release even a small portion of their ownership. This was not surprising at the low prices then prevailing and relatively easy availability of credit for family groups with ties or good relations with banks. On top of this, the political instability in neighboring Cambodia, Laos, and Vietnam alarmed many potential investors in Thailand and abroad. However, in 1977, trading and prices began a steep boom which ended in a speculative frenzy in 1978 and an equally sudden collapse in 1979. Several factors contributed to the widespread speculation, overbought market, and inevitable crash which was finally triggered by the failure of Raja Finance, a popular finance company (also one of the "hottest" stocks) because of fraud. First, the SET and brokers had been unprepared for the meteoric increase in trading activity and settlements, despite frantic efforts to catch up and set up systems. Moreover, investors were inexperienced and tempted by easily available margin finance (officially up to 70% of the purchase price but in practice often as high as 100% because the brokers were unable or unwilling to monitor their exposure). And finally, manipulation and insider trading were rampant because of inadequate legislation, confusion among regulatory authorities, insufficient monitoring systems, a breakdown of settlement methods, and inefficient registration methods. All of these are common problems in emerging markets at comparably early stages of development.

Table 7-1   Historical Perspective on Key Market Statistics for Thailand

Year	Listings	Market Capitalization ($$ Million)	Trading Volume ($ Million)	Turnover (%)	New Issues	Year-end P/E	Year-end P/BV	SET Index U.S. $ (%)	IFC Thai Index U.S. $ (%)	Exchange Rate U.S. $ (%)
1991	279	35,815.0	30,089.0	102.2	65	14.3	3.2	18.1	36.1	1.8
1990	214	23,895.9	23,089.1	92.6	102	13.8	3.6	-30.3	-19.5	1.2
1989	175	25,647.9	13,451.7	78.5	78	26.4	2.1	127.3	126.9	-1.6
1988	141	8,811.3	5,597.8	78.6	N/A	12.0	3.8	35.7	42.5	0.0
1987	125	5,485.1	4,633.2	111.7	N/A	9.3	3.9	37.5	37.9	3.7
1986	98	2,877.9	1,133.4	47.8	N/A	12.3	4.3	53.5	79.9	2.0
1985	100	1,855.8	568.4	31.2	N/A	9.6	8.2	-5.1	2.0	1.9
1984	96	1,720.4	433.9	22.0	N/A	7.2	9.1	5.8	-1.0	-15.3
1983	88	1,487.9	380.7	25.6	N/A	6.5	7.0	8.9	22.1	0.0
1982	81	1,259.6	238.3	18.9	1	11.8	8.5	15.8	35.1	0.0
1981	80	1,002.5	108.1	10.2	3	9.5	9.6	-14.5	-29.5	-10.3
1980	77	1,206.2	307.8	25.3	8	6.4	9.4	-16.5	-16.3	-1.0
1979	69	1,344.2	1,066.9	79.3	9	5.8	9.2	-42.2	-40.0	0.0
1978	61	1,567.1	2,630.9	167.4	21	8.5	5.7	41.8	1.4	0.0
1977	39	899.7	1,277.1	141.9	14	6.1	3.9	122.0	116.3	0.0
1976	25	337.1	48.0	14.2	6	5.8	7.3	-2.4	-2.6	0.0
1975	21	253.4	26.9	10.6	21	5.0	10.2	—	—	0.0

Source: Securities Exchange of Thailand IFC EM Database; Researched by Emerging Market Management

The decade-long rise of the Thai stock market in the 1980s was, unlike the speculative frenzy of the late 1970s, built on a solid economic base although it ended, as stock market booms usually do, in a period where foreign and local investors began to outbid each other in a speculative climate. The 1980s were characterized by Thailand's emergence as one of the newly industrializing countries (NICs) with the following: (1) on average GNP growth of 8% (culminating in 12%-13% growth in 1988-1989); (2) a drop in inflation from double digits to 2%-3% in 1986-1987 followed by a modest rise to the 6% level by 1990-1991; (3) continuous high savings and investment rates (above 20%); (4) strong growth in foreign investment (especially from Japan and increasingly also other Asian countries); and (5) a turnaround in government finance from budget deficits to surpluses, enormous export growth averaging over 20% annually, and a boom in corporate earnings. This was accompanied by a decline in interest rates (until the late 1980s). Rates remained, however, positive in real terms and thus discouraged over-lending in favor of a spate of new offerings which reached a peak of 102 new issues in 1990.

After the collapse of trading volumes and prices in 1979, accompanied by a decline of the market p/e from over 21x to 6x and a rise of the dividend yield to 14%, it took the SET three years to begin its fairly steady, decade-long recovery which was interrupted only by one down year (in 1985) and a temporary drop in late 1987 after the crash in New York. Local enthusiasm and a heavy influx of liquidity from newly established Thai funds entangled the market in a growing speculative atmosphere which was bound to lead to a major correction. Finally, it was the worldwide domino effect on equity markets of the New York Crash which took the steam out of local market fever. The SET Index tumbled 52% from its high within a few weeks. The recovery already began before the end of 1987 as it became clear that the worldwide market crash had not significantly dented the economic dynamism in South East Asia. It was only interrupted by relatively minor technical corrections until August 1990 when Kuwait was invaded causing a second worldwide shockwave which Thailand did not escape. Earlier, the SET Index had reached a peak as a democratic government was elected in early 1990, companies showed strong earnings growth and foreign exchange controls were liberalized.

After their disastrous experience with the boom in 1978, brokers were now ready for the vastly increased volume. There was much more institutional investment (mostly from funds but also from increased participation by provident funds), and margin loans played only a marginal role. The rise in the market made it more attractive for companies to offer their shares to the general public, while the rapid industrial expansion required a major infusion of funds for new investment. Moreover, professional management gradually took over from the original founders as day-to-day managers and corporate owners became more sophisticated in maintaining control without majority ownership and, thus, less fearful of losing control to outside shareholders. As a result of all of these developments, and supported marginally by modest tax incentives for listed companies, the major Thai corporations increasingly listed their shares and did rights issues to increase their equity base.

However, speculative pressures remained. Taiwanese and Hong Kong investors entered the Thai market after their own markets collapsed. Manipulation by a few major players remained an endemic problem without serious efforts to control it, earnings forecasts by companies (especially those related to real estate) and brokers were often inflated, and profits from early successes in real estate investment added to the speculative atmosphere until the condominium craze in Bangkok began to go sour. The invasion of Kuwait was no more than the "straw that broke the camel's back" because at the same time more fundamental problems should have led to a market correction. Economic growth began to slow down as the expansion bumped up against infrastructural barriers, a tighter monetary policy caused higher interest rates as the authorities became concerned about inflation and the current account, and a slowdown in corporate earnings momentum raised questions on expanded p/e multiples and high prices in comparison with underlying book values (Figure 7.1).

The Thai market adjusted to these new, more sober realities in late 1990, although it moved up again in early 1991 as the war in the Middle East was ended relatively quickly and with only temporary impact on the world economy. In February 1991, a military coup ended Thailand's democratically elected government, but it became quickly evident to most informed observers that there was no fundamental change in political direction. The traditional balance between King, technocrats, business, and the military remained intact, but this short-term reversal from democracy was aimed at cleaning up rampant corruption and pushing through a number of long overdue structural reforms in anticipation of a new constitution which would establish a sounder basis for elected government. The Thai market went into the dolldrums again in mid-1991 which brought it to the most attractive valuation levels in several years. While it is no longer the "flavor of the month" among international investors, the Thai market has become a small but relatively steady part of major internationally oriented portfolios as it has become better known and researched.

Structure of the Market

The major listings represent a broadly diversified cross-section of the Thai economy. Financial institutions and industrials each have a one-third share of total market capitalization with services and others making up the remainder. Banks dominate the financial institutions, but there is also active trading in finance and insurance companies. Among the main industrials are conglomerates, food, agribusiness, textiles, and footwear. Services include hotels and newspapers while

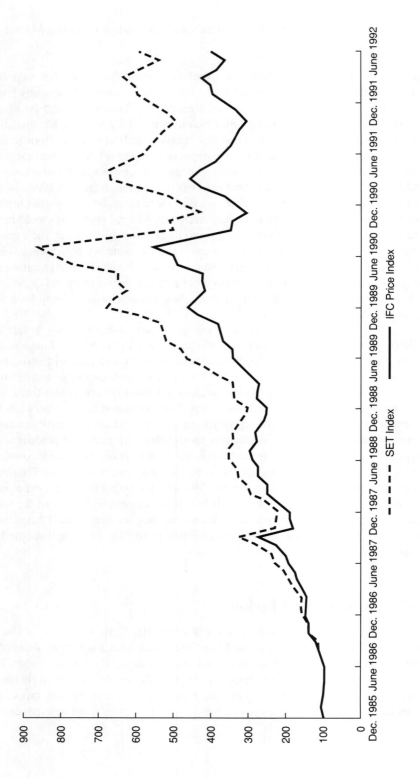

Figure 7-1 Thailand Market Performance

Dec. 1985 June 1986 Dec. 1986 June 1987 Dec. 1987 June 1988 Dec. 1988 June 1989 Dec. 1989 June 1990 Dec. 1990 June 1991 Dec. 1991 June 1992

- - - - SET Index   ——— IFC Price Index

Table 7-2   Stocks Ranked by Market Capitalization in Thailand

Ranking	Company	Industry	Market Capitalization (U.S. $)	Country Weight	December 1991 P/E
1.	Bangkok Bank	Banking	2,748	6.4%	4.99
2.	Siam Cement	Cement and Glass Products	2,299	5.3%	17.30
3.	Thai Farmers Bank	Banking	1,281	3.0%	7.25
4.	Tanayong	Real Estate	1,203	2.8%	—
5.	Siam Commercial Bank	Banking	997	2.3%	9.53
6.	Siam City Cement	Cement and Glass Products	789	1.8%	23.13
7.	Krung Thai Bank	Banking	702	1.6%	19.74
8.	Krisada Mahanakorn	Real Estate	664	1.5%	—
9.	Bank Ayudhya	Banking	663	1.5%	9.97
10.	Land and House	General Building Contractors	624	1.4%	32.87
11.	Finance One	Credit Agencies Other Than Banks	598	1.4%	—
12.	TPI Polene	Petroleum Refining & Related Products	598	1.4%	13.92
13.	Shinawatra Computer	Communications	468	1.1%	49.53
14.	Dsfsco	Credit Agencies Other Than Banks	419	1.0%	17.39
15.	Phatra Thanakit	Credit Agencies Other Than Banks	416	1.0%	37.46
16.	CP Feedmill	Agricultural Production–Livestock	412	1.0%	10.95
17.	Asia Credit	Credit Agencies Other Than Banks	327	0.8%	13.73
18.	Thai-German Ceramic	Cement and Glass Products	318	0.7%	18.83
19.	IFCT	Credit Agencies Other Than Banks	312	0.7%	8.20
20.	Union Asia Finance	Credit Agencies Other Than Banks	297	0.7%	23.02
21.	1st Bangkok City Bank	Banking	290	0.7%	21.12
22.	Tisco	Credit Agencies Other Than Banks	288	0.7%	9.16
23.	Siam Pulp & Paper	Paper and Allied Products	276	0.6%	14.21
24.	Siam City Bank	Banking	275	0.6%	10.22
25.	New Imperial Hotel	Hotels and Other Lodging Places	265	0.6%	47.23

Source: IFC Emerging Markets Database

several mines and major distributors of consumer goods are also listed. Table 7-2 shows the breakdown of market capitalization and trading volume by sector.

Investors

Traditionally, the Thai market has been dominated by individual investors among whom female buyers were a particularly important group. The Thai brokers are geared toward the retail market by having mini-duplicates of the trading floor in their offices where price quotations were adjusted on the boards through direct radio links with the SET, enabling clients to follow market events (and excitement) very closely. Domestic institutional investors did not play an important part until recent years. Insurance companies were constrained in their buying of shares by government regulation and risk aversion, although they have been more active in recent years. Pension funds were virtually absent from the market until 1988 (when antiquated Provident Fund legislation was finally changed) because neither contributions nor return on investment were tax deductible (as they are in many other countries). And finally, the development of a mutual fund industry was blocked by the monopoly given to the Mutual Fund Company (MFC), an affiliate of the semi-governmental development bank, for managing investment funds and later even for acting as the sole domestic adviser to "on-shore" country funds. The only traditional major domestic institutional investors were the Crown Property Bureau which has a stake in many Thai bluechips and the banks which—directly or through their founding families—have significant stakes in many companies. Table 7-3 lists the 20 most actively traded shares by Market Value, SET, in 1991.

Foreign Portfolio Investment

Until the mid-1980s, Thailand was virtually unknown among international investors. In fact, the Bangkok Fund, Thailand's first country fund offered by Merrill Lynch in August 1985, barely raised $10 million initially. Its excellent performance disproved the hesitations of many international investors who still looked upon Thailand with suspicion as a small casino. Even more important was the success of the NYSE-listed Korea Fund in 1984 which gradually created a new "fashion" among international investors. In December 1986, the $30 million Thailand Fund was offered, with MFC as local adviser ensuring status as a "local" investor rather than as a foreign investor subject to foreign investment restrictions. Beginning in February 1988, 11 other on-shore country funds and two other off-shore country funds were offered in rapid succession over the next two years, raising a total of over $1 billion as Thailand basked in its newly found popularity. Foreign portfolio investors have not only participated through these country funds, a large number of regional funds and several global emerging markets funds have also

**Table 7-3   The Twenty Most Actively Traded Shares
by Market Value, SET, 1991**

Ranking	Company	Market Value (Baht Billion)
1.	Siam Cement	69.60
2.	Bangkok Bank	43.80
3.	Thai Farmers Bank	29.68
4.	Siam City Cement	25.16
5.	Krung Thai Bank	18.96
6.	Shinawatra Computer	17.46
7.	Land and House	16.50
8.	Thai-German Ceramic	11.85
9.	Phatra Thanakit	9.40
10.	Asia Credit	8.26
11.	Tisco	8.18
12.	1st Bangkok City Bank	7.79
13.	Padaeng Industry	7.40
14.	Saha-Union	7.38
15.	Dahana Siam Finance & Securities	7.10
16.	Siam City Bank	7.09
17.	Asia Securities Trading	5.85
18.	Union Asia Finance	5.59
19.	National Finance & Securities	5.55
20.	General Finance & Securities	4.08

Source: IFC Emerging Markets Database

invested actively in Thailand during the past few years. A select group of European, U.S., and Japanese pension funds, investment funds, and insurance companies have also invested directly in various Thai stocks, mostly on a long- term basis, while (mostly individual) investors from Hong Kong and Taiwan have also drifted into and out of the Thai market occasionally. Detailed information on the country funds is provided in Table 7-4 and statistics on annual foreign portfolio investment flows and the share of trading activity as well as the percentage ownership by foreigners can be found in Table 7-5.

In 1988, a special "foreign board" was established for trading in those shares that are registered in foreign names and may be purchased within the foreign ownership limit of certain companies. A number of companies have no such limitations, but the Banking Law restricts ownership in banks to 49% while other laws limit ownership in finance companies also to 49% and in a number of other companies to 50%. Moreover, there are more stringent limitations in the articles of association (sometimes as low as 25%) of many other companies, including many of the blue chips and several with excellent growth prospects, limiting foreign involvement. As a result, a foreign premium has developed for many stocks which may range between 10% and 70% but which has fluctuated over time depending on Thailand's popularity among international investors. The premiums were highest in the period before the August 1989 drop in prices and, because of an absence of

Table 7-4   Country Funds in Thailand

On-Shore Funds, 1990

	The Thailand Fund	The Thai Fund	The Thai-Euro Fund	The Thailand Growth Fund	The Thai Prime Fund	The Thailand International Fund
1. Investment money						
-Fund value	US $30m	US $115m	US $75m	US $50m	US $155m	US $75m
-Par value	-	-	US $10	-	-	-
-Offering price (per unit)	US $10.375	US $12.00	US $10.70	US $10.10	US $10.00	US $10.67
-Placement	Institutions in Europe & America	60% in USA, the rest in Europe & Japan	Europe	Japan	Europe, Japan, and Singapore	Europe
2. Registration	Thailand	Thailand USA	Thailand Guernsey	Thailand	Thailand Singapore	Thailand Cayman Islands
3. Parties involved	IFC Vickers da Costa Morgan Stanley BIL MFC	Salomon Brothers IFC Deutsche Bank Capital Morgan Stanley MFC	Lloyds Investment Manager Hoare Govett MFC Phatra Tanakit	Nikko Securities Asian Development Bank Nikko Merchant Bank (Singapore) MFC	Nomura Securities Co., Ltd (Japan) IFC Singapore Nomura Merchant Banking MFC	Swiss Bank Corp. Investment Banking Fidelity International Ltd. MFC
4. Investment adviser	Morgan Stanley Asset Management	Morgan Stanley Asset Management	Lloyds Bank Fund Management	Nikko International Capital Management (NICAM)(Singapore)	Nomura Capital Management	Fidelity International Ltd.
5. Management company	MFC	MFC	MFC	MFC	MFC	MFC
6. Custodian	Krung Thai Bank	Thai Farmers Bank	Thai Farmers Bank	Siam Commercial Bank	Bangkok Bank	Bangkok Bank
7. Listing	London	New York	London	Tokyo	London Singapore	London
8. Launching date	December 1986	February 1988	May 1988	May 1988	September 1988	November 1988
9. Life	25 years	25 years	50 years	25 years	25 years	25 years
10. Type	Open-end	Closed-end	Closed-end	Closed-end	Closed-end	Closed-end

Table 7-4   (Continued)

	The Thai-Asia Fund	The Thai Asset Fund	The Thai-Equity Fund	The Thailand Capital Fund	The Thai Equity Growth Fund	The Thailand Emerging Fund
1. Investment money						
–Fund value	US $50m	US $50m	US $50m	US $69m	US $75m	US $150-200m
–Par value	US $10	US $10	US $10	—	US $10	US $10
–Offering price (per unit)	US $10.00	US $10.68	US $10.50	US $12.00	—	—
–Placement	Asia-Pacific	Asia, Australia, and Hong Kong	Singapore	World-wide	Europe and America	Japan
2. Registration	Thailand Cayman Islands	Thailand Guernsey	Thailand Singapore	Thailand USA	Thailand	Thailand UK
3. Parties involved	Scimitar Asset Mgmt Ais Ltd. Standard Chartered Asia Limited Chintung Limited MFC	Elders Finance Group Elders Finance Pacific Ltd. MFC	DCBC DBS Bank MFC	Daiwa Securities (USA) Merrill Lynch Daiwa International (HK) MFC	Credit Swiss First Boston MFC	Normura Securities MFC
4. Investment adviser	Scimitar Asset Management Asia Limited	Elders Finance Pacific Limited	Capital International Limited	Daiwa International Capital Management (HK) Ltd.	—	—
5. Management company	MFC	MFC	MFC	MFC	MFC	MFC
6. Custodian	Standard Chartered Bank Bangkok	Siam Commercial Bank	Thai Farmers Bank	Bangkok Bank	—	—
7. Listing	Hong Kong	Hong Kong Australia	Singapore	New York	New York	London
8. Launching date	November 1989	November 1989	March 1990	May 1990	—	—
9. Life	25 years	25 years	20 years	25 years	25 years	25-50 years
10. Type	Closed-end	Closed-end	Closed-end	Closed-end	Closed-end	Closed-end

Source: The Thai Partners International Limited

Table 7-5 Off-Shore Funds, 1990

	Bangkok Fund	Siam Fund	Thai Investment Fund
1. Investment money			
-Fund value	U.S. $67m	U.S. $95m	US $30m
-Offer price (per unit)	—	U.S. $13.75	US $10.40
-Placement	Europe and North America	Europe	Europe and Japan
2. Registration	Singapore	Cayman Islands (through Singapore)	Guernsey Island
3. Participants	First Overseas Bangkok Investment (Merrill Lynch & Cazenove)	Banque Indosuez (Geneva branch)	Yamaichi International (Europe)
4. Investment adviser	Bangkok First Investment and Trust	Asia Securities Trading	Asia Securities Trading
5. Management company	First Overseas Bangkok Investment	Indosuez Asia Investment Services	Yamaichi Capital Management (Guernsey)
6. Listing	London	London	London
7. Launch date	August 1985 (U.S. $10m) November 1986 (U.S. $15m) March 1988 (U.S. $17m)	December 1987 (U.S. $40m) April 1988 (U.S. $55m)	April 1988
8. Life	50 years	50 years	50 years
9. Type	Open-end	Closed-end	Closed-end Open-end (starting from 1988)

Source: The Thai Partners International Limited

trading in several stocks, they sometimes adjusted to more realistic levels only slowly, creating distortions which only those who followed the market closely recognized.

Technical Market Details

Stock Exchange and Trading System

The Securities Exchange of Thailand (SET) is Thailand's only stock exchange with trading hours from 9:00 a.m. to noon Monday through Friday. Recently a second trading session was added, expanding the trading hours. All trading in listed securities must take place through the SET by the 35 member securities companies. Members may not trade listed securities outside the SET. Short selling is not allowed. Prices may not move more than 10% up or down from the previous day's close and may not open the next day by more than four price "spreads."

Starting in May 1991, the SET began fully computerized trading operations which eliminated the need for a trading floor. Until that time, a trading floor system similar to that of many other Asian markets was used. Bids and offers of individual stocks were displayed on individual boards along the walls of the trading floor around which the brokers gathered. Trading was by open auction. Floor brokers quoted their bids in a buying column and their offers in a selling column together with their firm's identification. The floor broker on the opposite side of the trade was obliged to take the first quote on the board which corresponded with his or her bid or offer. The selling member was responsible for executing the sales record and having it signed by both parties, filling out the sales contract in triplicate and delivering the third copy to the SET officials who entered the trades into the SET's computer system for clearing and setttlement. Separate boards were used for transactions in "foreign registered" shares, odd lots (typically less than 100 shares or Baht 10,000), and block trades in excess of Baht 10 million or 10% of the company's registered paid-up capital. Such block trades required special SET approval.

The address of the SET is as follows:

Securities Exchange of Thailand
Sinthon Building, 2nd floor
132 Wireless Road
Bangkok 10500 Metropolis
Telephone: (66) 2-250 00018
Fax:
Telex: 84063 CHASE FX TH (SET)
Cable: SECEXTHAI

Commissions and Other Costs

Commissions are generally as follows:

- 0.5% of the traded amount for shares, preferred shares, debentures, and mutual funds.

- 0.1% for government and state enterprise bonds.

- Regional brokers (through whom most transactions for international investors take place) typically add another 0.5% on top of the local commission.

Taxation, Foreign Investment, and Foreign Exchange Regulations

The following regulations apply:

- *Dividend withholding tax:* 15% except for countries with double taxation treaties which may be subject to a lower account.

- *Capital gains withholding tax:* 25% for non-Thai institutional investors (juristic entities), except for investors incorporated in countries with bilateral tax treaties. In certain tax treaties, a differentiation is made between investments in companies involved in real estate and other investments in listed stocks.

- Maximum foreign ownership in banks: 49%

- Other companies: 50%-100%

- Articles of Association often limit foreign ownership.

Since a major liberalization in the spring of 1990, foreign investors in listed stocks may transfer up to $500,000 in capital gains and dividends per transaction without central bank approval.

Settlement Procedures

All transactions are cleared through the SET's computerized clearing system and settled on the third day following the trading day. Physical transfer of stock certificates (for which the SET serves as registrar) is gradually being replaced by the Share Depositary Centre, a centralized computer system maintained by the SET.

Legislation, Regulation, and Disclosure

The Securities Exchange of Thailand Act, which is undergoing major revision, prohibits insider trading which is liable to both criminal prosecution by the Thai authorities and civil action by the injured party. Officers and auditors of all listed companies as well as SET officials are required to disclose changes in their shareholdings (including shares held by their spouses and children) on a semiannual basis.

Takeovers or mergers of public companies are subject to shareholders resolutions which must be passed with a 75% majority. Shareholders who object to a merger have the right to force transfer of their shares to parties to be found by the company at the most recent price quoted on the SET or the registered price, whichever is higher. Companies in Thailand are not allowed to hold treasury stock or take them in pledge.

Listing requirements are different for "listed" and "authorized" companies. A listed company must have paid-up capital of at least Baht 20 million, a minimum of 300 shareholders each owning no more than 0.5% and collectively owning at least 30% of paid-up capital. Authorized companies must have a minimum number of at least 200 shareholders owning collectively — at least 25% of the paid-up capital. Any proposed changes in capital must be submitted for approval to the SET accompanied by a detailed memorandum outlining the use of proceeds together with financial projections and pro-forma balance sheets and income statements.

Reporting requirements of listed and authorized companies include audited reports on an annual basis within three months of the end of the company's fiscal year (usually December) and unaudited quarterly financial reports. Companies listed or authorized on the SET must also immediately report in writing to the SET any event which may materially influence their share prices such as strikes, suspension of business, closure, serious damage to the company, board resolutions to increase or decrease the capital, dividend announcements or a decision to suspend dividends, mergers, and changes in management control. Within three days, companies must notify the SET of changes in directors, officers or managers, modifications to the Articles of Association, or moves of the company's principal office.

Requirements for new offerings were changed in July 1990. A detailed information book must contain at least the following data:

- Name and location of the company

- Purposes of the offer

- Clarification on whether the shares offered are existing shares or new shares and the beneficiary of the premium in the case of existing shares

- A detailed description of the offering including type and number of shares, par value and offer price, conditions of the offering, procedures of subscription and acceptance, procedure for allotments, names of those offering the shares, and commitments by underwriters to repurchase shares if listing application is denied

- Average cost per share

- Background information on the issuer including past capital increases of the past three years

- Dividend policy

- Detailed financial statements

- Data on directors, officers, and shareholders

- Name of auditor

- Articles of Association and Memorandum

- Date of publication of the information book, time and place of issue, and subsription documents

Research Sources

The SET publishes an annual fact book with extensive data on the market. Local broker research was virtually nonexistent until a few years ago when analysts of regional brokers began to cover the Thai market . It has taken a quantum jump since that time and continues to improve. Local research is available from Thai Securities which publishes a monthly research report as well as daily market comments, price information, and a press digest. Capital Securities and Asia Credit also maintain large databases on the market and individual stocks. However, the most extensive research is available from regional/international brokers (who often have close links with local securities companies) such as Crosby Securities, Baring Securities, W.I Carr, Hoare Govett, Credit Lyonnais, James Capel, and Jardine Fleming. Most regional brokers offer daily market comments, updates on earnings forecasts, company reports, and weekly or monthly market reviews with specific buy recommendations.

Company Profiles*

Alucon Manufacturing

Packaging.   Alucon Manufacturing (AM) is the largest manufacturer of rigid and flexible wall tubing products in Asia, after Japan, with an 80% market share in Thailand and a major presence in the Asian markets. Its strategic focus is the production of international standard tubing products to meet multinational customers' quality specifications where appearance and quality are of greater importance than

---

*Company profiles are provided by the editors.

price, although its products are 30% cheaper than Japan. Tubes are mainly for the cosmetic, pharmaceutical, and consumer areas where the tubes make up a relatively minor portion of total costs. It imports aluminum ingots, melts them into slugs, and then uses the slugs through an extrusion process to produce both flexible and rigid walled aluminum tubes, such as toothpaste tubes and aerosol cans. It operates two plants, one near Bangkok and one near Lam Chabang port. Alucon Manufacturing is 30% owned by the managing director and his wife.

Ayudhya Life Assurance

Life Insurance.   Ayudhya Life Assurance is a small company with about 2.5 market share of new premiums. It is controlled by the Ratanarak family, whose affiliated companies include Bank of Ayudhya and Siam City Cement. It has in its portfolio sizeable unrealized gains from its equity investments in affiliated companies, namely Ayudhya Insurance, Bank of Ayudhya and Siam City Cement.

Bangkok Bank

Banking.   Bangkok Bank (BB) was founded in 1944 and is currently the largest commercial bank in Thailand. It accounts for 27% of total assets and about 30% of foreign exchange transactions. Although its market share is decreasing, it is still twice as large as its nearest competitor. BB has over 400 on-line domestic branches with 15 overseas branches. It has a network of ATMs and is the leader of the large Bank Net pool. It has investments in financing, leasing and securities companies. The subsidiaries, most 10% owned, include Asia Credit, Union Asia Finance, Union Securities, Asia Securities, Bangkok First Investment Trust and Bangkok Insurance. BB is 20% owned by the Sophonpanich family and 4% by the Ministry of Finance.

Bank of Ayudhya

Banking.   Bank of Ayudhya (BAY) is the fifth largest commercial bank in Thailand with 7% of assets. It is a full-service commercial bank, with 6,200 employees and 211 domestic branches and one Hong Kong deposit taking company. Its loan portfolio is totally domestic, and consists of real estate (15%), manufacturing (25%), trade finance (23%), consumer loans (6%) and other (31%). It is the only bank that has 100% of its branches interconnected. BAY is managed by the Batanarak family who own at least 14% together with other companies in the group and its affiliates, Great Luck Equity and Bangkok Broadcasting and TV.

C.P. Feedmill

Agribusiness.   C.P. Feedmill (CPF) is part of the CP Group, is one of the leading Thai conglomerates and is the largest integrated agribusiness group in Asia with operations in Thailand (its original base), China, Hong Kong, Turkey and Indonesia.

Thailand is one of the world's five net exporters of food. CPF is becoming the major holding company for all Thai operations with controlling interests in CP Northeastern (CPNE) and Bangkok Agricultural Products (BAP), two other listed companies. The three companies have 3,700 employees. CP Feedmill's is the world's largest producer of shrimp food, accounting for over 50% of CP Feedmill's revenues, mostly for export to Japan. It also has its own shrimp farms, processing and cold storage facilities. The three companies annually produce over 500,000 tons of chicken (70%) and swine (30%) feed, 60 million day-old chicks, and 200-300,000 commercial pigs. The CP Group continues its diversification with a growing presence in retailing (Makro discount stores and the Kentucky Fried Chicken franchise) and a recent, massive telecommunications project. CP Pokphand, listed in Hong Kong and London, is the Group's major holding company and has a 25% stake in CP Feedmill.

IFCT

Banking. The Industrial Finance Corporation of Thailand (IFCT) was established in 1975 as Thailand's industrial development bank. A major dispute with the Thai government over its insurance of IFCT's losses on foreign loans was recently resolved and management reshuffled. The bank will move toward becoming a broader based financial institution and has established close ties with the government Savings Bank with its 500 branches. IFCT is the parent of the Mutual Fund Company which has a monopoly on managing domestic mutual funds and is adviser to many international country funds for Thailand. Major shareholders include the Ministry of Finance, Krung Thai Bank and various international banks.

Shinawatra Computer

Telecommunications. Shinawatra Computer Co. (SHI) was established in 1983 to supply IBM mainframe and minicomputers to government and state enterprises. With a view to fully exploiting the rapidly expanding markets for computers, telecommunications equipment and radio/TV broadcasting, SHIN acquired equity and/or entered into joint ventures in a number of companies. These include controlling interests in ICSI (sale and leasing computers, and providing programming and maintenance services); IBC (an operator of cable TV); Advance Info Service Ltd (with a 20 year concession to operate the 900 Mhz cellular telephone network); Digital Paging Services (with a 15 year concession to operate a digital display Phonelink paging service); Phonepoint (with 10 year concession to operate one-way telephone network), Datanet (installs AT&T data switching equipment in government premises around Bangkok); and Samart Satcom (manufacturer of satellite dishes). The Shinawatra family (54%), company directors (17%) and Singapore Telecom (10%) are the majority shareholders of SHI which was listed on the exchange in August 1990.

Siam Cement Company, Ltd.

Construction Materials.   Siam Cement Company (SCC), established in 1921 and listed since the opening of the Thai Exchange, is the flagship of the Thai economy. It is the largest producer of cement and construction materials (which account for over 70% of the earnings and 64% of domestic demand with no exports at present because of capacity constraints) and has grown into the largest industrial conglomerate with subsidiaries in virtually all basic industries, modeled on the Japanese and Korean groups. Subsidiaries produce iron and steel, petrochemicals, diesel engines, paper and pulp products, tires, gypsum board, computers, telecommunications, and mosaic tiles. SCC also has a major trading company for exports and imports of group products and those of other Thai exporters. All of the subsidiaries were acquired as ailing firms and turned around to become profitable operations aided by: a strong economy, the deep financial pockets of SCC, forward or backward integration, and a highly professional management team. SCC is a mirror of the Thai economy.

Swedish Motor Corporation

Automobiles.   Swedish Motors Corporation (SM) is the sole distributor in Thailand of Volvo cars, trucks, and buses under concessionaire agreement from AB Volvo (Sweden). Its six subsidiaries are involved in the sales, service, leasing, and assembly of automobiles in Thailand. Swedish Motor Car Sales deals in used Volvos; Swedish Transport is responsible for sales of trucks and buses; Swedish Motor Service provides after-sales service; Swedish Leasing provides hire-purchase for sales; Thai Swedish Assembly (30% owned) assembles Volvo cars and other makes under contract; and TSA land (30%) owns the land where the factory is owned. SM and its subsidiaries each have separate concessionaire agreements with AB Volvo, which are due to expire in December 1992, rolling over thereafter on a one-year notice period. Volvo distributes two car models in Thailand, but enjoys the highest market share outside Sweden with 5.2% of the total passenger car market and 45% of the luxury car segment. It is the only assembler of top-of-the-line luxury cars in Thailand, and always has the most recent models from Sweden (currently the 940 and 960 series). All cars are imported completely knocked down (CKD), while trucks and buses are imported completely built up (CBU). SM is owned 21% by Volvo (Sweden) and 20% by Churirat and Simon Bonython.

Thai Farmers Bank

Banking.   Thailand Farmers Bank (TFB) is the second largest bank (in terms of assets) in Thailand with assets of over $10.6 billion, 331 branches, 13,660 employees, and a reputation for innovation and professional management. It has a market share of 14% of total domestic bank loans and 15% of deposits. TFB has been among the pioneers in the use of ATMs, electronic banking and credit cards in

Thailand and was the first to offer transferable CDs. It is effectively controlled by the Lamsam family, while it is 5% owned by Siam Cement, and 3% by the Crown Property Bureau (the royal family).

Thai Gypsum Products Co., Ltd.

Building Materials.   Thai Gypsum (TGP) is one of two domestic suppliers of gypsum with a 50% market share. It manufacturers gypsum board (80% of sales), plaster (10%), and metal studs and other construction materials (10%) which are sold both domestically and abroad. TGP is 8% owned by United States Gypsum (USG), which is helping to increase production quality and efficiency. Thai Gypsum is currently operating at 100% of capacity, although capacity is being increased through technological improvements. TGP is owned and controlled (40%) by the Kampanatsanyakom family, and Young brothers (8%).

Thai President Foods

Food and Beverage.   Thai President Foods (TF) manufacturers and distributes wheat-based noodle products and biscuits. It is a member of the Saha Pathana group, one of the largest consumer-related groups in Thailand. Its strategy is the production of items for the food industry, mainly staples, snack foods and beverages. Its main business is the production of 11 different varieties of "Mama" instant noodles, as well as "Jummum" brand noodles. Noodles account for 86% of sales, biscuits 13% and others 1%. Biscuits are sold under the Kristop, Nissin and Farmhouse brands, with only one local major competitor (Imperial). About 20% of sales are exported, with the U.S. and Hong Kong the largest markets accounting for over 25% of exports each. TF distributes Mama and Nissin products through Saha Pathanapibul, while most other brands are sold through Octa International.

Thai Wah Company, Ltd.

Conglomerate.   Thai Wah Co. Ltd. (TWC) is a manufacturer and exporter of agricultural commodities, mainly tapioca flour and hard pellets, as well as a major property owner and developer. The company exports tapioca flour to Taiwan, Japan and the U.S., and tapioca pellets to the EC. TWC has been emphasizing its property area, a spinoff from its large agricultural landbank, with the construction and management of the Thai Wah Tower office condominium in Bangkok, the first class Dusit Laguna Hotel in Phuket (52% owned), as well as other hotels also in the Phuket area. Moreover, the company has been accumulating prime real estate in the Bangkok area and a major land bank up-country to be developed into a variety of "integrated" tourist resorts. Thai Wah is 25% owned by the Singapore-based Wah-Chang International Corporation.

Thanulux

Textiles and Clothing.   Thanulux (TNL), one of the manufacturing arms of the Saha Pathana Group, was founded in 1975 and listed in 1984 to manufacture shirts for the domestic market under the Arrow trademark. It manufacturers a broad range of middle to up-market garments and leather products produced under established French and U.S. names such as Arrow, Guy Laroche, Absorba, Ellesse and others. Arrow holds a 40% market share in Thailand's brand named menswear market. Sales breakdown by product lines are shirts (41%), leather products (20%), children's wear (17%), and ladies garments, sportswear and others (22%). Domestic marketing is handled exclusively through International Cosmetics (ICC), another member of the Saha Pathana Group, whose strength allows TNL products to command prime display sites in department stores. TNL has 2,500 employees, comprising 90% production workers and 10% administrative staff. Labor accounts for 16% of production costs, raw materials 72%. Over 90% of raw materials are sourced in the domestic market. TNL is owned 48% by the Saha Pathana Group.

Source: Emerging Markets Management.

8

MALAYSIA

Nick Seaward, Research Director
Baring Securities
Kuala Lumpur, Malaysia

Although the Kuala Lumpur Stock Exchange (KLSE) is usually described as an emerging market, by some standards it can be considered well-developed. Market capitalization as a percentage of gross domestic product is around 125%, for instance, compared with around 60% for New York and 90% for Tokyo. Turnover as a percentage of market capitalization has for some time hovered around the orderly level of 2% per month—broadly comparable to Tokyo or Sydney.

These characteristics are attributed to two factors. First, securities trading in Malaysia can be traced back to the 19th century and the concept of equity is, therefore, well-entrenched in Malaysian society. Second, the market has always been open to foreigners and for many years offered the only exposure to the palm oil and natural rubber markets. More recently, together with Singapore, it has offered one of the best direct plays on the industrialization of Southeast Asia.

Having severed all its historical ties with the Stock Exchange of Singapore (SES) in January 1990, the KLSE is attracting increased interest from overseas institutions. Widely followed international indices, such as the FT Actuaries World Index, have begun to split the KLSE out from the SES, giving the market a separate—and enhanced—weighting. This process has been accelerated by a major expansion of its market capitalization, due largely to the Malaysian government's vigorous privatization policy.

The Stock Market

Brief History

Until 1990, the development of securities trading in Malaysia moved hand-in-hand with that of Singapore. The reason for this was historical: the British started to colonize the Malay peninsula in 1786, using Singapore as its administrative and commercial center from about 1830 onward.

The same currency was used throughout the Malay states and the Straits Settlements of Penang, Malacca, and Singapore. And when the Malayan Stock Exchange was formed in May 1960, companies registered in both Singapore and the Malay peninsula were traded, despite the fact that the two territories did not enter into formal political union until September 1963 with the creation of Malaysia.

In 1965, Singapore was expelled from the Federation of Malaysia, but the two countries retained a common currency until May 1973. It was only in 1973, with the enactment by Malaysia of its own Securities Industry Act, that the Stock Exchange of Malaysia and Singapore could formally split. The Kuala Lumpur Stock Exchange was established in July of that year.

Structure

The KLSE is a company limited by guarantee without a share capital and is incorporated under the Malaysian Companies Act of 1965. It is situated in the Damansara suburb of Kuala Lumpur, but since the end of the open outcry system of trading on November 13, 1989, and its replacement by a semi-automated system of trading, the location of the exchange itself has become increasingly irrelevant.

Trading hours on the exchange are from 10:00 a.m. to 12:30 p.m. and from 2:30 p.m. to 4:00 p.m., Monday to Friday. There are 49 active licensed stockbroking companies in Malaysia but another three firms are expected to begin trading soon. Foreign stockbrokers are not permitted to be members of the exchange but they may buy up to 30% of the equity of Malaysian stockbrokers. At a later date, this stake may be increased to 49% at the discretion of the KLSE.

Companies are listed on two boards—the Main Board and the Second Board—depending on various criteria at the time of listing. At the end of 1991, there were 287 companies listed on the Main Board and 31 companies listed on the Second Board. The total market capitalization was approximately M $155bn, or US $57bn. The top 20 KLSE stocks by market capitalization as of December 20, 1991 can be found in Table 8-1.

The average daily volume of the exchange has been running at around 65m units. Peak volumes, seen during the first quarter of 1990, exceeded those of New York with over 200m shares traded a day. In value terms, however, the KLSE bears no comparison with the established major markets. The average trading value has been about M $160m a day throughout 1991.

Table 8-1   Top 20 KLSE Stocks by Market Capitalization as of December 20, 1991

Stock	Sector	Market Capitalization (M $m)
Telekom Malaysia	Telecommunications	18,424.00
Sime Darby	Conglomerate	6,028.60
MISC	Shipping	5,201.20
Resorts World	Gaming	5,145.80
Genting	Gaming, plantations	5,052.10
Malayan Banking	Financial	4,964.00
Rothmans Malaysia	Tobacco	3,683.30
Tanjong	Gaming	2,790.10
Malaysian Airline System	Airline	2,310.00
Shell Malaysia	Refining	2,160.00
Kumpulan Guthrie	Plantations	2,090.00
Golden Hope	Plantations	1,920.40
Perlis Plantations	Sugar, flour milling	1,888.90
Tan Chong Motor	Vehicle assembly	1,787.50
United Engineers (M)	Construction, roads	1,766.70
Public Bank	Financial	1,689.50
Esso Malaysia	Refining	1,674.00
Malayan United Inds	Conglomerate	1,660.00
Renong	Conglomerate	1,656.60
Nestle Malaysia	Food manufacturer	1,629.80

Source: Baring Securities

In 1992, the market capitalization of the KLSE is expected to grow by some 30% to US $75bn, principally due to the privatization and flotation of several Malaysian government-owned companies. The most important of these will be the national car manufacturer, Proton, and the electricity utility, Tenaga Nasional. When listed sometime during the third quarter of 1992, Tenaga is expected to vie with Telekom for the largest stock by market capitalization on the KLSE.

Recent and Expected Structural Changes in the Stock Market

The Split with Singapore

Despite the split with Singapore, numerous Malaysian-registered companies remained listed on the Stock Exchange of Singapore and vice versa. In December 1985, the unsatisfactory nature of this arrangement was hammered home when the collapse of the Pan-Electric Industries group in Singapore forced the temporary closure of the KLSE.

In October 1989, the Malaysian government announced a January 1, 1990 deadline for 1982 Malaysian-registered companies to delist from the SES. At that time, these companies accounted for 37% of the SES's capitalization and 40% of the SES's average daily volume. The SES retaliated by forcing 53 Singapore-registered companies to delist from the KLSE, equivalent to 35% of the KLSE's market capitalization and 2% of the KSLE's average daily volume.

More damaging to the KLSE was the SES's decision to establish an over-the-counter (OTC) market, called Clob International, offering trades in 133 Malaysian companies. Clob will continue to trade a large volume of Malaysian shares until the KLSE manages to implement scripless trading, based on a central depository system (CDS), scheduled for June 1992.

Weighting in International Indices

Institutional investors have taken advantage of the fungibility of Malaysian and Singaporean stocks to reduce paperwork. Most global and international fund managers still tend to lump the two markets together in their portfolios, denominating all their stocks in Singapore dollars and using Singapore-based custodian facilities.

This practice has had two important effects. First, with their stocks denominated in Singapore dollars and lodged there, managers have tended to prefer to trade on the market providing quotes in the same currency and the least logistical problems with delivery. Second—due to this historical propensity to trade both Malaysian and Singaporean stocks in Singapore—some widely followed stock market indices have given Singapore and Malaysia a joint weighting. The Morgan Stanley Capital International (MSCI) allocates Singapore and Malaysia just 0.7% of its world index.

It can be argued that this joint weighting is disadvantageous to Malaysia. Fund managers are inclined to trade in the market they know better. Quantitative investors seeking to replicate the index in their portfolios can fill up the MSCI allocation with Singaporean stocks, or Malaysian stocks listed on the Clob International OTC market, without having to venture forth onto the KLSE.

When the MSCI does eventually split the two markets, Malaysia can expect to see a sharp inflow of funds as institutional investors are forced to trade on the KLSE. In April 1991, when the FT Actuaries World Index doubled its weighting for Malaysia, the KLSE Composite Index jumped by nearly 10%.

Trading Systems Development

The Central Depository System will be the culmination of a series of improvements to the actual trading and settlement implemented by the exchange since 1984 when clearing became fully computerized. In 1987, a real-time price reporting system was introduced, replacing closed-circuit television or telephone coverage of the actual trading board and enabling the new KLSE Composite Index to be updated instantaneously. Then, in 1989, the KLSE progressively switched over from the open outcry system to a semi-automated trading system called Score.

With Score, bids and offers are input by brokers via special terminals linked directly to the KLSE premises. There they are matched by computer operators isolated in quarantined conditions, and confirmation of trades are routed direct to the dealing rooms of the brokers. For the first time, investors were able to verify the exact time their orders were executed and the prevailing bid and offer prices on the market.

Score was followed in early 1990 with the implementation of a fixed delivery and settlement system. Previously, brokers had to deliver scrip to the central, semi-automated clearinghouse, called "Scans" in Malaysia, by the Wednesday of the week following the trade. This usually resulted in a flood of paper landing at Scans on the day of the deadline, instead of an orderly processing of trades day by day.

The unsatisfactory nature of this arrangement was hammered home during the first two months of 1990, when abnormally high volume of up to 210 million shares a day was pushed through the KLSE, partly as a result of the split from the SES. Scans proved unable to cope and brokers lost track of certificates worth around M $150m at one stage. Eventually the mess was sorted out with the help of a near doubling of settlement staff employed by the industry and the imposition of fixed delivery, which spread the paperwork evenly throughout the working week.

Settlement Terms

Under the new fixed delivery system, the seller must deliver certificates to his or her KLSE broker four market days after the date of the trade (T+4) and the broker to Scans five days after the date of the trade (T+5). Scans will then deliver the certificates to the broker of the buyer by T+6 and the broker to his or her client by T+7.

The KLSE has imposed these settlement terms rigorously. A selling client that fails to deliver to a broker will be brought in by the exchange on the next market day. This can prove expensive: the KLSE is entitled to buy in at 10 bids higher than the last-done price. For stocks trading at prices above M $10.00, a bid is 10 sen, so a failure to deliver Telekom Malaysia, for instance, could be penalized at the rate of M $1.00 per share.

Under current rules, short-selling and stock burrowing is not permitted. It is, therefore, advisable that until the introduction of CDS, investors use local custodian facilities and check before trades that their scrip has not been sent out for registration. Although the KLSE is bringing pressure on company registrars to speed up the process, registration of shares can take up to three months for some listed companies.

Transaction Costs

Commission charges are fixed by the KLSE and are not open for negotiation. Brokerage is payable by both buyer and seller. There is a minimum brokerage for all transactions of M $5.00 (Table 8-2).

Table 8-2   Brokerage Rates

	Less than 50 sen	50 sen to M$1.00	M$1.00 and above
Stocks, ordinary shares and preference shares	0.5 sen	1 sen	1%

Source: Baring Securities

Clearing fees are 0.05% of the transacted value and are payable by both buyer and seller. Stamp duty is payable at the rate of M $1 for M $1,000 or fractional part of the value of the shares. However, since May 1988, all contract notes between Malaysian brokers and foreign stockbrokers are exempt from stamp duty.

Central Depository System (CDS)

After several delays, due to development problems with software, it now looks as if the first operations of CDS will begin in July 1992. The depository is being set up by a limited company owned 55% by the KLSE, 25% by the Association of Banks in Malaysia, and 20% by a local peace foundation.

CDS will not replace share certificates, as do some other depository systems in operation around the world. Instead, the KLSE plans to immobilize progressively all share certificates, starting with new issues from July 1, 1992 onward. Buyers and sellers will simply see a change in the book entry in their statement of account.

Initially, share certificates will be held by broker members of the exchange, but eventually Malaysian banks are expected to be designated as authorized depositor agents. It is anticipated that some two or three years will be required before the system is fully operational. By 1995, it is hoped that CDS will be running smoothly enough for delivery-versus-payment terms to be introduced, and the delivery deadline brought forward to T+3.

Implication of CDS for Clob and ADRs

Until CDS becomes operational, it is hard to predict with any certainty what the effect on Clob International or the ADR system will be. Certainly, Clob will be more vulnerable, as there will be no physical scrip to trade on that OTC market and the Malaysian authorities could simply refuse to register any change of ownership between institutions that was not crossed on the KLSE. There are indications, however, that the Singapore-based banks may attempt to set up a system of Singapore Depository Receipts for Malaysian stocks prior to the completion of CDS. This would screen the bulk of Singapore transactions from scrutiny by the KLSE.

While the KLSE recognizes that ADRs (American Depository Receipts) are in the long-term interest of the Malaysian capital markets, the danger is that they may fall victim to the more urgent aim of claiming back from Singapore the business currently being lost to Clob. It would be difficult for the KLSE or the government to draft regulations that prevented the smooth operations of Singapore Depository Receipts without affecting American Depository Receipts as well.

Second Board and the Bumiputra Stock Exchange

Second Board

In November 1988, the KLSE launched its Second Board. This coincides with the raising of the minimum paid-up capital of new companies seeking a listing from M $5m to M $20m, which automatically disqualified a number of small up-and-coming companies from tapping the capital markets to fund their future expansion.

In order to maintain the access of smaller companies to equity financing, companies with a paid-up capital of between M $5m and M $20m can now apply to be listed on the Second Board. Second Board companies have to comply with all the corporate disclosure rules of their Main Board cousins, but they are given certain concessions in addition to the lower paid-up capital requirement.

These concessions include the prelisting requirement for a profit track-record of only two-to-three years, compared with the Main Board requirement of five year's unbroken profitability. Furthermore, Second Board companies are saved the expense of having to print their full prospectuses as advertisements in two local newspapers prior to the public offer: they need only print summaries of their prospectuses.

Bumiputra Stock Exchange

It is a little-known fact that there are two stock markets in Malaysia. In addition to the KLSE, there is also the BSE, the Bumiputra Stock Exchange. For anyone investing in the Malaysian market, it is important to understand the term "Bumiputra." In the Malay language, the word literally means "sons of the soil." It is used to distinguish the indigenous, mainly Malay, Malaysians from their ethnic Chinese and Indian fellow citizens who migrated to the country after the Malays.

After Malay resentment at the economic predominance of the Chinese erupted into open rioting in May 1969, the government implemented the "New Economic Policy" (NEP)—a program of positive discrimination in favor of the Bumiputras, which aimed to ensure that Bumiputras built up a stake of at least 30% of the equity of Malaysia-registered companies (both listed and unlisted). By 1990, the Bumiputras had increased their stake from 1% in 1970 to 20.3%, with probably an additional 2% to 3% held through racially unidentified nominees.

The government established the Bumiputra Stock Exchange in 1971. The idea was to have the shares of Bumiputra-owned companies traded without the risk of them falling into the hands of non-Bumiputra (i.e., foreign, or ethnic Chinese or Indian Malaysian) shareholders. Unfortunately, only eight companies are listed and trading is virtually nonexistent.

The Malaysian authorities have already indicated their intention to dissolve the Bumiputra Stock Exchange and to relist the eight stocks on the Second Board. However, they have to still address the problem of preventing non-Bumiputras from buying the shares once they are listed on the KLSE. One possibility would be to frank the shares "Bumiputra Only." This, of course, would lead to the creation of a Bumiputra Board on the KLSE, in the same way that a Foreign Board is already beginning to evolve.

Foreign Board and Foreign Portfolio Investment

Along with the implementation of the positive discrimination program in favor of the Bumiputras, the NEP also brought in strict controls on foreign holdings of Malaysian equity (listed and unlisted). These were aimed at reducing the foreign-held share of the Malaysian economy from around 55% at the beginning of the NEP in 1970 to 30% by 1990. In fact, this target was overshot by a considerable margin and at the end of 1990, foreigners held 25.1%.

From the point of view of the fund manager, however, that percentage figure is not so significant. Unfortunately, data on foreign holdings of Malaysian listed companies is not very precise, nor is it collected on a regular basis.

Foreign Holdings in Listed Companies

According to a survey conducted by the KLSE in 1990, foreign holdings of listed companies were 27.4% of the total paid-up capital at par value. There are no figures available for the foreign shareholdings by market capitalization; however, given the fact that foreign shareholders tend to be institutions investing in blue-chip stocks, it is believed that the percentage share would be higher than 27.4% based on this method of reckoning.

With the onset of the NEP in 1970, the government equipped itself with powerful mechanisms to force foreigners to sell off their equity. These mechanisms are still in place, despite the fact that foreign shareholdings are below the maximum desired limit. The key questions is: Will they be used in the future?

According to the KLSE, foreign ownership of listed companies is "generally restricted to 30%," but since 1986, several foreign controlled listed companies (Nestle, Guinness, and Rothmans, to name a few) have been permitted to restructure their equity in compliance with the Bumiputra requirements of the NEP while still retaining foreign majority control.

Guidelines issued by the Ministry of Finance indicate that the government will generally veto the acquisition by any one single foreign party of 15% or more of the voting rights of a Malaysian company, or the acquisition by aggregate foreign interests of 30% or more of the voting rights, unless they can demonstrate that such acquisition will lead to "net economic benefits" to Malaysia. This is open to widely differing interpretations and depends very much on the composition of the Foreign Investment Committee at the time.

The most recent policy pronouncement on this issue came in June 1991 with the publication of the Second Outline Perspective Plan, 1991-2000, which laid the framework for the successor to the NEP. In it the government stated that the future regulatory process would be, "based on the merits of each case and taking into account the importance of majority ownership to foreign and local investors." However, since then a new issue has been approved on the condition that foreign ownership be restricted to 30%!

Foreign Board

It is remarkable that so vital a point should be subject to so much confusion. If a general 30% foreign limit is to be enforced from here on, then a foreign board is a certainty. And given the bad experience that foreign investors have had with foreign premiums in other Southeast Asia markets (the Singaporean banks being an obvious example), some Malaysian brokers are concerned that foreign buyers will stay away from the market once the 30% limit has been reached.

Several companies already have a foreign limit on their share of ownership determined by their articles of association. This is particularly true of the financial services sector, where the central bank, Bank Negara Malaysia, restricts foreign ownership of licensed financial institutions to 30% as a matter of national security. Other companies impose the limit for tax reasons: Malaysian International Shipping Corporation (MSC), for instance, enjoys 100% tax-exemption on profits from shipping operations because of its status as Malaysia's national flag carrier and this status would be endangered if foreign shareholdings were to approach 50%.

Only two listed companies on the KLSE have reached their 30% foreign shareholdings limit: MSC and Public Bank. Initially, MSC operated a queuing system, whereby foreign buyers could only get their shares registered if an equivalent foreign registered holding were sold. Eventually, however, MSC followed Public Bank's example and requested a separate listing on the KLSE for its foreign-registered shares.

Generally, the foreign shares have traded at a premium of between 15% and 25%. But there have been occasions under certain market conditions (usually a panic sell-off) when the foreign shares have traded at a discount. These occasions are rare and short-lived, however, as local shareholders are entitled to buy foreign shares and register them as local.

Taxation of Foreign Shareholders

There is no capital gains tax in Malaysia. However, all dividends issued by Malaysian publicly listed companies have 35% corporation tax deducted at source. This deduction is treated as a tax credit when the shareholder files a tax return at the end of the financial year. Nonresidents are, therefore, not entitled to this tax credit.

Fixed-income securities are becoming increasingly important in Malaysia and more issues are expected to come to the market. Interest paid to nonresidents is subject to a 20% withholding tax. This is taxed at source for residents of countries that do not have a taxation treaty with Malaysia.

There is no restriction on the repatriation of capital and remittance of profits or dividends. However, for sums in excess of M $10,000 (US $1.00 = M $2.75), a form must be completed and approved by Bank Negara. Generally speaking, approval is automatically granted.

New Listings

Foreigners are not permitted to subscribe to public offerings of shares in companies being listed on the KLSE for the first time. The rationale for this restriction is never stated publicly but its clear intention is to provide a profit to Malaysian stags, who are able to subscribe at prices set artificially low by the Capital Issues Committee.

In the past, some local Malaysian brokers have obliged foreign clients by subscribing for new issues on their behalf. However, this practice is fraught with danger and foreign institutions have no legal redress in the Malaysian courts if anything goes wrong.

Indices

In the 1970s, indices which tracked the KLSE were very few. Probably the most widely followed index at that time was the Industrial Index compiled by the Singapore stockbroking firm of Fraser & Co. In 1987, however, the KLSE produced its own Composite Index, which has been adopted as the industry standard. The KLSE Composite is updated every 15 minutes. The KLSE Composite Index comprises 85 stocks and is computed by using the formula:

$$\frac{AMV1}{AMV0} \times 100$$

where AMV1 is current aggregate market value and AMV0 is base aggregate market value. A weighted average method is used.

In October 1991, the KLSE announced the creation of a new index, the Emas Index ("emas" is the Malay word for gold). The Emas Index comprises all stocks on the Main Board and is calculated on the same basis as the Composite Index. Although the KLSE has not stated this explicitly, it is widely believed that the Emas Index has been created to cater to the forthcoming Kuala Lumpur Options and

Financial Futures Exchange. With Telekom Malaysia accounting at the moment for 20.5% of the Composite Index, the opinion has been expressed in some quarters that the Composite Index is too vulnerable to single stock movements.

Regulatory Bodies

The regulatory structure of the KLSE, its stockbroking members, and companies listed on KLSE is somewhat complicated. The KLSE itself is regulated by the Ministry of Finance, which has the right to appoint the executive chairman and two other members of the nine-member board. Within these limitations, it is self-governing.

Stockbrokers are regulated by the Registrar of Companies (RoC)—a body which normally comes under the Ministry of International Trade and Industry (MITI)—but for the purposes of administering the Securities Industry Act 1983 it is governed by the Ministry of Finance. Meanwhile, the listed companies themselves are regulated by the RoC, but for this purpose the RoC operates under the auspices of MITI. However, to confuse matters even more, several Malaysian stockbrokers are now owned by licensed financial institutions and, therefore, come under the purview of the central bank, Bank Negara, which has the right to regulate all subsidiaries of the licensed financial institutions.

Capital Issues Committee

Looming over the entire industry is the feared Capital Issues Committee (CIC). The CIC has the power to approve, disallow, or amend the terms of any corporate exercise involving the issue of traded securities, whether by initial public offering, rights issue, bonus issue, or issue of shares for the purchase of assets.

This power extends to the pricing of IPOs and the number of new shares and the price of those shares that can be issued for the acquisition of assets by existing listed companies. Companies may appeal against a ruling but if that appeal is turned down, they must proceed with the issue on the CIC's terms or withdraw the proposal. As the period between the date of submission of proposals and the date of the CIC's decision can sometimes be as long as six months, this causes considerable problems with pricing.

Any public flotation of a company must be approved by the CIC and the CIC has the absolute right to determine the price at which the new issue can be offered to the public. Prior to 1987, the CIC used to set the maximum permitted price/earnings multiple for new listings at absurdly low levels of between three and five times gross earnings. With the market trading on an average multiple of some 25 times net earnings, this arbitrary valuation was enabling stags to triple their money overnight. It was scarcely surprising, therefore, that new issues were oversubscribed by as much as 40 times. Much has been done to improve this situation with the publication of several successive guidelines by the CIC, containing more realistic maximum permitted multiples (Table 8-3).

The CIC holds directors responsible for the profit forecasts contained in prelisting prospectuses. In the event of a deviation of more than 10% from the forecast (up or down), upon publication of the next set of results the CIC requires a full explanation from directors. If the CIC is dissatisfied with the explanation, it can censure publicly the directors and the company and in extreme cases of outright dishonesty, it can even delist the company from the KLSE.

Foreign Investment Committee

The Foreign Investment Committee (FIC) is one of the principal tools of the NEP, whereby the government implements the restructuring aspects of its positive discrimination policy in favor of Bumiputras. Although, as the name implies, the FIC was originally set up to keep the foreigners under control, these days the FIC is more of a general-purpose blunt weapon used to regulate the Malaysian corporate sector.

The FIC has the power to regulate any company with shareholder funds of more than M $2.5m or those with more than 75 full-time paid employees. More importantly, from the investor's point of view, the FIC has the power to prevent "any merger and take-over of any company or business in Malaysia whether by Malaysian or foreign interests; and any proposed acquisition of assets or interests exceeding in value of M $5m whether by Malaysian or foreign interests."

Table 8-3   Maximum Permitted Gross Multiples for New Listings

Sector	PE Multiple
Property	3.5 - 10.5
Services	4.0 - 11.0
Trading	4.0 - 11.0
Transportation	4.0 - 11.0
Contracting and construction	4.5 - 11.5
Tourism (including hotels)	4.5 - 11.5
Insurance	5.0 - 12.0
Manufacturing	5.0 - 12.0
Gaming	6.0 - 13.0
Finance companies	6.0 - 13.0
Stockbroking companies	6.0 - 13.0
Plantations	7.5 - 14.5
Utilities	8.0 - 15.0
Banks	8.5 - 15.5

Panel on Take-Overs and Mergers

The Panel was set up to administer the Malaysian Code on Take-Overs and Mergers, which came into force on April 1, 1987. In essence, the code is similar to similar regulations in other markets.

Associate company status is achieved with ownership or control of 20% of the paid-up capital of companies. Disclosure of a shareholding is required at 10% and the threshold for the mounting of a mandatory general offer comes at 33%. Where parties acting in concert hold more than 33% but less than 50%, and an additional 2% is acquired by those parties, a mandatory general offer is also triggered off.

Company Profiles*

Amalgamated Steel Mills Berhad

Conglomerate   Amalgamated Steel Mills Berhad (ASM) is Malaysia's largest steel manufacturer with an efficient, advanced and integrated steel mill in the Klang Valley, one of the fastest growing areas in Malaysia. ASM, its 52 subsidiaries (10 dormant) and 2 associates are in five major areas: steel manufacturing and trading, motorcycle assembly and marketing, food production, retailing, and financial services. ASM's strategy is to concentrate on the steel business while diversifying into strategic areas where they have related operations, have a strong market presence, and can purchase operations cheaply and turn them around. It has a history of buying undervalued companies and turning them into highly profitable operations. Steel manufacturing and trading currently represents 80% of revenues, which is expected to drop to 60% in three years. ASM is a family run operation owned by William Cheng (40%), Lion Corp. (29%), and L.T.A.T. (23%), the armed forces pension fund.

British American Life and General Insurance

Insurance   British American Life and General Insurance (BAI) was the fifth largest domestic life insurance company in 1989, and the ninth largest including foreign insurers, with a 5% share among domestic insurers and a 2% market share of total insurers. It is also the largest home service life insurer in Malaysia, with 70% of the home life service market. BAI has two main insurance areas, home life service and ordinary life. BAI was originally set up as a branch of British American Insurance in the 1960s, covering Malaysia and Singapore and offering both general and life insurance. They recently sold both their Singapore insurance companies, eliminated their general insurance areas, and have become solely a Malaysian life insurer. BAI is owned by John Hancock USA (29%) and its managing directors Steve and Melvin Wong (6%).

* Company profiles are provided by the editors.

Kian Joo Can Factory

Packaging   Kian Joo Can Factory (KJ) is one of the largest listed packaging companies in Malaysia engaged in the manufacture of aluminum and tin cans, polyethylene terephalate (PET) bottles, and corrugated fiberboard cartons. KJ is the only producer of aluminum cans in Malaysia, and one of the two main producers of tin cans. It is the only domestic producer of 2 liter PET bottles, and only one of two producers of the 1.25 liter size. It is among the top 5 producers of corrugated carton boxes. The can division contributes about 80% of group turnover, with the plastics division and carton division contributing 15% and 5% respectively. KJ's major competition is from Fima Metal Box (FMB) which produces 3 piece tin cans and is partially owned by the Malaysian government. KJ's overall market share has been increasing from 35% in 1984 to 45% in 1989.

Keck Seng

Property/Plantation   Keck Seng (KS) is a mixed housing and plantation company located in Johore. Its traditional business has been plantations, mainly palm oil (98%), cocoa and rubber. Recently, it has been gradually developing its huge plantation landbank in Johore, and has become the largest listed property company in Johore in terms of developable land. In 1989, plantation earnings accounted for 65% of the pre-tax profit, with housing development accounting for the remaining 35%. Housing development is expected to contribute 54% of pre-tax profit in 1990. Keck Seng is owned 50% by the Ho family and 9% by Lembaga Tabung Angkatan Tentera (Armed Forces Fund).

Malaysian International Shipping Corporation (BERHAD)

Shipping   Malaysian International Shipping Corporation (MISC) is a major international shipping company with 45 vessels with a combined tonnage of 1.27 million deadweight tons including 5 LNG tankers, 12 container ships, 4 cargo coasters, 1 woodchip carrier, 10 dry bulk carriers, 3 parcel carriers, 7 tankers and 3 supply carriers. Five new container ships are on order and should be delivered between 1991 and 1992. Close to half of MISC's revenues are secured until 2003 through contracts with Malaysia LNG Sdn. About 50% of sales are from LNG operation, with the remaining from other shipping and on-shore activities. LNG operations contribute 60% to net earnings, while the remainder contribute 40%. MISC is the third largest company in Malaysia (after Telekom Malaysia and Sime Darby). MISC is 59% owned by the government.

Metroplex Berhad

Property Developer   Metroplex (MB) was incorporated in Malaysia under the name Seacorp Realty Development Corporation Ltd. which was changed to

Metroplex Berhad in 1984. Metroplex is a holding company with subsidiaries and associates primarily involved in housing and property development. MB has also diversified into management services, leasing and financing, building construction and trading as well as made a bid for management of the Langkawi Resort Hotel and other properties in resort areas. Main businesses income includes sale and lease of its residential and commercial properties (52% of pre-tax profit in FY 1990), net interest income (25%), rental income (14%), and other income from subsidiaries (9%). The group's subsidiary companies include Metroplex Leasing & Credit Corp. (leasing, hire-purchase financing and money-lending), Metroplex Trading (trading in construction materials), and Metroplex Construction (building construction); Metroplex Centrepoint (property development), and Metroplex Project Management (property development). Metroplex is 83.1% owned by Mr. Dick Chan, his wife, and ???.

Samanda Holdings

Manufacturing   Samanda Holdings (SH) is an investment holding company with 11 subsidiaries and four associated companies engaged in the manufacture of adhesive tapes and labels, foil laminated paper, and rubber based products including latex gloves, rubber bands, and diving equipment, as well as trading, property development, and courier services. It is the largest adhesive tape manufacturer in the ASEAN region with a 70% dominance in the domestic market, with the bulk of Samanda's tapes consumed by the manufacturing sector. Samanda's trading subsidiaries handle mainly products manufactured by the group, but are expanding to include additional products. Samanda Holdings is 22% owned by Ngan Ching Wen, the Secretary General of the Chinese Chamber of Commerce, 22% by Ganda Holdings, also controlled by Ngan, and 10% owned by PNB, the government national investment trust.

Sime Darby

Conglomerate   Sime Darby (SD) is the largest conglomerate in Malaysia with the highest market capitalization of any company listed on the Kuala Lumpur Stock Exchange. It has four listed subsidiary companies in Malaysia (which contributed more than 55% to earnings), along with other unlisted companies. Consolidated Plantations (50% owned, 15% of 1990 pre-tax profits) is the fourth largest listed plantation company in Malaysia. DMIB (26% owned, 7% of pre-tax profits) manufactures tires for passenger cars, heavy equipment, and airplanes. Tractors Malaysia (72% owned, 24% of pre-tax profits) is the sole distributor for Caterpillar earth moving equipment and also the assembler of Ford, BMW, Suzuki and Land Rover motor vehicles. Sime UEP Properties (50% owned, 10% of pre-tax profits) is a major property developer with a huge landbank in the Klang Valley, Pasir Gudang, Johore, and Melaka. SD has other subsidiaries and affiliates in Malaysia in the packaging, insurance, medical, and engineering areas, with a total of 173 consolidated companies both in Malaysia and abroad. It also has subsidiaries under the Sime Darby name in Hong Kong (75% owned), Australia (81%), Philippines (56%), and Singapore (69%). Domestic operations accounted for 70% of group profits in 1990, with foreign operations the remaining 30%.

Sime Darby is 17% owned by Amanah Saham Nasional, 12% by MMC, and 6% by the KIO.

Tan Chong Motor Holdings

Automotive   Tan Chong (TC) was incorporated in 1972 by the Tan family, which has held the Nissan franchise in Malaysia and Singapore for more than 30 years. TC was the biggest seller in the market until the introduction in Malaysia of the Proton Saga, the government sanctioned national car, which currently has a 65% market share. TC group started diversifying into auto parts manufacturing in 1978 and is today the largest auto parts manufacturer in Malaysia, producing both for domestic and export markets. Besides the car industry, the group is also involved in the distribution of heavy equipment, industrial machinery, and cosmetics under the Japanese Shiseido brand name, which has become one of the best-known names for beauty and skin care products in Malaysia. Other operations include travel agencies, property investment and development, insurance, and hire purchase financing. The motor division contributed 65% of sales in 1989, which was split between Singapore 35% and Malaysia 30%. The remaining sales were from auto parts 15%, heavy equipment 10%, and others 10%.

Telekom Malaysia

Telecommunications   Telekom Malaysia (STM) was incorporated in 1984 to take over the operations of the Malaysian Telecom Department, which provided national telecommunications and related services in Malaysia. STM was listed in KLSE in November 1990 and was the first utility, and the largest government corporation to be privatized (1.4% of the Malaysian economy in 1989 and 10% of the current market capitalization). STM has an exclusive license to provide international and domestic telecommunications services until 2007. The breakdown of revenues in 1990 was: business phones Malaysia (53%), residential (31%), mobile devices (5%), telex (2%), leased circuits (3%), public pay phones (2%), data services (1%), and others (i.e., telefax, subscriber equipment) (4%). The majority of STM is owned by the Ministry of Finance and Federal Lands Commission (76%). The current foreign ownership limit is 25%.

Tractors Malaysia Holdings

Heavy Equipment   Tractors Malaysia (TM) is a distributor of Caterpillar Tractor heavy equipment (one of the top three distributors in the world), Ford cars and commercial vehicles, and ten other major heavy equipment manufacturers. Tractors is a major force in the heavy equipment industry in Malaysia, five times the size of its main competitor UMW Holdings. TM serves a broad base of industries, including forestry, construction, mining, and agriculture. It is the third largest car distributor in Malaysia, as well as a major property holder, with assets including Wisma Tractors, a 231,000 sq. ft. commercial property in Subang Jaya, and the adjoining lot on which it began developing a 250,000 sq. ft. building in 1991. Sales by division in 1990 were heavy equipment (64%) and automotive (36%), with the automotive division expected to surpass the heavy equipment as the major contributor to profits in two years. Sales by industry is estimated to be logging (50%), automotive and agriculture (30%), construction (15%), and mining (5%). Tractors is 71.7% owned by Sime Darby, Malaysia's largest conglomerate.

UAC BERHAD

Building Materials   UAC is a producer of three types of building materials: roofing materials, flagsheets/pattern sheets, and water pipe. The roofing materials area produces low cost roofing materials only for inexpensive government housing schemes. The flagsheets/pattern sheets are used for ceilings and partitions for houses and offices. UAC is the only asbestos-free producer in Malaysia. Finally, the pipe area produces one type of pipe for rural water supplies. Other divisions include brakepads for motor vehicles and production and installation of fire protection activities. None of these areas are price controlled. UAC is 22% owned by Boustead Holding and 9% by Arab Malaysian nominees.

INDONESIA: ONCE ASLEEP, NOW NEWLY EMERGED

John R. Niepold
Senior Investment Analyst, Crosby Securities
Jakarta, Indonesia

Although Indonesia established its first stock exchange in 1912, it has only been since 1989, following the "Pacto" and "Pakdes" deregulation packages of 1987, 1988, and 1989, that the stock market has awoken and the value traded has increased from US $4 million in 1988 to US $4 billion in 1990. Since 1988, the market capitalization has grown from US $253 million to US $6.8 billion in December 1991 (based on "listed" shares only; when considering all shares, the market capitalization is three times higher). During the same period, the number of companies listed has grown from 24 to 141 (See Table 9-1).

This explosive growth has been the result of numerous deregulation packages the government enacted since 1987, which encouraged the entire private financial sector of the economy to grow dramatically. These measures coupled with strong economic growth, prudent industrialization management to encourage nonoil exports, a stable political climate, and a dramatic increase in foreign investment have helped fuel the expansion of the economy and of the entire financial sector.

Although the Indonesian market grew very quickly in 1989 and 1990 and trading has increased dramatically, the market mechanism itself has not kept pace. Liquidity and settlement are better but remain difficult. Regulation practices are being improved, but the process is slow and they remain less than adequate. Research has also increased dramatically in the past two years, but given the limited track records of most of the listed companies and relatively poor disclosure, research sophistication is also behind the more developed markets in the region.

Table 9-1   Summary of Stock Market Data

Year	Listings	Market Capitalization ($ millions)	Trading Volume ($ millions)	Turnover (percent)	New Issues	Year-End P/E	Year-End P/BV	JSE Index US $ (percent)	Exchange Rate US $ (percent)
1991	141	6,823	2,981	40.1	13	13.7	2.0	-40.4	-4.0
1990	125	8,081	3,992	75.8	67	24.0	4.2	-1.0	-5.8
1989	57	2,254	541	38.7	37	46.0	7.5	27.2	-3.8
1988	24	253	4	2.5	0	19.0	—	264.9	-4.9
1987	24	68	3	4.2	0	5.3	3.5	17.9	-0.5
1986	24	81	1	1.4	0	-7.3	3.6	-41.1	-45.9
1985	24	117	3	2.9	5	3.0	3.5	0.0	-4.7
1984	24	85	2	2.2	5	6.2	3.8	-30.7	-8.0
1983	19	101	11	10.1	6	3.1	5.0	-65.6	-43.5
1982	14	144	19	17.1	6	28.6	6.5	-13.2	-7.5
1981	8	74	12	17.5	2	7.8	0.9	-6.0	-2.8
1980	6	63	9	14.9	6	6.6	1.1	—	0.0

Sources: BAPEPAM, IFC Emerging Mkts. Databases, Crosby Securities

Market Size and Trading Activity

As of December 1991, the capitalization of the Jakarta Stock Exchange (JSE) totaled Rp 13.5 trillion or US$6.8 billion. However, these figures represent the "listed" shares only. In Indonesia not all issued shares are actually listed on the exchanges, and most companies only have a portion of their total issued shares listed. The market capitalization for all shares (which is generally more comparable with other markets in Asia) is much higher. In October 1991, the market capitalization for all shares was Rp 28.6 trillion or US$14.5 billion. As a percentage of GNP, the stock exchange in Indonesia is very small given the country's size and economic potential. As the fifth largest country in the world, in terms of population and with the largest economy in Southeast Asia, the long-term potential of the market is enormous. Many believe that eventually the Indonesian stock market, if properly managed, could become the largest in the Pacific Basin outside Japan.

Although market volumes have risen substantially, liquidity remains poor. Since 1989, new issue growth has been dramatic with 37 companies going public in 1989, 67 in 1990, and 13 more in 1991. Given the government's tight money policy which began in 1990, turnover has slowed and was US$3.0 billion in 1991 versus US$4.0 billion in 1990. The reduction is also the result of reduced foreign interest in the market given its foreigners had dominated trading since 1988, although actual statistics are not available because there is no organized foreign board in Indonesia.

History

The first securities market, the Vereeniging voor den Effecten Handel (Securities Brokers Association), was established in Jakarta in 1912 by the Dutch. This market, along with two others in Surabaya and Semarang, established in 1925, traded shares primarily of Dutch East Indies government agencies and other Dutch companies (mostly plantations). The three exchanges remained open until 1942 when they were closed at the outset of WWII.

Following Indonesia's independence in 1949, the stock market in Jakarta reopened in 1952 and was operated by the Association of Money and Securities Traders which consisted of three Dutch private banks, two Dutch brokers, and two Indonesian banks. The Bank Indonesia (the central bank) served as an advisor to the market at that time. During this period, trading was not very active and most of the listed securities were either state bank bonds or prewar listed securities.

In 1957 and 1958, most Dutch companies were nationalized and as a result, many of the listed companies either delisted or suspended trading. This led to the demise of the stock exchange and for all practical purposes, the Indonesian stock market was again closed in 1958.

In the 1960s and early 1970s, government policies made a stock market unnecessary. Generally, financing was provided by the various state banks which channeled the country's oil revenues into Indonesian businesses at subsidized rates. In order to discourage capital flight, in 1968 the government eliminated income tax on interest income received from time deposits. Although the exchange was reopened in the 1970s, and several companies listed during the 1970s and early 1980s, the fact that interest income was tax free discouraged investment in instruments other than time deposits.

It was not until 1977, following the creation of several capital market agencies, that the stock market was again opened and supported by the government. In 1977, the government established Badan Pelaksana Pasar Modal, (BAPEPAM), the Capital Market Executive Agency. BAPEPAM was created to establish, regulate, and operate the stock market and to oversee new listings. A second agency, PT (Persero) Danareksa (Danareksa), was also created to support the market by providing small denomination investment certificates (mutual funds) to individual investors. Danareksa also served to support and maintain stability in the market. Originally, half of each new issue had to be offered to Danareksa. As a result, the agency virtually controlled the prices on the exchange.

Although the Ministry of Finance did not at this time remove the tax-free status of time deposit interest, it did encourage companies to go public by offering tax incentives and allowing for the revaluation of assets. Foreign companies could also use the exchange as a means to satisfy requirements that they divest various percentages to Indonesians. During this period the government also offered some tax advantages to shareholders of newly listed companies, but generally the exchange grew not so much because it provided a source of cheap funds or created an attractive investment alternative to the public, but rather because it allowed the listing companies to lower their tax burden.

Semen Cibinong was the first company to go public in August 1977 and by 1984, 24 firms were listed. Although the market rose roughly 15 percent in rupiah terms in 1978 (this was countered by an almost 50 percent rupiah devaluation that year), it declined slowly but steadily through 1984. Between 1977 and 1983, most public companies were foreign joint ventures. Given the exclusion of tax on deposits, poor liquidity, and a general lack of education on what drives a stock market, share prices were driven primarily by yield, not capital appreciation potential. To encourage subscription of shares in this yield-guided market, two companies, PT Bayer Indonesia and PT Hotel Prapatan, issued preferred shares in 1982 and 1983 respectively, offering dividend yields (based on par value) of one percent above prevailing deposit rates. Clearly, the market was artificially supported by the government's tax incentives rather than by typical investment or finance criteria. Consequently, it is not surprising that the stock market experiment which began in 1977 was not successful until further reforms were introduced.

Beginning in 1983 as oil prices fell, the government attempted to restructure the Indonesian economy and move away from its dependence on oil revenues which supplied roughly 80 percent of export earnings. In 1984, the government eliminated controls on interest rates and tax incentives received from investing in shares were removed. The banking sector grew and deposit and lending rates soared. This ended the growth in new issues due to the yield orientation of the exchange, as the costs to companies of going public made such an endeavor uneconomic without the previously allowed tax breaks. From 1984 until 1989, there were no additional companies offering shares, and yields averaged well over 15 percent. Trading during these five years was virtually nonexistent, averaging less than US$5 million per year. During this entire period (1977–1987), foreigners were not allowed to invest in listed shares.

Major market reforms heralded a new era beginning in December 1987. The first deregulation package liberalized listing, underwriting, and trading regulations. Share price movements were no longer limited (previously there was a daily price movement limit of four percent). The listing requirements and conditions were simplified and foreigners were allowed to purchase shares in eight nonjoint venture companies. During this time, the Bursa Parallel (Over the Counter Market) was also established, possessing fewer listing requirements than the main stock exchange.

Despite the changes, no new companies went public in 1988. One already listed company however, Jakarta International Hotel, raised Rp 23 billion (US$13.6 million) in a second issue which was extremely successful and largely subscribed for by foreigners. Immediately following this issue, the government further deregulated the financial sector by allowing all banks to offer savings accounts and by allowing both foreign and domestic banks to open more branches. In order to encourage lending, bank reserve requirements were lowered from 15 percent to 2 percent. Perhaps the most significant ruling was the imposition of a 15 percent tax on bank time-deposit income. For the longer term, this made investment in shares a more attractive option for local investors.

In December 1988, more deregulatory measures were announced. The most significant included: private exchanges outside Jakarta were allowed, insider trading rules were defined, and licensing requirements for banks were simplified. Following the measures, the Surabaya Stock Exchange was opened in June 1989. The new regulations also allowed for the establishment of many new types of local and joint venture financial institutions, including securities companies. Following the deregulatory measures in December 1988, the market soared. The JSE index, which had languished in previous years, shot up from 123 to 442 in just three weeks in December before falling back to 305 by the end of the year. Total volume for the month increased dramatically to US$12.3 million. Although this figure was still small, it was a substantial increase over previous levels. This strong showing from the local and foreign investment community suddenly brought attention to Indonesia as a market that could potentially "emerge" and one which could be effectively used by private companies to raise inexpensive capital.

Trading volume picked up somewhat in early 1989 but exploded in August following several new listings and new legislation which further opened the market to foreign investment. The legislation allowed foreigners to purchase up to 49 percent of all companies' listed shares, including the foreign joint ventures but excluding banks. In the past, foreigners could only purchase shares in 8 of the 24 listed companies. Following the legislation, foreigners could buy shares in any listed company except the then listed Panin Bank. Between July 1989 and the end of the year, 37 companies went public raising just over US$1 billion. As a result of the new issues and a 31 percent rise in the JSE index, the market capitalization of the shares of listed companies made available for stock tradings rose ten-fold from US$253 million at the end of 1988 to US$2.3 billion at the end of 1989. The market capitalization for all shares was US$9.8 billion.

Although education and the market mechanism remained poor in Indonesia, local investors who were given priority for new issues subscribed for shares in order to sell them quickly to foreigners. This activity worked well between July 1989 and October 1989 but slowed just prior to the listing of Indocement on December 5, 1989 as some new issues were undersubscribed and supply outgrew demand. Indocement was the largest and most controversial new issue in Indonesia at the time. The company which raised US$335 million was allowed to go public despite not satisfying all listing requirements. (Indocement had not been profitable for two years which is a requirement to list on the "main board.") Indocement, which represented roughly one-third of the market capitalization at the time, was "digested" but not easily. For the first time, underwriters, who were not highly capitalized, began to get nervous and the new issue supply slowed in late December 1989 and into early 1990. In December 1989 there were only two new issues.

At the outset of 1990, demand was again higher than supply as new issues slowed while Indonesian country funds managers began to invest in Indonesia. The country funds for Indonesia had raised roughly US$250 million in 1989. The short-term weight of money was too large given the supply of scrip and the market soared reaching a high of 682 on April 4, 1990.

As is often the case, underwriters overreacted to the increased demand. Given the renewed interest in the market, underwriters again brought more new issues to market beginning in March 1990 when over US $500 million worth of scrip was offered. Although this scrip was taken up and was generally offered at reasonable prices, similar cash calls continued in April, May, and June. Because earlier issues had been tremendously oversubscribed and many new foreign joint venture firms had recently opened up, underwriters began "bidding up" prices on new issues without slowing the supply of new offerings. By May, demand weakened following a poor local subscription to INCO while nearly US $700 million worth of expensive stock came to market. The combination of oversupply at relatively expensive prices and the impact on liquidity of the requirement that half of each issue had to be subscribed for by local investors hurt the market for the remainder of the year. The weakening demand and reduced liquidity was further exacerbated by BAPEPAM, which instituted a new "lot" trading system on May 1, 1990. Settlement, which was already poor, slowed even more as many older stock certificates had to be split or combined into board lots of 500 shares.

Following May 1990, volumes dropped and investors became less interested given the already high market P/E ratio of 30X. For the remainder of the year, the market fell generally on reduced volumes. Confidence in the market was also hurt by the Bank Duta scandal in October 1990 when it was discovered that the bank had lost US $420 million in foreign exchange trading. The losses were made up by shareholders (primarily foundations headed by President Soeharto), but the bank had gone public just five months earlier and no mention was made of the open foreign exchange position in the financial statements. Given the bank's capital base, by Indonesian law Bank Duta was only allowed to have a net open foreign exchange position of just under US $25 million.

In December, the market rose, most likely because local financial institutions took advantage of poor liquidity to push up prices prior to the year end. In total, 67 companies went public in 1990 in Indonesia (mostly in the first half of the year), making the market one of, if not the fastest growing stock market in the world. In total, roughly US $2.9 billion was raised by companies going public in 1990. This figure is particularly staggering given the trading value for the year of US $4.0 billion. In 1989, the amount raised by new issues was roughly twice the traded value during the year. By the end of 1990, the market capitalization had risen to US $8.1 billion (for listed shares of 125 companies) from US $2.3 billion at the end of 1989.

The year 1991 was difficult for Indonesia's stock market, falling 40 percent (62 percent from the high reached in April 1990) as local investors became wary of the stock market given very high local interest/deposit rates. Although Indonesia experienced an economic "boom" in 1990 with high GDP growth of seven percent, an ever widening current account deficit and higher inflation forced the government to continue its tight money stance which began in the summer of 1990. With interest rates on deposits well over 20 percent, investors stayed away from the capital market and trading volume was much lower in 1991 than in 1990. Despite some strength in February and March of 1991, generally the market has been weak with the decline increasing in June through October before recovering somewhat in November.

The lack of interest was not helped by the poor performance of a widely held stock, PT Argo Pantes, a textile company. In August 1991, PT Argo Pantes released results which were far below forecasts made by the company previously. The controversy resulted as the company did not properly disclose its difficulties to investment analysts, BAPEPAM, or to one of its major minority shareholders, the International Finance Corporation (IFC). The poor results further eroded confidence in the regulatory system governing the exchange and in listed companies. This reduced confidence, coupled with short-term economic difficulties, has put a brake on the stock market's development. Until the market begins to recover, large capital raisings will most likely be restricted to offshore convertible and warrant issues. Such a hiatus in new issues and steep price falls are not unique to Indonesia at this stage of its development.

Outlook for the Near Future

As in other emerging markets, it is likely that Indonesia will continue to feel "growing pains." It is expected that the market will eventually be privatized and that regulation and disclosure enforcement will improve. Efforts are being made in these areas, but change is very slow. In this country, policy regulations are quickly passed, but implementation is often slow. Research is also improving as more brokers are now in place. Like other markets which became popular upon "emergence," Indonesia's capital market popularity has waned somewhat following its dramatic growth in 1989 and 1990. From a regional perspective, however, the Indonesian market is now large enough that it is now considered a "core" market by most Southeast Asian and emerging stock market institutional investors.

Structure of the Market

Although this has not always been the case, the listings in Indonesia are reasonably representative of the nonoil Indonesian economy. Although there are small oil- and gas-related companies listed, their weightings are very small. Cement companies represent the largest weighting as a sector followed by manufacturing, pulp and paper companies, and banks. Conglomerates are also large but represent primarily Astra International. Table 9.2 provides data on the largest stocks in the Indonesian market. Table 9.3 shows the breakdown of the Indonesian market by sector as of October 1991.

Investors

Following the opening up of the Indonesian exchange to foreigners partially in 1987 and then fully in 1989 (except for banks), trading has been dominated either by foreigners themselves or by local speculators who generally follow or anticipate foreign buying. Unlike the Thai market where individual investors provide solid liquidity, much of the trading in Indonesia is institutional or conducted by larger investors. This is partially why liquidity and turnover are low given the market's size. Bank shares may eventually be purchased by foreigners, but they are currently only open for investment by Indonesians.

Table 9.2 Indonesian Stock Market Capitalization, October 31 1991

Company	Industry	Market Capitalization Total Shares (Rp million)	Market Capitalization Total Shares (US $ million)	Market Capitalization Traded Shares (Rp million)	Market Capitalization Traded Shares (US $ million)	Percent of Total Market Capitalization	Percent of Traded Market Capitalization
1. PT INDOCEMENT	Cement	4,521,552	2,287	678,233	343	15.8%	5.9%
2. PT ASTRA INTERNATIONAL	Conglomorate	2,543,100	1,286	575,453	291	8.9%	5.0%
3. PT GUDANG GARAM	Tobacco	2,020,292	1,022	404,058	204	7.1%	3.5%
4. PT INDAH KIAT PAPER	Pulp/Paper	1,072,422	542	281,340	142	3.7%	2.4%
5. PT UNILEVER	Consumer	1,001,233	506	150,262	76	3.5%	1.3%
6. PT INTI INDORAYON	Pulp/Paper	931,500	471	931,500	471	3.3%	8.0%
7. PT POLYSINDO	Textile	846,400	428	220,800	112	3.0%	1.9%
8. PT INCO	Mining	558,900	283	111,784	57	2.0%	1.0%
9. PT BRANTA MULIA	Manufacturing	525,000	266	157,500	80	1.8%	1.4%
10. PT PABRIK KERTAS TJIWI	Pulp/Paper	513,360	260	513,360	260	1.8%	4.4%
11. PT BANK BALI	Bank	490,053	248	490,053	248	1.7%	4.2%
12. PT SEMEN GRESIK	Cement	444,864	225	210,000	106	1.6%	1.8%
13. PT BANK DANAMON	Bank	425,600	215	45,600	23	1.5%	0.4%
14. PT DHARMALA SAKTI SEJAHTERA	Financial	405,000	205	135,000	68	1.4%	1.2%
15. PT GAJAH TUNGGAL	Manufacturing	374,000	189	374,000	189	1.3%	3.2%
16. PT SEMEN CIBINONG	Cement	348,269	176	348,269	176	1.2%	3.0%
17. PT UNITED TRACTORS	Manufacturing	338,100	171	221,833	112	1.2%	1.9%
18. PT BANK INTL INDO	Bank	322,000	163	322,000	163	1.1%	2.8%
19. PT BANK UMUM NASIONAL	Bank	318,500	161	63,700	32	1.1%	0.6%
20. PT KALBE FARMA	Pharmaceutical	310,000	157	124,000	63	1.1%	1.1%
21. PT GREAT GOLDEN STAR	Textile	308,450	156	119,400	60	1.1%	1.0%
22. PT HANJAYA MANDALA S.	Tobacco	306,000	155	76,500	39	1.1%	0.7%
23. PT BDNI	Bank	299,200	151	299,200	151	1.0%	2.6%
24. PT MODERN PHOTO	Consumer	275,900	140	62,000	31	1.0%	0.5%
25. PT INDORAMA	Textile	274,365	139	104,650	53	1.0%	0.9%

Exchange Rate (Rp/US $)   1,977
Source: Crosby Securities

Table 9.3   Indonesia, October 1991, Sectors Ranked by Market Capitalization

Sector	Total Capitalization Weighting* Percent
Cement	18.55
Manufacturing	14.35
Banks	9.45
Conglomerates	9.07
Pulp/Paper	8.79
Textiles	8.24
Tobacco	8.24
Consumer	6.04
Property	4.61
Financial	2.08
Mining	1.95
Pharmaceutical	1.62
Electronics	1.47
Hotels	1.42
Beverage	1.27
Insurance	1.00
Miscellaneous	0.94
Plantations	0.77
Food	0.14
Total	100.00

*Note: The Capitalization figures are based on all outstanding shares.
Source: Crosby Securities

Although local pension funds are large and invest modestly in new issues, generally they are mostly invested in debt instruments and real estate. Given their long-term outlook and the fact that they are cash rich, government pension funds typically do not bring any secondary market liquidity. This is expected to change soon as new pension fund laws are currently being voted upon in the legislature. The new laws may encourage pension funds to invest more in the market by setting up guidelines for investment (currently there are no guidelines). The new laws will also set final guidelines for local fund management firms to follow and will allow these firms to manage pension fund money as well as offer domestic mutual funds. Currently, only Danareksa, the state-owned underwriter and fund management company, is allowed to offer mutual funds to local investors.

Locally, banks and other financial institutions have also invested in the market. Their roles are expected to be reduced in the long term, following government regulations that they must divest shares over the next several years.

Foreign Portfolio Investment

Despite its small size, numerous funds have been started to invest in the Indonesian market. This was linked not only to the promise of the market itself, but also to the timing of the stock market deregulation. During late 1989 and 1990, country funds became increasingly popular. As a result, many offshore Indonesian funds exist with listings in New York, London, Hong Kong, Singapore, and Amsterdam. The total amount raised for these dedicated funds has been roughly US $570 million.

Currently, foreigners are allowed to purchase up to 49 percent of all "listed shares" of any company except for banks. Unlike most markets, the number of shares issued may differ from those actually listed. Where some companies have all issued shares listed, others do not. When companies choose to list more shares, it effectively opens up more shares to foreigners. The difference between listed and nonlisted shares creates confusion and likely results in reduced liquidity.

Foreign investment is also made difficult because there is no foreign board in Indonesia as there is in other Asian markets. As a result, only local prices are actually quoted despite the fact that some shares have a foreign premium of up to 50 percent. In the longer term, it is expected that an organized foreign board will be created once the exchange is privatized and computerized.

Technical Market Details

Stock Exchange Trading System

There are currently two exchanges in Indonesia—one in Surabaya and one in Jakarta—although trading is dominated by the Jakarta market. All companies except for those listed on the OTC market are listed on both exchanges. The Surabaya exchange which is privately owned is fully computerized and generally more efficient. However, almost all foreign trades are conducted in Jakarta, as that is where the scrip usually is located. Trading in Surabaya remains very small and localized.

The Jakarta Stock Exchange (JSE) is open Monday through Friday with trading completed in two sessions Monday through Thursday (10:00 a.m. to 12:00 p.m. and 1:30 p.m. to 3:00 p.m.) There is only a morning session from 9:30 a.m. to 11:00 a.m. on Fridays. All trades must be conducted through exchange members of which there are now nearly 300.

Trades are conducted manually on the trading floor and are generally completed in 500 share lots. Originally, there was no specified lot size as the capital market was intended to be open to all investors even if the investor could purchase only one share. When settlement became increasingly difficult as share certificates could be in any denomination, BAPEPAM introduced a lot system into the market effective May 1, 1990. At the time, BAPEPAM broke shares into three categories: odd-lots (less than 500 shares), lots of 500 shares, and blocks (more than 10,000) shares.

Subsequently, the size of blocks has been increased to trades of more than 200,000 shares to encourage more lot trading. Following the rule change, trading slowed as many share certificates had to be reregistered into lots. Much of this has now been completed and the trading system is not smooth but has improved.

Trading

Bid and offer prices along with a broking firm identification number are placed on separate columns on white boards on the JSE trading floor. Bids must be submitted to a BAPEPAM official first, but once bid and ask prices match, brokers must return a transaction slip to an exchange official on the floor who then registers the trade. Settlement is conducted by the brokers by the fourth trading day after the transaction has occurred (there is no central clearing). Should settlement take longer, the broker will be assessed one percent of the transaction amount per day. There is no central clearing/settlement system in Indonesia currently.

Although there are foreign ownership limits of 49 percent of listed shares, there is not an organized foreign board as of yet. As a result, foreign premiums do exist but are not officially quoted by the exchange. Each day, BAPEPAM publishes a foreign ownership list showing how many shares are currently available for foreign ownership. This list is made available to each active member firm.

For odd-lot transactions there are separate boards and each listed company is assigned an odd-lot dealer. As dealers are not required to make markets in shares, however, odd-lot transactions can be very difficult. Block trades and large lot trades are typically completed off exchange but then crossed in the market.

Trading on the Bursa Parellel (OTC) exchange is completed differently. The market itself is only open from 9:00 a.m. to 10:00 a.m. each day with each market maker required to post bid and ask prices for a minimum of 100 shares. However, trades do not have to be completed during market hours. Trading is typically very slow. Recently, trading has been reduced even more as two companies (Zebra Taxi and Wisma Dharmala Sakti) have moved their listings to the JSE. Currently, there are only two companies listed on the OTC market. Typically, foreigners have not been active on the OTC market given its poor liquidity and the fact that shares are in bearer form.

The addresses for the Jakarta Stock Exchange and the Surabaya Stock Exchange are as follows:

The Jakarta Stock Exchange
Jalan Medan Merdeka Selatan No. 14
P.O. Box 1439
Jakarta Pusat 10110
Indonesia

Telephone: (62-21) 365509
Fax: (62-21) 350442
Telex: 45604 BAPEPAM IA

The Surabaya Stock Exchange
Jalan Pemuda No. 29-31
Surabaya, Indonesia

Telephone: (62-31) 510646
Telex: 510 823 SURABAYA

Brokers, Securities Firms, and Fund Management Companies

In November 1990, the Ministry of Finance approved new regulations regarding the stock market. In the new rulings, the ministry allowed for three types of firms to actively participate in the stock market. Only securities companies and broker dealers were allowed formerly. In the new regulations, increased capital requirements for these firms and more regulations governing their activities were announced. In addition, a new type of firm, Investment Manager (Fund Management) was created. Below is a listing of the three types of firms:

Securities Companies	Securities companies must have a paid up capital of Rp 5 billion. Securities firms may perform stockbroking, underwriting, and investment advisory functions.
Broker-Dealer	Stockbroking firms must have a paid up capital of Rp 500 million. These firms may perform stockbroking activities.
Investment Manager	Fund management firms must have paid up capital of Rp 500 million. These firms may manage local investment funds.

For all these firms, foreign companies may enter into joint ventures and own up to 85 percent of the company. Foreign joint venture firms must have paid up capital twice that of the local firms (the above figures refer to local firms).

Commissions and Other Costs

Local stockbrokers may charge a commission up to a maximum of 1 percent of the transaction value. Foreign brokers may or may not add commission to the local commission.

Exchange members must pay a transaction fee of 0.1 percent on all trades to the JSE. In addition, there is a stamp duty of Rp 1,000 assessed on each transaction.

Taxation and Other Foreign Investment Regulations

Dividends.   Dividends and other interest income are subject to a 20 percent with-holding tax for nonresidents and 15 percent for residents. The tax is deducted by the company paying the dividend. It is expected that these tax rates will rise in 1992.

Capital Gains Tax.   Capital gains tax is not imposed on securities dealings con-ducted by foreign investors. There are currently capital gains laws regarding Indonesian investors. However, these are not enforced as the administration remains poor.

Foreign Ownership (applies to shares listed on the exchange)

Maximum foreign ownership in banks: 0 percent
Other companies: 49 percent

(Note: Bank ownership regulation is now, however, being voted upon by the legislature. In the future, bank shares may be open for foreign investment.)

Currency Restrictions.   Currently, there are no currency restrictions in Indonesia. The currency is completely convertible and profits may be repatriated.

Settlement Procedures.   Settlement is currently conducted by the exchange members (brokers) and physical share certificates must be transferred. Custodian services are available within Indonesia.

Legislation, Regulation, and Disclosure

Listing Requirements.   Listing requirements differ for the Bursa Efek Indonesia (JSE and Surabaya exchanges) and the Bursa Parallel (OTC exchange). Basically, the requirements are as follows:

	Bursa Efek	**OTC**
Company	Limited Liability	Limited Liability
Domicile	Indonesia	Indonesia
Minimum Paid up Capital	Rp 200 million	Rp 100 million
Profitability	2 years	No requirement
Financial Statements	3 years	3 years or life of company, whichever is less

Other: Banks must be classified as "sound" by the Bank Indonesia (central bank) for the last year and "sufficiently sound" for the past two years. The bank must also meet capital adequacy requirements set by the Bank Indonesia.

Financial statements must be audited by a registered public accountant (or state accountant for state-owned companies) with an unqualified opinion.

The stock offered for registration must have a minimum nominal value of Rp 100 million with at least a Rp 1,000 par value per share.

Recent regulations have placed more responsibility on Managing Lead Underwriters to confirm that all information and disclosure in the prospectus is correct. In the past,, this responsibility was held by BAPEPAM.

Other Obligations.   Although there is not currently a central information authority in Indonesia, listed companies must submit yearly financial statements to BAPEPAM within 120 days after the close of the fiscal year. Mid-year results are also required to be filed. Both statements must be published in at least two national newspapers in Indonesia.

Research Sources

Some official information is available from BAPEPAM and through other government economic publications but it is minimal. Research is available from local stockbroking firms and some statistical information can be obtained from the Institute for Economic and Financial Research which supplies the IFC with yearly stock market data.

The most detailed research and statistics, however, concerning companies and the stock market is available from the many international broking firms which now follow the Indonesian market such as Crosby Securities.

Company Profiles

PT Unilever Indonesia

Consumer Products   Unilever went public in early 1982 and became the ninth company listed on the Jakarta Stock Exchange. Under its technical assistance agreement with Unilever N.V, the Indonesian company has the right to use all Unilever patents and trademarks in Indonesia. The company produces three broad categories of goods: foods, detergents, and cosmetics. Demand for consumer products as a whole in Indonesia is increasing at approximately 20 percent annually due to an increase in the labor force of 3 percent annually, increased frequency of use, larger amounts used per application of many items, and increased market segmentation. Unilever Indonesia itself is primarily a product producer, but through its massive distribution network Unilever products are sold in over 400,000 outlets throughout Indonesia.

Currently, Unilever is by far the largest foreign consumer product producer in Indonesia, and as such it is the most direct stock play on the growing consumer market in Indonesia with its more than 180 million people.

PT Astra Graphia

Electronics   PT Astra-Graphia is the business machine and electronics arm of PT Astra International (Astra International owns 80 percent) and is the sole distributor of Fuji Xerox copiers, Digital Computers, Goldstar PCs, fax machines components and monitors. Fuji Xerox has nearly a 40 percent market share in copiers in Indonesia.

Although the company plans to develop its core business, for the longer term Astra Graphia is investing in businesses through seven subsidiary companies which assemble electronic products including computers, distribute various value added products for computer systems, manufacture speakers and speaker boxes, sell telecommunications equipment, and develop financial software. The company's most recent investment was in Pt Astra Microtronics Technology, a company which began to assemble and test integrated circuits on Batam Island in the fall of 1991. Astra Graphia owns 25 percent of the company.

PT Astra International

Automobiles\Conglomerate   Astra International is the holding company for the Astra Group the second largest in Indonesia. Well over 70 percent of sales are derived from the company's automotive division which has roughly a 55 percent market share in Indonesia. Astra assembles and distributes Toyota, Daihatsu, BMW, Isuzu, Peugeot, and Renault automobiles as well as Nissan Diesel trucks. In addition, the company also manufactures, assembles, and distributes Honda motorcycles which have roughly a 60 percent market share in Indonesia. Through more than 40 subsidiaries, the company manufactures various automobile and motorcycle components used in its assembly operations.

In addition to its automotive operations, the company is involved in Heavy Equipment through its 60.7 percent holding in PT United Tractors (listed), Electronics through its 80 percent holding of PT Astra Graphia (listed), Financial Services, Wood-based Industry, and Agribusiness. The Astra Group is one of the more respected in Indonesia and the listed company is currently the only true holding company which is public. As the most liquid and diversified listed company, Astra is the most direct play on the Indonesian economy as a whole.

PT Indocement

Cement   Indocement is the largest cement producer in Indonesia and one of the largest in the world. Currently, the company has an installed cement capacity of 7.7 million tons per annum and has a market share of over 40 percent in Indonesia.

Indocement is controlled by the Salim Group, the largest business group in Indonesia, along with the Indonesian government. Recently the company issued a US $75 million euro-convertible bond. Indocement will use the funds generated to purchase PT Tridaya Manunggal Prakasa Cement, a cement company also controlled by the Salim Group with a capacity of 1.5 million tons.

As a tremendous generator of cash, Indocement may eventually develop into a large conglomerate by itself. Currently the company is expanding into more related products for its cement operations. As the largest company on the exchange, in terms of capitalization, and with a substantial market share in cement, Indocement is the most significant cement play in Indonesia.

PT Gudang Garam

Cigarettes   Gudang Garam is the largest clove cigarette (kretek) cigarette manufacturer in Indonesia. In Indonesia the cigarette industry is enormous and annually provides more than US $1 billion in excise and VAT taxes to the government. Gudang Garam has more than a 45 percent market share in Indonesia and last year produced nearly 60 billion kretek cigarettes.

PT Modern Photo Film

Fuji Film and Cameras   Modern Photo Film (MPF) is the sole distributor for all Fuji Photo Film Company's photographic products in Indonesia. Currently the company markets photographic film and paper, cameras, lenses, photo processing equipment (primarily minilabs), chemicals, microfilm, motion picture film, x-ray film, and graphic art products to independent retailers as well as to Modern Putra Indonesia (a 63 percent owned retailing subsidiary). The company enjoys an 85 percent market share in film, 37 percent share in camera sales, 61 percent in developing machines and 70 percent in color photographic paper in Indonesia. Through its four subsidiary companies, MPF is also involved in camera manufacturing, retailing, film/paper manufacturing, and film processing. One of its subsidiaries, Honorus Industries, manufactures 40 percent of Fuji's cameras worldwide. Modern Photo is a play on consumer demand, manufacturing, and tourism in Indonesia.

PT Inti Indorayon Utama

Paper Pulp   Indorayon is a long-fiber, short-fiber, and fluff pulp producer with a capacity of 165,000 tons per year and is controlled by the Raja Garuda Mas group in Sumatra. Currently the company is optimizing its plant to push production to 220,000 tons per year. Because the company has a large concession, 136,000 hectares, and replanted trees grow much more quickly than they do in Northern countries, Indorayon is one of the lowest cost producers in the world. Longer term the company is expanding into rayon production. Although there are environmental questions concerning the replanting of trees, many new pulp projects are planned in Indonesia. Recently Indorayon received a development loan to assist it with its reforestation program.

Figure 9-1 Indonesia Market Performance (in US$; December 1989 = 100)

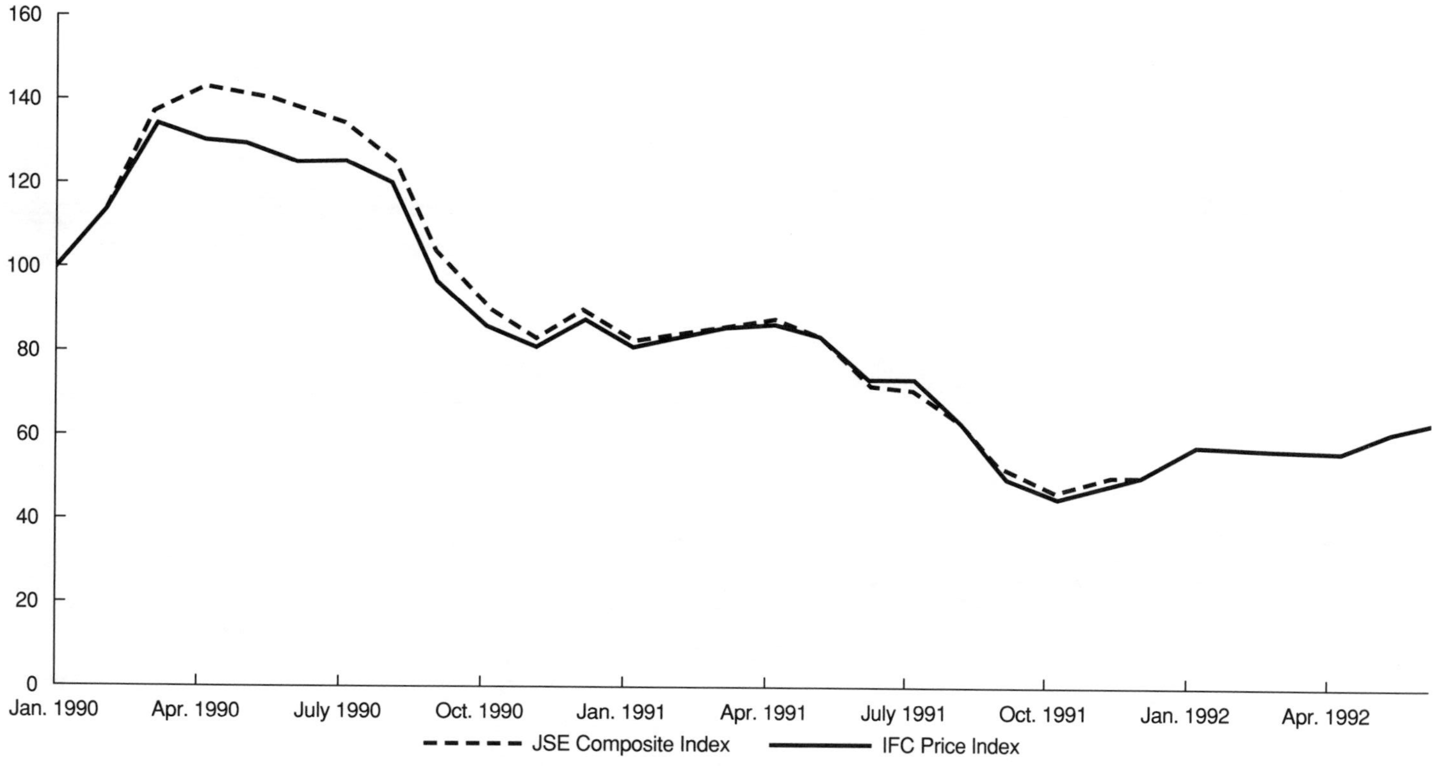

Source: IFC Emerging Markets Database

THE PHILIPPINES

Francisco Rodrigo, Portfolio Manager
Clemente Capital Corp.
New York, United States

The Philippine stock market is one of the oldest in Asia, dating all the way back to August 1927 when the Manila Stock Exchange was established. In the decades following its creation, the Manila Stock Exchange was arguably the premiere stock exchange in the Asian region. In fact, it was not until the early 1970s that the Hong Kong exchange overtook the Philippines in terms of market capitalization and turnover.

Over the years, however, political turmoil, scandals, and economic hardships have stunted the development of the Philippine capital markets. Today, despite its long history, the Philippine stock market remains small and relatively underdeveloped.

Total market capitalization as of the end of 1990 stood at US $6 billion (about 15% of GDP), making it one of the smallest in the Asia-Pacific region. Daily trading value averaged between U.S. $3 to U.S. $4 million for the year (Table 10-1).

Today there are over 150 companies listed on the Philippine exchanges (Table 10-2). Of these, however, only about 30 are actively traded and only a handful are liquid enough and fundamentally solid enough to be considered blue-chip stocks.

The Stock Market

A Brief History

Philippine equities are traded on two exchanges: The Manila Stock Exchange and the Makati Stock Exchange. The Manila Stock Exchange is by far the older of the two, dating back to 1927.

Table 10-1   Market Capitalization and Trading Statistics for Various Asia-Pacific Markets Ranked by Market Capitalization (as of December 31, 1990)

	Market Capitalization (U.S. $ bil)	Average Daily Trading Volume (U.S. $ mil)
Japan	2,830	5662
Australia	148	156
Taiwan	112	2873
Hong Kong	83	149
Malaysia	47	45
Korea	46	256
Thailand	24	101
Singapore	40	56
Indonesia	6	13
Philippines	6	4

Source: Clemente Capital Corporation

Table 10-2   Market Information

	1987	1988	1989	1990
Number of Listed Firms	138	141	146	153
MSE Composite	813.2	841.7	1104.6	651.4
Mkt Capitalization (U.S. $ bil)	2.9	4.2	11.8	5.8
P-E Ratio	15.9	19.1	16.8	14.3
Market Yield	2.9%	1.0%	2.8%	4.0%

Source: Clemente Capital Corporation

For about four decades following its creation, the Manila Stock Exchange was the only stock exchange operating in the Philippines. That changed in 1963, when a group of well-known businessmen conceived of a second stock exchange to be located at the heart of the nation's new premiere business district, Makati.

Opposition to the creation of the new Makati exchange was fierce at first. What followed was two-and-a-half years of legal discussions and court cases that culminated in a Supreme Court ruling, which not only allowed the new Makati Stock Exchange to operate but also allowed it to trade securities already listed on the Manila Exchange. On November 16, 1965, the Makati Stock Exchange officially began operations.

As the years progressed, operations of the two exchanges came to be more and more coordinated. Commission rates were unified and a joint listing agreement was signed mandating that any security listed on one exchange also be listed on the other.

Up until about the early 1970s, trading on the Philippine stock exchanges had been dominated by mining stocks. In 1978, however, the discovery of oil in the southern region of the country caused oil counters to come to the forefront. For a while, trading activity soared, dominated by speculators anticipating the next big oil strike.

As the 1970s drew to a close, however, conditions started to deteriorate. Oil prospects turned out to be greatly exaggerated and many small investors suffered heavy losses. A credit squeeze in 1979 led to the failure of several prominent brokerage firms. In 1981, a respected banker named Dewey Dee absconded with millions, undermining the people's confidence in the nation's financial system. The combined effects of these events shook the capital market to its foundations. By mid-1982, stock prices had fallen to less than half of their 1978-1980 peak levels and for a while market activity dwindled to almost nothing.

The stock market had only begun to recover from these traumatic experiences when it suffered yet another major blow. In 1983, Benigno Aquino, President Marcos's chief political rival, was assassinated on his way back to the country after years of exile in the United States. Aquino's death threw the entire nation into chaos. The economy went into a tailspin, and both capital and manpower began to flee the country. As a result, stock prices again went into freefall.

Interest in the equity markets did not return until 1986, when Marcos was ousted from office by a People's Power revolution spearheaded by Aquino's widow. Mrs. Aquino's rise to office seemed to mark a new era for the Philippines. The economy took off, foreign investments began to pour into the country, and Filipinos who had fled the nation during the Marcos' years began to flock home. Reflecting this new enthusiasm, the local stock market skyrocketed, this time with commercial and industrial companies spearheading the advance. Even the occasional political hiccup seemed incapable of dampening investor sentiment, and by 1989 the Philippine stock market was setting record highs.

Towards the end of 1989, however, things once again took a turn for the worse. A year-end coup attempt put an end to the market's three-year bull run. Since then, a series of political snafus and natural disasters have once again raised doubts about the nation's future, dampening investor confidence. Sterling earnings performances by some of the nation's leading companies like PLDT and PNB have helped prop up the market, in general, but many of the second-line stocks continue to languish at levels well below their 1989 peaks. Figure 10-1 gives an overview of the stock market's performance during 1990 and 1991.

The Structure of the Stock Market

As stated earlier, Philippine equities are traded on two exchanges: the Manila Stock Exchange and the Makati Stock Exchange. Although these exchanges operate inde-

Figure 10-1 Market Performance (1990–1991)

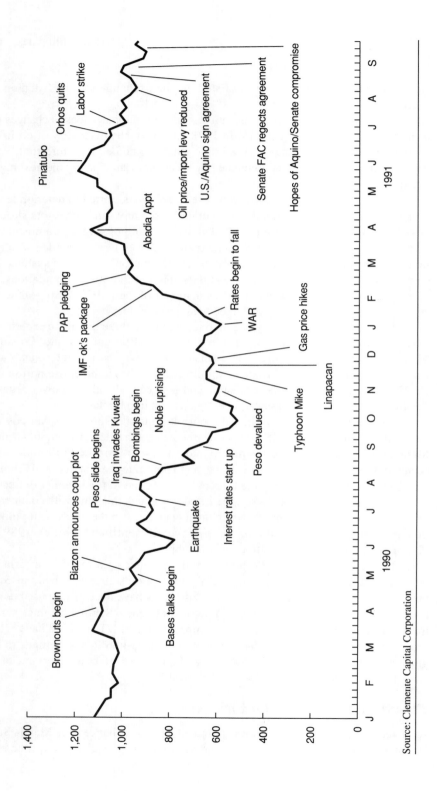

Source: Clemente Capital Corporation

Table 10-3   Top Philippine Companies Ranked by Market Capitalization

	Market Capitalization ($ mil)	Trading Volume ($ mil)	Description of Business
Ayala Corp	2011	36.54	Conglomerate
Ayala Land	1276	*	Real Estate Development
San Miguel	1121	30.93	Food and Beverage
PLDT	845	119.39	Telecommunications
PNB	742	91.46	Banking
PCI Bank	418	2.11	Banking
BPI	245	0.25	Banking
Metro Bank	112	0.54	Banking
Lepanto Consolidated	75	2.53	Mining
Philex Mining	71	3.46	Mining
Benguet Corp	71	2.82	Mining

*Ayala Land did not list until the second half of 1991.
Source: Clemente Capital Corp.

pendently of one another, their roster of stocks is identical. Current Philippine law requires that any company listed on one exchange also be listed on the other. Consequently, any firm wishing to issue securities through the exchanges must be screened by a joint listing committee composed of members of both exchanges.

Because the two exchanges operate independently of one another, it is possible for the price of a particular issue to differ from one exchange to the next. Such discrepancies, however, are usually eliminated by arbitragers within a relatively short period of time.

There are currently over 150 companies listed on both exchanges. Of these 150 companies, however, only about 30 are actively traded and only a handful can be classified as blue-chip stocks.

The major blue-chip issues are Ayala Corporation, Philippine Long Distance Telephone (PLDT), Philippine National Bank (PNB), and San Miguel (Table 10-3). As of June 1990, these four companies accounted for almost 60% of the market's total capitalization and about 95% of daily trading volume.

Trading on the Philippine equity markets has traditionally been dominated by a relatively small number of institutions and professional individuals. Among the institutions that actively participate in the market are the Social Security System, the Government Services Insurance System, and the Armed Forces Retirement Fund. In addition, there have been a number of dedicated country funds that have been established in recent years. These include the First Philippine Fund, the JF Philippine Fund, and the Manila Fund. (A brief description of each fund is provided below.)

The First Philippine Fund
Listed on the New York Stock Exchange
Date of Listing: November 1989
Total Shares Outstanding: 8.98 million
Investment Advisor: Clemente Capital, Inc.
Annual Fee: 1%
Special Features: Only foreign fund allowed to purchase "A" shares. (See following section for explanation of "A" and "B" shares.

The JF Philippine Fund
Listed in London
Date of Listing: November 1989
Total Shares Outstanding: 7.5 million + 1.5 million warrants
Investment Advisor: Jardine Flemming Investment Mgmt (Hong Kong)
Annual Fee: 1.75%

The Manila Fund
Listed in London
Date of Listing: October 1989
Total Shares Outstanding: 5 million
Investment Advisor: Indosuez Investment Services (Hong Kong)
Annual Fee: 1.875% of first $50 million, 1.5% of the next $50 million, and 1.125% on anything above $100 million.

Types of Shares

Filipino law restricts foreign ownership in certain areas of business, such as media, education, banking, utilities, and natural resources. Companies that fall into these restricted areas generally classify their shares into two categories: "A" shares and "B" shares. "A" shares are generally reserved for Filipino nationals, while "B" shares can be purchased by anyone foreign or local.

It must be noted, however, that not all companies follow this "A" share/"B" share convention. Exceptions include:

(a)   companies that are not involved in restricted areas of business and do not own land (e.g., Saniwares, a manufacturer of bathroom fixtures, and Sime Darby Pilipinas, a tire manufacturer) and

(b)   companies that float a sufficiently small percentage of their shares so that even if all those floated shares were purchased by foreigners it would not violate foreign ownership restriction. Examples of such firms include RFM Corp. and almost all banks.

Stock Market Operations

Trading hours.   Trading at both the Manila and Makati Stock Exchanges is conducted between the hours of 9:30 a.m. to 12:00 noon. A 15-minute extension (12:00-12:15) is provided to allow brokers to complete unexecuted orders, provided said orders were received before closing and are executed at the 12:00 noon closing price.

Trading methods.   Both the Manila and Makati Stock Exchanges are double-auction markets, where both buyers and sellers are represented by stockbrokers. Trading is conducted by posting bid and ask prices on blackboards with the broker's initial posted along side.

If an order is to be executed at market price, the broker calls the first posted seller or buyer. When a broker receives both a buy and sell order for a given stock at the same price, he or she places his or her initials under both the buy and sell columns and crosses the orders at the given price.

Transactions are invoiced via confirmation slips, which are sent to clients on the day that the trade is executed. Payment must be made upon receipt of confirmation.

Price freezing limits.   SEC regulations limit the amount by which the price of a given security can move on a given day. If the price of a given stock rises by 50% or falls by 40%, the price of that security is automatically frozen, unless there is an official announcement from the company or some government agency that would justify such a price fluctuation. (Movement of the stock for purposes of price freez-

---

Table 10-4   Guide to Minimum Fluctuations and Lot Sizes of Philippine Equities

Price Range (in Pesos)	Minimum Fluctuation (in Pesos)	Lot Size (in Shares)
0.001 - 0.005	0.0002	200,000
0.0055 - 0.01	0.0005	200,000
0.011 - 0.025	0.001	100,000
0.026 - 0.05	0.001	50,000
0.0525 - 0.10	0.0025	20,000
0.105 - 0.25	0.005	10,000
0.26 - 1.00	0.01	5000
1.02 - 2.50	0.02	2000
2.55 - 5.00	0.05	1000
5.10 - 10.00	0.10	500
10.25 - 25.00	0.25	100
25.50 - 100.00	0.50	50
101.00 - 250.00	1.00	10
252.50 - 250.00	2.50	5

Source: Clemente Capital Corporation

ing is based on the last closing price or the last posted bid price, whichever is higher.)

Board lots and fluctuations.   Board lots are defined as the minimum number of shares an investor is normally required to buy or sell. A fluctuation is the minimum increment by which the price of a stock can rise or fall. Both the size of the board lot and the price fluctuation vary according to the base price and nature of the individual issue. Table 10-4 below provides a general guide to the normal lot size and fluctuations of individual stocks. It is possible to transact odd-lot sales or purchases. Odd-lot transactions are carried out on a board specifically designed for such trades.

Settlement and clearing of transactions.   Settlement date, in the case of regular transactions, falls on the fourth trading day following the transaction. Certificates sold must be delivered by the selling client before then. Payment for the purchase of stock is due upon receipt of confirmation from the broker and must be received no later than the settlement date.

All brokers tabularize their daily transactions and submit a summary to the clearing agent of the Stock Exchange four days later. New stock certificates are issued by the clearing agent and are delivered to the client by the broker as soon as they are received from the clearing agent. Be advised, however, that the issuance of new stock certificates can sometimes take several weeks.

Table 10-5   A List of Some of the Larger, More Active Philippine Securities Firms

Manila Stock Exchange	Makati Stock Exchange
All Asia Securities	AGJ Securities
Anscor-Hagedorn Securities	Belson Securities
Barcelon Roxas Securities	BPI Securities
Baring Securities, Philippines	Citicorp Vickers, Phils
James Capel, Philippines	Equitiworld Stock Brokers
Jardine Flemming, Philippines	I Ackerman & Co.
R. Coyiuto Securities	Jardine Flemming Exchange Capital
Sun Hung Kai Securities	Papa Securities
	Peregrine, Philippines
	Philippine Asia Equity
	Pryce Securities
	Urbancorp Investments

Source: Clemente Capital Corporation

Brokers and Commissions

The Manila and Makati Exchanges have a total of 181 members—90 in Manila and 91 in Makati. Of these 181 members, a total of 93 are active—20 in Manila and 73 in Makati. Many of these member firms, however, represent individuals trading for their own accounts. Table 10-5 lists some of the larger, more active brokerage houses that foreign investors may want to call if they intend to do business in the Philippines. Please note that the inclusion or exclusion of any securities firm in Table 10-5 is not in any way indicative of the quality of that firm. Nor is the table meant to be a comprehensive list of all the active brokerage houses in the country. It merely reflects the author's experience and his knowledge of the larger securities institutions involved in the Philippine stock market.

Philippine brokers generally charge a standard rate of up to 1.5% on all trades, subject to a minimum of 45 pesos. More often than not, however, many brokers are willing to offer discounts to large clients.

In addition to the brokerage fee, stock sales are also subject to a transfer tax equal to 1/4% of the gross selling price. There is also a documentary stamp tax of 50 centavos for every 200 pesos par value or fraction thereof. This documentary tax, however, is customarily absorbed by the broker.

The Regulatory Environment

The Securities and Exchange Commission of the Philippines

Established in 1936, the Securities and Exchange Commission of the Philippines (SEC) is responsible for regulating the local securities industry. The SEC's responsibilities include:

- the registration and regulation of both stock exchanges;

- the licensing of securities brokers and dealers;

- the promulgation of rules and regulations on securities trading and

- the issuance of opinions and rulings pertaining to the application of the Corporation Code of the Philippines, the Revised Securities Act and other statutes.

The SEC is a quasijudicial government agency under the administrative supervision of the Office of the President of the Philippines. It is composed of a chairman and four associate commissioners, all appointed by the president for staggered terms of seven years.

Any company wishing to issue securities to the public must file a sworn registration statement with the SEC. This registration statement must contain detailed information about the company, its business, and its management and must be prepared in accordance with the principles of full and fair disclosures.

Information contained in the registration statement must be updated periodically. Registered companies are required to submit periodic financial and operational reports. Furthermore, they are obliged to keep the SEC, the exchanges, and the general public informed of any and all material facts that may affect its stock price as soon as they occur. Public companies are also prohibited from releasing any material information that may affect the price of its security via press conference or interview, unless a representative of the SEC is present.

The Securities Investors Protection Fund (SIPF)

The SIPF was created to help protect investors against fraud and the possible failure or insolvency of stock exchange members. The organization, however, is geared more towards small local investors and, from a practical standpoint, is of little use to large institutional and individual players. The SIPF reimburses customers of registered securities firms for losses of up to 10,000 pesos ($370) in the event the securities firm is forced to liquidate. The SIPF is administered by a Board of Trustees composed of members of the SEC, the exchanges, and the public.

Rules on Insider Trading and Stock Manipulation

Both insider trading and stock manipulation are considered illegal in the Philippines. Rules and regulations pertaining to these activities are generally patterned after those of the United States. The Philippine SEC has conducted investigations into such activities in the past, but as of yet no convictions have been handed down.

Margin Trading

Under the Revised Securities Act, the use of credit for the purchase of securities is limited to the larger of the following: (1) 65% of the security's current market price or (2) 100% of the lowest price of the security during the preceding 36 months, but not more than 75% of the current market price.

Rules Governing Foreign Investors

Foreign investors are prohibited from purchasing "A" shares.

Purchases of Philippine equities by foreign entities and nonresidents must be registered with the Central Bank in order to qualify for repatriation of dividends and proceeds resulting from the subsequent sale. If the investor has a local custodian, it is the custodian who issues the necessary registration documents. In the absence of a local custodian, the broker usually sees to the registration requirements. (Note: stocks handled by brokers will usually be held in street name.)

Even if Central Bank registration requirements are met, repatriation of dividends and proceeds of sale may take a while, usually anywhere from three to eight weeks, depending on the broker used and the nation's foreign currency situation at the given time.

Table 10-6 Withholding Tax Rates Imposed by the Philippine Government on Dividends for 19 Major Countries

Australia	15	(a)
Austria	10	(b)
Belgium	15	(c)
Canada	15	(b)
Denmark	23.32	(d)
Finland	15	(e)
France	15	(b)
West Germany	10	(f)
Indonesia	15	(f)
Japan	10	(h)
Korea	10	(f)
Malaysia	15	
New Zealand	15	
Pakistan	15	(g)
Singapore	15	(g)
Sweden	23.32	(d)
Thailand	15	(e)
United Kingdom	15	(b)
United States	20	(g)

(a) If rebate or credit is given to recipient; otherwise effective rate is 25%.

(b) If recipient holds 10% of the voting shares of the paying corporation (payor), or in the case of Austria, also if the recipient holds 10% of the shares issued by the payor during the six months preceding the dividend payment date. Otherwise the rate is 25%.

(c) If the dividend is tax exempt in Belgium; otherwise the rate is 20%.

(d) Equivalent to two-thirds the regular tax and is applicable upon compliance with certain requirements.

(e) If recipient owns 10% of the voting shares of the payor or, in Thailand's case, 15%.

(f) If recipient holds 25% of the capital of the payor (15% in the case of Germany) or, in the case of Korea, if the dividend is paid by a BOI-registered preferred pioneer enterprise; otherwise, the rate is 20%.

(g) If recipient holds at least 25% (10% in the case of the United States and 15% in the case of Singapore) of the capital of the payor during part of the payor's taxable year preceding the dividend payment date and during the prior year; otherwise, the rate is 25%.

(h) If the recipient holds 25% of the voting shares of the payor or of the shares issued by the payor during the six months preceding the dividend payment date, or if the dividend is paid by a BOI-registered pioneer enterprise; otherwise, the rate is 25%.

Foreign investors are subject to withholding taxes on dividends. The tax rate on dividends varies anywhere from 10% to 25%, depending upon the domicile or citizenship of the investor and the percentage of the company owned by the foreign investor. (A table of applicable tax rates for the various countries is attached.)

There is no withholding tax on capital gains, but investors are subject to the following charges:

1. A tax equal to 1/4 of 1% of the gross selling price on any stock sold.

2. A 10% VAT on the broker's commission, which the broker will usually pass on to the seller.

Table 10-7   Components of the Manila and Makati Stock Exchange Composite Indexes

	"A" Share Market Capitalization (pesos, Mil)	Index Weighting
Commercial-Industrial		
ANSCOR	751.6	0.7%
Ayala Corporation	36093.8	33.8%
First Philippine Holdings	637.0	0.6%
Globe-Mackay	603.5	0.6%
Philippine Long Distance	26758.2	25.1%
Philippine National Bank	7582.3	7.1%
Philrealty	640.9	0.6%
Robinson Land	856	0.8%
San Miguel Corporation	22687.5	21.3%
SM Fund	1286.9	1.2%
Subtotal: Commercial-Industrial	*97897.8*	*91.8%*
Mining		
Apex Mining	57.3	0.1%
Atlas Consolidated Mining	807.8	0.8%
Benguet Corporation	983.2	0.9%
Dizon Copper-Silver Mines	901.9	0.8%
Lepanto Consolidated	1359.6	1.3%
Manila Mining	122.9	0.1%
Philex Mining	1250.8	1.2%
Surigao Consolidated	50.5	0.0%
Vulcan Industrial	209.9	0.2%
Subtotal: Mining	*5744.1*	*5.4%*
Oils		
Basic Petroleum	164.9	0.2%
Oriental Petroleum	1447.6	1.4%
Philodrill	1048.9	1.0%
Seafront Resources	217.9	0.2%
Trans-Asia Oil	144.9	0.1%
Subtotal: Oils	*3024.2*	*2.8%*
Total	106666.2	100.0%

Source: Clemente Capital Corporation

Dividends and capital gains may or may not be subject to income tax, depending upon the prevailing tax treaty between the Philippine government and the country of the investor.

Table 10-6 is a tabular summary of withholding tax rates imposed by the Philippine government on divideds for 19 major countries.

The Manila and Makati Stock Exchange Composites

Although they each publish their own stock market composite index, both the Manila and Makati Exchanges calculate their respective indexes in similar manners.

The indexes of both exchanges are based on the "A" share price movements of 24 key companies, weighted by market capitalization. (See Table 10-7 for a list of the 24 companies.) These 24 companies are then subdivided into three groups, Commercial-Industrials (C-Is), Mines, and Oils. These groups in turn constitute the basis for calculating the C-I, Mining, and Oil subindexes.

Because of their size relative to the other counters that make up the composites, four stocks (Ayala Corporation, Philippine Long Distance, San Miguel Corporation, and Philippine National Bank) tend to dominate the movements of the index (Table 10-7).

Appendix

The address and some basic information for the Manila Stock Exchange and the Makati Stock Exchange is listed below:

The Manila Stock Exchange
Manila Stock Exchange Building
Prensa St. cor Muella de la Industria
Binondo, Manila
Philippines
Tel: 632-408-867

Number of Members: 90
Of which are active: 20

Trading Activity: 9 mos 1991
Shares: 106.9 million
Value: PHP 12.3 billion

The Makati Stock Exchange
Ground Floor
Makati Stock Exchange Bldg.

*Company profiles are provided by the editors.

Makati, Metro Manila
Philippines
Tel: 632-810-1145

Number of Members: 91
Of which are active: 73

Trading activity: 9 mos 1991
Shares: 81.5 million
Value: PHP 15.1 billion

Company Profiles*

Ayala Property Ventures

Real Estate   Ayala Property Ventures Corporation (APVC) was organized by the
Ayala Corporation in 1988 to offer the public a vehicle by which to directly participate in real estate projects initiated by the Ayala Corporation or any of its subsidiaries. APVC has the charter to undertake projects including land banking for
long-term capital appreciation; develop properties for sale and/or leasing; and purchase real estate for eventual sale at a profit. Ayala Land, a subsidiary of Ayala
Corporation, is the General Manager. APVC pays a .50% management fee to Ayala
Land, payable quarterly, based on book value of the assets. APVC became a publicly owned company in February of 1989. Ayala Corporation owns 25% of the outstanding shares.

Benguet Corporation

Mining   Benguet, founded in 1903, is one of the world's leading producers of gold
and chromite, with an annual production of 235,584 ounces of gold (down 17%
compared to 1989), 103,563 tons of chromite (-10%), 307,000 ounces of silver
(-9%), and 36 million pounds of copper (-10%). It also has a 54% stake in Itogon-
Suyoc, a publicly-traded mining company whose gold production stood at 16,000
ounces in 1990. Forty percent of Benguet's gold is extracted from underground
mines, and contribution of open pit mines will further increase starting at the end of
1991. Benguet wholly owns Benguet Management Corporation (which has stakes in
non-mining companies of foundry work, fresh fruit, cocoa, forestry and land/sea
transport) and Benguet International (mining). Benguet also has minority stakes in
Engineering Equipment (construction—40%), Petrofield Exploration (40%), Asian
Bank (28%). Benguet employs 13,000 personnel, and it is one of the most actively-
traded stocks on the Manila/Makati exchanges, representing 1% of the index. Its
shares have been listed on the New York Stock Exchange since 1949.

Philippine National Bank

Banking   Philippine National Bank (PNB) is the official depository of the Republic of the Philippines and is the country's largest commercial bank. PNB was restructured in 1986, when the government acquired P47B of its non-performing loans and P55B of liabilities, and was privatized in 1989, when the government sold 30% of the outstanding shares to the public. The government remains PNB's single-largest customer, accounting for 40% of deposits. PNB is the leading bank in the Philippines by almost all measures, with a 9.7% market share of total deposits (up from 8.9% in 1986), 12.9% of loans (up from 8.6%), and 14% of the assets in the banking sector. It has an extensive banking network, serving even the remote areas of small provinces with 185 domestic branches and 6 foreign, with plans of adding another 6 domestic and 2 foreign by year-end 1990. The Republic and the Philippines

The Philodrill Corporation

Conglomerate   Philodrill, founded in 1969 as an oil-exploration company, is one of the leading conglomerates in the Philippines, with interests in petroleum (15% of revenues), real estate, mining, venture capital, and financial services (where equity in earnings from affiliates in these fields represented 7% of revenues in 1989). Interest and dividends were 20% of revenues and gain on sale of marketable securities was 58%. The company has diversified into non-oil related fields because oil reserves at its existing wells are now 90% depleted. Its present investment portfolio consists of a 36% ownership in Philrealty, a property development company, 28% of Surigao Mining, a gold mining company, 4% of Atlas Consolidated Mining, the country's leading copper supplier, 13% of Seafront Resources, an oil exploration company with interests in chrome mining and smelting, 15% of Pacific Rim and Export Holdings (Primexport), which owns 9 export-oriented companies, 30% of Trafalgar Holdings, a partnership with Asian Oceanic Group (Hong Kong) to invest in Philippine companies on the stock exchanges, and 93% of General Credit Corporation, a leasing company with the license to operate a bank.

Philodrill is one of the most liquid shares in the Philippines. ADRs, which will be traded over-the-counter, will be issued on April 15, 1990.

Philippine Long Distance Telephone (PLDT)

Telecommunications   PLDT is the principal supplier of local and long-distance telephone service in the Philippines, with 94% market share. It has a major expansion and modernization program underway to meet the growing demand for telephones. It will add 130,000 new telephone lines in 191, with plans of having 1.5 million telephones in service by 1993, from only 1 million today. PLDT has enhanced its long-distance service capability by recently installing a fourth international gateway. Interconnection by other carriers into the PLDT network will add to

PLDT's growth. PLDT is the third-largest listed company in the Philippines, accounting for 9% of the index.

San Miguel Corporation

Food and Beverage   San Miguel is the largest food and beer producer in the Philippines, with 35,700 employees and a market capitalization of U.S. $1 billion. It is best known for its "Pale Pilsen" beer and has a leading market share in fruit juice and soft drinks, ice cream and dairy products, feeds/livestock and aquaculture products, coconut oil, coffee, and packaging materials. Beverages are 65% of revenues, food and agribusiness 20%, and packaging 15%. San Miguel has brewery operations in Hong Kong and China. Exports are 14% of sales. Nestle, Coca-Cola Bottlers, Ramie Textiles, and La Tondena Distillers (hard liquor) are affiliated companies of San Miguel.

11

PAKISTAN: A SMALL MARKET WITH POTENTIAL*

Khalid A. Mirza
Division Manager
International Finance Corporation
Washington, D.C.

The stock market has grown rapidly in recent years essentially on the back of progressive measures to liberalize and deregulate the economy, notably the removal of barriers to foreign investment and the increasing reliance placed on private initiative. Notwithstanding the market's sharp rise, share prices still represent excellent values. Also, a large pool of entrepreneurial talent underscores the high potential for growth in commercial activity which is fundamental to a healthy stock market. However, the institutional structure remains weak and future prospects are, to some extent, clouded by a deteriorating law and order situation, rising inflation, the inability to enforce debt due to inadequacies of judicial recourse (lowering the real cost of debt), and deficient regulation.

History

During the two decades preceding independence and the establishment of Pakistan in 1947, the city of Lahore (Northern Pakistan) witnessed the formation and demise of several stock exchanges beginning with the Lahore Stock Exchange in 1934 which subsequently merged with the Punjab Stock Exchange Limited incorporated in 1936. Dramatic expansion in incomes of the Lahore business community during the war years led to the setting up of another three stock exchanges, namely, the

---

*Sources of information on Pakistan include IFC's Emerging Markets Database publications; Annual Reports of the State Bank of Pakistan, the Karachi Stock Exchange, the Lahore Stock Exchange, and the Investment Corporation of Pakistan; Ready Board Quotation Sheets of the Karachi Stock Exchange; and speeches of the President, Karachi Stock Exchange.

Punjab Share and Stock Brokers Association Limited, the Lahore Central Exchange Limited, and the All-India Stock Exchange Limited. These exchanges suffered badly in the depression after the war. Except for one exchange that migrated to Delhi and merged with the Delhi Stock Exchange, the rest closed down when the subcontinent was partitioned in 1947. During this time most of Lahore's prominent business families were displaced.

After independence, Karachi being the chief port and designated capital attracted an influx of immigrants from all over the subcontinent and became the hub of business activity in the fledgling state. Deprived of access to the Bombay Stock Exchange, a group of entrepreneurs got together and rented a room in downtown Karachi to trade in shares and securities. The Karachi Stock Exchange (KSE) thus came into existence on September 18, 1947, and was incorporated as a company limited by guarantee on March 10, 1949. Although at the time of its incorporation KSE had as many as 90 members, only five or six were active brokers. Also, KSE then had a mere 13 companies listed with paid-up capital aggregating Rs 108 million (US $33.6 million).

Following the KSE, stock exchanges also emerged in two other important cities—Dacca and Lahore. The Dacca Stock Exchange was set up in 1954 as KSE's counterpart in East Pakistan (now Bangladesh). In the late 1950s, a feeble attempt to revive a stock exchange in Lahore on the debris of the four stock exchanges existing there prior to independence (under the title of Pakistan Stock Exchange Limited), floundered and made no headway. Much later, in 1970, the present Lahore Stock Exchange (LSE) was formed and began functioning in May 1971. Apart from the obvious handicap of being a newcomer and well behind the already established KSE, it had an inauspicious start. Soon after its formation, business in general, and stock market activity in particular, got bogged down in a minefield of adverse political and economic developments, namely, the outbreak of hostilities with India; the separation of the country's eastern province to form Bangladesh; the induction of a socialist government which rapidly nationalized large segments of industry, insurance, banks, and shipping; recessionary conditions following the oil crisis of 1973; and a drastic 120 percent devaluation which greatly enhanced the debt servicing burden of industries catering to the domestic market.

Starting literally from scratch with a rather small entrepreneurial class, a rudimentary infrastructure, and an almost nonexistent industrial base, Pakistan's economy—and with it the stock market—made steady progress in the 1950s. Pragmatic policies seeking a healthy mix of private initiative and government involvement made this possible; this was all the more remarkable considering the disruption of economic links with India and the huge refugee problem the country was saddled with. As a result, during 1949 to 1960, listings on KSE rose to 81 companies in 1960 representing an aggregate paid-up capital of over Rs 1.0 billion (US $267.2 million), the market capitalization being about Rs 1.9 billion (US $511.6 million).

Having survived the initial difficult years of its existence, Pakistan made rapid economic strides in the 1960s, notably in the first half of the decade, against the backdrop of political stability fostered by an authoritarian government. These were clearly boom years with Pakistan being referred to by international agencies as a "model for development." It was also a period of considerable stock market growth, although this was marred by periods of decline arising as consequence of the 1965 Indo-Pakistan War and the sociopolitical unrest during most of 1966–1970 which dampened economic activity. While the central bank's share price index (SBP Index)[1] rose by only 16.3 percent over the decade, the market broadened, and by 1970, listings had nearly quadrupled to 318 and market capitalization had doubled to Rs 4.25 billion (US $892.5 million). Annual turnover also increased sharply in the second half of the decade; more than 15.4 million shares changed hands in 1970 which was 3.5 times more than 4.4 million in 1965. After a rapid increase in members to a total of 200, KSE ceased to admit new members in 1966 and also rationalized its operations; this included the setting up of a "clearing house" in 1969 to facilitate settlements.

Concentration of economic power as well as an acute sense of political alienation engendered by an authoritarian government unleashed strong sociopolitical forces. The backlash of a popular socialist movement in West Pakistan and a widely supported separatist movement in the country's Eastern wing destabilized the economy as well as polarized the country politically. The fruits of an ill-conceived attempt at a military solution and another round of Indo-Pakistan hostilities were the establishment of Bangladesh in 1971 and, at the same time, the ushering in of a socialist government in what is left of Pakistan. Other than perhaps the last two years, the 1970s were largely dismal for private business activity and for most of these years the stock market fared rather poorly. Overall, by 1980, the number of companies listed was 314, which was about the same as in 1970. Market capitalization was only 50 percent higher at Rs 6.36 billion (US $642.4 million), this being about 20 percent lower than the aggregate paid-up capital! The annual turnover of 25.8 million shares in 1980 was also only 67 percent higher than in 1970.

The 1980s began with the policy of greater reliance on private enterprise to achieve economic goals firmly reinstated. Until today, successive governments have only reaffirmed as well as strengthened this policy, despite rearguard opposition by vested bureaucratic elements. While there have been more plans to divest than actual divestments achieved, the shift away from the public sector was concrete enough to rekindle business confidence and encourage private investment with a most favorable impact on stock market activity. Emphasis on the private sector led the government to recognize—for the first time during the mid-1980s—the importance of the stock market as a vehicle for capital formation and the need to develop it (see Figure 11-1). The 1984–1986 budget was watershed inasmuch as incentives in the shape of a 15 percent tax differential favoring listed companies as well as

[1] State Bank of Pakistan's General Index of Share Prices (SBP Index).

Figure 11-1 Pakistan Market Performance (in US $; December 1985= 100)

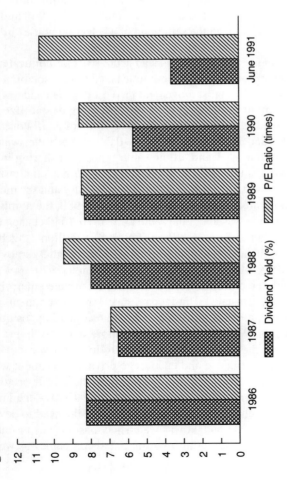

exempting dividends from tax were prescribed. These measures, recently withdrawn in part, were largely responsible for the considerably heightened pace of listings and new issue activity during 1986–1990. The 1980s as a whole saw stock market progress on all counts: listings in 1990 were 487 (after 33 de-listings due to mergers and other reasons, as compared to 314 in 1980); market capitalization went up more than ten times to Rs 64.8 billion (US $2.98 billion) this being more than twice the aggregate paid-up capital; and annual turnover also rose nearly ten times to 252.9 million shares (i.e., an average of over a million shares traded daily) representing a traded value of nearly Rs 5 billion (US $230 million). Also, as compared to 1980, the SBP Index in 1990 was 83 percent higher at 308.53.

Recent Developments

KSE's recent performance (from 1984 to June 1991) is summarized in Table 11-1 and Figure 11-2.

The stock market's performance in 1990 was clearly a marked improvement over 1989 in terms of listings (+47), market capitalization (+21 percent), turnover (+21 percent), and stock market indices i.e., SBP Index (+9.2 percent) and IFC Total Return Index (+11.4 percent). This is impressive considering that 1990 started with highly aggravated tensions with India and then saw the following: (1) a change of government and the uncertainties of an election, (2) the Gulf crises with adverse consequences on the balance of payments, and (3) a lackluster economic situation worsened by suspension of US aid on political grounds, as well as denial of an IMF disbursement for failure to meet economic targets. Although there were bouts of depression, on the whole the market sentiment during 1990 did not suffer. Seemingly, the market took heart from privatization moves (including sale of 10 percent shares of Pakistan International Airlines to the public raising an equivalent of US $12.7 million) and significant steps taken to liberalize the economy, including opening the economy for foreign investment.

Measures to liberalize and deregulate were further augmented in the first half of 1991. Barring few exceptions, industrial approvals are no longer necessary, barriers to foreign investment have been removed, and the Rupee is in effect, freely convertible. Two of the smaller government-owned banks have been privatized—one of them sold by auction to a combine of 12 business houses and the other by way of an employee buy-out—and firm plans have been announced to privatize 115 public sector enterprises. As expected, the stock market has responded positively to this significant opening up and deregulation of the economy, in particular the new liberal framework for foreign investment in shares of listed Pakistani companies and the removal of constraints to the repatriation of investment proceeds, gains, and dividends.

Table 11-1   KSE's Recent Performance

Year	Listings	Market Capitalization (US $Mill.)	Trading Volume ($ Mill.)	Turnover Ratio* (%)	New Issues (No.)	Year-end P/E	Year-End P/BV	SBP Index Change (local currency)	IFC TR Index Change (US $) (%)	Exchange Rate Change (US $) (%)
1991	542	7,326	645	12.6	17	16.2	5.0	132.8	172.3	-13.30
1990	487	2,850	231	8.7	49	8.5	2.0	11.3	11.4	-2.16
1989	440	2,457	193	8.0	38	8.4	1.8	5.5	6.5	-12.94
1988	404	2,460	177	8.0	26	9.4	1.7	15.0	14.6	-5.41
1987	379	1,960	162	8.8	18	6.8	1.7	14.3	6.7	-1.43
1986	361	1,710	155	10.0	9	8.2	1.9	20.1	20.8	-7.36
1985	362	1,371	236	18.4	17	—	—	-1.1	17.8	-3.88
1984	347	1,226	180	14.8	20	—	—	0	0	-12.11

*Total value traded divided by average market capitalization for the period in local currency
Sources: IFC Emerging Markets Database; KSE (for new issues)

Figure 11-2 KSE Dividend Yield and P/E Ratio

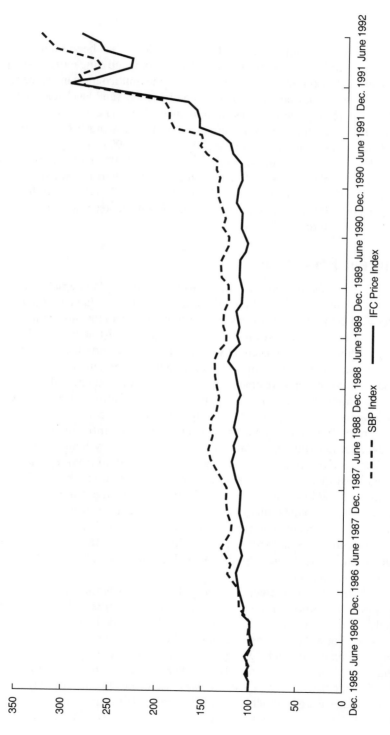

350

300

250

200

150

100

50

0

Dec. 1985 June 1986 Dec. 1986 June 1987 Dec. 1987 June 1988 Dec. 1988 June 1989 Dec. 1989 June 1990 Dec. 1990 June 1991 Dec. 1991 June 1992

- - - - SBP Index   —————— IFC Price Index

Source: IFC's Emerging Markets Database

Foreign investment in listed Pakistani shares has been taking place since March and April of 1991, primarily by Hong Kong and Singapore-based portfolio managers and institutional investors. At least one multicountry investment fund has already invested substantially and one small country fund has been floated with at least two more on the anvil. These developments have far out-weighed the negatives viz strong inflationary pressures arising from the growing fiscal imbalance and a deteriorating law and order situation. By year-end 1991, listings had risen to 542 (after delisting six companies), and as compared to 1990, market capitalization had more than doubled to US $7.4 billion, turnover had almost doubled to 12.6%, and the value traded also more than doubled to US $645 million. The SBP Index rose by 133 percent in local terms and the IFC Total Return Index rose 172 percent respectively in dollar terms.

Current Perspective

Assuming satisfactory political solutions to the country's internal ethnic conflicts and its external disputes with neighboring countries (India and Afghanistan), the underlying environment for stock market growth is favorable insofar as government policies are supportive of the private sector and investment, both domestic and foreign. This is further bolstered by the presence of a reservoir of progressive entrepreneurs that have emerged over the years. In the longer term, however, it would not be possible to sustain investment activity and stock market growth if rampant lawlessness cannot be curbed and the rising tide of inflation (principally caused by widening fiscal deficits) cannot be brought down to acceptable levels.

Presently material reductions in lawlessness and inflation appear difficult to achieve. Further, although Islamization of the banking system produced the desirable impact of essentially freeing financial rates of return from regulatory controls, the real cost of debt is very low (or even negative) since the cumbersome and extremely slow judicial processes effectively prevent enforcement through the courts. Extensive availability of "low cost" bank debt has been and continues to be an important disincentive to the raising of equity capital from the public. Pampered by banks and financial institutions, creditworthy companies are also reluctant to issue debenture stock, the cost of making debenture issues being in any case higher than obtaining a loan.

There are several other regulatory, legal, and operational aspects that constitute stumbling blocks in the way of the market's progress. First, companies are unable to achieve market clearing prices for their public issues; despite liberalizing trends, pricing of new issues still remains under government control. This strongly dissuades companies from "going public" and results in the present anomalous situation where out of approximately 25,000 registered companies in Pakistan only about 500 are listed. Second, lack of clarity as regards to convertibility has prevented the emergence of publicly issued convertible debenture stock, which, owing to the flexibility this instrument entails for both issuers and investors, has been the engine powering the strong growth of the neighboring Indian market. Apparently, under the Companies Ordinance 1984, only noninterest bearing securities are convertible. Third, absence of suitable company law provisions that permit, on a fair and orderly basis, hostile takeovers of closely-held companies means that minority shareholders suffer since managements having access to the real cash flow and benefits are not interested in share prices which the market rationally determines to reflect the "official" cash flow made available to the world at large. A fall in share prices too far below real values would be worrisome for managements if faced with appropriately defined takeover provisions. Fourth, improving stock exchange operations (in relation to trade executions, settlements, and dissemination of market information) as well as strengthening the regulatory framework (particularly with respect to mergers and acquisitions, prevention of insider trading, and to ensure market transparency) are also essential for the stock market to enhance its credibility, attract investors, and deepen.

In sum, the future appears bright for Pakistan's stock market provided inflation and crime can be checked, the court processes to enforce debt are made more effective, new issue pricing/underwriting commissions are fully decontrolled, due provisions are stipulated to make possible hostile takeovers of closely held companies, and appropriate regulatory as well as procedural improvements are implemented.

Market Structure and Characteristics

Relatively, the Pakistan stock market is quite small since in terms of capitalization it is a mere one percent of all emerging stock markets (as of December 1991). It is also heavily concentrated in a few stocks both in terms of capitalization and turnover, and the securities listed are often closely-held. This obviously means a small float, lack of liquidity, and considerable price volatility. Also, the market's current strong growth could lead to trading fluctuations, difficulties in recording and settling transactions, and difficulties in interpreting and applying relevant regulations. Further, although the far-reaching economic reforms and liberalization measures announced are largely being acted upon, it remains to be seen whether the motivating political will (or economic necessity) will persist to ensure that the announcements made are fully implemented and legislated.

KSE is the only active stock exchange in Pakistan; LSE is comparatively somewhat dormant. All companies listed on LSE are also listed on KSE (except The Punjab Bank which is only listed on LSE). There are 80 more listings on KSE as compared to LSE. Stock brokers in Lahore appear to pass most of their orders to Karachi for execution; the transactions actually booked on LSE are immaterial in the overall scheme of the stock market. Transactions on LSE aggregated 22.4 million shares during the year to June 30, 1990, as compared to 252.9 million shares traded on KSE during 1990. The opening of a stock exchange in the capital city of Islamabad has been only recently approved (August 1991) and this has yet to commence operations. Both KSE and LSE are similarly regulated and run, and it is expected that the new exchange in Islamabad will also follow the same operating pattern. The following paragraphs describe the regulation and operation of the stock markets in Pakistan essentially with reference to KSE.

Basic Regulatory Framework

Regulation of the stock market and securities business in Pakistan is principally governed by the Securities and Exchange Ordinance 1969, (SEO), and the rules pre-scribed pursuant to this enactment. The regulatory body entrusted with the powers conferred on the government under this law is the Corporate Law Authority (CLA), an agency constituted under the Companies Ordinance 1984, which is responsible for not only supervising stock exchanges and their members but also licensing investment advisors, regulating the contents of prospectuses, and enforcing legisla-tion pertaining to both companies and corporate securities. There is a also fair element of self-regulation. Stock exchanges are responsible for establishing stan-dards for listing and dealing in securities, regulating the conduct of stock exchange members, and organizing the smooth clearing and settlement of trades executed. Acting as a dealer in a listed security outside the exchange where it is listed is pro-hibited, thereby technically preventing the development of a market in listed securi-ties outside the stock exchanges. In reality, there is a substantial unofficial market of transactions that occur outside the exchanges. Some are subsequently reported by brokers to the exchanges whereas others are ostensibly direct transactions between principals. New issues of securities are regulated under the SEO and generally require the consent of the Controller of Capital Issues (CCI)[2] in the Ministry of Finance (although functionally CCI is placed under CLA); in granting consent to a new issue, CCI can impose such conditions as may be deemed necessary under the circumstances. In addition, CLA is legally empowered to suspend trading on a stock exchange, override its board of directors or cancel its registration. Trading on KSE or in certain securities has been, on occasion, suspended in the public interest.

Membership

Until recently, stock exchanges in Pakistan only permitted individuals or partner-ships of close relatives as members. Corporate members with a minimum paid-up capital of Rs 20 million (US $800,000) were only recently allowed by KSE through an amendment in its constitution in June 1990, and at present there are only two cor-porate members—Jahangir Siddiqui & Co. Limited and Khadim Ali Shah Bukhari & Co. Limited—both of which are looking to further broaden their shareholding through foreign institutional investment. Several other KSE members intend to

---

[2] The Control of Capital Issues Act, under which the office of CCI was created, was essen-tially a measure of the Imperial British Government of India during World War II to ration capital and get Indians to subscribe to war bonds instead of company stocks.

convert to corporate status. There is clearly a need to encourage adequately capitalized corporate membership to enable brokers to reach out to the vast untapped
market in smaller towns, take on underwriting obligations responsibly, and develop
research facilities to adequately inform their clientele—the latter is conspicuously
absent in Pakistani stock brokerage houses.

Membership of the stock exchanges is fixed; KSE has 200 members of which
about 130 are active through trading and is mostly dominated by 15 to 25 members.
It is only possible to become a member by buying an existing seat (or "card" in
common parlance). The transaction requires approval of the exchange which has
been stipulated to ensure that membership is not acquired by unsuitable persons.
The price of a card is now around Rs 5 million (approximately US $200,000),
having appreciated markedly in recent years. Pressure is growing on the exchanges
to open up to new members; one proposal is that each exchange should annually
determine the number of additional members to be admitted based on predetermined
criteria reflecting increase in activity and size, and new cards should be sold at the
going market price (possibly by auction). The proceeds of such card sales could be
usefully utilized to improve the exchange's facilities.

Names and addresses of a few leading stockbrokers are given below:

Name	Address	Telephone	Facsimile
Jahandir Siddiqui . & Co. Ltd	90 KSE Bldg. Karachi	241 9491/ 241 9001	241 8106
Khadim Ali Shah Bukhari & Co. Ltd.	95 KSE Bldg. Karachi	241 9210/ 241 2914	241 5762
Amin Issa Tai	615 KSE Bldg. Karachi	241 9381/ 241 1722	242 3469
Firozuddin A. Cassim	26 KSE Bldg. Karachi	241 5459/ 241 1933	241 4742
Aziz Fida Hussein	4 KSE Bldg. Karachi	241 5076/ 241 6051	241 5042
Sarmad Husseini	4 LSE Bldg. Lahore	63768	56950
N.F. Dastur	LSE Bldg. Lahore	57666/ 57777	56950

Commissions

Brokerage commissions are not left to negotiation between brokers and their
clients but are fixed by the exchange. The commission rates vary with the market
price of the shares bought or sold. KSE's schedule of commission rates is shown
in Table 11-2.

Table 11-2   KSE Brokerage Commissions

Price per Share	Rate for Financial Institutions	Rate for other Clients
Rs 0.01–19.99	Rs 0.09	Rs 0.10
Rs 20.00–29.99	Rs 0.13	Rs 0.15
Rs 30.00–49.99	Rs 0.16	Rs 0.25
Rs 50.00–74.99	Rs 0.24	Rs 0.36
Rs 75.00–99.99	Rs 0.40	Rs 0.80
Rs 100.00–plus	Rs 0.64	Rs 1.50

Source: Korachi Stock Exchange

New Issues

Ordinarily, capital can be privately placed if the company's paid-up capital does not exceed Rs 100 million (US $4 million approximately). Any company issuing capital or envisaging in its financial plan the issue of capital exceeding Rs 100 million is required to make a public offering of its shares and obtain a listing; a company proposing to issue shares such that its capital exceeds Rs 100 million is also required to proceed accordingly (converting itself to a public company if it does not already have this status). Irrespective of the Rs 100 million limit, all public issues or offers of sale of shares require CCI consent. Usually, CCI's consent stipulates that the shares offered to the general public must not be less than half the paid-up capital excluding capital subscribed by foreign associates. In its discretion, CCI may reduce the public offering by the amounts to be invested by development finance institutions (DFIs), effectively deeming DFIs as part of the public. Another CCI condition is that 20 percent of the public issue must be offered to the National Investment (Unit) Trust (NIT), an open-ended mutual fund. The prospectus or offer document also needs to be cleared by CCI and CLA, the latter to ensure that the Companies Ordinance 1984 has been adhered to. In addition, the prospectus is to be approved by the stock exchanges on which the security is to be listed.

Previously, new issues could only be made at par value, although rights shares as well as shares offered when converting a private company to publicly listed status could be made at a price not more than book value. This has been achieved in successive stages over several years. In a dramatic departure from past practice, the government recently notified its intention to allow new issues of shares at prices reflecting a premium above par if so warranted by management quality and earnings growth potential, and the government will also permit existing companies to offer shares at prices above book value if it can be reasonably justified by earnings capacity, dividend record, and market/replacement value of assets. Although the step is still short of allowing the full interplay of market forces, it is a move in the right direction and will encourage companies to make public issues of capital. New issue pricing restraints have resulted in huge over-subscriptions, a lottery-type culture (since minimum level subscriptions usually far exceed the amount offered and are, therefore, balloted to determine allotments), and some degree of investor disaffection with the entire process. During 1985 to June 1991, 123 new issues offered US $255.2 million equivalent in the aggregate against which the subscriptions received grossed US $2.26 billion, i.e., nearly nine times the amount offered.

Listing Criteria

The commercial incentive to seek a stock exchange listing is negligible since (1) bank debt is the primary source of finance; it has a low effective cost and is readily available; (2) entrepreneurs are unable to issue shares at a market clearing price; and (3) closely owned family businesses are reluctant to part with control. A listing is sought only to comply with the requirements imposed on financial institutions, and the Rs 100 million capital limit, and then only after all avenues have been exhausted to circumvent this limit, including corporate spin-offs. The tax incentive viz a tax rate of 45 percent for listed companies as against 55 percent for unlisted companies is marginal in the Pakistani circumstances. Each stock exchange has published its listing regulations which are similar and not very detailed, the principal criteria for listing being: (1) a minimum paid up capital of Rs 20 million (approximately US $800,000); (2) a public issue resulting in at least 250 subscribers; (3) approval of the prospectus or offer for sale document by CCI, CLA, and the stock exchange. Apart from provisions relating to disclosure as set out in the Companies Ordinance 1984, stock exchanges can and do seek additional information in terms of their own rules and regulations. These rules also address procedural aspects of new issue allotments, share transfers, dividend payments, holding of annual general meetings, and the circumstances in which a listing may be suspended or canceled.

Company Reporting Requirements

Each stock exchange has specified several reporting requirements for compliance by listed companies. KSE requires each company *inter alia* to do the following:

1. Submit its half-yearly and annual financial statements as soon as these are approved by the board. (This is in addition to half-year unaudited financials plus annual audited reports sent to shareholders directly.)

2. Notify change of directors, material business changes, all major asset acquisitions, and liquidations including relevant supporting information.

3. Notify in advance the date and time of any board meeting called to consider accounts and declare shareholder entitlements to benefits.

4. Notify board decisions regarding proposed changes in capital including issue of bonus shares, rights issues, or capital refunds.

5. Notify board recommendations as regards dividends and other entitlements accruing to its listed securities.

Dealing and Settlement Procedures

Trading on KSE takes place five days a week, Saturday to Wednesday, from 10:15 a.m. to 2:00 p.m. under an open outcry system. Each listed security is called out and traded in sequence. Members' clerks shout out bids and offers with transactions occurring when these match. Transactions are noted by a KSE representative, recorded on a board, and also communicated to members via closed circuit monitors. Settlement for shares dealt on a "ready" basis, takes place through a centralized clearinghouse. Clearing usually takes place once a week, generally on a Sunday, with clearing dates posted in advance. Shares traded in any week from Saturday through Wednesday are thus settled on the Sunday of the following week. On any clearing day, settlement essentially involves payment by the purchaser by 11:30 a.m. with the share certificates being delivered the same day. In the event of default (which rarely, if ever, occurs) KSE "squares" the deal through an open-market purchase or sale at the erring member's cost. KSE's trading and settlement structure is similar to the London Stock Exchange's "account" dealing system. Trading can also take place on a "spot" basis in which case settlement is directly effected between the buying and selling members within 24 hours. Forward trading permitted on KSE is limited to only five widely held shares: ICI (Pakistan) Limited, Pakistan Engineering Corporation, the Ravi Rayon Limited, National Motors Limited, and Pakistan National Shipping Corporation. Forward trading takes place on the basis of delivery and settlement at the end of each month. Trading for the new month generally starts around the 20th of the previous month.

KSE is seriously considering plans to automate settlement and dealing, but no firm schedule of implementation has been set so far. A study arranged by IFC in 1986 revealed that with only procedural changes (such as an increase in trading hours and a switch in trading style from trading tables to zone or board style) the level of trading activity carried out then—about 1,200 trades per hour—could be quadrupled without an expansion in facilities. Trading activity has actually grown nearly 400 percent since 1986; existing facilities have very little cushion left to allow further expansion in dealing, and a degree of automation is clearly necessary. Even greater pressure is being felt in the clearing system; its automation should receive priority if KSE wishes to avoid inordinate delays in settlement or a breakdown of the settlement system (experienced by stock markets which did not take appropriate measures to cope with increasing business volumes). Clearing is, of course, simpler to automate and to manage being essentially a batch data processing operation as compared to an on-line, real time, inquiry system.

New issues of securities approved for listing are not formally listed and traded until 15 days after confirmation is received that the allotment letters have been dispatched. To regulate the unofficial kerb trading that used to often develop in new issues after the subscription period closed until formal listing took place, KSE now grants provisional listing to new issues approved for listing one day after the ballot is held to determine allotment. Settlement of such trades does not take place on the usual clearing days but on the date the securities are listed on the ready section.

Price Movements

Certain limits are imposed under KSE's regulations on permitted price movements within any clearing period. If the price of a security dealt with on a "ready" basis fluctuates by 50 percent or Rs 5, whichever is higher in any clearing period, trading in the security is suspended until all outstanding contracts in respect of that period have been settled. Trading in that security may, however, continue on a "spot" settlement basis. As regards to provisionally listed securities, trading is suspended until official listing in the event the price moves by more than 100 percent from the clearing rate at the end of the first day of trading as a provisionally listed security.

Market Capitalization

As of December, 1991 there were a total of 542 companies listed on KSE with a total market capitalization of US $7.3 billion equivalent. In Table 11-3, KSE's market capitalization has been sectorally broken down as of December 31 in each of the years from 1987 to 1990 and as of June 30, 1991, along with the number of companies in each sector as of the latter date.

Around a quarter of the market's capitalization is attributable to multinational companies where the foreign parent has a controlling equity and interest. Multinationals are consistently the best performers insofar as dividend payouts are concerned—probably used by the parent company as a means to maximize repatriation of profits. The 15 largest companies on the basis of market capitalization as of June 30, 1991 (i.e., only 3 percent of the number of companies listed) accounted for 35.8 percent of the total market capitalization. These companies are listed in Table 11.4 ranked by market capitalization represented by each as of June 30, 1991.

The market's credibility is hurt by the large number of ostensibly unprofitable companies that do not pay any dividends (more than 150) but somehow continue to exist and remain listed. The lack of confidence in stock investments thus engendered has had an overall adverse impact on share values.

Types of Corporate Securities

Apart from common equity, termed "ordinary shares," the Companies Ordinance 1984 does not permit any other type of equity. The shares are issued for a par or face value which is usually Rs 10 but can also be Rs 5, Rs 100, and Rs 50. Preference shares issued prior to 1984 have been mostly redeemed and only four issues remain listed. It is possible to list Participating Term Certificates (PTCs) and Term Finance Certificates (TFCs)—both Islamic financial instruments that profess to eschew interest—but these have been thus far privately placed with banks and financial institutions and not offered to the public. PTCs essentially involve a return to the holders based on the proportionate share of profits attributable to the amount invested which is then contractually fixed (say 17 percent) in consideration of the holders giving up the right to higher profits. TFCs notionally involve the holders buying a

Table 11-3 KSE Market Capitalization by Sector (Rs Million)

	1987	1988	1989	1990	1991	Number of Companies (June 1991)
Finance Companies, Mutual Funds, and Banks	3,053.83	2,557.50	3,995.71	5,982.10	8,820.70	52
Insurance	1,271.39	1,527.13	1,345.86	1,831.74	2,015.40	30
Cotton Textile	3,991.24	5,300.03	7,824.79	9,961.52	13,498.50	151
Woolen Textile	177.84	176.71	177.21	185.67	198.80	8
Synthetic and Rayon	248.29	236.71	323.50	1,942.84	5,867.50	14
Jute	391.84	423.73	513.37	563.63	786.10	10
Sugar and Allied Industries	2,770.28	3,562.94	3,889.35	4,521.71	4,437.60	30
Cement	1,440.55	1,964.07	1,993.38	1,767.51	2,325.30	10
Tobacco	780.47	906.18	1,149.00	1,255.45	1,403.80	7
Fuel and Energy	6,991.66	7,789.14	9,862.32	10,725.64	14,618.80	11
Engineering	786.63	1,031.11	1,083.13	883.93	1,145.90	15
Auto and Allied Engineering	1,280.85	1,630.67	1,708.48	1,909.18	2,686.30	18
Cables and Electric Goods	797.45	747.99	970.35	995.42	1,424.50	14
Transport and Communication	6,160.52	3,310.23	3,166.29	2,134.82	2,809.80	3
Chemicals and Pharmaceutical	13,499.52	7,227.18	8,128.01	9,189.46	11,740.00	34
Paper and Board	1,105.32	1,207.79	1,101.51	1,243.38	1,754.30	12
Vanaspati and Allied Industries	1,425.02	996.75	426.13	443.76	536.70	16
Construction	43.30	67.84	43.73	56.35	68.10	4
Leather Tanneries	634.21	729.95	883.24	941.03	1,003.50	6
Food and Allied Industries	n/a	1,068.28	2,960.81	3,827.07	4,957.70	18
Glass and Ceramics	n/a	406.00	420.81	389.46	445.30	8
Miscellaneous	1,796.53	662.28	818.67	998.64	1,425.40	27
Total	38,646.74	43,530.21	52,785.65	61,750.31	83,970.00	498

Sources: KSE, Investment Corporation of Pakistan

Table 11.4   KSE Largest Companies Ranked by Market Capitalization (June 1991)

Company	Market Capitalization (Rs Million)
1. Lever Brothers (Pakistan) Limited	3,143.30
2. ICI (Pakistan) Limited	3,023.60
3. Dewan Salman Fibres Limited	2,931.50
4. Pakistan Oilfields Limited	2,798.64
5. National Refinery Limited	2,465.64
6. Karachi Electric Supply Corporation	2,447.97
7. Pakistan International Airlines Corporation	1,964.80
8. Rupali Polyester Limited	1,727.45
9. Sui Northern Gas Company	1,608.60
10. Sui Southern Gas Company	1,606.68
11. Pakistan State Oil Corporation	1,364.11
12. Glaxo Laboratories (Pakistan) Limited	1,362.30
13. Pakistan Tobacco Company	1,229.56
14. Dawood Hercules Limited	1,217.64
15. Exxon Chemical Limited	1,138.18

Source: Investment Corporation of Pakistan

piece of the borrower's business and a sale back to the borrower at a higher price (i.e., at a marked-up price) which is then paid back over the tenor of the financing in equal installments. This is very similar to repayments by way of equated installments of principal and interest. Some uncertainty as to the rights of TFC and PTC holders in the event of losses and the fact that these instruments cannot be made more attractive through a plausible conversion feature has prevented their development as listed securities. However, the "modaraba," the other Islamic instrument introduced in Pakistan, has recently become quite popular. Compared to only 7 in the beginning of 1991, as many as 17 modarabas stood listed on KSE as of June 30 representing a market capitalization of Rs 3.74 billion (US $154.78 million) viz 4.5 percent of the market. By the end of August, 1991, a total of 25 modarabas were listed on KSE, having raised an aggregate of Rs 1.99 billion (US $82.4 million) their total market capitalization being Rs 4.43 billion (US $183.4 million). Modarabas are regarded as akin to mutual funds in that a two-tier structure with a separate management company is stipulated. A significant difference is that modaraba management companies are only paid fees out of the profits earned by the modaraba not exceeding 10 percent thereof. Also, the management company is invariably expected to invest at least 10 percent in the modaraba managed by it. Modarabas have a number of other interesting features such as exemption from tax if more than 90 percent of profits are distributed and the ability to leverage up to 10 times paid in equity (although the gearing in vogue is rather low and well within the permissible limit). The strict regulatory controls exercised by the Registrar of Modarabas (under CLA), the inability to raise funding through commercial paper issues, and the inability to borrow foreign exchange loans on interest basis are compelling negative aspects,. but these have not detracted the public from investing in modaraba certificates.

Public Debt Securities

Foreign Exchange Bearer Certificates issued by the federal government in exchange for foreign currency deposits are the most actively traded public debt securities. These are issued in three-year maturities but may be encashed in foreign currency on demand. There is very little trading in other federal and provincial government listed debt securities, which are mostly held by banks and institutional investors until maturity. The two largest categories of listed public debt securities are: (1) bonds aggregating Rs 15.6 billion in face value issued by the parastatal, Water and Power Development Authority, in three series; and (2) Bearer National Fund Bonds (about Rs 44.1 billion outstanding as of April 1, 1991) issued by the federal government in one- to three-year maturities, the latest issue having been made in 1990.

Major Investors

The guidelines for public issues have been so framed as to attempt a wide distribution of securities. In addition, the public participates through NIT, the Investment Corporation of Pakistan (ICP), and insurance companies. Individual shareholders are estimated to be around 500,000 or about 0.40 percent of the population. An analysis of the broad ownership pattern of corporate equity is shown in Table 11-5. The "individuals" component in the table includes management holdings in the names of family members and friends. The usual ownership pattern of a medium-sized listed company is that the sponsors hold about 50 percent, directly or indirectly, and financial institutions about 30 percent. The "float" is generally less than 20 percent and for the market as a whole it is probably less than 15 percent.

Turnover

Institutional investors tend to hold on to shares for longer periods as compared to individuals who are more speculative and tend to dominate trading. The average daily turnover of shares on KSE is now more than twice the level of one million shares a day in 1990. Total traded value in 1990 represented approximately 8.5 percent of the average market capitalization for that year. Trading in 1991 more than doubled to $645 million and the turnover ratio increased to 12.6 percent. Trading tends to concentrate on a handful of securities; the ten most actively traded compa-

Table 11.5   Ownership Patterns of Equity (Percent)

Individuals	27.8%
Financial Institutions	33.0%
Government and Semi-Government Bodies	17.5%
Joint Stock Companies	20.2%
Other	1.5%
	100.00%

Source: KSE

**Table 11-6   List of Largest Traded Shares During
July 1990–June 1991**

Name of Company	Turnover Number of Shares
1. L.T.V Capital Modaraba	27,507,900
L.T.V Capital (R)	1,118,100
2. Dewan Salman Al.	15,042,000
3. 2nd Prudential Modaraba	10,494,000
4. 1st Sanaullah Modaraba	9,280,900
5. 1st Prudential Modaraba	8,903,120
6. Raza Textile	7,222,900
7. B.R.R 2nd Capital Modaraba	6,481,600
8. Agriautos	5,807,800
9. Khalid Siraj Al.	5,754,900
10. 1st Habib Bank Modaraba	5,708,300

Source: KSE

nies accounted for 26.8 percent of turnover in 1990. Table 11-6 lists the ten most actively traded stocks during 1990–1991.

Recent trading in modaraba certificates has been quite heavy. During the first half of 1991 an estimated 16 percent of the turnover booked related to modaraba certificates.

Institutional Structure

This is weak. Generally, stock brokers offer a very basic service, essentially carrying out client orders and providing informal, largely intuitive, advice. Research facilities at brokerage houses are practically nonexistent and brokers seldom publish research material whether for clients or the public. Some new issue management is done by the more active KSE members as also a limited degree of underwriting.

The first real institutional underpinning came to the market with the setting up of NIT in 1962, the only open-ended mutual fund in Pakistan. NIT enjoys 20 percent preferential allotment of new issues; this privilege is under attack. It has grown in size, and in 1990, NIT had about 64,000 unit holders and Rs 9.3 billion (US $428.2 million) invested. The offer and repurchase prices are fixed in relation to net asset value, although in computing this, assets are valued at cost rather than market value on grounds of market illiquidity. Also, since it follows a "buy and hold" strategy and little capital gains are realized, distributions to unit holders primarily comprise dividend receipts; the units are, therefore, viewed as bond equivalents.

The second capital markets institution is the Investment Corporation of Pakistan (ICP), the brainchild of a Harvard professor. Originally conceived as an investment bank, it still engages in the same lines of activity it was originally established in 1966 to carry out. They include viz underwriting securities issues, placement of debentures, managing investment accounts of individuals (the Investor's Scheme), floatation and management of closed-end mutual funds, and managing its own portfolio of investments. Additionally, it has also been a big player in the provision of bridge loans to be repaid from the proceeds of public issues made after start of production. As of April 1991, ICP had 12,300 Investor's Scheme accounts with assets aggregating Rs 681 million (US $31.35 million); it had floated 21 mutual funds having raised a total capital of Rs 570 million (US $26.2 million) these being successful income-oriented funds that had paid dividends for 1990 of between 14 percent–43 percent on par; and had its own portfolio amounting to Rs 562 million (US $25.9 million). ICP has made a contribution towards broadbasing equity ownership and creating an awareness of the capital market. There is only one private mutual fund, Golden Arrow, which has performed poorly and perhaps only one modaraba, the recently established First Inter Fund Modaraba (FIM), which has confined itself solely to investments in shares employing sophisticated techniques with apparently a fair degree of success.

Standby underwriting, without subsequent distributions of shares taken up, has been mostly provided by ICP-led consortia; to a lesser extent, other DFIs, in particular Bankers Equity Limited, have also organized underwriting consortia of the same kind. National Development Finance Corporation (NDFC) took the innovative step of organizing a club of brokers to subunderwrite public issues underwritten by it. The scheme has not made much headway, perhaps because of unconfirmed reports of disaffection arising from NDFC's inability to show all its deals to the club. Brokers are becoming more active in underwriting and some of the new investment finance companies are actively looking for underwriting business.

Stock Market Publications

Until recently, the only sources of information on the stock exchange and listed securities available to the general public were daily newspapers and *The Business Recorder* which every day publishes a reasonably detailed write-up on at least one listed company in addition to general stock exchange news and analysis. While ICP has been periodically dispatching research notes on listed securities to its investment account holders, there is only one professional investor's information service, Hafiz Investors Service, which commenced a few years ago that regularly provides data and analysis on listed companies to subscribers. In addition, FIM has recently begun to publish a weekly paper devoted to providing information of interest to investors called *The Stock Scanner*. Also, KSE has a daily Ready Board Quotations Sheet distributed amongst members, financial institutions, and key stock market players. In addition to giving closing prices and transactions recorded, it contains relevant corporate disclosures and announcements.

Stock Market Indices

Basically, KSE and the State Bank of Pakistan (SBP) calculate and publish indices to measure stock market performance. The KSE Index is a simple arithmetic average of 50 selected, most actively traded, shares with necessary adjustments for differences in par value. SBP has two indices. The first, a "general" index (the SBP Index), covers all listed shares and is a composite weighted average of ten sectoral indices which are arithmetic averages of share prices in each sector, the weight given to each sector being proportional to the total paid-up capital of the companies in each sector. On the same basis but covering only selected, actively traded shares, is the SBP Sensitivity Index which has significantly reduced time comparability since the shares included are revised every year. SBP and KSE indices have provision to adjust for bonus and rights. Besides these indices, FIM also calculates and publishes the FIM General Index which covers all ordinary shares listed on KSE weighted by the paid-up capital of each company. The FIM General Index is calculated by a two-step formula: first the calculation of sectoral indices weighting each company in proportion to its paid-up capital within each sector; second, combining the sectoral indices into one index weighting each sector in terms of the sector's total paid-up capital relative to the paid-up capital of the entire market. The approach in this case is predicated in the belief that low capital shares are closely held and distort the picture by fluctuating a lot on low trading. It takes into consideration the effect of bonus/rights shares and also allows new companies to be included immediately in the index. Lastly, IFC's indices for Pakistan are weighted by market capitalization. Based on the chained Paasche method, these indices measure the change in the value of 54 component stocks (that cover about 56 percent of the market, and have been selected on the basis of capitalization, liquidity, and sectoral diversity) adjusted for capitalization and for addition or deletion of stocks. The IFC Total Return Index makes a further adjustment for total cash dividends and the implied stock dividend in rights issues (derived from the cum-rights price as compared with the rights issue price) to fully measure the market's performance.

The Foreign Investment Regime

As a result of a series of reform measures taken by the present government, foreign investment has been substantially liberalized; effectively, there is no restriction on foreigners or nonresident Pakistanis purchasing shares of a listed company or subscribing to public offerings of shares. Currently, some approvals from the Investment Promotion Bureau (IPB), the government's project sanctioning and foreign investment regulatory body, and the exchange control restrictions of the SBP are occasionally needed.

IPB approval is now needed only for foreign investment in an undertaking which is not an industrial project or an industrial undertaking engaged in any one of the four restricted industries (arms and ammunition, security printing, currency and mint, high explosives, and radioactive substances), and that, too, *only if* the foreign investor is a sponsor or promoter of the project. All other investments by foreigners, including subscriptions to public offerings as well as purchases listed shares in the secondary market, do not require IPB approval.

For the purposes of exchange control, SBP consent for foreign investment is needed in the case of (1) corporate securities other than shares, (2) purchases of existing shares of unlisted companies; and (3) issues of new shares by unlisted non-manufacturing companies. Furthermore, permission of SBP is required *if* the consideration is not paid in foreign exchange or, in the case of a listed company, it is less than the quoted price, and also if the buyer is a local branch of the foreign company. Subscriptions to new shares in unlisted manufacturing companies, secondary market purchases of shares on a stock exchange, and subscriptions to public offerings of shares do not require SPB approval for exchange control purposes.

CCI consent for the issue of shares to foreign investors is only needed in the case of an unlisted company engaging in one of the four restricted industrial categories, and for this purpose CCI can be expected to take the same position as IPB. As stated earlier, public issues of shares by companies whether or not having foreign equity investment need CCI approval. However, foreign investors can subscribe to all public offerings as explained above.

Foreign investors, if nonresidents, are liable to tax in Pakistan only on income, profits, and gains sourced in Pakistan. However, capital gains derived from sales of listed shares are currently exempted from tax until June 1993 when the exemption will be due for renewal (it has been renewed from time to time in the past). Capital gains derived from sale of unlisted securities are also subject to a reduced tax rate of 27.5 percent if the shares are held for more than 12 months. Dividend income, too, is separately taxed at the rate of 15 percent plus a surcharge of 10 percent of the tax if the total income exceeds Rs 100,000 [effectively 16.5 percent]. All other income is taxed at normal rates; a foreign company would pay an effective rate of 55 percent.

Company Profiles*

Lever Brothers

Household Items.   Lever Brothers is a subsidiary of Unilever plc, London, with 65 percent shareholding in the Pakistani company. It produces and sells margarine (Blue Band), cooking oil (Dalda), soap (Lux, Rexona & Lifebuoy), detergents (Surf) and personal products (Signal Toothpaste, Sunsilk Shampoo and Gibbs Saving Cream). Recently, the company has established a factory to produce hydrogen. As a result of the worldwide takeover, Lipton Pakistan's operations of tea blending, packing of dates and shrimp farming were merged in 1988. The company's net sales revenue has increased from Rs. 1.1bn in 1984 to Rs. 5.5bn in 1990. In the same period, the company's net profits increased from Rs. 28.9mn to Rs. 257mn.

* Company profiles are provided by the editors.

ICI

Chemical Products.   ICI manufactures and sells polyester, staple fibre, soda ash, paints and specialty chemicals. Additionally, it sells imported agrochemicals, pharmaceutical and general chemicals. In 1989, the Polyester fibers and Soda ash capacities were raised by 40 percent and 28 percent respectively. In 1990, ICI's total assets employed were over Rs. 1.0 billion. The company's net sales revenue has increased from Rs. 877mn in 1984 to Rs. 2.9bn in 1990. In the same period, its net profit increased from Rs. 27.3mn to Rs. 202mn. New Soda ash and agrochemicals formulation plants will be operational in 1992. ICI Pakistan is a subsidiary of the British multinational, Imperial Chemical Industries, with 60 percent share in the Pakistani company.

Pakistan Oilfields

Energy.   Pakistan Oilfields is a government-controlled enterprise engaged in the exploration, drilling, production and transmission of Crude Oil, Gas, LPG and Sulphur Solvent. In addition, the company has a share in exploration venture of other organizations such as Oil and Gas Development Corporation and Occidental Oil. The company's sales increased from Rs. 499.5mn in 1984 to Rs. 928.6mn in 1990. In the same period its net profits increased from Rs. 173mn to Rs. 360mn.

National Refinery

Petroleum Products.   National Refinery is a mainly state owned company engaged in the production of petroleum products. The Company's main products are motor spirit, naphtha, furnace oil, asphalt, lube base oil and middle distillates. It has three separate refineries i.e., two lube and one fuel refineries. In 1990, the fuel refinery produced 2.3 million metric tons of fuel and the two lube refineries produced 678 thousand metric tons of lube. State Petroleum Refining and Petrochemical Corporation and Islamic Development Bank of Jeddah are the largest shareholders in the company. The company is currently constructing a fuel refinery to expand its refining capacity.

Karachi Electric

Electricity.   Karachi Electric is a government-controlled enterprise providing electricity service for the city of Karachi. In view of the growing demands of the city, the company has been expanding its electricity generating and distribution capacities. At present, a number of expansion projects estimated to cost over Rs 1.5 billion are underway. The corporation's sales revenue has increased from Rs. 2.9bn in 1984 to Rs. 6.3bn in 1990. In the same period, its net profits increased from Rs. 156mn to Rs. 231mn.

Rupali Polyester

Textile.   Rupali Polyester is engaged in the production of polyester yarn and fibre. Incorporated as a public company in 1980 and listed on the Karachi Stock Exchange in May 1990, Rupali is the largest producer of polyester staple fibre in Pakistan. In 1990, Rupali produced 8.3 million tons of yarn and 19.3 million tons of fibre. Its sales increased from Rs. 1.2bn in 1989 to Rs. 1.5bn in 1990. The company is owned by the Feeresta family and the general public with 90 percent and 10 percent shareholding respectively.

Sui Northern Gas

Natural Gas.   Sui Northern Gas is engaged in the purification, transmission and distribution of gas and in the construction of pipelines in the northern areas. Fifty-one percent of its shares are owned by the government, 6.74 percent by Burmah Oil, Glasgow, 3.62 percent by the general public and the balance by institutional investors. The company's sales were under one billion rupees in 1981 but were nearing Rs.4 billion in 1990.

Sui Southern Gas

Natural Gas.   Sui Gas Transmission Co. Ltd. & Southern Gas Co. Ltd. were merged in 1988 & renamed as Sui Southern Gas Company. At present, a primarily government-owned company, Sui Southern is engaged in the purification, transmission and distribution of gas and in the construction of pipelines in the southern areas. In 1990, its paid up capital was Rs. 419mn. The same year, it recorded net sales and profits amounting to Rs. 2.2bn and Rs. 28mn respectively.

Pakistan State Oil

Petroleum and Related Products.   Pakistan State Oil (PSO) was originally formed in 1974 as the Pakistan Development Corporation (PSDC), to promote the development of petroleum products storage in Pakistan. In 1975, ESSO Pakistan's assets were sold to the government, and then transferred to PSDC, which was renamed State Oil. In 1976, the new State Oil, Pakistan National Oil and Dawood Oil were merged as Pakistan State Oil Company Limited. At present, PSO has an extensive storage and distribution network and enjoys over 65 percent of the market share in Pakistan. Its net profits increased from Rs. 131mn in 1984 to Rs. 194mn in 1990. PSO is managed by Ministry of Petroleum and Natural Resources although the government's direct shareholding is only 25.5 percent.

Glaxo Laboratories

Pharmaceutical.   Glaxo Laboratories is a subsidiary of Glaxo Group of U.K. with 60 percent shareholding in the Pakistani company. It manufactures and sells pharmaceutical and lead products. In pharmaceuticals, it is strongly placed in the anti-ulcer market (Zantac, dermatologicals) and Betnovite range and antibiotics (mainly Ceporex). In recent years, Glaxo has invested heavily in facilities to manufacture raw materials utilized in formulation of drugs and medicines.

Pakistan Tobacco

Tobacco.   Pakistan Tobacco is the largest private sector industrial company in Pakistan engaged in the manufacture and marketing of cigarettes and tobacco. Its main brands are Gold Leaf, Capstan, Wills, Player's No.6 and Embassy. Pakistan Tobacco is a subsidiary of Imperial Tobacco, a British company with a shareholding of 65 percent. The company's net sales increased from Rs. 4.2bn in 1986 to Rs. 7.9bn in 1990. In the same period its net profits increased from Rs. 84mn to Rs. 127mn.

Dawood Hercules

Agrochemicals.   Dawood Hercules established in 1968 is a joint venture of Hercules of USA and the Dawood Group. The company manufactures and markets urea fertilizer. Currently 80 percent of the company's shares are owned by Dawood Industries and Hercules USA, 10 percent by IFC and the rest by the general public. The company enjoys 20 percent of the fertilizer market in Pakistan. The company's production capacity has increased from 345 thousand metric tons in 1984 to 382 thousand metric tons in 1990. In the same period, its net profits increased from Rs. 33mn to Rs. 137mn. The company is currently constructing an additional urea pro-ducing plant with a capacity of 548,000 metric tones/year.

Exxon (Engro) Chemical

Agrochemicals.   Exxon Chemicals, the oldest ammonia-urea manufacturer in Pakistan was incorporated in 1965 as a subsidiary of the U.S. multinational Exxon (75 percent holding). However, in early 1991, Exxon sold its shareholdings in a management buyout and the company changed its name to Engro Chemicals. At present Engro is primarily owned by Engro's Management and staff, IFC, CDC and AFIC with 27 percent, 15 percent, 10 percent and 7.5 percent shares respectively. The company has an annual capacity of 268 thousand metric tons of urea produc-tion, which is expected to increase to 330 thousand metric tons by 1992.

SRI LANKA

Michael McLindon and Richard Samuelson
Emerging Markets Research
Washington, D.C.

Marianne Page and Niall Shiner
Smith New Court
Colombo, Sri Lanka

History of the Stock Market

The history of the Colombo Stock Market dates back to 1896. It started principally as a trading arena for tea, rubber, and other agricultural products. Since World War II, turnover levels in the exchange have been low. In fact, turnover really started to pick up only in 1989. The exchange, as it is currently formed, was set up in 1985 as the Colombo Securities Exchange. This name was changed to the Colombo Stock Exchange in 1990. The major reasons for the increase in interest in the stock exchange are a program of economic reforms introduced by President Premadasa and the termination of various political problems which had been responsible for economic chaos between 1986 and 1989. President Premadasa's decision to abolish a 100 percent tax on foreign investment in Sri Lankan equities and to allow foreign investors to remit their proceeds from sale out of Sri Lanka dramatically affected the stock market.

Sources of information: Crosby Securities Ltd Beijing, Crosby Reasearch Ltd Hong Kong, Shanghai Securities Exchange and Shen Zhen Securities Exchange.

Following these changes, trading volume, which had averaged approximately US $50,000 a day before these reforms, has now risen to approximately US $750,000 a day; on some days it has soared to as high as US $2 million. A principal reason for this increase has been foreign institutional investors buying into the market.

In addition, share prices have increased substantially because of a significant increase in corporate earnings due to their improved economic position, and a re-rating of the market after foreigners were able to invest. The outlook of the market in the next two to three years depends on three elements: (1) creation of a domestic institutional investing base; (2) the government's program of privatizing state-owned industries and listing them on the stock market; and (3) the willingness of overseas investors to acquire shares in Sri Lanka given its market rating and the Tamil Tiger civil war in the northeast.

Economic Restructuring Since 1977

The economic record of Sri Lanka's first 30 years was mediocre. Policies were highly protectionist and money was channelled to social programs which, while suc-cessful, allowed few funds to be directed toward either industrialization or modern-ization of the traditional agricultural sectors. The private sector's role in Sri Lanka's development was decidedly limited, while the government's role continued to grow and command increasing proportions of the GDP.

With the election of the Jayawardene administration in 1977, economic policy became more liberal. Import restrictions and price controls were reduced, and foreign investment was actively encouraged. The state's overwhelming presence in the economy was also somewhat reduced.

As a result of these changes, GDP growth from 1978 to 1983 reached an average of 6 percent, a marked improvement over the 2.9 percent average for 1971 to 1977. While growth in the 1980s continued to be impressive, budgetary difficul-ties, civil disturbances, and looser monetary policy have somewhat dampened eco-nomic performance.

A major objective of the Premadasa administration has been to promote priva-tization and development of the capital markets. More broadly, a greater role has been promised to the private sector in driving the economy.

Overall, the economy has long-term promise. The financial system is relatively sophisticated, the savings rate is above average compared with that of other countries at similar levels of national income, basic legislation for private corporations is in place, and accounting standards are good for a country at this stage of development.

History of the Colombo Stock Exchange

To better appreciate the extraordinary transformation that has occurred at the Colombo Stock Exchange over the last two years, one should consider its condition prior to 1990. Only recently, in 1985, was the perennially moribund stock market reorganized as the Colombo Securities Exchange. (It is now called the Colombo Stock Exchange, or CSE.) In 1987, the Securities Council Act created, for the first time, a regulatory body charged with ensuring orderly markets and protecting buyers of listed equity and debt securities. The Securities Council, (now called the Securities and Exchange Commission or SEC) also advises the government on the development of the capital markets.

Operations on the Colombo Stock Exchange were initially slow and cumbersome, mainly because they were manual and paper-based. This limited the efficiency and timeliness of share transfers. Even before the recent rise in trading in 1990 and 1991, the CSE experienced settlement difficulties.

Other, more daunting, problems were of a structural nature. Many Sri Lankan companies were unwilling to list, thus limiting the supply of shares on the market and reducing liquidity. Interest rate and tax policies actually encouraged companies to favor debt over equity financing. Most of the companies that did list did not trade actively, and there was little float in the market. None of the brokers operated outside of Colombo, and the services they provided to clients were limited. Investment research and portfolio management skills were virtually nonexistent.

The demand for shares was also severely limited. The Sri Lankan public was generally unaware of the potential benefits of investing in shares. Those who were aware frequently lacked confidence in the market and tended to prefer less risky, albeit lower-yielding, bank deposits. Institutional investors, which should have been a significant source of demand, were typically government owned, and served as captives for low-yielding (in real terms) government debt. Foreign portfolio investment was effectively eliminated by a 100 percent tax on purchased shares.

Recent Developments

Since 1990, the changes at the exchange have been dramatic, both technically and in terms of trading activity. In other areas, particularly with respect to regulatory and institutional development, the process has been more evolutionary.

In 1990, the CSE was the second best performer in the world after Venezuela and has continued to appreciate strongly since then. Both the CSE All Share Index and the CSE Sensitive Shares Index have risen over 70 percent as of September 1991. The average PER was 18.1 on September 30, 1991, which indicates that stocks are no longer undervalued as in previous years.

This, combined with the currently uncertain political atmosphere following an attempted impeachment of the president, probably augurs flatter performance for the foreseeable future. Yet this is no cause for alarm, given that it is a typical pattern among fledgling markets. Indeed, a number of observers are relieved to see the CSE enter a period of consolidation, for fear that a protracted speculative rise would lead to a market collapse.

More important, as far as the long-term development of the market is concerned, is that despite the recent consolidation, the domestic appetite for new equity remains strong. This is clear from the oversubscription greeting relatively large recent share issues such as that of the Development Finance Corporation of Ceylon (DFCC).

Several government decisions were vital to the market's "takeoff." The most important of these occurred in June 1990, when the government liberalized foreign portfolio investment by abolishing the 100 percent tax on share purchases by foreigners (subject to the limitation that their aggregate shareholding not exceed 40 percent of the shares issued).

This almost immediately triggered a surge in foreign interest in the market. It captured the attention of both the domestic brokerage firms and the Sri Lankan investing public and led to a rapid rise in previously undervalued shares. Officials at the CSE report that there are now over 50 foreign funds approved to invest in the market.

Market Structure

Market Size

There is one stock exchange in Sri Lanka, the Colombo Stock Exchange. There are currently 178 listed securities. Liquidity, however, is concentrated in approximately 30 of these. In terms of market capitalization, the market has grown from Rs 21 billion (US $500 million) in 1990 to Rs 62 billion (US $1.5 billion currently).

Despite recent increases in turnover, liquidity is still low. Frequently, large blue-chip conglomerates like John Keells Holdings do not trade on a full day. Liquidity tends to be concentrated in several of the recently listed local banks and recently privatized government corporations such as Merchant Bank of Sri Lanka and Ceylon Oxygen.

Stock Market Indices

Two indices are quoted by the Colombo Stock Exchange:

1. The All Shares Price Index, which is a weighted index of all quoted shares.

2. The Sensitive Price Index, which consists of a weighted index of the top 30 stocks by market capitalization. (See Figure 12.1.)

Figure 12-1 Columbo Stock Exchange Indices (1st January 1985–30th September 1991)

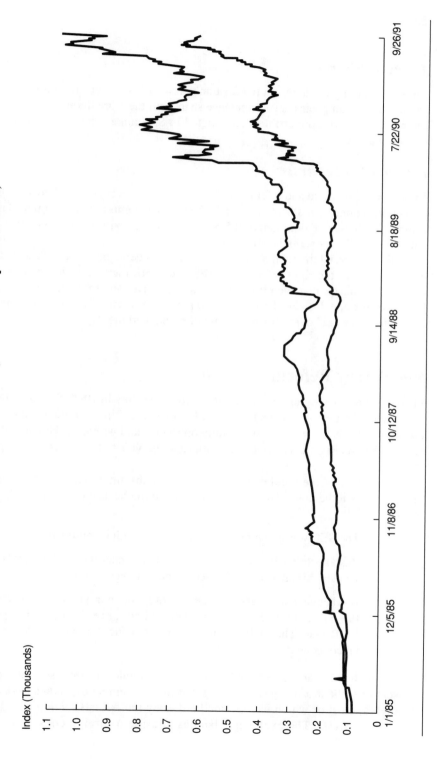

Index (Thousands)

Types of Shares

The vast majority of shares on the Sri Lankan Stock Exchange are ordinary voting shares. A few companies have preference shares but these are illiquid. As yet, there are no warrants or convertible shares listed in Sri Lanka. There is no futures or options market.

Dealing Procedures

Brokers write their bid and offer prices for each stock on a board for all to see. Order execution is done by matching bids and offers. The commission rate for trades is on a sliding scale with a minimum of 0.5 percent. Trading hours are 9:30 a.m. to 11:30 a.m. Short selling of script is not allowed.

For a material transaction, which is defined a s being more than US $100,000, each broker has the right to hold over the trade until they have shown it to their clients. This means that even if there is an agreed buyer and seller, the trade can be held over for one day. Furthermore, if 10 percent or more of a company is introduced, it can be held over for a maximum of seven working days.

Regulatory Reforms in 1990

In addition to opening up the market to foreign investors in 1990, the government implemented other supportive measures. For example, it revised the capital gains tax, abolished the ad-valorem stamp duty on shares, and withdrew the withholding tax on 15 percent on dividends, and withdrew the wealth tax on listed company shares.

Progress on the regulatory front was also substantial during 1991, though more remains to be done. The key amendments to the Securities Act were the following:

- The SEC was given responsibility for regulating unit trusts.

- Responsibility for insider trading was put under the SEC, whereas previously this area was addressed in the Companies Act.

- A takeovers and mergers code was drafted, approved by the MOF and the FTC, and in September 1990 was being reviewed by the Legal Draftsman. This code is expected to help reduce instances of "creeping" takeover abuses.

Both the SEC and CSE have had the benefit of guidance from several foreign advisors over the last few years. During that time, a number of studies have been completed, most of which were funded either by the Asian Development Bank (ADB) or USAID. The exchange also has a resident foreign consultant, Mr.

Bradford Warner, who advises on a daily basis. These resources combined have had a marked impact on keeping the technical, regulatory, and institutional development of both the SEC and the exchange on track.

A study by Robert Bishop, formerly with the New York Stock Exchange, recommended specific rule changes for the stock exchange and proposed a method for implementing a compensation fund. Mr. Bishop also compiled all exchange and stock exchange regulations into one book, entitled *Consolidated Sri Lanka Securities Regulations*.

A study by Estella Tang included recommendations for both licensing brokers and ensuring compliance. The latter includes reporting requirements for brokers, conduct of business rules, and suggestions for inspections of brokers and surveillance of the exchange. Ms. Tang also made preliminary recommendations for reorganizing the SEC.

More recently, the ADB completed a comprehensive study of the existing regulatory functions of the SEC, the Registrar of Companies, and the CSE. The study recommends a more appropriate regulatory framework and proposes a plan for organizing the staff of the SEC.

The ADB is apparently willing to direct significant resources to assist the SEC in its regulatory role, although the current status of this potential project is not known. One issue that should be addressed is finding ways to better fund SEC activity. The SEC is funded by the government and needs a bigger budget allocation if it is to undertake significant enforcement activities. A major concern is that low government salary scales will not permit the SEC to attract high caliber enforcement personnel.

A number of other areas also need to be addressed. One area concerns accounting standards. Currently, auditors' opinions are not required for the financial statements of listed companies. Support is growing in the financial community for making the opinions mandatory. Listed companies should also begin to move toward using internationally accepted accounting standards. The World Bank has noted this need as well.

Consolidated tax returns should be permitted so that losses in one subsidiary can offset gains in other subsidiaries. Likewise, loss carry forwards should be permitted in order to survive an acquisition. This would make it easier for a stronger entity to take over a weaker one and help in handling over-leveraged situations and bailouts. Also, companies should be permitted to pay dividends out of pretax earnings so that they are taxed on one level only, namely, in the hands of the recipient. (Intragroup dividends from subsidiary to parent should not be taxed.)

Another area that should be addressed and was noted in the ADB study concerns the lengthy time required for the subscription and allotment process in Sri Lanka. Presently, the process is both serial and fraught with delay. The four steps required include the following.

1.   Distribution of the prospectus,

2. A subscription period during which investors submit applications for shares and checks are cleared,

3. Input of data from applications so that the subscriptions can be analyzed,

4. Refunding of monies for oversubscriptions and delivery of stock certificates.

Thereafter, the shares are listed on the exchange. In efficient markets, this process takes place more rapidly, provides flexibility in pricing, and does not tie up investor funds.

Finally, more than one broker objects to the current rule regarding the sale of large blocks of shares. In instances where the CSE considers a block to be large, this rule requires seven days before a transaction is closed. This allows blocks to be bid up during the waiting period and exposes brokers to the risk of losing deals that they thought were closed. Brokers want the period shortened. The Takeovers and Mergers Code should improve the current system because it calls for reporting on only 10 percent portions and above.

Share Trading Activity

As shown in Table 12.1, the number of shares traded, daily market trading by value, and market turnover (or the value of shares traded divided by market capitalization) all point to a dramatic increase in share trading. At the same time, despite this improvement, with a 6 percent level of market turnover, the exchange must be classified as a relatively illiquid market, even by emerging market standards.

Table 12.2 shows that the number of companies newly listed on the CSE has increased by seven over the last three years. However, during that time, other companies have decided to delist. Consequently, the total number of listed firms has remained almost constant.

It should be noted that in 1990 the government imposed a "broad basing" requirement for a listed company to retain its advantageous tax rate (40 percent versus 50 percent). There is a two-year window within which to restructure. Presently, some 135 out of 179 currently listed companies would "fail" the broad-basing test and may have an incentive to delist.

Privatization in Sri Lanka

With the help of foreign advisors, most notably USAID, the government has mounted an aggressive privatization program. In fact, privatization through share offer has accounted for most of the increase in listed companies. It has also helped

Table 12.1 Number of Shares Traded, Daily Market Trading by Value, and Market Turnover

Years	Millions of Shares Traded	Daily Market Trading (Thousands)		Market Turnover (Percentage)	Market Capitalization	
		Rs	US$		Rs millions	US$ millions
1991	53.3*	16,599**	414,975**	4.7**	62.5*	1,523.2*
1990	41.7	6,567	146,797	4.2	36.9	922.0
1989	12.2	1,075	29,404	1.3	17.1	529.5
1988	13.2	1,610	50,635	2.4	15.7	493.5
1987	17.3	1,459	49,542	1.8	18.5	626.9
1986	6.1	603	21,513	1.2	11.8	421.6
1985	4.8	332	12,233	0.8	9.9	363.5

* Through September 30, 1991
**Through September 30, 1991 (6.3 percent annualized)

Source: CSE

Table 12.2   New Listings on the Colombo Stock Exchange

	1985	1986	1987	1988	1989	1990	1991*	Total
New Listings	2	6	4	8	2	1	4	27
Delistings	0	5	9	0	2	2	0	18
Net New Listings	2	1	-5	8	0	-1	4	9
Total Number of Companies Listed	172	173	168	176	176	175	179	

*As of September 30, 1991

Source: CSE

Table 12.3   Privatization by Share Offer

Enterprise	Close of Offer	Number of Applications*
United Motors	September 1990	1,605
Merchant Bank of Sri Lanka	November 1990	9,146
Ceylon Oxygen	April 1991	15,049
Pugoda Textiles	June 1991	30,973
DFCC	September 1991	41,033

*Note that because of the problem with multiple applications, the number of applications overstates the number of individual shareholders applying for the share offers.

Source: Merchant Bank of Sri Lanka

to broaden the base of share ownership. In July 1990, it was estimated that there were about 24,000 shareholders in Sri Lanka. In the wake of the five share offerings shown in Table 12.3, this number roughly doubled to 50,000 within the last year. Given that there are some 17 million inhabitants in Sri Lanka, the percentage of the population owning shares remains minuscule. Nevertheless, it is clear that the potential for Sri Lanka's privatization program to supply shares to the market has only been lightly tapped.

The overall growth of the market was captured in Table 12.1 by the impressive growth in market capitalization. The 15 largest companies (in terms of market capitalization) are summarized in Table 12.4.

Supply of Shares

While demand for shares in Sri Lanka has grown steadily, the supply, with the exception of those created through privatization, has lagged. The CSE is attempting to encourage as many new companies as possible to list. The accounting firm Ernst & Young in Colombo is undertaking a survey among listed and unlisted companies to determine what the impediments to listing are.

As in other markets, Sri Lankan companies must consider the benefits and costs in deciding whether to list or not. There is a direct fiscal incentive to list, namely, a corporate tax rate in Sri Lanka of only 40 percent for listed companies, as compared with 50 percent for private companies.

The difficulties in getting companies to list are not different in Sri Lanka from other emerging markets at this stage of their development. Generally, there is widespread reluctance to widen the ownership of family-owned and run companies for fear of loss of control. Certain firms also fear the disclosure requirements of being listed, especially in instances where they have a history of underpaying their tax obligations. In Sri Lanka, as elsewhere, these concerns have limited new company listings and the availability for sale of shares held by family members in existing

Table 12.4 Market Capitalization of the Top 15 Companies

Company Name	Number of Issue Shares	Last Price (Rs)	Market Capitalization (Rs)	Percent of Total Market Capitalization	Shares for Non-Nationals
1. Hayleys Ltd.	7,500,000	560.00	4,200,000,000	7.37	2,042,638
2. Ceylon Tobacco Ltd.	68,266,700	50.00	3,413,335,000	5.99	nil
3. John Keells Holdings Ltd.	10,000,000	315.00	3,150,000,000	5.53	1,806,955
4. Commercial Bank	10,000,000	250.00	2,500,000,000	4.39	nil
5. Aitken Spence Co Ltd.	5,100,000	455.00	2,320,500,000	4.07	767,993
6. Hatton National Bank	6,000,000	360.00	2,160,000,000	3.79	2,331,624
7. Grain Elevators Ltd.	15,000,000	135.00	2,025,000,000	3.55	nil
8. Trans Asia Hotel Ltd.	50,000,000	35.00	1,750,000,000	3.07	14,173,200
9. Haycarb Ltd.	9,000,000	180.00	1,620,000,000	2.84	3,503,672
10. Asian Hotels Corp., Ltd.	29,326,000	52.50	1,539,615,000	2.70	7,181,660
11. DFOC Corp.	1,000,000	1,300.00	1,300,000,000	2.28	61,404
12. Property Development Ltd.	66,000,000	18.50	1,221,000,000	2.14	26,343,808
13. Nestle Lanka Ltd.	50,000,000	22.00	1,100,000,000	1.93	nil
14. Dipped Products Ltd.	6,000,000	165.00	990,000,000	1.74	1,851,000
15. Lanka Orix Leasing Ltd.	4,500,000	200.00	900,000,000	1.58	nil

Source: Colombo Stock Exchange

listed companies. Another significant problem in Sri Lanka (and many other developing countries) is the distortion created by the relative cost of debt and equity finance. After allowing for inflation, the net-of-tax real cost of debt has often been negative. (The easy availability of debt and poor debt recovery legislation are additional factors favoring debt financing by firms.) Equity financing, on the other hand, can be quite expensive. An additional constraint in Sri Lanka is that the corporate finance skills needed to take a company public are as yet poorly developed. Many companies are still poorly informed about both the process and benefits. As other countries have demonstrated, however, some of the reasons for reluctance begin to ease once prices on the stock market begin to increase.

Demand for Shares

Domestic brokers generally contend that foreign investors have been the driving force behind the exchange during the last year. They describe their domestic clients as "speculative." That is, they do not invest on the basis of the fundamental value or earnings potential of a firm. Thus, to date they have seen little need to undertake research on the market. The result is that, outside of firms such as John Keells, Forbes and Walker, and the Merchant Bank of Sri Lanka, local research is still not available. However, given the strong foreign interest in the market, there is a growing incentive for local brokerage firms to develop these capabilities. Gradually that seems to be happening. The main constraint at this point is a severe shortage of trained securities analysts. Sri Lanka needs the equivalent of a Chartered Financial Analyst program.

Investors

Investors in the Sri Lankan stock market can be broken down into four categories: directors and controlling shareholders of public companies, overseas multinationals, overseas institutional investors, and retail.

Directors and controlling shareholders of public companies. As much as 65 percent of the market capitalization of the Colombo Stock Exchange is owned by controlling shareholders of public companies.

Overseas multinationals. For historic reasons, overseas companies such as ICI, BAT, BATA, and Nestles have controlling stakes in large Sri Lankan companies. These stakes prevent other foreigners from investing in these companies.

Overseas institutional investors. It is estimated that since the market opened up in 1990, approximately US$40 million has been invested by institutional fund managers predominantly based in Hong Kong.

Retail.   Retail investors now account for the approximate US $500,000 of daily turnover that occurs, unless there are significant foreign purchases in the market.

Because of the above factors, the free float within the market is exceptionally small by international standards. This will improve due to the following reasons:

- Controlling shareholders becoming willing to sell down their stakes.

- The government's privatization program.

At the time of this book's publication, there is no Sri Lankan country fund, no domestic unit trusts, and no internal fund management industry. However, a more institutionalized domestic fund management industry is expected to develop in the next three years.

Institutional Investors

Still missing from the demand side of shares are domestic institutional investors. The largest pension funds in the country are the Employees Provident Fund (EPF) and the Employees Trust Fund (ETF). These are still captive instruments of government policy. EPF is by far the larger of the two. The labor commissioner estimates that the EPF collects roughly 400 million rupees per month. Currently, both EPF and ETF invest all their funds in either treasury bills or government-owned corporations.

Although technically these funds could diversify, both are subject to directives from the Ministry of Finance which basically determines investment policy. To give an idea of how dependent the government is on the EPF, its director estimates that the EPF funds make up 60 percent of the government deficit. In that light, it seems unlikely that the investment policy will be allowed to change soon. Unfortunately, both funds earn a negative real return on their investments, which is likely to create problems for the budget deficit in the longer run. Moreover, this is unfair to the beneficiaries of these funds. Ironically, the directors of both funds readily acknowledge that the situation should change.

There are some provident funds that predate the ETF and EPF but compared to the EPF they are very small. Although there are about 150 accounts in total, the aggregate inflow of funds per month is less than 100 million rupees. Unlike the EPF, these funds can invest in high yield securities but not entirely freely. Every year, for example, the labor commissioner must approve the accounts to ensure they are sound investments. It is noted that in the past there have been instances where funds have been mismanaged.

The government has begun to address the exchange's obvious need for greater institutional participation by recently passing legislation permitting the formation of unit trusts. The trusts are expected to play an important role in generating demand. Several firms, including the DFCC and Capital Development and Investment

Corporation, Ltd. (CDIC), are applying for licenses to set up unit trusts. The incentives offered under the legislation include a five-year tax holiday, no capital gains tax, and no withholding tax.

Private insurance companies are just beginning to invest in the CSE, but these firms are still small and subject to limitations on the percentage of paid-in capital they are allowed to commit to equity. Meanwhile, the two largest insurers remain state owned and, like the state pension funds, are captives of government policy with respect to their investment decisions.

Clearly, rules governing the investments of private sector insurance companies need to be adjusted to allow more equity investment. The public insurance companies can and should be privatized, and pending that, their investment policies should be changed to permit greater equity in their portfolios.

Taxation, Foreign Investment, and Foreign Exchange Regulation

There is a 15 percent withholding tax on dividends. Investments held by a foreigner of over one year are not subject to capital gains tax. If disposal is made at a profit within one year, a capital gains tax of 20 percent is withheld unless the beneficial owner of the share is registered in the United Kingdom or Canada.

There is a maximum limit of 40 percent on foreign holdings in all Sri Lankan listed equities. It is possible that this limit will be revised or even abolished in the near future. This rule was introduced in June 1990 and some companies such as Ceylon Tobacco, which is 80 percent owned by BAT, are, therefore, not currently available for foreign investment.

Brokers

There are currently 11 licensed stock brokers on the Colombo Stock Exchange. No foreign brokers have established a presence in Sri Lanka yet. Currently, turnover is dominated by two large established brokers, Forbes and Walker and John Keells Ltd., who account for approximately 60 percent of market turnover.

Brokers and others readily admit that modern corporate finance is still not well understood in Sri Lanka, but they have begun to take an interest in developing that capability. Domestic securities firms basically earn all of their revenues from brokerage. In response to the rising trading volume, these firms expanded rapidly during 1991 in terms of staff, business volume, and number of offices. Asia Securities, for example, has gone from one to six employees in six months. It now claims to handle 16 percent to 17 percent of volume on the exchange. Similarly, John Keells is rapidly expanding. It plans to open five offices outside of Colombo by the end of 1992, in cities such as Galle and Kandy. If more brokers follow suit, this would be the ideal way of addressing the problem of distributing shares outside of Colombo and is bound to stimulate more activity in the stock market.

As of July 1991, the CSE began tracking the financial condition of the brokers on a periodic basis. In fact, new rules were put in place in 1991 requiring brokers to file monthly accounts. These reports pass through the CSE into the SEC.

Settlement Procedures

Settlement in Sri Lanka operates on a period account basis. Settlement occurs twice monthly with the buying broker settling on the first Wednesday of the month and the selling broker the first Friday of the month.

The Central Depository System (CDS) went into operation on September 2, 1991. It is being trumpeted as the eighth such automated system to be installed worldwide. Five companies are being rapidly added to it. In September 1992, there were 17 in the system. The share prices of all companies can be readily viewed on any of several terminals. The system also provides investors with monthly account statements. Information generated by the CDS is sent to individual companies on an as-needed basis, for example, when dividends need to be paid. Moreover, because the CDS records the time sequence of trades, as well as the identity of which brokers are transacting those trades, the CSE has unprecedented ability to monitor insider trading.

Remote access to quotations is now available to all eleven brokers. The system is still undergoing finetuning and further developments. Ultimately, it should be capable of linking banks, brokers, and investors. Still farther down the road, the current open outcry system of share trading could be automated.

As a control on price movements on the CSE, bid and quoted prices are not allowed to go up or down more than 10 percent. This is monitored carefully by CSE officials.

Sources of Information

With the exception of a comprehensive guide to the Sri Lankan economy (which includes brief summaries of the individual major companies by Mackinnon and Keells Financial Services Ltd., distributed internationally by Smith New Court), local brokers have as yet to develop research products. Several international brokers have written overviews of the Sri Lankan stock market. The Colombo Stock Exchange handbook gives an annual breakdown of the balance sheets, profits and loss statements, and other information of all listed companies on the Colombo Stock

Exchange. Baring Securities has published a detailed handbook on the market and listed companies.

Company Profiles*

Several of the largest companies in Sri Lanka—such as Ceylon Tobacco, which is controlled by BAT; Ceylon Industrial Chemicals, which is controlled by ICI; or Bata Shoes, which is controlled by Bata—are unavailable for foreign investment because of the 40 percent limit on foreign equity holdings.

Hayleys

Hayleys is Sri Lanka's leading conglomerate. Its major activities are the manufacture and export of activated carbons and rubber products, primarily gloves. It is expanding its manufacturing activities to areas such as brushes, agricultural products, and electrical goods. The company has also targeted the hotel and tourist industry and high value added agriculture, such as seeds and mushrooms, as areas of future growth.

Hayleys owns extensive property holdings in Colombo and around Sri Lanka. Because of over capacity in its core businesses like activated carbon and rubber gloves, earnings growth will lag behind those of its major competing conglomerates.

John Keells Holdings

John Keells Holdings is a diversified conglomerate whose major activities are hotel, tourism, and property investment. It is also engaged in financial services and various agency businesses. It is not exposed to export based manufacturing.

The group owns seven hotels and also controls Walkers Tours, which is the largest travel agency in Sri Lanka. The recent acquisition of Whittal Boustead has added further hotel interests and soft drink interests to the group.

Aitken Spence Ltd.

Aitken Spence is the third of a trio of large Sri Lankan conglomerates. Its major activities are shipping, freight forwarding and container operations, travel agency and hotel management and ownership, services in the form of insurance and property development, manufacturing, printing, agriculture, and textiles.

It is approximately halfway between John Keells assets based businesses and Hayleys export based manufacturing businesses.

---

*Company Profiles are provided by the editors.

Central Finance

Central Finance is Sri Lanka's leading hire purchase company. It has an extensive product network throughout Sri Lanka and unlisted property development and hotel interests. It has two listed subsidiaries, Central Industries, a plastic pipe manufacturer, and Central Securities, a stock broker.

Hatton National Bank

Sri Lanka's banking industry is dominated by two large state owned banks, Bank of Ceylon and Peoples Bank. Hatton National Bank, which is controlled by the Browns Group, is the largest private bank.

Its origins date back to the 19th century. It owns extensive property in Colombo and other provincial cities. Of all the Sri Lankan banks, it has the greatest exposure to nonrupee banking because of its recent takeover of the Emirates Bank.

Seylan Bank

Seylan Bank was established in March 1988. The Bank is part of the Ceylinco Group which is controlled by the Kotelawala family.

The bank has expanded rapidly by winning deposits and market share from the moribund state sector. Deposits have grown from nothing in March 1988 to a level of 2.6 billion rupees at the end of 1990.

The bank is very liquid with only 50 percent of its deposit base being lent out. By the end of 1991, the bank estimates that it will have a branch network of 35 branches.

Korea Ceylon Footwear Ltd.

Korea Ceylon Footwear is Sri Lanka's leading footwear manufacturer and exporter. Its major markets are Italy and France and only 2 percent of its products are sold internally. Korea Ceylon's advantages are its labor cost rate which is approximately US $0.20 an hour, and the fact that the majority of its raw materials, mainly rubber, are locally produced in Sri Lanka.

Because of its status as a Greater Colombo Economic Commission (GCEC) company, it is exempt from all import and export tariffs and pays no profits tax.

Lanka Milk Foods

Lanka Milk Foods has 40 percent of the Sri Lankan dried milk market. Because of its nutritional qualities, dried milk is a major food item in Sri Lanka.

Simplistically, the company imports dried milk, mainly from the Milk Marketing Board in the U.K., packages it and distributes it under its Lakspray brand name. In the past, Lanka Milk Food's profits have been volatile as the price of milk powder in Sri Lanka is controlled by the government. However, the price of its major raw material, dried milk, fluctuates on the open market, a problem aggravated by currency depreciation. Last year price controls were removed from dried milk.

The company's packaging is done on an 8.5 acre production site outside of Colombo which is currently underutilized.

The government, which currently controls 60 percent of the stock, is in the process of selling down its stake.

Cargills

Cargills is the Harrods of Sri Lanka, occupying prestigious Victorian premises in the center of Colombo as well as similarly prestigious branches in other provincial cities.

Cargills has extensive agencies for foreign goods. The company has diversified into a new area in Sri Lanka, supermarkets. There are already four "Food City" retail supermarkets established and the company expects to double this within the next two years.

CHAPTER **13**

CHINA

Xu Yao Ping
Crosby Securities and *The New York Times*
New York

Entrepreneurship fits well into the Chinese character. Traditionally, it used to be a filial duty that sons leave home to make their fortune and be an asset to their family. This custom largely accounts for the family control of wealth in Hong Kong, Southeast Asia, and particularly Taiwan where two-thirds of the households invest through the stock market.

Now a stock market is born in China. The public's enthusiasm has been eruptive about this venue of investment. Just three years ago, at a time of renewed Communist rigidity towards a market-oriented economy, stock exchanges were synonyms of capitalism. However, many economists predict that a large bourse will emerge in China within a decade. The central government, too, has fully recognized the nation's need for a capital market and is trying to foster it in spite of their philosophical ambivalence. On the one hand, it needs to keep a lid on the crater of market forces for fear of disorder. On the other hand, it is pressured to provide a market which can help alleviate the nation's economic plight by channelling stagnant savings into capital-hungry industries.

The Shanghai Securities Exchange was inaugurated in December 1990. A second market, the Shen Zhen Securities Exchange was established in April 1991. New brokerage firms have been created, the number of companies applying for listing has reached hundreds, and demand for new shares has been tremendous. As much as China's leadership prefers caution, it has publicly expressed the aspiration of rebuilding an international financial center within this century.

Sources of information: Crosby Securities Ltd Beijing, Crosby Research Ltd Hong Kong, Shanghai Securities Exchange and Shen Zhen Securities Exchange.

China is also planning to allow foreign investors to participate in the Shanghai and Shen Zhen exchanges. For fear of losing control to foreigners, only 25 percent of a state enterprise's shares can be issued as B shares. In a belated effort to tap overseas portfolio capital, China has realized the need to race against the new bourses springing up around the world. An example of this flexibility is its willingness to accommodate foreign investors with B shares within just a year. In all probability, joint ventures and foreign-capital ventures in China will come to the market much sooner than most domestic companies. China is expected to gradually include foreign institutions among its stock market investors.

The History: One Year Versus 100 Years

Dating back to the days of the Shanghai Sharebrokers Association, founded in 1891, or the years of the Shanghai Stock Exchange between 1904 and 1949, Shanghai was truly the largest securities market in the Far East. With its members from 236 brokerage firms and 194 listed stocks, the exchange is credited for the city's past glory and prosperity. It is also the setting for many tales about crooks, adventurers, and capitalist tycoons which fascinate as well as worry the Chinese today.

Yet, neither of the present exchanges is a resurrection of the old bourse. Rather, both were born out of the test tubes of economic reform with distinct socialist birthmarks.

Beginning in 1981, government bonds were issued and compulsorily allocated to individuals. Since 1984, when reforms challenging egalitarianism expanded from the rural communes to the urban enterprises, 800 companies have issued corporate bonds and stocks. Prior to 1985, however, securities were not transferable. Roughly 69 percent of the corporate securities were issued to employees, 24 percent to outside corporations, and only a symbolic 7 percent to the public; almost none of these securities, which guaranteed a minimum interest return of 16 percent, were common stocks. In a stricter sense, an equity market did not exist.

As economic growth continued, China experienced a geometric leap in the increase of individual savings. Much of this money became stagnant because of a lack of investment vehicles which threatened the nation with inflation. Resistance to the compulsory Treasury bonds was breeding dissatisfaction across the nation. The issued corporate bonds and stocks became a de facto bonus for employees, hence arousing complaints from the public about unfairness. Unable to back off from its funding needs, the state decided in 1985 to make all securities transferable by creating a secondary market and adopting new standards for common stocks. Banks and financial institutions began to set up securities companies through their affiliates and subsidiaries.

Over-the-counter transactions took place in scant volumes and yet provided no solution to the paradox of increased savings and the shortage of capital. In early

1990, total savings was estimated to be over RMB 600 billion (versus a gross value of RMB 380 billion for consumer goods available) and inflation was in double digits. An austerity program was implemented, which forced one-third of the factories in many provinces to suspend production for lack of working capital. At the same time, the successful capitalization of the recently listed companies and the obvious quality improvement of such companies began to convince the leadership that a capital market would be a way to channel "idle money" to finance the other parts of economy.

In December 1990, a nationwide bond trading system (STAQ) was launched by a professional team of returnees from abroad, the Beijing Securities Exchange Executive Council, who had played with the plan of a stock market since early 1988 when such an idea was not yet conceivable to the leadership. In the same month, Shanghai officials received approval from Beijing to start the first exchange and restore the city to its position as an international financial center. Although many cities applied to develop their regional stock exchanges in the next five years, only the Shen Zhen Securities Exchange was set up in 1991. Besides the fact that other cities lacked adequate preparation, China's leaders also seem to be cautious about the unforeseen challenges that stock markets might bring against the socialist regime.

Recent Developments

Major cities such as Guang Zhou (in the South), Xiamen (Southeast), Shen Yang (Northeast), and Wu Han (Central) will probably establish their own securities exchanges within five years. Realistically, with only a handful of listed stocks and rules and regulations still being tested out in the existing markets, these cities will not be able to make a stock exchange operational in the next two years. Companies from other provinces are, however, allowed to seek listings in Shanghai, which is meant to be a national market, rather than Shen Zhen's regional exchange. Moreover, to meet strong public demand, all domestic investors are allowed to purchase shares in these exchanges.

Currently, bonds make up about 90 percent of the securities traded in China. Although bonds may continue to dominate the market for a few years, attention is now increasingly focused on the issuance of common stocks. During the last quarter of 1991, the state set a target for Shanghai and Shen Zhen to issue new shares amounting to RMB 200 million, a 30 percent to 40 percent increase in the combined par value. In addition, a foreign board has been set up to allow direct foreign participation. Fifteen issues of B shares, which are available to foreign investors only, have been listed as an experiment to tap a new source of overseas investment. If successful, approval will be given to dozens of selected companies to issue B shares in 1992. It is also expected that foreign companies and joint ventures currently operating on Chinese soil will be introduced into the Shanghai and Shen Zhen markets to improve liquidity.

Although still embryonic in form, these two exchanges are regarded as pioneers of the Chinese securities business. Directly led by a National Administrative Committee of Securities (including heads of the State Planning Commission, the Ministry of Finance, the State Commission of Economic Reforms, and the central bank's Administration of Exchanges Control), the exchanges are supervised by committees consisting of equivalent entities at the local level. This structure is designed not only to prevent malpractice such as insider trading, but also to control the pace of their expansion in the face of public enthusiasm about equity investment. Guidelines and regulations covering various aspects of an exchange—from membership qualification to listing requirements—have been formulated under the same supervision. This has proved extremely helpful in building the credibility of these exchanges.

Market Performance

Although the bond market and the equity market are both immature, they have taken two entirely different paths. Due to the compulsory nature of the Treasury bonds and the absence of a secondary market, bonds were traded without regulations among individuals in early 1980s. Because all securities companies were forced to buy more than they could sell, Treasury bonds were traded at a 40 percent to 50 percent discount to the issuing price. From the end of 1989, market liquidity increased dramatically, with the 1990 issue volume tripling the aggregated volume of RMB 9 billion over the previous three years. With an average nominal yield of 8 percent to 9 percent, Treasury bonds and government revenue bonds in particular have become popular with the public. In October 1991, RMB 700 million Beijing Municipal Revenue Bonds were sold within one week. Ownership of securities per household in the major cities of China is estimated to be around RMB 450.

In contrast, shareholders were beneficiaries of preferential issues in the beginning. Since their public listing, the prices of all initially issued stocks—six in Shen Zhen and eight in Shanghai—have risen sharply. To highlight, Shen Zhen stocks shot upwards 27 times of their par value, from a total market value of RMB 270 million to RMB 7 billion between March and November 1990. In the ensuing three months, however, market value fell to a low of RMB 5 billion. Analysts attribute the drop to uncertainty about the state's attitude towards approval of the then unofficial exchange which triggered panic selling. It must be noted, that the market had been ridden with frauds in taxation, registration, and price manipulation before its plunge.

The Shanghai market, in comparison with Shen Zhen, has been less speculative, even though similar regulations, such as the now-lifted one percent limit on daily price fluctuation, were applied to both exchanges.

Market Structure

Because stocks are relatively new compared with bonds in the securities market, the most actively traded securities at the OTC sites as well as the exchanges are government bonds and corporate bonds. Table 13.1 is a breakdown of different of securities as of December 1991.

Market Size

Nearly 50 listed stocks have been traded on the exchanges, 17 in Shanghai and 26 in Shen Zhen, with market capitalization totalling around RMB 66 billion. But these numbers are constantly changing. More than 500 companies including joint ventures and those from Hong Kong are queuing up to issue shares. Due to many companies insufficient preparation of documentation, only several dozen of them were authorized by the exchanges in the first half of 1992.

Newly listed stocks on the Shanghai exchange are No. 5 Steel Co., Pudong Volkswagen Taxi Co., Zhongcheng Property Co., Special Steel Pipes Co., and Pudong Taxi Co. Those in Shen Zhen include Southern Glass Co., Wuye Property Co., and Konka TV. Many of these listed companies have issued B shares recently. Table 13.2 indicates the size of the listed stocks in both exchanges.

While the Shen Zhen exchange has surpassed the Shanghai exchange in market capitalization, no one is sure which market will grow faster. According to officials in Beijing, the Shanghai exchange will eventually outgrow Shen Zhen and live up to its status as the national market. Shanghai plans to enlarge the number of listed stocks to at least 30 before the end of 1992. Given its exposure to the nearby Hong Kong stock market, however, Shen Zhen might find it much easier than its Shanghai counterpart to list joint venture companies, new domestic companies with a standardized balance sheet, and even Hong Kong companies.

Table 13.1   Breakdown of Securities

Type	Issuer	Par Value (US$ billion)	Percentage of Total
Total		48.2	100
Treasury Bonds	Ministry of Finance	24.1	50
Government Revenue Bonds	Planning Commission	9.6	20
Financial Bonds	People's Bank of China	9.4	19
Corporate Bonds	Companies	4.8	10
Stocks	Companies	0.5	0.1
Listed Stocks	Companies	0.2	0.03

Source: Crosby Securities

Table 13.2   Listed Stocks in China (As of July 3, 1992)

Company	Date of First Issue	Number of Shares (1,000)	Par Value	Market Capitalization (RMB1,000)	Earnings Per Share (1991)	P/E (1991)
Shanghai Exchange						
Yanzhong Industrial	January 1985	2,000	10	34,900	0.58	300.86
Vacuum Electron	January 1987	2,000	100	434,800	11.82	183.93
Xinye Property	September 1988	2,000	10	72,596	2.0	178.81
No. 2 Textile	March 1992	17,899	10	450,689	n.a.	114.98
Light Industry	February 1992	16,516	10	284,901	n.a.	410.71
Jiafeng Cotton	February 1992	7,063	10	156,096.3	n.a.	181.15
United Textile	February 1992	6,177	10	140,518.3	n.a.	130.00
Special Tubing	December 1991	3,611	10	75,732.3	n.a.	246.76
Feile Acoustics	December 1984	500	10	20,050	1.61	249.07
Aishi Electronics	January 1985	270	10	9,178.7	0.33	1030.20
Shenhua Electric	January 1987	1,000	10	39,050	3.35	116.57
Feile Corp	September 1987	4,866	10	90,021	0.73	253.42
Yuyuan Markets	March 1988	65	100	58,516.3	106.10	
Phoenix Chemical	March 1989	2,467	10	89,781.3	1.73	210.40
Subtotal		1,075,170		20,077,077		
Shenzhen Exchange						
Development Bank	May 1987	134,630	1	5,513,100	1.255	43.80
Jintian Industry	February 1988	53,400	1	1,767,540	0.66	37.61
Wanke Enterprise	November 1988	92,360	1	2,142,750	0.367	70.30
Anda Transportation	December 1989	29,250	1	666,900	0.33	57.00
Champaign Inudstrial	March 1990	90,000	1	859,500	0.358	24.81
Baoan Holdings	March 1988	264,040	1	7,393,120	0.55	21.88
Southern Glass	November 1991	71,590	1	1,557,080	0.26	83.65
Southern Glass B	November 1991	35,590	1	431,400	0.26	51.15
Konka Electronic	November 1991	80,500	1	1,923,950	0.50	48.19
Konka B	January 1992	58,370	1	963,110	0.50	33.27
Wuye Properties	November 1991	227,510	1	5,574,000	0.26	92.80
Wuye B	February 1992	30,000	1	462,000	0.26	58.33
China Bicycles	November 1991	80,500	1	1,875,650	0.46	50.32
China Bicycle B	January 1992	58,370	1	1,865,850	0.46	32.40
Saige Dashen	April 1989	21,230	1	702,710	0.70	55.17
Zhengye	August 1989	25,310	1	1,232,600	0.98	49.69
Huafa Electronic	November 1991	122,900	1	2,261,360	0.18	102.22
Huafa B	February 1992	70,130	1	701,300	0.18	55.56
Petrochemical	November 1991	123,900	1	2,812,530	0.31	73.23
Petrochemical B	February 1992	15,000	1	210,000	0.31	45.16
Jinxing	November 1989	23,760	1	558,360	0.42	66.38
Huayuan Electron	November 1991	26,560	1	594,940	0.32	70.66
Victor Onward	November 1991	74,920	1	1,438,460	0.19	100.21
Victor Onward B	March 1992	52,160	1	521,600	0.19	52.08
Zhongchu	November 1991	74,350	1	1,583,660	0.22	95.09
Zhongchu B	March 1992	12,000	1	135,600	0.22	50.45
Subtotal		2,026,710		45,870,270		

Source: Crosby Securities

Regulatory Framework

The Shanghai Securities Exchange and the Shen Zhen Securities Exchange resemble each other in that both are experiments for a capital market with Chinese characteristics. The Administrative Committee of Securities headed by the governor of the People's Bank supervises the two markets directly. Omnibus laws and regulations come directly from this committee and apply to both Shanghai and Shen Zhen, although the former is preferred as a national exchange and the latter a regional one.

Regulations governing the exchanges include trading guidelines and listing requirements. To illustrate, listing requirements include the following:

- Registration or at least approval by the exchange.

- A paid-up capital of at least RMB 20 million which is certified by a China-registered accountant.

- Profitability in the most recent fiscal year and improvement in profitability over the previous year.

- A net capital representing at least one-third of total assets.

- A minimum of 1,000 shareholders whose combined shareholding should amount to 20 percent of the total issued shares.

- A two-year track record.

No definition is made of the items on the balance sheets or income statement. There is also no requirement that a share have a nominal value.

The qualifications for a member broker include the following:

- Authorization by the People's Bank of China with a license to conduct securities business.

- A capital exceeding RMB 10 million.

- Two years of experience conducting the securities business with a qualified staff.

Differences between the Shanghai Securities Exchange and the Shen Zhen Securities Exchange

Despite the regulatory similarity, the two exchanges have also shown features that will differentiate them in the near future. In Shanghai, 52 outlets of securities trading agencies with some 1,300 staffers have been formed to handle the securities business. Some of these agencies are allowed to trade for their own account while others can only act as agents. Among the 25 members of the Shanghai exchange, 16 are from Shanghai and the rest are from other major cities. The exchange plans to admit some 80 members nationwide later this year. With approval from Beijing, it is also planning to start the trading of futures and options in 1992.

The Shen Zhen exchange, while similar in structure, has only 13 members so far. As a special economic zone, however, this new city is just miles from the affluent and sophisticated capital market, Hong Kong, and it is in Guangdong province which is the most rapidly growing region of China. Already merging, the two territories' close economic and cultural relation will probably help develop the Shen Zhen market at a faster pace. With Shanghai's Pudong area yet having to break ground for new skyscrapers, foreign companies may well choose to establish themselves in the special economic zone rather than in Shanghai.

Turnover and Liquidity

Before more high-quality companies are introduced into the market to enhance choices, liquidity will remain a serious problem for both exchanges. Another fact accounting for illiquidity is the large positions held by state-owned entities. Because of the insignificant size of the equity market relative to the bond market, the scarce records of market turnover in both exchanges usually include bonds as well as equity shares. Since the exchanges were opened, however, turnover has significantly increased and indices for the equity market will soon be made available. In Shanghai, for example, annual turnover of traded securities exceeded RMB 8 billion in 1991 compared with only RMB 2.4 billion for the total of 1990. Annual turnover of the listed shares reached RMB 1.5 billion in 1991 or 25 times of the aggregate turnover of OTC transactions in the previous five years. In May 1992, the city's exchange recorded a monthly equity trading volume of RMB 4.1 billion (see Figure 13.1).

Composition of Market Capitalization by Industry

Given the short list of stocks, a sectoral breakdown can not be very comprehensive. In Shen Zhen, a development bank stock occupies 12 percent of the market, leaving the other 15 stocks divided among property development, transportation, trading, and manufacturing. Likewise in Shanghai, two companies from the electronic and radio industry represent 85 percent of the market. However, sectoral diversity has obviously become a factor in the selection of new listings. Among the six newly listed Shanghai stocks, three new industries are represented—steel, property, and transportation (see Table 13.3).

Figure 13-1 Weekly Trading Volume 1991 for Shanghai and Shen Zhen Exchanges

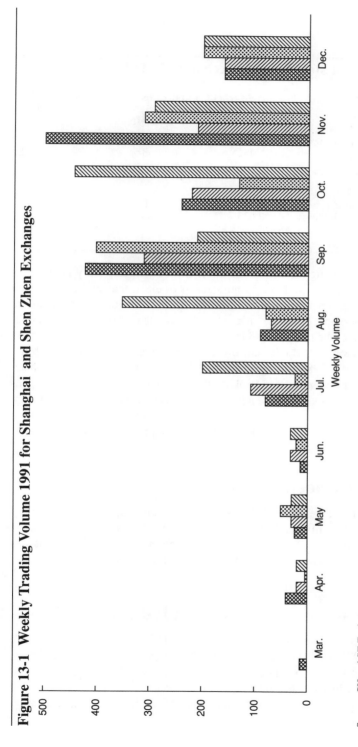

Weekly Volume

Source: SH and SZ Exchanges

Table 13.3   Largest Stocks (As of December 27, 1991)

Stocks Listed on Shanghai Exchange	Market Capitalization		Percent of Local Market
	RMB MN	**USD MN**	
Shanghai Vacuum (A) (Zhenkong)	435	66	21
No. 2 Textile	451	68	22
Stocks Listed on Shen Zhen Exchange			
Development Bank(Fazhan)	2,979	550	40
Baoan Industrial Group Holdings	2,633	485	35

Shanghai's Zhenkong (Shanghai Vacuum) and Feiyin (originally Feile) were the first issues in Shanghai. Both are manufacturers of electronic appliances which have grown into conglomerates over the past decade of economic modernization. The two groups now own a dozen factories after they purchased some ailing companies in the market over the past three to four years.

Fazhan (Development Bank) and Baoan are relatively new issues, with the former issuing shares in 1989 and the latter in 1991. Fazhan started out as a branch of Guangdong's government-owned bank by the same name and became independent when Shen Zhen was given more autonomy as a special economic zone. Baoan, which is also the name of a county with a large overseas Chinese community, was a new conglomerate engaged in retail, manufacturing, and property businesses.

Most Actively Traded Stocks

In Shanghai, Yanzhong (retail) and Zhenkong (electronics) are the most actively traded stocks with monthly trading volume of 12,000 shares and 25,000 shares respectively. In Shen Zhen, Wanke and Jintian are the most actively traded stocks with a monthly average volume of between 2 million and 2.5 million shares.

Composition of Local Stock Market Indices

The Shen Zhen Index, based on six stocks, was made public in April 1991. The price on April 3, 1991 was 100. The index is market weighted. The Shanghai Index, based on eight stocks, was made public in July 1991. Prices of December 19, 1990 represented 100. The index is also market weighted.

Figures 13.2 and 13.3 illustrate the index performance of both the Shanghai and the Shen Zhen exchanges.

Figure 13-2 Shanghai Index (July 1992)

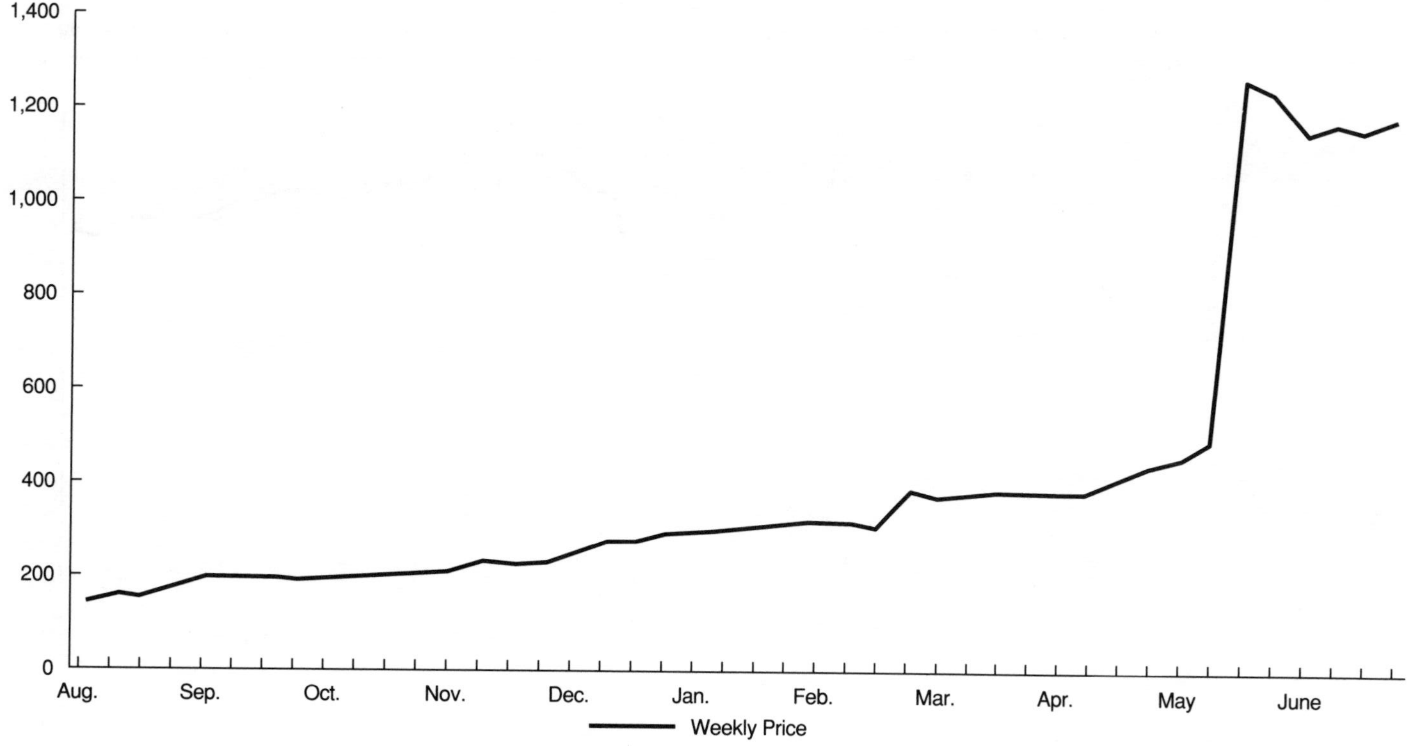

Source: SH Securities Exchange

Figure 13-3 Shen Zhen Index (July 1992)

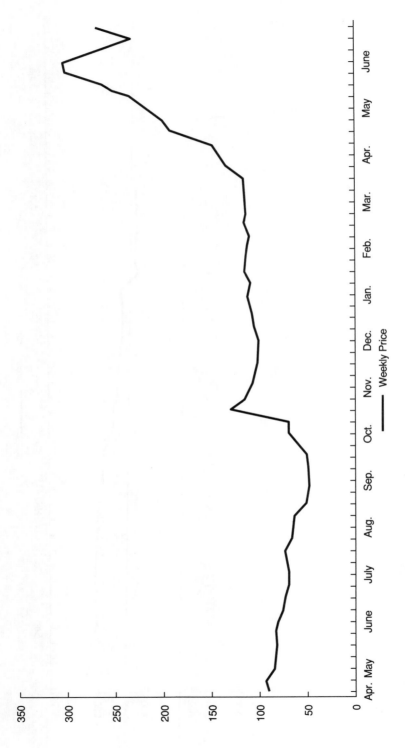

Source: Shen Zhen Securities Exchange

Types of Shares

All listed stocks on the exchanges are common shares. As stated earlier, most shares issued prior to 1989 were preferential shares with more bond features and debenture features. While most companies are not yet prepared to issue warrants, standard preferential shares or shares with other features, neither are the domestic investors ready to accept any new concept than common shares. As the market matures, diversification of share types will naturally increase.

P/E Ratio

Table 13.4 lists stock market performance for 1990 through mid-1992. P/E went from 45.9 in 1990 to 123 in July 1992.

Dealing Procedures and Settlement

Dealings by Brokers

When a customer enters into the market to buy or sell securities, he or she must select a member company's broker to execute the order. He or she must also open an account with the broker. Execution instructions can be both "market" orders and "limit" orders. Validity of the order can be extended from one day to five days. Only spot trading is allowed. The trading amount must be in a set board lot or its multiple. Brokers are obliged to trade according to the principle of time priority and price priority.

Table 13.4   Stock Market Performance in China

	1990	1991	1992 (July)
Market Capitalization (RMB)	5.8 bn	9.0 bn	66 bn
(USD)	1.2 bn	1.5 bn	13 bn
Trading Volume (RMB)	n.a.	3.5 mn	3.2 bn
Number of Listings	13	14	43
Currency Devaluation (%)	9.6	1.0	8.0
P/E	45.9	112	123
Dividend Yield	3.7	3.2	3.5

Source: Crosby Securities

Settlement and Delivery

Trades must first be balanced by brokers on both sides of the transaction according to the net amount payable and receivable. The settlement departments then are responsible for collecting the net amount receivable or payable and preserving it until the trade settles and the shares are registered. Transfer of ownership can only be carried out by the settlement department of a brokerage firm. The regular way of settlement is trade date plus two business days.

Investors and Ownership

Listed companies are a novelty to the Chinese system. In this socialist economy, all enterprises are owned by the state and local governments or collective groups affiliated to a larger entity. These entities are linked and controlled by a vertical line of political leadership and are responsible for almost all employee benefits from housing to health care and grain rations. Although ownership of personal properties and even self-employment have always existed, it was a decade of reform that helped the nonstate sector grow from zero to a proportion of nearly 48 percent of the entire economy, thus ushering in the diversification of ownership.

Along with the emergence of an entrepreneur class, more and more individuals are becoming legal owners of any company whose shares they hold. Shen Zhen residents hold savings in excess of RMB 5 billion and most of them are willing to invest. In Shanghai where 12 million people live, one out of every 13 people has participated in the securities market. Individuals from distant provinces have swarmed into these two cities with stacks of bill notes to purchase stocks. Individual investors and institutions provide 60 percent and 40 percent respectively of the publicly raised capital in China.

The savings pool is an indication of the huge potential of the Chinese capital market. However, it is often ignored that ownership has been governmental. Therefore, institutional investors representing government property and state enterprises will participate in the market as major players.

Domestic Securities Industry

Securities companies were products of haste. They were set up on the order of Beijing as part of an effort to develop a secondary market, much like temples in history were built nationwide at the imperial decree. Trading became active only in 1990 partly due to a lack of expertise. For the same reason, stock market development was slower than some had wished. The Shanghai Securities Exchange officials readily admit that the exchange will not function normally until more professionalism is introduced into the securities companies as well as the administrative bodies.

Between 30 and 40 independent securities companies and some 300 investment and trust companies are dealing in securities in China. All of them started as a subsidiary of banks and government institutions but became independent in 1989 to avoid conflicts of interest.

The leading securities houses in China include the following:

- International Securities Co. (former Shanghai Trust and Investment affiliate)

- Shen Yin Securities Co. (former affiliate of the People's Bank Shanghai)

- Finance Securities Co. (former affiliate of Shanghai Finance Bureau)

- Hai Tong Securities Co. (former affiliate of the Communications Bank)

- Shen Zhen Securities Co. (former affiliate of People's Bank Shen Zhen)

Issues and Regulations Concerning International Investors

China began to consider tapping new sources of overseas investment, such as the portfolio capital, as early as late 1989. Lacking experience, the government has been cautious in the process of launching a stock market and opening it up to the world. It has spent two years pondering over solutions to the problems that might arise in the introduction of foreign shares.

To limit foreign ownership, the central bank only allows a maximum of 25 percent of a company's entire issue to be B shares. Unlike Indonesia or Thailand where individuals are allowed to purchase local shares and have them registered as foreign shares through a local sponsor, B shares are available to and freely traded among foreign investors only. To further differentiate, the listed companies with B shares are entitled to favorable tax treatment and more freedom of import and export as specified by the joint venture laws. As yet, the government is still looking for proper ways of listing foreign companies in the Chinese exchange.

Denominated in the inconvertible RMB, B shares had been technically impossible until 1991 when devaluations of the local currency made the official exchange rate almost at par with the black market price of hard currencies. To protect foreign shareholders against some aspects of currency risk, their stock certificates will allow them to convert RMB proceeds at the official rate at the government-run swap markets now functioning in the major cities of China.

For years, the Chinese leaders were troubled by the unnecessary fear that overseas institutional investors would take over the management of Chinese companies. It may yet take some time before they can pave a smooth road for this new vehicle of foreign investment, but it is clear that China will need more foreign capital to finance its economic growth. Studies by official delegations have been conducted in Thailand, Hong Kong, the United States, and other capital markets.

Academic conferences attended by international securities businesses have become frequent events in an effort to improve the draft laws and regulations regarding shareholders rights, standardized accounting, disclosure procedures, trading of securities, and the qualification of personnel, which are either crude or short of clear definitions.

In theory, Chinese leaders wish to issue as many B shares as possible. After Shanghai Vacuum and Shen Zhen's Jintian Industries and Wanke Enterprises were authorized to issue B shares, envious companies across the nation demonstrated great enthusiasm to follow suit. But among the hundreds of applicants, the central government in Beijing chose to exert caution by allowing only a few companies at a time to come to the market. Towards the end of 1991, joint ventures of United Textiles and Huanqiu Toys in Shanghai, and Southern Glass and Wuye Property in Shen Zhen, were notified to prepare for issues of A shares first, apply for listings, then issue B shares. By the end of 1992, China will have about 25 issues of B shares.

Conclusion

To sum up, experimentation with the stock market sometimes shows justifiable caution. At other times, experimentation is an excuse used by bureaucrats to gloss over inefficiency. The healthy development of stock markets in China may require the removal of some ideological as well as technical obstacles. But changes that have already occurred over the past decade, especially in the last two years, provide ample evidence that this country is indeed emerging as a new economic superpower.

Shanghai Company Profiles*

Yanzhong Industrial Ltd.

In the company's six-year history, Yanzhong has expanded rapidly, acquiring three domestic companies, launching three Sino-foreign joint ventures, and completing a 5,600 square meter office building. The group consists of seven factories that manufacture a variety of consumer products such as furniture, perfume, and cosmetic ornaments. The company also manufactures packaging machinery and office automation devices. With its additional equity capital raised in 1991, excellent profit is expected in 1992.

---

*Company Profiles are provided by the editors.

Shanghai Vacuum

Vacuum is the largest stock listed in the Shanghai exchange. The company also ranks among the 500 largest state-owned enterprises in China. It is involved in the manufacture of the core component for televisions. The TV manufacturing industry has seen a 20-fold growth in the last 10 years. Vacuum itself is planning to move to the higher growth area of color televisions, an area where potential demand may be as great as 140m sets in the 1990s. With its recent issue of B shares making up 25 percent of its total equity, Vacuum will lower raw material costs by 25 percent, total costs by 10 percent, while the international issue will lower the company's tax charge by between 50 percent and 75 percent. Generally speaking, Vacuum is a good play on a high-growth economy.

Feigu Holdings

Also known as Shanghai Feile Holdings, Feigu was the first company to issue common shares in China. The company manufactures audio-systems and their various accessories. It is only recently that Feigu has become a manufacturer of telecommunications products. With the government recently restricting the import of consumer goods, Feigu is experiencing a quick expansion of its domestic market demand. Many of its 19 products are beginning to gain a foothold in the overseas market as well. Currently, the number of employees is 2,678.

Feiyin Audio-System Corp.

Mainly held by its parent Feigu and its own employees, Feiyin provides distribution and maintenance services for Feile products. Since its retail site was opened, its business has expanded to the sales of foreign brand electronic audio systems as well as stage lighting and sound equiment such as Ross of the United States and Yamaha of Japan. Profit growth of 29 percent and 49 percent are recorded for 1989 and 1990 respectively. The number of employees is 53.

Shanghai Aishi Electronic Equipment Co.

With only 35 employees, Aishi was brought to the market as an example of a good quality stock with 15 percent dividend yield in the last few years. The company specializes in the distribution of the products manufactured by its parent company, Shanghai Wireless Equipment Factory. With its aggressive management style, Aishi also represents many manufacturers of electric adaptors, domestic appliances, and new electronic products. It is planning to start a factory in the new development area, Pudong, for the manufacturing of television components.

Shenhua Electric Technology United Co.

Shenhua started out as a collective run by a suburban county of Shanghai. With the reform policies favoring non-state enterprises in terms of autonomy, Shenhua brought up a management team that rendered the business a great success, expanding from a shop into five stores specialized in the sales of electric equipment, metal materials, plastic products, computer components, and even a hotel. With its additional capitalization in December 1990, Shenhua completed one phase of its expansion plan by building and investing in several factories, thus linking up a chain of production, supply, and distribution. In Shanghai, the company now is referred to as the Shenhua Group.

Fenghuang Chemical Holdings

Fenghuang is the Shanghai exchange's only company from another province, Zhejiang. It is also the only medium- to large-sized state enterprise that has issued shares in Zhejiang. Privileged with the excellent management experience of its parent, Lanxi Chemicals Co., Fenghuang is exposed to not only the domestic but the international market as well. Its main cosmetic products, ranging from soap to detergent, include a few which have enjoyed stable sales abroad. It has a few major projects in line for the next two years which will bode well for the company's long-term development.

Yuyuan Garden Market Holdings

With its majority holder being the state, the company has 63 retail stores all located in the prime commercial and tourist area of urban Shanghai. Its business contacts include more than 2,000 manufacturers and suppliers nationwide. During the economic slowdown resulting from the austerity program, Yuyuan proved exceptionally resilient. According to its five-year business plan, the Yuyuan Garden area will be built into the largest shopping center and tourist spot in Shanghai. The number of employees is 1,105.

Shen Zhen

Development Bank (Fazhan)

The Development Bank was originally a group of six credit agencies in Shen Zhen restructured into a holdings company in 1987. Now, its 616 employees operate the head office, 9 branches, and 63 outlets across the whole special economic zone. Besides the main business function as a bank, it is also associated with several finance and property development companies in other areas including Hong Kong. By the end of 1990, deposits totalled RMB 2.3 billion and loans RMB 2 billion. It is also authorized to conduct business in foreign currencies. With its influence and experience in the area, the bank will continue to be a direct beneficiary in the high-growth economy in Shen Zhen as well as in Southern China.

Wanke Industrial Holdings

The original Wanke was established in 1984 as an exhibition center of modern science and technology. It came to the market in 1988 as the first Chinese commercial enterprise that went public by international standards for equity companies. In the ensuing years, Wanke's management style has changed dramatically from its old bureaucratic style. The last six years have seen the company grow from a distributor specialized in technological and office equipment into a conglomerate involved in trade, manufacturing, real estate, and mass media. Its 321 employees come from 27 provinces of China and more than a quarter of them are college graduates. The company is planning to further expand its business into international trading, printing, finance, garment, and other new fields.

Jintian Industrial Holdings

Jintian used to be the affiliate of a state-run textile manufacturer in Shen Zhen. Since its public issue of shares in 1988, Jintian's expansion has been phenomenal. It started as a textile and dying company with some foreign trade on the side. Now the company's business is diversified into property development, tourism, transportation, and textile. The company is known in Shen Zhen for its good credibility as well as aggressive expansion capability. Overseas offices of Jintian include those in Hong Kong, Thailand, and Warsaw.

Anda Transportation Ltd.

Located in the industrial area of Shekou, Anda Transportation has been a beneficiary of the quick improvement of infrastructure in the special economic zone. While diversification features the growth of many other Shen Zhen companies, Anda seems to have expanded rapidly in its own specialized area. It started out as a small fleet of pickup trucks and minibuses, Anda now is a major transportation company with a network of cargo transport, vehicle repair and automobile parts sales. It owns a parking area of 10,000 square meters and a fleet of 108 vehicles. With a long-term contract signed with the Shekou port authority, Anda will enjoy steady income growth in the next few years.

Yuanye Industrial Holdings

Yuanye is a state-enterprise turned shareholding company in joint venture with a Hong Kong textile company. When it came to the market in 1988, its main shareholders included a few other Hong Kong textile companies which helped in the diversification and export of Yuanye's products. Since 1989, the company has made acquisitions not only in the special economic zone but in Australia as well. With 1,216 employees, Yuanye now fully owns 20 enterprises ranging from textile, trading, and real estate to tourism facilities. International activities are clearly the highlight of Yuanye's business project.

Baoan Industrial (Group) Ltd.

Representing the county by the same name, Baoan has been a conglomerate in the very beginning of its eight-year history. It has benefited directly from the area's vicinity to Hong Kong, participating in trading, tourism, and labor supply. The group now fully owns 11 companies and has built office buildings, hotels, and retail stores among its other investments in railways and 12 other companies in the region. The main areas the company is involved in include the manufacture of car radios and record players, video tapes, packaging materials, and telecommunication equipment—of which 70 percent are exported. The company's growth potential is huge, considering its extensive business contacts and capability of funding in the still-backward context of China.

LATIN AMERICA

14

MEXICO

Felicia Morrow
Emerging Markets Management
Washington, D.C., United States

Overview of Market

The Mexican stock market has been one of the best performing markets in the world since 1982, rising by over 8,900% in U.S. dollar terms from its trough in December 1982 through October 1991. Today it is the largest market in Latin America, measured by market capitalization. The dramatic growth represents recovery from Mexico's economic collapse in 1982.

The bull market began in 1983 and continued through 1987, when the price index hit a then-record high in early October of 1987 (Figure 14-1). At the same time, price-to-book value reached 3.1x, and the average price-to-earnings ratio peaked at 35x. Investors gradually returned to the market in 1988, as Mexico's future looked brighter and investors recovered from the shock of the New York crash. The 1987 index high was surpassed in 1990 and continued its rise through October 1991. With market capitalization representing only 28% of GDP, the Mexican market still offers significant growth potential.

As domestic and foreign money has poured into the stock market, the market has become more expensive, rising from a price-to-earnings ratio of 5.0x in 1988 to 12.3x in 1991. With strong earnings growth, however, the overall market in 1991 has risen over 93% in U.S. dollar terms through October, while the market P/E has increased only 3%. Investors increased their investment in the market over the past ten months, and market capitalization has doubled. Attracted by availability of equity financing, many firms have made initial and secondary offerings, both in Mexico and international capital markets.

Market returns could continue to be impressive, although they are likely to be lower than levels achieved this year. The outlook for continued strong earnings

Figure 14-1 Mexican Market Performance (in U.S. \$; December 1985=100)

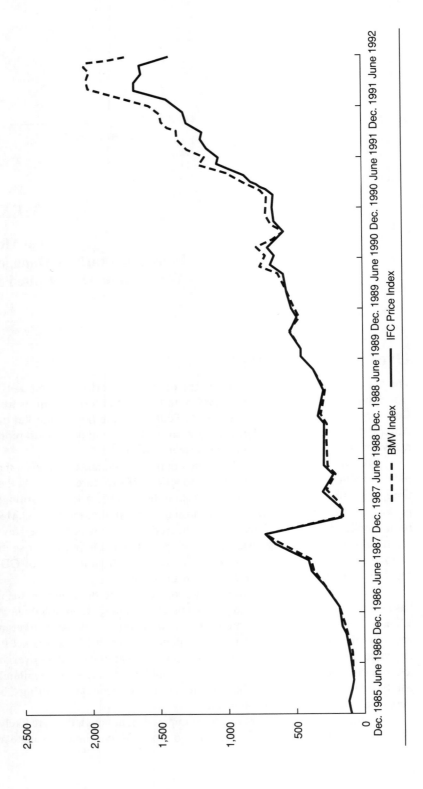

2,500

2,000

1,500

1,000

500

0

Dec. 1985 June 1986 Dec. 1986 June 1987 Dec. 1987 June 1988 Dec. 1988 June 1989 Dec. 1989 June 1990 Dec. 1990 June 1991 Dec. 1991 June 1992

– – – BMV Index   ——— IFC Price Index

Table 14-1   Mexican Stock Market Annual Return (Dollars)

1983	1984	1985	1986	1987	1988	1989	1990	1991*
234%	26.5%	30.1%	106.7%	-7.8%	94.1%	69.4%	36.7%	93%

*Through September 1991
Source: Acciones y Valores

growth is good, because firms have become competitive on an international scale, are positioning themselves to maximize opportunities offered by the Free Trade Agreement of North America, and will benefit from rising per capita income. Also, listing on the New York Stock Exchange has meant a major revaluation for Telefonos de Mexico (Telmex), a trend which could affect other Mexican issues and result in a higher multiple for the overall market.

Recent History

The current performance of the Mexican market was started by the recovery of the index from its lowest level in 30 years in December 1982. Until 1982, Mexico had enjoyed 50 years of growth, with annual average GDP growth of 6%, reaching 8.3% and 7.9% in 1980 and 1981 respectively. In 1982, growth stalled as Mexico was pushed to the brink of bankruptcy following a sharp rise in interest rates and lower oil prices.

Through the 1970s, the country had become dependent on oil revenues and debt to finance heavy expenditures and allowed industry and agriculture to operate in a heavily protected environment. In the early 1980s, when oil price fell, the government was forced to increase borrowing, which shot up to 9.7% of GDP in 1981 from 2.5% in 1980. When interest rates rose, Mexico exhausted its foreign exchange reserves and could no longer meet its debt-service obligations.

Investors bailed out of the market, as the 1982 return plummeted to a negative 87.4%, and Mexico's private sector confronted its own debt crisis. Private sector debt had increased by 266% between 1978 and 1982 with the expectation that growth would continue. As economic growth halted—declining 0–6% and 4.2% in 1982 and 1983 respectively—and the peso was devalued by 65%, consumer demand dried up and the peso cost of debt repayment rose sharply. Many firms were forced into bankruptcy, as inflation soared close to 100%.

Mexico took swift and effective action, led by President de la Madrid, who took office in 1982. The country reduced its public sector deficit, which fell from 17% of GDP in 1982 to less than 9% in 1983, lowered real wages, and continued to devalue the peso. Inflation declined to 80% in 1983. The stock market took notice and soared in August 1983, yielding an annualized dollar return of over 100% and closing the year up 234%.

Although Mexico experienced difficult years in the period between 1982 and 1988, with inflation reaching 160% in 1987 and real per capita GDP 14% in 1987 from the 1980 level, its current strong economic performance is based on reforms introduced under de la Madrid. Forced by the loss of oil revenues, the government recognized the need to foster the competitiveness of its nonoil sector and began the process of opening the economy that has transformed domestic firms—firms that had been highly protected and inefficient through 1982— to become internationally competitive.

De la Madrid made headway, until his government turned to a more expansionary policy in 1985, increasing public spending and easing monetary policy. The September 1985 earthquake, the 1986 plunge in oil prices, and a consequent rise in the fiscal deficit to 16% of GDP forced the government to increase its borrowings. GDP declined 3.7% in 1986.

In early 1987, however, Mexico's economic prospect appeared to be brightening. Mexico joined GATT in August 1986, and the government moved forward on reducing state interference in the marketplace, eliminating remaining subsidies on export financing, reducing subsidies to parastate companies, and strengthening efforts to privatize state enterprises. The balance of payments was improving and Mexico had successfully renegotiated a debt package with private foreign creditors. Exports were rising and the current account was showing a surplus.

Investors—large and small—began to rush into the market, partly due to the modestly improving fundamentals and negative real interest rates, but fueled by speculative hopes for unrealistically high corporate profits. As the annualized return reached over 300% by April 1987, the trading value rose 285% from January to April. By August, the annualized return was 517%, and total trading value for the month peaked at U.S. $2.78 billion, a trading value not seen again until August 1991.

The promise of recovery soon faded. As inflation reached 160% in 1987, the market plunged, triggered by the U.S. market crash in October 1987. The index's annualized dollar return was a negative 8% in 1987.

Under the Salinas' administration, which took office in 1988, economic growth has resumed and inflation declined. GDP grew by 3.9% and 3.6% in 1990 and 1991 respectively, while inflation dropped to 18.8% in 1991 from 29.91% the year before. This resurgence of economic growth and lower inflation, accompanied by critical structural changes geared toward establishing a free market economy, including the promised passage of the Free Trade Agreement of North America by 1993, ignited the market. Market capitalization rose to U.S. $101.7 billion by the end of 1991, up tenfold since December 1987, as daily trading volume of shares rose 76% in the same period.

The specific achievements of the Salinas' administration provide a continuing basis for economic growth. The government's objectives were clearly laid out in the Pact for Stability and Economic Growth (PECE), which established wage, price, and exchange rate controls and continued reforms of de la Madrid including the opening of the economy with acceleration of privatization. Salinas' major achievement has been the establishment of strict control over government finance; in 1991 the public deficit fell to 1.6% of GDP, excluding privatization proceeds. This contrasts sharply with the financial deficit of 16.9% in 1982 when public expenditures had been used to drive economic growth.

Most important in reducing government expenditures has been the successful renegotiation of external debt under the Brady plan in 1989, reducing foreign debt from 75% of GDP four years ago to 35% in 1991 and lowering external debt servicing from 6% to only 2.5% of GDP. Higher oil revenues, reduced expenditures, and tax reforms that enlarged the taxable base have also contributed to this reduction.

Government policies have successfully fostered development of a free market economy and supported improved corporate performance. Tax reforms have reduced taxes to internationally competitive levels, with corporate rates lowered from 42% in 1986 to 35% in 1991 and personal taxes from 60.5% to 35%. Privatization, initiated in 1982, has proceeded smoothly with over 860 firms privatized or in the process to date. Over the same period, Mexico has continued to liberalize trade, with tariffs now averaging 10% to 15%, down from 27% in 1982, and the value of import permits declining from 100% in 1983 to 14% in 1990.

Foreign portfolio investment, which reached $18.59 billion or 18.3% of the market's capitalization at the end of 1991, has played a critical role in the economy and the market's growth, stimulated by policies that have removed restrictions limiting foreigners to minority ownership and improved foreign investors' access to the stock market. Most important was the approval of the Regulation to Promote Mexican Investment and Regulate Foreign Investment in May 1989, which established a new legal framework guaranteeing foreign investors' rights and simplified administrative rules and procedures. One of the more important aspects of the new regulation was that it authorized foreign investors, who had been limited to a maximum ownership of 49% of capital stock—or less in certain industries—to hold a majority share in the capital stock of many sectors.

Recent Stock Market Performance

The stratospheric rise in the Mexican market in 1991 has been led by rocketing returns in telecommunications (i.e., Telmex) and construction (i.e., cement companies). All sectors have performed well in 1991 except for mining, which has yielded negative returns over the past two years (Table 14-2).

Table 14-2   1991 Market Returns (Dollar Terms)

Sector	1991
Mining	2.5%
Industrials	39.7%
Construction	205.2%
Commerce	64.8%
Communications	227.3%
Services	86.7%
Holding	53.2%%
Market	**118%**

Source: Comision Nacional de Valores, 1991 Annual Report, Secretaria de Hacienda y Credito Publico

Led by Cemex, 12 companies on the exchange showed U.S. dollar returns that exceeded 100% (Table 14-3).

Looking at returns over a longer period, 1983 through 1991, the ranking of companies with highest U.S. dollar returns is different (Table 14-4). Vitro ranks at the top and, except for Alfa, Cemex and Cifra, is followed by less well-known and less liquid stocks.

As investors have poured money into the market, it has become more expensive on a price to earnings basis, reaching a prospective P/E of 12.3x in August 1991 and P/BV of 2.1x.[1] Table 14-5 lists market ratios from 1986 to 1991.

These levels represent only a 3% increase over 1990s year-end P/E, however, and remain far below the peaks in 1987. The rise in the market P/E has been moderated by strong earnings growth, up 26% in real terms in the second quarter of 1991. Although sales growth reached only 5.3% in real terms in the second quarter of 1991 versus 15.5% in the same period in 1990, net profits improved as operating

Table 14-3   Dollar Returns Over 100%

Cemex (Cement)	312%
Telmex (Communications)	236%
Tremec (Autoparts)	218%
Ttolmex (Cement)	216%
Sidek (Steel/Tourism)	179%
Spicer (Autoparts)	162%
Banoro (Banking)	145%
Grupo SyR (Retail)	129%
Texel (Textiles)	125%
Serfin (Banking)	111%
Banamex (Banking)	108%
Cifra (Retailing)	102%

Source: Acciones y Valores

[1] Excluding Telmex, which has usually traded at multiples below the market average, the 1991 market P/E rose to 13.2x.

Table 14-4   Dollar Returns from 1983-1991

Company	Dollar Return 1983–1991	Company	Dollar Return 1983–1991
Vitro (Glass)	36,035%	Cydsasa (Chemical)	14,867%
Nacobre (Autoparts)	32,872%	Visa (Holding)	13,775%
Alfa (Steel/Chemicals)	20,038%	Gissa (Autparts/Construction)	12,576%
Cemex (Cement)	17,680%	Cifra (Retailing)	12,514%
		Sidek (Steel/Tourism)	12,514%
		GPTT (Retailing)	12,432%
		Ericson (Telecommunications)	12,190%

Source: Acciones y Valores

margins expanded, with slowing inflation and enhanced operating efficiencies, and interest costs declined sharply. For example, interest costs fell 12.3% in real terms in the second quarter of 1991 versus a 6.3% increase in the second quarter of 1990. Net profits of several firms, including Cemex, have also benefited from extraordinary gains, particularly from the sale of treasury stock.

The P/BV ratio has shown a larger increase than the P/E, rising 49%, reflecting the relatively stronger growth in earnings than net worth, and the willingness of investors to give greater weight to the former.

Even after its run-up, the Mexican market remains cheaper than many developed and other major Latin American markets, except Brazil. At the same time, many Mexican firms continue to promise strong earnings growth, based on rising per capita income, increased trade, capacity expansion, lower inflation, and improved competitiveness. The latter was forced upon them following several years of operating under high inflation and price controls, accompanied by a gradual opening of the borders.

Dividend Yield

Dividend yield has been relatively low in Mexico, hovering around 2% to 3% (Table 14-6). In 1991, the trend has been down from comparable quarters in 1990, probably reflecting increased uses for funds internally.

Table 14-5   Market Ratios

	1986	1987	1988	1989	1990	1991
P/E	10.5	6.2	5.0	10.7	11.9	12.3
P/BV	1.0	0.8	0.7	1.0	1.41	2.1

Table 14-6   Dividend Yield

1987	1988	1989	1990 Q1	1990 Q2	1990 Q3	1990 Q4	1991 Q1	1991 Q2
3.9%	3.0%	2.1%	2.8%	2.5%	3.1%	3.4%	2.5%	2.2%

Source: IFC

Market Size

With the increasing need for and availability of equity financing, the 205 issues listed on the exchange at the end of 1990 gradually increased to 237 by October 1991, with more to be listed.[2] As of fall 1991, 16 new companies were registered for listing and are expected to raise approximately U.S. $1.5 billion.

A growing number of Mexican firms have turned to international capital markets for equity financing for both initial and secondary offerings. Telmex's successful issue in May 1991 raised a record $2.2 billion in the United States, Europe, and Japan. As of the end of 1991, 14 firms issued ADRs (American Depository Receipts) and an estimated 12 more issuances are planned before the end of the year. Through August 1991, total ADRs were valued at U.S. $9.8 billion. The 14 firms are listed on the U.S. stock exchanges.

- Cemex
- Cifra
- Femsa
- Gigante
- San Luis
- Synkro
- Telmex
- Vitro
- Ceramic
- GCarso
- Ponderosa
- Sidek
- Tamsa
- Tolmex

[2] Many companies have more than one issue.

The growing presence of ADRs in the U.S. market are having a profound influence on Mexican equity values. As more companies begin to trade on the U.S. exchanges and become better known to non-Mexican investors, they are being revalued and increasingly influenced by the performance of the U.S. exchanges. Some analysts expect that demand for shares and arbitrage between the markets will result in appreciation in Mexican stocks and that the higher earnings growth of the Mexican companies, estimated at 20% to 25% compared with 5% in the United States, will influence prices favorably as well.

The best example has been Telmex, which historically traded at low multiples. Beginning with the privatization in December, the firm has seen a major revaluation, moving up sharply in anticipation of the large offering in May 1991 when it began trading on the New York Exchange and again surging forward in early July, as international investors revalued the company in light of its expected earnings growth and relatively low valuation level, compared to other telecommunication companies worldwide. In January 1991, before the Gulf war, Telmex was trading at a prospective P/E of approximately 5.5x. Today, the company is trading at a multiple of approximately 12.3x.

Trading Volume

Trading volume has soared over the past 12 months. The total value traded daily averaged U.S. $120 million in 1991, up from U.S. $46 million in 1990 (Table 14-7). Total value traded in 1991 was 2.6 times 1990 levels.

Trading activity remains highly concentrated. Ten stocks dominate trading volume, accounting for 83% of total activity; five stocks account for 63% of the total. Consequently, the market remains thin, and liquidity continues to be a constraint for many investors. However, an increasing number of closely held firms are finding means to increase liquidity as they seek access to new equity sources.

Market Capitalization

At U.S. $101.7 billion, Mexico's market capitalization was the largest in Latin America at the end of 1991, surpassing that of Brazil, then at an estimated U.S. $36 billion, and Spain's at U.S. $61.6 billion. The market capitalization increased by over 1,000% since 1987.

The IFC (International Finance Corp.) quotes the market capitalization without including government shares, partly because they were not very significant in the mid-1980s. As the market values grew and privatization efforts continue, the percentage of government-held shares increased as well. However, this percentage decreased sharply in 1991, following the sale of Telmex and the first banks, especially Banamex (Table 14-8).

Table 14-7   Annual Trading Value (in millions of U.S. Dollars)

1983	1984	1985	1986	1987	1988	1989	1990	1991
873	1,880	1,911	3,409	14,743	5,681	6,075	12,138	31,559

Source: Acciones y Valores

Table 14-8   Market Capitalization

	1985	1986	1987	1988	1989	1990	1991
Total (US billion)	3.9	5.5	9.1	14.9	26.6	41.7	101.7
Government. Held	.09	.12	.7	1.2	4.1	9.0	5.6
Government % Total	2.2%	2.1%	7.9%	7.8%	15.3%	21.6%	5.5%

Source: IFC

The telecommunications sector (i.e., Telmex) represents the largest percentage of market capitalization, accounting for 26% of the total, followed by manufacturing, banking, conglomerates, and retail (Table 14-9).

The ten largest stocks by market capitalization on the exchange rank as shown in Table 14-10.

Stock Market Index

The Mexican Stock Exchange Index—Indice de Precios y Cotizaciones de Bolsa Mexicana de Valores (IBMV)—is composed of a representative number of stocks, selected for liquidity and weighted by market capitalization. The index is revised every two months, primarily on the basis of trading volume. It is heavily dominated by Telmex, which accounted for 32.3% of the index in December 1991, following the issue of the L shares in May 1991. Four other companies, Cemex, Banacci, Cifra, and Gcarso, account for another 34% of the index. To reduce Telmex's weighting, the Telmex A series was eliminated from the index, effective September 1991. As of December 1991, the index was composed of the listed issues weighted by market capitalization (Table 14-11).

Telmex and other large market capitalization stocks, such as Cemex and Cifra, give a distorted view of the market's overall performance, because of their heavy weighting and astronomical returns in 1991. The rate of the market rise for Mexican companies, after eliminating the effects of relative market capitalizations, is reflected in the new index designed by Banamex, called the BANAMEX-30. The index gives equal weight to each share, so that an investor has a means to measure returns, irrespective of the size of the firms in which he is investing. The BANAMEX-30 is composed of 30 stocks of high or medium marketability, similar to those on the

---

Table 14-9   Sector and Divisions Market Capitalization

Sector	Percentage of Market Capitalization
Communications	30
Banks	13
Conglomerates	11
Retail	11
Construction	10
Financial Group	7
Food	7
Chemical	2
Paper	2
Brokerage Houses	2
Autoparts	1
Electronics	1
Mining	1
Tourism	0.3

Source: Accidaes y Velores

Table 14-10   Ten Largest Firms by Market Capitalization (U.S. millions)

Telmex	$19,548.58	26%
Banamex	4343.1	6%
Cifra	3849.63	5%
Cemex	3786.18	5%
Bancomer	2913.38	4%
Vitro	2728.64	4%
Femsa	2562.87	3%
Ttolmex	2117.13	3%
Kimber	1622.7	2%
Alfa	1238.06	2%
Total: Top Ten	44,708.23	59%
Total Market	76,000.00	100%

IBMV, and uses December 28, 1990 as a base date, using 628.79, which was the value of the Mexican Stock Exchange Index (Table 14-12). Since each series is weighted equally (3.33%), the Banamex index registered returns of 80% in 1991.

Marketability

Stocks are ranked according to their liquidity by a marketability index. Classification ranges include four categories: minimal, low, medium, and high marketability and is based on value and volume of shares traded, number of transactions, capitalization value, share lots traded, and trading days.

Table 14-11 Price Index Mexican Stock Exchange, February 1992

Issuer	Series	Percent of Index
Telmex	L	32.26%
Gcarso	A1	7.09%
Cemex	A	5.57%
Banacci	ACP	5.38%
Vitro	NVO	4.90%
Femsa	B	4.79%
Cemex	B	3.81%
Banacci	BCP	3.36%
Bancomer	B	3.35%
Cifra	B	3.25%
Cifra	A	3.10%
Alfa	A	2.98%
Cifra	C	2.02%
Ttolmex	B2	1.99%
Kimber	A	1.69%
Bimbo	2	1.61%
Gigante	BCP	1.45%
Contal		1.16%
Penoles	A2	0.86%
Gmexico	A2	0.83%
Apasco	A	0.80%
Tamsa		0.78%
Desc	A	0.71%
Comerci	B2	0.71%
Serfin	B	0.69%
Desc	B	0.67%
Cydsasa	A	0.64%
Maseca	A2	0.52%
Comrmex	B	0.44%
Codumex	A	0.42%
Ericson	B	0.40%
Gfobsa	BCP	0.27%
Gfobsa	ACP	0.27%
Banorte	ACP	0.27%
CMA		0.23%
Somex	BCP	0.23%
Banoro	B	0.20%
Intenal	B	0.19%
Texel		0.08%
Sanluis	A-2	0.04%
Total		100%

Source: Accionos y Valonres, "El Mercado", p.40.

The number and percentage of companies in each category has changed in 1991, with stock series accounting for high marketability increasing by 45% and medium marketability by 42%. The total number of series in each category, some of which are different series for the same firms, was as shown in Table 14-13 in 1990 and 1991.

Table 14-12 Returns in U.S. Dollars

	1990	Jan.	Feb.	Mar.	Apr.	May	June	July	Aug	Sept.	Oct.	Nov.	Dec.	1991
BMV	37%	-1.0%	6.0%	21.0%	12.0%	21.0%	-4.0%	12.0%	5.0%	0	9	0	3	118
BMX	45.0%	-3.0%	8.0%	16.0%	8.0%	21.0%	2.0%	1.0%	-4.0%	-1	10	4	1	80

Source: Banamex

Types of Shares

Mexican equities can be purchased directly or through mutual funds, ADRs, or the Nafinsa Trust. The types of shares available for purchase fall into one or more of the following categories:

- "A" shares carry full economic and corporate rights and can be owned directly only by Mexican citizens.

- "B" shares also carry full economic and corporate rights and are open to all categories of investors. Most firms have 40% to 49% of their shares in "Bs".

- "N" shares are stripped of voting rights but carry full economic rights and can be held by all investors.

- "Limited" shares carry economic rights and limited corporate rights.

The private banks—which were auctioned in 1991 and 1992—are open to a limited 30% foreign ownership, which could be increased, and have a different structure:

- "A" shares may be acquired only by Mexican citizens, the Federal Government, development banks, the "Bank Fund for the Protection of Savings," and the holding companies of financial conglomerates and will represent 51% of capital.

Table 14-13 Stock Marketability

Marketability	1991 Series		1990 Series	
	Number of Firms	Percentage	Number of Firms	Percentage
High	29	12%	20	9%
Medium	44	22%	31	16%
Low	44	22%	57	29%
Minimal	38	19%	42	21%
Cancellation in Process	52	25%		
None			49	25%
Total	207		199	100%

- "B" shares may be held by those eligible for "A" shares and by Mexican corporations and can represent up to 49% of total capital.

- "C" shares will be available to foreigners as well as Mexicans and can represent up to 30% of total capital.

Price-to-Earnings and Price-to-Book Value Ratios

The rise in sector P/E ratios—compared on the basis of August 1990 and 1991 prices over last twelve month's earnings—has been most dramatic in food, telecommunications, paper, and retailing. The P/E in the food sector rose 52%, in telecommunications 56%, in retailing 24%, and in paper 22%. P/BVs are up more sharply in a broader range, including retailing, up 109%, industrials 91%, steel 85%, and telecommunications 78%, reflecting the slower rise in a company's net worth as compared with earnings growth. Table 14-14 lists P/E ratios and P/BVs for August 1990 and August 1991.

Dealing Procedures

Trading hours were extended in 1992 to 8:30 a.m. - 4:30 p.m. Mondays through Fridays, except for national holidays, to allow for increased trading volume. To control price volatility in a relatively illiquid market, the Bolsa suspends trading for one hour when change in the price of a given share exceeds 5% of the last price.

Trading on the floor takes three forms: verbal agreement, crossdealing, and firm order. The verbal agreement is through outcry of a buy or sell offer and is closed when a trader accepts the deal. Crosses are possible when a broker has two orders for the same issue, series, and price. To close the deal, the trader on the floor must announce the transaction through a microphone without having other traders interject with better offers. A firm order occurs when a trader has a buy or sell offer at a fixed price. He places the order in the trading floor and states the issue, series, and price. His order is listed in chronological order and closes the operation when another brokerage house has a complimentary offer. Firm orders take precedence over verbal and cross deals.

All transactions are settled in cash within 48 hours. Indeval, the central depositary agency, provides physical custody, using the Central Bank's vaults. Registration of securities is prompt, with Indeval recognizing computer registration over physical possession. Brokerage houses, Mexican commercial banks, and the Citibank branch in Mexico are all eligible to hold securities at Indeval. As of December 1989, Indeval began providing custody services directly to foreign financial institutions and global custodians under their name. Fees vary, ranging from .0125% per month to 0.0%.

Table 14-14 P/E Ratios and P/BVs for August 1990 and 1991.

BANAMEX*	Banking	6.21x	12.1x	95%	1.29x	3.03x
CIFRA	Retailing	11.8x	21.9x	86%	2.7x	4.8x
CEMEX	Construction	8.6x	13x	51%	.98x	2.5x
BANCOMER	Banking	7.14x	9.55x	34%	1.03x	2.0x
VITRO	Glass	6.0x	11.7	95%	.7x	1.1x
FEMSA	Food	12.6x	14.1x	12%	.8x	1.3x
TTOLMEX	Construction	8.6xx	11.82x	37%	.8x	1.75x
KIMBER	Consumer	13.3x	12.2x	-8%	1.9x	2.3x
ALFA	Steel/Petro	7.97x	7.53x	-6%	.73x	.76x
MASECA	Food	10.8x	15.4x	43%	2.3x	4.9x
PENOLES	Mining	7.6x	7.7x	1%	.6x	0.4x
TAMSA	Steel	94.5x	17.9x	-81%	.4x	0.5x

Source: EMM/Vector/Barings
*Banamex became Banacci in August 1991, after privatization and a successful offer led by Acciones y Valores, a major brokerage house.

The National Securities Commission announced its decision to deregulate commissions and fees charged by brokerage houses on September 17, 1991. Commissions and fees for stocks, custody, and clearance, as well as for management and supervision of mutual funds, became negotiable on November 1, 1991. As of August 1991, actual fees were below the official rates of 1.7% plus VAT for transactions under $200 million pesos (US $65,600) and 1.0% plus VAT for transactions above that amount. Generally, foreign institutional investors were paying 0.5% to .85% and retail investors 1% to 1.5%, depending on amount traded. Following deregulation, commissions for institutional investors ranged from a low of .3% to .5%.

After the 1987 crash, margin accounts and futures trading were discontinued. As the National Securities Commission intends to increase market liquidity, however, new instruments are being introduced, such as options and warrants. In September 1991, option trading on Telmex began, and warrants had been issued for Telmex, Cifra, and Femsa shares. Short selling has also been recently approved, but the procedures have proven so complicated that it had not yet been instituted as of end 1991.

Major Investors in the Market

Major investors in the market include approximately 140 institutional investors, including insurance companies, banks, pension funds, mutual funds, and foreign investors, and a broad number of small investors.

Structure of Local Securities Industry

The Bolsa Mexicana da Valores, S.A. de C.V. (BMV), was established in 1907 and is today the only stock exchange in Mexico. The Comision Nacional de Valores (CNV) was organized in 1946 to regulate stock market activity. In 1975 a legal framework for securities transactions was established with passage of the Securities Market Law.

The Bolsa operates as a private corporation, owned by 25 brokerage firms, which have exclusive rights to trade on the floor and must be Mexican-owned corporations. The stock exchange and brokers are regulated by CNV through representatives from the Tesoreria de la Federacion (Treasury), Banco de Mexico, Secretaria de Comercio y Fomento Industrial (the Ministry of Commerce and Industrial Promotion), Nafinsa (the largest development bank), and four private sector advisors.

To ensure the financial stability of brokerage houses and safeguard investors' accounts if a brokerage house fails, a contingency fund was set up in 1985. In 1990 a securities rating institute was organized to rate Mexican debt instruments traded on the Bolsa.

Equity trading in the securities industry is concentrated among a small number of firms. The top four account for 54% of the trading volume and the top ten account for 81%. Names and addresses are included at the end of this chapter. Brokers provide a range of services, including trading, investment counseling, research, and, in some cases, custody. They can also provide investment banking and management of investments funds, which include fixed-income funds, mutual funds, or venture capital funds. Banks and investment advisors are also authorized to provide brokerage services, but they are not permitted a seat on the exchange.

The structure of the brokerage industry recently changed, as several brokerage houses purchased majority ownership of newly privatized banks and are forming financial groups. The largest among these is now Banacci, representing the merging of Banamex and Acciones y Valores. Operations in many houses are being consolidated.

The quality of research from Mexican brokerage houses has improved dramatically in the recent past. Mexican analysts are now publishing information based on interviews with company executives and making forecasts for annual earnings. Most houses are still reluctant to make sell recommendations, however, because they do not want to jeopardize their company relationships.

Issues and Regulations Concerning Foreign Investors

Foreign ownership restrictions.   The 1989 revision of the 1973 Law to Promote Mexican Investment and Regulate Foreign Investment has relaxed restriction on foreign ownership. Foreigners can now own up to 100% in 73% of Mexico's 754 economic sectors, including cement, pharmaceuticals, most manufacturing, electronics, computers, and tourism, without the need for prior authorization. Sectors such as agriculture, livestock farming, publishing, maritime services, construction, and legal, accounting, and auditing services require the approval of the National Commission on Foreign Investment. In 36 other sectors previously closed to investment, including insurance companies, foreigners can hold up to 49%. Foreigners are now restricted to 30% ownership of Mexican banks, but could eventually be allowed to hold a larger percentage.

To facilitate foreign investment, the government established the Nacional Financiera (Nafinsa) Foreign Investment Trust in 1989, as a vehicle for foreigners to buy Certificates of Ordinary Participation (CPOs), representing "N" or "A" shares, of which the latter had been previously restricted exclusively to Mexican ownership. CPOs have full economic rights but no voting rights. They are negotiable instruments issued and held by a Mexican trust. The trust has grown considerably to $1.8 billion in October 1991. Ten issues account for 75% of the Trust's value (Table 14-15).

ADRs constitute the single largest source of foreign capital, accounting for over 70% of total foreign capital invested in Mexican companies. Fourteen companies had issued ADRs through the end of 1991. Investment in free subscription shares is the next most important vehicle, followed by investments held by Nafinsa (Table 14-16).

Trust mechanisms, in addition to the Nafinsa Trust, have also been established to permit majority ownership by foreigners in regulated industries and to extend the term of ownership of property in coastal and border areas, now permitted for an initial period of 30 years with possible extensions at 30 year intervals.

Taxes.   There are no capital gains taxes on the sale of equities. Cash dividends are also exempt, if they are paid out of profits that have already been taxed at the corporate level. Otherwise, the tax is 35%. Share dividends are not taxed.

Exchange rate.   Currently, Mexico operates with a pegged exchange rate, devaluating 2% annually against the dollar or 20 centavos per day. The controlled rate applies to import and export of certain goods and certain private and public loan transactions. The free market rate, which has been at or close to the controlled rate for several years, applies to all other transactions, including dividend or distribution payments. Investors interested in dollar appreciation, therefore, must obtain returns greater than the rate of devaluation to maintain the dollar equivalent.

Table 14-15 Nafinsa Trust

Issue	Amount (Pesos)	Percentage of Total	August/January 1991: Percentage Change (Value)
Kimber A	909,630.48	22.07%	41.72%
Vitro NVO	613,809.07	14.89%	655.92%
Cemex A	431,871.31	10.48%	1104.54%
Apasco A	410,648.65	9.96%	106.74%
Cifra ACP	406,462.65	9.86%	102.36%
Maseca A2	165,775.1	4.02%	N/A
Alfa A	148,628.59	3.61%	7.37%
Codumex A	121,983.19	2.96%	-5.05%
Desc B	121,251.55	2.94%	62.12%
Tamsa RES	105,511.39	2.56%	25.19%
Others	686,561.34	16.66%	63.19%
Total	4,122,133.32	100.00%	105.58%

Source: Mexican Stock Exchange/ InverMexico

The government is expected to fix the peso to the U.S. dollar, reducing slippage to 0% in 1992.

The rate of peso devaluation vis-a-vis the U.S. dollar has been below the rate of inflation since 1986. Devaluations that occurred in 1982 and again the in the mid-1980s, however, were so substantial that real appreciation since 1987 has brought the real effective exchange rate, as of July 1991, to only about 11% below the 1978 average, which is used as a benchmark for peso equilibrium (Table 14-17). The strong inflow of dollars into the country and high foreign reserves is expected to provide continuing support for the peso at current levels.

Patents and trademarks. A new Industrial Property Act was expected to take effect before year-end 1991 and will ensure that patents and trademarks are respected. Patents will be protected for 20 years and trademark protection will be extended from five to ten years.

Table 14-16 Foreign Investment in Equities (October 1991)

Vehicle	Value (millions of dollars)	Percentage of Total
ADRs	9,924.0	72.0%
Mexico Fund	485.9	4.0%
Free Subscription Shares	1,974.4	14.0%
Nafinsa Trust	1,357.3	10.0%
Total	13,741.0	100.0%

Source: Mexican Stock Exchange/Invermexico

Table 14-17 Rate of Peso Devaluation Vis-a-Vis the Dollar

Year	Inflation (%)	Peso Devaluation versus Dollar (%)	Simple Differential (%)
1981	28.7	12.8	15.9
1982	98.9	466.2	-367.3
1983	80.8	8.7	72.2
1984	59.2	30.1	29.1
1985	63.7	113.1	-49.4
1986	105.7	104.5	1.2
1987	159.2	143.4	15.8
1988	51.7	3.1	48.6
1989	19.7	16.7	3.0
1990	29.9	10.2	19.7
1991	18.8	5.0	13.8

Source: Banco de Mexico

Company Profiles*

Telefononos de Mexico (TELMEX)

Telecommunications   Telefonos de Mexico, privatized in December 1991, is the sole provider of telephone service in Mexico. Telmex owns all public exchanges, a nationwide network of local lines and the principal public long-distance telephone transmission facilities and has a 70% market share of the cellular market. Under a concession granted by the government through 1996, Telmex has been permitted to increase tariffs subject to an aggregate "price cap" and is required to increase number of lines in service at a minimal average annual rate of 12%. Given a market where only 6.6 access lines per 100 citizens are installed, an existing backlog of approximately one million lines, and new demand sparked by rising business activity, Telmex has substantial opportunity for growth. The company expects to finance at least 70% of investment needs through internally generated funds, following successful negotiations with suppliers to reduce costs in 1991 and 1992.

Banco Nacional de Mexico (Banamex)

Banking   Banamex, founded in 1884, is the largest bank in Mexico, with assets over U.S. $26 billion, market capitalization of U.S. $470 million (38.9% of the total banking sector market cap) at the end of August 1991, and approximately 31,797 employees. Banamex has 10 billion accounts and over 745 branches in Mexico, 13 offices abroad, and correspondent-banking relationships with approximately 1,300 financial institutions.   The bank is active in five areas: finance and banking support, commercial banking, international banking, corporate and investment banking, and retail banking. The bank has shown a high return on equity, reaching 25% in April

* Company profiles are provided by the editors.

1991. In August 1991, Banamex was privatized, with a group of investors led by Roberto Hernandez and Alfredo Harp of Acciones y Valores purchasing 50.72% of the capital stock for $3.2 million equivalent to 2.62x book value.

CIFRA

Retailing   Cifra is the largest retailer in Mexico of apparel, household goods, and food. By end 1991 the firm expects to have total sales area of 553,000 square meters in five major divisions: 36 Almacenes Aurreras, which sell food, clothing, and general merchandise; 33 Superamas, food stores that appeal to the high income shopper; 21 discount Bodegaurreras targeted at low-income consumers; and 27 Suburbias, specializing in clothing for the middle income segment. Cifra also operates a chain of restaurants with 16,954 seats, including 56 Vips—cafeteria-style restaurants—and 18 El Porton and specialty restaurants, catering to higher income consumers. Cifra plans to expand sales area by 16% over the next two years and entered into a joint venture with Walmart in July 1991 with the intention of opening at least three new stores similar to Sam's Club in the United States.

CEMENTOS MEXICANOS (Cemex)

Cement   Cemex, founded in 1906, is the fourth largest cement producer worldwide and the largest in Mexico, with a 64% domestic market share.   The company has a total capacity of 24.3 million tons with 19 cement plants in Mexico and 10 terminals and three mixing plants in Texas, Arizona, and California. It also has extensive distribution networks. Grey cement accounts for 60% of total sales, premixed concrete 12%, and clinker 3%. Cemex is internationally competitive, having achieved low production costs of U.S. $26/ton and serves a market growing at an anticipated 10% annually. In October 1991, Cemex announced plans to increase production capacity by 35%, investing $1 billion over the next four years to add 8.8 million metric tons. The company intends to finance the expansion through both internal and external funding and will benefit from a continued low tax rate, since it is allowed by law to depreciate up to 70% of new investments in the first year.

BANCOMER

Banking   Bancomer, founded in 1932, is the second largest bank in Mexico and is engaged in commercial and investment banking activities domestically and internationally.   Bancomer's total assets represent 25% of total assets in the Mexican banking system. With 740 branches, the bank has the largest retail customer base in Mexico. 39% of 1990 sales were generated by credit operations, and 55% by commissions and premiums. Bancomer was sold in October 1991 to Vamsa, which acquired 53% of the stock at 2.99x book value for U.S. $2.54 billion.

VITRO

Conglomerate   Vitro, established 1909, is a multinational engaged primarily in the production of glass containers in the United States (42% of total sales) and Mexico (23% of sales). Over the past year it has also seen major growth in its flat glass and appliance divisions, each of which generate 10% of company sales. 55% of the company's assets are located in Mexico; 45% in the United States. Vitro is positioning itself for the opening of the borders with an aggressive expansion program and a recent agreement with the U.S. market leader Corning. Vitro is currently investing in increasing appliance production by January 1992, generating an additional $150 million in export sales, doubling flat glass capacity, expanding windshield output, and building a new glass container plant in Mexicali, with two-thirds of output targeted for export. In 1991 alone, Vitro invested U.S. $392 million. The Corning agreement will merge consumer houseware divisions of both firms to allow for sale of complimentary products through established distribution systems.

FEMSA

Beverage   FEMSA is the largest consumer products company in Mexico with sales in beverage and packaging. Beer accounts for 74% of sales, including such brand names as Carta Blanca, Superior, Dos Equis, Tecate, and Bohemia; soft drinks 15% of sales, generated by five Coca Cola bottling and distributorship franchises, two of which together constitute the world's largest Coca Cola bottling operation, as measured by population served; mineral waters division 5% of sales; and packaging 6% of sales. FEMSA's products are market leaders, with beer holding a 52% market share, Coca Cola 54% in Mexico City and 71% in Southeastern Mexico, and mineral waters 58%.

TTOLMEX

CementTtolmex was founded in 1989 through the merger of two cement companies, Empresas Tolteca de Mexico and Cegusa. Cemex, which holds 75% of Ttolmex's outstanding shares, is planning a 64% expansion in Ttolmex's capacity by 1994.   Ttolmex operates nine plants and an established distribution network, with its primary market in the northern part of Mexico and the southern United States. Industrywide, cement demand is expected to grow slightly over 10% in 1991 and 1992 and increase to 12% by 1993.

KIMBERLY CLARK DE MEXICO

Paper Products   Kimberly Clark is a consumer products company manufacturing consumer and business paper products. Kimberly operates four mills located near Mexico City and manufactures for consumer use (59% of total sales): bathroom and kleenex tissues, paper napkins and towels, feminine hygiene products, and disposable diapers; and for industrial consumption (31%): writing, printing, and facsimile papers. Exports to the United States represent 10% of sales. Kimberly Clark Corporation (U.S.) holds 43% interest. Kimberly is making a $500 million investment in a new plant in the northeast of the country.

ALFA

Steel   Alfa, founded in the late 1800s as part of the "Monterrey Group" and established as a holding company in 1974, is a producer of steel (37% of 1990 sales; 12% of exports), petrochemicals (35% of sales; 78% of exports), and food (12% of sales). Total exports account for 19% of sales. Initially, a steel producer, Alfa diversified and overexpanded until 1982 when it encountered insurmountable problems with high leverage, which were not resolved until 1989 when creditors subscribed to 45% of the company's capital.   Alfa sells its products in the steel, petrochemical, paper and packaging, food, carpets, and automotive parts sectors.

DESC

Holding Company   Desc, established 1973, is a holding company with interests in Spicer (50% of total 1991 revenues), an autoparts manufacturer; Novum, a petrochemicals (carbon black and synthetic rubber) and food (poultry) company; Girsa, a petrochemicals firm (adhesives, resins, and latex); and Dine, a real estate developer. Exports represent 19% of sales, with Girsa exporting 50% of its total volume and Novum 30 to 40%. Twenty percent of Spicer's sales are direct exports. Desc's holdings are all major players in their sector: Spicer is one of the leading autoparts suppliers in Mexico and invested U.S. $50 million in 1991 to increase capacity in wheel, heavy duty transmissions, and constant velocity joints; Univasa, the poultry subsidiary, is the fourth largest producer in Mexico with a 50% market share in the southeast and is expanding production; and Novum is the only domestic producer of carbon black.

EL PUERTO DE LIVERPOOL

Retailing   Liverpool, founded in 1847, owns eight "Liverpool" stores located in high income areas: five in Mexico City and one each in Villahermosa, Monterrey, and Tampico. In 1988, the firm acquired 51% interest (accounted for on a consolidated basis, representing 12% of total sales) in eight stores in eastern Mexico under the name Las Fabricas de Francia: three are in Guadalajara and five in surrounding areas. Liverpool stores, with an average of 20,000 square meters of floor space per store, specialize in clothing (20% of sales), furniture (18%), and electronics and appliances (18%) targeted at the high income consumer; Las Fabricas stores are smaller, having an average of 8,000 to 10,000 square meters per store. Liverpool owns prime retail space in Mexico, including three commercial centers, in which it

operates stores and generates rental revenue. Currently, it is developing the largest
commercial mall in Mexico City.

GRUPO CARSO

Holding Company   Grupo Carso is a holding company with majority ownership
in Nacobre, a producer of aluminum and copper products and automotive parts;
Cigatam, a cigarette manufacturer; Frisco, a zinc and copper mining operation; and
Sanborn's, a food/retail chain. It also owns 10.4% of Telmex, in conjunction with
other Mexican investors.

BIMBO

Food   Bimbo has over 40 subsidiaries engaged in the production of food and beverages. The firm is in the final stages of investing U.S. $400 million to expand the
production capacity of existing plants. The firm intends to maintain and expand its
90% market share in white bread and is looking for a joint-venture partner in its
potato chip and snacks product lines.

APASCO

Cement   Apasco is the fourth largest cement producer in Mexico, with a 13%
market share. With the opening of its fourth plant in northern Mexico in June 1991,
Apasco has capacity to produce 4.3 million tons of cement annually and has entered
the market previously dominated by Cemex. The new plant's total output will reach
1.1 million tons/year in 1992, after a start-up of 300,000 tons through the end of
1991. The new plant is state-of-the-art technologically; Holderbank, one of the
world's largest cement companies, owns 49% of Apasco and has provided technological assistance. Apaso is also investing to expand and upgrade two older plants.
The industry outlook is positive, given the eight years of stagnation that followed
the debt crisis in 1982 and the importance of infrastructure in the country's development.

PENOLES

Mining   Penoles is the world's leading producer of primary silver, bismuth and
sodium sulphate, and a market leader in Mexico, with 52% of sales generated by
exports and at least a 50% market share in its products. The firm is engaged in the
exploration and development, smelting, refining, and manufacturing of non-ferrous
metals and chemical products. Refractory sales, now 8% of total revenues, represents the company's fastest growing segment. Penoles' cost structure consists of
35% in raw materials, 30 to 35% in electricity, 10 to 15% in labor, and 10% fuel. In
1991 and 1992, Penoles expects to invest $100 million in zinc and gold mines and

$30 million in expanding its zinc smelter. Penoles has 19 mines with 12,000 employees. The primary shareholder is Mr. Alberto Bailleres.

TAMSA

Steel Tubing   Tubos de Acero de Mexico (TAMSA), founded in 1952, is Mexico's only producer of seamless steel pipe. Since 1987, Tamsa has been fully integrated, producing iron ore, sponge iron and steel scrap for use in final products, which are primarily used in oil drilling and transport. Specialty steel products are sold to the oil, automotive, and mining industries. Tamsa's operations are located near Pemex's major oil fields and Veracruz, a major port. Its total pipe production capacity is 660,000 metric tons and steel production 950,000 metric tons. In 1991, Tamsa began to recover from its near bankruptcy in December 1988, as its financial position improved. Once dependent on Pemex as its primary customer, Tamsa successfully diversified its customer base to maintain sales volumes when Pemex slowed purchases—exports represented 81% of 1990 sales, up from 60% in 1986. As Pemex has renewed purchases, Tamsa is continuing to serve export markets, but exports have declined in importance, representing only 54% of total sales through June 1991.

CYDSA

Petrochemicals   Cydsa is one of Mexico's largest petrochemical and chemical products companies with 1990 revenues of $793 million. The firm holds interests in 20 subsidiaries engaged in the production and marketing of over 200 products and services. Primary products include acrylic fibers (34% of total assets), PVC resins and products (19%), flexible packaging (17%), caustic soda and chlorine (9%), and water treatment chemicals, equipment, and services. The company is a major exporter, with 23% of 1990 sales sold to over 50 different countries. Vitro holds 49.9% interest in the firm.

CONDUMEX

Diversified   Condumex, established in 1952, has three major divisions: 1) the automotive parts division (29% of total sales); 2) electromanufacturing, producing cables for telecommunication (14%) and power transmission (39%), transformers, and electric motors (11%); and 3) plastics, manufacturing PVC and pipes for use in agriculture, construction, and packing (7%). 1991 earnings suffered, as did those of most telecommunications suppliers, from a temporary halt in purchases by Telmex in the first half of the year, due to large inventories, and to price reductions, negotiated by Telmex's new owners. Principal customers include the Federal Electricity Commission, Telmex, Pemex, and the private sector. Pirelli holds a 20% interest.

Key Contacts in Mexico

Mexican Investment Board (MIB)
Paseo de la Reforma 915
Lomas de Chapultepec
11000 Mexico, D.F.
Tel: (5) 202-78-04
Fax: (5) 202-79-25

Banks

Bancomext
Camino a Santa Teresa 1679
Col. Jardines del Pedregal
01900, Mexico, D.F.
Tel: (5) 652-88-21/86-20/84-22
Fax: (5) 652-94-08

Nafin
Insurgentes Sur 1971, piso 10
Torre Sur
Col. Guadalupe Inn
01020 Mexico, D.F.
Tel: (5) 550-16-16.550-69-11
Fax: (5) 550-31-32

Banca Contia
Paseo de la Reforma 450, P.H.
Mexico, D.F.
Tel: (5) 514-69-45/67-85
Fax: (5) 208-58-21.208-58-81

Banca Cremi
Paseo de la Reforma 93, piso 15
Mexico, D.F.
Tel: (5) 535-24-19.546-02-32/07-21
Fax: (5) 592-7854.592-67-28

Banco del Atlantico
Hidalgo 128
Col. del Carmen, Coyoacan
Mexico, D.F.
Tel: (5) 544-53-12/53-96.689-80-66
Fax: (5) 544-50-96

Banco BCH
Paseo de la Reforma 364, piso 2
Mexico, D.F.
Tel: (5) 533-04-34/04-35
Fax: (5) 207-07-08

Banco de Credito y Servicio
Paseo de la Reforma 116, piso 18
Mexico, D.F.
Tel: (5) 535-26-85/46-99/99-49
Fax: (5) 703-06-05

Banco Internacional
Paseo de la Reforma 156, piso 3
Mexico, D.F.
Tel: (5) 535-25-71.566-91-93
Fax: (5) 566-60-44

Banco Mexicano Somex
Paseo de la Reforma 211, piso 17
Mexico, D.F.
Tel: (5) 535-61-79.546-20-90
Fax: (5) 566-84-93

Banco Nacional de Mexico
Isabel la Catolica 44, piso 1
Mexico, D.F.
Tel: (5) 709-09-20.518-90-20
Fax: (5) 5-12-25-94

Bancomer
Av. Universidad No. 1200
Mexico, D.F.
Tel: (5) 534-00-34
Fax: (5) 621-32-00/01/02

Multibanco Comermex
Blvd. M. Avila Camacho 620, piso 3
Mexico, D.F.
Tel: (5) 395-50-32/51-89.520-53-17
Fax: (5) 202-62-26

Multibanco Mercantil de Mexico
Montes Urales 620, piso 3
Lomas de Chapultepec
Mexico, D.F.
Tel: (5) 596-68-05.520-36-43
Fax: (5) 259-15-14

Banca Promex
Av. La Paz 875
Guadalajara, Jalisco
Tel: (36) 13-49-16/11-88/07-79
Fax: (36) 13-09-37
In Mexico City:
Paseo de la Reforma 199, piso 1
Tel: (5) 566-09-10.592-40-07
Fax: (5) 592-18-04

Banca Serfin
Padre Mier Oriente 134, piso 9
Monterrey, Nuevo Leon
Tel: (83) 42-79-44.40-17-60
Fax: (83) 43-48-44
In Mexico City:
Insurgentes Sur 1931, piso 8
Tel: (5) 548-43-13/37-47/48-93
Fax: (5) 550-06-88

Banco del Centro
Venustiano Carranza 235
San Luis Potosi, San Luis Potosi
Tel: (481) 2-26-03.2-46-09.2-73-53
Fax: (481) 4-30-94
In Mexico City:
Paseo de la Reforma 195, piso 1
Tel: (5) 566-72-59.535-93-16
Fax: (5) 703-35-02

Banco Mercantil del Norte
Zaragoza Sur 920
Monterrey, Nuevo Leon
Tel: (83) 40-56-70.45-10-30
Fax: (83) 44-83-22
In Mexico City:
Madero 22, Mezzanine
Tel: (5) 510-18-77.512-74-40
Fax: (5) 512-36-85

Banoro
Obregon y Angel Flores
Culiacan, Sinaloa
Tel: (671) 3-40-62.3-80-30
Fax: (671) 5-38-71
In Mexico City:
Insurgentes Sur 819, piso 5
Tel: (5) 543-21-34/34-67
Fax: (5) 543-04-73

Banco del Oriente
Avenida Dos Oriente 10
Puebla, Puebla.
Tel: (22) 41-67-52/42-51
Fax: (22) 42-04-13
In Mexico City:
Paseo de la Reforma 506, piso 20
Tel: (5) 286-86-25/81-76/85-30
Fax: (5) 286-83-54

Banpais
Hidalgo 250 Poniente
Monterrey, Nuevo Leon.
Tel: (83) 42-83-83.43-60-30
Fax: (83) 44-39-78
In Mexico City:
Insurgentes Sur 1443 piso 1
Tel: (5) 563-44-38/74-59.598-66-49
Fax: (5) 563-33-12

Brokerage Firms

Abaco
Montes Rocallosos 505 Sur
Col. Residencial San Agustin
Garza Garcia
66260, Monterrey, Nuevo Leon
Tel: (83) 35-29-11.35-35-86
Fax: (83) 35-04-51

Acciones Bursatiles
Hamburgo No. 190
Col. Juarez
06600 Mexico, D.F.
Tel: (5) 533-06-25 al 34
Fax: (5) 207-39-44

Acciones y Valores de Mexico
Paseo de la Reforma 398
Col. Juarez
06600 Mexico, D.F.
Tel: (5) 584-29-77
Fax: (5) 208-50-48.584-29-77
ext. 1552

Afin
Periferico Sur 4355
Col. Jardines de la Montana
01900 Mexico, D.F.
Tel: (5) 652-92-44.652-94-88
Fax: (5) 652-63-98

Arka
Emilio Castelar No. 75
Chapultepec Polanco
11560, Mexico, D.F.
Tel: (5) 255-21-55.203-40-34
Fax: (5) 203-52-87

Bursamex
Fuente de Piramides 1 pisos 6 y 7
Lomas de Tecamachalco
53950 Naucalpan, Estado de Mexico
Tel: (5) 294-63-44/61-58
Fax: (5) 294-76-13

C.B.I.
Insurgentes Sur 1886
Col. Florida
01030 Mexico, D.F.
Tel: (5) 575-31-33
Fax: (5) 534-96-67.534-88-46

Cremi
Paseo de la Reforma No. 144, piso 1
Col. Juarez
06600 Mexico, D.F.
Tel: (5) 566-62-11
Fax: (5) 566-62-11 ext. 1525

Estrategia Bursatil
Camino al Desierto de los Leones 19
Col. Guadalupe Inn
01020 Mexico, D.F.
Tel: (5) 550-71-00
Fax: (5) 550-71-00 ext. 4018

Fimsa
Jaime Balmes 11
Edificio B, Piso 6
Col. Polanco
11510 Mexico, D.F.
Tel: (5) 395-73-33/76-05
Fax: (5) 395-70-18

Grupo Bursatil Mexicano
Paseo de la Reforma 382-2
Col. Cuauhtemoc
06600 Mexico, D.F.
Tel: (5) 207-02-02
Fax: (5) 208-49-11

Interacciones
Paseo de la Reforma 383
Planta Baja
Col. Cuauhtemoc
06500 Mexico, D.F.
Tel: (5) 264-18-00.208-00-66
Fax: (5) 525-39-42

Inverlat
Bosques de Ciruelos 120
Col. Bosques de las Lomas
11700 Mexico, D.F.
Tel: (5) 596-62-22/25-55
Fax: (5) 596-25-55 ext. 1051

Invermexico
Blvd. Manuel Avila Camacho 170
Col. Lomas San Isidro
11620, Mexico, D.F.
Tel: (5) 570-70-00.570-50-22
Fax: (5) 202-10-70

Inversora Bursatil
Paseo de las Palmas 736
Planta Baja
Lomas de Chapultepec
11000 Mexico, D.F.
Tel: (5) 259-15-42.202-11-22
Fax: (5) 540-74-92

Mexico
Paseo de la Reforma 231
Col. Cuauhtemoc
06500 Mexico, D.F.
Tel: (5) 584-99-22
Fax: (5) 511-27-46

Mexival
Paseo de la Reforma 359 piso 1
Col. Cuauhtemoc
06560, Mexico D.F.
Tel: (5) 208-20-44
Fax: (5) 208-52-15.202-21-07

MultiValores
Blas Pascal 105
Col. Morales Polanco
11510 Mexico, D.F.
Tel: (5) 557-62-55/28-33
Fax: (5) 557-62-55 ext. 3720

Operadora de Bolsa
Rio Amazonas 62
Col. Cuauhtemoc
06500 Mexico, D.F.
Tel: (5) 592-69-88
Fax: (5) 592-69-88 ext. 2821

Prime
Paseo de la Reforma 243
Torre B, piso 3
Col. Cuauhtemoc
06500 Mexico, D.F.
Tel: (5) 533-59-70
Fax: (5) 207-01-81

Probursa
Blvd. Adolfo Lopez Mateos 2448
Col. Altavista
01060 Mexico, D.F.
Tel: (5) 660-11-11/13-35
Fax: (5) 660-11-11 ext. 2235

Valores Bursatiles de Mexico
Insurgentes Sur 670. Piso 6
Col. de Valle
03100 Mexico, D.F.
Tel: (5) 536-30-60/687-90-11
Fax: (5) 510-89-80

Valores Finamex
Rio Amazonas 91
Col. Cuauhtemoc
06500 Mexico, D.F.
Tel: (5) 525-90-20.208-00-33
Fax: (5) 208-17-56

Value
Liverpool 54
Col. Juarez
06600 Mexico, D.F.
Tel: (5) 207-27-26.525-46-00
Fax: (5) 207-27-26 ext. 3323

Vector
Av. Roble 565 Oriente
Col. Valle del Campestre
Garza Garcia
66265 Monterrey, Nuevo Leon.
Tel: (83) 35-67-77.35-77-77
Fax: (83) 35-78-97

Other Key Contacts

CANADA

Montreal
*Place Bonaventure
Etage F Allee Farnham 18
Montreal PQ
H5A 1B4 Canada 305
Tel. (514) 393-1758
Fax: (514) 393-3340

Toronto
*2 Bloor St. East, Suite 3032
Toronto, Ontario
M4W 1A8 Canada
Tel. (416) 922-5548
Fax: (416) 922-1746

Vancouver
*Granville Street 1365-200
Vancouver, B.C.
V6C 1S4 Canada
Tel. (604) 682-3648
Fax. (604) 682-1355

UNITED STATES:

Atlanta
*229 Peachtree St., N.E.
Cain Tower, Suite 917
Atlanta, Georgia 30303
Tel. (404) 522-5373, 522-5374
Fax: (404) 681-3361

Chicago
*225 N. Michigan Ave., Suite 708
Chicago, Illinois 60601

Tel. (312) 856-0316. 856-0318.
856-0319
Fax: (312) 856-1834

Dallas
*277 Stemmons Freeway Suite 1622
Dallas, Texas 75207
Tel. (214) 688-4096. 688-4097
637-0233
Fax: (214) 905-3831

Los Angeles
*8484 Wilshire Blvd., Suite 740
Beverly Hills, Ca. 90211
Tel. (213) 655-6422. 655-2760
655-6421
Fax: (213) 852-4956

Miami
*New World Tower
100 N. Bicayne Blvd., Suite 1601
Miami, Florida 33132
Tel. (305) 372-9929
Fax: (305) 374-1238

New York
*150 East 58th Street, 17th floor
New York, N.Y. 10155
Tel. (212) 826-2916/2919/2921
Fax: (212) 826-2979
**450 Park Avenue, Suite 401
New York, N.Y. 10022
Tel. (212) 753-8030.753-8031
Fax: (212) 753-8033

San Antonio
*1100 N.W. Loop 410 Suite 409
San Antonio, Texas 78213
Tel. (512) 525-9748
Fax: (512) 525-8355

Seattle
*Plaza 600 Bldg.
600 Stewart Street-Suite 703
Seattle, Washington 98101
Tel. (206) 441-2833. 441-2834
Fax: (206) 441-3553

Washington, D.C.
**1615 L. Street N.W., Suite 310
Washington, D.C. 20036
Tel (202) 338-9010. 338-9017
Fax: (202) 338-9244

LATIN AMERICA

Argentina
*Esmeralda 715, 4th Floor B.
Buenos Aires, Argentina 1007
Tel. (541) 394-3602. 394-3571
Fax: (541) 322-5619

Brazil
*Rua Paes de Araujo No. 29
Conjuntos 94,95 y 96
ITAIM-BIBI
Sao Paulo, S.P. 04531
Tel. (5511) 820-7672/9870
Fax: (5511) 820-7717

Chile
*San Sebastian 2807
4th Floor, 413-414
Comuna de los Condes
Santiago, Chile
Tel. (562) 233-5600/5472
Fax: (562) 231-6302

Venezuela
*Asociacion Bancaria de Venezuela
4th Floor, office 44
Ave. Venezuela, El Rosal
Caracas, Venezuela 61-181
Tel. (582) 951-6078. 951-5147
Fax: (582) 951-2494

EUROPE

Austria
*Passaurplatz 5
Viena, Austria 1010
Tel. (431) 533-7260. 533-7368
533-7450
Fax: (431) 535-3396

Belgium
*164 Chaussee de la Hulpe 1st Floor
Brussels, Belgium 1170
Tel. (322) 660-2906. 660-2907
Fax: (322) 675-2692

France
*4 Rue Notre Dame, Des Victoires
Paris, France 75002
Tel. (331) 4020-0731, 4261-5180
Fax: (331) 4261-5295

Germany
*Internationales Handelszentrum
Buro 643, Friedrichstrasse
1086, Berlin, Germany
P.O. Box 11-04-11
W-1000 Berlin 11, Germany
Tel. (4930) 2643-2594/2595
Fax: (4930) 2643-2572
*Adenauerallee 100, D-5300
Bonn 1, Germany
Tel. (49228) 22-30-212
Fax: (49228) 21-11-13

Italy
*Centro Della Cooperazione
Internazionale
Largo Africa 1
Milan, Italy 20145
Tel. (392) 43-6076. 43-6711
Fax: (392) 43-6450

Spain
*Basilica 19, 6th Floor A
Madrid, Spain 28020
Tel. (341) 597-4767. 597-3033.
597-4033
Fax: (341) 597-0039

Sweden
*Kungsgatan 18, 5th Floor
Stockholm 111-35, Sweden
Tel. (468) 723-0230
Fax: (468) 663-2420

United Kingdon
*60/61 Trafalgar Square, 2nd Floor
London WC2N 5DS, England
Tel. (4471) 839-7860. 839-6586.
839-6587
Fax: (4471) 839-4425
**99 Bishopgate, 17th Floor
London, E.C. 2M-3XD
England
Tel. (4471) 628-0016. 374-0140
Fax: (4471) 374-0716

AUSTRALIA

*135-153 New South Head Rd.
Edgecliff NSW 2027
Sidney, Australia
Tel. (612) 362-4270. 362-4271
Fax: (612) 362-4392

ASIA

Hong Kong
*Street 1809 World Wide House
Col 19 des Voeux Road Central
Hong Kong, Hong Kong
Tel. (852) 521-4365
Fax: (852) 845-3404

Japan
*2-15-2 Nagata-Cho
Chiyoda-Ku
Tokyo, Japan 100
Tel. (813) 3580-0811. 3580-0812
Fax: (813) 3580-9204
**Kokusai Building 918
1-1, Marunouchi 3-Chome
Chiyoda-Ku
Tokyo 100, Japan
Tel. (813) 3284-0331. 3284-0332
Fax: (813) 3284-0330

Korea
*The Korea Chamber of Commerce and
Industry
Bldg. No. 642, 6th Floor 45
4-KA, Namdaemun-Ro, Chung-Ku
Seoul, Korea
Tel. (822) 775-5613
Fax: (822) 775-5615

Singapore
*152 Beach Road
No. 09-01 Gateway East
Singapore 0718
Tel. (65) 296-8281
Fax: (65) 298-5825

Taiwan
*International Trade Building
Suite 2692, 26 Fl.
333 Keelang Rd. Sec. 1
Taipei, Taiwan, R.O.C.
P.O. Box 109-0994
Tel. (886) 2757-6526-28
Fax: (886) 2757-6180

Representative Offices:
*Trade Commission of Mexico
(Bancomext)
**Nacional Financiera (Nafin)

15

BRAZIL

André Pires de Oliveira Dias
Banco Geral do Comercio
San Paulo, Brazil

History of the Market

The Brazilian stock market began in 1877 with the creation of the Bolsa de Valores do Rio de Janeiro. Rio de Janeiro was the capital of the country at that time, as well as the most important city. Trading was concentrated in federal bonds and used to finance the government, which at that time was a monarchy.

In 1890, the Bolsa Livre de Valores was established in Sao Paulo, a city that was beginning to grow in economic importance due mainly to strong coffee production and exports. This stock exchange was closed in 1891 as a consequence of over-expansion which resulted in bankruptcy. In 1895, a new stock exchange, the Bovespa, was founded in Sao Paulo. Its aim was to be a mechanism to transfer resources from the agricultural sector to the rapidly growing industrial sector. This stock exchange operated on the pattern of European stock exchanges, initially trading in metals, government bonds, currency exchange, and commercial loans.

Until 1940, government bonds represented the major portion of transactions, but with the new companies law announced that year, the scenario changed. In 1956, under the government of Juscelino Kubitschek, industrial activity increased greatly, contributing to the expansion of trading volume at the exchange. At the same time, the financial system experienced structural changes with the creation of the National Monetary Council. In 1965, "Law #4728" authorized the stock exchange to regulate itself, under the supervision of the National Monetary Council. In 1967, income tax incentives were introduced to stimulate stock purchases through investment funds called "Fundos 157." Under this regulation, 10 percent (later 12 percent) of income tax owed could be invested in the purchase of shares of a Fundos 157. The portfolios of these funds could be invested one-third in already listed shares and two-thirds in new issues. At this time, 134 brokerage houses had seats at the Bovespa Stock Exchange.

The Bovespa index was first calculated in 1968 and went online in 1972. In that year, for the first time, the volume traded at the Bovespa surpassed that traded at the Rio de Janeiro Stock Exchange. In 1976, the CVM (Securities and Exchange Commission) was created together with a new companies law. In 1978, the Central Bank announced a regulation obliging insurance companies to invest part of their technical reserves in the stock exchange. In 1980, the Bovespa began a massive investment in a data dissemination and services network, through the introduction of the broadcast system, which enabled the exchange to offer online/real-time services to its member firms. In June 1990, the Bovespa introduced the Computer Assisted Trade System (CATS), licensed by the Toronto Stock Exchange.

In terms of investors, by 1983 the general public accounted for 36 percent of the total volume traded at the Bovespa, institutional investors for 13 percent, companies for 23 percent, financial institutions for 20 percent, and others 8 percent. Today, the general public is responsible for only 25 percent, institutional investors 23 percent, companies 12 percent, financial institutions 35 percent, and others 5 percent. After 1986, when the general public entered the market heavily and a sharp decline occurred, fundamental analysis (rather than market rumor and speculation) became gradually more important for evaluation of the market and of the economy as a whole. This became even more important with the entry of small numbers of foreign investors in the market in 1988 and more active foreign involvement since 1991.

Trading volume has become more concentrated on a small group of stocks in the last few years. In 1979, the five most actively traded stocks represented 26 percent of the total volume, while they represented 58 percent in 1990. Also, the issuing of new shares has been rare in Brazil in recent years. In 1980, there were 426 listed companies, while in 1985 there were 541 and as of 1991 there were 574 (see Table 15.1).

Past and Present Performance

After the economic boom of the 1970s, when Brazil experienced a rapid increase in economic activity, the 1980s began with a deep recession. The stock market also followed this trend, with the Bovespa index performing poorly in 1980, 1981, and 1982. In 1983, when the country began to leave the recession behind, the stock market followed. The Bovespa index increased 120 percent in U.S. dollar terms that year, 68 percent in 1984 and 52 percent in 1985. Volume traded also jumped from U.S. $1.7 billion in 1980 to U.S. $10.9 billion in 1985 (see Table 15.1 and Figure 15.1).

At the start of 1986, with the inflation rate increasing, the government announced the Cruzado Plan. With prices frozen, a sharp decrease in interest rates, and growth in real wages, the stock market experienced the strongest boom of its

Table 15.1 Market Statistics

	Market Capitalization (US$ millions)	Trading Volume (US$ millions)	Number of Listings	Return US$ (percent)	Currency Depreciation (percent)	P/E	P/BV	Dividend Yield (percent)
1991	44,110	9,221	574	291.61	-516.93	9.19	0.80	5.29
1990	15,973	3,749	581	-72.73	-1,397.27	5.47	0.27	7.65
1989	44,141	9,912	592	24.06	-1,401.29	8.92	0.70	3.70
1988	31,067	10,899	589	151.14	-955.01	6.95	0.52	6.15
1987	16,942	5,948	590	-72.00	-381.60	4.43	0.30	11.79
1986	40,988	17,910	592	-0.45	-41.94	7.72	0.83	4.81
1985	42,765	10,855	541	52.23	-229.46	7.59	0.93	6.55
1984	26,994	6,299	522	67.51	-223.58	5.30	0.59	4.70
1983	15,100	3,255	506	120.44	-289.44	5.60	0.51	5.30
1982	10,261	2,211	493	-17.10	-97.71	2.40	0.27	12.40
1981	12,577	1,310	488	9.58	-95.11	3.40	0.33	10.60
1980	9,221	1,745	426	-6.38	-54.01	3.20	0.39	12.80

Notes:
1. 1991 = Until December.
2. In 1986 the currency was divided by 1,000.
3. In 1989 the currency was divided by 1,000.
4. Market capitalization in US$ is based on the year-end US$ rate.
5. Trading volume (cash market) in US$ is based on the average US$ rate.
6. Turnover = market capitalization/trading volume
7. Number of listings = number of companies traded at Bovespa
8. P/E and P/BV – from 1980 to 1984 source = Unibanco
9. P/E and P/BV – from 1985 to 1991 source = Geral Do Comercio
10. Dividend yield – from 1980 to 1981 source = IFC
11. Dividend yield – from 1982 to 1984 source = Euromoney Magazine/FIBV
12. Dividend yield – from 1985 to 1991 source = Geral Do Comercio

Source: Bovespa, IFC Emerging Markets Data Base (unless otherwise noted)

Figure 15-1 Bovespa Index (Quarterly Data in US$ Terms)

December 1979 = 100%

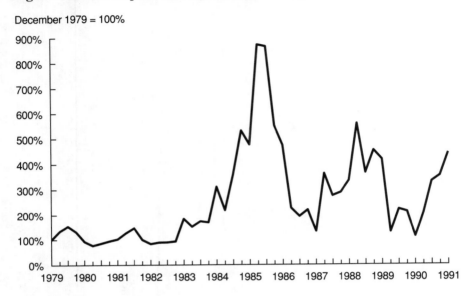

history. The general public became the most important investors in the market again, and in May 1986 the average P/BV of the Bovespa reached 2.8x, while the average P/E reached more than 10x. As the plan began to fail in the second half of 1986, however, the stock market experienced a sharp drop and closed the year with a 0.5 percent negative performance in U.S. dollar terms. This bear market lasted until the end of 1987, during which the Bovespa index decreased 72 percent in U.S. dollar terms.

In 1988 the market began to recover again. The Bovespa index was very undervalued and for the most part stocks were very cheap. At the same time, foreign investors began to enter the market through foreign investment funds. In that year the market increased 151 percent in U.S. dollar terms. The year 1989 began with a major question concerning the first election, after 25 years of military dictatorship. It also began with another economic plan, the "Summer Plan," which once again attempted to reduce inflation through the freezing of prices and wages. Even with this troubled scenario, the stock market increased 24 percent in U.S. dollar terms.

The year 1990 began with great expectations concerning the new government. With President Collor de Mello taking office on March 15, the new government announced a radical economic plan. Besides the freezing of prices and wages, the government also froze 80 percent of all citizens' and companies' money. The money was to stay blocked at the Central Bank for 18 months and then to be returned. With this money frozen, the stock market decreased sharply, and the

Bovespa index decreased 73 percent in U.S. dollar terms. Liquidity also declined, with volume traded falling from U.S. $9.9 billion in 1989 to U.S. $3.7 billion in 1990.

At the beginning of 1991, the stock market was again very undervalued. The average P/E of the market was 5.5x in December 1990, one of the lowest levels ever. Despite an unraveling of the economic policies and a lack of economic growth, the market began to recover. In May 1991, the CVM (Brazilian SEC) gave authorization to foreign institutional investors to invest directly in the Brazilian stock market, which contributed further to the Bovespa's good performance. The stock market increased 191 percent in U.S. dollar terms by June 1991, and 291 percent by year end, and market capitalization jumped from U.S. $15 billion in December 1990 to U.S. $44 billion in December 1991. However, the Bovespa index, which is heavily weighted toward a small group of actively traded shares, exaggerated market performance. The IFC index for Brazil (which market weights 60 of the most actively traded shares) was up 148 percent.

Market Structure

Market Size

The Bovespa had 574 listed companies as of December 1991. In recent years, the number of listed companies has not increased much and new issues are not frequent due to the volatility of the market, the high inflation rate, and the low price/book value ratios.

The Stock Exchanges

Brazil has nine stock exchanges. However, only Sao Paulo (Bovespa) and Rio de Janeiro (BVRJ) have satisfactory liquidity, with Sao Paulo responsible for 65 percent of the total volume traded in the country and Rio de Janeiro responsible for 30 percent. The other regional stock exchanges are together responsible for only five percent of the volume. The six other exchanges are: BVES (Santa Catarina and Rio Grande do Sul), BVPR (Parana), BVPP (Pernambuco and Paraiba), BOVMESB (Minas Gerais, Espirito Santo, and Brazilia), BVBSA (Bahia, Sergipe, and Alagoas), Bolsa Regional do Ceara (Ceara, Rio Grande do Norte Piaui, Maranhao, Para, and Amazonas) and BVS (Santos).

Main Industries and Stocks

In terms of market capitalization, telecommunications (18 percent), followed by electric utilities (16 percent), and banking (11 percent) have the highest representation in the Bovespa. Also important are food and beverage (9.6 percent), mining (7.6 percent), oil (7.5 percent), holding companies (7.2 percent), and pulp and paper (5.5 percent). (See Table 15.2.)

Table 15-2   Market Capitalization by Industry

Industry	Market Capitalization (US$ 1,000)	Participation (percent)
Telecommunications	7,860,467	17.82
Energy/Electronic Materials	7,062,070	16.01
Banks	4,953,594	11.23
Mining	3,347,977	7.59
Oil	3,308,278	7.50
Holding	3,175,946	7.20
Beverages	3,158,302	7.16
Pulp and Paper	2,430,481	5.51
Building Materials	1,614,439	3.66
Steel	1,499,752	3.40
Chemical/Petrochemical	1,226,268	2.78
Food	1,067,471	2.42
Auto Parts	816,042	1.85
Electric-Electronic	688,122	1.56
Civil Construction	396,993	0.90
Textiles	357,294	0.81
Matallurgic	308,773	0.70
Commerce	211,730	0.48
Mechanic	198,497	0.45
Airlines	167,619	0.38
Others	127,920	0.29
Computers	70,577	0.16
Fertilizers	39,699	0.09
Agricultural Equipment	13,233	0.03
Toys	8,822	0.02

Source: Bovespa

The largest Brazilian stock by market capitalization at year end 1991 was Telebras with $5.0 billion (11.4 percent), followed by Electrobras with $4.1 billion (9.2 percent), Petrobras with $3.3 billion (7.5 percent), and Vale do Rio Doce with $2.6 billion (5.9 percent). It is worth noting that the five largest companies listed on the Brazilian exchange are all partially owned by the government (see Table 15.3).

Most Actively Traded Stocks

In 1991, Petrobras lost its traditional status as the most actively traded stock. That year, Telebras led the most actively traded stocks, followed by Petrobras and Vale do Rio Doce (Table 15.4).

Bovespa Index Composition

The Bovespa index is composed of 57 stocks, chosen and weighted according to the volume traded in the previous six months. Thus, the weight of each stock changes in computing the index. The composition of the index is changed each quarter. In the Bovespa index, calculated in January 1992, (see Table 15.5), the stock with the

Table 15.3   Ten Largest Stocks (December 1991)

Company	Market Capitalization (US$ 1,000)	Participation (percent)
1. TELEBRAS	5,032,742	11.41
2. ELETROBRAS	4,086,300	9.26
3. PETROBRAS	3,301,485	7.48
4. VALE DO RIO DOCE	2,597,959	5.89
5. TELESP	1,908,793	4.33
6. SOUZA CRUZ	1,475,227	3.34
7. BRAHMA	1,456,847	3.30
8. BRADESCO	1,253,518	2.84
9. SUZANO	956,190	2.17
10. BANCO DO BRASIL	951,704	2.16
Subtotal (10 Companies)	23,020,796	52.19
Total (570 Companies)	44,110,367	100.00

Source: Bovespa

Table 15-4   Ten Most Actively Traded Stocks (1991)*

Company	Trading Volume (US$ 1,000)	Participation (percent)
1. TELEBRAS PN	2,946,159	31.98
2. PETROBRAS PP	1,141,917	12.40
3. VALE DO RIO DOCE PP	593,521	6.44
4. PARANAPANEMA PN	379,362	4.12
5. VALE DO RIO DOCE PN	297,515	3.23
6. ELETROBRAS PNB	148,357	1.61
7. TELESP PN	104,516	1.13
8. BANCO DO BRASIL PN	73,580	0.80
9. BRAHMA PN	65,386	0.71
10. BRADESCO PN	63,325	0.69
Subtotal (10 Companies)	5,813,638	63.11
Total (570 Companies)	9,211,235	100.00

*Cash Market
Bovespa Index Composition

highest participation was Telebras with 31 percent, followed by Vale do Rio Doce with 16 percent and Petrobras with 14 percent.

Types of Stocks

In Brazil there are two types of stocks: common stocks, which have voting rights, and preferred stocks, without voting rights but with priority concerning dividend payments and reimbursements in case of company extinction or bankruptcy. Due to

Table 15-5 Composition of the Bovespa Index

Company	Participation (percent)
1. ACOS VILLARES PN	0.93
2. AGROCERES PP	0.09
3. ALPARGATAS PN	0.34
4. AGUATEC PP	0.06
5. ARACRUZ PPB	0.30
6. BANESPA PN	1.63
7. BELGO MINEIRA ON	0.29
8. BELGO MINEIRA PN	0.55
9. BOMBRIL PN	0.38
10. BRADESCO PN	1.22
11. BRAHMA PP	0.89
12. BANCO DO BRASIL ON	0.24
13. BANCO DO BRASIL PN	2.40
14. CEMIG PN	0.82
15. CEVAL PN	0.44
16. CIA HERING PN	0.21
17. CIM., ITAU PN	0.25
18. COFAP PP	1.23
19. COPENE PNA	1.83
20. DURATEX PP	0.71
21. ELECTROBRAS PNB	5.05
22. ESTRELA PN	0.20
23. FNV PN	0.09
24. FERRO LIGAS PN	0.63
25. IPIRANGA PET., PP	0.17
26. ITAUBANCO PN	0.66
27. ITAUSA PN	0.50
28. KLABIN PP	0.16
29. LUXMA PP	0.04
30. MANNESMANN ON	0.24
31. METAL LEVE PP	0.46
32. PAPEL SIMAO PN	0.92
33. PARAIBUNA PP	0.20
34. PARANAPANEMA PN	8.68
35. PETROBRAS ON	0.10
36. PETROBRAS PN	13.65
37. PIRELLI ON	0.09
38. PIRELLI PN	0.09
39. REFRIPAR PN	0.18
40. RIPASA PP	0.21
41. SADIA CONCORDIA PN	1.13
42. SHARP PPA	0.14
43. SID. RIOGRANDENSE PN	0.10
44. SOUZA CRUZ ON	0.34
45. SUZANO PP	0.28
46. TELEBRAS PN	30.58
47. TELESP PN	1.61
48. TUPY PN	0.18
49. UNIPAR PNB	0.71
50. VALE DO RIO DOCE PP	15.81
51. VARIG PN	0.28
52. VIDR. STA. MARINA OP	0.31
53. WHITE MARTINS ON	1.32
Total	100.00

Source: Bovespa

the concentration of control with family groups or conglomerates, preferred shares are the most actively traded types of stocks in Brazil. Historically, both preferred and common stocks could be registered or bearer, but beginning in 1992, all stocks will have to be registered.

Dealing Procedures

Trading on the Brazilian Stock Exchange requires the intermediation of brokerage houses, which execute orders given by their clients through one of their representatives on the trading floor. Trading can be followed via a sophisticated terminal network operated by the stock exchanges, mainly the Bovespa. In June 1990, the Brazilian securities commission (CVM) authorized the use of the CATS (Computer Assisted Trading System) licensed by the Toronto Stock Exchange to the Sao Paulo Stock Exchange (Bovespa), to be operated together with the traditional system of operation. Brazil's market is highly automated by emerging markets standards.

Settlement

The two types of settlement are physical delivery and financial settlement. Physical delivery corresponds to the delivery of securities to the stock exchange by the brokerage house. It occurs on the first working day (D + 1) after the trade. The stocks are available to the purchaser after settlement. In practice, most shares are held in the central custody system of the stock exchange.

Financial settlement corresponds to the payment of the total value of the operation, by the brokerage house of the purchaser, and the respective receipt, by the seller. It occurs on the second working day (D + 2) after the trade.

Beginning in September 1991, only half of the brokerage fees will be set by the stock exchanges, while the other half will be negotiated between the brokerage houses and the investors. The intention of the CVM is that from 1992, all of the brokerage fees will be negotiated freely.

Structure of the Securities Industry

Until the mid-1960s, there were basically no instruments of long-term financing in the economy, due to a law that established the ceiling for interest rates at 12 percent per annum. The need for other instruments increased due to the fast industrialization process that began in the mid-1950s.

In 1964, a new law led to great changes in the structure of the financial and capital markets, diversifying and widening the types of financial assets, stimulating savings, increasing the number of developing institutions, allowing mergers and acquisitions among banks, and stimulating the development of the stock market. The financial system, after the changes, includes commercial banks, investment banks, consumer finance and credit companies, leasing companies, equity and fixed-income mutual funds, foreign capital funds, and brokerage firms. This law also created the National Monetary Council, to establish credit and currency policy and the Securities and Exchange Commission—Comissao de Valores Mobiliarios. The CVM is responsible for regulating the capital markets and companies according to corporate law, registration of companies traded on the stock exchange's public offerings, and registration of independent auditors, consultants, and securities analysts.

Equity trading is done by brokers and securities dealers. The securities dealers generally operate in the retail market, putting together small orders and trading these as a block through a brokerage firm, since they cannot have seats on the stock exchange. There are about 100 brokerage firms operating in the Sao Paulo and Rio de Janeiro markets. The brokerage firms can basically be classified into "independent" brokerage firms and brokerage firms controlled by banks. The latter have an important market share due to their greater capacity to support the volatility of the Brazilian market, which as a result has caused banks to dominate the money market business. Banks also dominate the market in administering foreign funds.

The top ten brokerage houses typically contribute approximately 25 percent of total volume traded in the market. The positions change considerably from month to month. The top ten during 1991 are listed in Table 15-6.

Foreign Investment Regulation

Until July 1991, foreign portfolio investors could invest in Brazil only through the Brazil Fund (listed on the New York Stock Exchange) or more than 24 other specialized funds set up by international fund managers in Brazil under Resolution 1289, promulgated by the CVM in March 1987, or Decree 4131 of September 1962, which first allowed foreign portfolio investment. These funds required CVM approval, a local administrator (typically a bank or brokerage house), a minimum investment period of 90 days, and a minimum investment of 70 percent of the total portfolio in listed stocks. Despite the heavy concentration of trading in only a few stocks, limitation in any single stock was limited to 10 percent of the portfolio which hampered those with strong convictions on particular stock choices as well as those who attempted to mimic the Bovespa returns.

Since July 1991, institutional investors are also allowed to set up "omnibus accounts" which are essentially portfolios of one or more shares held in local custody and involving the appointment of a local financial institution as administrator. The minimum holding period (of 90 days) and portfolio diversification restrictions were abolished for the new omnibus accounts as well as for the funds as long as the foreign institution can demonstrate that it represents a bona fide (group of) institutional investor(s).

Table 15.6   Composition of Trading Volume by Top Ten Brokers

Company	Percent of Total
1. SN CREFISUL S/A SC	3.60
2. CITIBANK CCTVM S/A	3.50
3. TENDENCIA CCTVM S/A	3.10
4. NOVINVEST S/A CVM	3.01
5. BRADESCO S/A CTVM	2.94
6. BANCOCIDADE CVMC LTDA.	2.53
7. VETOR	2.49
8. RMC S/A SC	2.30
9. DIGIBANCO CCVM S/A	2.25
10. LIBERAL	2.18
Subtotal (10 Companies)	27.90
Total (95 Companies)	100.00

Source: Bovespa

It is also expected that Telebras, Aracruz, Vale do Rio Doce and other leading Brazilian companies will issue ADRs or IDRs some time in 1992. Moreover, investment for foreign retail investors is also expected to be eased.

Distributions of dividends are subject to a 15 percent withholding tax, but capital gains are tax exempt.

16

CHILE

Jaime Valenzuela
Citibank
Chile

Overview of the Chilean Stock Market

The Chilean stock market dates from the end of the last century. The country's first securities exchange was founded in 1873. Until the 1930's the market grew substantially, fostered by the economic progress of the liberal Chilean economy of those years. Then a period of gradual deterioration followed which coincided with the establishment of an economy closed to foreign trade and with increasing intervention of the state. Transactions reached their trough during the Marxist government of Salvador Allende (1970-1973) (Table 16-1).

**Table 16-1 Growth of Annual Trading Value
(in millions of U.S. dollars)**

Period	Traded Amount
1930-1939	89.9
1940-1949	81.0
1950-1959	70.2
1960-1969	22.6
1970-1979	52.2
1980-1989	359.3
1990	779.4
1991	4,824.0

Source: Bolsa de Comercio de Santiago

After the September 1973 coup, the military government headed by General Pinochet began to apply the principles of a free market economy again. The role of the securities market was strengthened by policies aimed mainly at encouraging private enterprise. The stock market rose, responding to improvement in the economy and the performance of companies. Later, with the deep recession suffered by the Chilean economy in 1982, there was a downturn in the market. Since 1985, the stock market has had its best period in history.

The amount traded has increased from US $ 67.4 million in 1985 to US $779 million in 1990, representing an average compound annual growth rate of 63%. At the same time, share prices have increased significantly. Indeed, the weighted average return of the 30 most actively traded stocks reached a yearly average in US dollar terms of 78.8% during the period 1985-1990 and was 102.6% during the first six months of 1991.

The reactivation of the stock market since 1985 is largely explained by the following reasons.

The Country's Strong Economic Growth.   GDP's real annual average growth rate was 5.7% during the period 1984-1990, a fact that places Chile in a privileged position in Latin America.

The Good Performance of Chilean Corporations.   This is reflected in higher profitability and a better financial position (see Table 16-2). This good performance has enticed the entrance of new investors to the stock market, including foreign ones.

Table 16-2   Financial Ratios as of December 31

	1984[1]	1985	1986	1987	1988[2]	1989	1990
Return on sales (%)	2.9	−0.5	14.7	19.5	32.5	28.9	23.7
Return on equity (%)	2.4	−0.5	15.2	19.5	24.4	28.9	14.3
Current liquidity ratio (times)	1.27	1.54	1.37	1.43	1.76	1.66	1.64
Debt to equity ratio (times)	0.86	0.90	0.80	0.54	0.46	0.45	0.45

[1]Sample of 113 corporations between 1984-1988.

[2]Sample of 115 corporations since 1988.

Source: Bolsa de Comercio de Santiago

Privatization of the Most Important State-Owned Companies.   This process started slowly in 1984 but gathered considerable momentum in the following years, adding an important new supply in the stock market. It is important to underline the fact that before these companies became part of the stock exchange, most trading was in shares of corporations which were largely held either by a foreign group or by Chilean families.

More Intensive Use of the Stock Market to Raise Equity Capital.   Table 16-3 lists the number of new issues from 1984 to 1990.

Increasing Participation of Institutional Investors.   These include pension funds, life insurance companies, foreign capital investment funds, and mutual funds in the stock market (Table 16-4).

Table 16-3   New Equity Issues in Chilean Stock Market (From 1984 to 1990)

Year	New Issues (Millions of U.S. $ of December 1990)
1984	97.0
1985	185.1
1986	314.5
1987	1,127.0
1988	624.6
1989	306.7
1990	253.2

Source: Bolsa de Comercio de Santiago

Table 16-4   Institutional Investor's Assets Under Management (Millions of U.S. $ of each year)

	Pension Funds	Life Insurance Companies	Mutual Funds	Foreign Funds
1986	2,833	833	260	
1987	3,027	1,000	336	
1988	4,073	1,193	422	
1989	4,836	1,463	538	250
1990	6,654	1,847	434	512

Source: Superintendencia de Valores y Seguros .

Progress in the area of regulation and information.   This has allowed investors to have better and more timely information on the stock exchange and the registered companies. These companies must submit quarterly financial statements (audited yearly) to the Superintendency of Securities, and therefore, to the public.

Performance of the Chilean Stock Market

Given the characteristics of the market and the availability of data, the analysis of the market's performance will be divided in two periods: 1961-1980 and 1981-1991.

Period between 1961 and 1980

As this Table 16-5 illustrates, there is enough data on market size for these years, but there is no data on market return. The best proxy for market return is the real change in the General Stock Price Index (IGPA). This is only a proxy of return because it does not include dividend payments. The word "real" means adjusted by domestic inflation.

During the 1960s, total stock market value, trading volume, and real change in IGPA showed a negative trend. The main reason for this poor performance was the increasing intervention of the government in the economy, which deterred both private initiative and the efficient allocation of resources through the market.

During the government of the Marxist Salvador Allende the stock market reached its trough. The year 1972 was the worst year in terms of market capitalization and return and the second worst in traded volume.

The liberalization process implemented during the period of military regime which took over the government in 1973 had an immediate positive effect on the stock market. Indeed, since that year a sustained recovery in both stock prices and trading volume began. This strong cycle lasted until 1980.

Period Between 1981 to Present

Starting in 1981, more and better stock market data are available. In Tables 16-6 and 16-7, two new indicators of return were added: the change in the Selective Stock Price Index and the weighted average return of the 30 most-traded stocks. The former is a price index formed by the 40 most-traded stocks (not adjusted by dividend payments) and the latter is the average return (including dividends and capital gains) of the 30 most-traded stocks weighted by the volume traded in each stock during the year.

Other data such as price/earnings, price/book value, and dividend yield became available in 1984.

Table 16-5 History of the Equity Market

Year	Market Capitalization U.S. $ Millions December 1990	Trading Volume U.S. $ Millions December 1990	Turnover Ratio %	Number of Listed Companies	Real Change in IGPA Index
1960	540.6	22.2	4.1	339	N.A
1961	437.0	19.3	4.4	343	−18.15
1962	489.5	26.6	5.4	339	22.09
1963	628.1	41.0	6.5	342	31.69
1964	609.2	36.2	5.9	341	-8.45
1965	457.2	29.7	6.5	352	−36.09
1966	361.8	14.2	3.9	346	−12.36
1967	316.1	10.9	3.4	369	−21.47
1968	273.0	12.0	4.4	393	16.18
1969	266.3	14.3	5.4	378	21.00
1970	193.6	14.1	7.3	368	−51.40
1971	185.6	5.8	3.1	345	53.73
1972	127.7	6.7	5.2	336	−36.44
1973	486.8	13.1	2.7	335	392.30
1974	368.2	24.9	6.8	352	−11.65
1975	544.7	25.0	4.6	350	20.29
1976	706.0	29.6	4.2	347	31.73
1977	2,276.7	79.1	3.5	283	109.55
1978	2,732.6	142.3	5.2	208	46.57
1979	4,401.3	181.5	4.1	232	51.97
1980	6,836.7	398.6	5.8	263	39.92

Source: Bolsa de Comercio de Santiago .

The previous tables show the bullish market of the 1970s which ended in 1981. In that year the Chilean economy began to be affected by the international recession of the early 1980s. Already burdened with a record level of external debt, the recession caused a big fall in Chile's terms of trade. Together with the sudden stop of external capital inflows, this forced the country to make a huge adjustment in its economy. The worst year was 1982, when real GDP fell 14.1%. This recession, which lasted until 1983, seriously affected the stock market. Indeed, during 1981 and 1983, all of the stock market's return indicators fell, and volume traded dropped more than 60%.

In 1984, the recession ended and an impressive recovery of the stock market began. Since 1985 all return indicators, either in US dollar or real peso terms, have

Table 16-6 Stock Market Data

Year	Number of Companies Listed on the Stock Exchange	Stock Market Value U.S. $ Mill December 1990	Stock Transaction U.S. $ Mill. December 1990	Stock Turnover Ratio Percentage	Stock Market Value Percentage of GDP	Stock Dividends U.S. $ Mill. December 1990	Dividends and Distributions U.S. $ Mill. December 1990	Stock Paid for at Market Value U.S. $ Mill. December 1990	Total Stockholders of Companies listed on the Exchange
1981	241	4,781	248.7	5.3	22.9	632.1	266.9	223.0	—
1982	212	4,652	116.7	2.6	25.9	215.0	186.0	196.8	348,038
1983	211	2605	58.6	2.2	15.0	7.1	101.8	149.3	350,413
1984	208	2,523	47.3	1.9	13.6	9.3	137.0	97.0	371,778
1985	215	2,729	67.4	2.5	14.4	51.4	226.6	185.1	435,389
1986	215	5,219	380.3	7.3	26.0	16.3	294.6	314.5	478,628
1987	211	6,415	612.4	9.5	30.3	44.7	564.5	1,127.0	497,039
1988	203	8,083	737.5	9.2	35.1	23.9	877.3	624.6	571,688
1989	213	10,750	925.2	8.7	42.5	0.0	1,273.8	306.7	629,321
1990	216	13,636	779.4	5.7	53.3	0.0	1,071.7	253.2	569,956
1991	221	27,984	1,900.0	8.8	93.0	—	—	—	—

Note: Exchange rate as of December 1990 U.S. $ = 337.09

Source: Bolsa de Comercio de Santiago and SFC Emerging Markets Data Base

Table 16-7 Stock Market Data

Year	Change in IGPA		Change in IPSA		Weighted Average Return of 30 Most Traded		Price to Book Value	P/E Ratio	Dividend Yield
	Real	U.S. $	Real	U.S. $	Real	U.S. $			
1981	(31.02)	(24.47)	(42.18)	(37.38)	(25.63)	(18.56)			
1982	(27.28)	(53.38)	(24.93)	(51.88)	(11.54)	(43.29)			
1983	(30.75)	(28.49)	(10.32)	(7.39)	10.55	14.15			
1984	(8.92)	(23.53)	(12.35)	(26.41)	12.53	(5.52)	0.37	15.72	5.26
1985	37.78	21.47	61.80	42.65	126.29	99.50	0.39	0.00	8.98
1986	102.53	113.53	139.33	152.33	169.85	184.51	0.68	5.38	10.79
1987	7.88	12.70	31.83	36.88	36.96	43.08	0.70	5.17	10.82
1988	18.73	28.89	35.65	47.32	70.58	85.17	0.71	3.60	13.67
1989	35.72	36.96	35.91	37.16	68.01	69.55	0.78	4.86	15.96
1990	20.97	35.85	29.62	45.56	40.49	57.77	1.00	7.50	10.06
*1991	57.18	64.56	84.38	98.05	93.45	102.54	N.A.	N.A.	N.A.

*Up to June 30, 1991

Source: Bolsa de Comercio de Santiago

been positive. In addition, volume traded has steadily grown, in 1990 reaching a level of almost twice that of 1980 (the peak in the previous positive cycle).

The performance of the stock market has been even better during 1991. During the first six months the weighted average return of the 30 most-traded stocks was 102.54% in US dollar terms. If nothing unexpected happens during the second half, 1991 should be a record year for the stock market in both return and volume traded.

There are long-term factors that lead to optimism about the future of the stock market. Some of these factors include the following:

- The strong position of the Chilean economy.

- The fact that Chile has overcame the difficult hurdle of re-establishing a multiparty democracy while maintaining the principles of a free market economy.

- The growth potential created by sizeable investments being made by private corporations in important industries such as mining, energy, forestry, and fisheries.

- The depth and demand that should continue to be added to the stock market by institutional investors (for example, assets of private pension funds should double their size by the year 2000).

- The strong financial and competitive position of Chilean corporations, which puts them in an advantageous position to tap the current world-wide trend toward liberalization of trade and integration of the world-wide and regional economies.

Market Structure

Market Size

Over the past six years, the number of listed companies has remained virtually unchanged (215). Nevertheless, total stock market value, in U.S. $ and as a percentage of GDP, has increased significantly (from US $2.8 billion and 14% of GDP in 1985 to US $13.6 billion and 53% of GDP in 1990). With only a limited amount of new issues and hardly any stock dividends (except in 1987), the growth of the stock market is explained almost exclusively by price increases.

Trading volume has also shown an important increase over the last six years (from US $67.4 million in 1985 to US $779.4 million in 1990, with a peak of U.S. $925.2 million in 1989). However, the stock turnover ratio has remained stable.

It is important to underline the fact that stock transactions are highly concentrated in a few companies. Table 16-8 shows the percentage of total amount traded in the 10 and 30 most-traded stocks.

Table 16-8   Percentage of Total Traded Volume

Year	10 Most-Traded Stocks	30 Most Traded Stocks
1981	55.89	81.22
1982	58.27	79.78
1983	47.78	61.43
1984	39.32	58.14
1985	53.64	75.37
1986	69.34	86.74
1987	70.77	83.35
1988	72.88	86.99
1989	68.22	83.90
1990	57.81	78.61

Source: Prepared by the author with data from the Bolsa de Comercio de Santiago.

As it can be observed, the market is very concentrated in the 30 most-traded stocks, which represented almost 80% of total transactions in 1990. Furthermore, only ten stocks represented almost 58% of total transactions in the same year.

Stock Exchanges

There are three stock exchanges in Chile: The Bolsa de Comercio de Santiago, the Bolsa de Valores, and the Bolsa de Comercio de Valparaiso. By far the most important is the Bolsa de Comercio de Santiago. This stock exchange had a monopoly since 1982, until a few years ago when the Bolsa de Valparaiso (the least important) and the Bolsa de Valores started operations.

Two industries, forestry and public utilities, represent more than 50% of total market capitalization (Table 16-9), another example of the high concentration of the Chilean Stock Market. Another industry with a high percentage of total market capitalization is financial services and investments, but this is influenced by the fact that investment companies which own the largest blue chips are included in this category. Table 16-10 and 16-11 list ten largest and most traded companies of the Chilean equity market.

Stock Market Indices

There are two price indices: the Selective Stock Price Index (IPSA) and the General Stock Price Index (IGPA). The IPSA is composed of the 40 most-traded stocks. The IGPA index includes all listed stocks. Both indices are a weighted average of closing prices without adjustment for dividend payments. The weight of each stock in the index is based on market capitalization, amount traded, and turnover. Since 1990, a series of the IPSA adjusted by dividends is also available.

**Table 16-9   Main Industries by Market Capitalization
As of December 1990**

Industry	Percentage of Total Market Capitalization
Mining	2.7
Forestry[1]	23.1
Agriculture Products	0.4
Food, Beverage, and Wines	5.1
Fishing	2.0
Industrial	13.9
Financial and Investments	18.4
Shipping	3.0
Public Utilities	30.0
Other	1.5
Total	100.0

[1]Includes cellulose and paper production (COPEC is included).

Source: Prepared by the author with data from Bolsa de Comercio de Santiago

---

Table 16-10 Top Ten Chilean Stocks Ranked by Market Capitalization

Company	1991 Market Capitalization (U.S.$ MM)	% of Total Market Capitalization
Endesa	3,903	14%
Copec	3,010	11%
Telefonos/OCTC	2,650	9%
Enersis	2,500	9%
Cartones	2,083	7%
Chilectra	1,090	4%
Vapores	868	3%
CCU	809	3%
CCT	735	3%
Minera	701	3%

Source: Bolsa de Comercio de Santiago

These two indices are published daily by the Bolsa de Comercio de Santiago (Table 16-12).

Table 16-11 Top Ten Chilean Stocks Ranked by Value Traded

Company	1991 Value Traded (U.S.$ MM)	% of Total Value Traded
Endesa	322	17%
Enersis	166	9%
Telefonos/OCTC	147	8%
Chilgener	140	7%
CAP	72	4%
Entel	72	4%
Iansa	67	4%
Chilectra	59	3%
Cartones	53	3%
Mantos Blancos	49	3%

Source : Bolsa de Comercio de Santiago

Table 16-12 Stock Market Indices as of December 30 of Each Year

		Index Value				
		IGPA			IPSA	
Year	High	Low	Close	High	Low	Close
1985	43.5	33.1	43.5	54.2	34.5	54.2
1986	88.2	45.4	88.2	129.8	57.9	129.8
1987	118.9	81.4	95.2	217.1	129.2	170.1
1988	113.3	90.9	113.1	230.8	159.1	230.8
1989	153.4	121.1	153.4	320.4	255.0	313.6
1990	184.9	142.6	182.8	409.5	299.2	400.7

Source : Bolsa de Comercio de Santiago

Type of Shares

Almost 100% of stocks traded in Chile are common stocks. There are some few preferred stocks, mainly of commercial banks. During 1991, futures contracts on the IPSA index began being traded on the Bolsa de Comercio de Santiago. The maturity of the traded futures contract is three months. This market is still very small.

Dealing Procedures

Stock are traded both in open outcry and in electronic sessions. Only brokers who are members of the stock exchange may deal on the exchange. Brokers are allowed to acquire securities for their own account only after they have completed all orders for their clients. Brokers must be approved for membership by the board of the respective stock exchange. Members should adhere to a code of ethics and should maintain a minimum net worth. All brokers are regulated by the Superintendent of Securities ("Superintendencia de Valores y Seguros").
The main stock brokers are the following:

- Citicorp Chile S.A., Corredores de Bolsa, La Bolsa 64, 4th   floor, Santiago, Chile. Fax: (56 2) 695 70 98

- Larrain Vial S.A., Corredores de Bolsa, La Bolsa 88, Santiago, Chile. Fax: (56 2) 672 34 50

- Tanner ABN S.A., Corredores de Bolsa, Nueva York 25, 4th floor, Santiago, Chile. Fax: (56 2) 672 66 78

These brokers provide some economic, stock market, and company information. Nevertheless, the latter is mainly historic information. Until recently, there were only a very few providers of detailed industries and company reports (including earning forecasts). Now Citicorp, Baring Securities, and Larrain Vial have started to provide such information.

Settlement is on the second day after the trade date until a different date for settlement is agreed upon by the parties. Transaction costs in the Bolsa de Comercio de Santiago are the following:

- Stock Exchange Commission: Between 0.5% and 0.1% based on accumulated traded volume during the month.

- Broker Fee: This is freely negotiated between the client and the broker, but the most common range is 0.3% to 1%.

- A value added tax (VAT) of 18% is charged on both the Stock Exchange and Brokers fees.

Major Investors

Traditionally, most Chilean corporations which were not state-owned are controlled by a major economic group (Angelini, Matte, Claro, etc.). These are usually family groups. However, after the privatization program, an important group of companies with a different ownership structure appeared in the market. Based on their ownership, three kinds of corporations can be distinguished: controlled and illiquid, controlled but highly liquid, noncontrolled and liquid.

Controlled and Illiquid.   These include corporations controlled by one or two shareholder groups which own a high percentage of the stocks. These groups seldom sell; thus only the small portion not owned by the major shareholders is traded in the stock exchanges. The market for these companies is small and illiquid.

Controlled and Highly Liquid.   These corporations are controlled by a group, but the percentage of the shares which is not controlled is large enough to form a liquid market. The best examples of members of this group are Copec and Cartones.

Noncontrolled and Liquid.   These corporations are mainly the companies that were privatized in the 1980s.

The Chilean market is highly concentrated because a very high percentage of listed companies are controlled and illiquid. This is the reason why only ten companies represent more than 55% of total transactions.

As Table 16-13 shows, the participation in the stock market by the main institutional investors is still low but has shown an increasing trend over the last years.

How Foreigners Can Invest In Chile

In Chile, the capital account is not completely open. There are some special regulations for foreign investors interested in the Chilean Securities Market. Currently, the best alternative for these investors is to invest through a Foreign Capital Investment Fund (FCIF).

Law 18,657 governs the organization of FCIF. A FCIF should be a fund or trust set up outside Chile, and the Chilean Superintendency of Securities must give permission for its operations in Chile. This law imposes some restrictions to FCIF. Some of the most important include the following:

Table 16-13 Percentage of Total Stock Market Value

Year	Pension Funds	Foreign Funds
1987	3.24	
1988	4.13	N.A.
1989	4.79	N.A.
1990	5.53	2.63

Source: Prepared by the author based on information from the Superintendencia de AFP and the Superintendencia de Valores.

- Capital can not be redeemed during the first five years of operations. Realized dividends and capital gains may be redeemed at any time.

- The FCIF should have a local administrator.

- A FCIF may neither invest more than 10% of its assets in a single issuer nor own more than 5% of the voting capital of any issues.

Law 18,656 provides some benefits: a preferential tax rate (only a 10% withholding tax on redemption of dividends and capital gains) and guaranteed access to the formal Foreign Exchange Market through the signing of a Decree Law 600 (DL 600) Contract with the Chilean government.

Sources of Information

Some sources of information include the following:

- "Reseña Anual," Bolsa de Comercio de Santiago.

- "Boletin Mensual," Bolsa de Comercio de Santiago.

- "Informativo Diario," Bolsa de Comercio de Santiago.

- "Boletin Mensual," Banco Central de Chile.

- "Brief of the Chilean Economy," Citicorp Chile Administradora de Fondos de Capital Extranjero (private document).

- "Informe Trimestral," Citicorp Chile S.A., Corredores de Bolsa.

- "Revista de Valores," Superintendencia de Valores y Seguros.

- "Boletin Mensual," Superintendencia de AFP.

Company Profiles*

Copec:

Compañia de Petroleos de Chile (Copec) is the largest Chilean private company. It is a holding with investments in a wide variety of businesses: marketing and distribution of oil products, production and/or distribution of other products oriented to the domestic market (appliances, gas, electricity and others), fishing and forestry (cellulose production). Approximately 60% of Copec's earnings are from forestry. In

*Company profiles are provided by the editors.

1992-1993 Copec will double its production of cellulose. Fishing and forestry are oriented to exports. Copec is controlled by the Angelini Group.

Cartones:

Compañia Manufacturera de Papeles y Cartones (Cartones) is a producer of cellulose and paper products (paper, diapers, etc.). Almost 50% of its sales are from exports. In 1991-1992, it will almost double its production of cellulose through its affiliate Celulosa del Pacifico, of which it owns 46%. Cartones is controlled by the Matte Group.

Endesa:

Empresa Nacional de Electricidad (Endesa) is the main Chilean producer of electricity. During 1990-1991 Endesa has added important production capacity with the completion of two new hydroelectric plants. These plants will allow Endesa to increase its sales at a rate of at least 5% per year until 1995. In 1996 Endesa will begin operations of a new hydroelectric plant, which will be the largest in Chile. The company was state-owned and was privatized during the former government.

Telefonos:

Compañia de Telefonos de Chile (Telefonos) is the largest Chilean telephone company. It owns the concession to operate throughout the country, with the exception of only 2 regions (of a total of 13). At December 1990, it owned 812,000 telephone lines. Investment plans for the period 1991-1996 envisage a doubling to 1,782,000 lines. Total investment will be approximately U.S. $1,200 million. Telefonos was previously state-owned and was privatized during the former government. Telefonica of Spain owns 43.66% of its shares.

Enersis:

This is a holding company whose main investment is Chilectra, the largest Chilean electricity distribution company. It also owns 12.7% of Endesa, another utility. It was privatized during the former government.

Minera:

Minera Valparaiso (Minera) is an investment company which indirectly owns 19% of Cartones. It also has investments in electricity and real estate. It is controlled by the Matte Group.

Vapores:

Compañia Sud Americana de Vapores (Vapores) is the largest Chilean shipping company. It operates approximately 26 ships of which it owns 17. Its revenues are correllated with Chilean foreign trade. It is controlled by the Claro Group.

ARGENTINA

Eduardo Tapia
Baring Securities
Buenos Aires, Argentina

Founded in 1854, the Stock Exchange of Buenos Aires is the oldest in Latin America and was the first to establish a securities commission (1937). Highly integrated in the political and economic life of Argentina, it reached its heyday during the 1930s when it was comparable in size and activity to many European markets.

During the past three decades, however, its performance was unstable. Government overspending, high inflation rates, and problems with the currency eroded investors' confidence, leading to highly volatile stock prices. As a result, the number of listed companies, market capitalization, and trading activity diminished, making investors shift their assets to different financial instruments.

After going through many economic crises, however, Argentina may finally be entering a new era. Beginning in 1989, President Carlos Menem's government introduced structural changes in the economy that are changing its historical protectionist status. Deregulation, privatization, and fiscal discipline are the pillars of a new economic plan that drastically reduced inflation and interest rates, giving the Argentinean market a better foundation and better prospects.

Market Size and Trading Activity

President Raul Alfonsin's government (1983–1988) brought back democracy to Argentina, but the stock market performed poorly. Market capitalization fluctuated around U.S. $1 billion to $2 billion and daily traded value averaged U.S. $1.5 million. From 1989 onward, the market oscillated strongly, reaching U.S. $3 billion in capitalization and a daily traded value of U.S. $3 million in January 1991.

321

The lack of liquidity in the stock market was a consequence of undervalued prices and the erosion of corporate earnings over a decade. During the years of decline, most of the big companies were held by family groups which generally controlled 70% or more of the companies' market capitalization.

As of December 1991, 174 stocks were listed on the Stock Exchange of Buenos Aires with a market capitalization of U.S. $18.5 billion spread over the various economic sectors (Table 17-1).

During the last five years, the stock market's free-float fluctuated between 15% and 34%. After a virtual absence for several decades, foreign investors began entering the market in 1991.

After the currency was tied to the dollar, the stock market began to reflect investors' expectations of an economic turnaround and triggered an avalanche of foreign portfolio investment. The market reached new records of index and volumes with daily trading reaching a peak of over $100 million on August 23, 1991.

The number of listings is likely to grow since market capitalization represents only 10% of GNP and investors are hopeful about the structural economic reforms, the economy's expansion, and the privatization of the public sector which may bring back home U.S. $50 billion of Argentinean flight capital.

History

All through its history, the Stock Exchange of Buenos Aires has reflected the inconsistency of governmental policies and the frequent instability of the economic system. Created in 1954, the year following the constitution's decree, the exchange

Table 17-1   Industrial Sectors Represented in the Stock Market

Industry	Companies	Percentage
Petroleum	Astra, Perez, Companc, Comercial del Plata	25.8
Telephone	Telefonica de Argentina	18.5
Steel	Acindar, Siderca	13.4
Chemical/Petrochemical	Atanor, Cia Quimica, Electroclor, Indupa, Ipako	5.6
Banking	Banco Frances, Banco Galicia, Banco Supervielle	4.7
Food	Bagley, Canale, Molinos Rio de la Plata, Terrabusi	4.6
Paper	Celulosa	3.7
Construction	Corcemar, Juan Minetti	2.4
Sugar	Ledesma, Ingenio Tabacal	1.1
Automobile	Renault	1.1
Remainder		20.0
Total		100.0

Source: Baring Research

Figure 17-1 Stock Index in U.S. \$, (September 1, 1988–December 30, 1991)

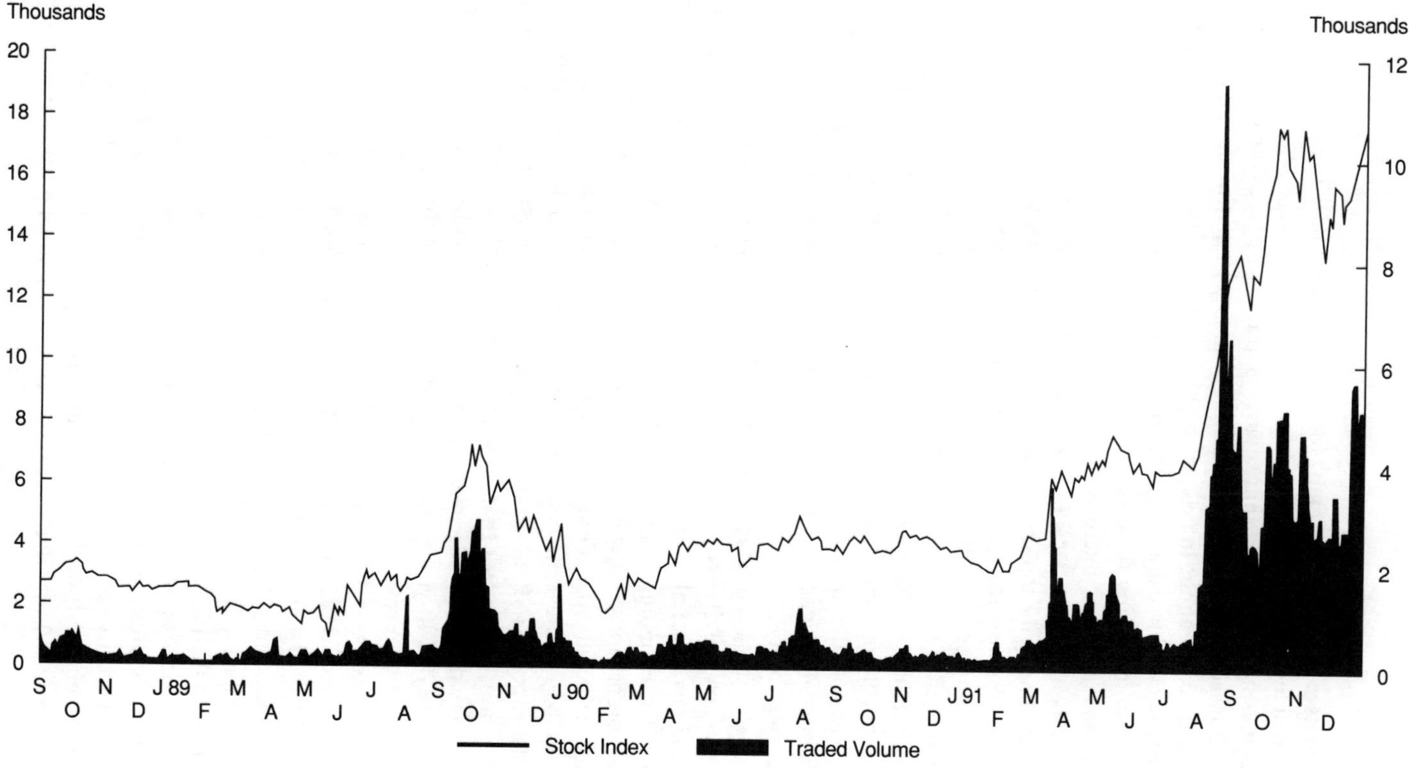

served in its early years as a "club" for wealthy merchants who exerted considerable influence in the country's political life.

It was not until 1872 that securities trading began. During the following decade, transactions were done primarily in mortgage certificates and shares of the National Bank. Dealings in private stocks did not exist until 1914, when the Stock Exchange decided to cease metals trading. In 1929, the Exchange and Bond Market (responsible for setting fixed income transactions, executing operations, and safeguarding the members' interests) was founded.

For the first three decades of the twentieth century, the Argentinean economy, which was among the top seven in the world, based its growth on a dynamic agricultural sector. Exports from the primary sector were close to 25% of GNP. Within an open economy perspective, imports fluctuated between 20% and 30% of GNP, growth ranged around 4% a year, and inflation averaged 2%.

Amid the world crisis of the 1930s and World War II, the comparative advantages of development based on agricultural exports broke down. The agricultural sector was not able to satisfy employment demand prompted by the immigration from Europe. Politically, the military's first coup d'etat was a prelude of 50 years of political instability.

Under the populist government of Juan D. Peron, the import substitution model (which heavily protected the industrial sector by taking advantage of cheap labor and raw materials from the agricultural sector) was chosen as the strategy for growth. The economic role of the state increased through the nationalization of private corporations (railways, energy, and communications) and the implementation of strict regulations. From 1940 to 1970, public expenditures went from 11% to 31% of GNP. In the same period, the ratio of imports/GNP dropped from 27% to 10%, the exports/GNP ratio, based on agricultural products, fell from 25% to 12%, and the industrial sector that grew from 16% to 25% did not generate exports. Annual growth fell to 3.2% and the average inflation climbed to 15% a year. The trademark of that 40-year period was a cyclical crisis in the balance of payments that caused recurrent recessions.

The crisis was also evident in the evolution of securities trading. In 1934, stocks represented only 4% of traded volume. Reaching a peak of 54% in 1948, the volume dropped consistently thereafter. Forty years later (1988), as a result of the massive placement of public bonds geared to fund the government deficit, the volume dropped to 5%.

During the 1950s, private stocks became significant and the number of listings increased from 266 in 1950 to 476 in 1959. In the early 1960s, Argentina went through a prosperous period. An industrial boom and a swift flood of investments in the stock market were followed by an increase in listings that reached 675 companies by the end of 1962. But economic instability, arising from high government expenditures (36% of GNP), resulted in a drop of stock prices and traded volume that lasted through the following years (Table 17-2).

Table 17-2 Number of Listed Companies Since 1960

Year	Number of Listed Companies	Year	Number of Listed Companies	Year	Number of Listed Companies
1960	552	1982	248	1987	206
1970	414	1983	238	1988	194
1975	322	1984	236	1989	184
1980	278	1985	227	1990	179
1981	263	1986	217	1991	171

In 1969, Law 17811, which regulates public securities offerings and the organization and operation of all stock exchanges, was enacted, creating the legal framework for the future development of the capital market. One year later, the Argentinean economy entered its worst period. From 1970 to 1989, the GNP per capita fell more than 10%, the inflation rate averaged 180% a year, the public expenditures/GDP ratio went from 31% to 50%, and from 1978 to 1982 the external debt increased greatly.

During the 1970s, the stock market went through two unprecedented speculative movements. The first one occurred in March 1976, just after the military coup against Isabel Peron's government. Stocks were at extremely undervalued prices and a new law, "Revaluos Contables," allowed accounting adjustment by inflation, creating a gap between prices and book values. The fabulous, and unrealistic, upward trend ended in August 1976 when the National Development Bank started selling its enormous holdings to a nonreactive market. In 1979, another short bull market cropped up before the settlement of a border conflict with Chile that almost started a war. The economic recovery lasted for only one year, and in 1980 a financial crack caused the bankruptcy of several banks.

The 1980s began with democracy, an economy in shambles, and an administration facing rising inflation, external debt, and recession. Unable and unwilling to tackle structural economic problems, the elected government tried to renegotiate its debt and external credits, and applied heterodox economic strategies to reduce inflation and stabilize economic activity which starved without investment. Along with wide alternatives regarding short- and medium-term hedging instruments in the form of inflation-adjusted mortgage bonds, the government flooded the market with dollar bonds (Bonex) and several types of certificates with diverse monetary adjustment formulas.

The government bonds represented strong competition to stocks, inducing a flat decade in terms of market capitalization (U.S. $1 billion to $2 billion), and daily traded value (U.S. $1.5 million). When domestic investors lost confidence in public bonds, the last financial source was depleted. At that point, the only available financing source was the inflationary tax. Argentina ended the last year of the decade with hyperinflation (4,927% in 1989).

From 1989 onward, oscillations in the market continued. Market capitalization reached U.S. $3 billion and in January 1991 the market saw a daily trading value of U.S. $3 million. When Cavallo's "Convertibility Plan" was introduced (April 1, 1991), confidence was restored and an entirely new age in the history of the Argentinean stock market began with a skyrocketing of prices, trading activity, and market capitalization. In 1991 the market showed a continuous upward trend, with a capitalization of U.S. $18.5 billion and an average daily traded value of U.S. $19 million.

Turning Point

After decades of economic mismanagement, the need for structural change was finally accepted by Argentina's leaders, its people, and the productive sectors, including businessmen and unions. In order to decrease hyperinflation, high interest rates, unemployment, and uncompetitive industries, President Menem's administration launched the most ambitious plan ever attempted in the country. The main reforms introduced by the government included the following:

- State Reform Law (September 1989)
    - Empowered the president to modify the legal status of state organizations and create new entities on the basis of a split, merger, liquidation, or transformation of existing companies.
    - Declared all public institutions in a state of emergency for a one-year term that was then extended for another year.
    - Announced all different forms of privatizations.
    - Suspended lawsuits against the state for two years.

- New Foreign Investment Regime (November 1989)
    - Equal treatment for national and foreign capital.
    - No need for previous approval (exceptions: financial sector, radio stations, and television channels).
    - No legal limits regarding the type or nature of foreign investments.
    - Introduction of a free exchange regime (free repatriation of capital investment and remittance of dividends and capital gains).

- Privatization

    As of July 1991, the Argentinean privatization process retired approximately U.S. $7.3 billion of the country's external debt through debt-to-equity-swaps. This amount represents approximately 12% of the Argentinean debt with commercial banks. The sale of 60% of the shares of ENTEL (telecommunications company) was the largest one-time transaction in external-debt reduction in Latin America (U.S. $5.0 billion).

    As of June 1991, the following companies were privatized, reducing public expenditures:

    - Petrochemical Industry: Polisur, Monomeros, Vinilicos, Petropol (30% state owned).
    - Telecommunications: Television Channels 11, 13, and 9 (100% state owned).
    - Concession of national highways (100% state owned).
    - Railways: Rosario-Bahia Blanca, Ferrocarrilo Urquiza; Tren de la Costa (100% state owned).
    - Telephone Companies: ENTEL (100% state owned) - 30% of the company was offered on the Stock Exchange of Buenos Aires Stock Exchange in December 1991.

    There are many other "targeted" companies in the process of privatization and there will be more in the near future. Among them are Gas del Estado (gas distribution), OSN (water supplier), Segba (electric generation and distribution), YPF (oil company), Agua y Energia (hydroelectricity), Ferrocarriles Argentinos (railways), YCF (coal), Subterraneos de Buenos Aires (subways), ELMA (Shipping), and ENCOTEL (postal service).

- Deregulation

    The energy sector (petroleum and gas), which was almost entirely under state control (from extraction and distribution to sale), began a process of deregulation in 1989. Since January 1991, there has been free access for private entities, and the government has already sold secondary areas by concession and central areas in association with the government. Until now, the government has generated over U.S. $500 million in cash by selling the rights of crude oil exploitation in four central areas.

    On November 1, 1991, President Menem signed an unprecedented and comprehensive decree that gave Argentina one of the most liberated economies in Latin America. The fiscal, internal commerce, ports, foreign trade, transportation, banking, and service sectors have been deregulated, reducing the state's expenditures as well as ending monopolies, red tape, and privileges in order to encourage the country and its economy to enter a phase of global competitiveness.

- Trade Agreements

Argentina, Brazil, Uruguay, and Paraguay recently signed an agreement of economic integration (MERCOSUR) that will become effective on January 1, 1995. The geographic area of these countries represents 60% of Latin America and includes 45% of its total population. This potential market of 190 million people, and labor force of 70 million, would create a GNP of U.S. $436 billion, exports of U.S. $44 billion, and import capacity of U.S. $26 billion (based on 1990 data). Given the fact that Brazil is the primary export market for Argentinean industry, the existence of complementary advantages between both countries would make Brazil a tailor-made partner for external demand. Expectations regarding this regional block and a possible improvement of relations with the United States point to the creation of a vast free trading region that will extend from Alaska to Tierra del Fuego.

- Cavallo's Convertibility Plan

The basic points of the convertibility plan are as follows:

- Reserves of the Central Bank back the monetary base with an exception rate of =A= 10,000/U.S. Dollar (or one Peso equals U.S. $1 as of January 1, 1992).
- Indexation is prohibited while outstanding debts may be adjusted at a maximum annual rate of 12%.
- New fiscal measures have been enacted, increasing taxes in order to balance the budget.
- Government employee's wages were frozen.
- The cost of utilities has been reduced, allowing for a reduction in prices as a concession from companies.

Inflation dropped dramatically from 37.9% per month in February 1991 to 0.4% in November 1991 as a result of these measures; interest rates decreased from an annual rate of 600% (March 1991) to 15% (November 1991). In addition, the government has managed to turn around its budget deficit from 13% of GNP in mid-1989 to a small surplus, partially from the revenues of privatizations.

- Liberalization of the Economy

   To further deregulate the Argentinean economy, on October 31, 1991, President Menem announced a decree introducing key changes in six fundamental areas:

   1.   Commercialization of goods and services:
      a) All restrictions on trading and limitations regarding quality of goods information are deregulated. Exceptions are activities related to Argentinean defense and security systems, public services that constitute natural or legal monopolies and are regulated by special laws, recently privatized telephone companies, airlines, and soon to be privatized utilities.
      b) Total deregulation of freight and transportation across the country.
      c) All fixed tariffs, fees, and commissions on professional services (legal, medical, financial, etc.) are removed, disallowing any impediment of free agreements.
      d) Any regulation that impedes the free practice of professional activities is abolished.
      e) Medical products can be sold anywhere without prescription and can be imported freely as long as the government deems them appropriate for public consumption. There will be no restrictions on dispensing locations as in the opening of new pharmacies.
      f) All restrictions on loading and unloading, service hours, and working days in ports are abolished. All existing regulations impeding commercial activities such as packaging, administration, and sales in ports are also abolished.

   As a result, freight costs are expected to drop 30% and professional fees 10%. Ports' trading costs are expected to drop, as will the price of medicine. The government expects that after these measures, prices will decrease 7% as a consequence of lower intermediary costs and reduction in bureaucracy.

   2.   Deregulation of foreign trade:
      a) All regulations on imports and exports are abolished except in those cases in which international agreements, public health, and the environment need to be preserved.
      b) New import tariffs: 5% (raw materials), 13% (intermediary goods), 22% (final products). No tariff is applied to capital goods that are produced outside of the country.

c) The 3% statistical tax on exports is abolished.

The benefits are likely to be greater access to capital goods from abroad and reduction in exporting costs.

3.   Dissolution of regulatory entities:

    a) The Junta Nacional de Carnes and the Junta Nacional de Granos, in charge of certifying quality of meat and grains respectively, are eliminated. Their functions will be taken over by the Agriculture, Cattle, and Fishing Ministry. Other institutions to be dissolved are the Instituto Forestal Nacional (Forestry), Mercado de Concentracion Pesquera (Fishing Products Exchange), Corporacion Argentina de Carnes (Meat Corporation), Instituto Nacional de Vitivinicultura (Wine Entity), and the Comision Reguladora de Produccion de Comercio de Yerba Mate (Yerba Mate Commission).

    b) Liniers Cattle Market will be privatized.

    c) All limitations imposed on wine, yerba mate, tobacco, and sugar production are abolished.

    d) The government has offered voluntary retirement plans to the employees of dissolved organizations.

The benefits include eliminating bureaucracies, allowing cost savings and providing a higher degree of efficiency.

4.   Fiscal and stock exchange reform:

    a) The stamp tax (0.2%) has been discarded from all transactions.

    b) The income tax on all bond and stock transactions for local and foreign individuals and institutions has been abolished.

    c) The transfer tax (0.5%) on stocks, bonds, and foreign exchange transactions has been abolished.

    d) Brokerage fees have been completely deregulated and will be negotiated freely.

    e) Cash dividends are exempt of any withholding tax.

A future benefit of this reform is that transaction expenses at the stock exchange will drop significantly as a consequence of growing competition among brokers.

5.   Wage deductions:

The Social Security System will absorb all funds previously destined for pensions and subsidies and will solely manage them.

6.   Salaries:

Previous legislation determined regulations for each industry and "collective agreements" with unions established salaries. These agreements will now be freely negotiated and modified between employers and employees.

For Argentina, the return to competitiveness implies seeing beyond the short term and the immediate distortions caused by economic reforms and focusing on its abundance of resources and the advantages of its climates and land. Many industries should enter a new period of long-term growth. They include:

- Oil and petrochemical
- Agriculture and agro-industry
- Food and beverages
- Light machinery
- Fishing
- Mining
- Automobile spare parts
- Construction
- Tourism
- Paper & pulp
- Telecommunications
- Consumer products

Structure of the Market

For the last two decades, the Argentinean capital market has been fundamentally centered on public bonds. Among them, the most outstanding have been the "Bonex," bearer public bonds denominated in U.S. dollars, which can be freely traded in the country or abroad. Bonex are quoted on the New York Stock Exchange and are largely traded in the OTC local market and in offshore marketplaces. Bonex prices were always a reflection of the political and financial unsteadiness of the country, and their appeal owes much to the former exchange controls as they represented the only mechanism to buy or sell foreign currency and remit funds abroad. In general terms, the internal return rate has always been attractive due to the country-risk factor, although historically they never defaulted on payments of interest or principal. The bonds' issues represent today U.S. $4 billion, equivalent to 7% of total Argentinean debt (Table 17-3).

Table 17-3

Series of Bonex

Bonex	1982	1984	1987	1989
Date issue	2/15/82	12/12/84	9/07/87	12/28/89
Term	10 years	10 years	10 years	10 years
Amount issued*	3,000	1,000	1,000	4,500
Term repayment	8 years	8 years	8 years	8 years
Maturity date	2/15/92	12/12/94	9/07/97	12/28/99
Interest rate	Libor	Libor	Libor	Libor
Interest paid	semi-annually	semi-annually	semi-annually	semi-annually

*U.S. $ millions

Evolution of Traded Volumes

	Stocks Percent	Public Bonds Percent
1979	56	44
1980	52	48
1981	11	89
1982	11	89
1983	22	78
1984	24	76
1985	28	72
1986	30	70
1987	12	88
1988	27	73
1989	51	49
1990	54	46
1991	80	20

Total Traded Volume by Market - 1990

	Buenos Aires Stock Exchanges	OTC Market	Offshore Market
Equities	800 million	12 million	0
Public Bonds	940 million	14 billion	80 billion
Corporate Bonds	7 million	17 million	0

Sources: Bolsa de Comercio de Buenos Aires Mercado Abierto Electronico

The 1990s bring a change to develop an attractive stock market in the region. As an indicator, the August 1991 rally pushed up the Price/Book Value ratio of leading companies to 1.3 after a long period during which stocks traded well below their book values. Also, leading shareholder groups are actually considering new issues, many private companies are considering going public, and placements of privatized companies would produce a significant increase in the amount of traded shares. The Argentinean market has also become more internationalized with the introduction of several ADRs and the successful issue of Telefonica, which exceeded the expectations of most market observers.

Several new policies favor the development of the capital markets, cutting away decades of unnecessary bureaucratic regulation. They include:

- Banks were authorized to participate in the brokerage business.

- A new corporate-bond tax law has been approved.

- No capital gains taxes for local or foreign investors.

- Brokerage commissions have been deregulated.

- No stamp tax.

- No foreign exchange controls.

- No tax on cash dividends.

- No minimum investment period.

- No restrictions on invested amounts.

- No restrictions on ownership.

The new president of the local Securities Exchange Commission, Martin Redrado, has been actively pushing the development of embryonic capital markets. His further plans include:

- Automatic authorization of technical revaluation of corporate capital.

- Creation of local institutional investors through private pension fund development.

- Internationalization of the market with ADR programs for local companies.

- Rating agencies to evaluate companies.

- New mutual funds laws.

- Private placements outside the country.

- Agreement with the U.S. Securities and Exchange Commission for exchange of information.

Types of Shares

Table 17-4 lists the leading stocks by market capitalization. As of December 1991, there were 174 listed companies in the stock market, of which 21 had issued common and preferred shares. Common shares represent 99.2% of the total.

Common shares may have either one or five votes. Upon distribution of share dividends, shareholders receive one voting share. When the capitalization of reserves is approved at the shareholders' meeting, each shareholder receives the same type of stock already held.

There are different kinds of preferred shares, including those with basic dividends and those with participation in additional dividends. These shares have no rights at the shareholders meeting except when there is a delay in cash dividend payment. These kinds of stocks are received by shareholders when inflation-adjustment reserves are capitalized.

Corporate bonds can be issued in both local or foreign currency, with adjustments to principal and with fixed or variable interest rates.

**Table 17-4   Leading Stocks by Market Capitalization
In U.S. $ Millions**

Companies	December 1990	December 1991
Perez Companc	487.5	3,402.7
Siderca	413.6	1,737.7
Celulosa	204.6	443.5
Astra	201.2	969.6
Indupa	189.7	450.9
Massuh	99.3	198.7
Ipako	99.0	383.0
Ledesma	93.2	233.7
Banco Frances	82.5	465.7
Aluar	73.4	256.9
Molinos	71.1	364.7
Alpargatas	61.7	438.7
Acindar	59.5	743.0
Comercial del Plata	43.6	401.8
Banco Shaw	42.6	93.2
Juan Minetti	38.9	255.2
Garovaglio	38.5	176.3
Renault	37.8	209.4
Banco Galicia	37.4	332.7
Total	2,375.2	14,982.7
Market Capitalization	74.60%	81.03%

Investors

As government policies consisted of a series of economic and political missteps, Argentina's basic individual investor's market became extremely small, highly concentrated, and notably unsophisticated in terms of research, thus discouraging local institutional investors who viewed the stock market as a sort of "casino."

Mutual funds, established in 1960 and still extremely underdeveloped (around U.S. $300 million), are managed by banks and financial entities. Pension funds, historically run by the government, are completely bankrupt, and insurance companies have had to use hedging instruments to survive devaluations.

The new stability established by the Cavallo plan has drastically changed the potential of existing investment alternatives and is beginning to refocus the attention of institutions on stock investments.

Foreign Portfolio Investment

Until 1985, the Argentinean stock market was completely unknown among international investors. In 1986 and 1987, the first global market funds appeared, investing in a market that traded U.S. $0.7 million a day. Fundamental investment yardsticks produced some excellent bargain hunting. During those years, when Argentinean macroeconomic indicators would scare any logical analyst, the best companies in the country were trading at a big discount (0.4 price/book value) and 2× price/earnings.

Under Menem's administration, and with the establishment of free market policies, a second wave of investors has entered the market. During 1991, new regional funds increased foreign participation in the market, amounting to about 4% of market capitalization.

The Deregulation Decree issued on October 31, 1991, which eliminated capital gains tax for foreigners, has transformed this market into one of the most liberal ones in the world. Without limitations on holdings, no restrictions on time of investment, free entrance and exit through the foreign exchange market, and no capital gains tax, an increasing interest among foreign institutional investors is expected.

Operations

Among the eleven Argentinean stock exchanges, Buenos Aires' is the most active. The other exchanges are: Bahia Blanca, Cordoba, La Plata, Mar de Plata, Mendoza, Rio Negro, Rosario, San Juan, Santa Fe, and Tucuman.

The address of the Buenos Aires Stock Exchange is:
25 de mayo 534
1002 capital Federal
Republica Argentina
Phone: 54-1-313-5231 or 33
Fax: 54-1-312-9332

Institutional Framework

Buenos Aires Stock Exchange (BASE)

The BASE is a nonprofit civil association in which representatives of diverse economic activities may participate. Its main functions are to: authorize the listings of corporate stocks; control the submitting of quarterly and annual reports and penalize the companies that fail to do so; publish corporate balance sheets and disclose related information; and publish daily the traded stock exchange securities prices.

The stock exchange has a computerized system to process operations at the trading floor. During trading hours (from 11:00 a.m. to 3:00 p.m., Monday through Friday) electric panels display quoted prices and trading volumes on each stock, coupon (in case of issue), public and corporate bonds, and options. Trading is performed through open auction with bids and offers on individual stocks. The selling broker is responsible for filling out the sales contract in triplicate and delivering the third copy to the stock exchange officials. The trade is then entered into the stock exchange's computer system for registration, clearing, and settlement.

Due to a significant increase in the traded volume, block trades are now placed more often among the brokers who trade for foreigners. A futures option market has been developed although short selling is not allowed.

Mercado de Valores de Buenos Aires (MVBA)

The MVBA is a corporation with 250 shares in stock capital. The holding of one share is required to be a stockbroker. The MVBA regulates brokers' activities, reviews their books, and defines and regulates subsequent transactions. It also guarantees trading between brokers.

Comision Nacional de Valores (CNV)

As an official agency representing the Securities Exchange Commission, its functions are to authorize the public offers of securities (after authorization companies must request permission from the stock exchange to be listed) and to control the compliance with the regulation of trading activities and accounting standards which corporations must follow.

Caja de Valores (CV)

The CV is the clearing house. Its main holders are BASE and MVBA (90%). The CV receives and keeps, on a collective deposit basis, securities negotiated at the stock exchange and securities under trust. Only stock exchange brokers, OTC brokers, financial agencies, and mutual funds can be depositors. Every depositor holds a subaccount registered with the CV.

Over the Counter Market (OTC)

Most financial agencies and money exchange offices operate outside of the BASE premises. Trading in counters is connected to each other through telephone extensions; these operations are heavily concentrated in government bonds. The participation in stock trading is insignificant.

Commissions and Other Costs

Commissions have recently been deregulated and today are established by individual brokers. They generally vary between .5% and .9% for institutional investors (Table 17-5). Transfer and stamp taxes have been abolished and duties are collected by the BASE and MVBA.

Table 17-5

	Commission	BASE* Duty	MVBA* Duty
Public Bonds			
Purchase	deregulated	0.02	0.02
Sale	deregulated	0.02	0.02
Equities			
Purchase	deregulated	0.2	0.2
Sale	deregulated	0.2	0.2
Corporate Bonds			
Purchase	deregulated	0.02	0.02
Sale	deregulated	0.02	0.02

*Reduced from March 1992.

Foreign Investment Taxation and Foreign Exchange Regulations

The Argentinean market has dropped its barriers to foreign investors to a minimum, as can be seen in Table 17-6. Since late 1991, it has been one of the most "open" emerging markets.

Settlement Procedures

Transactions are registered through BASE and cleared and settled by the MVBA, which guarantees all trades among brokers.

Ninety-five percent equity settlements are done on a 72-hour basis. Physical transfer of stock certificates has been gradually replaced by the Caja de Valores (CV), via book entry.

Legislation, Regulation, and Disclosure

Law #17811, known as the Statute of Public Offering (Ley de Oferta Publica), establishes the legal framework for public offering of securities in Argentina. The law provides disclosure requirements and its compliance is regulated by the Comision Nacional de Valores (CNV). The CNV oversees compliance requirements for those who issue publicly traded securities. The regulations require full disclosure of:

- legal aspects of incorporation or registration,

- names and personal data of directors, managers, controllers, and other officers of the issuer, and

- balance sheets and other economic and financial information on the issuer.

Table 17-6   Changes in Treatment of Foreign Investors

	Past	Present
Foreign Ownership Regulation	2% of stock capital or U.S. $2 million	No limits
Capital Repatriation	Restricted	No limit time
Capital Gains	36% of adjusted gain or 18% of net sales proceeds	Nonexistent
Foreign Exchange Control	Existent	Nonexistent
Transfer Tax	0.5	Nonexistent

Issuers are required to submit their balance sheets and any other material information to the CNV. Balance sheets must be published quarterly and audited annually. Public offerings must be made on the basis of a prospectus which must comply with specific disclosure requirements set by CNV regulations and approved by the CNV.

The Stock Exchange of Buenos Aires requires similar disclosure from quoted companies. Both the CNV and the Stock Exchange of Buenos Aires have legal power to enforce disclosure regulations and impose sanctions in case of noncompliance on the issuer and its managers. The sanctions range from fees to the prohibition of the securities' public offering.

Since December 26, 1991, General Resolution #190 of the CNV regulates insider trading and takeovers. It describes the duty of listed companies to disclose pertinent information as well as the duty of controlling shareholders to inform of all relevant trades. It also regulates other items related to the transparency and reliability of the securities market.

Research

Bolsa de Comercia de Buenos Aires publishes a daily bulletin and a weekly magazine. Instituto Argentino Mercado de Capitales, an entity belonging to the Mercado de Valores de Buenos Aires, provides corporate news.

Local broker research was nonexistent until a few years ago. At the present time, Banco General de Negocios, Compania de Servicios Bursatiles, Merchant Bankers Asociados, and Baring Securities Argentina are providing research for foreigners.

Brokers

MVBA ranking: (December 1991)

1. Compania de Servicios Bursatiles S.A.

2. Rabello y Cia. S.A.

3. Aldazabal y Cia.

4. Martorell y Cia.

5. Titulos Valores S.A.

6. Interacciones S.A.

7. M.B.A. Sociedad de Bolsa S.A.

8. Quilburs S.A. Sociedad de Bolsa

9. Mascaretti y Cia. S.A.

10. Tutelar Bursatil S.A.

Company Profiles[*]

Alpargatas

Textiles   Established in 1883, Alpargatas is a large textile company that possesses 23 plants and employs 14,500 people. Its operations are organized in two main divisions: textiles and footwear, which account for 45% and 55% respectively of total sales. Within the textile division, the share by products is the following: denim (cloth for jeans) 50%, color line (cloth for fabric) 15%, home line (towels, blankets, sheets, canvass) 15%, and exports (composed mainly of denim) 20%. In the footwear division, the product share is more concentrated: sport shoes 60%, casual shoes 25% and exports 15%. Since Alpargatas' brands are well recognized in Argentina, its domestic market share for its main product lines are high: denim 70%, color line 20%, home line 15% (but, in this segment, the market is very fragmented), sport shoes 42%, and casual shoes 26%. Estimated CY91 sales are $400 m, 17% of which is exported. The main export markets for Alpargatas' goods are: Germany (24% of exports), U.S. (18%), Brazil (15%), and Italy (12%). Alpargatas also participates in the insurance and fishing business through different subsidiaries. The San Remigio group controls 34.5% of the company, the Roberts group owns 17.5% and the remaining 48% is in the hands of 20,000 shareholders.

Astra

Oil/Petrochemicals   Astra is the second largest oil exploration company in Argentina. It sells all of its oil to YPF (the state oil company), at prices adjusted monthly to reflect changes in operating costs. It also has interests in petrochemicals, marine transport, and construction. Astra has a 50% participation in Pecten, an oil consortium involving Shell (U.S.A.) and Shell Argentina y Texaco (U.S.A.). Astra represents nearly 5% of the Argentinean index. The Gruneisen family owns a controlling interest, with float being only about 20%. Ten percent of the outstanding shares are listed in Zurich.

[*]Company profiles are provided by the editors.

Banco Frances

Banking   Established in 1875, Banco Frances (BF) is the fifth largest Argentine private commercial bank in terms of deposits ($250 mn) and the fourth largest based on net worth (with $163 mn, it ranks eighth among all the existing banks). In June 1991, the revenue breakdown was: commissions and fees (mainly from the use of automatic teller machines, credit cards, foreign exchange transactions, and savings accounts charges) 80% and interest revenues (spread) 20%. BF operates 58 branches (four have just been transferred from Banco Santander to BF in accordance with a purchase agreement established last year) and employs 1,500 people. It has representative offices in Uruguay and works closely with Banco Nacional in Brazil. BF controls an offshore company, Grand Cayman (net worth of U.S. $12 mn), and has minority stakes in Banelco (around 8%) and Visa S.A. It also manages a mutual fund which ranks fifth in terms of net worth ($4 mn). SudAmericana de Inversiones, which belongs to the Otero Monsegur family, has a 40% stake in the bank. Constantini, the owner of a financial company, recently acquired a 20% capital participation from Alpargatas. The remaining 40% is free floating.

Comercial del Plata S.A.

Holding Company   Founded in 1927, Comercial del Plata (CP) is a holding company involved in oil exploration and distribution, railways, engineering and construction, telecommunications, insurance, agribusiness, and investment management (in Zurich). About 30% of its outstanding shares are quoted in Zurich, most of them held in Swiss hands.

CP owns 230 gas stations throughout the country and operates an oil storage facility in Buenos Aires' Port which is used by third parties. CP has been active in the privatization process.

Galicia (Banco de Galicia y Buenos Aires)

Banking   Banco de Galicia y Buenos Aires, established in 1905, is a commercial bank, with 4,000 employees and 175 branches, of which 60% are concentrated in and around Buenos Aires. It also has four branches in the United States, Brazil, and Chile. Three families, Escasany, Ayerza, and Braun, hold 85% to 90% of the outstanding shares.

Garovaglio y Zorraquin

Petrochemicals   Garovaglio is a major petrochemical producer which also owns 61% of IPAKO, a major Argentinean polyethylene producer which, in turn has a major participation in Petroquimica Bahia Blanca, the only producer of ethylene in Argentina. Garovaglio also has a polypropylene joint venture with Shell which started operations in 1992. Garovaglio also owns 40,000 hectares for cattle raising and agricultural production and owns Inter-American, S.A., the 15th largest insurance company in Argentina.

IPAKO

Petrochemicals   Established in 1956, IPAKO is engaged in the production and marketing of petrochemicals, holding a 76% market share in polyethylene. The company owns an ethylene and polyethylene plant in the Buenos Aires province (capacity: 15,000 tons/year) and interest in two major affiliates, Petroquimica Bahia Blanca (PBB) and Polisur. PBB, Argentina's largest supplier of ethylene, is 21% owned by IPAKO, 51% by the state and the balance held by other private firms (11% Electrocolor, 5.5% Indupa, 9.5% Japanese C.Itoh, and 2% Induclor). Polisur produces low-density polyethylene (capacity 210,000 tons/year) using ethylene from PBB. After acquiring the remaining 30% stake in the hands of the government in 1990, IPAKO then sold 10% to the IFC, thus currently holding 90% of Polisur. In association with Shell, IPAKO (51% ownership) is completing the Petroken project aimed at producing 100,000 tons/year of polypropylene. The firm also has interests in companies engaged in trading, mining, financial services, and timber. FY91 unconsolidated sales amounted to $109 m. The Garovaglio group controls 60% of IPAKO. The remaining capital is diversified among the IFC 3.85%, foreign funds 7%, domestic funds 3%, and other investors 26%.

Juan Minetti

Cement   Juan Minetti is the second largest cement producer in an oligopoly market composed of seven firms. The company has five plants, three of which are currently operating (Malagueno in Cordoba, Puesto Viejo in Jujuy, and Panqueua in Mendoza) while the remaining two have been shut down. The potential capacity of the operating plants is 1.4 million tons. The revenue breakdown is: portland cement 85% and special cement (used in masonry and in oil fields) 15%. Estimated sales for CY91 were around 830,000 tons (59% capacity), with a 19% market share. The cost structure is as follows: fixed production costs (related to maintenance of its plants and equipment) 70%, wages 14%, energy (gas and electricity) 11%, and raw material 5%. About 98% of the company's cement production is channeled into the domestic market whereas only 2% is exported to neighboring countries such as Chile and Brazil. Minetti currently employs 1,040 people (795 tons/employee). The Minetti family holds 80% of the company's shares. The float represents 20% (since August 1991, Salomon Brothers has acquired a 3%-5% stake).

Ledesma

Conglomerate   Ledesma is a leading manufacturer of refined sugar (50% to 55% of total revenues) and paper (35% to 40%). The company is also engaged in the production of an alcohol-based fuel, fresh fruit juices, corn syrup, horse breeding and cattle raising, insurance, transportation, and pension fund management. Exports currently account for over 45% of total sales. Established in 1914, Ledesma is one of the largest firms in Argentina, as measured by market capitalization. The Ledesma family controls 90% of the outstanding shares.

Molinos Rio de la Plata

Food Processing   Molinos Rio de la Plata, founded in 1931, is one of Argentina's leading food processing companies with total fiscal year 1988/89 sales of U.S. $377 million. The company's primary product lines include oilseeds (soybean, sunflower, and cotton) processed for export and domestic consumption (45% of total revenues), wheat products (41%), yerba, an Argentine beverage, (8%) and miscellaneous items (6%). Many of Molinos' domestic products are market leaders with strong brand recognition among consumers; Molinos' oilseed products hold a 40% market share, flour 20%-25%, rice 18%-20% and mayonnaise now 100%. Molinos employs 4,300 people and has twelve plants, ten storage facilities, and 16 food distribution centers throughout Argentina. Molinos is considered the food division of Bunge y Born, a large Argentine-based multinational, which owns majority interest in Molinos.

Perez Companc

Oil/Petrochemical   Perez Companc is Argentina's largest private sector group with main activities in oil exploration and petrochemical production and through its subsidiary, SADE, it is also involved in construction and telecommunications. The company has investments in forestry, finance, agriculture, supermarket, coffee, and chocolate industries. The company owns 20% of Carrefour, a supermarket chain.

Renault

Auto & Auto Parts   Renault, which began operating 20 years ago, is one of the three leading car manufacturing companies in Argentina. It has a 31% market share and has capacity to produce 70,000 cars/year. Spare parts accounted for 15% of sales, and exports during 1990 were expected to represent 23% of sales. The company owns a manufacturing plant in Chile which produces transmissions for all of the cars Renault manufactures in Argentina. Its traditional export markets include France, Uruguay, Chile, Venezuela, Colombia, Bolivia, U.S.A., and Mexico. In 1989, the company initiated exports of car bodies to Yugoslavia, traffic ambulances to Peru, R-12 and R-9 car models to Angola, and began selling car parts to General Motors in Brazil. Renault (France) owns 72% of the outstanding shares.

18

VENEZUELA

Luis Eduardo Muro
M.M. Fintec
Venezuela

Over the past decade, the Venezuelan stock market has developed from a small-sized emerging market into a medium-sized market. Its capitalization has grown from $ 2.7 billion to $ 11.2 billion, and its trading volume from $ 60 million to $ 3.2 billion, between 1980 and 1991.

During the 1980s, the Venezuelan market had six "up" years in inflation adjusted terms and four "down" years, exhibiting considerable volatility and net losses which were made up by a spectacular rise in 1990. For the period from 1980 through June 1991, the average market return was 44.0%, clearly above the average inflation and devaluation rates of 23.4% and 26.4% respectively.

Important changes have taken place in the Venezuela capital market, and some others are about to occur. In 1990, the market was opened to foreign investment and mutual funds started. A stronger privatization program is developing, the national pension fund system is expected to be replaced in the near future, and the Caracas Stock Exchange is being modernized. All these efforts and realities point to a consolidation and growth period for the Venezuelan capital market in the future.

Overview of the Market

History of the Stock Market

The first attempt to establish a stock exchange in Venezuela took place in 1805 when a group of businessmen founded the Commerce Exchange in Caracas which functioned until 1821.

More than 70 years later in 1893, the Caracas Chamber of Commerce adopted the constitution of the Caracas Stock Exchange, but it was not until April 1947, when activities really began with an initial listing of 18 stocks and six government bonds.

Today, the Caracas Stock Exchange is a private company which is administered by a board of directors consisting of five members who are elected every two years; three of these directors represent the stock exchange members and one is elected by the Chamber of Commerce, and one by the National Securities Commission. The director chosen by the Chamber of Commerce has traditionally also been nominated president of the stock exchange.

In June 1958 a second exchange, the Miranda State Commerce Exchange, opened in Caracas and caused a division in the market. Neither of the two exchanges had enough trading volume to justify their separate existence, but it was not until 1974 that the two exchanges were merged.

The overthrow of President Perez Jimenez in 1958 halved prices. However, the price index recovered somewhat during the 1960s. Only seven new issues were released between 1958 and 1965, bringing the total to 96 listings in 1965, of which fewer than 80 were ever traded. Share trading remained stagnant at about U.S. $8-12 million annually during the 1960s, with turnover declining from 28% to 7% in the same period.

The first Capital Market Law was enacted in January 1973, followed by a second in April 1975, in an effort to broaden share ownership, stimulate the market, and protect investors. The 1973 law established a National Securities Commission and introduced the concept of mutual funds, capital companies (SACA - Sociedad Anonima de Capital Autorizado), and stock companies (SAICA - Sociedad Anonima Inscrita de Capital Abierto) which must have at least 50% of their capital held by the public but pay a lower corporate tax rate, in exchage. During the 1970s, the stock market had a six-year period (from 1971 to 1977) of positive returns, but from 1978 to 1981 the stock index declined. A second growth period began in 1982 and ended in 1987.

In 1986, a change in the government's attitude towards the capital market was discernible. The National Securities Commission (NSC), without giving up its regulatory capacity, minimized procedures for new offerings of securities. In June 1986, the constitution of the Maracaibo Stock Exchange was approved and it began operations the same year after several years of preparation. However, volume has been far below that of the Caracas exchange, accounting for less than 1% of the Caracas Stock Exchange trading volume from 1987 to 1990.

In 1988 and 1989 the stock market reflected the problems in the country's economy. Prices and trading volume dropped in nominal as well as real or dollar-adjusted terms. After a new economic program was adopted following elections which brought President Perez back to power, the market had a spectacular rise in 1990 followed by a consolidation during 1991.

Recent and Expected Structural Changes in the Stock Market

In 1990, the regulations for foreign investments were modified. Decree No. 727, published in Official Gazette No. 34.397, allows free movements of capital and dividends in or out of the country without restrictions. Foreign investors can buy and sell shares on the Venezuelan stock exchanges as long as they register their investment with the SIEX (Superintendencia de Inversiones Extranjeras). Total opening is contemplated but, for the moment, the banking industry and some basic industries have maximum levels of foreign participation of 19.9% and 49.9%. Another important development is the creation of six mutual funds during the past two years.

Privatization is one of the most important goals of the new economic program and may increase the number of listed companies. Banco Occidental de Descuento is an example. It was privatized by mid-1990, and today is traded actively on the stock exchange. The government is also studying a new law which includes a change in the national pension system, creating privately managed pension funds and, along the lines of the Chilean system (see Chapter 16), allowing fund selection by employees. Estimates are for $2.6 billion in the first year and $11 billion in five years to be managed by the new pension system. All these movements are supported by the modernization of the Caracas Stock Exchange including headquarters, new computers and software, and new trading and clearance procedures to support the growth and credibility of the market.

Stock Market Performance

From 1980 to June 1991, the average market return was 44.0%, clearly above the average inflation of 23.4% and the average devaluation of 26.4%. Table 18-1 presents the evolution of the Caracas Stock Exchange Market Index, the change in the index, and the bolivar devaluation from 1980 to 1991.

Market Structure

Market Size

As of December 31, 1991, total market capitalization stood at $ 11.2 billion. The number of listed companies was 122 in 1990 versus 60 in 1989. Table 18-2 presents the evolution of total market capitalization in bolivars and dollars and the number of listed companies in the market from 1980 to 1991.

Table 18-1   Stock Market Performance (1980–1991)

Date	Market Index	Change in Index Percentage	Inflation Rate Percentage	Currency Devaluation Percentage
1991	29.316	63.9%	30.0%	22.2%
1990	17.891	589.3%	40.7%	17.2%
1989	2.754	–28.8%	–84.5%	–10.5%
1988	3.866	–1.6%	–29.5%	–28.2%
1987	3.928	87.9%	28.1%	43.6%
1986	2.090	155.7%	11.6%	42.3%
1985	.817	38.9%	11.4%	18.1%
1984	.588	43.9%	12.2%	1.8%
1983	.409	29.6%	6.4%	–188.4%
1982	.315	14.6%	9.8%	0.0%
1981	.275	–7.4%	–16.2%	0.0%
1980	.297	2.9%	–21.6%	0.0%

Source: Central Bank of Venezuela and Caracas Stock Exchange

Table 18-2   Stock Market Size (1980–1991)

Date	Market Capitalization Venezuelan Currency (billions)	$ U.S. (billions)	Number of Listings
1991	681.838	11.214	66
1990	415.893	8.391	66
1989	50.277	1.156	60
1988	67.546	1.816	60
1987	67.077	2.278	110
1986	34.275	1.510	108
1985	16.238	1.128	108
1984	—	—	116
1983	12.005	2.792	—
1982	10.368	2.415	98
1981	10.476	2.441	—
1980	11.407	2.657	—

Source: IFC - Emerging Stock Markets Factbook, Caracas Stock Exhange & M.M. Fintec

The Stock Exchanges

Until 1986, the Caracas Stock Exchange was the only stock exchange operating in the country. At that time, the Maracaibo Stock Exchange opened, but the trading volume has remained far below that of the Caracas Stock Exchange. Some brokers have been using the Maracaibo Stock Exchange to increase their services and clients, but the big difference between the two exchanges remains with the Caracas Stock Exchange keeping its leading position.

Both the Caracas and Maracaibo exchanges are open five working days. The Caracas Stock Exchange operates from 10:30 a.m. to 12:30 p.m. and the Maracaibo Stock Exchange from 11:00 a.m. to 12:30 p.m. The exchanges are not interconnected in real time, but are linked by Reuters. The addresses for both exchanges are listed below:

Bolsa de Valores de Caracas
Avenida Urdaneta
Santa Capilla a Carmelitas
Banco Central de Venezuela
Piso 19
Caracas, Distrito Federal
Tel: 81 51 41

Bolsa de Valores de Maracaibo
Calle 96, entre avenidas 4 y 5,
Banco Central de Venezuela
Piso 9
Maracaibo
Estado Zulia
Tel: 22 54 82 - 22 54 84

Dealing Procedures

On the Caracas Stock Exchange, trading takes place by open outcry around a circular desk. Bids and offers are repeated by the stock exchange official inside the desk closing trade by trade. Prices are then posted on blackboards around the trading room.

Since April 1991, any selling broker is obligated to present to the stock exchange a certificate of ownership for the traded shares to be able to settle a transaction. This procedure will disappear when all the closing and clearance steps take place automatically.

Depending on the time to settle the trades, six types of transactions are accepted on The Caracas Stock Exchange: "de hoy" to be settled the same day, "de contado" to be settled the next day, "de fuera," "de fuera a voluntad del vendedor," and "de fuera a voluntad del comprador" to be settled in eight days and "A # DIAS," to be settled in a maximum of 120 days.

All brokers have to apply the same brokerage commissions for stock trading. The board of directors of the Caracas Stock Exchange establishes brokerage commissions but requires the approval of the National Securities Commission. The brokerage commission is calculated as follows:

Amount of the Trade (Bolivars)	Commission (% + Bolivars)
A. <= 20,000	0.90%
B. > 20,000 and <= 40,000	0.85% + 10 Bs
C. > 40,000 and <= 60,000	0.75% + 40 Bs
D. > 60,000 and <= 80,000	0.65% + 90 Bs
E. > 80,000 and <= 100,000	0.55% + 160 Bs
F. > 100,000	0.50% + 200 Bs

Source: Caracas Stock Exchange.

Market regulations do not forbid insider trading; however, the Caracas Stock Exchange does. The penalty for a trade made with inside information is that a third party may ask to have the trade annulled. It is doubtful, however, that cancellation can be enforced by law. Insider trading rules are expected to be enforced, and the access of foreign investors to the Venezuelan capital market will be broadened in order to make these markets more attractive.

All Venezuelan stockbrokers must post a bond of 100,000 bolivars which serves as indemnification to customers of any broker who has lost money because of fraud or misdealings. The amount of this bond is considered insufficient in normal practice in Venezuela, although it has not been increased by the NSC. There is no other form of compensation, except for direct action against the broker.

The Venezuelan Capital Market Law permits stock transfer agents although they are not compulsory and are used by very few companies. In those cases where a company has a stock transfer agent, the risks and responsibilities for the transfers of securities are in the hands of the transfer agent as well as the broker.

Turnover

From 1980 to 1989, the average annual trading value and turnover was $82 million (or less than $500.00/day) and 4.9% respectively, but during 1991 the trading value and turnover ratio increased to $3.2 billion and 33%. Table 18-3 presents the evolution of the total market capitalization in dollars, trading volumes, and turnover statistics from 1980 to 1991.

Table 18-3   Stock Market Trading Volume and Turnover (1980 – 1991)

Date	Market Capitalization U.S. $ billion	Trading Value billion	Turnover
1991	11.214	3.240	33.1%
1990	8.391	2.232	43.0%
1989	1.156	.093	6.1%
1988	1.816	.221	10.9%
1987	2.278	.148	8.1%
1986	1.510	.052	4.1%
1985	1.128	.031	—
1984	—	.027	—
1983	2.792	.059	2.3%
1982	2.415	.082	3.4%
1981	2.441	.047	1.8%
1980	2.657	.060	2.3%

Source: IFC - Emerging Stock Markets Factbook, Caracas Stock Exchange and M.M. Fintec

Composition of Market Capitalization by Industries

In Venezuela there is no formal publication that clearly divides or groups the companies listed in the stock market by industries. Table 18-4 gives an approximate estimate of the composition of the market capitalization by industries at the end of 1990. The table is prepared following the basic structure of the Caracas Stock Exchange Index and a few sources of information available in the market.

Ten Largest Stocks by Market Capitalization

One of the basic conditions for the listing of companies is a minimum paid-up capital of 20 million bolivars. The top ten stocks in Venezuela's market represent more than 65% of total market capitalization. Tables 18-5 and 18-6 present the ten largest stocks in the first half of 1991 and at the end of 1990.

Ten Most Actively Traded Stocks

The ten most-traded stocks in the Caracas Stock Exchange accounted for more than 90% the past 18 months (1990-June 1991). Tables 18-7 and 18-8 present the ten most actively traded stocks in the first half of 1991 and during 1990.

Table 18-4   Market Capitalization By Industry (December 1990)

Industry	Weight
Financial Industries	
Banking and Financial Services	50.7%
Investment Companies	3.1%
Stock Exchange	0.5%
Real Estate Companies	0.2%
SUBTOTAL (FINANCE)	54.5%
Nonfinancial Industries	
Construction	18.8%
Conglomerates and Manufacturing Companies	10.9%
Utilities	8.1%
Agriculture and Food	3.0%
Textile	2.9%
Pulp and Paper	1.8%
SUBTOTAL (NONFINANCE)	45.5%
TOTAL	100.0%

Source: Caracas Stock Exchange and M.M.Fintec

Table 18-5   Top Ten Venezuelan Stocks Ranked by Market Capitalization

Company	1991 Market Capitalization (U.S.$ MM)	% of Total Market Capitalization
1 ELECTRICIDAD	1,515	14%
2 BCO DE VENEZUELA	1,414	10%
3 BCO PROVINCIAL	932	8%
4 SIVENSA	561	5%
5 VENCEMOS	425	4%
6 BCO MERCANTIL	415	4%
7 BCO VEN. CREDITO	357	3%
8 CORIMON	294	3%
9 FIVENEZ	293	3%
10 SUDAMTEX	211	2%

Table 18-6   Top Ten Venezuelan Stocks Ranked by Value Traded

Company	1991 Value Traded (U.S.$ MM)	% of Total Value Traded
1 ELECTRICIDAD	1,058	33%
2 SIVENSA	545	17%
3 BCO DE VENEZUELA	365	11%
4 BCO PROVINCIAL	304	9%
5 MANTEX	190	6%
6 FIVENEZ	124	4%
7 BCO MERCANTIL	107	3%
8 VENCEMOS	85	3%
9 VENEPAL	64	2%
10 SUDAMTEX	33	1%

Table 18-7   Ten Most Actively Traded Stocks From January-June 1991

Company Name	Trading Billion Bolivars	Value Million U.S. $	Percentage of Total Trading Value
1. Electricidad de Caracas	59.768	1,057.7	32.6%
2. Sivensa	30.809	545.2	16.8%
3. Banco de Venezuela	20.603	364.6	11.3%
4. Banco Provincial	17.173	303.9	9.4%
5. Mantex	10.717	189.7	5.9%
6. Fivenez	7.012	124.1	3.8%
7. Banco Mercantil	6.050	107.1	3.3%
8. Vencemos	4.786	84.7	2.6%
9. Venepal	3.626	64.2	2.0%
10. Sudamtex de Venezuela	1.879	33.3	1.0%
Subtotal	165.375	2,926.7	90.3%
Total	181.688	3,240.0	100.0%

Table 18-8   Ten Most Actively Traded Stocks In 1990

Company Name	Trading Billion Bolivars	Value Million U.S. $	Percentage of Total Trading Value
1. Electricidad de Caracas	21.102	456.3	20.4%
2. Banco de Venezuela	18.534	400.7	18.0%
3. Banco Provincial	18.314	396.0	17.7%
4. Sivensa	14.170	306.4	13.7%
5. Vencemos	9.137	197.6	8.9%
6. Mantex	5.288	114.3	5.1%
7. Sociedad Financiera Vzla.	3.357	72.6	3.3%
8. Venepal	3.275	70.8	3.2%
9. Banco Union	2.181	47.2	2.1%
10. Cerveceria Nacional	1.980	42.8	1.9%
Subtotal	97.344	2,104.6	94.3%
Total	103.236	2,232.0	100.0%

Source: Caracas Stock Exchange and M.M.Fintec

Composition of the Local Stock Market Index

The Caracas Stock Exchange Index is calculated with 17 of the principal stocks traded on the stock exchange. The index is composed of 35% financial stocks and 65% of nonfinancial stocks. This index was established in 1989 and its base is January 1971 = 100. Table 18-9 presents the actual composition of the stock market index.

Types of Shares

Two types of shares are traded on the Caracas and Maracaibo stock exchanges— common shares and preferred shares. The main type of stock listed on the Venezuelan stock market is the common share type, but a few cases of preferred shares exist. Almost all shares are in bearer form. All types of shares are regulated by the Venezuelan Commercial Code and by the Venezuelan Capital Market Law.

Table 18-9   Composition of Stock Market Index

Stock	Weight
Financial Stocks	
1. Arrendadora Banvenez	2.5%
2. Banco Mercantil	7.5%
3. Banco Provincial	7.5%
4. Banco de Venezuela	7.5%
5. Sociedad Financiera de Venezuela	5.0%
6. Banco Venezolano de Credito	5.0%
Subtotal (Financial Stocks)	35.0%
Nonfinancial Stocks	
7. Ceramica Carabobo	2.5%
8. Cerveceria Nacional	2.5%
9. Corimon	7.5%
10. Electricidad de Caracas	7.5%
11. Mantex	5.0%
12. Protinal	2.5%
13. Sivensa	7.5%
14. Sudamtex de Venezuela	7.5%
15. Telares Palo Grande	7.5%
16. Venezolana de Cementos (Vencemos)	7.5%
17. Venepal	7.5%
Subtotal (Nonfinancial Stocks)	65.0%
Total	100.0%

Source: Caracas Stock Exchange

Table 18-10 P/E, Dividend Yield and P/BV (1980 - June 1991)

Date	P/E Ratio	Dividend Yield	P/BV Ratio
December 1991	30.5	0.5%	5.5
1990	29.3	0.7%	3.4
1989	6.4	2.2%	5.9
1988	11.4	1.1%	1.4
1987	16.9	0.5%	2.3
1986	9.4	1.3%	3.2
1985	—	3.9%	3.6
1984	—	—	—
1983	—	—	—
1982	—	—	—
1981	—	—	—
1980	—	—	—

Source: IFC-Emerging Stock Market Factbook, Caracas Stock Exchange and M.M.Fintec

Price Earnings Ratio, Dividend Yield, and Other Market Information

The average P/E and P/BV ratio from 1986 to 1989 were 11.0 and 2.6 respectively. Strong increases during 1990 led to high levels of 29.3 and 5.9 for the P/E and P/BV at the end of 1990. Table 18-10 presents the evolution of the price/earnings (P/E) ratio, the dividend yield, and the price/book value (P/BV) ratio from 1980 to 1991.

Major Investors in the Market

Typical investors in the Venezuelan market are banks, mutual funds, insurance companies, investment firms, and brokers who dominate trading volume in the stock market. Private individuals have participated only for periods of time.

Mutual funds appeared two years ago and have been growing very fast. In June 1991, six mutual funds were operating in the market and this number is expected to increase in the short term.

Mutual Funds In The Market

1. Fondo Mutual de Venezuela
2. Fondo Mutual Provincial
3. Fondo Mutual la Ceiba
4. Fondo Mutual Bancor
5. Fondo Mutual Profimerca
6. Fondo Mutual J.D. Cordero

Foreign investors have been active since 1989 when the new economic program began, and restrictions on foreign investment almost disappeared with Decree No. 727 except for trading in bank stocks.

Structure of the Securities Industry

The securities industry in Venezuela has two principal components, the investment banking firms and the brokerage houses, most of them related or integrated with a banking group.

List of Principal Investment Banks

Investment banking firms appeared in Venezuela in 1989. Some of them include brokerage houses, but others prefer to have relations with a group of brokers working on a transaction basis. Some of the principal Venezuelan investment banks include the following:

- Financorp
  CCCT, Sector Yarey, Mezz.2.
  Chuao. Tel: 959 00 02.

- Finantrust-Capitales Noroco
  Torre Banhorien, PH-A, Av Casanova
  con Las Acacias. Tel: 781 74 44.

- M.M.Fintec
  Av. Andrés Bello, Urb. Mariperez,
  Edificio Las Fundaciones, Piso 4.
  Caracas. Tel: 573 69 22.

- Merinvest
  Av. Andrés Bello, Urb. Mariperez,
  Edf. Fondo Comun, Piso 13.
  Caracas. Tel: 574 97 11.

- Oberto, Sosa Y Asociados
  Av. Francisco de Miranda, Urb. Los
  Palos Grandes, Edif. Mene Grande, Mohedano,
  Piso 2. Tel: 285 50 80.

- Venezuelan Asset Management
  Av. Los Chaguaramos, Urb. La Cas-
  tellana, Centro Gerencial Mohedano,
  Oficina 3-D. Tel: 761 07 10.

List of Principal Brokers or Brokerage Houses

There are 55 brokers in the Caracas Stock Exchange, most working with financial groups. Some of the principal brokers include the following:

- Alcantara V. Rafael, Cavelba S.A.
  Edf. Sudameris, piso 9 Ofc.902, Av
  Urdaneta. Tel: 562 13 33.

- Bancaracas Casa de Bolsa C.A.
  Edf. Ibarras, Piso7, Esq Ibarras, Av.
  Urdaneta. Tel: 561 63 21.

- Bancor Mercado de Capitales C.A.
  Torre Europa, Nivel oficinas, Av. Fco
  de Miranda. Tel: 951 00 18.

- Banguaria Mercado de Capitales C.A.
  Torre K.L.M., Piso 12, Av. Romulo
  Gallegos. Sta Eduvigis.Tel: 2835545.

- Banvenez Mercado de Capitales C.A.
  Edif. Bco de Venezuela, Piso 18, Esq.
  Sociedad, Av. Universidad. Tel: 5638055.

- C.A.Sofimara Mercado De Capitales
  Casa de Bolsa "Sofimerca."
  Edf. Grupo Financiero Bancomara
  Av Bolivia. Tel: 781 78 77.

- Capitales Noroco-Casa De Corretaje,C.A.
  Torre Banhorien, PH-A Av Casanova c/Las
  Acacias. Tel: 781 55 33.

- Coronado, Fernando
  Edf. Citibank, Mezzanina, Carmelitas
  a Altagracia. Tel: 82 58 22.

- Escotet Valores C.A.
  Torre Orinoco, P.H, Cruce Calle Orinoco
  c/Veracruz. Las Mercedes. Tel: 920131.

- Financorp Valores C.A.
  C.C.C.T., Sector Yarey, Mezz.2, Of.
  M-2, Chuao. Tel: 959 08 56.

- Flores R., Victor Julio
  Edf. Karam, Piso 4, Ofc.421, Pelota a
  Ibarras, Av. Urdaneta. Tel: 5635039.

- Incorp Casa De Bolsa S.A.
  Edf. Ferrer Palacios, Piso 3, El Rosal
  Tel: 952 34 72.

- Intercambios Valores
  Parque Cristal Oeste, Piso 11, Ofc.
  Top 11-3. Av. Fco de Miranda.

- Intervalores Casa de Bolsa, S.A.
  Centro Gerencial Mohedano, P.H.-B Calle
  Los Chaguaramos, La Castellana.
  Tel: 561 72 08.

- Inversiones y Valores Union
  Torre Grupo Union, Piso 19, Esq. El
  Chorro, Av Universidad. Tel: 5018819

- J.D. Cordero y Asociados
  Edf. Centro Mercantil San Francisco
  Piso 2, Esq. San Francisco, Av. Universidad.
  Tel: 41 24 11.

- Marino Recio Valores C.A.
  Torre Bco Lara, Piso 1, Esq de Mijares
  Tel: 83 55 55.

- Merinvest Sociedad de Corretaje
  Edf. Fondo Comun, Piso 13, Av.Andres
  Bello c/calle Fidel. Tel: 5749711.

- Monteverde Santiago
  Ctro Profesional Eurobuilding, Piso 7
  Ofc. 7-A, Calle La Guairita, Chuao.
  Tel: 92 14 57.

- Morles Gustavo
  Edif. Centro Valores, Piso 7, Ofc 7
  -3, Esq. Luneta Tel: 561 34 87.

- Multinvest Operadora de Bolsa C.A.
  Plaza La Castellana,Torre Multinvest
  Piso 5, La Castellana. Tel: 2633680.

- Profimerca
  Edf. Torre America, Piso 2,Of.2-7
  Esq.Veroes, Av. Urdaneta. 5634054.

- Provincial De Valores
  Ctro. Financiero Provincial, Piso 7,
  Av. Este O, San Bernardino. Tel: 5740911.

- Valores Cavendes
  Torre Cavendes, Piso 16, Av. Fco de
  Miranda. Tel: 284 82 90.

- Valores Latino Casa de Bolsa
  Ctro.Financiero Latino, Piso 13,Ofc.1,2
  y 3. Av. Urdaneta . Tel: 563 92 59.

- Valores Vencred S.A.
  Edf. Centro Mercantil San Francisco
  Piso 4, Ofc.4-7, Esq. San Francisco
  Av. Universidad. Tel: 8011836.

Issues and Regulations for International Investors

Since the beginning of 1990, Venezuelan foreign investment regulations have undergone substantial reforms. Today, a foreign investor can register an operation under guidelines that reduce paperwork to a minimum. It essentially grants the foreign investor the same rights as a domestic investor.

All restrictions on foreigners dealing on the Caracas and Maracaibo Stock Exchanges have been removed, including operations on the exchanges and purchase of shares. The government approved the creation of brokerage firms. As of January 1990, corporations chartered in Venezuela can get authority to act as a broker and can also purchase seats on the Caracas and Maracaibo exchanges.

Decree 727 eliminated limits on repatriation of profits, reinvestment, and the need for prior authorization to invest or to establish subsidiaries or affiliated companies. Furthermore, the new rules mark an end to many of the previous restrictions on the activities of foreign companies; however, some areas such as banking, oil, steel, media, security, and public utility remain subject to special laws as reserved sectors. Furthermore, multinational corporations (i.e., those more than 50% foreign-owned) can now access the capital markets for short- and medium-term debt funding.

The tax on dividends (previously 20%) was eliminated September 1, 1992. At that date the capital gains tax was reduced from a maximum of 50% to a maximum of 30%.

Company Profiles

Banco de Venezuela

Banking   Banco de Venezuela, established in 1890, is the third-largest commercial bank in Venezuela in terms of deposits and second in terms of net worth. It has a 12% market share in lending and 12% in deposits. It operates a nationwide banking system with 162 branches and also operates a branch in New York. Lending operations account for 51% of total income, banking services 10%, treasury 11%, banking services 8%, and other incomes 20%. Banco de Venezuela provides collection and payment services to the government.

Banco de Venezuela's Financial Group includes a mortgage bank (Banco Hipotecario de Venezuela), an industrial leasing company (Arrendadora de Venezuela Banvenez), an investment and financial company (Sociedad Financiera de Venezuela), a bank in Curacao (Banco de Venezuela N.V.), and a bank in Miami (Banco de Venezuela Internacional).

Banco Latino

Banking   Banco Latino, established in 1950, is the second-largest commercial bank in Venezuela in terms of deposits and fourth in terms of net worth. It operates 84 branches throughout the country, has a 12% market share in loans and deposits, and it has been the bank that has grown most in 1990. Lending accounts for 80% of its total income, banking services 8%, treasury operations 4%, and other 8%. It has an affiliated mortgage bank (Banco Hipotecario de Occidente) and a leasing company (Arrendadora Latino).

Banco Mercantil

Banking   Banco Mercantil, established in 1925, is the fourth-largest commercial bank in Venezuela in terms of deposits and third in terms of net worth. It has a 9% market share in loans and 10% in deposits. It operates a nationwide banking system with 107 branches and has operations in London, Frankfurt, New York, Bogota, Lima, Sao Paulo, Panama, Curacao, and Miami. It is the strongest in the retail banking segment. Lending accounts for 67% of its total income, banking services 14%, treasury 17%, and other incomes 2%. The Vollmer Family owns a controlling participation in the bank. Banco Mercantil has several associated companies, including Banco Hipotecario Mercantil, a mortgage bank; Arrendadora Mercantil, an industrial leasing company; and Sociedad Financiera Mercantil, an investment and financial services company.

Banco Provincial

Banking   Banco Provincial is the largest commercial bank in Venezuela in terms of deposits and net worth. It has an 18% market share in loans and 17% in deposits. It operates a nationwide banking system, with 113 branches and branches in Panama and Curacao. Loan operations account for 68% of total income, banking services 7%, treasury operations 8%, and other incomes 17%. Banco Provincial provides collection and payment services to the government.

Banco Provincial is part of a financial group which owns several companies, including an industrial leasing company (Arrendadora Provincial), and an investment and financial company (Sociedad Financiera Provincial).

Banco Union

Banking   Banco Union, established in 1946, is the fifth-largest commercial bank in Venezuela in terms of capital and deposits. It has an 8% market share in loans and deposits. It operates a nationwide banking system with 154 branches and has operations in Panama, New York, Sao Paulo, and Bogota. Lending accounts for 66% of its total income, banking services 16%, treasury 6%, and others 12%.

Banco Union is affiliated with a mortgage bank, an industrial leasing company, and an investment and financial services company.

Corporacion Industrial Montana (CORIMON)

Conglomerate   CORIMON, established in 1949, is one of the ten largest conglomerates in Venezuela. It has broadly diversified operations, with revenues coming from construction (paint and roofing materials) 31%, basic chemicals (resins) 31%, beverage (fruit juice) 20%, and packaging 18%. The company has more than 4,000 employees.

Electricidad de Caracas

Electric Utility   Electricidad de Caracas, established in 1895, is the sole provider of electricity in Caracas, the largest city in Venezuela. Its fuel mix consists mostly of oil and gas. Its distribution transmission network is connected to the nationwide electricity network, providing access to additional power when needed. The company has a capacity of 1,975.5 MW and its operating rate is 86%. Electricity demand is composed of industrial and commercial 61%, residential 36%, and other 3%. The company has approximately 5,240 employees. In 1991, Electricidad de Caracas acquired 5.2% of CANTV, the privatized telecommunications company in an effort to become involved in a broader array of services which may eventually also include the financial management of water and garbage collection companies which are being privatized.

MANTEX

Textile   MANTEX, established in 1951, is one of the Venezuela's largest textile companies. The principal products of MANTEX are artificial and synthetic fibers and filaments for textile industries and material for cigarettes filters. The company's exports account for 29% of total sales in 1990.

Siderurgica Venezolana. (SIVENSA)

Steel   SIVENSA, established in 1948, is the largest private steel company in Venezuela. It derivates 57% of its sales domestically and 43% from exports (mainly to the United States, Korea, and Taiwan). The construction industry represents 35% of the domestic business, replacement auto parts 22%, wire cord market 18%, the oil industry 13%, and original equipment for the car industry 12%. SIVENSA has more than 7,000 employees.

Venezolana de Cementos (VENCEMOS)

Cement   VENCEMOS, established in 1943, is the largest cement company in Venezuela, with a 40% market share domestically and 70% in exports. It has a capacity of 3.5 million tons/year and is operating at 98% of capacity. VENCEMOS exports to the United States (East Coast) and the Caribbean markets, has more than 4,000 employees, and is part of the Mendoza Group, one of the leading industrial groups in the country.

Venezolana de Pulpa y Papel (VENEPAL)

Pulp & Paper   VENEPAL, established in 1954, is Venezuela's largest pulp and paper company, with a 38% share of the domestic market. It has seven plants in Venezuela and a paper manufacturing plant in San Juan, Puerto Rico. The principal products of VENEPAL are writing and printing paper, cardboard, paper bags, special types of paper including waxed paper, plastic containers for milk, and packaging products. VENEPAL is part of the Mendoza Group.

Sources of Information

The major sources of information on the stock market are the National Securities Commission, the Central Bank of Venezuela, and the Caracas and Maracaibo stock exchanges.

All companies which have either shares or bonds or any other type of security authorized for public offering by the NSC, must comply with ordinary reporting requirements under the Securities and Exchange regulations.

In addition to presentation of audited financial statements on an annual basis and unaudited statements semiannually, companies must inform the NSC of salaries and shareholding of the board of directors, dividends, important financial information, and other factors which could affect, in a material manner, the operations of the company. The NSC has adopted a policy of suspending trading of shares of companies which find themselves in financial difficulties.

Since 1990, some financial newspapers, magazines, and TV programs appeared on the market, which continuously present information and analysis about the stock market and its development. Names, addresses, and phone numbers of some helpful institutions and companies which can provide information about the Venezuelan market are listed below:

- Caracas Stock Exchange:

  Avenida Urdaneta de Santa Capilla a Carmelitas. Banco Central de Venezuela. Piso 19. Caracas, Distrito Federal. Tel: 81 51 41

- Maracaibo Stock Exchange:

  Calle 96, entre Avs.4 y 5. Banco Central de Venezuela. Piso 9. Maracaibo, Estado Zulia. Tel: 22 54 82 - 22 54 84

- Central Bank of Venezuela:

  Avenida Urdaneta, de Santa Capilla a Carmelitas. Edificio Banco Central de Venezuela, Caracas, Distrito Federal. Tel: 801 51 11 - 801 53 56

- National Securities Commission: Avenida Urdaneta, de Santa
                                     Capilla a Carmelitas, Edificio
                                     Banco Central de Venezuela,
                                     Caracas. Tel: 81 93 83

- IFC (International Finance Corp.):   1818H Street, N.W. Washington
                                        D.C. 20433, U.S.A.
                                        Tel: 47 71 23

- M.M. Fintec, C.A.:   Avenida Andrés Bello, Urb.
                        Mariperez, Edificio Las
                        Fundaciones, Piso 4. Caracas,
                        Venezuela.
                        Tel: 5736922, 5736299.
                        Fax: 5735620.

- Invest Analysis - A biweekly guide to the Venezuelan Equity Market
                        Apartodo Postal 76.634, El
                        Marqués, Caracas 10 Ave
                        Abraham Lincoln 174 Boulevard
                        de Sabana Grande Edif. Gran
                        Sabana. Piso 1

SECTION **IV**

EUROPE

19

GREECE

Nicolas Bornozis, President
CCF International Finance Corporation
New York, United States

Greece is located at the tip of the Balkans and lies at the southern end of Europe. The country covers 132,000 square km. It is predominantly mountainous. About 70% of the land surface is used for agriculture and 17% is wooded. Greece has a population of 10 million with 58.1% being urban, 11.6% semi-urban, and the remaining 30.3% agricultural. Athens is the capital, with three million inhabitants. In addition, there are about four million Greeks living in Europe, North America, and Australia.

The country's political system is a parliamentary democracy and has been since 1975, when a national plebiscite absolved the previous system of constitutional monarchy.

Since 1981 Greece has been a full member of the European Economic Community.

Political Stabilization

Between 1981 and 1989 Greece was under Socialist administration. This was followed by a period of political instability, as two inconclusive elections in 1989 produced coalition governments. Finally, the elections of April 1991 brought the conservative party back to power with 46.8% of the vote. The current government has a majority of 152 out of the 300 members of the Parliament. National elections are scheduled to take place with a span no longer than every four years. The last elections were in April 1990.

Economy

The stabilization and restructuring of the economy is the top priority of the current government. Greece's economic performance in the 1980s has been mediocre. The economy has been characterized by high inflation (22% in 1990), a large public-sector deficit (20.9% of GDP in 1990), and a growing current-account deficit (5.4% of GDP in 1990).

The government has adopted a three-year plan (1991-1993) aimed at reversing the economic decline and removing the structural imbalances inhibiting growth in the economy. This plan has two main elements.

The first element is a stabilization program that aims to increase revenues and decrease expenses. On the revenue side, new taxes have been imposed, the tax base is being expanded by gradually including groups that were not subject to income tax (such as the farmers), and the tax collection system is being overhauled to curtail the substantial tax evasion. On the expense side, the automatic wage indexation was abolished in 1991, and the government budget has been reduced.

The second element of the plan addresses the fact that Greece's problems are primarily structural, reflecting the concessionary and interventionist policies of several previous administrations. To counteract this, in 1990 the government passed an economic infrastructure law whose objective is to reduce the size of the public sector, decrease government intervention, and liberalize the economy.

The new law introduced a range of sweeping changes. The public sector was redefined, opening several of its activities to the private sector. Banking is no longer part of the public sector, which means that financial institutions will eventually be allowed to operate under market conditions. The problematic companies that have drained the country to the toll of U.S. $1 billion annually are slowly privatized or liquidated. New investment incentives were provided in the form of tax allowances tied to the performance of the investment. In addition, the labor market was partly liberalized and the stock exchange reforms that were passed in 1988 were further expanded in 1991.

This strategy sets the stage for a gradual economic rebound and, if pursued consistently, can lead to a long-lasting recovery. Its implementation has been slower than was hoped. Nevertheless, it continues despite strong opposition from several groups. The government has the support of the population, as confirmed by the October 1991 municipal elections, and after almost a year and half in power it appears increasingly stable.

These efforts, which are steps in the right direction, receive strong support from the EEC. In February of 1991, EEC approved an ECU 2.2 billion (U.S. $2.97 billion) loan to Greece, which will be used to finance several infrastructural and developmental projects. The first tranche of ECU 1 billion was transferred in February. The disbursement of the second tranche of ECU 600 million in early 1992 is contingent on satisfactory progress achieved on the economic front.

The government's targets are quite ambitious. By 1993, they expect to bring inflation from 22% down to 7%, reduce the balance of payments deficit from 5.4% to 3.0% of GDP, and reduce public sector borrowing from 20.9% to 3.0% of GDP. In 1994, Greece plans to join the EMS.

The results so far have been encouraging. Given the restrictive monetary and fiscal policies to stabilize the economy, domestic demand is in decline and overall GDP growth is slow. Inflation was projected at 17.5% by the end of August 1991, with the expectation that it would be lowered to 16% by year end from 22% last year. Despite the adverse effects of the Gulf crisis on oil prices and tourism, the situation in the balance of payments has been improving. In the first half of 1991, the current account deficit shrank to $2.2 billion, compared to $2.8 billion for the same period last year. It is expected that in 1991 it will be reduced to $2.6 billion from $3.6 billion in 1990. Furthermore, it is anticipated that the deficit will be covered by private capital inflows eliminating the need for additional foreign borrowings. The reduction in the PSBR has been lower than expected due to the slower progress of the privatization program.

Looking to the future, the strategy formulated by the Greek government is the appropriate one. If it is implemented, then Greece has a good chance for an economic rebound.

The Upturn of the Private Sector

In spite of the demise of the public sector and its effects on the overall economy, the private sector managed to achieve an economic upturn that began in 1989. This started with an economic stabilization program implemented by the previous administration in 1987. At the same time, generous sector grants partially provided by the EEC boosted private investment for the first time in many years. Most sector grants went to the replacement of obsolete machinery and equipment. The relaxation of credit for housing resulted in increased residential construction activity. Finally, the recovery in real household income spurred private consumption. All these factors contributed to an increase in the activity of the private sector and, coupled with productivity gains and lower wage costs, resulted in sharply improved profitability. European companies were attracted and started buying minority or majority stakes in several Greek corporations.

Greece is currently in a period of slow growth and the priority is to combat the structural imbalances of the economy (Table 19-1 and 19–2). Therefore, the gains by the private sector will not come from expanded economic activity. They could come, however, from the deregulation and liberalization of the economy.

Table 19-1   Percentage Change on Annual Total Investment

	Greece	EEC	USA
1961-1973	10.0	5.7	4.5
1974-1982	-1.9	-0.5	-0.6
1983	-1.3	0.0	8.8
1984	-5.7	1.3	15.9
1985	5.2	2.4	6.9
1986	-6.2	3.8	2.0
1987	-7.8	5.5	4.1
1988	9.0	8.4	5.4
1989	8.6	6.8	1.6
1990e	2.9	4.4	-0.4
1991e	2.9	2.9	-1.0
1992e	4.7	4.2	3.3

Source: EEC

Table 19-2   Real Unit Labor Costs (1980 = 100), (Nominal unit labor costs divided by DGP deflator)

	Greece	EEC	USA
1961-1970	104.4	96.8	96.9
1981	100.0	100.0	100.0
1981	106.3	100.7	98.6
1990e	103.5	93.0	99.0
1991e	101.3	92.8	100.4
1992e	98.0	92.2	100.3

Source: EEC

Changing Picture of the Greek Economy

The following briefly explains the changing picture of the Greek economy. These are the most active industries and the ones that will be most affected by the new economic reality in Greece.

Banking and Finance

The banking sector has been dominated by a number of state-controlled banks operating within a system of strict and protectionist regulation. Two banks have been owned by the private sector and recently several new privately-owned banks have been established. There is also a large number of foreign banks, which control only a small portion of the Greek market.

Commercial banks in Greece have been obliged to channel the bulk of their deposits to the financing of the public sector. The primary reserve requirement reached 56.5% of the deposits, with part of it blocked at rates set by the Bank of Greece. The needs of the problematic companies and of other categories of subsidized borrowers absorbed another important part of their resources. Furthermore, until 1987, interest rates on loans and deposits were set by the Bank of Greece, and a number of profitable activities such as residential loans and consumer lending did not exist or were restricted. Finally, the inclusion of banks in the public sector led to overstaffing and low productivity.

The government has embarked on a program to liberalize and eventually privatize the banking sector. Several smaller state-controlled banks are passing to private ownership and several new bank charters have been granted. The bigger banks are proceeding with a restructuring and privatization of their industrial holdings, which will allow them to stop the drain on their resources and allocate funds to profitable activities. This will also have a positive impact on their balance sheets and profitability.

To a large extent, interest rates have been freed. Despite this, the spread between deposit and lending rates has remained very big (close to 12%) as the result of tight monetary policy mainly aimed at the private sector. Banks realized a profit windfall from this temporary situation.

Banks are entering a number of new activities that will create new sources of revenue in the future. These activities include mortgage financing, leasing, consumer lending, private banking, investment banking, and asset management. Banks in Greece can enter any field of the financial services industry.

Insurance Sector

The insurance sector is undergoing transformation, as many of the bank-owned insurance companies are privatized. Less that 10% of the population carries life insurance, indicating this sector has bright prospects. Insurance companies have also entered the asset management business and have started offering individually-funded retirement benefit plans, which is a new concept for most Greeks, who depend on state-funded plans for their retirement.

Agriculture

Agricultural production accounts for 15.8% of GNP and its exports amount of 28% of the total value of exports. Since 1981, with the assistance of subsidies and low-interest loans from the EEC, agricultural investment has been strong, and farming income has been increasing continuously. Future problems may arise from the fragmentation of farmland into small plots, which prevents efficient use of modern technology and thus limits productivity.

Shifts in consumer preferences, both in Greece and other EEC countries, offer new opportunities in a variety of commodities. Opportunities will be encountered in the manufacture of standardized food items, deep frozen, and preserved foods. It is worth noting that a substantial portion of the agricultural production comes from cooperatives. These will no longer enjoy the magnitude of subsidies of the previous administration, which will force them to be transformed into more efficient units or close down.

Manufacturing

Industrial production in total accounts for 56% of the total value of exports and 43.3% of GNP. It experienced rapid growth in the 1960s and 1970s, while the 1980s was a period of contraction. Greece's industrial production is mainly concentrated in light manufacturing and processing. Currently, the government is placing priority on sectors of high technology, such as telecommunications and information systems.

Greece is the only member of the EEC that produces cotton on a large scale. This accounts for the importance of the textile sector in the country. Since 1984, food, beverage, and chemical industries have fared above average. The one industry that has constantly outperformed the national average and is ranked as the most successful is the cement production sector. Greece is one of the largest exporters of cement in the world, exporting over 50% of its production. The privatization in this sector has drawn substantial attention from the major European firms.

After a boom in the 1970s, construction went into recession in the early 1980s as consumers rushed to sell their real estate holdings as a result of concerns related to socialist government policies. Lately, however, the trend has been reversed. Real estate prices surged upwards in response to housing shortages and the liberalization of home financing. Furthermore, real estate prices were adjusting to higher EC levels. Another factor contributing to the construction boom is the necessity for infrastructural development such as new highways, railroad lines, bridges, power generation plants, a new airport, and the Athens Subway system. Several of these projects are supported by EC funds.

Tourism

Greece, along with the southern coast of Spain, France, and Italy, monopolizes the tourist flow from the rich industrial countries of the north. Tourism generates on average 8 million visitors per year and in 1989 accounted for 21.5% of invisible earnings. The focus now is not on new capacity but rather on improving the infrastructure of the existing units. Despite problems in the short term from the Middle East crisis, tourism maintains very bright prospects for further development in Greece.

Shipping

The position of Greek shipping has always been one of dominance in the international arena. Due to a global crisis that hit shipping from 1975 to 1985 with a temporary break in 1981, the survivors of today are among the best-run shipping companies in the industry worldwide. It is estimated that the Greek-owned fleet surpasses 80 million deadweight tons, placing Greece among the top three shipowning countries in the world. Shipping inflows account for about 20% of Greece's invisible earnings. Piraeus, already one of the main international shipping centers, strives to become a major shipping finance center as well. The "Posidonia Exhibition," hosted in Piraeus every two years, is considered to be the largest maritime exhibition in the world.

Table 19-3   Basic Economic Statistics of Greece

Employment

Total employment, 1989, in 000	:	3,671
By sector (in percentage):		
- Agriculture	:	25.3%
- Industry & construction	:	27.5%
- Other (mainly services)	:	47.2%
Unemployment rate, 1990	:	7.7%

Production

GNP, 1989, in billion drachmae	:	8,713.2
GNP, 1989, in billion U.S. $	:	53.7 (1989, 1 US $ = 162.4 drs)
GNP per capita (1989, in U.S. $)	:	5,359.0
1990 GNP growth (constant prices)	:	
Gross fixed investment		
(as percent of GNP in 1989)	:	18.7%
GDP Composition, 1989	:	
- Agriculture	:	17.0%
- Mining & manufacturing	:	21.1%
- Construction	:	6.0%
- Services	:	55.9%

:	Transport. & communication	: 11%
	Banking & insurance	: 16%
	Other	: 28.9%

Foreign Trade

Exports of goods and invisible receipts, as percent of GNP, 1990	28.9%
Imports of goods and invisible payments, as percent of GNP, 1990	34.3%
Current account deficit, as percent GNP, 1990	(5.4)%
Trade deficit as percent GDP, 1990	(18.1)%
Invisibles balance as percent GDP, 1990	12.7%
Tourism earnings (percent of GNP) :	3.8%
Emigrant remittances (percent of GNP) :	2.7%
Shipping earnings (percent of GNP) :	2.6%
Current account deficit, as percent GDP, 1990	(5.4)%

The Government
(figures as percent of GDP)

Government revenues	27.0%
Government expenditures	44.6%
Government deficit	(17.6)%
Deficit of other public sector activities	(3.3)%
Public Sector Borrowing Requirement	(20.9)%

The Currency

Monetary unit	:	Drachma (Drs)		
Parity rates	:		Average 1990	June 1991
		1 U.S. $ =	158.52 Drs	195.00 Drs
		1 DM =	98.24 Drs	109.30 Drs
		1 FF =	29.16 Drs	32.20 Drs
		1 BP =	272.75 Drs	321.20 Drs
		1 ECU =	202.00 Drs	224.60 Drs

(source : Bank of Greece)

Interest Rates
Bank Rates (end September 1991)

	Deposits	Lending
Short-term rates	16%	27 - 29%
Medium-term rates	18 - 22%	25 - 27%
Government Securities		
Treasury Bills	3 months	19%
	6 months	22%
	12 months	23.5%
Treasury Bonds	2 and 3 years	24.0 - 24.5%

Source: For most of the information, the source is OECD.

Table 19-4   Composition of Greek Trade (1989)

Exports

Food and beverage	23 %
Tobacco	2 %
Raw materials and semifinished products	4 %
Minerals and ores	7 %
Petroleum products	6 %
Manufacturers	57 %
Other	1 %
Total	100 %

Imports

Food items	15 %
Consumption raw materials	8 %
Construction raw materials	8 %
Fuel and lubricants	13 %
Capital goods	24 %
Manufactured consumer goods	32 %
Total	100 %

Source: Bank of Greece

Table 19-5   Composition of Greek Export Manufacturers (1989)

Textiles	43 %
Metal articles	11 %
Aluminium and alumina	7 %
Steel plate	7 %
Chemicals and pharmaceuticals	6 %
Cement	4 %
Furs	2 %
Other	20 %

Source: Bank of Greece

Table 19-6   Greece's Trading Partners (1989)

	Imports	Exports
EEC	59 %	62 %
Other Europe	8 %	6 %
East Europe	5 %	4 %
Total Europe	72 %	72 %
OPEC	7 %	3 %
USA	12 %	14 %
Japan	3 %	1 %
Other	6 %	10 %
Total	100 %	100 %

Source: Bank of Greece

Table 19-7   Annual GDP Growth Rate (In Constant Prices)

	Greece	EEC	USA
1961-1973	7.7	4.8	4.0
1974-1982	2.7	1.9	1.6
1983	0.4	1.6	3.9
1984	2.8	2.3	7.2
1985	3.1	2.5	3.8
1986	0.8	2.6	2.8
1987	-0.1	2.9	3.7
1988	4.0	3.8	4.6
1989	2.6	3.3	3.0
1990e	1.0	2.9	1.0
1991e	1.0	2.2	0.3
1992e	1.5	2.5	1.0

Source: EEC

Table 19-8   Inflation Rate (GDP Deflator)

	Greece	EEC	USA
1961-1973	4.5	5.2	3.6
1974-1982	17.2	12.0	8.1
1983	19.1	8.5	3.4
1984	20.3	6.9	3.6
1985	17.7	6.0	2.7
1986	18.8	5.5	2.5
1987	14.2	4.1	2.9
1988	14.5	4.5	3.2
1989	15.5	5.1	4.1
1990e	20.8	5.7	4.2
1991e	17.7	5.5	5.5
1992e	15.1	4.8	5.7

Source: EEC

Table 19-9   Balance on Current Account as Percent of GDP

	Greece	EEC	USA
1961-1973	-2.9	0.4	0.5
1974-1982	-2.0	-0.4	0.2
1983	-5.0	0.1	-1.0
1984	-4.0	0.3	-2.4
1985	-8.2	0.7	-2.9
1986	-5.3	1.4	-3.2
1987	-3.1	0.7	-3.4
1988	-1.7	0.2	-2.4
1989	-4.8	0.2	-1.8
1990e	-5.1	-0.3	-1.7
1991e	-5.1	-0.8	-1.8
1992e	-4.5	-0.7	-1.4

Source: EEC

Table 19-10   Annual Growth Rate of Exports and Imports

	Exports	Imports
1974-1981	5.5	0.4
1982-1988	9.9	8.9
1989	3.8	10.6
1990e	4.4	5.2
1991e	4.5	3.4
1992e	5.3	4.2

Source: EEC

Table 19-11   The Evolution of the Drachma Against Other Currencies(Average Fixing Prices)

Year	U.S. Dollar	Deutsche Mark	French Franc	Pound Sterling	European Currency Unit
1985	138,197	47,516	15,448	179,557	105,711
1986	139,954	64,626	20,232	205,232	137,469
1987	135,429	75,393	22,544	221,781	156,165
1988	141,861	80,783	23,820	252,298	167,584
1989	162,420	86,460	25,487	265,898	178,825
1990	158,515	98,240	29,162	282,746	201,996
1991 June	176,450	108,020	31,880	317,550	222,222

Source: Bank of Greece Basic Economic Statistics of Greece
(for most of the information the source is OECD)

The Development of the Greek Stock Market

The stock market has become an important investment vehicle and source of capital over the last few years. Traditionally, Greek corporations have raised capital mainly from bank financing and, to a lesser degree, from equity, which came primarily from family sources. As a result, activity and prices on the stock exchange remained low. In 1988 and 1989, the austerity program implemented by the Greek government led to improved performances in the private sector. Investors, first from overseas, took advantage of the relative undervaluation of Greek companies in comparison to international standards by investing in the Athens Stock Exchange and purchasing minority or controlling stakes in Greek corporations.

This activity took place at a time when the private sector's need for capital was increasing in preparation to meet the challenges presented by Europe's unification. Banks could no longer meet the needs of the private sector, as they had to devote most of their resources to the financing of the large public sector deficits. This situation pushed Greek companies to the stock market for equity capital, thereby contributing to the rapid evolution of the market.

The development of the Greek stock market has been a success on an international scale. Investment returns have been quite attractive. In the three years ending in 1990, the ASE index increased by 242% in drachma terms. In 1990 alone, the Greek market was the second-best performer in the world, increasing by 90% in U.S. dollar terms. The market went through a structural transformation. The number of companies listed increased sharply, new individual and institutional investors were attracted, market liquidity improved, and a new stock market law provided a modern and adequate regulatory framework. The automation of the stock exchange and the establishment of a central depository, both of which are imminent, will substantially improve the transparency of the transactions as well as the clearing and settlement process.

With a market capitalization representing only 25% of GDP, the Greek stock market has potential for further progress. Greece's membership in the EEC and its proximity to the Middle East and Eastern Europe are strategic assets. The implementation of the current government program to restructure and liberalize the economy will benefit the private sector in several ways and will have a positive impact on the development of the stock market.

Market Performance

The market has soared since April of 1990 when the conservative party won the elections. This increase reflected the expectation that the new government would confront and resolve the country's economic problems. A robust earnings growth by several companies increased the level of investor confidence and sent prices to high levels, reaching P/E ratios over 30. The arrival of the Gulf crisis and Greece's failure to win the 1996 Olympics had a sharp negative effect on the market.

Downward pressure was further exacerbated by concerns over the deterioration of public sector finances. It was temporarily reversed when the government announced a 10% taxation of interest income. In the first six months of 1991, the Greek market experienced one of the sharpest declines (22%) among both emerging and developed markets. This correction brought prices and P/E ratios to attractive levels. Table 19-12 lists the ASE composite share price index. Table 19-13 lists the index on a monthly basis.

Table 19-12   ASE Composite Share Price Index (In Local Currency Terms 1980 = 100)

Year	Index
1985	70.95
1986	103.86
1987	272.47
1988	279.65
1989	459.43
1990	932.00
1991	954.38 (June 28, 1991)

Table 19-13   The Movement of the Index on a Monthly Basis (In Local Currency Terms, 1980 = 100)

Month	Year	Index
July	1989	330.51
August		373.19
September		516.71
October		504.70
November		473.17
December		459.43
January	1990	540.51
February		595.36
March		646.31
April		973.55
May		1,077.49
June		1,553.43
July		1,521.01
August		1,379.26
September		1,150.30
October		972.66
November		882.14
December		932.00
January	1991	906.53
February		1,291.72
March		1,242.88
April		1,158.49
May		1,019.36
June		954.38

Source: ASE Statistical Bulletin

Table 19-14 Comparison of Total Return Among Share Price Indexes (in U.S. $ December 1984 = 100)

	IFC Emerging Markets Composite	S & P 500	MSCI EAFE	Greece
1984	100.0	100.0	100.0	100.0
1985	128.3	131.7	156.7	103.4
1986	144.1	156.2	266.3	157.7
1987	166.2	164.4	332.7	397.8
1988	267.3	191.5	472.9	252.4
1989	414.7	251.9	474.1	454.8
1990	297.0	244.1	364.1	899.6
1991 (June)	344.0	279.0	370.4	784.2

Source: IFC
Note: Total Return also includes dividends paid.

Table 19-15 Comparison Among Major International Share Price Indexes (in U.S. $) (1984 = 100)

	IFC Emerging Markets Composite	S & P 500	MSCI EAFE	Greece
1984	100	100	100	100
1985	121.6	126.3	153.0	91.5
1986	129.2	144.8	255.2	129.0
1987	137.8	148.2	314.3	304.5
1988	208.5	166.1	398.1	167.9
1989	305.9	211.3	434.8	280.3
1990	209.6	197.5	327.4	531.1
1991 (June)	232.8	221.9	329.7	419.2

Source: IFC

Market Structure

Investing in the ASE

There is only one stock exchange in Athens (ASE) quoting two markets. The "official market" is for larger companies, while the newly established "parallel market" is for smaller ones. The official market accounts for 99.2% of ASE's capitalization. Transactions can take place only through licensed stockbrokers.

ASE lists both stock and bonds, most of which are government bonds. In the primary market, bonds account for over 90% of capital raised. The situation is reversed on the secondary market, where equities represent 92% of total activity.

Companies Listed and Market Capitalization

The Greek stock market was not an important source of capital to corporations until 1990, when the number of companies listed increased substantially. That year the private sector experienced the most severe credit crunch from bank sources. Encouraged by brisk investor interest in the stock market, Greek companies turned to the ASE for their capital needs. There was a flurry of new listings accompanied by capital increases of companies already listed. Subsequently, the government was also attracted to the market through public bond issues, most of which are denominated in ECU.

Initially, the issue price of new equity issues had to be guaranteed by the underwriters for a period of six months. The price guaranty was abolished in 1991, and underwriters have no further obligations to the investors or the issuer once the placement is concluded and the syndicate is disbanded.

Overall, the Greek market is characterized by a high degree of concentration. Four sectors account for 80.3% of the market. The financial sector (banking, insurance, investment, and leasing companies) represents 49% of the total market capitalization. Then comes the metallurgical sector (12.1%) and cement and building materials companies (10.5%), followed by the food, beverage, and flour companies (8.7%). It is interesting to note the strong presence of the textile sector (5.1%).

The ten largest companies listed (five banks, two cement companies, two metallurgical companies, and one food company) represent 50% of the total market capitalization. This figure increases to 69% when the 20 largest companies are included.

The existing concentration will be alleviated over time, as more companies come to the stock market. Greek corporations, which developed as family-owned enterprises, are in the process of opening up their capital and management structures. With a market capitalization representing only 25% of GDP, the potential for further growth is obvious.

Table 19-16 ASE Market Capitalization (In Billion Drachmas and Billion USD) (1 U.S. $ = Drs 195)

Year	Bonds		Stocks		Total	
	Drachmas	U.S. $	Drachmas	U.S. $	Drachmas	U.S. $
1985	291.4	1.5	113.1	0.6	404.5	2.1
1986	444.9	2.3	156.6	0.8	601.5	3.1
1987	789.5	4.1	565.6	2.9	1,355.1	7.0
1988	1,785.9	9.2	598.4	3.1	2,384.3	12.3
1989	2,763.2	14.2	996.6	5.1	3,759.8	19.3
1990	3,895.3	20.0	2,429.0	12.5	6,324.3	32.5
1991 June	4,125.7	21.2	2,479.3	12.7	6,605.0	33.7

Source: ASE

Table 19-17 Number of Companies Listed on the ASE

1981	111
1982	113
1983	113
1984	114
1985	114
1986	114
1987	116
1988	119
1989	119
1990	145
1991	152 (end of June)

Source: ASE

Table 19-18 Total Capital Raised Through the ASE (Includes New Listings and Capital Increases of Listed Companies) (In Billion Drachmas and Million US $)

Year	Bonds		Stocks		Total	
	Drachmas	U.S. $	Drachmas	U.S. $	Drachmas	U.S. $
1985	189.8	973	2.3	12	192.1	985
1986	275.0	1,410	4.9	25	279.9	1,435
1987	384.1	1,970	95.3	489	479.4	2,459
1988	1,417.1	7,267	41.9	215	1,459.0	7,482
1989	1,499.1	7,688	7.1	36	1,506.2	7,724
1990	2,083.4	10,684	190.8	978	2,274.2	11,662
1991 June	1,415.4	7,258	98.6	506	1,514.0	7,764

Source: ASE

Table 19-19 A Profile of the ASE: Companies Listed, Number of Listings, and Market Capitalization by Sector (As of end of June 1991) (1 U.S. $ = 195 Drachmas)

Sector	Number of Companies	Number of Listings	Market Capitalization (Billion Drachmas)	Market Capitalization (Million U.S. $)	Percent Total Market Capitalization
Official Market					
Banks	14	17	953.6	4,890	38.5%
Insurance	4	4	104.8	537	4.2%
Investment Companies	8	13	118.4	607	4.8%
Leasing	3	3	35.7	183	1.4%
Metallurgical	15	32	299.6	1,536	12.1%
Cement & Building	6	10	260.8	1,337	10.5%
Wood & Timber	3	6	46.8	240	1.9%
Food & Beverage	13	21	186.6	957	7.5%
Flour Companies	5	6	29.5	151	1.2%
Textile	16	29	125.5	644	5.1%
Tobacco	3	5	75.3	386	3.0%
Hotels	3	5	54.1	277	2.2%
Mining	1	1	50.2	257	2.0%
Chemical	7	10	32.7	168	1.3%
Paper	1	2	1.8	9	0.07%
Transport	1	1	1.3	7	0.05%
Cold Storage	1	1	0.3	2	0.01%
Commercial & Miscellaneous	19	33	81.1	416	3.3%
Suspended Listings	23	29	n/a	n/a	0.0%
Total Official Market	145	228	2,458.1	12,606	99.13%
Parallel Market	7	14	21.2	109	0.87%
Total ASE	152	242	2,479.3	12,714	100.00%

Source: ASE Monthly Statistical Bulletin

Table 19-20   The 20 Largest Companies in Terms of Market Capitalization (as of June 28, 1991) (1 U.S. $ = 195 Drachmas)

Company	Market Capitalization (Billion Drachmas)	Market Capitalization (Million U.S. $)	Percent Total	Sector
National Bank of Greece	215.9	1,107	8.7 %	Bank
Credit Bank	164.3	843	6.6 %	Bank
Heracles General Cement	154.0	790	6.2 %	Cement
Commercial Bank of Greece	142.3	730	5.7 %	Bank
Ergo Bank	131.4	674	5.3 %	Bank
Intracom	128.2	657	5.2 %	Metal/Telco.
Titan Cement	86.1	442	3.5 %	Cement
Ionian Bank	84.2	432	3.4 %	Bank
Delta Dairy	72.7	373	2.9 %	Food
Aluminium of Greece	68.5	351	2.8 %	Metallurgical
Ten Largest Companies	1,247.6	6,399	50.3 %	
Mortgage Bank	61.0	313	2.5 %	Bank
Piraiki Patraiki	53.5	274	2.2 %	Textiles
Papastratos	50.5	259	2.0 %	Tobacco
Financial Mining Industries	50.2	257	2.0 %	Mining
Astir Insurance	48.0	246	1.9 %	Insurance
Viohalco	45.6	234	1.8 %	Metallurgical
Ionian Hotel Ent.	42.1	216	1.7 %	Hotels
Hellenic Investment Co.	42.0	215	1.7 %	Invest. Company
Bank of Greece	35.4	182	1.4 %	Bank
ETEVA - National Ind. Dev. Bank	33.6	172	1.4 %	Bank
Total	461.9	2,368	18.6 %	
Total 20 Companies	1,709.5	8,767	68.9 %	

Source: ASE Monthly Statistical Bulletin

Yield, Earnings Growth, and P/E Levels

Calculation of Greek P/Es.   The calculation of Greek P/Es has two main particularities. First, financial research in Greece is in its early stages. Therefore, in most cases, P/Es are calculated based on historic rather than expected earnings. This distorts the comparison with other markets where P/Es may be calculated on expected earnings. It also fails to capture the high earnings rate of certain companies, which would make the P/Es much lower.

Secondly, at this point most brokers calculate P/Es on the basis of profits before tax (PBT). This makes it difficult to compare them with other markets where P/Es are calculated based on profits after tax (PAT). It must be noted that even though the statutory corporate income tax rate is 48%, the effective one is between 20% and 30%. This is mainly due to the existence of generous tax allowances that were established to encourage investment. Corporate profits distributed as dividends are subject to withholding at source at the rate of 42% for bearer and 45% for registered shares. This withholding takes care of the tax liability of individual investors.

Table 19-21   Average P/E Ratios and Dividend Yield of Listed Companies by Sector (P/Es : Prices of 6/28/91 Over 1991e Earnings Before Tax- (Dividend Yield Based on 1990 Dividends)

Sector	P/E	Dividend Yield
Banks	12.4	3.8 %
Insurance	113.2	0.3 %
Investment Companies	8.5	8.8 %
Cement Building	22.8	1.0 %
Metallurgical	17.8	3.6 %
Textile	16.1	3.0 %
Chemical	14.5	1.7 %
Food & Beverage	24.0	1.6 %
Commercial Companies	16.8	5.2 %
Wood & Timber	12.3	3.8 %
Tobacco & Paper	108.1	3.5 %
Miscellaneous Companies	12.6	3.7 %
Parallel Market	11.7	5.5 %

Source: N.D. Devletoglou Securities S.A., Athens, Greece

Table 19-22   Distribution of P/E Ratios (By Number of Companies)

Range of P/E Ratio	Number of Listings in Range	Percent of Total Listings
Negative	38	19.1%
0 - 6	5	2.5%
6 - 8	21	10.6%
8 - 10	29	14.6%
10 - 12	17	8.5%
12 - 18	38	19.1%
18 - 25	17	8.5%
Over 25	34	17.1%

Source: N. D. Devletoglou Securities S. A., Athens, Greece

**Table 19-23 The Earnings Growth of Listed Companies
by Sector (Earnings After Taxes)**

Sector	1989/1988	1990/1989	1991e/1990
Banks	74.5%	100.5%	63.4%
Insurance	(46.3)%	(136.6)%	n/a
Investment Companies	n/a	139.6%	(71.7)%
Cement Building	130.8%	17.6%	18.9%
Metallurgical	49.7%	0.8%	14.2%
Textile	(10.3)%	24.4%	(33.1)%
Chemical	(223.0)%	(24.0)%	(63.9)%
Food & Beverage	21.9%	56.5%	84.0%
Commercial Companies	41.7%	(13.2)%	61.3%
Wood & Timber	(137.4)%	(22.7)%	(53.6)%
Tobacco & Paper	(13.3)%	(48.1)%	n/a
Miscellaneous Companies	16.7%	78.8 %	97.3%
Parallel Market	190.2%	313.1%	80.6%

Source: N. D. Devletoglou Securities S. A., Athens, Greece

Market Liquidity

Market liquidity has improved substantially. The daily number of shares traded and the value of transactions has increased considerably (Table 19-24). ASE's turnover compares quite favorably with the rest of the emerging markets.

The ten most active stocks account for 64.8% of the total value of transactions and 30.7% of the total volume of shares traded. The 20 most active stocks represent 76.6% and 47.4% of value and volume respectively (Table 19-25).

The annual turnover (number of shares traded as percentage of total capital of companies listed) increased from 10.9% in 1989 to 36.3% in 1990. This is quite satisfactory, particularly given that the average float of listed Greek companies is around 30%-35%. The largest stocks are quite liquid, with an average daily volume between 10,000 and 15,000 shares.

Table 19-24 Average Daily Turnover of the ASE (Amounts in Millions) (1 U.S. $ = 195 Drachmas)

	Equities		Bonds		Total	
	(Drachmas)	(U.S. $)	(Drachmas)	(U.S. $)	(Drachmas)	(U.S. $)
1987	242.4	1.2	8	0.04	250.4	1.2
1988	177.5	0.9	19	0.10	196.5	1.0
1989	357.7	1.9	22.3	0.10	380.6	2.0
1990	2,590.1	13.3	950.1	1.28	2,840.2	14.6
1991	2,349.0	12.1	202.1	1.00	2,551.1	13.1

Volume of Shares Traded on ASE
(In Thousand Shares)

1987	17,546
1988	15,799
1989	27,113
1990	91,450
1991	56,181 (6 months)

Source: ASE

Table 19-25 The Most Active Stocks on the ASE (During the First Six Months of 1991)

Company	Value Traded Drachmas Billion	Value Traded $ Million	As Percent of ASE's Total	Shares Traded Thousand	As Percent of ASE's Total	As Percent of Company's Total Shares	
National Bank of Greece	39.4	202	13.4	2,050	3.7	16.8	Bank
Commercial Bank	35.7	183	12.2	3,034	5.4	20.9	Bank
Ergo Bank	25.0	128	8.5	2,915	5.2	16.1	Bank
Credit Bank	24.0	123	8.2	1,344	2.4	13.6	Bank
Ionian Bank	14.8	76	5.0	1,703	3.0	15.4	Bank
Titan Cement	13.1	67	4.5	757	1.4	14.6	Cem.
Intracom	11.6	59	4.0	869	1.6	12.8	Meta.
Mortgage Bank	10.4	53	3.5	907	1.6	11.2	Bank
Heracles Cement	8.7	45	3.0	2,428	4.3	4.8	Bank
Delta Dairy	7.3	37	2.5	1,153	2.1	9.3	Food
Total	**190.0**	**973**	**64.8**		**30.7**		
Bank of Attica	5.3	27	1.8	3,654	6.5	20.3	Bank
Nibid Bank	4.8	25	1.6	259	0.5	11.4	Bank
Aluminium of Greece	3.6	18	1.2	137	0.2	3.8	Meta.
Petzetakis	3.6	18	1.2	1,092	2.0	19.6	Chem.
Pisteos Inv.	3.3	17	1.1	531	1.0	17.7	Inve.
Progress Fund	3.3	17	1.1	1,440	2.6	23.2	Inve.
Elais	3.1	16	1.0	241	0.4	10.7	Food
Ethniki Ins.	2.9	15	1.0	618	1.1	9.9	Insu.
St. George Mil	2.8	14	0.9	928	1.7	25.5	Food
Alpha Leasing	2.8	14	0.9	371	0.7	10.3	Leas.
Total	**35.5**	**181**	**11.8**		**16.7**		
Total	**225.5**	**1,156**	**76.6**		**47.4**		
ASE Total	**293.6**	**1,506**	**100.0**	**56,181**	**100.0**		

Source: ASE Statistical Bulletin

Investor Profile

It is difficult to obtain precise data regarding the participation of each class of investors in the Greek stock market. In general terms, it is estimated that foreign investors account for 25% of the activity (occasionally this has gone up to 40%), domestic institutional investors for 45%, and Greek individuals for 30%.

Foreign investors were initially drawn to the market as the result of the undervaluation of Greek companies in comparison to international standards. Their involvement, however, has become more strategic and long-term oriented. This stance is due to a variety of factors that include the ongoing interest of European firms to acquire stakes in Greek corporations, the efforts to restructure the economy, and the strong earnings progression of the private sector.

The majority of foreign investment in the Greek market has come from European investors. Most invest through mutual funds managed outside Greece. However, as of 1990, portfolio managers increased their direct participation in the Greek market. In addition, American investors exhibited a stronger interest, which is expected to intensify with time. Japanese interest is still at its early stages.

Greek institutional investors are investing in closed- and open-end mutual funds. Pension funds are not yet very active. Many experience financial difficulties and those with surplus assets have been investing pension funds primarily in government paper. EEC directives stipulate that pension funds must be freed from government intervention regarding the choice of their investments. Asset management is making strong inroads in Greece. As a result, it is expected that pension funds will become more active in the future and have a positive impact on the stock market.

Most mutual funds have been established since 1989 and are managed by banks and insurance companies. At the end of June 1991, there were eight closed-end funds (investment companies, quoted on the ASE). Their market value of 118.4 drachmas (U.S. $607 million) equaled 4.8% of ASE's total capitalization. Contrary to other markets, in Greece, the majority of closed-end funds trade at a substantial premium to their book value. There were 12 open-end mutual funds with a total net asset value of 163.8 billion drachmas (U.S. $840 million).

Individuals have a strong presence in the Greek stock market, either directly on their own or through mutual funds. They have been attracted to the stock market for a variety of reasons. Besides bank deposits and other hard assets (such as real estate and cars) they did not have a big variety of investment alternatives. Given the strong returns of the stock market, they viewed it as a hedge against inflation. The recent taxation of bank deposits intensified interest in the stock market.

Until recently, Greek mutual funds could invest up to 20% of their assets overseas. Individuals were restricted from investing internationally by foreign exchange controls. As the result of EEC directives, the foreign exchange restrictions were lifted in the summer of 1991 for investments in EEC countries.

The Operation of the ASE

Institutional Setup

The Athens Stock Exchange (ASE) was established in 1876 and is a self-managed public institution. It is under the supervision of the Ministry of National Economy (Capital Markets Committee).

It is governed by a council comprised of nine members appointed by the Ministry of National Economy following recommendations by the ASE's member firms, the companies listed, the investment funds, ASE's employees, and the Ministry of National Economy.

Types of Listings

The ASE lists both stocks and bonds. Stocks listed are common or preferred shares, which can be either in bearer or registered form. In accordance with this, most Greek companies have more than one listing.

By law, shares of banks, insurance, investment, real estate, and defense companies must be in registered form.

The majority of bonds listed are government and other public-sector loans. The corporate bond market in Greece is currently at the very early stages of its development. Recently, Greek corporations have shown an active interest in the issuance of convertible bonds. It must be noted that activity in the secondary market for bonds is quite small.

Listing Requirements

Listings on the ASE must be approved by the Stock Exchange Council. The criteria for admission were harmonized in line with the EEC Directive 79/279. (See Table 19-26.) Once a portion of securities of a certain class is listed, then all securities of the same class are considered listed and can trade on the exchange without any restrictions.

Shares must be distributed to the public through an underwriter. The companies must publish a prospectus, which has to be approved by the Stock Exchange Council before its publication

Table 19-26 Listing Requirements

Criteria for Equity Listing	Official Market	Parallel Market
• Minimum equity capital	170,000,000 Drachmas (equals U.S. $870,000)	100,000,000 Drachmas (equals U.S. $510,000)
• Years of profitable operation prior to listing (exceptions are possible for newly formed companies)	5	3
• Proceeds to a capital increase of and distribute it to the public	25%	15%

Criteria for Bond Listing	Official Market	Parallel Market
• Minimum equity capital	100,000,000 Drachmas (equals U.S. $510,000)	100,000,000 Drachmas (equals U.S. $510,000)
• Years of profitable operation prior to listing (exceptions are possible for newly formed companies)	5	3
• Amount of bond issue cannot exceed of company's net equity capital	50%	50%
• Issue to be distributed to the public through an underwriter		

Trading Hours of the Stock Exchange

At present, transactions can take place only on the floor of the stock exchange during the hours of operation. The official market is open from 8:30 a.m. to 12:30 p.m., Monday through Friday. The parallel market is open from 12:30 a.m. to 1:00 p.m., Monday through Friday.

Method of ASE's Operation

At present, ASE is a double-auction market by the outcry system. Stockbrokers fill customer orders only on an agency basis without taking positions for themselves. Matching of buy and sell orders on the same stock received by the same broker from different clients is not allowed, and each order must be executed separately through the exchange.

Commission Rates

At present, commission rates are fixed on a sliding scale, as follows:

Order size	Commision rate
up to 1,000,000 drs. (equal to U.S. $ 5,100)	1.00%
1,000,001-3,000,000 (equal to U.S. $ 5,101 - $ 15,500)	0.75%
over 3,000,000 (equal to U.S. $ 15,501)	0.50%

Stock Exchange Taxes and Transfer Fees

There is no tax on stock exchange transactions. Registered shares are subject to a transfer fee of 0.30% paid separately by both the buyer and the seller.

Type of Transactions

At present, only cash transactions are allowed.

Settlement

Currently, all transactions are scheduled to settle within 48 hours. A Central Depository was recently established and will go into operation shortly. This will render the previous system of physical delivery of securities obsolete.

Imminent Changes

The automation of the ASE is underway. Once completed, it is expected that ministerial decrees will activate provisions of the stock market law that allow market making by qualified stockbrokers as well as the consummation of transactions outside of the stock exchange either concurrently with exchange hours or for a limited time before and after the official market.

Commissions will be liberalized and margin trading is envisioned. Derivative instruments (warrants, options, etc.) are under study for introduction.

The Stockbroking Industry

The stock market law of 1988 abolished the monopoly on stockbroking licenses. At the same time the law introduced the formation of stockbroking firms, whose range of permissible activities is dependent upon their level of capitalization, as follows:

Equity Capital	Activities Permitted
70,000,000 Dollars (equal to U.S. $ 360,000)	Agency broking only
200,000,000 Dollars (equal to U.S. $ 1,025,000)	Plus market making
1,000,000,000 Dollars (equal to U.S. $ 5,130,000)	Plus market making and underwriting

Prior to the law of 1988, commercial banks had been allowed to establish stockbroking firms that could be involved in all aspects of the financial markets. Individual stockbrokers in existence prior to 1988 were allowed to continue operations without forming stockbroking firms. Their activities, however, have been restricted to agency broking. Most individual brokers opted to establish stockbroking firms, as is indicated below:

	1989	1990	1991 (June)
No. of individual stockbrokers	32	27	11
No. of stockbroking firms	-	13	38
Total	32	40	49

By June 1991, four stockbroking firms were bank subsidiaries, with the remainder owned by former stockbrokers and new entrants to the market.

Issues Concerning International Investors

Investment Restrictions

Although there are no restrictions, buyers who accumulate 10% of a company's stock must notify the ASE and the Capital Markets Committee. Currently, this applies only to companies with registered shares. There is legislation pending to extend it to companies with bearer shares as well and to provide notification for other accumulation levels as well (20%, 33%, 50%, 66.6%).

Taxation and Repatriation of Earnings

There is no capital gains tax.

For domestic investors, dividend income is tax free up to 50,000 drachmas (U.S. $256) annually for dividends received from one company. The amount goes up to 200,000 drachmas (U.S. $1,025) per investor for dividends received from more than one company. Dividends in excess of 200,000 drachmas annually are taxed at 42% if they come from registered shares and at 45% if the shares are bearer. Interest income from fixed income securities is tax-free.

International investors (from any country, EEC or not) who imported foreign currency to invest in the Greek stock market can repatriate their capital and earnings converted in foreign currency without any restrictions whatsoever. No minimum holding period exists for investments in the stock market.

The repatriation of dividend and interest income is subject to withholding taxes. There are bilateral tax agreements between Greece and several countries to avoid double taxation. Withholding taxes are established as follows:

U.S. AND EEC INVESTORS

Dividends	42 % for registered shares
	45 % for bearershares
Interest	10% on corporate bonds
	0% on government bonds

Financial Information Released by Companies

Greek companies listed on the ASE must release audited financial statements annually and unaudited statements semi-annually.

Custody and Settlement

International investors must have a custody account with a Greek bank either directly or through their own global custodian.

Greek Companies with International Listings

Currently, the only Greek company with an international listing is Boutaris. The company maintains a sponsored American Depositary Receipt program with Citibank. The ADRs trade over the counter in New York.

Sources of Information

Investors can obtain information regarding the stock market by contacting the following:

    The Athens Stock Exchange
    10, Sofokleous Street
    Athens, Greece
    Telephone: (01) 3211-301
    Fax   : (01) 3213-938
    Telex   : 215820 BURS GR.
    President : Dr. Nikitas Niarchos

Prices and information on the Athens Stock Exchange can be obtained through REUTERS and TELERATE pages, as follows:

    REUTERS : ATXA - ATYZ
    TELERATE : 9095 General Index Page

Company Profiles[*]

ALUMINUM DE GRECE

Mining/Smelting   Aluminum de Grece (ADG) was founded in 1961 with Pechiney, France, as majority owner for the production and sale of aluminum and alumina. ADG benefits from its localized production facilities, which are close to bauxite mines and next to the ocean with their own deep sea port. The company mines the bauxite, refines it into alumina and aluminum, and ships the finished product from a single location. ADG has sufficient bauxite reserves until 2004, with no technical problems in extraction. ADG is 51% owned and operated by Pechiney, France, which is among the largest aluminum producers in Europe.

[*]Company profiles are provided by the editors.

BOUTARIS WINE

Food and Beverage   Boutaris Wine Company (BWC) is one of the major wine producing companies in Greece, and is expanding its operations in the food sector. It was founded in 1879 and went public in 1987. Boutaris has production plants in four regions, two bottling plants (in Naoussa and close to Athens), 133 acres of wholly-owned vineyards and contracts with 1,000 acres of neighboring vineyards. Six red wines (including a "Grand Reserve"), five white wines, and two more wines are produced. High-quality wines account for 30% of sales and 50% of profits, and table wines account for the remaining 70% of sales. Grapes for the high-quality wines are grown in owned or contracted vineyards, and the table wine grapes are purchased from various vineyards. Eighty percent of exports (10% of sales) go to the European community where Germany is the largest market (30%), with the remainder to the United States and Canada. Boutaris Wines are owned 72% by the Boutaris family and 15% by the National Investment Bank of Greece.

CREDIT BANK

Banking   Credit Bank (CB) is the third-largest commercial bank in Greece and the largest of the private sector banks, with 9% market share and more than 115 branches (including 9 mobile units) throughout the country. Its targeted customers are upscale, dynamic, and well educated people who require more than traditional Greek banking. In addition to retail and corporate banking, other areas of business include consumer credit (VISA and ATMs) and leasing and merchant banking, which it performs through affiliated companies. CB also provides services needed by international businessmen and has a reputation as a pioneer and innovator. CB is known as the most dynamic bank in Greece, run by a new breed of young, educated Greek bankers. CB is majority owned by the Costopoulos family.

DELTA DAIRIES

Food and Beverage   Delta Dairies (DD) was established in 1952 and is the market leader in the Greek dairy products industry. It processes around 450,000 liters of milk daily and produces a full range of products, including more than 80 brands of ice cream, yogurt, milk, and dairy desserts. In 1989 it launched the "LIFE" range of natural fruit juices, which were very successful. In 1988 it acquired two companies, Froza, engaged in frozen foods, and Evrotrofes, engaged in the production of animal feeds. In terms of market share, Delta controls ice cream (45%), fresh cream (80%), fresh milk (47%), total milk (22%), yogurt (30%), and fruit juice (30%). Fresh dairy products are 45% of sales, ice cream 30%, and juices 25%. Delta Dairies is 80% owned by the Daskalopoulos family.

ERGO BANK

Banking   Ergo Bank (EB) is a privately-owned bank organized in 1975. It is the only bank in Greece not owned by the public sector or a large industrial group and is considered the most professional, profitable, and well-run bank in Greece. Deposits, assets, and profits have grown steadily and rapidly over the past five years and its return on assets is the highest of any bank in Greece, as well as high by international standards. EB has a strong company culture that emphasizes productivity and accountability, initiated by an entrance exam. It has 53 domestic branches plus a London branch, is expanding into Italy, and will be adding 10 new branches in 1991.

EB is partly employee owned, with no person owning more than 3%, and is relatively liquid by Greek standards. It is one of the few banks in Greece that is fully computerized.

FOURLIS BROTHERS, S.A.

Consumer Durables   Fourlis Brothers was established in 1950 as a manufacturer and distributor of consumer durables. It has since discontinued most of its manufacturing activities, except for kitchen range hoods and some TV assembly (20% of sales), and has instead become a major importer of consumer durables, mainly TVs, stoves, refrigerators, and air conditioners. The company's main suppliers are General Electric, Telefunken, NEF Hausgeraete, and RCA. The company also maintains business ties with other suppliers throughout the world. Selling is on a wholesale basis only, through a distribution network of over 1,000 dealers and retailers, which is considered one of the best in Greece. Fourlis Brothers is 72% owned by the president and his three brothers.

GREECE FUND LIMITED

Country Fund   This is a new, closed-end fund with a target amount up to $20 million offered by Schroders and Salomon Brothers. It will be listed in London and is incorporated in Jersey. Its purpose is to invest in the securities of Greek companies listed on the Athens Stock Exchange, but it may also invest in unquoted stocks that are likely to be listed. The fund will not invest in start-up ventures. Before being fully invested, the fund will invest in money market instruments denominated in dollars or other freely convertible currencies. Total front-end commissions are 5% (4% for investments over $1 million). According to Schroders, its allotment is 95% subscribed.

Management: Schroders Investment Management, which manages $27 billion including several European and small-company funds, will be the Investment manager; Ergoinvest, a Greek investment company that has significantly outperformed the market in five of the seven past years, will be the investment adviser. Total management and advisory fees will be 1 3/8% less $40,000.

HELLENIC BOTTLING COMPANY

Food and Beverage   Hellenic Bottling Company (HBC) was established in 1969 by the Coca-Cola Company and was sold to Kar-Tess, S.A. (also known as the Leventis-Ioannou Group) in 1981 after a number of unprofitable years. A 25% share of the company was floated on the Greek market in July 1991. HBC is the leading soft drinks bottler in Greece, with a 66% market share, and is also the fourth largest company in the country in terms of total sales. Eighty percent of sales are from soft drinks, with the remainder of sales comprised of fruit juices (10%), mixers (5%), and mineral water (5%).

INTRACOM S.A.

Telephone/Telecommunications Equipment   Intracom (IC) was founded in 1977 and is the leading Greek manufacturer of telecommunication equipment and systems. The company was first offered on the market in early 1990 and now represents 5% of the Athens Stock market capitalization. The main products of the company are telephone exchanges, analog and digital transmission systems, and telephone sets, although many other related products are also manufactured. IC is 69% owned by Mr. Kokalis and other large individual shareholders, 12% by Ericsson S.A. (Sweden), and has a 19% free float.

MICHANIKI (MC)

Construction   Michaniki (MC), established in 1974, is currently the third-largest construction company in terms of assets (among 80), accounting for 6% of the public construction market. It is almost exclusively in public projects such as plant/buildings (35% of ongoing contracts in 1990), earth moving and energy projects (11%), highway and bridges (44%), tunnelling (7%), and port (3%). It employs 640 employees. Twenty percent of the shares were listed in the stock exchange in July 1990, and after the recent capital increase, free float increased to 35%. The majority shareholder is Mr. Emfietsoglu, who is also the CEO.

NATIONAL BANK OF GREECE

Finance Holding Company/Bank   The National Bank of Greece (NBG) is the largest banking institution and conglomerate in Greece. Without its unconsolidated subsidiaries and affiliates, it is three times larger than the next largest bank and represents 14% of the capitalization of the Greek market as the largest stock. It also has a controlling interest in nine other banking institutions (in Greece and various other countries with large Greek communities), two investment funds (Delos Mutual Fund and The National Investment Company), two insurance companies, a hotel company, a shipyard, and a warehouse company. In addition, it owns a large amount of real estate and minority participations in numerous listed companies. The bank is indirectly controlled by the government through various public enterprises.

N. LEVENTERIS S.A.

Wire and Cables   N. Leventeris S.A. (NL) was established in 1932 as a handicraft operation producing sailing items. The company was incorporated in 1948 as an importer of wire ropes and related attachments. In 1972, the company was listed and a new factory was opened to produce hard steel wires. The company has over 50% of the domestic market share for wire cables, with no local competition. Production is used mainly in the shipping, fishing, and electrical transmission industries. The company has continued to grow and expand and currently produces hundreds of different sizes and types of light and heavy wire cables, as well as being a distributor for many nonmetal ropes and cables to broaden its domestic product line. Leventeris is 62% owned by the general manager, the son of the founder.

A.G. PETZETAKIS S.A.

Plastics and Rubber   A.G. Petzetakis (PET) was established in 1963 and listed in 1973. It is the largest plastics and rubber manufacturer in Greece and one of the three largest industrial groups in Europe in the field of manufacturing of plastic pipes, parts, and integrated irrigation systems. It produces three main types of pipes, namely polyvinyl chloride (PVC) (65%), polyethylene (34%), and rubber (1%). Major users of PET products are divided equally among the construction, agriculture, and food production industries. A.G. Petzetakis is owned 50% by the Petzetakis family and 7% by the Greek government.

TITAN CEMENT

Building Materials   Titan Cement (TC) was founded in 1911 and is the largest private company in the cement industry and the second-largest exporter of cement in Greece (behind Aget Iraklis, which is 90% state-owned). Greece is the largest exporter of cement in the world (and the 20th-largest producer), a testimony to the international competitiveness of this industry. Titan's activities include mining, manufacturing, marine and land transportation, worldwide marketing, and research. It has four plants with a production capacity of 5.5 million tons a year and two port facilities. It has 43% market share of the domestic market and 33% market share of the Greek export market. Major export markets are the United States (42%), Saudi Arabia (14%), and Italy (13%).

20

PORTUGAL

John R. Reinsberg*
Lazard Freres & Co.
New York, United States

Overview of the Market

Although the first regulation of the Lisbon Stock Exchange was announced on October 10, 1901, it was not until the mid-1970s that a series of laws were established governing the organization and functioning of the stock exchanges. Today, Portugal's economy is one of the smallest in Europe. In 1990, the population of 11 million produced $56 billion in GDP.

After World War II, Portugal's GDP doubled between 1955 and 1969. It continued to expand at an annual rate of about 8.5% between 1970 and 1974. However, after oil prices soared and Portugal suffered a democratic revolution in 1974, the government suspended all securities transactions, effectively closing down the stock exchanges. The Lisbon exchange was closed for three years and the Oporto for six years. Significant trading on the Lisbon Stock Exchange did not commence again until 1977. (Table 20-1)

During the mid-1980s, the market grew moderately until a spectacular, if not euphoric, 21-month period between January 3, 1986 and October 9, 1987. Mainly due to Portugese entry into the EC and the deregulation and reform of the financial and public sectors, the Lisbon B.T. &A. Price Index (the Portugese benchmark) leaped from 572.9 to 6749.8, or over 1000%. (The index uses a 1977 base rate of 100.)

* Michael A. Bennett, M.B.A., Finance, 1992, University of Chicago, assisted Mr. Reinsberg with this chapter.

Table 20-1 Equity Market Overview

	Market Capitalization		Trading Volume (For Lisbon and Porto Examples)		Turnover Ratio	
	Lisbon Escudo (millions)	U.S. $ (millions)	Lisbon Escudo (millions)	U.S. $ (millions)		
1980		10.13	67.3		0.7	
1981		10.00	69.5		0.8	
1982	26	8.20	92.0	65	1.0	0.7
1983	25	11.00	84.0	135	1.0	1.4
1984	23	12.30	73.0	476	3.0	6.1
1985	24	30.20	192.0	851	5.0	6.0
1986	63	223.50	1,150.0	9,041	60.0	7.1
1987	143	150.30	8,857.0	213,941	1,518.0	31.1
1988	171	1,052.20	7,172.0	163,384	1,136.0	14.8
1989	182	1,588.40	10,618.0	300,374	1,912.0	22.8
1990	181	1,257.20	9,210.0	240,449	1,687.0	16.9
1991	180	1,284.40	9,613.0	406,159	2,818.0	32.0

Source: IFC Emerging Markets Data Base; Bolsa de Lisboa.

Since the "1987 Crash," the Portugese stock market is one of the few world markets that did not regain its precrash luster. In 1988, strong domestic demand, foreign capital, and consumption overheated the market. Imports grew as exports suffered, leading the government to act on inflation problems and the trade deficit by introducing tax reform. As of mid-1991, the price index stood at only one-third of late 1987 level, at about 2230, with fading momentum. (Table 20-2, Figure 20-1, Figure 20-2)

In 1991, the Portugese market was adversely affected by the Gulf war. The effect of surging oil prices on inflation and economic growth scared foreign investors out of the market. Since 60% of the Portugese market float is owned by foreigners, this had an even greater effect on the Portugese market than other countries. Additionally, the economic downturn was heightened in Portugal because of its reliance on the paper and pulp industry, a cyclical sector.

On a positive note, domestic demand has been resilient and the government's privatization program has been a major factor in attracting foreign capital. As a result of the recent underperformance of the Portugese market, the P/E ratio fell to a low level despite the fact that earnings are expected to grow above the European average over the next few years. The market P/E was only 11 on 1991 earnings. Earnings growth was about 12% in 1990 but slowed in 1991.

Government

The Cavaco Silva government was reelected in the October 1991 elections. Fiscal policy (spending cuts) is taking over monetary policy in efforts to solve the budget deficit and inflation problems. Monetary policy has been tight since 1987, which has helped inflation drop below an estimated 10% in 1992. As a result of the spending cuts, market forces should push interest rates down. Because the Portugese government has joined the EMS, the government seems more concerned with fighting inflation than maintaining growth.

As a result, some believe that the Portugese economy will not pick up as strongly as the other OECD countries. Since inflation was well above the European average, inflation fighting and spending cuts will take center stage at the expense of higher economic growth. Because interest rates have been forced so high to combat inflation, a plethora of foreign capital has continued to pour in, seeking those high rates. This influx has more than tripled foreign currency reserves; another matter hurting inflation numbers is that Portugal has one of the lowest unemployment rates in the world. As a result, wages have skyrocketed as internal demand remains strong. This wage inflation is adding to the overall inflation rate.

Nevertheless, the Cavaco Silva government still needs to encourage foreign investment to stimulate private enterprise and Portugal's membership in the European Community. Foreign investors have been drawn to Portugal by recent

Table 20-2   US\$ BT&A Return & Currency Valuation

	BTA Index	Market Return (Pesetas)	FX	Valuation Percentage (U.S. $)
1980	235.1			
1981	203.5	-14.5		
1982	190.5	-6.4	89.0	
1983	187.0	22.6	131.5	
1984	249.7	33.5	169.0	
1985	566.4	126.8	160.5	
1986	1202.0	112.2	146.2	
1987	2990.3	148.0	129.9	-11.15%
1988	2355.9	-21.2	146.4	12.70%
1989	3287.0	39.5	149.8	2.32%
1990	2143.4	-34.7	136.6	8.80%
1991	1977.7	-7.7	133.6	22.0%

Source: IFC Emerging Markets Data Base.

Figure 20-1 Lisbon BT&A Weekly Price Index
(August 16, 1985 to August 16, 1991)

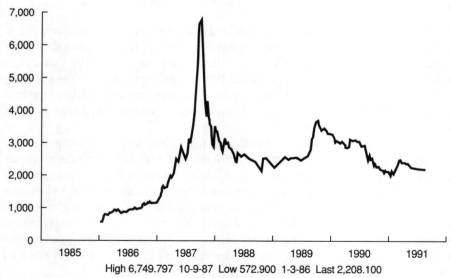

High 6,749.797 10-9-87 Low 572.900 1-3-86 Last 2,208.100

Source: Datastream

Figure 20-2 Portugese Escudo to U.S. Dollar Weekly Exchange Rate

Source: Datastream

economic growth, the easing of foreign investment laws, and an effective and low-cost labor force. As a result, the government is continuing its efforts to promote investments in Portugal.

Market Structure

Portugal's two stock exchanges are located in the country's two largest cities. The capital and largest city is Lisbon, with a population of almost one million. Oporto, the second largest city, has a population of less than 500,000. At the end of 1991, the market capitalization of the 180 stocks listed on the Bolsa de Valores de Lisboa, (Lisbon Stock Exchange), was 1,284 billion Portugese escudos or US $9.6 billion (See Table 20-1). There are two exchanges - the Bolsa de Valores de Lisboa in Lisbon and the Bolsa de Porto in Oporto. Most securities listed on the Oporto exchange are also listed on Lisbon.

There are two trading sessions on the Lisbon Stock Exchange. The morning session opens at 10:15 a.m. and closes at 1:45 p.m. and the afternoon session runs from 2:30 p.m. to 5:00 p.m. The afternoon session only includes trading of the most-liquid 35 shares and 20 bonds of the prior week. Other securities during the afternoon session are allowed to list in the computerized trading. The Oporto exchange also has two sessions from 10:00 a.m. to 2:00 p.m. and from 2:30 p.m. to 4:30 p.m. A similar afternoon process of specific stock and bond trading also takes place. In

1991, systems were implemented to merge the two exchanges through an electronic linkup to match prices and ease broker access.

The securities markets of Portugal have substantially less volume than the securities markets of the United States, and companies are significantly less liquid and more volatile than securities of comparable U.S. companies. As a result, these markets may be subject to greater influence by adverse events generally affecting the market and by large blocks of securities.

The benchmark index of the Bolsa de Valores de Lisboa is the Banco Totta & Acores Index (BT&A). This market cap-weighted index was introduced in 1987 and is a selection of stocks listed on the exchange (Table 20-2). Banco Totta, a Portugese bank, is responsible for picking the stocks and calculating the index. Figure 20-1 shows a weekly price index. Figure 20-2 shows a weekly exchange rate.

As of December, 1991, the ten biggest companies in the index represented more than 67% of the total index weight. The largest company by market cap is Soporcel-Sociedad de Celulose, with 16% of the total. The company controls almost 40% of the paper industry. Celulose Ciami, the third-largest company, has another 22% of the paper sector, suggesting the importance of the paper manufacturing industry to stock market activity. Sonae, the chemicals and financial management holding company, is the second largest. (Table 20-3, 20-4) This chapter is followed by brief profiles of the main companies listed in Portugal.

Major Investors

At the end of 1990, Portugese share capital was worth about US $9 billion. Portugese families and the government account for about 55% and 15% of the total market capitalization, respectively. Only 30% of the share capital, or US $2.6 billion, is free-float. More than 60% of this float, or US $1.6 billion, is owned by nonresidents. The U.K. institutions, alone, represent 25% of total foreign investment. Although non residents own a majority of the free float, they own less than 20% of the total market capitalization. Due to the apparent lack of interest by Portugese private investors, these statistics display the importance of foreign investment in Portugal. Not only is the Portugese apathy to the stock market evident in the aforementioned statistics, but also in the excessive weight of fixed income securities in the portfolios of Portugese institutional investors.

Structure

Listed securities are divided into two market sections. The "official" market lists bonds, shares, and other securities with substantial public ownership levels. The "unofficial" market lists shares of companies that do not have the public share own-

**Table 20-3   Top Ten Portugese Stocks Ranked by
Market Capitalization**

Company	1991 Market Capitalization (US$ MM)	% of Total Market Capitalization
1 BCP	1,259	13%
2 BTA	977	10%
3 BPI	758	8%
4 SOPORCEL	371	4%
5 MARCONI	290	3%
6 J. MARTINS	273	3%
7 UNICER	267	3%
8 SONAE INVESTIMENTOS	229	2%
9 MAGUE	158	2%
10 CISF	146	2%

Table 20-4   Top Ten Portuguese Stocks Ranked by Value Traded

Company	1991 Value Traded (US$ MM)	% of Total Value Traded
1 BCP	217	8%
2 BTA	120	4%
3 LISNAVE	73	3%
4 MARCONI	66	2%
5 BPI	50	2%
6 SONAE INVESTIMENTOS	38	1%
7 J. MARTINS	23	1%
8 MAGUE	20	1%
9 C. AMORIM	18	1%
10 SOFINLOC	18	1%

ership levels required for the official market but do meet the minimum require-ments. This market is similar to the over-the-counter market in the United States. Although most traded shares are in bearer form, some companies do have registered shares. Liquidity has always been and remains a problem on both exchanges.

Clients must place orders through only seven official brokers. These brokers are regulated by the Ministry of Finance under Portugese securities law and are supervised by executive committees of the respective exchanges. Membership on the exchange is not open to foreign nationals or organizations. Although there is a forward and options market, there are no index derivatives traded in Portugal. However, stocks not listed on the stock exchange can be traded outside the exchange. Stockbrokers trade these securities similar to "pink sheets" in the United States. Daily security prices are established by the official brokers who match buy and sell orders. Official brokers cannot deal for their own account. There is a 5% limit on daily price changes. Physical receipt of share certificates is necessary, as most of the shares are in bearer form.

Issues and Regulations

Foreign ownership of Portugese securities is monitored by "The Instituto do Comercio Externo de Portugal." The stock exchanges are regulated by the Internal Stock Exchanges Regulation. Transactions must be reported monthly by the owner's banks to the Portugese central bank. Foreign ownership is prohibited in utilities and communications and in other areas where the public sector exercises a monopoly. The government has been encouraging the establishment of joint ven-tures in industries where foreign capital and technical resources are needed. A commission is currently reviewing legislation concerning the capital markets in response to the freedom of capital movements by 1992.

Foreign investors are not liable to Portugese capital gains taxation. However, dividends are taxed at 20%. While interest and capital gains are repatriated, Portugal has a double-taxation agreement with most European countries. The country also has limited withholding tax treaties with Austria, Belgium, Brazil, Denmark, Finland, France, Germany, Italy, Norway, Spain, Switzerland, and the U.K.

Portugal joined the EC in 1986, agreeing to eliminate all barriers. In addition, Portugal is a member of the UN, NATO, OECD, and IMF, as well as the International Bank for Reconstruction and Development and the International Finance Corporation. The country is also a party to the General Agreement on Tariffs and Trade.

Business projects which involve investments greater than US $70 million and significantly affect exports and the balance of payments qualify for substantial tax and financial benefits which are negotiated on a case-by-case basis.

21

TURKEY

Peter Bennett
Morgan Stanley Asset Management
London, United Kingdom

Investment Background

Turkey is situated between Europe, Asia, and the Middle East and borders Greece, Bulgaria, Georgia, Armenia, Iran, Iraq, and Syria. It is larger than any Western European country with a total land area of 776,980 square kilometers as well as 7,126 kilometers of Mediterranean coastline. The population of Turkey is 5.8 million people and is growing at 2.3% per year and estimated to reach 7 million by the year 2000. Over 50% of the population lives in urban areas.

The Republic of Turkey was established by Mustafa Kemal Ataturk in the 1920s. Ataturk instituted many crucial changes that laid the foundations for Turkey to mature as a parliamentary democracy. By separating church and state, Ataturk developed the first secular country in the Islamic world. Ataturk also introduced the phonetic alphabet and to this day soldiers are required to remain in the army until they can demonstrate the ability to read and write. This helps explain Turkey's high literacy rate of 70%.

Over the past five years GNP growth has averaged 5.2% per year, which is the highest average annual rate of the OECD countries. Since 1980, economic policy has moved away from state control and has instead supported free market initiatives. At first there was some resistance to this shift in economic policy; however, now that many reforms have had time to make an impact, there is widespread support. For example, the platforms for the three political parties that competed in the general election of October 20, 1991, were very similar. Each party supported free market reform, and included in its economic agenda the continued privatization of state assets, the gradual reduction of tariff barriers, and a more laissez faire approach to business. This similarity in campaign platforms illustrates that there has been an ideological shift in attitudes over the past ten years. There are few clamors for the nationalization of industry or protectionism. Turkey is no longer an insular nation striving to be fully self-sufficient.

The three most prevalent political parties are the Motherland Party (ANAP), the True Path Party (DYP), and the Social Democratic Party (SHP). ANAP was founded by President Turgut Ozal and is now led by Prime Minister Mesut Yilmaz. DYP is being led by Suleyman Demirel, who was a prime minister during the 1970s. SHP is being led by Erdal Inonu and is the most liberal party. ANAP and DYP have more conservative biases and have similar objectives. They both support the rapid development of infrastructure. The SHP would prefer Turkey's resources to go toward protecting the rights of individuals. All parties believe that the further privatization of state assets will be an integral part of funding their objectives.

The price that Turkey has had to pay for such strong GNP growth has been high inflation. In 1990, more than half of the economic activity could be attributed to the State Economic Enterprises (SEEs). These companies have been rapidly developing infrastructures since ANAP came to power in the early 1980s. Turkey now sports extensive highway and telecommunication networks, natural gas pipelines in urban and industrial areas, and three dams at the mouths of the Tigris and Euphrates in Eastern Anatolya. In order to finance these developments, the Treasury increased the money supply rapidly throughout the 1980s. As a result, inflation has not fallen below 20% for more than a decade. Now that much infrastructure is in place, and goods and services can travel more easily throughout Turkey, the government has the opportunity to reduce its infrastructure investments and bring down inflation.

Turkey has been an associate member of the EC since 1964 and its application for full membership will be reviewed in 1993. The EC member countries accounted for 53.1% of Turkish exports and 41.8% of imports in 1990. Turkey and the EC are preparing for customs union by 1996, which will open up new markets for Turkish goods and at the same time force Turkish industry to invest in modernizing its production facilities in order to remain competitive.

Turkish Capital Markets

The Capital Markets Board

Due to the relative infancy of the Turkish capital markets, it is worthwhile to examine their foundations before exploring the Istanbul Stock Exchange (ISE) itself. In 1981 Parliament passed the Capital Market Law and one year later the Capital Markets Board (CMB) was established. The CMB is the governmental authority responsible for the development of Turkey's capital markets.

Between 1982 and 1986 the framework for establishing the Istanbul Stock Exchange was created. In 1983 the CMB issued a decree stating its intention to establish a stock exchange, and in 1984 a publication laying out the rules and regulations that would govern such an exchange was written and distributed by the CMB.

In 1986 the Istanbul Stock Exchange was opened. Originally 50 companies were listed. By September 1991 the number of quoted companies grew to 131. The Istanbul Stock Exchange supervises the trading of equities, corporate bonds, government bonds, treasury bills, and commercial paper. Originally there were two sections in the stock market, the first for new listings and the second for traded securities. In 1990 they were merged.

As a result of the rapid growth in the financial markets, there was a need to improve the existing legal framework and the Draft Code Law was introduced to expand the CMB's powers. Now the CMB is authorized to set the rules and regulations for establishing derivative markets such as options and futures. It is commonly believed that such markets would serve to reduce short-term speculation in the stock market, which currently has little depth due to the absence of institutional and pension fund money.

The main responsibilities of the CMB include:

1. Defining and instituting the rules and regulations governing the Turkish capital markets.

2. Reviewing and approving public offerings.

3. Supervising public companies.

4. Regulating and authorizing those institutions that operate in the Turkish capital markets.

Capital Increases

Before the ISE began operating in 1986, companies relied heavily on bank loans for their financing needs, which were expensive due to the comfortable oligopolies that maintained banks. Since the establishment of the ISE, however, bank loans as a percentage of shareholders' equity have fallen sharply. Companies have used the privilege of their listings to raise capital through rights issues. The proceeds were used to pay down debt and finance investment plans. So far the CMB has rarely refused the request of a listed company to increase its capital. For this reason, some companies have abused the privilege of their listing to raise their capital more than needed, and occasionally the capital raised is invested in a project that does not yield the investors a return that is above the risk-free rate of government bonds. Often, the proceeds obtained through a rights issue were used for working capital needs instead of long-term investments. The CMB has recognized this problem and is now making the requirements for floating rights issues more stringent in order to restrict this abusive behavior (Figure 21-1).

Figure 21–1

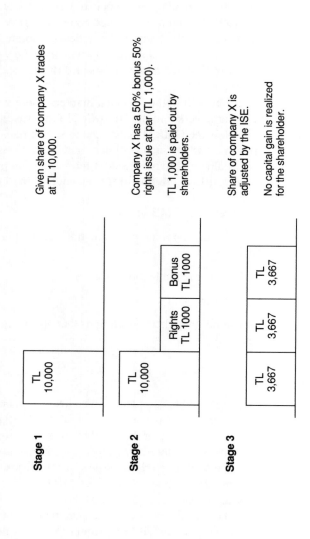

Stage 1

TL 10,000

Given share of company X trades at TL 10,000.

Stage 2

TL 10,000 | Rights TL 1000 | Bonus TL 1000

Company X has a 50% bonus 50% rights issue at par (TL 1,000).

TL 1,000 is paid out by shareholders.

Stage 3

TL 3,667 | TL 3,667 | TL 3,667

Share of company X is adjusted by the ISE.

No capital gain is realized for the shareholder.

In Turkey, shares are issued at par value (TL 1,000). Dividends are usually paid at the same time; however, shareholders must immediately relinquish these dividends in order to purchase rights. In the past shareholders believed that by having the opportunity to purchase shares at par value they were receiving an immediate profit, since the shares could be sold on the ISE at more than par value. Now shareholders are beginning to understand how these rights issues are diluting their share of a company's profits.

In order to attract investors to the stock market, in 1986 the CMB established a regulation that forced companies listed on the ISE to pay out at least 50% of their net income in the form of dividends. Now that investors have become more sophisticated in their valuation techniques, they are becoming more interested in companies with low price/earnings ratios as opposed to companies with high dividend yields. Currently, in order to finance themselves, companies float rights issues and take back dividends as they are paid out. This constant stream of rights issues serves to dilute earnings per share. Since it is currently impossible to trade preemptive rights, the investor is forced to take up the rights. The CMB is aware of this inefficiencies that have emerged and has introduced a bill to Parliament that, if enacted, would effect three changes. First, the rule forcing companies to pay out at least 50% of their net profits would be either abolished or relaxed. Second, prospectuses stating the reasons for a rights issue would be supplied to investors on a timely basis, and finally, it would be possible for shareholders to sell unwanted rights in the market. These changes would help the ISE become as an efficient, equity raising mechanism.

Taxation and Legislation

Over the past five years there have been some important changes in Turkish tax law. Withholding tax on dividends for individuals and domestic mutual funds has been abolished, and foreign investment funds no longer have to pay corporate taxes on capital gains. These changes have encouraged more foreign and domestic investors to participate in the market.

In 1988, Article 15 of Decree 32 paved the way for foreign, nonresident investment funds to invest directly in the ISE. They are not subject to any prior permission to purchase and sell securities that are listed on the ISE, and those securities that (although not listed on the ISE) have been issued with either the permission of the CMB or other government entities.

The purchase or sale of these securities must be done through banks or other intermediary institutions that have been authorized by the CMB. Nonresident investment funds are also free to transfer abroad any income generated by capital gains, dividends, or liquidation of such securities, as long as the transfer is executed by a bank or authorized intermediary.

In order for a nonresident investment fund to exercise the right of management participation either through seats on the board of directors of a company or through shareholder meetings, the nonresident entity must obtain prior approval from the Foreign Investment Directorate (FID) of the Undersecretariat for the State Planning Organization (SPO).

Since 1986 foreign investment in the ISE has grown rapidly. There are currently two foreign investment funds fully devoted to Turkish equities. The Turkish Investment Fund, Inc. is listed on the New York Stock Exchange while The Turkey Trust, Limited is listed on the London Stock Exchange. Overall, foreign investors represent a small portion of equity ownership in Turkey, as local investors still dominate the exchange.

The Public Participation Authority

The Public Participation Authority (PPA) was given the task of privatizing state assets and using the proceeds to develop infrastructure and construct affordable housing. Privatization is viewed as an important part of government activity by each of the three major political parties, since it serves to generate funds as well as decrease the burden that the State Economic Enterprises (SEEs) put on the budget. The PPA hopes that eventually the privitization process leads to quotations on foreign stock markets, as domestic companies develop the need to become globally competitive. In the past, in order to distribute shares, the PPA has used the extensive branch networks of both the public and private sector banks. Lately, due to domestic dissatisfaction with how the privatizations were handled, the PPA is now concentrating on selling blocks to interested parties.

The first privatization of public shares on the ISE was in 1987 when the PPA sold 28% of Teletas, a telecommunication concern. In 1989, the PPA sold five cement plants to Ciment Francais and sold off minority positions in Eregli Demir Celik (flat steel producer), Cukurova Elektrik (utility), Bolu Cimento (cement), Arcelik (white goods), and Celik Halat (steel cable and wire). In 1990, the PPA partially privatized Petkim (petrochemicals), THY (Turkish Airlines), Tupras (state oil refinery), and Petrol Ofisi (oil and gas distributor).

Istanbul Stock Exchange

The Istanbul Stock Exchange (ISE) is open from Monday through Friday from 10:00 a.m. to 12:00 p.m. Since the ISE is not owned by its members, the government appoints the chairman. There are four other members of the governing council that represent the following entities: brokerage houses, individual members, commercial banks, and a development bank. Only licensed members of the ISE are entitled to trade securities on the floor of the exchange. In order to obtain a seat on the exchange an individual or institution must demonstrate to the ISE its capital is sufficient; however, there is no fee that needs to be paid. There are currently over 150 members including banks, brokerage houses, and individuals. In order to transact securities on the ISE an investor must trade through a member.

At the end of September 1991, the total market capitalization of the ISE was TL52,388bn (U.S. $11bn). Along with the 131 companies quoted and traded, over 1,200 companies are listed on the ISE. Many companies obtain a listing but not a quotation in order to benefit from certain tax advantages. The total market capitalization of the exchange has risen from TL25,575bn in January 1991 to TL52,388bn in September 1991. At the same time the Turkish Lira has depreciated by 51.04% against the U.S. dollar. In January 1990 TL2,311.37 purchased U.S. $1, and at the end of September 1991 it took TL4,720.50 (Table 21-1).

Table 21-1   Turkish Stock Market Information

Years	Month	Market Capitalization Billions	P/BV	T. Equity
1989	January	2,070	0.78	2,646
	February	2,668	1.01	2,646
	March	2,566	0.97	2,646
	April	3,007	1.14	2,646
	May	2,749	1.04	2,646
	June	4,714	1.78	2,646
	July	4,586	1.73	2,646
	August	5,498	2.08	2,646
	September	9,526	3.60	2,646
	October	10,967	4.14	2,646
	November	10,270	3.88	2,646
	December	15,553	5.88	2,646
1991	January	25,585	4.40	5,814
	February	24,705	4.00	5,815
	March	23,172	4.20	6,176
	April	23,935	4.50	5,517
	May	27,709	4.90	5,319
	June	40,995	5.50	5,655
	July	70,289	7.50	7,454
	August	68,350	7.30	9,372
	September	70,924	7.90	9,363
	October	66,313	7.30	8,978
	November	52,638	5.60	9,084
	December	55,238	5.40	9,400
1991	January	65,004	6.30	10,318
	February	77,122	3.40	22,683
	March	69,128	3.30	20,948
	April	59,716	2.90	20,612
	May	61,290	2.90	21,134
	June	62,562	2.90	21,573
	July	56,202	2.60	21,616
	August	58,538	2.70	21,681
	September	52,655		

Source: TEB Research

Listing Requirements

Companies that wish to obtain a listing on the ISE must be approved by the CMB and the ISE. In order to obtain the approval of these two entities, a company must meet the following listing requirements:

- The company must have been in existence for three years and profitable for at least the previous two years. If over 25% of the company's capital is held by more than 100 shareholders, then the company could be only two years old to be considered.

- The company must be willing to float at least 15% of its capital and have reserves of more than Turkish Lira 200 million.

- The company must be in good financial condition, which means that the company must be adequately capitalized.

Listed Companies

Due to the relative immaturity of the economy, the market capitalization of the ISE is dominated by banks and holding companies, which make up 34% of the stock market. During the early stages of an emerging market, the lack of competition allows banks to form a comfortable oligopoly that sustains the above average margins on their loan portfolios. At the same time, holding companies are able to operate profitably in a diversified range of businesses due to their access to capital and stature in the business community. As a result, they tend to collect majority shareholding stakes in many unrelated businesses. Once free market reforms begin to take effect, both banks and holding companies will find that they must alter their strategies in order to survive in the increasingly competitive environment. Banks are the first to feel the pressure of competition since money is a transferable commodity, and competing banks can easily be established. Holding companies will find that they must sell off many of the companies in their portfolios and concentrate on one or two businesses in which they can add value and compete in the more competitive environment.

In the early stages of an emerging market, investors tend to value a stock market by its yield. Since investors can normally obtain higher yields by investing in bonds, they see little reason to invest in a stock market when dividend yields are below bond yields. For this reason, the common valuation multiples for stocks, such as the price/earnings and price/book value ratios, languish at levels far below the growth rates of their underlying companies. Turkey experienced the same market valuation anomaly when the ISE opened in 1986; however, as investors have become more sophisticated, valuation multiples rose, and the dividend yield fell.

Under current Turkish accounting standards, depreciation is included in the costs of goods sold making it difficult to assess the true cash flow of a company

Table 21-2   Sector Composition of Turkish Stock Market

Sector	Market Capitalization U.S. $ Thousands	Percent of Total
Automotive	831	7.15
Building Materials	57	0.49
Cables	71	0.61
Cement	453	3.90
Chemicals	1,812	15.58
Electronics	878	7.55
Financials	2,561	22.02
Foods	354	3.04
Glass	288	2.48
Holdings	1,366	11.75
Iron and Steel	920	7.91
Leisure	171	1.47
Machinery	7	0.06
Metallurgy	92	0.79
Pulp/Paper	226	1.94
Textiles	524	4.51
Utilities	635	5.46
Miscellaneous	383	3.29
Total	11,629	100.00

Source: TEB Research

through its audited accounts alone. Instead, it is necessary to rely on other sources of information such as brokerage research in order to obtain an adequate knowledge of a company. A list of research sources has been supplied at the end of this chapter.

Indices

There are three indices that are devoted to the Turkish stock market: The International Finance Corporation (IFC) Turkish Index, The Istanbul Stock Exchange Index (IMKB), and the Morgan Stanley Capital International (MSCI) Turkish Index. The IFC and MSCI indices are market capitalization-weighted. They both aim to hold a diversified range of companies that (when combined) make up at least 60% of the total market capitalization of the ISE. The IMKB index is free float-weighted and published daily by the ISE (Figure 21-2 and Table 21-3). The IMKB index is quoted in Turkish Lira and contains 75 companies. Since the free float of many quoted companies is so small, the IMKB is free float-weighted in an effort to reflect the actual volume of trading as well as the market capitalization of the ISE.

Figure 21-2 Monthly Performance of ISE Index

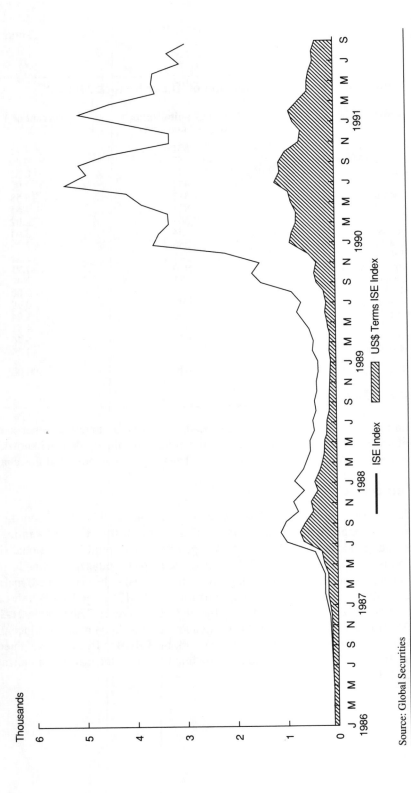

Source: Global Securities

Table 21-3 Monthly Levels of the ISE Index

Year	Month	ISE Index	U.S. $ Based ISE Index
1986	January	100	100
	February	119	117
	March	115	102
	April	112	100
	May	115	98
	June	115	99
	July	121	104
	August	138	119
	September	146	123
	October	150	119
	November	160	127
	December	170	133
1987	January	216	169
	February	260	201
	March	245	186
	April	269	199
	May	394	284
	June	446	309
	July	1012	680
	August	1149	757
	September	1029	651
	October	786	491
	November	890	542
	December	673	396
1988	January	857	454
	February	721	361
	March	635	307
	April	553	257
	May	553	247
	June	468	199
	July	492	202
	August	428	165
	September	455	163
	October	404	142
	November	405	135
	December	373	122
1989	January	379	119
	February	487	149
	March	465	136
	April	533	152
	May	653	184
	June	795	220
	July	701	194
	August	875	236
	September	1475	393
	October	1664	432
	November	1507	389
	December	2217	571
1990	January	3641	924
	February	3516	869
	March	3294	790
	April	3308	781
	May	3852	885
	June	4132	927
	July	5384	1201
	August	4939	1094
	September	5085	1108
	October	4507	967
	November	3256	690
	December	3255	662
1991	January	4213	825
	February	5102	912
	March	4519	728
	April	3554	538
	May	3626	533
	June	3587	496
	July	3041	413
	August	3301	428
	September	2937	371

Source: Global Securities

Settlement and Custody

At the moment, there is one-day physical settlement on every Thursday. The ISE is researching the possibility of developing a book entry system where all share certificates would be held in one central location. However, it is estimated that it will take at least 18 months to implement such a change. All shares traded on the ISE are bearer shares, which makes collecting dividends a laborious process since coupons must be clipped from each bearer share and sent to the company. One day settlement is particularly difficult for foreign investors since it takes two days to purchase Turkish Lira. This means that foreign investors are restricted from investing immediately given an investment opportunity. Once a central custodial facility is established, the ISE envisions the settlement day being extended to three days each week. The reason that it currently remains only one day is due to the ISE wanting to discourage the street trading that occurs on prop tables directly outside the exchange.

Trading on the ISE

The average daily trading volume of the ISE has increased dramatically over the past five years (Table 21-4). In 1986 the ISE turned over an average of U.S. $60,000 per day, and as of July 1991 it has traded an average of U.S. $32m per day (Table 21-5). Since the free float available is only about 17% of the total market capitalization of the ISE, it can still take time to accumulate a meaningful position in a stock.

Due to the volatility of the Turkish stock market, domestic institutions and pension funds have been loathe to invest. These investors believe it is safer to hold government bonds, which pay tax free interest than to venture into the stock market. Many studies indicate that equity investment can outperform bonds substantially over time due to the fact that bond yields tend to hover just above inflation, while a company must have a return on equity that is far above inflation in order to remain competitive in the long term. As the ISE matures, it is likely that domestic institutions and pension funds will begin to venture into the stock market and provide more depth. At the moment the stock market attracts short-term traders and speculators, which adds to volatility.

Table 21-4   Listed Companies and Trading Value

Year	Number of Companies Traded on ISE	Average Daily Trading Value (TL Billion)	Average Daily Trading Value (U.S. $ Million)
1986	80	0.03	0.06
1987	82	0.42	0.62
1988	79	0.59	0.41
1989	76	6.81	3.28
1990	110	61.99	23.55
*1991	129	119.99	32.52

*As of July 31, 1991.
Source: Global Securities

Table 21-5 Trading Volume, Market Capitalization, and Market Valuation

		Trading Volume (MIO TL)	U.S. $/TL Monthly Average	Trading Volume (MIO U.S. $)	Number of Shares Traded (000)	Market Capitalization (TL BIO)	Market Capitalization (U.S. $ BIO)	P/E	Dividend Yield
1989	January	7,168	1,848.11	3.88	2,711	2,000	1.08	2.3	20.8
	February	9,760	1,909.17	5.11	3,542	2,600	1.36	3	16.2
	March	26,115	1,978.11	13.20	9,456	2,500	1.26	2.9	16.8
	April	15,917	2,054.56	7.75	4,143	3,000	1.46	3.4	14.3
	May	36,827	2,067.35	17.81	7,130	3,700	1.79	4.2	11.5
	June	113,850	2,115.94	53.81	26,043	4,700	2.22	5.4	9.1
	July	45,440	2,139.46	21.24	7,302	4,500	2.10	4.6	11.6
	August	60,496	2,185.59	27.68	10,524	5,400	2.47	5.5	9.7
	September	245,222	2,240.54	109.45	26,171	9,500	4.24	9.6	5.5
	October	364,457	2,275.80	160.14	34,262	10,900	4.79	11	4.8
	November	241,631	2,312.33	104.50	24,412	10,200	4.41	10.3	5.2
	December	569,024	2,309.64	246.37	82,360	15,500	6.71	15.7	3.4
1990	January	1,128,273	2,328.53	484.54	104,245	25,500	10.95	18	2.5
	February	1,184,413	2,377.59	498.16	91,303	24,700	10.39	17.4	3
	March	649,658	2,452.73	264.87	61,026	23,100	9.42	16.5	3.2
	April	528,699	2,502.68	211.25	56,159	23,900	9.55	17	3.1
	May	1,383,897	2,547.48	543.24	138,057	27,700	10.87	19.7	2.7
	June	1,115,649	2,626.44	424.78	146,462	40,900	15.57	23.3	2.5
	July	1,556,685	2,662.18	584.74	171,487	70,200	26.37	30.7	1.9
	August	2,018,507	2,677.34	753.92	207,938	68,300	25.51	29.8	2
	September	1,512,348	2,715.79	556.87	130,585	70,900	26.11	30.9	1.9
	October	1,690,362	2,739.67	616.99	151,750	66,300	24.20	28.8	2.1
	November	1,200,453	2,773.78	432.79	126,435	52,600	18.96	22.8	2.7
	December	1,344,120	2,871.05	468.16	151,940	55,200	19.23	23.9	2.6
1991	January	1,644,689	2,980.50	551.82	183,655	65,000	21.81	15.1	4
	February	3,981,933	3,180.50	1,251.98	315,989	77,000	24.21	17.7	3.4
	March	2,753,075	3,531.00	779.69	218,396	69,100	19.57	15.5	3.9
	April	1,401,092	3,827.00	366.11	120,465	59,700	15.60	13.4	4.6
	May	2,960,069	3,983.50	743.08	242,675	61,200	15.36	13	4.7
	June	1,750,540	4,192.00	417.59	178,497	62,500	14.91	13.2	4.6
	July	2,621,531	4,362.50	600.92	336,292	56,200	12.88	11.4	5.4
	August	3,663,019	4,513.50	811.57	476,141	58,500	12.96	11.9	5.2
	September	1,957,669	4,655.00	420.55	400,893	53,600	11.51	10.8	5.8

Source: TEB Research

Table 21-6   Market Valuation Since 1986

Year	P/E	P/BV	Yield
1986	4.3	—	—
1987	19.8	—	2.9
1988	2.6	1.5	11.2
1989	17.6	7.2	3.6
1990	22.5	3.7	5.5
1991 - September	10.0	2.5	5.7

Source: IFC, Morgan Stanley Research

Table 21-7   Ten Largest Companies (October 4, 1991)

Name of Company	Price in TL as of October 4, 1991	1991 E P/E	Market Capitalization in U.S. $ millions	Market Capitalization in TL millions
Akbank	3,800	4	1,186	5,600,000
Koc Holding	10,750	14	907	4,280,000
Petkim	1,150	*	731	3,450,000
Eregli Demir Celik	3,700	4	602	2,841,600
Tupras	3,500	4	541	2,555,000
Arcelik	11,000	7	516	2,437,875
Tofas Oto Fab	11,500	23	390	1,840,000
Petrol Ofisi	4,300	5	328	1,548,000
T.Is Bank	1,323	5	322	1,519,450
Eczacibasi Ilac	9,900	12	315	1,485,000

Ten Most Active Stocks (October 4, 1991)

Name of Company	Value Traded in TL millions	Daily Volume Traded in TL millions	Value Traded in U.S. $ thousands	Percent of the Total
Cukurova Elektrik	68,293	13,659	14,467	15.0
Eregli Demir Celik	60,630	12,126	12,844	13.3
Tupras	57,477	11,495	12,176	12.6
Eczacibasi Ilac	34,615	6,923	7,333	7.6
Petrol Ofisi	32,745	6,549	6,937	7.2
Eczacibasi Yatirim	30,225	6,045	6,403	6.6
Arcelik	25,706	5,141	5,446	5.6
Adana Cimento	19,152	3,830	4,057	4.2
Sarkuysan	16,936	3,387	3,588	3.7
Mardin Cimento	9,781	1,956	2,072	2.1
Others	100,433	20,087	21,276	22.0
Total	455,992	91,198	96,597	100.00

Source: TEB Research

Company Profiles*

Akbank

Banking   According to a Euromoney survey, Akbank was the third most profitable bank in the world in 1990 in terms of its return on assets. However, even though Akbank's return on assets is high at 6.8%, it is important to note that the bank has not revalued its substantial industrial holdings, which are held at cost. These holdings are revalued to account for inflation but they are stated well below their current market value. Akbank is 95% owned by the Sabanci Group while the remainder is listed on the Istanbul Stock Exchange. Most of Akbank's industrial holdings are either directly or indirectly owned by the Sabanci Group as well. Akbank has 622 branches throughout Turkey, of which 510 are owned. Due to current regulations, banks in Turkey must keep 10% of their assets on deposit at the Central Bank. These are held in long-term (one year) treasury bonds. Akbank has ventured into credit cards and ATMs recently and is building up a nationwide computer system called Aknet. Akbank developed a joint venture in 1988 with Dresdner Bank of Germany and Banque Nationale de Paris called BNP-AK-Dresdner Bankasi A.S. in order to facilitate pan European transactions.

Arcelik

Electronics   Arcelik is the largest producer of household appliances in Turkey. The company is majority owned and controlled by the Koç Group, while 18.6% is floated on the Istanbul Stock Exchange. Arcelik holds the dominant market share in Turkey for refrigerators (52%) and washing machines (78%), while it has a strong presence in vacuum cleaners with 40% of the market. Arcelik produces its refrigerators, dishwashers, and washing machines under respective licenses from Bosch, Siemens, and General Electric. The company owns 27.5% of Bekoteknik, which manufactures brown goods under license from Toshiba and Hitachi. Bekoteknik is also majority owned by the Koç Group, however it has not yet been floated on the Istanbul Stock Exchange. Due to the high inflation in Turkey, people tend to spend their wages quickly, before the currency devalues. White and brown goods are particularly sought after, and Arcelik offers a payment plan to its customers to facilitate the purchase of its products. Arcelik has four plants: Cayirova plant in Istanbul produces air conditioners, dishwashers, and washing machines; the first Eskisehir plant produces refrigerators while the second manufactures compressors; and the Izmir plant produces vacuum cleaners.

Cukurova Elektrik

Utility   Cukurova Elektrik owns and operates four hydroelectric power plants and one thermal power plant. The company was established in 1957 to meet the growing

*Company Profiles are provided by the editors.

need for electricity in the Cukurova region; however, since 1978 demand for electricity has been above the company's production. As a result, Cukurova Elektrik has been required to purchase electricity from the state-owned National Electricity Authority (TEK). In 1990, Cukurova Elektrik purchased 55% of the electricity that it sold from the national grid. The company will complete the construction of a new dam in 1991 that, combined with ongoing modernization investments, will double production capacity by the end of the year. Much of the financing for these investments was organized by the World Bank. Demand for electricity is growing by over 7% per annum in the Cukurova region, which houses one of the two main industrial centers of Turkey. Cukurova Elektrik is also due to benefit from the increased demand for electricity in nearby Eastern Anatolya as the Greater Anatolian Project (GAP) comes online.

Eczacibasi Ilac

Pharmaceuticals   Eczacibasi Ilac is the dominant pharmaceutical producer in Turkey with an overall market share of 14%. The company holds the majority of the market in specialty areas such as oral hygiene, health, and beauty products. Eczacibasi Ilac manufactures 206 compounds, of which about half are produced exclusively. The company enjoys product licenses for 24 products from Astra, Schering, Takeda, and Fujisawa and has a joint venture with Rhone Poulenc. In Turkey, pharmaceutical companies are not allowed by law to have a net margin in excess of 15% of sales, and can be extended to 20% for certain products. Since a wholesaler of pharmaceuticals is allowed a 9% margin, Eczacibasi Ilac has developed an extensive distribution network to maximize its profit margin. The company is currently reviewing the possibility of establishing a network of retail outlets in the Soviet Republics. Over the last few years exports to the former USSR have been in excess of $50 million. Eczacibasi Ilac is majority-owned by the Eczacibasi group of companies.

Ege Biracilik

Brewery   Ege Biracilik is the largest brewer in Anadolu Endustri Holdings, which taken together produces over 40% of Turkey's beer. Founded in 1968, the company is located outside Izmir and brews the popular brand Efes Pilsen. Ege Biracilik also brews Lowenbrau under license. The company has a malt factory in Afyon that supplies the other two breweries under the Anadolu Endustri Holding umbrella: Guney Biracilik and Erciyas Biracilik. Even through Turkey is a Muslim country, the demand for beer has grown consistently. This growth had not only been due to the growing attraction of Turkey as a destination for tourists but also from strong demand among the younger generations. Ege Biracilik currently has an annual production capacity of 120 million liters, which is due to be expanded to 720 million liters under the investment program. Since Ege Biracilik has not abused the privilege of having rights issues, over the past few years its earnings per share has grown strongly. The company finances most of its investments out of cash flow. Ege Biracilik is majority-owned by Anadolu Endustri Holdings.

Eregli Demir Celik

Flat Steel   Eregli Demir Celik (known as Erdemir) is a flat steel producer that commands 25% of the Turkish steel market with its two million tons of annual capacity. Erdemir is currently investing $1.7 billion over the next four years to increase capacity by 50% to three million tons per annum and to modernize its existing production facilities. The investment program is called CIM, which stands for "Capacity Improvement and Modernization," and consists of 18 projects. The Public Participation Authority (PPA) still controls over 50% of Erdemir through direct holdings and those of affiliate companies. The management of Erdemir is currently suggesting that the PPA sell its stake to a foreign steel producer, which would enable Erdemir to obtain the cash and technology it needs as well as open up foreign export markets for its products. Even though both sales and profits were flat in 1990 due to decreased demand for steel in the world market and the subsequent fall in steel prices, demand in the domestic market remains strong.

Kordsa

Cord Fabric   Kordsa is the only manufacturer of cord fabric for tire production in Turkey, which makes it uniquely located to take advantage of the increase in automobile production to occur in the next few years as Toyota, Renault, and Peugeot begin production. The company also stands to benefit from the growing replacement market for tires, which, with Turkish roads in such disrepair, is a very buoyant market. By being located in the same industrial complex as Brisa, which is a joint venture with Bridgestone and the Sabanci Group in radial tires, and Dusa, which provides the raw material for cord fabric production, Kordsa is able to minimize transportation costs and benefit from vertical integration. As opposed to many production facilities in Turkey, Kordsa is not labor intensive. Heavy investment over the past few years has made the company's factory highly efficient and modern. Kordsa's shares have performed poorly in the past due to excessive rights issues that have diluted profits and disappointed investors. However, management now believes that its capital is adequate for its current investment plans and has acknowledged the dilative nature of previous rights issues. As a result, Kordsa does not plan to have a rights issue in either 1991 or 1992. Kordsa is majority-owned by the Sabanci Group.

Petkim

Petrochemicals   Petkim is the holding company for Alpet, which is located outside Izmir, and Yarpet, situated 200 kilometers east of Istanbul. Petkim is

Turkey's primary producer of petrochemicals and related products. Over 65% of sales are to domestic concerns. Demand for Petkim's products is growing strongly in line with investments that are currently being made in the electronics, automobile, and packaging industries. Petkim produces both low- and high-density polyethylene for plastics, as well as PCC compounds, PVC, and ammonium sulphate. Petkims's prices are still regulated by the government, which has put pressure on margins in the past. Petkim will need to invest in modernizing its production facilities if the company intends to compete in the global arena. The PPA successfully sold 19% of Petkim to the public in 1990 and still holds the majority of the company.

Teletas

Telecommunications   Teletas produces switching systems, digital exchanges, telephone sets, and radio link systems for use in the domestic market. The company exports only 3% of production. During the 1980s, Teletas benefitted strongly from government infrastructure spending on expanding Turkey's telecommunications network. The government has given emphasis to the modernization and development of the Turkish telecommunications system and now boasts the existence of telephones in even the smallest village in Eastern Anatolya. In the government's latest development plan Teletas has received a contract to install a fiber optic transmission network in Thrace as well as 1,450 television transposer units and transmitters throughout the country. Alcatel owns 39% of Teletas and provides the company with needed technology. Teletas was the first company that the PPA privatized and now 20% is floated on the Istanbul Stock Exchange.

Sources of Information

Broker and Bank Research

- TEB Research
  Meclis-i Mebusan Caddesi 35
  Findikli
  80040 Istanbul
  Tel: 901 151 2121

- Global Securities
  Halaskargazi Caddesi 368/11
  Cifkurt Apt.
  80220 Sisli
  Istanbul
  Tel: 901 132 3040

- Guris Securities
  Yapi Kredi plaza
  C/Blok Kat 9
  Levent 80620
  Istanbul
  Tel: 901 180 5000

- Iktisat Bankasi
  Buyukdere Caddesi
  80504 Esentepe
  Istanbul
  Tel: 901 174 7026

ISE Publications

- 1991 Yearbook of Companies

- 1990 Annual Factbook

- Quarterly Bulletin

- Monthly Bulletin

- Regulations of the ISE

- Istanbul Stock Exchange
  Rihtim Caddesi No. 245
  TR 80030 Karakoy
  Istanbul

  Tel: 901 151 5906

Other Publications

- CMB Monthly Bulletin

- Turkish Daily News (English)

- Capital Market Board
  Mesrutiyet Caddesi No. 24
  Ankara
  Tel: 904 125 3016

- Turkish Daily News
  Tunus Caddesi 50-A/7
  06680 Kavaklidere
  Ankara
  Tel: 904 128 2956/904 223 6263

MIDDLE EAST

JORDAN*
Thomas C. Sorensen
Charlottesville, United States

The Amman Financial Market (AFM)

The Hashemite Kingdom of Jordan—with few natural resources, even fewer substantial companies, a relatively small population (but more people than it can support without continuous outside help), and unfriendly neighbors—is not the country one would expect to have the most efficient, most sophisticated stock market in the Arab world. But it does. Egypt with its large population or Saudi Arabia with its great oil wealth would seem more likely candidates. Yet it is the Amman Financial Market (AFM) that leads the way in the vast Arab world that stretches from Morocco on the Atlantic to Iraq on the Iranian border.

Jordan's advantage lies in its well-educated, talented population (over two-thirds of whom are Palestinians, refugee immigrants from Israel and its occupied territories) and its relative stability in the turbulent Middle East: King Hussain has been on the throne, ruling as well as reigning, for nearly 40 years through three wars, one insurrection, and numerous diplomatic and economic crises. Credit for developing Jordan's bourse goes to Dr. Hashem Sabbagh, AFM's chairman from the outset, and his deputy, Ibrahim A. K. Balbeisi, who as Acting General Manager saw the market through Jordan's severe foreign exchange crisis of the late 1980s and the devastating economic consequences of 1990-91, when Jordanians openly backed Iraq's Saddam Hussain against most of the rest of the world.

---

*Sources of Information: Data was supplied by the Statistical Department, Amman Financial market. All interpretations, analysis, and comment are by the author, who is solely responsible for the contents of this chapter.

The resulting alienation from Saudi Arabia and Kuwait (Jordan's main aid donors), Jordan's over-dependence on trade with now-impoverished Iraq, its reliance on foreign aid, its loss of remittances from Jordanians working in the Gulf before the war, and the burden of finding work for the estimated 275,000 of them who returned to Jordan, make problematical any forecasts about the nation's economy or its stock market.

Economic Background

International Monetary Fund experts estimate that Jordan's Gross Domestic Product (GDP) declined 7.9% in 1990 instead of an expected real growth of 3%., and it is probably down another 15-20% in 1991, making Jordan a main victim, after Kuwait and Iraq themselves, of the Gulf war. Unemployment near 25% could engender social and political instability, especially in view of the growing appeal of Islamic fundamentalism among poorer Jordanians.

Moreover, most analysts forecast a slow comeback. Predictions by IMF experts are shown in Table 22-1.

Recent Developments

The stock market did recover with surprising ease from its 7% fall during the Gulf crisis. It may get another shot in the arm should the U.S.-sponsored Arab-Israel Peace Conference return the potentially prosperous West Bank to Arab rule and allow free flow of goods, money, and people across the Jordanian-Israeli frontier.

Table 22-1

	1990	1991	Change
Exports f.o.b.	1,063	1,250	+17.6%
Imports c.i.f	2,585	2,600	+0.6%
Remittances receivable	462	450	−2.6%
Remittances payable	71	70	−1.4%
Travel receivable	360	370	+2.8%
Travel payable	265	270	+1.9%
Investment income	67	60	−10.4%
Debt interest	599	622	+3.8%
Other services (net)	285	250	−12.3%
Foreign aid	547	406	−25.8%
New borrowing	545	391	−28.3%
Debt coming due	935	827	−11.6%

Note: Figures are in millions of dollars

But even under the most favorable circumstances, any real bull market appears far off if ever. Corporate profits were off 16% overall in 1990, with manufacturing companies—many dependent on exports to Iraq—off 26%. Profitability is almost certain to be slow coming back, especially as long as Unite Nations' sanctions on Iraq remain in place.

History

The AFM was created in 1976 by Law No. 31 and opened for business on January 1, 1978. Although technically a government agency under the Ministry of Finance, Law 31 gives the AFM legal, financial, and administrative independence (although, as in all matters Jordanian, the King has the final word).

Since its inception, the Amman Financial Market has shown resilience if not much else. It has been notably less volatile than most emerging markets, both up and down. Traders made (and lost) money over the past decade, but long-term investors did poorly, especially foreign investors penalized by sharp devaluations in the Jordanian Dinar (JD). The AFM Index (100 at 1/1/80) shows all too clearly Jordan's failure to participate in the great bull markets of the 1980s: It closed 1980 at 111.5, and in 1990 at 118.4, with an intervening year-end high of 203.5 (1982) and low of 106.5 (1986) (Table 22-2).

Before establishment of the AFM, securities trading was done on a hit-and-miss basis through real estate offices, banks, and unlicensed brokers scattered throughout Jordan. Except for a few stocks, liquidity was nonexistent, spreads between bid and asking prices were enormous, and many transaction prices were not disclosed. The AFM changed all that with the creation of a regulated auction market with full disclosure of bid and asking prices, instant reporting of all transactions, standardized listing requirements including periodic audited company reports, and the licensing of brokers.

Objectives set forth in Law 31 have essentially been met, including the following: (1) mobilization of savings by encouraging investments in securities (i.e., by implication, not in unproductive real estate or gold); (2) regulation and control of the issuance of and dealing in securities, to assure soundness, ease, and speed of transactions, in accordance with the financial interests of the country and the protection and interests of small investors; (3) and the gathering and publishing of "necessary data" to achieve these objectives.

An AFM Committee, appointed by the Minister of Finance, provides overall direction of the market, with day-to-day activities supervised by a general manager. In addition to him, the committee includes representatives of banks and specialized credit institutions, listed companies, Jordan's Central Bank, the Amman Chamber of Industry, the Federation of Chambers of Commerce, the AFM Brokers Association, the Controller of Companies, and the Ministry of Finance.

Table 22-2   Amman Financial Market Performance 1978–1991

Year	Listed Companies	Trading Volume (JDm)	Closing Index	Average Yield Percentage	P/E	P/BV Ratio	Market Capitalization (JDmm)
1978	57	5,616		3.8	10.5		283.2
1979	71	15,843		3.1	12.8		473.4
1980	71	41,431	111.5	3.7	11.1		495.5
1981	72	75,417	176.9	2.7	15.4		834.6
1982	99	128,289	203.5	3.0	15.8		988.3
1983	109	141,427	153.4	2.6	17.9		1,008.5
1984	115	59,327	119.5	3.8	13.6	1.9	886.0
1985	117	66,731	115.7	3.5	13.6	1.4	902.6
1986	115	69,523	106.5	3.1	13.7	1.3	877.2
1987	119	148,178	117.3	3.5	14.3	2.2	915.8
1988	120	132,625	124.4	3.3	11.5	2.1	1,085.6
1989	111	367,590	137.3	3.0	7.3		1,436.0
1990	108	268,886	118.4	4.5	7.2	1.3	1,280.8
7/91	107		132.9		8.3	1.3	1,407.2

Note: The AFM General Price Index, calculated daily, is an unweighted geometric average. Sector Price Indices (SPI) are computed first as follows: SPI=Inv. Log $\left(\frac{\sum \text{Log} \frac{x_i}{x_o}}{n} \right)$ (xi=current closing price, xo=base year opening price, n=number of companies in the sector). The General Price Index (GPI) = Inv. Log. $\left(\frac{\sum \text{Log} S_i}{n} \right)$ (si=Sector Price Index, n= number of sectors). The Bank & Financial Institution Index includes 10 companies, Insurance 5, Services 6, and Industrials 17, 38 in all.

Current uncertainties notwithstanding, the AFM is actively planning for the future. Some of the objectives include the following:

1. The licensing of two "specialist" market-making firms to improve liquidity and narrow spreads.

2. Creation of a Transfer & Depository Center to speed and improve settlement and clearing procedures.

3. Creation of one or more domestic mutual funds.

4. The extension of computerization to all departments.

5. Construction of a specially-designed building to replace current cramped quarters in the Housing Bank Building (*Mujamma Bank al-Iskan*) in Amman's Shmeisani district. Shmeisani has become Amman's financial district, with two luxury hotels within walking distance of the exchange.

Market Structure

In 1990, not a typical year because of the Gulf crisis, 136,054,317 shares were traded on the Amman Financial market with a total value of JD 268,885,973 ($390 million). As of mid-1991, there were 107 companies listed on the AFM, with a market capitalization of JD 1,407 billion (US $2.04 billion). That is over 50% of GDP, unusual for a developing country. But shares of Arab Bank alone accounted for JD 535 million or 38% of total market capitalization, a weighting not reflected in the AFM index. (Arab Bank also was the only major financial institution to close 1990 higher than a year earlier.)

As of December 31, 1990, market capitalization was divided among the various sectors as shown in Table 22-3.

Table 22-3

Sector	Market Capitalization		Percentage
	JDmm	**U.S.$ mm**	
Banks, financial companys	729.4	1,057.6	57
Insurance	39.4	57.1	3
Services	65.0	94.3	5
Industry	447.4	648.7	35
Totals	1,281.2	1,857.7	100

The ten largest stocks by market capitalization, as of December 31, 1991, are shown in Table 22-4. Table 22-5 lists the ten most actively-traded shares in 1991.

To be listed on the AFM, a company must meet the following criteria. A few companies that do not meet all requirements are allowed to trade on a "partial market" pending approval.

1.   Have paid-in capital of 50% or more of its shares' par value.

2.   Be at least one-year old.

3.   Publish annual reports with audited financial statements.

Table 22-4   Top Ten Jordanian Stocks Ranked by Market Capitalization

Company	1991 Market Capitalization (US$ MM)	Percentage of Total Market Capitalization
1. Arab Bank	781	31%
2. Phosphate Mines	196	8%
3. Cement Factories	125	5%
4. Petroleum Refinery	85	3%
5. Arab Pharmaceutical	63	2%
6. Arab Aluminum	39	2%
7. National Bank	37	1%
8. National Cable	35	1%
9. Islamic Bank	32	1%
10. Icaco	29	1%

Table 22-5   Top Ten Jordanian Stocks Ranked by Value Traded

Company	1991 Value Traded (US$ MM)	Percentage of Total Value Traded
1. Arab Bank	34	8%
2. Spinning and Weaving	23	5%
3. Arab Aluminum	21	5%
4. International Petrochem	15	4%
5. Icaco	12	3%
6. Arab Pharmaceutical	11	3%
7. Sulpho-Chemicals	10	2%
8. Cement Factories	9	2%
9. Cairo Amman Bank	8	2%
10. National Steel	7	2%

4. Publish stipulated significant information promptly, in at least two Amman newspapers for two consecutive days.

5. Be approved for listing by the AFM Committee.

6. Provide the AFM with copies of internal regulations and deed of association, a list of shareholders and directors, three copies of current financial statements and auditor's report, and a specimen share certificate.

A small secondary market in government, development agency, and corporate bonds also exists, but it is small. In 1990, only JD 3.1 million worth of bonds (55% of them corporate issues) were traded, an 86% drop from 1989's modest figure of JD 22.2 million.

Between 1982 and 1991, the number of brokerage firms licensed by the AFM was held at 27; in 1991, a 28th was added. Several are investment banks, but commercial banks are barred. Brokers generally also serve as custodians; Arab Bank acts in that capacity for some foreign investors. Eight of the licensed brokerage firms are publicly-traded companies with capital bases of JD 1.5 to JD 6 million. Eighteen are closely-held companies, mostly with capital of JD 500,000 (though four have under JD 100,000); two are partnerships with small equity.

Among those commonly used by foreign investors are Jordan Finance & Investment Bank, Arab Jordan Investment Bank, Jordan Finance House, and the Industrial Development Bank.

All orders for AFM transactions are handled by broker/dealers and are executed on continuous auction bases during trading hours. The market is open from 10:00 a.m. to 11:30 a.m. Jordan time (GMT+2), Saturday through Wednesday, and—to facilitate trading by foreign investors—from 5:00 p.m. to 6:00 p.m., Mondays through Wednesdays. Prices are quoted in Jordanian Dinars (JDs), and change by one or more Jordanian Piasters (100 Piasters=JD 1). From time to time, depending on market conditions or activity in a particular stock, the AFM imposes a 5% limit on daily price movement. Settlement and delivery are officially on a spot basis, but in practice the process may take as long as three days.

Company Profiles*

In examining companies whose shares are traded on the AFM, it is well to remember that most were the creations of one person or one family. The person or family may continue to play a dominant role in the companies and they usually have maintained control despite dilution in their shareholdings. Jordan is, after all, a relatively new country. It was carved out of the arid desert east of the Jordan River by the British after World War I to provide a throne for Prince Abdullah, son of Sherif

*Company profiles are provided by the editors.

Hussain of Mecca. A sleepy, impoverished land, it was energized by the waves of Palestinian immigrants who swept into the country after wars with Israel in 1948-1949 and 1967, and much of the nation's managerial talent is Palestinian.

There are 21 Jordanian banks and financial institutions traded on the AFM, but one towers over the field. Arab Bank Ltd. is the largest bank in Jordan (bigger than all the others combined), the oldest and largest wholly nongovernment business enterprise. It accounts for a disproportionate share of trading on the AFM. Arab Bank was founded in Jerusalem in 1930 by an ambitious young Palestinian, Abdul Hamid Shoman, who had emigrated to America, learned the banking business, then returned to the British Mandate of Palestine to start his own bank.

Shoman was a Palestinian nationalist before there was a Palestinian movement. Worried about losing control in the wake of massive immigration to the Holy Land by European survivors of the Holocaust, he decreed that non-Arab foreigners could not own Arab Bank shares—and with few exceptions that restriction remains. For nearly two decades, the bank has been run by his eldest son, Abdul Majeed Shoman, assisted by his brother Khalid. A namesake grandson of the founder, who perhaps is a future CEO, also sits on the bank's board.

A. M. Shoman was the first treasurer of the Palestine Liberation Organization (PLO), and Arab Bank has long been reputed to be "the PLO's bank." After the creation of Israel in 1948 and the loss of Arab Jerusalem to Israel in 1967's Six-Day War, the Shomans moved the bank's headquarters to Amman and have maintained good relations with Jordan's King Hussain, even when the PLO was unable to do so.

Arab Bank is a truly international institution with more dollar and sterling-denominated assets than those in JDs, more branches abroad (44) than in Jordan (40), and a 3,300 workforce that is nearly half non-Jordanian and non-Palestinian. (Palestinians in Jordan and many of those living in countries along the Gulf have been given Jordanian nationality.)

Arab Bank's assets exceed $10 billion, only a third of which are in loans, and two-thirds are in cash and money market instruments. Despite its extreme liquidity (or perhaps because of it), the bank has been consistently profitable, outperforming other Jordanian commercial banks and most nonfinancial companies with a return on equity in the mid-teens. No shareholder owns 10% or more of the 9.1 million shares outstanding, although collectively the Shoman family is assumed to have a controlling interest.

Jordan National Bank is 25 years younger than Arab Bank, with assets ($275 million) only a fraction of Arab Bank's, a fourth as many employees, and half the return on equity (although both banks earn just under 1% on assets). Mostly conservatively managed, the bank has weathered Jordan's difficulties reasonably well, although its branches in neighboring Lebanon have been hurt by the long civil conflict there. Abdul Kader Tash is Chairman and General Manager; day-to-day operations are supervised by Dr. Abder Rahman Touqan. Two members of the Mou'asher family represent that industrial clan on the board. Kuwait Investment Co., an investment bank 50% owned by the Kuwait government, is the only shareholder of record owning more than 10% of Jordan National.

Two investment banks are worth noting: Jordan Investment & Finance Bank and Arab Jordan Investment Bank.

Jordan Investment & Finance Bank, although small (assets equivalent to $123 million), is one of the best-managed financial institutions in Jordan. Its return on equity in the difficult year 1990 was 23.3% on assets 2.2%. In 1989, its best year (sixth since its inception), it earned 31.7% on equity and 2.9% on assets.

Although its exceptionally-able founding chairman, Basil Jardaneh, left to become Jordan's Finance Minister, the Jardaneh family continues to have two members on the board, including Chairman Nizar A. R. Jardaneh. The bank's Vice Chairman is the shrewd, long-time investment adviser to the Emirs of Kuwait, Khaled Abu Su'ud; the bank's only shareholder with 10% or more is Khalil Talhouni, who is also a director.

In addition, Mr. Talhouni is Chairman of Cairo Amman Bank, a joint venture of Jordanian investors with Banque du Caire. Assets are equivalent to $300 million. After producing good results in the mid-1980s, the 15-branch commercial bank has been hurt in recent years by weak loans and weaker earnings.

Arab Jordan Investment Bank is headed by Abdul Kadir Al-Qadi, who divides his time between Jordan and Qatar, where he helps manage the small, oil-producing Gulf sheikhdom's money. Day-to-day manager of AJIB is Jawad Hadid, another competent Palestinian. Five shareholders own more than 10% each; Mr. Qadi; Qatar National Bank; Arab Investment Co.; Libyan Arab Foreign Bank; and the Abu Dhabi Investment Authority (ADIA).

Commercial Bank of Jordan (27 branches), managed by Tawfiq Fakhoury, has done better than Cairo-Amman, but returns on assets and equity have not been impressive. The Housing Bank (86 branches) has thrived under the direction of Chairman and General Manager Zuhair Khouri. Some commercial banks are shareholders; the Kuwait Real Estate Investment Consortium has more than 10%.

In 1908, during construction of the legendary Hijaz Railway, phosphate deposits were discovered in what later became Jordan. The fortunes of Jordan Phosphate Mines Co. rise and fall with the world price of phosphate, as one would expect. But the company is 90%-owned by the Jordanian government, which puts a limit on JPM's profit by imposing special taxes and using it as an employer of last resort. This puts a cap on the upside without removing the downside risk inherent in any commodity.

JPM's market capitalization is less than a fourth of Arab Bank's, but well over twice that of Jordan Cement Factories. Also a government-dominated company, its heavy debt burden (made worse by devaluation of the JD) makes it less attractive than many cement producers in low-wage, developing countries. Downside protection is afforded by the government's guarantee of a JD 0.60 dividend.

The Jordanian government plays a major role, directly or indirectly, in a number of industrial companies, a legacy of the days when nearly all producing companies were monopolies or semi-monopolies, protected and often subsidized by the government. Today the companies are publicly traded, but investors must bear in mind that profits and dividends usually rank low among the government's priorities.

Among such companies are Jordan Tobacco & Cigarette, founded in 1931, whose competition comes chiefly from smuggled American cigarettes; Jordan Petroleum Refinery, which refines and markets oil imported from Iraq; and Jordan Electric Power, which generates and distributes electricity throughout most of the country.

Insurance was a late starter in Jordan, as in many Islamic countries, because its very concept challenges the pious Muslim's belief that God alone will protect and provide. Today there are 17 publicly-owned insurance companies in Jordan, most founded in the mid-1970s. Among those most actively traded in 1990, and of most interest to foreign investors are Jordan French Insurance (assets $10 million equivalent), partly owned by Compagnie Financiere du Groupe Victoire of France and Lincoln National Life of the United States; and Jordan Insurance (assets c. $20 million), founded in 1951, the oldest and largest in the group.

In Jordan as elsewhere, talented, dedicated management can make a difference. Sone of the successful companies where it has include the following:

- Arab Chemical Detergent Industries and its related Arab Sulpho Chemicals, built into the dominant position in soaps and detergents by Jamil Mu'asher.

- Arab Aluminium Industries, rescued from near collapse by Fuad Ayoub.

- Intermediate Petrochemical Industries, headed since its founding in 1980 by Abdel Malek Sa'id.

- Arab Pharmaceutical Manufacturing under General Manager Dr. Ma'an Shuqair.

But a word of caution to potential investors: All of these companies in the past have profited greatly from exports to Iraq, but as long as United Nations Security Council economic sanctions prevent Iraq from exporting its oil, Iraq will import little from anywhere—and Jordanian exporters will continue to suffer.

Ownership

As last measured in 1990, 85% of all publicly-traded Jordanian shares were owned by Jordanians, 13% by non-Jordanian Arabs, and only 2% by foreigners, chiefly institutions. Slightly more than 42% of shares were held by individuals, 23+% by companies, 29+% by the Jordanian government or government agencies; and 5% by others (including foreign institutions).

Latest available data from companies show some variation in percentages of shares held by Jordanians, Arab foreigners and non-Arab foreigners (Table 22-6).

Foreign Investment Restrictions

The Amman Financial Market treats Jordanian and non-Jordanian Arabs alike, both in subscribing to new issues and in trading. Non-Arab foreigners are also warmly welcomed to trade in the Jordanian market (including development and corporate bonds, as well as equities), and there are no restrictions on the repatriation of investment funds or income, including capital gains. Foreign investors are, however, required to adhere to the following restrictions:

1. Advance approval by Jordan's Prime Minister is required before any security is purchased for the first time. The approval process, which goes from the AFM to the Prime Minister's office via the Ministry of Finance, usually can be completed within two weeks. While this requirement appears to be almost amusingly onerous, in fact it is not. The wise foreign investor simply submits a list of all securities in which he or she might someday be interested (plus a few in which he or she is

Table 22-6

Company	Percentage of Shares		
	Jordanians	Arab Foreigners	Non-Arab Foreigners
Arab Bank	36%	63%	1%
Jordan National Bank	80	19	1
Housing Bank	34	55	11
Arab Jordan Investment Bank	53	47	*
Jordan Investment and Finance Bank	91	9	*
Jordan Insurance	94	6	*
Jordan French Insurance	78	1	21
Jordan Electric	96	3	1
Jordan Tobacco	86	12	2
Jordan Cement	95	4	1
Jordan Phosphate	75	25	*
Jordan Petroleum Refinery	82	18	*
Arab Pharmaceutical	93	7	*
Jordan Spinning and Weaving	78	22	*
Arab Chemical and Det.	93	2	5
Arab Aluminum	90	3	7
International Petrochemical	94	2	4
Jordan Sulpho Chemical	87	10	3

*Less than 1%

not, to avoid signaling his intentions too precisely), and after approval is obtained he or she is free to trade in any of them without further authorization.

2. A foreign investor may not own more than 49% of the outstanding shares of any company, except those involved in tourism, agriculture, or related services where foreign ownership may, as specified in the Encouragement of Investment Law of 1986, go as high as 99%.

Withholding Taxes

Jordan imposes no withholding or other taxes on dividends, interest, or capital gains.

Useful Names, Addresses, and Telephone and Fax Numbers

Amman Financial Market
P. O. Box 8802
Amman, Jordan
Tel. (962) 666-8404
Fax. (962)668-6830
Telex: 21711 SUKMAL JO
Dr. Hashem Sabbagh
Chairman and General Manager
Mr. Ibrahim A. K. Balbeisi
Assistant General manager

Arab Bank Limited
P.O. Box 950544 (Shmeisani)
Amman, Jordan
Tel. (962) 666-0115
Telex: 23091 ARABANK JO
Mr. Abdul Majeed Shoman
Chairman and General Manager
Mr. Khalid Shoman
Deputy Chairman

Arab Jordan Investment Bank
P.O. Box 8797
Amman, Jordan
Tel. (962) 666-4120, 666-4126, 667-1160
Fax. (962) 668-1482
Telex: 23590 AJIBGM JO
Mr. Abdul Kadir Al-Qadi
Chairman and General Manager
Mr. M. Jawad Hadid
Deputy General Manager

Central Bank of Jordan
(Bank al-Markazy)
Amman, Jordan
Tel. (962) 663-0289
Telex: 21250 BAKAZI JO
      21476 MARKAZY JO

The Housing Bank
P.O. Box 7693
Amman, Jordan
Bassam Atari, Dep. Dir. Gen.
Tel. (962) 666-7126/9
Telex: 21693 ISKAN

Industrial Development Bank
P.O. Box 1982
Amman, Jordan
Ziyad Annab, General Manager
Tel. (962) 664-2216/9
Telex: 21349 IDB JO

Jordan Investment & Finance Bank
P.O. Box 950601 (Shmeisani)
Amman, Jordan
Tel. (962) 666-5145/6
Fax: (962) 668-1410
Telex: 23182 JFBANK JO

Ministry of Finance
P.O. Box 17120
Amman, Jordan
H.E. Basil Jardaneh, Minister
Tel. (962) 662-308
Telex: 21424 JAMRK JO

INVESTMENT STRATEGIES AND RELATED ISSUES

COMPARISON OF EMERGING MARKET INDICES

Keith K. H. Park[1], Partner
Global Strategies Group
Los Angeles, United States
in collaboration with
Stephanie M. Atkins and Robert E. Ginis[2]
Emerging Markets Investors Corporation
Washington, D.C., United States

Introduction

As the 1990s continue, the globalization of institutional portfolios accelerates. The institutional interest in the emerging equity markets in the late 1980s is now being put into practice on a significant scale. In the 1990s, the investment in these markets is expected to grow in leaps and bounds and play an important role in international equity programs of pension sponsors.

As it is the case with the developed equity markets, investment in the emerging markets offers the distinctive benefits of international equity investment: diversification of market risks and enhancement of returns.[3] Given the growing investment in the emerging markets, pension sponsors are bound to search for ade-

[1]Park would like to express his sincere appreciation to Kate Jonas at Morgan Stanley Capital International and Peter Wall at International Finance Corporation for their objective and illuminating comments, and would also like to thank Peter Labonte and Sanjai Madan of MSCI and Don Lee of IFC for their assistance in other important ways.
[2]Park would like to credit and thank Atkins and Ginis for compiling a significant portion of the data presented in this chapter and state that the content of the chapter is not the view of Atkins, Ginis and Emerging Markets Investors Corporation. This chapter could not have been completed without the contribution of Park's co-authors and their editorial suggestions.

quate benchmark market indices for these markets in order to properly track local market movements and measure the performance of fund managers.

Currently, two emerging market indices are subscribed to by pension sponsors and fund managers: IFC Indices and MSCI Emerging Markets Indices (EMI). IFC Indices are published by International Finance Corporation in Washington, D.C., and MSCI EMI are published by Morgan Stanley Capital International in Geneva and New York. Because local market indices of the emerging markets use different criteria for index construction, market indices such as IFC Indices and MSCI EMI which use uniform construction criteria for the various markets are needed for the consistent benchmarking of all emerging markets.

This chapter compares the following characteristics of IFC Indices and MSCI EMI:

- Calculation

- Construction

- Market Weightings and Capitalizations

- Constituent Shares and Market Coverage

- Industrial Composition

- Performance

In its conclusion, the chapter attempts to assist pension sponsors and fund managers to select proper benchmark market indices for their emerging market investment programs.

Calculation of the Indices

There exists no fundamental difference in the principle underlying the calculation of the two indices. Both IFC Indices and MSCI EMI are market capitalization-weighted indices—the market capitalization of a constituent share is calculated by the multiplication of its market price and the number of its shares outstanding. Consequently, the share price change of a larger capitalization constituent will exert a heavier impact on the Indices than the same price change of a small capitalization constituent.[4] If there is any difference in their market capitalization weighting scheme, IFC Indices use the Paache formula whereas MSCI EMI uses the Laspeyres concept of a weighted arithmetic average.

The rationale behind the index weighting scheme by market capitalization is modern portfolio theory (MPT) that an efficient portfolio reflects the equilibrium of present asset supply and demand—that is, an efficient portfolio should represent a market portfolio. Therefore, a larger capitalization asset should be held in a greater proportion in an efficient portfolio.

As we can see in Table 23-1, both IFC and MSCI EM Indices are calculated in local currency and U.S. dollar terms. Also, IFC and MSCI offer total return indices as well as price return indices.[5] The difference in the calculation of the Indices is that whereas MSCI calculates its emerging market indices daily, IFC compiles them weekly and monthly. Moreover, the constituent shares of the Indices are updated periodically in the case of MSCI EMI whereas IFC reviews any change in the constituent shares once a year.

Construction

Table 23-2 compares the construction criteria of the three indices, and Table 23-3 presents their other characteristics such as constituent countries, shares, regional indices, and index base dates. As in Table 23-2, both IFC Indices and MSCI EMI seek to replicate local market industrial composition with constituent shares, the liquidity of which is adequate. However, MSCI EMI differentiates the open markets from the closed ones by publishing two separate indices: MSCI EM Free and MSCI EM Global Indices. MSCI EM Free Indices contain only those shares which can be purchased by non-local investors whereas MSCI EM Global Indices contain investible shares as well as those shares which can be purchased only by local investors. All three emerging market indices seek to have a 60% market coverage of each constituent country. For instance, MSCI EM Free Indices cover 60% of the investible total market capitalization of each constituent country.

As is the case with MSCI EM Global Indices, IFC Indices include non-investible as well as investible shares. However, IFC Indices are broader and more comprehensive than MSCI EM Global Indices in the sense that they include more markets which are either opened on a restricted basis or closed to non-local investors—Table 23-4 presents the current status of the market openings of the

Table 23-1   Calculation of Emerging Market Indices

	IFC Indices	MSCI EMI
Publication of Index Values	Indices are calculated weekly. and monthly.	Indices are calculated once a day with the closing prices of the previous day.
Currencies of Calculation	Local currencies and U.S. dollar	Local currencies and U.S. dollar
Total Return Indices	Available	Available (gross and net dividends)*
Update of Constituent Shares	Constituent shares are updated once a year.	Constituent shares are updated on aperiodic basis as necessary.

*The total returns of MSCI EMI will be available beginning in September 1992.
Source: International Finance Corporation and Morgan Stanley Capital International

Table 23-2   Comparison of Construction Criteria

	IFC Indices	MSCI EM Global Indices	MSCI EM Free Indices
Liquidity	Actively traded shares. Investibility by foreign investors is not considered.	Liquid shares. Investibility by foreign investors is not considered.	Liquid shares. Investibility is an important considera-tion for the inclusion.
Industry Composition	Broad diversification by industry.	Replication of the local industry composition in each constituent country.	Replication of the local industry composi-tion in each constituent country.
Market Capitalization	Approximately 60% of total market capitalization at the end of each year.	Aim for 60% coverage of the available total market capitalization of each constituent market.	60% coverage of the investible total market capitalization of each constituent market. MSCI EM Global Indices' coverage minus non-purchasable shares by foreign investors.

Source: International Finance Corporation and Morgan Stanley Capital International

Table 23-3   Comparison of Constituent Countries, Shares, Regional Indices, and Base Dates (as of January 1992)

	IFC Indices	MSCI EM Global Indices	MSCI EM Free Indices
Constituent Countries	20 countries	14 countries	13 countries*
Constituent Shares	877	537	477
Regional Indices	IFC Composite Index IFC Asia IFC Latin America	EMG Index EMG Far East EMG Latin America	EMF Index EMF Far East EMF Latin America
Base (Inception) Date	Dec. 31, 1984	Dec. 31, 1987	Dec. 31, 1987

*Korea was added to MSCI EM Free Indices in January 1992. Because of the significant restrictions after the market opening, the market coverage of Korea is limited to 20%.

Source: International Finance Corporation and Morgan Stanley Capital International.

Table 23-4   Market Weightings of Emerging Market Indices (as of June 30, 1992)

	Status of Market Opening	Total Universe*	IFC Indices	MSCI EM Global Indices	MSCI EM Free Indices
Argentina	Free entry	3.4%	4.9%	3.3%	5.1%
Brazil	Free entry	6.8%	5.5%	9.9%	14.3%
Chile	Free entry	5.0%	6.2%	7.2%	11.1%
Colombia	Restricted opening	0.7%	1.2%	0.0%	0.0%
M xico	Free entry	17.3%	14.3%	21.4%	25.5%
Venezuela	Restricted opening	1.2%	1.7%	0.0%	0.0%
Latin America		**34.4%**	**33.8%**	**41.7%**	**55.9%**
Korea	Restricted opening	11.5%	12.4%	11.4%	3.7%
Taiwan	Restricted opening	18.2%	19.6%	20.6%	0.0%
Malaysia	Free entry	10.5%	10.7%	10.7%	16.5%
India	Special funds only	9.4%	6.6%	0.0%	0.0%
Thailand	Free entry	5.9%	5.5%	6.7%	10.3%
Philippines	Special classes of shares only	2.1%	2.5%	1.8%	2.8%
Indonesia	Restricted entry	1.1%	1.4%	1.2%	2.1%
Pakistan	Free entry	1.1%	1.1%	0.0%	0.0%
Asia		**60.3%**	**60.8%**	**53.2%**	**36.3%**
Greece	Restricted entry	1.8%	1.9%	1.8%	2.7%
Turkey	Free entry	1.6%	1.4%	1.6%	2.4%
Portugal	Free entry	1.5%	1.5%	1.5%	2.3%
Jordan	Free entry	0.4%	0.4%	0.2%	0.4%
Nigeria	Closed	0.2%	0.2%	0.0%	0.0%
Zimbabwe	Special classes of shares only	0.1%	0.1%	0.0%	0.0%
Europe/Mid East/Africa		**5.6%**	**5.5%**	**5.0%**	**7.8%**

*The figures for the market total are from the IFC Emerging Markets Data Base.

Source: International Finance Corporation and Morgan Stanley Capital International

world's emerging markets. As we can see in Table 23-3, the number of constituent countries for IFC Indices is 20 whereas the number for MSCI EM Global Indices is 14—MSCI EM Free Indices have 13 constituent countries. In case of constituent shares, IFC Indices has 877 whereas MSCI EM Global and Free Indices contain 537 and 477 respectively.

All three emerging market indices offers three regional indices: the composite indices of the world, Asia's and Latin America's emerging markets. Although all three Indices include Greece, Turkey, and Portugal, they do not provide a composite index for the European emerging markets. Among the three, IFC Indices have the longest history. Their inception date was December 31, 1984 whereas MSCI EM Global and Free Indices, December 31, 1987.

Market Weightings and Capitalizations

Tables 23-4 and 23-5 compare the market weightings and capitalizations of the three emerging market indices. In both tables, the figures for "Total Universe" (the market total) are calculated from the IFC Emerging Market Data Base (EMDB). As we can see in Table 23-4, according to the IFC EMDB, Asia accounts for some 60% of the total market capitalization of the world's emerging markets, and Latin America accounts for 34%. The other 6% is located in Europe, the Middle East and Africa. The regional market weightings of IFC Indices are similar to the composition of the IFC EMDB's regional market capitalizations. However, in the case of MSCI EM Free Indices, their weighting of Latin America is larger than IFC Indices' and that of Asia is smaller than IFC Indices'.

Table 23-5   Comparison of Market Capitalization and Constituent Shares (as of June 30, 1992)

	Total Universe*	IFC Indices	MSCI EM Global Indices	MSCI EM Free Indices
Global				
Number of Constituent Shares	7,214	878	535	476
Market Capitalization	US$747bn	US$412bn	US$292bn	US$218bn
% of Total	100%	55%	39%	29%
Asia				
Number of Constituent Shares	5,128	487	302	249
Market Capitalization	US$450bn	US$251	US$157bn	US$97bn
% of Total Market Capitalization	100%	56%	35%	22%
Latin America				
Number of Constituent Shares	1,324	236	135	129
Market Capitalization	2.1%	2.5%	1.8%	2.8%
% of Total Market Capitalization	1.1%	1.4%	1.2%	2.1%
Europe/Mid-East/Africa				
Number of Constituent Shares	762	155	98	98
Market Capitalization	US$41bn	US$23bn	US$15bn	US$15bn
% of Total Market Capitalization	100%	55%	36%	36%

*The figures for the market total are from the IFC Emerging Markets Data Base.

Source: International Finance Corporation and Morgan Stanley Capital International

As we can see in Table 23-4, the market openings of Latin American countries are freer than Asian countries. Because MSCI EM Free Indices accounts for only investible shares, their Latin American weighting (56%) is substantially larger than their Asian market weighting (36%). Moreover, the Latin American weighting of MSCI EM Free Indices (56%) is larger than IFC Indices' 34%, and the Asian market weighting (36%) is smaller than IFC Indices' 61%.

Looking at the individual constituent countries, Taiwan, Mexico, and Korea of IFC Indices have the three largest market capitalization weightings of 20%, 14%, and 12% respectively. In the case of MSCI EM Global Indices, the order of the three largest market capitalization-weighted countries is Mexico (21%), Taiwan (20%) and Korea (11%). Given their emphasis on investibility, the three largest market capitalization-weighted constituent countries of MSCI EM Free Indices are Mexico (26%), Malaysia (17%), and Brazil (14%). Zimbabwe and Nigeria of IFC Indices have the smallest weightings of 0.1% and 0.2% respectively. Jordan and Indonesia are the smallest constituent countries in MSCI EM Global and Free Indices; they are weighted 0.2% and 1.2% respectively for MSCI EM Free Indices and 0.4% and 2.1% for MSCI Global Indices. Two of the world's largest emerging markets, Taiwan and Korea, are located in Asia and have restricted market openings. Because of its restricted market openings, Korea only accounts for 3.7% of the total market capitalization of MSCI EM Free Indices and Taiwan is not even included in MSCI EM Free Indices.

In addition to MSCI EM Free Indices' exclusion of Taiwan, MSCI EM Global and Free Indices do not include countries such as Colombia, Venezuela, India, Pakistan, Nigeria, and Zimbabwe which are the constituent countries of IFC Indices. Except for Nigeria, whose market is closed to inward international investment, the other countries allow the participation of foreign investors even though their market openings are rather restricted.

According to the IFC Emerging Market Data Base (EMDB), the total market capitalization of the world's emerging equity market as of June 1992 is US$747 billion—Morgan Stanley Capital International calculates the total market capitalization of the world's developed markets to be US$5.5 trillion. The total market capitalization of IFC Indices is US$412 billion whereas those of MSCI EM Global and Free Indices are US$292 bn and US$218 bn respectively. IFC Indices cover 55% of the total market capitalization of the IFC EMDB's world's emerging markets whereas MSCI EM Global and Free Indices cover 39% and 29% respectively.

The IFC EMDB estimates that 7,214 shares are listed in the world's emerging stock markets. IFC Indices have 878 constituent shares whereas MSCI EM Global and Free Indices have 535 and 476 respectively. As we can see in Table 23-5, even though the market capitalization weighting of the Latin American portion (56%) of MSCI EM Free Indices is larger than the Asian portion (36%), MSCI EM Free Indices have more constituent shares in Asia (249) than in Latin America (129).

Consequently, the average market capitalization of MSCI EM Free Indices' Asian constituent shares is much smaller than that of the Latin American counterparts.

Constituent Shares and Market Coverage of Each Constituent Country

As we can see in Table 23-6, Korea, Taiwan, and Brazil of IFC Indices have the largest number of constituent shares of 91, 70, and 69 respectively; Venezuela and Zimbabwe have the smallest of 17. In the case of MSCI EM Global and Free Indices, Korea, Thailand, Malaysia, and Brazil have the largest number of constituent shares of 89, 62, 61, and 57 respectively; Argentina and Philippines have the smallest of 15 and 17 respectively.

Table 23-6   Comparison of Number of Constituent Shares of Each Constituent Countries (as of June 30, 1992)

	Total Universe*	IFC Indices	MSCI EM Global Indices	MSCI EM Free Indices
Argentina	177	29	15	15
Brazil	570	69	57	57
Chile	228	35	25	25
Columbia	80	20	0	0
Mexico	203	66	38	32
Venezuela	66	17	0	0
Latin America	**1324**	**236**	**135**	**129**
Korea	688	91	89	89
Taiwan	239	70	53	0
Malaysia	343	62	61	61
India	2649	62	0	0
Thailand	300	51	62	62
Philippines	166	30	17	17
Indonesia	147	63	20	20
Pakistan	596	58	0	0
Asia	**5128**	**487**	**302**	**249**
Greece	129	32	19	19
Turkey	140	25	33	33
Portugal	183	30	26	26
Jordan	101	27	20	20
Nigeria	146	24	0	0
Zimbabwe	63	17	0	0
Europe/Mid East/Africa	**762**	**155**	**98**	**98**

*The figures for the market total are from the IFC Emerging Markets Data Base.

Source: International Finance Corporation and Morgan Stanley Capital International

Except for Mexico and Taiwan, MSCI EM Global and Free Indices have the same number of constituent shares for their constituent countries. As we can see in Table 23-7, this is because Morgan Stanley Capital International calculates the available total market capitalization (construction criterion for MSCI EM Global) and investible total market capitalization (construction criterion for MSCI EM Free) to be same for these countries—see Table 23-2 for the construction criteria of MSCI EM Global and Free Indices. In the case of Korea, MSCI limits the investible total market capitalization of MSCI EM Free Korea to 20% of the available total market capitalization of MSCI EM Global Korea, and uses the same number of constituent shares for both MSCI EM Global and Free Indices.

MSCI EM Global Mexico has 38 constituent shares whereas MSCI EM Free Mexico has 32. Also, as we can see in Table 23-7, MSCI EM Global Mexico covers 49% of the total Mexico market capitalization calculated by the IFC EMDB whereas

Table 23-7   Comparison of Market Capitalization Coverage (as of June 30, 1992)

	Total Universe*	IFC Indices	MSCI EM Global Indices	MSCI EM Free Indices
Latin America				
Argentina	100%	79%	38%	38%
Brazil	100%	45%	54%	54%
Chile	100%	69%	69%	69%
Colombia	100%	95%	0%	0%
Mexico	100%	46%	49%	38%
Venezuela	100%	76%	0%	0%
Asia				
Korea	100%	60%	41%	8%
Taiwan	100%	59%	44%	0%
Malaysia	100%	56%	40%	40%
India	100%	39%	0%	0%
Thailand	100%	52%	45%	45%
Philippines	100%	64%	34%	34%
Indonesia	100%	87%	49%	49%
Pakistan	100%	57%	0%	0%
Europe/Mid-East/Africa				
Greece	100%	59%	38%	38%
Turkey	100%	49%	39%	39%
Portugal	100%	53%	37%	37%
Jordan	100%	61%	29%	29%
Nigeria	100%	68%	0%	0%
Zimbabwe	100%	47%	0%	0%

*The figures for the market total universe are from the IFC Emerging Markets Data Base.

Source: International Finance Corporation and Morgan Stanley Capital International

MSCI EM Free Mexico covers 38%. Because of its restricted market opening, Taiwan is not included in MSCI EM Free Indices.

An interesting statistic to note in Table 23-6 is the number of listed shares in India. According to the IFC EMDB, India has the largest number of listed shares (2,649) which is greater than the total number of shares listed in Latin America (1,324). However, India is not even included in MSCI EM Global and Free Indices. Most of the shares listed on the 20 different Indian stock exchanges are small-capitalization, illiquid stocks—given that India's market capitalization is US$70 bn, the average market capitalization of these shares is a mere US$26 million. Currently, these shares cannot be bought directly by foreign investors. Foreign investors can only invest in the Indian stock market indirectly by buying special country funds. Even if the Indian government liberalizes its market to foreign investment, most of these shares are non-investible for institutional-size international investors. If we take into account the market impact which a large international institutional investor will create to buy these shares, the transaction cost for these shares is quite substantial.

Industrial Composition

Figure 23-1 presents the industrial composition of the three emerging market indices. MSCI EM Free Indices are more heavily weighted in the telecommunication sector than IFC Indices and MSCI EM Global Indices. The electrical and electronic sectors have a larger weighting in IFC Indices than in MSCI Global and Free Indices. In the case of the banking industry, its weighting in IFC Indices and MSCI EM Global Indices is heavier than that in MSCI EM Free Indices.

Performance

Because the total returns for MSCI Emerging Markets Global and Free Indices are not currently available, the price returns of the three emerging market indices and MSCI EAFE (Europe, Australia and Far East) Index are compared in Figure 23-2 and Figure 23-3. As we can see, all emerging market indices (IFC Composite, MSCI EM Global and MSCI EM Free) outperformed EAFE Index during the four and one-half year period from December 1987 to June 1992. In addition to the diversification of portfolio, emerging market investing offers the enhancement of returns.

As it can be seen in Figure 23-2, MSCI EM Global Index consistently outperformed IFC Composite Index. In the case of MSCI EM Free Index, it had been lagging behind IFC Composite Index until April 1990. After that point, MSCI EM Free Index has been showing returns exceeding both IFC Composite and MSCI EM

Figure 23-1

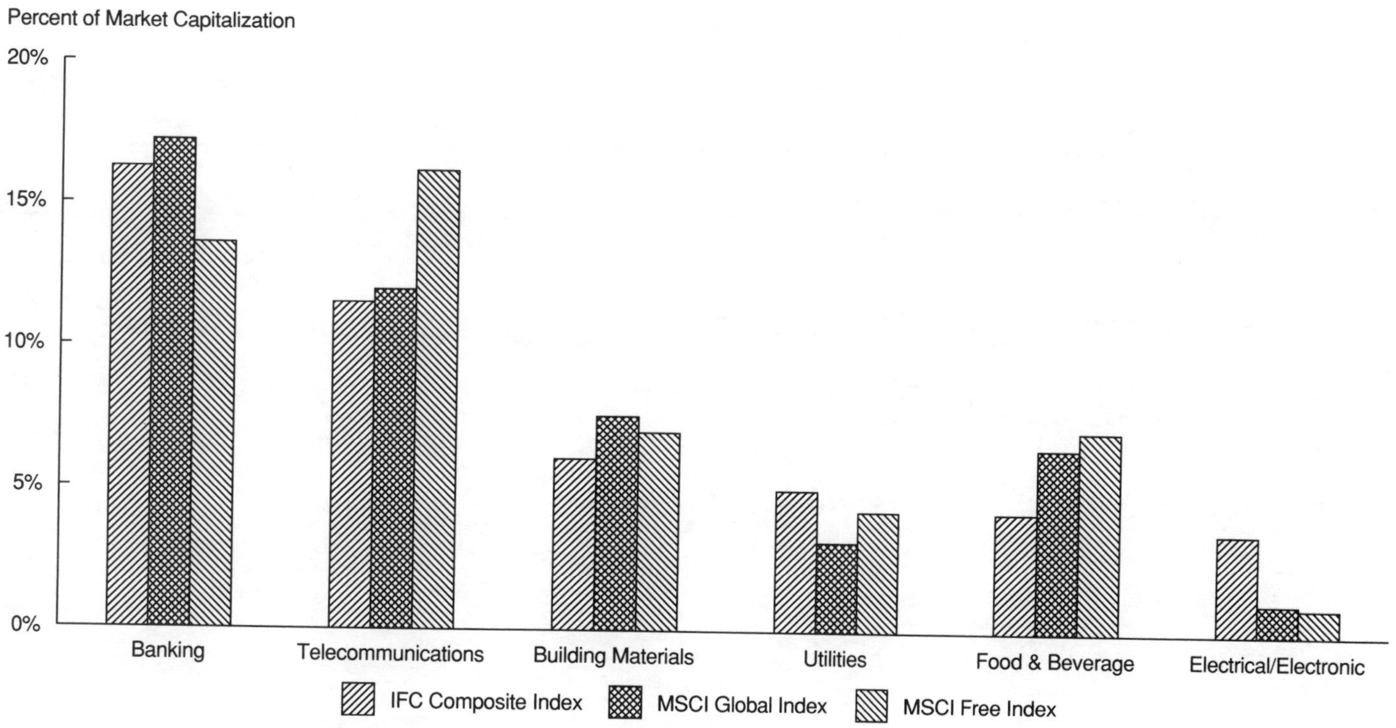
Percent of Market Capitalization
20%
15%
10%
5%
0%
Banking
Telecommunications
Building Materials
Utilities
Food & Beverage
Electrical/Electronic
IFC Composite Index
MSCI Global Index
MSCI Free Index

Figure 23-2

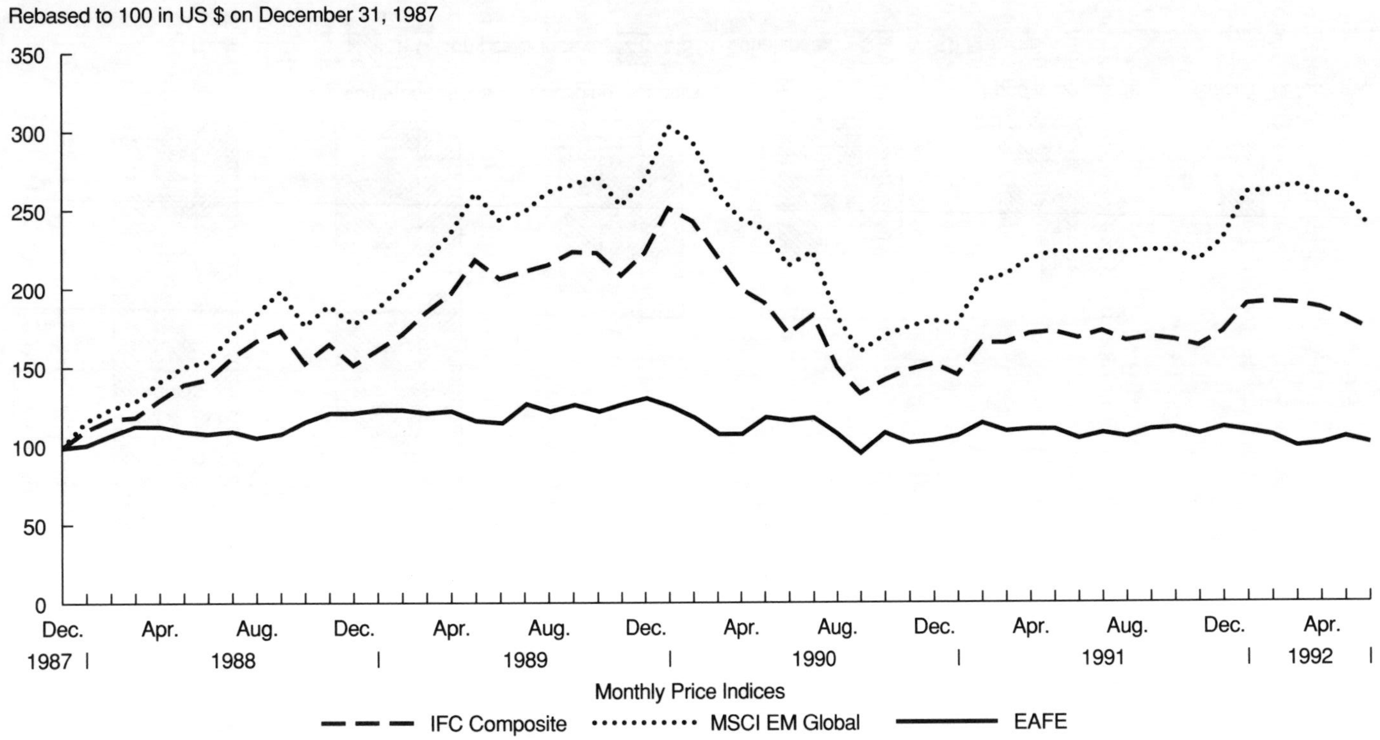
Rebased to 100 in US $ on December 31, 1987
350
300
250
200
150
100
50
0
Dec.
Apr.
Aug.
Dec.
Apr.
Aug.
Dec.
Apr.
Aug.
Dec.
Apr.
Aug.
Dec.
Apr.
1987
1988
1989
1990
1991
1992
Monthly Price Indices
IFC Composite
MSCI EM Global
EAFE

Figure 23-3

Rebased to 100 in US $ on December 31, 1987

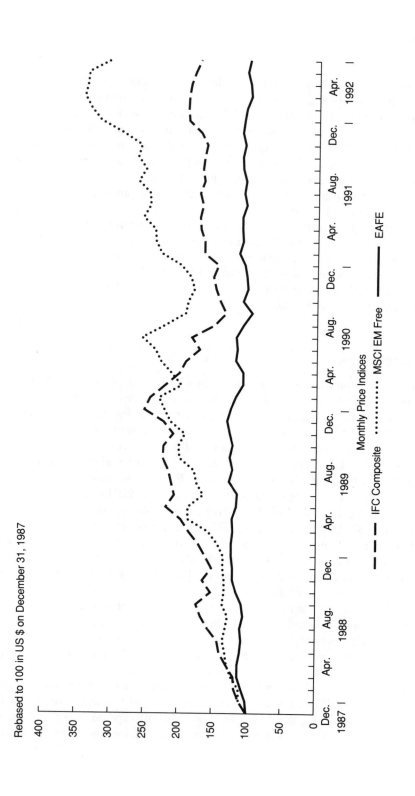

Global Indices—see Figure 23-3. These divergences in the performance of the emerging market indices could be attributed to the concentration of large capitalization shares in MSCI EM Global and Free Indices. A small number of largely-capitalized shares tend to dominate the market movements in the emerging markets. For instance, in 1990 four blue chip shares (Ayala Corporation, Phillippine Long Distance Telephone, Phillippine National Bank, and San Miguel) accounted for about 95% of the daily trading volume in the Phillippine equity market. In the case of Mexico, ten largely-capitalized shares accounted for about 83% of the 1991 total trading volume. Furthermore, in the case of most of the Latin markets such as Mexico, the participation of foreign investors has been largely responsible for the major market movements. Foreign investors tend to buy largely-capitalized shares of well-recognized companies due to liquidity and investment security. Consequently, large capitalization shares have been leading the market movements of the emerging markets, and this could be the major reason why MSCI EM Free has outperformed MSCI Global and IFC Indices.

Conclusion

Given that fund managers can only invest in the open markets, MSCI EM Free Indices appear to be the proper benchmark market index for measuring the performance of fund managers.[6] However, as more emerging markets are expected to open their doors to foreign investment, all emerging markets should be researched and monitored so that investment opportunities due to market opening can be seized immediately—for instance, Korea liberalized its equity market in January 1992 and was then added to MSCI EM Free Indices. For the purpose of research and broad monitoring of emerging markets, IFC Indices and MSCI EM Global Indices are constructed better than MSCI EM Free Indices. As we have seen in Table 23-2 through Table 23-7, the universe of IFC Indices is more extensive than that of MSCI EM Global Indices. Given its depth, IFC Indices will be the most superior for emerging market research. Also, some fund managers have found ways to invest in certain closed markets, and they might see IFC Indices as a better benchmark index for their investment portfolio.

If there is any one drawback of IFC Indices it is that they are calculated weekly rather than daily as in case of MSCI EM Global and Free Indices. Because the small capitalization shares of the emerging markets are traded quite infrequently, the accurate valuation of their daily price is not an easy task. Also, for IFC Indices whose universe is more extensive, getting all the necessary prices and other relevant data from the markets such as Zimbabwe on a timely daily basis will require substantial technological and labor resources. These liquidity and resource issues probably are the main reasons for the weekly rather than daily update of IFC Indices. One might claim that for the benchmarking purpose, whether the index calculation is weekly or daily will not make a significant difference. However, in the case of severe market volatilities which we happened to witness in the Latin American markets in the summer of 1992, the daily calculation of the benchmark indices will be important information to pension sponsors and fund managers who would like to closely monitor the status of their portfolios during the time of important market development.

Also, because the constituent shares of IFC Indices are updated only once a year, any change in the local market before the annual update of constituent shares will not be appropriately reflected in IFC Indices. If the measurement of performance is done only once a year, the annual update of constituent shares by IFC Indices will not present much problem. However, if the measurement of performance is conducted more frequently (for instance, quarterly), MSCI EM Free Indices whose constituent shares are updated periodically might be the better barometer of the local markets.

APPENDIX

The following are the mathematical algorithms used in calculating market capitalization-weighted indices:

A. Value of Index in Time 1 (the Inception of Indices)

$$IDX_1 = \frac{MV_1}{B_1}\left(= \frac{\text{Market Value in time 1}}{\text{Base Market Value in time 1}}\right)$$

$$MV_1 = \sum_{n=1}^{N} P_{n,1}S_{n,1}$$

B_1 $= MV_1 / 100$

IDX_1 = index value in time 1

N = the number of constituent stocks in index

$P_{n,1}$ = the price of constituent stock n at time 1

$S_{n,1}$ = the number of shares outstanding for constituent stock n at time 1

B. Value of Index in Time T

$$IDX_t = \frac{MV_t}{B_t}\left(= \frac{\text{Market Value in time t}}{\text{Base Market Value in time t}}\right)$$

$$= \frac{\sum_{n=1}^{N} P_{n,1}S_{n,1}}{B_t}$$

IDX_t = index value in time t

N = the number of constituent stocks in Index

$P_{n,t}$ = the price of constituent stock n at time t

$S_{n,t}$ = the number of shares outstanding for constituent stock n at time t

B_t = base market value in time t; $B_t = B_{t=1}$ when there is no change in capitalization structure of constituent stocks between time t and time $t-1$. Otherwise, base market value must be adjusted. The adjustment of base market value is explained below.

C. Adjustment of Base Market Value (B_t)

B_t will be equal to B_{t-1} if there is no change in capitalization structure of constituent stocks between time t–1 and time t. For instance, if there has been no change in capitalization structure of constituent stocks between time 1 and time t, B_t will be equal to B_1. Otherwise, B_t will be adjusted in the following way (Formula A):

$$B_t = B_{t-1} \times \frac{MV_{t-1} + C_t}{MV_{t-1}}$$

C_t = market value change due to a change in capitalization structure

The corporate actions affecting capitalization structure that will necessitate the adjustment in base market value are:

1. New share issuance
2. Stock repurchase
3. Rights issuance
4. Addition of a new constituent stock
5. Deletion of a constituent stock

(Note that such corporate actions as stock split and stock dividend will not entail an adjustment in base market value because they do not change the net market capitalization of company.)

The above five corporate actions will change the market capitalization of the affected constituent stock without changing the value of investment in that stock.

Index should only reflect the market trend which affects the value of your investment. Therefore, the market value change due to such an event as rights issuance, which does not affect the value of your investment but only the level of Index, must be offset. This offsetting is done by adjusting base market value as explained in Formula A above.

In Formula A, the ratio of $(MV_{t-1} + C_t)$ and (MV_{t-1}) measures the proportional change in market value in time t vis-a-vis time t–1. Moreover, the multiplication of the above ratio to the previous base market value, B_t, calculates the new base market value vis-a-vis the old value.

The calculation of the new market base market value vis-a-vis the old value is an offsetting adjustment which insures that an increase or decrease in market value due to the change in capitalization structure will have no impact on the level of index.

This method of adjustment of base market value maintains: 1) the comparability of the index values in different time periods; 2) the continuity of the index in tracking the stock market trend over a long period of time.

D. Calculation of Index Value in U.S. Dollar

IDX_{tLC} = index value in local currency in time t

IDX_{tUS} = index value in U.S. dollar in time t

MV_t = market value in local currency in time t

B_t = base market value in local currency in time t

C_t = market value change in local currency in time t due to the change in capitalization structure of constituent stocks

X_t = U.S. Dollar per Local Currency in time t

$$IDX_{1LC} = \frac{MV_1}{B_1} = \frac{MV_1}{MV_1/100} = 100$$

$$IDX_{1US} = \frac{MV_1 \times X_1}{B_1 \times X_1} = IDX_{1LC} = 100$$

$$IDX_{2US} = \frac{MV_2 \times X_2}{B_1 \times X_1 \times \dfrac{MV_1 \times X_1 + C_2 \times X_1{}^7}{MV_1 \times X_1}}$$

$$= \frac{MV_2 \times X_2}{B_1 \times X_1 \times \dfrac{(MV_1 + C_2) \times X_1}{MV_1 \times X_1}}$$

$$IDX_{2US} = \frac{MV_2 \times X_2}{\left(B_1 \times \dfrac{MV_1 + C_2}{MV_1} \right) \times X_1}$$

$$IDX_{3US} = \frac{MV_3 \times X_3}{B_2 \times X_1{}^8 \times \dfrac{MV_2 \times X_2 + C_3 \times X_2}{MV_2 \times X_2}}$$

$$IDX_{3US} = \frac{MV_3 \times X_3}{B_2 \times X_1{}^8 \times \dfrac{MV_2 \times X_2 + C_3 \times X_2}{MV_2 \times X_2}}$$

$$= \frac{MV_3 \times X_3}{\left(B_1 \times \dfrac{MV_1 + C_2}{MV_1}\right) \times X_1 \times \dfrac{(MV_2 + C_3) \times X_2}{MV_2 \times X_2}}$$

$$= \frac{MV_3 \times X_3}{\left(B_1 \times \dfrac{MV_1 + C_2}{MV_1}\right) \times \left(\dfrac{MV_2 + C_3}{MV_2}\right) \times X_1}$$

$$= \frac{MV_3 \times X_3}{B_2 \times \left(\dfrac{MV_2 + C_3}{MV_2 \times X_2}\right) \times X_1}$$

Therefore, it can be concluded that:

$$IDX_{tUS} = \frac{MV_t \times X_t}{B_{t-1} \times \left(\dfrac{MV_{t-1} + C_t}{MV_{t-1}}\right) \times X_1}$$

$$= \frac{MV_t}{B_{t-1} \times \left(\dfrac{MV_{t-1} + C_t}{MV_{t-1}}\right)} \times \frac{X_t}{X_1}$$

[3]For a detailed discussion of the risk/return benefits of investment in the emerging markets, see Keith K.H. Park, Chapter 1, "Enhanced Efficiency of Global Portfolio Diversification Through Emerging Market Investing."

[4]See the Appendix for the mathematical algorithms used for calculating market capitalization-weighted indices.

[5]When this article was being finished in the spring of 1992, MSCI informed the author that it would offer the total return indices of MSCI EMI beginning in September 1992.

[6]Because MSCI EAFE Index includes shares which cannot be purchased by foreign investors, its non-investibility has been pointed out as a major drawback against adequately benchmarking local markets. Responding to this criticism, Morgan Stanley Capital International later introduced EAFE Free Index. In constructing emerging market indices, MSCI took into account pension sponsors and fund managers' response to non-investibility and has created both MSCI EM Free and Global Indices.

[7]Note that C_2 is multiplied by X_1. The reason for this is that the ratio of $(MV_1 + C_2)$ and (MV_1) is intended to measure the proportional change in market value in time 2 vis-a-vis market value in time 1. Consequently, the proportional change in time 2 is measured in time 1 currency terms. Extending this reasoning, it can be concluded that in converting the index value in local currency to that in U.S. dollar, Ct should always be multiplied by X_{t-1}.

[8]$B_2 X_1$ is obtained from the denominator of IDX2US, which is mathematically explained on the previous page.

24

CLOSED-END EMERGING COUNTRY FUNDS REVIEW

Michael T. Porter
Vice President
Smith Barney, Harris Upham & Co.
New York, United States

The Case for Emerging Markets

Over the past few years, investor interest in the world's emerging markets has expanded significantly. This interest has been fueled by the relatively high returns recorded by emerging markets and by their perceived potential for large returns in the future. This chapter outlines the case for emerging markets and profiles the U.S.-listed country funds, which have been popular avenues of investment in emerging markets.

The world's emerging markets are shown in Figure 24-1 and include such exotic places as Pakistan, Sri Lanka, Turkey, Jordan, and Venezuela.

However, investors traditionally have had few means of entering LDC markets. Buying foreign stocks is cumbersome and expensive, complicated by multiple commissions and custodial fees. Other impediments include a shortage of stock, inadequate financial disclosure, ownership limits, and foreign exchange controls. The easiest way has been to put away money in closed-end single- or multi-country funds. Since the inception of **Mexico Fund** in 1981, the number of emerging country funds listed in the New York Stock Exchange has grown to 22 (see Figure 24-2).

Figure 24-1 The World's Emerging Stock Markets, 1990 (Market Capitalization in US $)

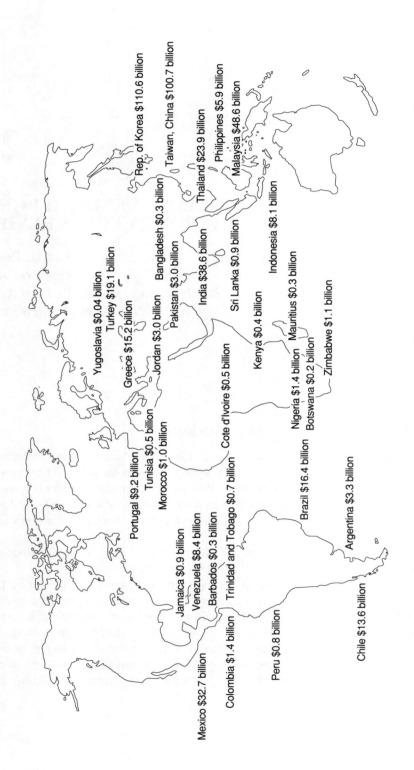

Figure 24-2 U.S.-Listed Closed-End Country Funds, Initial Public Offerings 1980–1990 (In U.S. $ Millions)

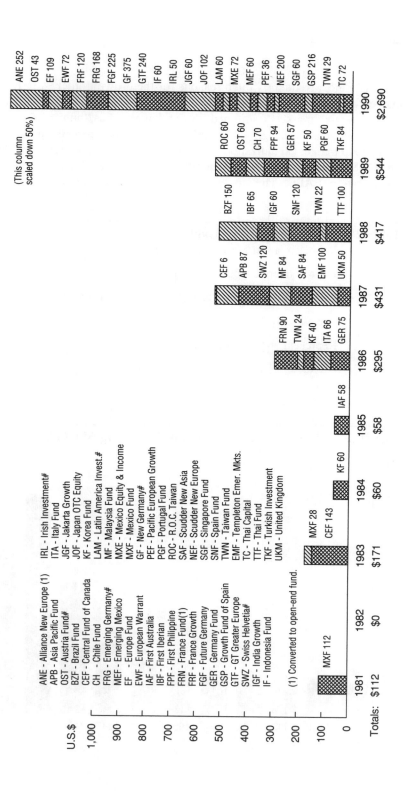

The most frequently cited reasons for the growing interest in LDC equity markets are shown in Table 24-1.

Emerging markets traditionally were thought of as "mini-markets" or "little casinos," but that is changing. Currently, there are more than 30 emerging markets, with a total market capitalization of around $522 billion at present, up 500 percent since 1980 (see Figure 24-3), and equivalent to 15 percent of non-U.S. world market capitalization (EAFE). The top 20 represent $1.8 trillion in gross domestic product

---

Table 24-1   Why Emerging Markets?

- Represent a fast growing part of the world economy

- Have delivered superior returns

- Provide further diversification of global portfolios

- Are attractively valued

- Represent huge marketplaces

- Are underweighted in global portfolios

Figure 24-3 Eleven Years' Growth of Emerging Markets

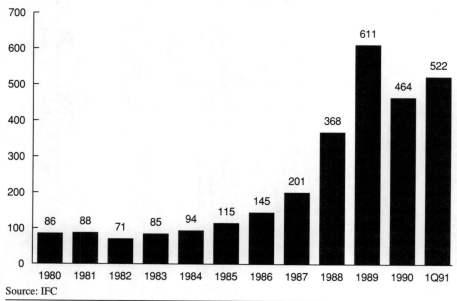

Source: IFC

(GDP). Taken together, emerging markets are bigger than the markets of Germany, France, and Canada (see Figure 24-4). Investors gradually are turning their attention to this increasingly important asset class.

One of the main reasons for putting money into LDC markets is the potential strength of corporate earnings. Emerging markets represent a very dynamic part of the world economy (see Figures 24-5 and 24-6). In the 1965–1989 period, developing nations grew at a 4.7 percent average annual rate, compared with 3.1 percent for the industrialized countries. Collectively, emerging nations should continue to experience growth rates exceeding those of industrializing countries, as the time it takes to double per-capita incomes in the early stages of industrialization has fallen dramatically. In theory, higher economic growth rates translate into higher corporate profit growth rates and share prices.

Emerging markets have delivered superior returns and offer potential high returns. Generally, over one-, two-, five-, and ten-year periods, emerging markets have outperformed developed markets. For example, markets in Mexico, Thailand, Taiwan, Venezuela, Malaysia, and Singapore have experienced growth of more than 100 percent (in dollar terms) since year-end 1988, compared with 54 percent for the United States and 7 percent for the EAFE Index (see Figure 24-7 and Appendix F).

Emerging markets can provide further diversification of global portfolios. Emerging markets have exhibited above-average returns with enormous volatility

Figure 24-4 Emerging Markets versus Major Markets Year-End 1990

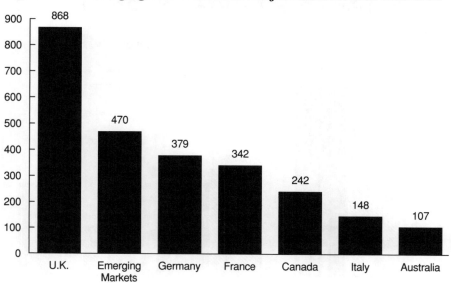

Source: IFC, MSCIP

**Figure 24-5   Gross Domestic Product Growth Rates
Annual Percentage Change**

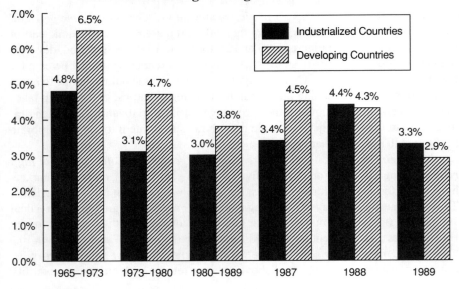

Source: World Development Report, 1991

Figure 24-6   Growth of GNP per Capita (Average Annual Percentage Change)

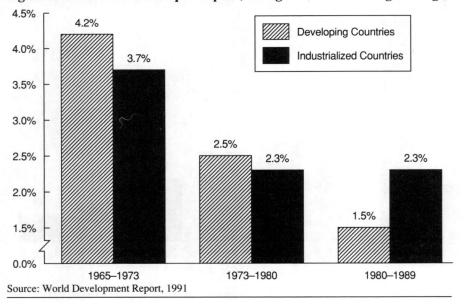

Source: World Development Report, 1991

**Figure 24-7 Cumulative Returns Through March 31, 1991
(In U.S. $; Dec. 1984 = 100)**

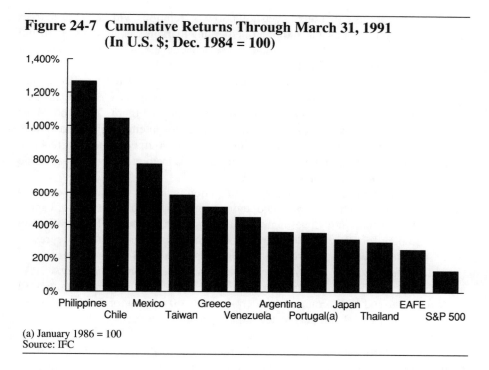

(a) January 1986 = 100
Source: IFC

**Figure 24-8 Correlation Coefficients: Emerging Markets versus
S&P 500 (Five Years Ending March 31, 1991)**

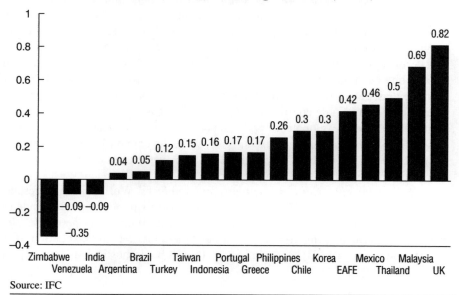

Source: IFC

individually, yet these markets have shown low correlations with the U.S. market and with each other. Thus, the addition of emerging markets can help raise portfolio returns while spreading risk. Correlations for selected developing markets versus the S&P 500 are shown in Figure 24-8.

Besides having good growth characteristics, emerging markets offer attractive equity valuations when measured by the yardsticks used in developed markets, such as price-to-earnings and price-to-book value ratios. Figures 24-9 and 24-10 show selected market averages. In general, rising ratios in emerging markets have offered opportunities for significant capital appreciation. In countries where share prices are low, the potential expansion in multiples is even greater than that of the growth in the nation's economy as a whole.

Another characteristic of a developing nation is that its capital market structure takes time to catch up with its economic progress. The structural lag of capital markets behind economic development is illustrated in Figure 24-11. Developing nations account for 12 percent of world gross domestic product, yet they represent only 5 percent of world market capitalization. This gap should narrow over time.

There is significant potential for further development of emerging markets. As a percentage of GDP, capitalization of the 20 largest emerging markets was 32 percent at year-end 1990, compared with 50 percent–60 percent for developed countries. Many of the stock markets in developing countries are very small in relation to the countries' economies, as seen in Figure 24-12.

Future liberalization of their financial markets, relaxation of foreign investment barriers, privatization, and the transition away from small, privately-held companies to public corporations could fuel high stock market expansion in developing countries in the 1990s. This would be positive for the country funds that invest in them.

Developing countries are overcoming historical objections to foreign investment. Increasingly, developing countries are coming to appreciate the benefits of open markets and private initiative. Many are recognizing that equity markets are integral to economic development and that foreign investment can act as a source of long-term capital. This trend should continue as long as the world's commercial banks consider themselves overextended in developing countries. Chile, for example, has shown what a Latin American economy can do if free enterprise is given a chance and state controls are dismantled. It has converted foreign debt to equity, encouraged development of private pension funds, and amended tax laws to provide greater investment incentives. As a result, the country has enjoyed strong growth since 1985. Mexico, Turkey, and Brazil are examples of countries that have opened up and seen their stock markets surge.

Developing countries represent huge marketplaces. World Bank projections suggest that by the year 2025, 85 percent of the world's population will reside in developing countries. Yet, industrialized countries account for 74 percent of the world's GDP. Developing countries will have huge markets to be satisfied. It is forecast that much of LDC economic growth will be domestic-led—not export

Figure 24-9   Comparative Price-Earnings Ratios (March 31, 1991)

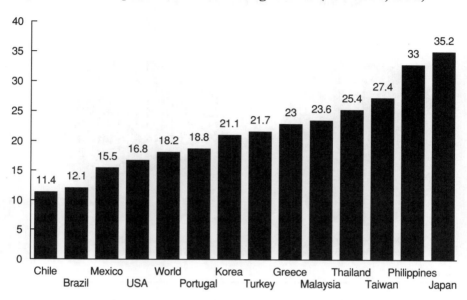

Figure 24-10   Comparative Price-Book Ratios (March 31, 1991)

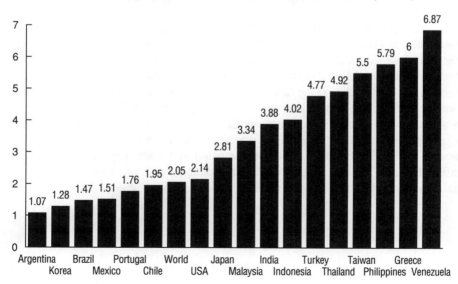

Source: IFC, MSCIP

**Figure 24-11   Structured Lag of Capital Markets
Behind Economic Development**

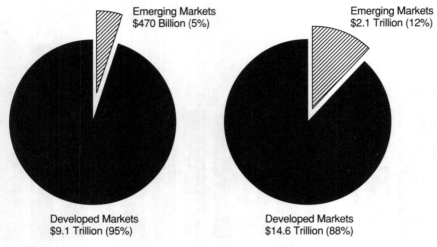

Emerging Markets
$470 Billion (5%)

Emerging Markets
$2.1 Trillion (12%)

Developed Markets
$9.1 Trillion (95%)

Developed Markets
$14.6 Trillion (88%)

Source: IFC

based. Many large Third World countries, including India, Brazil, and China, will
not need to export to grow. At the same time, they should see their standard of living
climb but still remain low enough that wages are competitive with those of industrialized countries. Consequently, they present exciting opportunities for early
investors.

Emerging markets are underrepresented in global portfolios. As noted earlier,
emerging markets' share of world GDP is 12 percent, but they account for only 5
percent of world market capitalization. This gap is likely to narrow over time,
because domestic demand—not foreign demand—traditionally has been the force
behind the past performance of developing stock markets. As global investors
become aware of the tremendous opportunities in Third World markets, the flow of
new equity from capital exporting countries such as Japan should increase. While
growing, foreign equity investment in emerging markets currently is believed to
amount to only $10 billion–$15 billion, compared with a total capitalization of $500
billion for those markets. Supply of capital should not act as a constraint on potential development of the emerging markets, as suggested in Table 24-2.

**Figure 24-12   Emerging Markets Equity Capitalization as a
Percentage of 1989 GDP/GNP (December 31, 1990)**

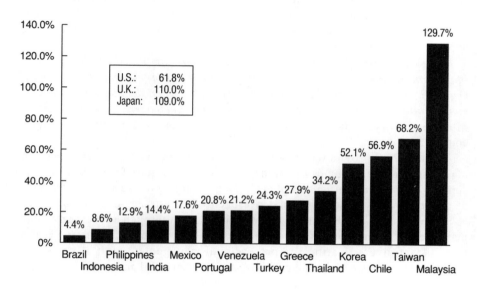

Source: IFC

Table 24-2   Assets in Emerging Markets

	1989 $ billion (Estimated)	2000 $ billion (Illustrative)
A. Total Assets of Institutional Investors	7,500	20,000
B. Of Which Assets in Foreign Equities as a Percentage of Total Assets (A)	750 (10%)	3,000 (15%)
C. Assets of Nonresidents in Emerging Markets	15	100
D. Total Capitalization of Emerging Markets	620	1,800

Source: Wider (No. 5)

Emerging Market Country Funds

There is a nice distribution of U.S.-listed funds that target every important emerging market. This distribution permits investors to take advantage of declines in some markets while others are going up. In other words, the investor can move from funds that target markets that are high into funds that target markets that are low, and hopefully catch the moves as they shift.

Despite these advantages, single-country funds can be risky because a very important factor—the question of timing—is left to the investor. Fortunately, regional emerging market funds also are available when the market timing and country allocation decisions are left to the investment manager. Another advantage of multi-country funds is that they may invest in markets for which no single-country funds exist.

Table 24-3 provides a rundown of the advantages of closed-end funds. A major attraction of the funds is that they offer the opportunity for investors to circumvent the practical difficulties of getting into emerging markets. Funds also may be used to diversify existing portfolio investments. For restricted-market funds, such as South Korea, India, Brazil, and Taiwan, investment through a specialized fund may offer the optimal way to overcome investment restrictions. Country funds also give instant diversification and professional management with a very small minimum investment. The country funds are SEC-registered and trade on the New York Stock Exchange, so they can be easily bought and sold.

Because closed-end funds issue a fixed number of shares, they trade at a premium, parity, or discount to their net asset values. Whether a fund sells at a discount or premium, the investor has two sources of risk and return. The first is associated with net asset value movement and the second is related to any shift in the discount or premium. Consequently, emerging market country funds can be more

---

Table 24-3   Advantages to Closed-End Country Funds

- Instant, wide diversification

- Country allocation vehicles

- Lower minimum investment

- Active professional management

- NYSE liquidity and SEC accountability

- Cost-effective access to restricted markets

- Attractive discount/premiums

---

volatile than, say, the U.S. or U.K. stock markets. The key, then, is to identify funds (1) that invest in attractive markets or regions, and (2) whose shares trade at lower-than-usual premiums or steeper-than-normal discounts.

In general, if a premium narrows (or, alternatively, a discount widens) while an investor is holding closed-end fund shares, there will be a reduction in performance relative to net asset value return. By the same token, if a premium expands (or discount narrows), the fund's share price will outperform the net asset value. Because investors tend to overreact to both good and bad news, the size of a fund's discount often is a reliable signal of when to buy or sell it. Table 24-4 gives some of the variables that affect the valuations of country funds. The most common interpretation is the degree of accessibility offered by the host market of a fund. Closed- or restricted-market funds (e.g., South Korea, Brazil, and Taiwan) often are associated with premiums, reflecting their scarcity value and supply/demand imbalances. The valuations of a fund's portfolio companies also are important, as is the track record of the fund and the perceived potential of the underlying market.

As Figure 24-13 suggests, there appears to be a correlation between discounts, market direction, and investor sentiment. Premiums prevail at equity market tops, while large discounts are seen following sharp market corrections. In general, it has been significantly more profitable to sell shares in country funds selling at narrow discounts, or premiums, and to buy them at large discounts.

Table 24-4   Discount-Premium Considerations

- Open, semi-open, and closed markets
- Insufficient research coverage
- Valuations of comparable funds
- Tax selling
- Underlying market valuation and direction
- Liquidity of underlying portfolio
- Performance record of fund
- Reputation of manager and/or advisor
- Management fees and expenses
- Foreign exchange rate movements
- Open-ending provisions

Figure 24-13 Closed-End Country Funds (Average Premium/Discount)

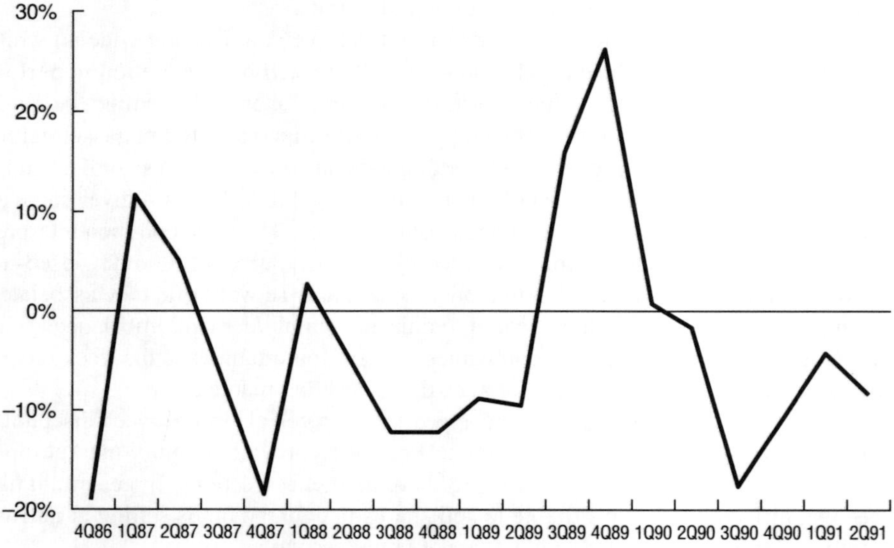

Table 24-5 provides details on the Latin American funds. This year, Latin American markets have outperformed, reflecting investor enthusiasm over the region's trends toward democracy, privatization, economic liberalization, and fiscal discipline.

The portfolios of the Latin funds are profiled in Appendix E. (Additional data on share price, net asset value, and premium/discount history are found in Appendix D.)

Table 24-5   Latin American Emerging Market Funds

Single Country	Symbol	Manager/Advisor
Brazil Fund	BZF	Scudder Stevens & Clark
Chile Fund	CH	BEA Associates
Emerging Mexico Fund	MEF	Santander Management Inc.
Mexico Fund	MXF	Impulsora del Fondo
Mexico Equity and Income Fund	MXE	Acci Worldwide SA/Advantage Advisors

Regional

Latin America Investment Fund	LAM	BEA Associates/Salomon Bros. Asset Mgmt.

Of the European emerging markets, only Greece is unrepresented in the United States. (There is a Greece Fund listed in London.) Austria Fund# is included because it has bought into Hungarian investments. No Eastern European funds have been launched in the United States to date. These countries do not have established equity markets, making investment opportunities available mostly through private placements and joint ventures (see Table 24-6).

Appendix F provides updated fact sheets on the European emerging markets funds.

The popularity of Asia is reflected in the large number of vehicles that invest in this dynamic region. In several cases, such as Taiwan, Thailand, and Indonesia, the investor has more than one fund to choose from.

Refer to Appendix G for updated fact sheets on the Asian emerging markets funds in our universe.

Fortunately, there are attractive multi-country funds that target Asian markets (see Tables 24-7 and 24-8). These vehicles have been good performers and are espe-

Table 24-6   European Emerging Market Funds

	Symbol	Manager/Advisor
Austrial Fund	OST	Alliance Capital Mgmt.
		Girozentrale Capital Mgmt.
Portugal Fund	PGF	BEA Associates Sociifa & Beta
Turkish Investment Fund	TKF	Morgan Stanley Asset Mgmt.
		TEB Ekonomi Arastirmalari

Table 24-7   Asian Emerging Market Funds

Single Country	Symbol	Manager/Advisor
First Philippine Fund	FPF	Clemente Capital/PNB Investment Ltd.
India Growth Fund	IGF	Unit Trust of India
Indonesia Fund	IF	BEA Associates/Jantes Capal (Far East) Ltd.
Jakarta Growth Fund	JGF	Namura Capital Management
Korea Fund	KF	Scudder Stevens & Clark/Daswoo Capital Management
Malaysia Fund	MF	Morgan Stanley Asset Mgmt./Arab Malaysian Consultant Sda Bhd.
ROC Taiwan Fund	ROC	International Investment Trust
Singapore Fund	SGF	DBS Asset Mgmt./Daiwa Int'l Capital Mgmt.
Taiwan Fund	TWN	China Securities Inv. Trust Corp./Fidelity Int'l Inv. Advisors Ltd.
Thai Capital	TC	Mutual Fund Co. of Thailand/Daiwa Int'l Capital Mgmt.
Thai Fund	TTF	Morgan Stanley Asset Mgmt./Mutual Fund Co. of Thailand

Table 24-8   Asian Emerging Market Funds

Regional	Symbol	Manager/Advisor
Asia Pacific Fund	APB	Baring Int'l Investment (Far East) Ltd.
Scudder New Asia Fund	SAF	Scudder Stevens & Clark

Global

Templeton Emerging Markets Fund	EMF	Templeton, Gailbraith & Hansberger Ltd.

cially suitable for investors who wish to avoid making market timing or country allocation decisions. The portfolios of these funds concentrate on Southeast Asian economies, which are benefiting from regional growth trends in manufacturing, as well as from strong investment flows from Japan.

In the United States, there is only one publicly-traded *global* emerging markets fund: Templeton Emerging Markets Fund. This fund allows investors to play emerging markets as an asset class—as a growing part of the global economy and world market capitalization.

In conclusion, emerging markets are coming of age and country funds are both a practical and economical way to access them. Global opportunities should not be ignored, and there currently are vehicles in place that can give investors access to those opportunities, with a much greater degree of confidence than in the past. *

*Please see Appendices A through G at the end of this book for the detailed emerging market performance statistics and closed-end country fund data. Appendices A through G are reprinted with permission from *Closed-End Emerging Country Funds Review* by Michael T. Porter, Smith Barney, Harris, Upham & Co.

ADRs AND OPPORTUNITIES FOR INVESTMENT IN THE EMERGING ASIAN AND LATIN AMERICAN EQUITY MARKETS

John R. Evans, Vice President
Miguel Martinez-Blank, Vice President
Bank of New York, New York, United States

Because greater diversification of institutional and portfolio assets is one of the major objectives for investment in the emerging Asian and Latin American equity markets, the demand for issuers with American Depositary Receipt or ADR programs has increased significantly. In addition to being rewarded with above average returns, ADR investors typically enjoy greater liquidity since the ADR trades in both the United States and the issuer's own stock market in ordinary share form and benefit from lower handling costs as global custodian charges are eliminated.

Advantages of Investing With ADRs

An ADR is a certificate that represents ownership in a non-U.S. company's publicly traded securities that may be traded on either a U.S. exchange such as the New York Stock Exchange or on the over-the-counter market or "pink sheets." Some of the major hurdles investors face in investing in the Asian and Latin American emerging markets that can be overcome by using ADRs include:

- Lack of information in English.

- Extended settlement periods.

- Lack of technically sophisticated custodian networks.

- Absence of favorable tax treaties or partially blocked currencies.

- Delays in receiving corporate action notices for dividends, annual general meetings, etc.

In each instance, ADR facilities are structured to provide maximum information flow and liquidity while also resolving the macroimpediments of investing in these markets.

Scope of Comparison

The focus of this chapter will be on the ADR programs of Asian and Latin companies from the non-Japan and Australia equity markets in the Pacific Rim including Hong Kong, Indonesia, Korea, Malaysia, the Philippines, Singapore, Taiwan, and Thailand, and those in Latin America including Argentina, Brazil, Chile, Mexico, and Venezuela.

Examples abound where ADR facilities have been established to resolve many of the aforementioned impediments and include issuers from Thailand, Chile, and Venezuela. In Thailand, where there is no applicable double taxation treaty, the ADR serves to eliminate a 20% capital gains withholding tax at the source, enabling investors to receive the full value of their investment while retaining the benefits of beneficial ownership—a requirement of many U.S. institutional investors. In Chile, the value-added aspect of the ADR facility enables the investor to have access to the official rate of exchange in settling ordinary and ADR share trading, allowing for a more efficient equity trading market to develop. In Venezuela, the establishment of the first ADR program for Sivensa has created a more favorable investment climate due to certain modifications of the country's tax code with regards to capital gains treatment.

Issuer Motivations

Today, a parade of Asian and Latin American companies are using ADRs to enhance shareholder value, raise equity or quasi-equity by way of a U.S. public offering or private placement under Rule 144A, and enhance the corporate profile for the issuers' products, services, and financial instruments. Such situations provide U.S. investors with interesting opportunities to profit from some of the fastest growing equity markets in the world. As Table 25-1 at the end of this chapter indicates, the variety and industry diversity of issuers with ADR programs is quite evident.

In addition to raising capital, issuer motivations for pursuing a U.S. ADR public offering include name recognition, enhanced liquidity, and broadened investor base. Such companies include Hong Kong Telecommunications, The Chilean Telephone Company, and more recently, Telefonos de Mexico. On the other hand, particularly among Latin issuers, many companies are looking to solve an immediate capital requirement by placing shares privately among qualified institutional investors under Rule 144A. Issuers in this category include Empaques Ponderosa, Grupo Carso, and Vitro, the latter which also recently listed its shares on the New York Stock Exchange.

Comparatively, Asian issuers that have tapped the 144A market in the United States by means of an ADR or Global Depositary Receipts (GDR) facility have done so for a variety of reasons, including a preference for equity rather than debt funding, a desire to avoid extensive public disclosure, and image enhancement from access to the international equity markets. GDRs are securities that are issued both in the United States and in European equity markets. The principal feature of the GDR is that it is fungible among the aforementioned markets and may be settled according to regional preferences as well as the issuer's home market. Issuers in this category include Samsung Company and Samsung Electronics in Korea and Keppel Corporation in Singapore. In the near future, issuers from Taiwan will also fit into this category as local regulations evolve to permit depositary receipt programs.

It should be noted that as the global equity capital markets embrace more uniform securities regulations and clearing systems, it is anticipated that international or global depositary receipt offerings will become more widespread. Some of the recent innovations include the structuring of global offerings, which initially are placed in the United States under Rule 144A and permit public trading of such securities in the over-the-counter markets after 40 days (as governed by Regulation S). This development effectively enables issuers to access the U.S. capital markets while permitting subsequent trading of those securities (through a Level-I ADR facility) without registration under the 1933 Securities Act and 1934 Exchange Act.

Case Studies

Although ADRs in both Asia and Latin America have been in existence since the 1960s in unsponsored form, it is only recently that Asian and Latin issuers have begun to establish sponsored ADR programs. Unsponsored ADRs typically are created by U.S.-investor demand without the consent of the issuer, as compared to sponsored ADRs, which are established by a non-U.S. issuer and are required for an exchange or NASDAQ listing. Inherent problems with unsponsored ADRs include fees charged by depositary banks for distributing dividends, lack of voting rights, and little or no information flow to investors and issuers. For such reasons, unsponsored ADRs have not been established since 1984.

Asia

In January 1991, Asia Fiber, a publicly-listed company on the Securities Exchange of Thailand, announced its intent to establish the first Sponsored Level-I ADR program for a Thai issuer. (A Sponsored Level-I program is an ADR facility that is traded on the over-the-counter market, where the depositary bank is formally appointed to act as its U.S. intermediary for providing service to the issuer's U.S. investors.) Asia Fiber, whose nylon and nylon-related products are sold in a variety of markets throughout Asia, Europe, and the United States, desired to diversify its shareholder base to balance its product sales. Faced with increasing competition for its commodity-oriented products, management sought to integrate its operations vertically by building a caprolactum plant—an essential ingredient in nylon filament production.

An important goal of the ADR was to achieve international recognition and investor interest in Asia Fiber in order to fund the development of this plant. At the time of the announcement of the ADR program in January, Asia Fiber's shares were trading at 52 Baht per share. Once the ADR program was declared effective by the SEC in May 1991, Asia Fiber's shares had appreciated to 110 Baht per share, more than double the price at the time of initial announcement. Subsequently, Asia Fiber conducted a rights offering in July 1991 at a price of 93 Baht per share.

In the June 1991 edition of *Asiamoney* magazine, Asia Fiber was ranked as having the best investor relations program for a Thai company due to the establishment of its ADR program[1]. This is particularly noteworthy considering traditional Thai reluctance toward corporate disclosure.

Hong Kong Telecom established a Level-III ADR program listed on the New York Stock Exchange in December 1988 and offered 180.7 million ADRs at a price of U.S. $17.50 to the U.S. public. The purpose of the offering was to increase Hong Kong Telecom's local and overseas shareholder base and reduce the parent's and the Hong Kong government's equity investment in the company in line with the latter's stated policy. Hong Kong Telecom is a principal subsidiary of Cable and Wireless, plc, a U.K. telecommunications company, which incidentally also has its ADRs listed on the New York Stock Exchange. Given the size of the offering and the relative weighting of Hong Kong Telecom in the Hang Seng index, an ADR offering was essential to the shareholders' objectives of achieving maximum value and liquidity for its investment.

Latin America

In 1989, the first Latin American ADR established in the post-debt crisis was Grupo Sidek, a Mexican issuer. Grupo Sidek followed a more traditional method of creating a presence in the U.S. financial marketplace by establishing a Sponsored Level-I ADR facility. By enlarging the market for its shares through an ADR program, Grupo Sidek has been able to expand and diversify its U.S.-investor base while rewarding its shareholders with a 67% return since the program's inception.

Grupo Sidek's aims were to enlarge the market for its shares through expanded and more diversified exposure, to take advantage of the low-cost entry into the

U.S. financial marketplace, and to enhance the image and understanding of the company's products, services, and financial instruments.

At the time of the launch of the ADR, Sidek's shares were severely undervalued, and there was very little liquidity in the Mexican market, since investors holding Sidek's shares were unwilling to sell due to the then-prevailing low share market price. Once the ADR program went into effect and the U.S. marketmakers were able to fulfill a few relatively small orders, the price edged upward and existing holders were willing to sell, thus adding liquidity and fueling additional ADR transactions. As of November 1991, Sidek had over 11.0 million shares placed in the United States in the form of ADRs. Recently, the company successfully completed a Rule 144A ADR offering valued at U.S.$90.0 million for one of its subsidiaries (SITUR).

In July 1990, The Chilean Telephone Company established a Sponsored Level-III ADR program, which brought about a New York Stock Exchange listing and a public offering of 6.5 million shares at an ADR price of $15.125. The primary reason for CTC's offering was the company's pressing need to meet expanding demand for telephone lines as the country's economy continues to grow. CTC estimates capital requirements for the next eight years to be approximately U.S.$2.0 billion in order to triple service to 1.6 million lines and more than 2.0 million telephones. Thus, the need to access a larger capital market through ADRs was imperative for continued growth.

No matter what the route is, it is clear that Asian and Latin American companies are finding ADRs to be a very useful financial tool to achieve a variety of corporate financial objectives. A listing of the ADRs issued by the companies of emerging Asian and Latin American countries appears at the end of this chapter.

Performance

In evaluating performance, we have chosen listed ADRs that represent shares of Hong Kong Telecom (HKT) and the Chilean Telephone Company (CTC). These two companies were chosen since they are easily comparable: i.e., non-U.S. telecommunications companies in growing markets, financial disclosure under U.S. GAAP, trading on the New York Stock Exchange, and representation as the largest market capitalization stocks in the Hong Kong and Chilean stock markets respectively. Below are the total return and compounded annualized returns of these ADRs since their listing on the NYSE.

Returns[2]	Total	Average
HKT	96%	19.82%
CTC	186%	67.40%

It is important to note that the price of the ADR compared with the price of the shares in the home market tends to trade at a near-equilibrium price, factoring in ADR creation and cancellation costs. One explanation for this factor is that arbitrage between the respective markets tends to keep ADR/ordinary prices in line between the markets. This is particularly apparent for ADR issues that are listed on the New York Stock Exchange, where there is almost an efficient market for information flows. It seems that ADR issuers, particularly listed ones, enjoy better price stability for their shares due to the investors' ability and discretion to buy and sell in two equity markets.

Conclusion

We foresee a trend where more issuers from these rapidly-growing economies will list on the major U.S. exchanges and seek to diversify their shareholder base by using ADRs. This is in view of investor demand for higher returns offered by investing in the emerging markets of Asia and Latin America, and evidence that listed ADR programs promote share price stability, corporate recognition, and funding access to the largest and most liquid equity capital market in the world. We also envision that international offerings of Depositary Receipt (DR) programs will become more prevalent in order to achieve a global shareholder base. As the variety and quality of ADRs and DRs available increases, fund managers and investors will be able to draw from a wide spectrum of investments that offer higher returns, reduced transaction costs, and the convenience of dealing in dollar-denominated securities.

Endnotes

[1]*Asiamoney* Magazine. June 1991.
[2]Returns are based on NYSE closing prices on November 22, 1991.

Table 25-1 ADRs Issued by Companies of Emerging Markets

Issue	Exchange	Status	Ratio	Depositary
Chile				
Compania De Telefonos De Chile (CTC)	NYSE	Sponsored	1:17	BNY
Hong Kong				
Asia Orient Company Limited	OTC	Unsponsored	1:500	
Carrian Investments Limited	OTC	Unsponsored	1:10	
Cathay Pacific Airways Limited	OTC	Unsponsored	1:5	
Cheung Kong (Holdings) Limited	OTC	Unsponsored	1:1	
China Light and Power	OTC	Unsponsored	1:1	
Chuangs Holdings Limited	OTC	Unsponsored	1:5	
Conic Investment Company Limited	OTC	Unsponsored	1:5	
Evergo Holdings Company Ltd.	OTC	Unsponsored	1:5	
Hang Lung Development Company	OTC	Unsponsored	1:10	
Hang Seng Bank	OTC	Unsponsored	1:1	
Henderson Land Development Co.	OTC	Unsponsored	1:5	
Hong Kong and China Gas Co., Ltd.	OTC	Unsponsored	1:1	
Hong Kong Electric Holdings	OTC	Unsponsored	1:1	
Hopewell Holdings Limited	OTC	Unsponsored	1:5	
Hutchison Whampoa Limited	OTC	Unsponsored	1:5	
New World Development Co. Ltd.	OTC	Unsponsored	1:5	
Sino Land Company Ltd.	OTC	Unsponsored	1:20	
Sun Hung Kai & Co., Limited	OTC	Unsponsored	1:5	
Sun Hung Kai Properties Ltd.	OTC	Unsponsored	1:1	
Swire Pacific Limited "A"	OTC	Unsponsored	1:2	
Television Broadcasts Limited	OTC	Unsponsored	1:1	
TVE (Holdings) Ltd.	OTC	Unsponsored	1:5	
Wah Kwong Shipping & Invest Co.	OTC	Unsponsored	1:5	
Wharf Holdings Ltd., The	OTC	Unsponsored	1:1	
Winsor Industrial	OTC	Unsponsored	1:5	
Applied International Holdings	OTC	Sponsored	1:200	BNY
C.P. Pokphand Co., Ltd.	OTC	Sponsored	1:5	BNY
Dairy Farm International Holdings Ltd.	OTC	Sponsored	1:5	BNY
First Pacific Company Limited	OTC	Sponsored	1:50	BNY
Hong Kong Land Holdings Ltd.	OTC	Sponsored	1:5	BNY
Hong Kong Telecommunications	NYSE	Sponsored	1:30	BNY
Hysan Development	OTC	Sponsored	1:10	CIT
Jardine Matheson Holdings Limited	OTC	Sponsored	1:1	BNY
Jardine Strategic Holdings Limited	OTC	Sponsored	1:2	BNY
Johnson Electric Holdings Ltd.	OTC	Sponsored	1:10	BNY
Mandarin Oriental International Ltd.	OTC	Sponsored	1:10	BNY
Playmates International Holdings Ltd.	OTC	Sponsored	1:10	CIT
Indonesia				
P.T. Indah Kiat Pulp and Paper	OTC	Sponsored	1:4	BNY
P.T. Indocement Tunngal Prakarsa	OTC	Sponsored	1:3	BNY
P.T. Inti Indorayon Utama	OTC	Sponsored	1:3	BNY
Korea				
Samsung Company 144A GDR	144A	Sponsored	1:1	CITI
Samsung Electronics 144A GDR	144A	Sponsored	1:1	CITI
Malaysia				
Bandar Raya Developments Berhad	OTC	Unsponsored	1:1	
Boustead Holdings Berhad	OTC	Unsponsored	1:1	
Genting Berhad	OTC	Unsponsored	1:1	
Kuala Lumpur Kepong Berhad	OTC	Unsponsored	1:1	
Malayan United Industries Berhad	OTC	Unsponsored	1:1	
Perlis Plantations Berhad	OTC	Unsponsored	1:1	
Selangor Properties Berhad	OTC	Unsponsored	1:1	
Sime Darby Berhad	OTC	Unsponsored	1:1	
Supreme Corporation Berhad	OTC	Unsponsored	1:1	
Berjaya Corp. Berhad	OTC	Sponsored	1:1	CIT
Inter-Pacific Industrial Group Berhad	OTC	Sponsored	1:10	CIT
Kesang Corporation Berhad	OTC	Sponsored	1:5	BNY

Table 25-1   *(Continued)*

Issue	Exchange	Status	Ratio	Depositary
Resorts World Berhard	OTC	Sponsored		CIT
Mexico				
CIFRA, S.A. De C.V.	OTC	Unsponsored	1:1	
IEM SA (Industria Electrica de Mexico)	OTC	Unsponsored	1:1	
Telefonos De Mexico S.A. De C.V. Ser A	NAS	Unsponsored	1:1	
Corporacion Industrial Sanluis Ser A	OTC	Sponsored	1:10	MGT
Corporacion Industrial Sanluis Ser A-1	OTC	Sponsored	1:10	MGT
Corporacion Industrial Sanluis Ser A-2	OTC	Sponsored	1:10	MGT
E.P.N., S.A. De C.V.	OTC	Sponsored	1:10	BNY
Empaques Ponderosa 144A	144A	Sponsored	1:4	BNY
Femsa, S.A. de C.V. 144A GDR	144A	Sponsored	1:1	CIT
Grupo Gigante, S.A. Dec. V	144A	Sponsored	1:10	CIT
Grupo Sidek, S.A. De C.V.	OTC	Sponsored	1:2	BNY
Grupo Synkro, S.A. De C.V.	OTC	Sponsored	1:1	BNY
Internacional de Ceramica 144A	144A	Sponsored	1:1	MGT
Ponderosa Industrial, S.A. De C.V.	OTC	Sponsored	1:10	BNY
Telefonos De Mexico S.A. De C.V. Ser L	NYSE	Sponsored	1:20	MGT
Tolmex, S.A. De C.V. "B" Shares	OTC	Sponsored	1:10	CIT
Tolmex, S.A. De C.V. 144A (Conv. Bond)	144A	Sponsored	1:1	CIT
Tubos De Acero De Mexico, S.A.	AMEX	Sponsored	1:1	MGT
Vitro, S.A. De C.V.	NYSE	Sponsored	1:1	CIT
Philippines				
Philodrill Corporation, The	OTC	Sponsored	1:2000	BNY
San Miguel Corp. ADR	OTC	Sponsored	1:10	MGT
Singapore				
Citi Developments Limited	OTC	Unsponsored	1:1	
Cycle and Carriage Limited	OTC	Unsponsored	1:1	
Development Bank of Singapore Ltd., The	OTC	Unsponsored	1:1	
Inchcape Berhard	OTC	Unsponsored	1:1	
Malayan Credit Limited	OTC	Unsponsored	1:1	
Overseas Union Bank, Limited	OTC	Unsponsored	1:1	
Sembawang Shipyards Limited	OTC	Unsponsored	1:1	
Singapore Land Limited	OTC	Unsponsored	1:1	
United Overseas Land Limited	OTC	Unsponsored	1:1	
GB Holdings	OTC	Sponsored	1:5	BNY
Keppel Corporation Ltd.	OTC	Sponsored	1:2	CIT
Keppel Corporation Ltd. 144A	144A	Sponsored	1:2	CIT
Neptune Orient Lines Ltd.	OTC	Sponsored	1:4	CIT
United Overseas Bank Limited	OTC	Sponsored	1:2	BNY
Thailand				
Advanced Info Services	OTC	Sponsored	1:2	BNY
Asia Fiber Company Limited	OTC	Sponsored	1:2	BNY
C.P. Feedmill Co.	OTC	Sponsored	1:2	BNY
Shinawatra Computer & Communications	OTC	Sponsored	2:1	BNY
Venezuela				
Ceramica Carabobo C.A.	OTC	Sponsored	1:1	BNY
Corimon	OTC	Sponsored		MGT
Mantex	OTC	Sponsored	1:4	BNY
Siderurgica Venezolana Sivensa (Sivensa)	OTC	Sponsored	1:3	BNY
Venepal	144A	Sponsored	1:3	BNY

GROWING PAINS OF THE KOREAN EQUITY MARKET

Keith K. H. Park, Partner
Global Strategies Group
Los Angeles, United States

The excellent investment opportunities offered by the Asian emerging equity markets will continue to attract the attention of prudent pension sponsors in the 1990s. From the pension sponsors' perspective, the low correlations of the Pacific Rim emerging equity markets with the major developed markets such as the United States, the United Kingdom, France, and Germany serve as a superb means for achieving a solid diversification of their portfolios, and consequently, lowering the risk of their portfolio[1] — see Table 26-1.

**Table 26-1   Correlations of Asian Emerging Markets
with Major Developed Markets***

	U.S.	U.K.	FRANCE	GERMANY
KOREA	0.1	0.1	0.1	0.1
TAIWAN	−0.2	0.0	0.0	0.2
THAILAND	−0.1	0.0	0.2	0.2
MALAYSIA	−0.2	0.1	0.1	0.2
INDONESIA	−0.1	0.0	−0.1	0.1

*Correlations of biweekly U.S. $ returns from January 1988 to September 1990.
Source: Morgan Stanley Capital International

---

[1]For a detailed discussion of the risk/return benefits of global equity investment, see Keith K. H. Park, "Reduction of Risk and Enhancement of Return through Global Equity Diversification," *The Global Equity Markets*, (Chicago: Probus Publishing Company, 1991), and "Enhanced Efficiency of Global Portfolio Diversification Through Emerging Market Investing," *The World's Emerging Stock Markets*, (Chicago: Probus Publishing Company, 1992).

Moreover, as we can see in Figure 26-1, four out of the six Asian emerging equity markets outperformed S&P 500 and MSCI EAFE (Europe, Australia, Far East) Indices in U.S. dollar terms during the six-year period between 1985 and 1990. For instance, the Korean market showed a 559.3% return during this period whereas EAFE and S&P 500 Indices, 264.1% and 144.1% respectively. Consequently, pension sponsors, who have allocated assets in the Asian emerging markets, have been able to enhance the returns of their portfolios.

In the 1990s, the economic expansion of the Asian economies will continue to fuel the robust growth of the equity markets in the region. For instance, as we can see in Figure 26-2, at the end of 1990 72% of the world's emerging equity markets were located in Asia, whereas only 43% were in the region in 1981. The total market capitalization of the Asian emerging markets increased by 839% from $36 billion in 1981 to $338 billion in 1990. The growth of the Korean market has been extraordinary as well. At the end of 1990, the Korean market accounted for 23% of the total market capitalization of the world's emerging markets, up from 5% at the end of 1981. The market capitalization of Korea grew 1,400%, from U.S. $7.4 billion in 1981 to U.S. $110 billion in 1990, and became the largest among those of the world's emerging markets.

In January 1992, the largest emerging market will open its door to direct foreign investment, and pension sponsors will be able to directly own a piece of the miracle economic machines of Korea, which have transformed the once war-destroyed country into a newly-emerging, industrial powerhouse.

However, despite the rosy expectation for the performance of the Asian emerging markets in general, the Korean market began 1992 with various uncertainties and difficulties. The final year of the 1980s was quite disappointing for international institutional investors holding the Korean papers. The Korea Composite Stock Price Index (KCSPI), which stood at 100 in early 1980, broke 1,000 briefly in April 1989 but then drifted lower, finishing the year with a mere gain of 0.28%. As its currency appreciated and labor cost rose, Korean export faltered in 1989 and the export-oriented economy grew at half the rate of the previous three years. In 1990, the bearish trend continued and the market fell 23.5%.

The first half of the 1990s will become the most crucial period for the Korean economy, which is currently going through a metamorphosis into an advanced industrial economy. Moreover, as other Asian economies become advanced industrial economies in the 1990s, Korea's current uncertainties and problems could indicate future dilemmas for these countries.

This chapter will examine the current state of the Korean economy and the consequent implications for the Korean equity market. In addition, the close examination of the Korean equity market might break the myth that the fundamental norms of a developed equity market are not applicable to the Asian equity markets such as Japan, and convince some to reconsider their valuation of the Asian markets.

Figure 26-1 Total U.S. Dollar Returns From Asian Emerging Equity Markets

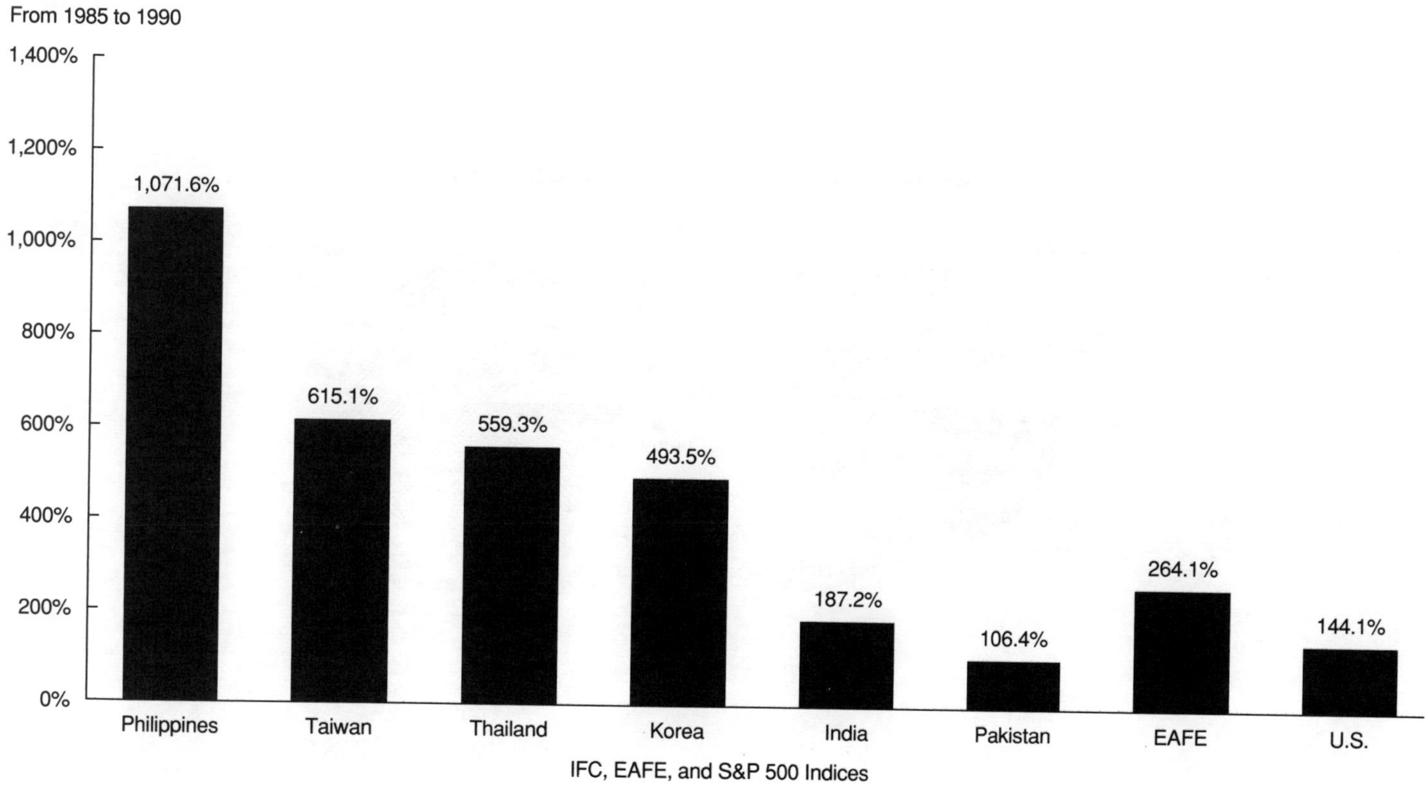

From 1985 to 1990

IFC, EAFE, and S&P 500 Indices

Philippines	1,071.6%
Taiwan	615.1%
Thailand	559.3%
Korea	493.5%
India	187.2%
Pakistan	106.4%
EAFE	264.1%
U.S.	144.1%

Source: International Finance Corporation

Figure 26-2 Composition of World Emerging Markets

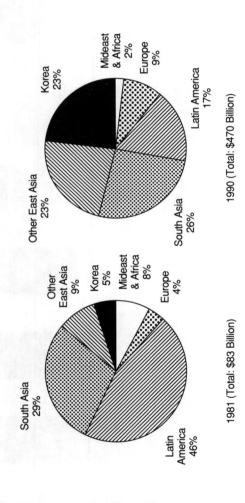

Korea
23%

Mideast
& Africa
2%

Europe
9%

Other East Asia
23%

Latin America
17%

South Asia
26%

1990 (Total: $470 Billion)

Other
East Asia
9%

Korea
5%

Mideast
& Africa
8%

Europe
4%

South Asia
29%

Latin
America
46%

1981 (Total: $83 Billion)

Source: International Finance Corporation

Economic Overview

Impressive Past Growth

In 1985, Korea had $46 billion of external debt — the fourth largest among the developing countries behind Mexico, Brazil, and Argentina. However, at the end of 1988, the Korean Ministry of Finance made the last payment for the loan from the International Monetary Fund (IMF). As a sign of the further turnaround for the Korean economy, two state-owned Korean banks, Korea Development Bank and KEB (Asia) Finance Ltd., which is the Hong Kong subsidiary of Korea Exchange Bank, announced in November 1989 that they would be participating as lead managers in a major sovereign loan syndication, which would lend $400 million to Indonesia. Since only one U.S. bank, Chemical, was involved in the syndication, the Korean participation impressed a number of foreign bankers. This dramatic metamorphosis of Korea from a borrower to an arranger of major international loans was made possible by its fast-growing trade surplus in the second half of the 1980s.

The export-oriented industrial strategy was superbly effective in the 1980s in turning Korea into a manufacturing powerhouse which exports steel, petrochemicals, textiles, consumer electronics, automobiles, ships, computers, and semiconductors. This industrial strategy enabled Korea to achieve the stupendous real growth rates of gross national product (GNP): an average rate of 12.6% from 1986 to 1988. During this period, the export growth brought about $28.3 billion current account surplus, which measures trade in goods and services as well as some unilateral transfers — see Figure 26-3. This impressive economic growth fueled the Korean equity market to rise 455.6% between 1986 and 1988. Without a doubt, the second half of the 1980s was a significant and giant step forward for the Korean economy; the per capita GNP of Korea, which was a mere $87 in 1962, grew to $4,040 in 1988.

However, as the Korean economy approached the end of the 1980s, it began to show the strains of its rapid growth. For instance, 1989 was an agonizing year for the Korean economy. The current account surplus fell by 64%, from $14.1 billion in 1988 to $5.1 billion in 1989. Also, the real GNP growth rate slowed down to 6.8% in 1989 from the two-digit growth rates of the previous three years. As the performance of an equity market is closely tied to that of its own economy, the Korea Composite Stock Price Index, which is the market capitalization-weighted index of all the companies listed on the Korean Stock Exchange, ended 1989 with a mere gain of 0.28%.

Current Economic Problems

The Korean economy exported an average of $46.6 billion between 1986 and 1988; the corresponding annual nominal GNP was $133.4 billion during this period. In other words, the Korean economy exported about one-third of its GNP each year

Figure 26-3 Current Account Balances and GNP Growth Rates of Korea

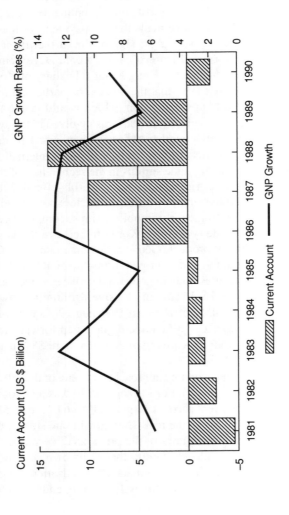

Source: Ssangyong Research Institute

since 1986, and in 1988, became the tenth-largest trading nation in the global economy. The trade surplus grew to $11.6 billion in 1988, up from $4.2 billion of 1986. As its trade surplus mushroomed, trade friction with the United States and Europe became a sensitive and sticky issue. In 1989, Korea was told by the United States and Western Europe that its growing significance in the world economy makes it no longer feasible to further rely on an unbalanced large trade surplus for its economic expansion and that its large trade surplus creates a distorting impact on the world economy.

Furthermore, in 1989 Korea was accused of: (1) artificially manipulating its currency in order to make its manufactured products unfairly competitive in the global marketplace; and (2) fortressing its domestic market with trade barriers in order to protect internationally uncompetitive domestic industries and constrain imports. The U.S. pressure for the rectification of the accused unfair trade practices was most demanding and vocal.

Nonetheless, Korea was able to spare itself from the trade sanctions of the so-called Super 301 clause of the 1988 trade bill, which named Japan, Brazil, and India as unfair trading partners. However, Korea came to a rude awakening in 1989 that its unbalanced export-oriented strategy would no longer be a viable industrial policy in the 1990s.

Under the heavy pressure from the United States and Europe, at the end of 1989 the Korean won had appreciated 24% against the U.S. dollar since the end of 1985 — most of the appreciation (14%) occurred in 1988. Combined with the currency appreciation, the labor cost — which had risen 20% annually from 1986 — elicited the declining competitiveness of Korean manufactured goods in the major world markets.

As Korea more widely embraced democracy, the labor activism, which had been severely repressed under the previous authoritarian regimes of Presidents Park and Chun, became vocal and active. During the first half of 1989, numerous rowdy labor strikes demanding higher wages and broader rights of workers ensued. These strikes had such a crippling impact on normal manufacturing operations that it was estimated to cost the Korean economy more than U.S. $1 billion of export. Furthermore, according to a survey in 1988, the currency appreciation and wage increase forced some 400 Korean companies to declare bankruptcy that year.

The industrial development of the Korean economy is a classical case of how the Asian NICs (Newly Industrialized Countries) such as Taiwan, Hong Kong, Singapore, and Korea have upstaged advanced, western industrial nations. After initially achieving highly efficient economies of scale in their domestic markets, which had been heavily protected from foreign competition, the firms from the Asian NICs entered the major world markets in the 1980s. Subsequently, they enlarged their market shares by driving the established firms of advanced industrial nations out of the market by undercutting prices, which was mainly possible by their low-cost domestic labor. The dominance of the Asian NICs' manufacturers in the 1980s was usually in low-end manufacturing sectors. However, the Korean manufacturers came to realize in 1989 that this strategy would not work any longer.

Remedies

The effective strategic response by manufacturing firms in advanced industrial nations, when their markets were flooded with low-priced goods exported from the Asian NICs, was to move into more specialized, higher-technology manufacturing sectors. After the economic setback in 1989, the Korean manufacturers sought to upgrade their products — it seems that history always repeats itself. Otherwise, Korean manufacturers could lose out to the new Asian NICs such as China, Thailand, Indonesia, and Malaysia. In February 1989, the Ministry of Science, announced that the government would invest U.S. $1.5 billion (won 1 trillion) over the next five years in electronics, information technology, and biotechnology research and development. Furthermore, the government sought pushing manufacturers to increase their spending on research and development, and increased investment in R&D from 2% of GNP in 1987 to 3% in 1991. Nonetheless, the effort to upscale products has been modestly successful. In 1990, the Korean economy recorded a trade deficit — $4.8 billion — for the first time since 1985.

The urgency to increase capital investment in R&D in the 1990s will require the Korean equity market to play a critical role in assisting the growth and survival of the Korean economy. It must be able to provide the low-cost capital Korean manufacturers badly need to upscale their products. The government has been making a serious attempt to nurture an efficient equity market by imposing heavy pressure on corporations to move away from bank loans and rely more on equity financing. Furthermore, the government, which does not want the corporate financing of the Korean firms to be limited to the shallow pocket of the domestic equity market, has been steadily masterminding the liberalization of the market, which will occur in the beginning of 1992.

The Korean Equity Market

Past Corporate Financing

In the English-speaking countries such as the United States, Britain, and Australia, the well-developed equity markets have been the traditional source of corporate financing. In addition, shareholders have exerted strong control over the governance of corporations. In contrast, West German and Japanese firms have often relied on loan financing provided by banks, which in turn, have maintained a strong relationship with the management of the borrowing corporation.

Until the first half of the 1980s, Korean corporations raised capital in a way somewhat similar to their West German and Japanese counterparts. Their corporate financing need was mostly met by the low-cost bank loans subsidized by the government, which in turn, had a strong say in the management and destiny of corporations.

In the 1970s, the government formulated an industrial development policy to nurture chemical and heavy industries. Following the policy of the government, the state-owned commercial banks provided huge low-cost loans to major business conglomerates called chaebols in order for them to implement the industrial planning of the government. This government subsidy, combined with the high inflation of the 1970s, enabled the chaebols to fund their growth with negative real interest rates.

However, some of the development projects subsidized by the government turned out to be less than what had been aimed for, and they incurred a massive amount of nonperforming loans in the books of state-owned commercial banks. As of June 1989, it was estimated that the top five commercial banks had some $3.8 billion of bad and doubtful loans in their books. These problematic loans contributed to high interest rates in Korea, well above the world average.

Ironically, the government subsidy which funded the initial expansion of the Korean conglomerates is now haunting the beneficiaries by creating a high financing cost. Because the Korean corporate borrowers have to put up a large amount of interest-free deposit to be eligible for bank loans, the Korean firms are estimated to pay real interest rates three times as high as those paid by their foreign competitors

Changes in Corporate Financing

The government has sought to reduce the chaebols' reliance on bank loans by pressuring them to use equity financing to meet their urgent need for investment in R&D. Also, the chaebols have been told to deleverage their balance sheets, which are loaded with huge debt due to the easy, low-cost credit provided by the government in the past.

In 1988, the Korean Ministry of Finance required 177 companies with debts of more than $30 million (won 20 billion) to repay them through equity financing. As a further move to wean the chaebols from dependence on the government-subsidized bank loans, the Ministry ordered 598 of the chaebols' affiliated companies to repay bank debts with funds to be raised in the capital markets in 1989. Also, the banking regulations have been amended in several ways that will force large corporations to raise money directly in the capital markets. For instance, the borrowing limit has been lowered from 75% of equity capital to 50%. Moreover, large corporations will not be allowed to acquire a controlling interest in banks.

The efforts of the government to nurture the equity market brought about some solid results. For instance, the Korean firms raised $21.6 billion through equity issuance in 1989, more than a twenty-fold increase from $970 million of 1986, and the number of the listed companies on the Korean Stock Exchange grew from 355 in 1986 to 626 in 1990.

The rising equity market in the second half of the 1980s created an ideal environment for the Korean firms to raise capital by floating equities. For instance, the

Korean corporations met 63% of their 1988 corporate financing need in the equity market. Before then, the equity financing hovered around 20%–30% of the total. However, as the Korean equity market began heading south in the spring of 1989 and fell 23.5% in 1990, equity issuance decreased dramatically in 1990. The Korean corporations raised $4.1 billion in 1990, which is an 81% decrease from 1989

As equity financing becomes difficult to acquire and the economy slowed down, the average debt amount of the top ten Korean chaebols rose and was running at 335.5% of their equity in 1991, a 10.5% increase from the 1990 level. As the outlook for the Korean equity market has gotten murkier, the Ministry of Finance which had been delaying the liberalization of its capital markets, is now bravely marching forward to open its equity market to direct foreign investment in order to prop up the market.

Internationalization of Corporate Financing

In addition to the high cost of the domestic bank loans, there has traditionally been a severe shortage of capital in Korea because, except for the second half of the 1980s, the Korean economy has never generated a significant amount of trade surplus. As a result, Korean firms used to have no choice but to substantially rely on foreign bank loans for their growth.

Consequently, since the early 1980s Korean firms have been trying to tap the international capital markets as a cheaper and more efficient source of corporate financing. For instance, as early as November 1981, Korea International Trust — an investment trust — was established to encourage foreign investors to indirectly participate in the Korean equity market.

Until 1985, the majority of foreign investment in the Korean equity market had been implemented through investment trusts managed by three Korean investment trust companies — Korea Investment Trust Co. (KITC), Daehan Investment Trust Co. (DITC), and Citizens Investment Trust Management Co. (CITMC). Table 26-2 details the investment trusts managed by the above three for foreign investors.

Most of the funds are traded in the form of International Depository Receipts. Most of the investment trusts are open-end funds. However, they are actually closed-end funds because the managers do not have freedom to issue new units without the approval of the Korean Ministry of Finance. The managers have to wait until the pre-existing units are redeemed before issuing new units. Because the Korean government currently determines the amount of foreign investment entering into the Korean equity market, the funds will not truly become open-ended until the liberalization of the market, scheduled to occur in the beginning of 1992.

The most well-known vehicles for indirect foreign investment in the Korean equity market are two exchange-listed, closed-end country funds: the Korea Fund, traded on the New York Stock Exchange and the Korea Europe Fund on the London Stock Exchange (LSE). In July 1990, the Korea Asia Fund was listed on the LSE and the Hong Kong Stock Exchange. Table 26-3 contains information on the above

Table 26-2   Korean Investment Trusts for Foreign Investors

Name	Value (in U.S. $)	Inception Date	Manager	Type*	Premium 11/26/91
Korea Int's Trust	25m	11/81	KITC	O	−2.85%
Korea Trust	25m	11/81	DITC	O	−2.26%
Korea Growth Trust	30m	3/85	CITMC	C	−2.09%
Seoul Int'l Trust	30m	4/85	KITC	O	−3.11%
Seoul Trust	30m	4/85	DITC	O	−2.29%
Korea Small Companies Trust	2m	12/85	KITC	C	n/a
Korea Emerging Companies Trust	3m	3/86	DITC	O	n/a
Korea 1990 Trust	50m	4/90	CITMC	C	−3.35%
Korea Equity Trust	n/a	5/90	KITC	O	−3.12%
Daehan Korea Trust	n/a	5/90	DITC	O	−2.74%
Daehan Asia Trust	100m	6/90	DITC	C	−18.97%
Seoul Asia Index Trust	n/a	7/90	CITMC	O	−15.08%
Korea Pacific Trust	n/a	7/90	KITC	O	−17.48%

* "O" for open-ended and "C" for close-ended
Source: Hanshin Securities Co. and Dongsuh Securities Co.

Table 26-3   Offshore Korean Closed-End Funds for Foreign Investors

Name	Value (in U.S. $)	Inception Date	Manager	Premium(%) 11/26/91
Korea Fund	100m	8/84	Scudder	19.44
Korea Europe Funds	60m	3/87	Korea Schroder Fund Management	11.99
Korea Asia Fund	n/a	7/90	Korea Asia Fund Management	6.77

Source: Hanshin Securities Co.

closed-end funds. The Korea Fund is not allowed to hold more than 5% of the total outstanding shares of a listed company; the Korea Europe Fund, 3%. Both funds may not invest more than 5% of their net asset value in one share, or more than 25% of their NAV in one industrial sector.

In December 1985, the Korean corporations whose operation had become more international began raising capital abroad and repatriating it by issuing convertible bonds in the Eurobond market. Table 26-4 lists Korean corporate convertible and warrant bonds, and depositary receipts offered to foreign investors.

The final step toward the internationalization of Korean corporate financing will be opening its domestic equity market in 1992. The Ministry of Finance is implementing the market opening after making a few policy blunders.

Table 26-4   Korean Convertible and Warrant Eurobonds and Depositary Receipts

Name	Amount (in U.S. $)	Issuance Date	Coupon Rate	Conversion Begins	Premium 11/26/91
SAMSUNG ELECTRONICS (CB)	20m	12/19/85	5%	10/19/87	12.56%
DAEWOO HEAVY INDUSTRIES (CB)	40m	5/23/86	3%	11/23/87	8.32%
YUKONG (CB)	20m	7/15/86	2%	1/15/88	78.11%
GOLDSTAR (CB)	30m	8/11/87	1.75%	2/11/89	102.70%
SAEHAN MEDIA (CB)	30m	10/04/88	1.75%	4/04/90	103.93%
SAMMI STEEL (BW)	50m	11/08/89	1.25%	3/08/91	313.15%
STC (CB)	30m	1/03/90	1.25%	7/03/91	299.00%
DONG AH CONSTRUCTION (CB)	50m	2/14/90	1.25%	8/14/91	191.02%
HYUNDAI MOTOR (BW)	70m	2/23/90	1.00%	8/23/91	130.13%
SAMIC (BW)	n/a	3/08/90	n/a	n/a	299.61%
MIWON (CB)	n/a	7/11/90	n/a	n/a	110.96%
SUNKYONG IND. (CB)	n/a	9/14/90	n/a	n/a	76.89%
SAMSUNG CO. (DR)	40m	12/18/90	—	—	8.77%
JINDO CO. (CB)	SFR 25m	2/28/91	6.00%	8/28/92	33.33%
SAMSUNG ELEC. (DR)	100m	3/09/91	—	—	10.58%
ANAM IND. (CB)	SFR 45m	3/11/91	6.00%	9/11/92	23.35%
KOLON (CB)	28.5m	3/14/91	4.00%	9/14/92	11.40%
SUNKYONG (CB)	65m	5/16/91	4.75%	2/16/92	12.61%
SAM BO (CB)	30m	6/04/91	3.5%	3/04/92	n/a
DAEWOO TELECOM (CB)	50m	6/18/91	3.5%	3/18/92	26.32%

Source: Hanshin Securities Co. and Dongsuh Securities Co.

Policy Blunders

In the beginning of 1989, the Korean government noticed that an accelerating money supply was creating severe inflationary pressure in the economy. Its large trade surplus was mainly responsible for the 18.8% growth of M2 in 1988, which was 11.8% in 1985 — M2 includes cash in circulation, savings, and time deposits. In 1988, the consumer price index jumped 7%, which was a two-fold increase from 3% in 1987. The strict foreign exchange controls, which prevented the mounting trade surplus from flowing outward, did not help lessen the excessive liquidity despite the government's tight reign on money supply. Alarmingly, in the first 25 days of January 1989, M2 increased at an annualized rate of 19.9%. In order to restrain money growth, the government reversed its earlier position on the market liberalization and imposed strict restrictions on the Korean corporations' new issuance of convertible bonds in Europe. The government even required the capital raised from floating Euro-CBs to be used only for foreign operations.

Although this blocked the Korean corporations' access to the international capital markets, in early 1989 the Korean government actively encouraged corporations to tap the domestic equity market. Maybe, given the bull market at that time, the Korean government believed that the pocket of the domestic equity market was deep enough to fund corporate financing need. However, the bull market did not last forever.

In the first three months of 1989, the Korea Composite Stock Price Index impressively rose 11%, but after the first quarter, began heading south. As the Korean economy stumbled due to lackluster export, the stock prices started reflecting the bleak outlook for Korean corporations. In November 1989, the government heavily intervened in order to prop up the slowing economy and sagging equity market. Despite the inflationary threat, the Bank of Korea lowered the discount rate, and the government decided to offer $1.5 billion (won 1 trillion) low-interest loans to companies. However, it did not bring about the intended economic cure, and instead, the equity market continued to sag.

The Korean government believed that the oversupply of shares was responsible for the downward market trend and ordered the brokerage houses to postpone new share issuances until 1990. It reversed its earlier position that actively encouraged domestic equity financing. Due to the shrinking trade surplus, there was less money available to flow into the equity market. Furthermore, as the Korean corporations, which relied heavily on export for their growth, struggled, the shares of the Korean firms were no longer a good investment choice. Despite the repeated intervention of the government, the invisible hand of Adam Smith dominated the market.

Discounting the realities of the Korean economy and corporations, share prices continued their downward trend. In mid-December 1989, the equity market hit its yearly low, and the Korea Composite Stock Price Index closed at 844.76, which was about a negative 7% change from the close of 1988. As the equity market appeared to collapse, the government once again aggressively intervened. It announced that an unlimited amount of bank funds would be supplied to investment trust firms intending to purchase equities. Furthermore, in order to bring back investors, the Korean government increased the discount on newly floated shares from 10% to 30%.

As for foreign investors, the government indicated that it would enlarge the Korea Europe Fund from $60 million to $110 million, and allow three new domestic investment trusts of $30 million each to be created for foreign investors. Also, it announced its intention to encourage the Korean corporations to issue more convertible bonds and bonds with warrants in the Eurobond market. Furthermore, the Ministry of Finance even hinted that it might liberalize the market to direct foreign investment before the targeted 1992.

Basically, the government decided to reverse its policy again after less than 12 months, realizing that the pocket of the domestic equity market was not deep enough to sustain the market rally of the 1980s, and that the domestic market needed foreign capital. Aided by the active support from the government, which wanted to see the market finish the year higher than the previous year's close, the market briefly surged. However, showing no sign of reversing its gradual downward trend, the equity market ended 1989 with a mere gain of 0.28%.

The Korean equity market showed in 1989 that it had grown too big to be managed by the bureaucrats of the government. Despite the government's effort to prop up the equity market, the market continued its bearish trend in 1990 and fell 23.5%. In 1990, the market signaled its loss of confidence in the Korean corporations' ability to sustain their previous export-oriented growth as the currency appreciation and rising labor cost adversely affected their global competitiveness. Furthermore, the economy managed by the government showed its limitations as well.

Liberalization Outline

According to the liberalization outline announced by the Korean government, Korean industries will be categorized by **limited** and **nonlimited**. Foreign investors will be permitted to invest up to 10% of the market capitalization of companies in **nonlimited** industries, and up to 8% of the market capitalization of companies in **limited** industries such as public utilities, defense, shipping, transportation, finance, and communication. Furthermore, a 3% limit is imposed for the maximum amount of investment in one company by any one foreign investor. Also, foreign investors will not be permitted to purchase the shares of POSCO (Pohang Iron & Steel) and KEPCO (Korea Electric Power Company).

Equities held by the investment trusts listed in Table 26-2 and those converted from the Euro convertible bonds listed in Table 26-4 will not be counted in calculating foreign investment limit. According to the liberalization outline, foreign investors need to acquire an investment identification card.

At the end of 1990, the foreign ownership of Korean equities via indirect investment accounted for almost 2% ($2.2 billion) of the total Korean equity market capitalization.

Outlook for the 1990s

Japanese firms were extremely successful in coping with the dramatic appreciation of the yen and the rising trade barriers abroad in the mid-1980s. They have upscaled their products and transplanted manufacturing facilities around the globe. The Japanese automakers are a good example. In contrast, the Korean chaebols displayed an enormous inertia in 1989 and 1990 to cope with the changes in the global trading place. Basically, they are now confronting the same problems which Japanese firms had to resolve. However, their bloated size and historical dependence on the government for guidance has created bureaucracy that does not help them to be responsive and innovative.

The rapid growth of the chaebols in the 1980s mandates them to develop an efficient management structure in order to sustain their global expansion and preserve their competitiveness in major world markets. How the Korean stock market fares in the 1990s will depend on how well the Korean firms strategically position themselves to stay globally competitive. The equity market will not support the companies which try to cling to the status-quo despite the rapidly changing market environment.

The Korean corporations, which are now making sincere efforts ω stay competitive in the global marketplace, cannot be ignored or forgotten. Differing from Taiwan, Singapore, and Hong Kong, the Korean economy has nurtured a significant number of substantial-sized multinational corporations. Consequently, these Korean companies, who have achieved significant economies of scale, are better prepared for the global competition of the 1990s. As a result, in the long run they will outperform the small-sized Taiwanese, Singapore, and Hong Kong companies. Therefore, the current economic problems, if they are properly resolved, will end up making the Korean firms more efficient and competitive, and better prepared for the global competition in the 1990s.

The problems the Korean economy currently confronts depict what could lie ahead for the fast-growing economies of Asia in the 1990s as they try to become advanced industrial economies. Definitely, the developing Asian economies are not a homogeneous economic group. However, some of Korea's economic problems will be commonly seen during their transitional period. Moreover, we will also observe the similar type of uncertainty and volatility seen at the Korean bourse in the other Asian emerging equity markets during their transitional period.

The transformation the Korean economy has to make in the 1990s will not be an easy task. However, its equity market can surely assist the transformation if a constructive environment and leadership is provided by the government. The Korean equity market is no longer an up-and-coming market, but rather a came-and-to-be-seen one.

Concerning the investment opportunities in Korea, the current uncertainty and bearish trend have created interesting buying opportunities for savvy investors. A wise and selective buying of undervalued shares will bring about handsome returns when the dust settles. Investors should look for companies making solid progress in transforming themselves to high-end manufacturers. Also, companies gearing themselves up to take advantage of booming domestic consumption for their future growth will do well in the 1990s as the Korean economy becomes more consumption-oriented and less export-oriented.

EMERGING ASIAN FUTURES AND OPTIONS MARKETS*

Keith K. H. Park, Partner
Global Strategies Group
Los Angeles, United States
Steven A. Schoenfeld, President
Intellicorp, Ltd.
Washington, D.C., United States

Bold Initiatives for a Promising Future

A dramatic financial evolution is spreading throughout the Asia-Pacific region, particularly outside of the region's major international financial centers. Recently, the expansion of capital market activities and structural liberalizations have often been more extensive in the less-developed regional financial centers. Furthermore, international fund managers from the developed world, who were able to enhance returns and reduce market risks by investing in the more-established Asian equity markets in the 1980s, are aggressively venturing into the emerging markets of the region in the 1990s. As a result, the less-developed Asian financial centers will be able to deepen their capital markets and will seek to develop risk management tools in order to further accelerate incoming foreign investment as well as domestically-generated investment. This chapter discusses some of the numerous changes that are bringing these emerging markets closer to the development of significant derivative market activity.

The emerging Asian financial markets have little in common except for geographical proximity. Some, like Taiwan and Korea, are on the threshold of building

*This chapter is an excerpt from Keith K.H. Park and Steven A. Schoenfeld, *The Pacific Rim Futures and Options Markets*, Probus Publishing Company, 1992.

capital markets of international standard, while others, like Mongolia and Vietnam, are decades away. In addition, their significance to regional derivative markets is varied. For instance, financial centers such as Korea and Taiwan have the potential to become a major source of business for regional or international exchanges in the near term. In the long term, a number of these financial markets could develop both vibrant futures and options markets at home, and send significant activity abroad.

In viewing these markets, it is essential to note that capital market development will be the basic prerequisite for financial futures activity. Although many countries in the region, such as Vietnam and China, are still on the lower portion of the development curve, the rapid economic growth in the region has greatly accelerated capital market development in the countries that are further up on the learning curve. As recently as the mid-1980s, it would have been unimaginable to consider financial futures markets in countries such as the Philippines and Malaysia. However, the Philippines established a financial futures exchange in 1990, and Malaysia is on the verge of doing so. Thus, even though it still strains one's imagination to envisage active financial derivative markets in countries such as Thailand and Indonesia, the dynamic metamorphosis of the region has surprised many observers before. Both of these countries could have derivative markets by the second half of the decade.

The common thread between the following countries is therefore more than geographical. Most of the Asian emerging financial markets can be characterized as demonstrating increasing awareness of derivative products, and possessing major long-term potential as either markets or sources of activity.

In this chapter, markets and financial developments in the Philippines, Malaysia, Taiwan, Korea, Thailand, Indonesia, China, Mongolia, and Vietnam are discussed. As mentioned above, the Philippines has a functioning financial futures market, and Malaysia will soon have one. The near-term prospects for Taiwan and Korea are uncertain but it will not be a surprise to see them trade financial futures and options in their domestic markets by the mid-1990s. Thailand and Indonesia both have rapidly maturing capital markets, and are likely to follow closely behind Taiwan and Korea in their emergence on the derivatives scene. China, Mongolia, and Vietnam still need to establish very basic infrastructures for capital markets based upon free market principles, and their development of financial futures and options lies on the distant horizon. However, given the rapid collapse of communism in Eastern Europe and the Soviet Union, upcoming regulatory and financial reforms in these three countries will likely be extensive. The financial terrain is certain to change dramatically during the 1990s.

Developed Equity Markets of the Asia Pacific and their Futures and Options Contracts

As global equity investment expanded dramatically, the Asia-Pacific region has been a prime beneficiary. This has occurred both because its equity markets showed stellar performances in the second half of the 1980s, and also because they offer an excellent means for the diversification of market risks due to their low correlations with U.S. and European equity markets.

As Figure 27-1 demonstrates, from 1985 to 1990 the Pacific Basin Index of the FT-Actuaries World Indices generated a total U.S. dollar return of 176.46% whereas the FT-Actuaries Europe and U.S. indices generated 169.00% and 97.94% respectively. Figure 27-2 shows the total return of each constituent country of the FT-Actuaries Pacific Basin Index between 1985 and 1990 vis-a-vis the FT-Actuaries U.S. Index. They all surpassed the performance of the U.S. market.

Also, as visible in Table 27-1, the Asian equity markets have low correlations with the major European and U.S. markets. Therefore, investment in the Asian equity markets offers an excellent means for diversifying the market risks inherent in a global portfolio.

As demonstrated above, investment in Asia-Pacific equity markets has been unquestionably consistent with the essential goals of institutional global investing: the reduction of market risks and the enhancement of returns.[1] Furthermore, given the significant size of the Asian equity markets, global investors cannot ignore the investment opportunities offered by these markets. As Asian economies expanded dramatically in the past decade, their equity markets have grown significantly as well. Whereas the Asia-Pacific region accounted for 23% of the total market capitalization of the FT-Actuaries World Index at the end of 1980, it accounted for 35% at the end of 1990—see Figure 27-3. At the end of 1990, Japan's market capitalization

---

Table 27-1   Correlations of Asian Equity Markets with Major European and U.S. Markets*

	U.K.	France	Germany	U.S.
Japan	0.39	0.35	0.39	0.39
Australia	0.58	0.35	0.44	0.33
Hong Kong	0.36	0.27	0.36	0.22
Singapore	0.57	0.31	0.42	0.40
New Zealand	0.47	0.27	0.39	0.37

*Correlations of local currency returns from January 1986 to December 1990.
Source: FT-Actuaries World Indices Group of Goldman, Sachs & Co.

---

[1] For a detailed discussion of the risk/return benefits of global equity investing, see Keith K.H. Park, "Reduction of Risk and Enhancement of Return through Global Equity Diversification," *The Global Equity Markets*, (Chicago: Probus Publishing, 1991).

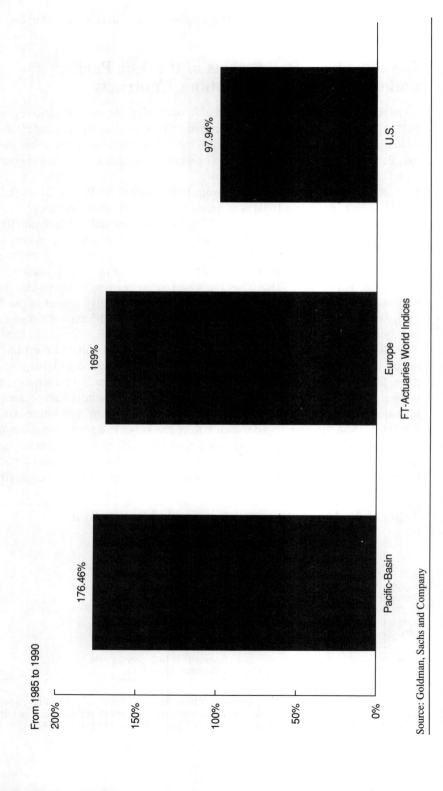

Figure 27-1 Total U.S. Dollar Returns from Regional Equity Markets

From 1985 to 1990

176.46%

169%

97.94%

Pacific-Basin

Europe
FT-Actuaries World Indices

U.S.

200%

150%

100%

50%

0%

Source: Goldman, Sachs and Company

Figure 27-2 Total U.S. Dollar Returns from Pacific-Basin Equity Markets

From 1985 to 1990

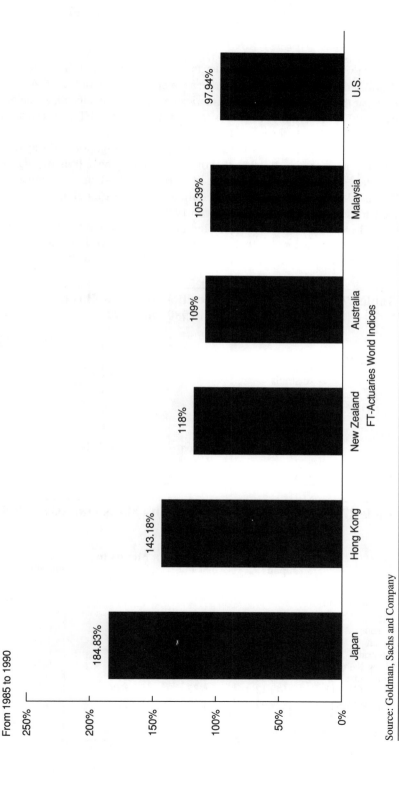

Source: Goldman, Sachs and Company

was the world's second largest after the U.S., comprising 33% of the FT-Actuaries World Index—the U.S. equity market accounted for 35% of the FT-Actuaries World Index at the end of 1990. When American equities are excluded, Japan accounts for over 50% of international shares, as measured by the FT-Actuaries Europe and Pacific (EuroPac) Index as well as other major indices.

Equity markets in Australia, Hong Kong, Singapore, Malaysia, and New Zealand are much smaller than that of Japan, but they have been popular with global investors seeking the diversification of market risks and the enhancement of returns. Table 27-2 shows the market capitalization weighting changes within the FT-Actuaries Pacific Basin Index between 1980 and 1990.

Tables 27-3 and 27-4 detail the investment in the Asian equity markets by major global investors in 1988 and 1989. The global investment in the Asian-Pacific equity markets has increased from $385 billion in 1988 to $545.71 billion in

Table 27-2   Percentage Composition of Pacific-Basin Equity Markets in 1980 and 1990

	1980	1990
Japan	73%	93.0%
Australia	14	4.0
Hong Kong	8	2.5
Singapore	2	1.0
Malaysia	2	0.3
New Zealand	1	0.2
Total Market Capitalization	US $403 bn	US $2,188 bn

Source: FT-Actuaries World Indices Group of Goldman, Sachs & Co.

Table 27-3   Gross Cross-Border Equity Flows into Asia in 1988 (U.S. Dollars in Billions)

	Japan	Australia	Market to Hong Kong	Singapore	Investor Total
Investor From:					
U.S.	US $66.96	4.87	5.34	1.36	78.53
Europe	120.49	13.58	7.83	0.95	142.85
Japan	—	3.32	4.50	1.00	8.82
Australia	3.50	—	2.50	0.25	6.25
Hong Kong	85.00	2.69	—	0.50	88.19
Singapore	2.00	0.00	1.00	—	3.00
Rest of World	49.12	6.82	0.96	0.15	57.0
Market Total	327.07	31.28	22.13	4.21	384.69

Source: Salomon Brothers Inc.

Figure 27-3 Percentage Composition of World Equity Markets

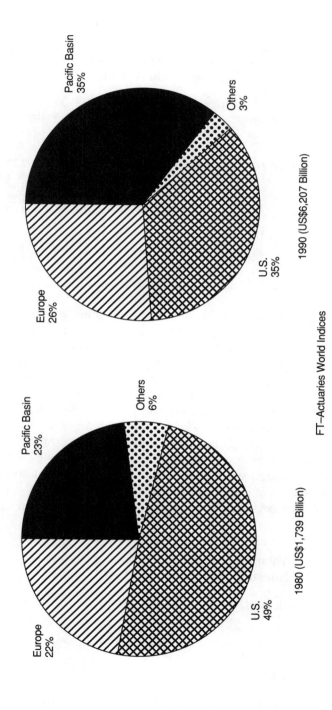

Pacific Basin
35%

Others
3%

U.S.
35%

Europe
26%

1990 (US$6,207 Billion)

Pacific Basin
23%

Others
6%

U.S.
49%

Europe
22%

1980 (US$1,739 Billion)

FT–Actuaries World Indices

Source: Goldman, Sachs and Company

Table 27-4   Gross Cross-Border Equity Flows into Asia-Pacific in 1989 (U.S. Dollars in Billions)

	Japan	Australia	Market to Hong Kong	Singapore	Investor Total
Investor From:					
U.S.	US $84.16	5.47	7.26	3.23	100.12
Europe	142.98	14.86	17.48	6.98	182.30
Japan	—	2.90	17.44	5.16	25.50
Australia	4.07	—	3.30	1.25	8.62
Hong Kong	19.98	9.80	—	7.17	36.95
Singapore	8.31	2.25	2.25	—	12.81
Rest of World	173.36	1.62	3.71	0.72	179.41
Market Total	432.86	36.90	51.44	24.51	545.71

Source: Salomon Brothers Inc.

1989— a 42% increase. This significant amount of investment in the Asian equity markets has been enhanced by the availability of risk management products.

As is visible in Table 27-5, the Asian equity markets are particularly volatile. Thus, as the Asia-Pacific region now comprises a significant portion of global institutional investors' portfolio, the risk management of investments in the region has become an essential part of global investment strategies.

For instance, when the price-earnings ratio of the Japanese equity market reached breathtaking heights in late 1988 and 1989, American, European, and Asian investors were increasingly becoming defensive with regard to their investment in Japan. As fear of a collapse in Japanese stocks became a reality in the beginning of 1990, the risk management of investment in Japan was more indispensable than ever before, and the use of index futures and options soared. Table 27-6 lists the currently-traded Asian stock index futures and options contracts and their exchanges.

Table 27-5   Volatilities of Pacific-Basin and Major International Equity Markets*

Japan	17.5%
Australia	15.9
Hong Kong	27.1
Singapore	18.8
New Zealand	22.4
U.S.	15.2
U.K.	13.2

*Measured by annualized standard deviations of local currency returns between December 1987 and September 1990.
Source: Morgan Stanley Capital International

Table 27-6   Currently Traded Asian Equity Index Futures and Options

	Exchange*	Listing Date
Japan		
Nikkei Stock Average Futures	OSE	9/88
Nikkei Stock Average Options	OSE	6/89
Topix Index Futures	TSE	9/88
Topix Index Options	TSE	10/89
Nagoya Options 25	NSE	10/89
Australia		
All Ordinaries Index Futures	SFE	2/83
All Ordinaries Index Futures Options	SFE	6/85
Options on Australian equities	ASX	1976
Singapore		
Nikkei Stock Average Futures	SIMEX	9/86
Hong Kong		
Hang Seng Index Futures	HKFE	6/86
New Zealand		
Barclays Share Price Index Futures	NZFOE	1/87
Barclays Share Price Index Options	NZFOE	2/89
Options on New Zealand equities	NZFOE	10/90

*OSE: The Osaka Securities Exchange
TSE: The Tokyo Stock Exchange
NSE: The Nagoya Stock Exchange
SFE: The Sydney Futures Exchange
SIMEX: The Singapore International Monetary Exchange
HKFE: The Hong Kong Futures Exchange
NZFOE: The New Zealand Futures and Options Exchange
ASX: The Australian Stock Exchange

In the 1990s, the development of new equity index futures and options contracts is expected in Asia's emerging stock markets. The Asia-Pacific region has the largest emerging equity markets in the world. As is visible in Figure 27-4, in 1990 the Asian emerging equity markets accounted for 73% of the capitalization of the world's emerging markets.

In the 1990s, institutional investment in these markets is expected to rise dramatically. As in the case of more established Asian equity markets, emerging markets in Asia have low correlations with major world equity markets—see Table 27-7. Furthermore, they have recorded superb performances during the past five years, as shown in Figure 27-5. As a result, the emerging equity markets of Asia offer excellent means for diversifying market risks and enhancing returns.

However, the Asian emerging equity markets are highly volatile, as can be seen in Table 27-8. In order to attract a significant amount of international investment, these markets need to develop adequate risk management tools. In the following section, the current efforts by the financial centers to establish financial futures and options markets are discussed.

Figure 27-4 Percentage Composition of World Emerging Equity Markets in 1990

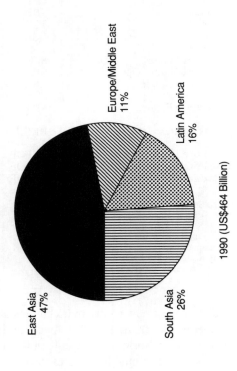

East Asia
47%

Europe/Middle East
11%

Latin America
16%

South Asia
26%

1990 (US$464 Billion)

Source: International Finance Corporation

Table 27-7   Correlations of Emerging Asian Equity Markets with Major European and U.S. Markets*

	U.K.	France	Germany	U.S.
Korea	0.1	0.1	0.1	0.1
Taiwan	0.0	0.0	0.2	−0.2
Thailand	0.0	0.2	0.2	−0.1
Malaysia	0.1	0.1	0.2	−0.2
Indonesia	0.0	−0.1	0.1	−0.1

*Correlations of biweekly US $ returns from January 1988 to September 1990.
Source: Morgan Stanley Capital International

Table 27-8   Volatilities of Asian Emerging and Major International Equity Markets*

Korea	22.4%
Taiwan	44.2
Malaysia	20.0
Thailand	26.7
Indonesia	43.4
U.S.	15.2
U.K.	13.2

*Measured by annualized standard deviations of local currency returns between December 1987 and September 1990.
Source: Morgan Stanley Capital International

Part 1: The Philippines

Although it is neither the largest nor most significant Asian-Pacific emerging financial center, the Philippines has already established a financial futures exchange. The Manila International Futures Exchange (MIFE) started trading commodity futures in 1986, and has since expanded its range of products to the interest rate and currency complexes. It now lists a total of eight contracts, four of which are financial futures. (See Table 27-9). The others are contracts on copra, coffee, sugar, and soybeans.

The MIFE has 13 Full Trading Members, all of whom are Philippine-registered companies. In addition, there are 13 Foreign Trade Affiliated Members. (See Table 27-10 for a list of Full Trading members.) The exchange is regulated by the Philippine Securities and Exchange Commission, and the Central Bank of the Philippines also has oversight for financial futures trading. The MIFE has its own clearing facilities—The Manila International Futures Clearing House Inc.—which acts as the ultimate guarantor of all trades on the exchange.

Figure 27-5 Total U.S. Dollar Returns from Asian Emerging Equity Markets

From 1985 to 1990

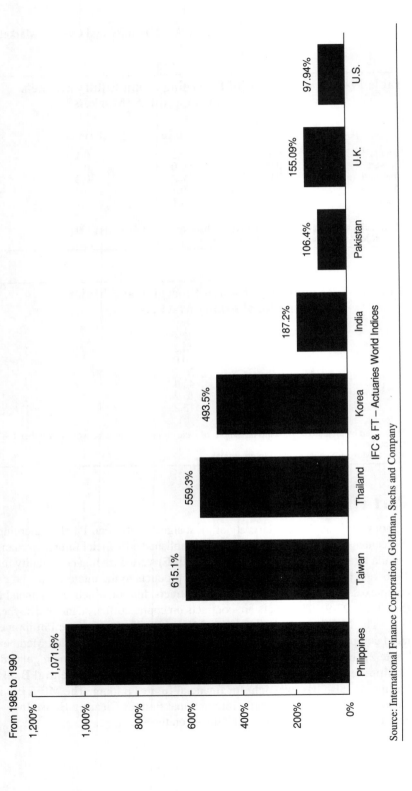

Source: International Finance Corporation, Goldman, Sachs and Company

Table 27-9   Currently Traded Financial Futures Contracts at the MIFE

Financial Futures	Inception
91-Day Philippines Treasury Bill Futures	10/90
British Pound/U.S. Dollar Futures	3/91
U.S. Dollar/Yen Futures	3/91
U.S. Dollar/Deutschemark Futures	3/91

Source: The Manila International Futures Exchange

Table 27-10   Corporate Full Trading Members of MIFE

Billion Gold Futures, Inc.
C.B. Master Commodities Futures, Inc.
C & T Global Futures, Inc.
Everich International Commodities, Inc.
Golden Commodities Corporation
Goldwell Commodity Traders, Inc.
Imperial Commodities, Inc.
Kingly Commodities Traders & Multi-Resources, Inc.
Pan-Asia International Commodities, Inc.
Queensland-Tokyo Commodities, Inc.
Solidlink Futures, Inc.
Trustcom Futures, Inc.
Uniwell Commodities, Inc.

Source: The Manila International Futures Exchange

In October 1990, MIFE launched its 91-day Philippine Treasury bill interest rate futures, and in March 1991, it began trading futures on US$/Yen, US$/Deutschemark, and British Pound/US$ foreign exchange rates. Both the interest rate and currency contracts are traded on the MIFE floor, but through very different trading methods.

The three currency contracts are traded by traditional, open outcry, whereas the interest rate futures use a unique combination of two different methods. Four times a day, the Peso rate contract trades through a "one-price group trading system," which gathers all buyers and sellers who indicate their orders in a manner similar to the London gold fix. When supply and demand is equalized, a single price is reached, and all orders transact at that price. At other times of the day, the short-term Peso interest rate contract trades—infrequently—through a board-trading system.

Trading on these new contracts is light, averaging less than 700 per day for all of the currencies in May 1991, and about 100 lots per day for the interest rate contract in the same month. On active days, however, currency volume can surge to over 1,000 lots. Open interest for the interest rate contract averages about 2,000 positions, while the currency contracts achieved an impressive total open interest of

5,800 positions by their third month of trading. Of the currency contracts, the U.S. Dollar/Yen is the most active. (See Tables 27-11 and 27-12 for volume and open interest figures.) Financial futures participants are predominantly Philippine financial institutions and corporations, with a small amount of activity emanating from Singapore, Hong Kong, Taiwan, and Indonesia.

In the near future, MIFE hopes to introduce a Philippine stock index contract but has a number of substantial hurdles to overcome. Aside from the need to secure regulatory approval from both the Central Bank and the Securities and Exchange Commission, MIFE must convince stock exchange officials and members to support the market, and will need to attract international members. There should be a natural core group of interested foreign participants for a Philippine stock index futures contract as Philippine equities have gained popularity with international fund managers.

In its very short experience with financial futures, MIFE has succeeded in attracting regional, as well as local, user bases for its currently traded contracts. This growing critical mass could serve as the foundation of liquidity for upcoming contracts such as Philippine stock index futures.

Table 27-11 Monthly Trading Volumes of MIFE's Financial Futures

	Interest Rate	Sterling	Yen	Deutschemark
10/90	1,134	n/l*	n/l	n/l
11/90	2,756	n/l	n/l	n/l
12/90	2,292	n/l	n/l	n/l
1/91	2,826	n/l	n/l	n/l
2/91	2,550	n/l	n/l	n/l
3/91	2,372	2,828	2,884	2,852
4/91	2,258	3,262	3,508	3,446
5/91	2,154	4,314	4,972	4,292

*Not Listed
Source: The Manila International Futures Exchange

Table 27-12 Month-end Open Interest of MIFE's Financial Futures

	Interest Rate	Sterling	Yen	Deutschemark
10/90	816	n/l*	n/l	n/l
11/90	2,392	n/l	n/l	n/l
12/90	2,518	n/l	n/l	n/l
1/91	2,876	n/l	n/l	n/l
2/91	3,338	n/l	n/l	n/l
3/91	3,222	1,250	1,216	1,258
4/91	2,852	1,594	1,674	1,656
5/91	1,974	2,082	2,842	2,106

*Not Listed
Source: The Manila International Futures Exchange

91-Day Philippine Treasury Bill Futures

Contract Unit: The weighted average of interest rates of the 91-day Treasury bills issued by the Central Bank of the Philippines.

Trading Month: Spot month plus three trading months.

Trading Hours: 9:30 a.m. to 11:30 a.m.
1:30 p.m. to 3:30 p.m.
(Manila time)

Contract Size: The contract price multiplied by 10,000 Pesos.

Last Day of Trading: The third Thursday of the trading month.

Settlement Day: The Monday immediately following the last trading day.

Settlement: All open positions will be settled by the cash settlement price on the settlement day.

Settlement Price: The weighted average of interest rates of the 91-day Treasury bills determined by the Central Bank of the Philippines on the third Friday auction of the trading month will be the basis for calculating cash settlement price.

U.S. Dollar/Japanese Yen Futures

Contract Unit: 12,500,000 Yen

Trading Month: Spot month plus three consecutive months.

Trading Hours: 8:30 a.m. to 11:30 a.m.
2:00 p.m. to 5:00 p.m.
9:00 p.m. to 4:00 a.m.
(Manila time)

Last Day of Trading: The third Tuesday of the trading month.

Settlement Day: The business day immediately following the last trading day.

Settlement: All open positions will be settled in Philippine Pesos.

Settlement Price: The average to the second decimal point (not rounded-up) of four hourly spot U.S. Dollar/Yen quotations by the banks and institutions designated by the Executive Committee on the last trading day.

U.S. Dollar/Deutschemark Futures

Contract Unit: 125,000 Deutschemark.

Trading Month: Spot month plus three consecutive months.

Trading Hours: 8:30 a.m. to 11:30 a.m.
2:00 p.m. to 5:00 p.m.
9:00 p.m. to 4:00 a.m.
(Manila time)

Last Day of Trading: The third Tuesday of the trading month.

Settlement Day: The business day immediately following the last trading day.

Settlement: All open positions will be settled in Philippine Pesos.

Settlement Price: The average to the fourth decimal point (not rounded-up) of four hourly spot U.S. Dollar/Deutschemark quotations by the banks and institutions designated by the Executive Committee on the last trading day.

Contract Unit: 62,500 British Pounds.

Trading Month: Spot month plus three consecutive months.

Trading Hours: 8:30 a.m. to 11:30 a.m.
2:00 p.m. to 5:00 p.m.
9:00 p.m. to 4:00 a.m.
(Manila time)

Last Day of Trading: The third Tuesday of the trading month.

Settlement Day: The business day immediately following the last trading day.

Settlement: All open positions will be settled in Philippine Pesos.

Settlement Price: The average to the fourth decimal point (not rounded-up) of four hourly spot British Pound/U.S. Dollar quotations by the banks and institutions designated by the Executive Committee on the last trading day.

Part 2: Malaysia

Beginning of a New Era

In 1990, the International Monetary Fund (IMF) told Bank Negara, the central bank of Malaysia, that its capital markets are not yet ready for financial futures. The Kuala Lumpur Commodity Exchange (KLCE) has gone nowhere with its professed intention to list financial contracts. The Kuala Lumpur Stock Exchange (KLSE) is preoccupied with refining its clearing and settlement system and has done little to develop options markets. This would not appear to be a conducive environment for a bold initiative for establishing derivative trading in Malaysia.

Yet, a group of well-connected Malaysian firms are trying to lead their capital markets to a new era of financial futures and options. With the implicit backing from the Ministry of Finance, the Kuala Lumpur Options and Financial Futures Exchange (KLOFFE) is currently being set up to enhance the growth of the Malaysian capital markets. The organizers of the exchange have ambitious goals and an optimistic timetable.

KLOFFE will be the stepchild of necessity—or at least perceived necessity. Malaysia's former Finance Minister, Datuk Paduka Daim Zainuddin, was committed to increasing Kuala Lumpur's potential as a financial center, not in order to capture international activity, but to support the country's economic development. The Malaysian government has major privatization plans in the works and recognizes the need to develop liquidity in its capital markets. Futures and options markets are integral to such an objective. When hedging and asset allocation facilities exist, investors can hold larger debt and equity positions and as a result, enhance the liquidity of the market.

Bold Move by Private Organizers

Since some of Malaysia's biggest privatization issues such as Telekoms and the National Electricity Board are slated for the near future, the agility in developing the derivative market is a high priority. Daim stated that "KLCE officials were dragging their feet" in bringing about needed changes, and he was widely known to disapprove of the way in which the KLSE handled the surge of volume after Malaysian shares were officially delisted from Singapore in 1989. Daim's well-known preference for shock therapy was apparent when, in December 1990, the Ministry of Finance and the Capital Issues Committee granted "approval in principle" to the private sector organizers of the KLOFFE for both futures and options trading.

The government's move stunned Kuala Lumpur Commodity Exchange officials who had always taken for granted that new financial contracts would be listed on the KLCE. Even the Ministry of Primary Industries, which oversees commodity trading, was taken by surprise. However, their shock is difficult to justify, considering that they had over three years to develop financial futures markets, and neither ideas nor actions had been forthcoming from them.

Clearly, there were different interpretations of the IMF report. After the IMF ruled out the KLCE, a group of five private institutional organizers of the KLOFFE decided to look into it themselves. Renong Bhd., the New Straits Times Press, Rashid Hussain Bhd., and Zalik Securities commissioned a M$100,000 feasibility study on the prospects for the Malaysian financial futures and options markets. Renong Bhd. in conjunction with its partially-owned subsidiary, the New Straits Times Press, will likely hold a controlling interest in the Kuala Lumpur Options and Financial Futures Exchange. Renong's chairman, Halim Saad, is considered by many observers to have represented Daim's viewpoint within the KLOFFE organizing group.

The Plan

The initial feasibility study was conducted by Commerce International Merchant Bankers Bhd. and relied heavily on outside consultants, especially from the existing foreign exchanges. The Stockholm Options Market (OM) is one such contributor. The first phase of the study was completed in early 1991, and its conclusions have sufficiently bolstered KLOFFE's organizers to move ahead with the project. Specific proposals were then submitted to the Ministry of Finance.

The organizers have set realistic goals for the exchange and have no starry-eyed vision of becoming a major regional futures trading center. According to the head of a Malaysian securities house with close ties to the organizers, KLOFFE's priority is to develop a derivative market that complements the Malaysian equity market. The organizers are also attempting not to make the same mistake that the KLSE made by modeling itself on the world's largest exchanges. They are looking at smaller exchanges as their role models, not to Chicago or London.

While the trading systems of both the New Zealand Futures and Options Exchange and the Swiss Options and Financial Futures Exchange (SOFFEX) have been studied, KLOFFE is planning to use Stockholm OM technology. The Swedish exchange organization has already successfully transferred its system to London and other financial centers and is rapidly expanding its international activities. The second phase of the study addresses more complex technical and legal aspects of KLOFFE's development. From these early plans, one can discern the rough contours of the market.

The exchange will be structured as an independent, profit-making company, with the aforementioned Malaysian organizing institutions as its main shareholders. It has not yet been decided whether memberships will represent partial ownership in the exchange, or simply convey the right to trade in the markets. It is also unclear whether membership will have tiered categories and privileges.

Membership is expected to be open to any firm which meets exchange requirements, which are yet to be formulated. This, however, does not guarantee that foreign firms can join KLOFFE independently. Foreigners may have to form joint-ventures with local banks or brokerage houses as they must for the Malaysian stock market. A high level member of the organizing group states that the KLSE members will be among the first to join the new exchange. Skeptics have noted, however, that KLOFFE is infringing on the stock exchange's turf, and that some members may be less than eager to join the new exchange.

Regulatory turf is also being contested. It remains undecided whether KLOFFE will be supervised directly by the Ministry of Finance or through a reorganized Commodity Trading Commission. So far, the Commissioner of the commodity regulatory board appears to be out of the decision-making loop. This issue may remain unresolved until other legal changes are enacted, but the Ministry of Finance holds most of the political cards.

The organizers have decided upon an automated trading system for more than the obvious overhead savings that come from not having a trading floor. A proven, off-the-shelf system will save software development costs and, moreover, will not be prone to costly and time-consuming debugging. KLOFFE will probably use a modified version of the Stockholm OM technology. The system will enable KLOFFE to establish an electronic trading system for futures and cash or futures options, with integrated clearing facilities. Furthermore, the Swedish system can accommodate telephone-based block orders, which could be built into the KLOFFE system or added at a later date when volume or type of contract necessitates it. The organizers see screen-based systems as more viable for the size of the Malaysian market, and also regards it as the wave of the future.

The Products

KLOFFE intends to concentrate on equity-related products at the onset. This meshes with the government's privatization and capital market plans and is expected to attract the broadest possible group of users. The relative familiarity of stock index futures will also smooth the KLOFFE's major educational and marketing tasks.

Southeast Asian equity markets have attracted significant regional and foreign interest, but the region needs local risk management products. For instance, many overseas fund managers fear liquidity drying up in the local markets and thus long for a viable hedging mechanism. Local index futures will lessen this fear, and consequently, enhance the inflow of investment.

While in many ways index futures are the logical place to start, it also will require numerous changes in existing legal and market structures if KLOFFE is to succeed. Liquidity in Malaysian derivatives—and the added liquidity that would flow into the cash market—is only possible if arbitrageurs and market makers can operate freely in both markets.

This means having to take short positions in the KLSE, which is currently prohibited. Arbitrageurs' difficulty in shorting stock has greatly handicapped the recovery of the Hong Kong Futures Exchange's Hang Seng index futures contract after the stock market crash of 1987. Regulators from Tokyo to Jakarta are naturally wary of relinquishing the control that they feel prevents speculators from driving markets down. However, they do not realize that they are hobbling the long-term development of genuine liquidity.

The KLOFFE organizers have recognized the need for changes in the cash market. According to an official at an organizing firm, the third phase of the feasibility study provides detailed recommendations on modifications for the stock market. One organizer states that KLSE restrictions on short selling need to be addressed and solved, preferably before they launch the contract.

The KLOFFE promoters are not waiting for the government machinery to act on their requests. They have brought in international lawyers with futures regulation expertise to prepare a proposal for modifying the existing Malaysian laws. The organizers then intend to submit their proposal and founding charter as a single package to the Parliament, backed by their ties to the government.

For instance, the authorities justifiably fear manipulation of an index in either direction—although there is a clear preference for upward movement. Also, the KLOFFE feasibility study indicates a need to find an appropriate index on which to base the futures contract. Malaysian market analysts and the exchange's organizers agree that the current benchmark for the KLSE—the New Straits Times Industrials (NSTI)—is inadequate. With only 30 components, it is subject to manipulation and does not reflect the overall Malaysian market. Even a senior official at the New Straits Times Press, which compiles the index, admits the shortcomings of the widely-followed NSTI. While the KLSE has a broader-based index, the KLOFFE organizers have indicated that they may create their own all-share index.

Regardless of the benchmark index that is to be eventually chosen, stock index futures are almost certain to be KLOFFE's first product. Even if there are teething pains, index futures will eventually enable institutional investors to rapidly hedge or adjust their Malaysian equity positions, and thus make them more willing to take larger holdings. These same risk management needs might also increase their appetite for options.

KLOFFE's "approval in principle" from the Ministry of Finance includes the right to list options on stocks as well. Just as the complacent Malaysian commodity industry had assumed that it would be given the chance to list financial futures, the Kuala Lumpur Stock Exchange always thought that options were its domain. But the authorities thought otherwise. KLOFFE is now giving a high priority to options on stocks as well as stock index futures. The initial study and inclination of the organizers favor options on a handful of the highest market capitalization and most actively-traded equities.

The exchange's proposed start-up plans—attracting members, educational programs, marketing efforts, launching index futures, and eventually options—are highly ambitious. Nevertheless, KLOFFE's organizers are looking beyond this first stage of development. Even though the August 1990 IMF report which cautioned against the early introduction of financial futures included interest rate and currency futures among the instruments that were not yet viable, it is in this direction that KLOFFE intends to eventually move. Products under consideration for the mid-1990s include: medium or long-term bond futures; short-term ringgit interest rate futures; the Malaysian ringgit/the U.S. dollar currency futures; and possibly the ringgit/the yen and the ringgit/the Singapore dollar contracts. Bond and interest rate futures would dovetail with the Ministry of Finance's efforts to cultivate active and sophisticated markets for government and corporate bonds, and commercial paper.

Potential Obstacles

The linkage between the development goals for KLOFFE and Malaysia's capital markets—along with the backing of the Ministry of Finance—should provide a solid foundation for the new exchange. KLOFFE is intended to play an integral part in the growth of Malaysia's domestic markets. Furthermore, the government's bold privatization plans should work to its advantage. However, establishing active futures and options markets will be substantially more difficult than attracting investors into the equity market.

Although a successful modification of the trading restrictions for the cash market would remove a major structural hurdle for KLOFFE and allow arbitrageurs to trade both sides, many traders question whether an active stock index future market can develop in Malaysia. Liquidity requires market makers and substantial pools of risk capital in addition to arbitrageurs.

The KLOFFE decision to opt for a screen-based system, while cost-effective, may inhibit the development of market depth. Electronic trading tends to function smoothly in normal market environments, but it exhibits a serious structural weakness at times of market stress. The presence of the on-screen market makers with their bids and offers cannot be guaranteed in a wildly volatile market. This has been demonstrated by the frequent pauses in trading—and occasional lock-ups—in Japan's Nikkei and Topix stock index futures and options contracts.

In contrast, the Singapore International Monetary Exchange's (SIMEX) Nikkei 225 futures trade continuously even during the most violent sessions. The difference is the constant bids and offers on the trading floor by "locals" who risk their own capital on a minute-by-minute basis. It has taken SIMEX much time and effort to build its own pool of locals, but it now stands as one of the exchange's major achievements and sources of strength. Also, SIMEX has long desired to launch Singapore stock index futures, and the KLOFFE's debut may hasten that moment.

KLOFFE, however, does not have time to develop a pool of locals. It might have to concentrate on getting as many market makers as possible and encourage arbitrageurs with clearing fee rebates and other incentives. But will Kuala Lumpur become an environment conducive to developing a futures market expertise?

Much depends on how open the KLOFFE truly is to foreign membership and participation. One reason Singapore has become a center of derivative expertise is that SIMEX strongly encourages foreign membership. This facilitates the transfer of hedging, trading, and market-making technologies. On this issue, Kuala Lumpur should look to its neighbor for a successful example.

KLOFFE Moves Ahead

Is Malaysia ready for a financial futures and options markets? In 1990, the IMF said "not yet." Or did they only mean that the KLCE was not yet ready for derivative trading, as a Renong official implied in January of 1991? Whatever the conclusion of the IMF report—which is now gathering dust on a bookshelf of the Central Bank of Malaysia—was, KLOFFE is currently sprinting ahead with the Ministry of Finance's endorsement.

"Sure, it's a bold move to grab the derivative turf from the KLCE and KLSE, but how else will it happen here?," a foreign broker in Kuala Lumpur said. There are bigger stakes involved, particularly the government's economic goals, and they are clearly a top priority.

So far, KLOFFE's organizers have taken an impressively realistic approach toward setting up the market. They have done their homework and are not aiming too high as other regional futures exchanges did in the mid-1980s. With strong underlying fundamentals and firm political support, KLOFFE could soon be another well-known acronym on the lips of Asian market participants.

Part 3: Taiwan

By some measures, Taiwan is Asia's second richest country, and it has the fourth largest equity market of the region after Japan, Korea, and Australia. According to the Emerging Market Indices of International Finance Corporation, the total market capitalization of Taiwan was U.S. $100 billion at the end of 1990. The country also has an extraordinarily high level of public speculation. Over 20% of the population has a stock trading account and the Taipei Stock Exchange has the world's second highest turnover, even after its 64% drop between February and July of 1990. This volatility has sparked a recognition of the need for risk management tools, but has equally elicited a greater public appetite for new speculative vehicles.

Until a government crackdown in 1989 and 1990, a huge, underground futures trading environment existed in Taiwan, generating over U.S. $1 billion in daily activity. Trading took place mostly at night since the illegal trades tended to price off of Chicago and New York markets. As many as 30,000 to 50,000 orders were sent abroad daily, and many more orders —100,000 to 150,000—never left Taiwan. These latter trades took place in "bucket shops," so named because most of the orders never made it to the exchanges, but were thrown into the house's "bucket" and netted off each other. As recently as early 1991, another type of bucketing activity was prevalent. Known as "Trading in the Air," brokers would accept bets on the future price movement of the local stock index or individual shares.

The government has closed down the biggest brokers in these activities, and forced others — many of whom have legal stockbroking operations — to curtail their business. A new law, sponsored by the Ministry of Economic Affairs, that will clarify the status of the futures industry and set up a regulatory structure, is now working its way through the Yuan (Taiwan's legislature), and will have its reading in the spring of 1992. The bill gained the support from various Taiwan business associations, securities firms, and overseas exchanges. Futures trading in Taiwan will thus be legalized by the end of 1992.

If the new law passes in its current form, Asian and U.S. futures industry leaders expect greatly increased Taiwanese business to flow to regional futures exchanges. Trading activity will be initially directed to the markets which are familiar to Taiwanese investors, such as Hong Kong, Singapore, and Japan. In addition, U.S./Taiwanese equity investment in those countries is expected to continue expanding, as well as investment in Thailand, Malaysia, Indonesia, and even the infant stock exchanges in China.

Futures brokerage firms from the United States and Japan have begun exploratory operations in Taipei, and their number is expected to grow. A few firms have already established joint ventures with local financial brokers or institutions.

Although the pending legislation is designed first to regulate futures brokerage activity in Taiwan which is geared to outward order flows, the development of domestic futures activity is likely to occur by the middle of the decade. Stock Exchange officials, Taiwan academics, and brokerage officials have all initiated research on a local stock index future, and there can be little doubt that Taiwan's risk-loving investors would welcome such a product. Any financial community that can devise and sustain "trading in the air," is certainly a ripe market for exchange-listed equity derivatives.

Furthermore, under a major infrastructure and financial development plan announced in early 1991, Taiwan set a timetable for broad reforms to make the island one of Asia'a main banking centers. Eased restrictions on foreign banks, internationalization of the New Taiwan dollar, and the establishment of a gold market have been proposed. The Finance Ministry also plans to develop Taiwan's bond market by floating over US $40 billion in bond issues by 1996, and privatizing scores of state-run enterprises.

These major capital market reforms, as well as the public's huge demand for speculative activity in the equity and commodity markets, will ensure a strong underlying foundation for the growth of Taiwan's derivative markets. By the end of the decade, Taiwan's financial strength will be close to catching up with its industrial prowess.

Part 4: Korea

As the Korean equity market declined over 23% between 1989 and 1990 after a rise of about 550% between 1985 and 1988, sharp volatility occured in the Korean securities such as closed-end country funds, investment trusts, convertible bonds, and bonds with warrants. These Korean securities have been the only investment vehicles available to international investors who wish to participate in the Korean equity market — direct access to the Korean market by international investors will not be possible until early 1992.

The Korea Fund listed on the New York Stock Exchange — a brainchild of the International Finance Corporation in Washington, D.C. — was the first exchange-traded, closed-end country fund ever created, and has been quite popular among international investors since its inception in August 1984 as the Korean equity boomed in the second half of the 1980s. Other funds, such as the Korea Europe Fund and the Korea Asia Fund, followed quickly behind.

From March to June of 1989, the Korean market fell some 15%. This kind of volatility convinced international investors of the need for risk management tools for their Korean investment, and the American Stock Exchange (AMEX) explored the feasibility of listing options on the Korea Fund in 1990. However, the insufficient daily trading volume of the Fund presented a problem of market manipulation, and options on the Korea Fund were never listed.

The Koreans themselves have begun to recognize the need for risk management tools after their market demonstrated that stock prices can also come down. The Korean Ministry of Finance announced its plan in 1990 to establish a stock index futures market and made its plan more specific in 1991 by including Korean stock index futures in its five year capital market restructuring plan. However, the Ministry's projected establishment of financial futures market faces a number of obstacles.

In case of stock index futures, the Korean government must be able to convince itself that the equity market should be driven by free market forces. The Korean government has sought to prop up the market on a number of occasions since 1989 without much success. An efficient stock index futures market cannot be formed if the government tries to boost the cash market whenever the underlying market heads substantially southward. At the end of 1989, the Korean government persuaded the three largest Korean investment companies to purchase declining Korean equities by offering them low-interest U.S. $3 billion bank loans. Despite the injection of U.S. $3 billion, the Korean equity market fell 23% in 1990 and incurred huge losses to the three investment companies — Korea Investment Trust, Daehan Investment Trust, and Citizens' Investment Trust. These losses are known to have put these three investment companies under serious financial stress despite the fact that they were considered blue chip firms throughout the 1980s.

The Korean Ministry of Finance has yet to deregulate interest rates and foreign exchange trading. These liberalizations will be the first steps toward establishing futures on interest rates and currencies. The complete deregulation of domestic interest rates and foreign exchange trading is not expected until the mid-1990s.

Furthermore, in order to establish futures markets, the education of the Korean financial community will be essential. However, the Korean securities houses and institutional investors are not currently allowed to trade financial futures overseas. Instead, Korean corporations have been permitted to trade commodity and currency futures in international futures markets for hedging purposes only since 1975. Currently, five foreign-owned and one Korean-owned commodity brokerage firms are operating in Korea: Gerald Commodities Ltd., Korean Commodities Inc., Cargill Investor Services Korea, Paribas Commodities Inc., Credit Lyonnais Rouse, and MG Commodities.

Korean corporations are required to report their international futures positions to the Ministry of Finance. Despite this disclosure requirement, it is well known that Korean corporations have been speculating in international currency derivative markets. For instance, a bank located in Southwestern Korea wiped out two-thirds of its total net worth by taking reckless positions in international currency derivative markets during the two-year span between 1989 and 1990. Since then, the Ministry of Finance has been taking more cautious steps in allowing Korean institutions to trade in international futures markets. This will further delay the entry of Korean financial institutions into international futures markets.

In 1990 Korean economy was the 15th largest in the world in terms of GNP. As the Korean economy completes its transformation into an industrialized nation in the 1990s, its capital markets need to catch up with the prowess of the Korean manufacturers in order to support their continuing growth. After the Iraqi invasion of Kuwait in 1990, Korea, which relies heavily on imported oil, purchased a substantial amount of crude oil at its peak price (over U.S. $40/barrel) at the end of 1990, anticipating a further surge in the oil price. Although the Gulf crisis ended in the spring of 1991 and oil prices declined to pre-war levels (U.S. $20/barrel), in May 1991 Korea was still taking the delivery of oil priced in late 1990. Korean industrial companies cannot maintain their competitiveness against their foreign counterparts if they have to consume higher priced oil. This energy fiasco has further convinced Korean institutions of the need for sophisticated hedging operations.

Korea faces a number of problems which it must overcome in order to establish a financial and commodity futures industry and markets. However, it seems to have recognized the importance of developing them in order to nurture a balanced economy. The Ministry of Finance and Korean securities houses have been patiently studying international futures markets since the mid-1980s. Korean industrial companies have rapidly overcome many obstacles in a short period of time on a number of occasions to become world class steel manufacturers, shipbuilders, computer chip makers, and automobile manufacturers. Furthermore, in a four-year period between 1985 and 1989 the Korean equity market saw its total market capitalization grow approximately 1,900% to U.S. $141 billion from U.S. $7 billion in 1985; it became the tenth-largest equity market in the world, surpassing Switzerland. Thus it would not be surprising if Korea develops significant financial and commodity futures activity and markets by the mid-1990s.

Part 5: Thailand

In the mid-1980s, Thailand was one of the Asian emerging financial markets whose readiness for a domestic financial futures market was highly questionable. While the development of such markets still lies in the distant future, it is now a much more realistic possibility than would have been believed just a few years ago. Substantial growth and maturation is anticipated for the Thai capital markets in the 1990s, and this could lay the foundation for financial futures and options. Furthermore, as the economic growth of the country continues its remarkable progress, the Thai financial futures market could play a significant role.

Fueled by stellar economic growth throughout the 1980s, the Thai equity market boomed and attracted both domestic and international investors. According to the Emerging Market Indices of the International Finance Corporation, at the end of 1990 Thailand's total market capitalization was U.S. $24 billion. This represented a 1,200% growth in five years from U.S. $1.9 billion in 1985, yet there is still much room for further expansion. Upcoming government privatization plans will continue to increase market capitalization and broaden the base of shareholders in Thailand. The widely discussed liberalization of investment guidelines for domestic institutions should also deepen the equity market.

The Ministry of France is expected to authorize stock warrants and convertible bonds in 1992. These are the first steps toward equity derivative activity. Other steps include the Stock Exchange of Thailand's development research into both index futures and stock options. Overseas derivative exchanges have been approached for consultation and feasibility studies.

The Ministry of Finance has also expressed its desire to expand the ability of financial institutions and corporations to issue debt, and to nurture the development of the secondary bond market. These efforts to create a favorable infrastructure for capital formation will include tax reform and the lifting of asset allocation restrictions on life insurance companies and mutual funds. As capital market development proceeds, it will create domestic demand for risk management tools, and might open the way for both equity and bond futures trading in Thailand.

The path toward derivative activity in Thailand is not clear, and is strewn with many political and economic uncertainties, such as the February 1991 military coup. However, the country's phenomenal economic growth, increasing financial strength, and active role in the Southeast Asian economic development, will likely make it a key economic force in the Asian-Pacific region in the coming years. Thailand's hosting of the World Bank/IMF annual meeting in 1991 is only the first indication of its emerging prominence within the world financial community.

Part 6: Indonesia

The Indonesian financial markets have made enormous strides since the sweeping liberalization of October 1988, known as "Pakto." The reforms allowed new banks and foreign joint venture banks to open for the first time in 20 years, and liberalized foreign exchange trading and offshore borrowing. As a result, both the number of banks and the level of deposits have more than doubled.

Capital market activities have grown even more dramatically. New listings on the Jakarta Stock Exchange (JSE) boomed, with over 150 companies going public since the reforms took effect. According to the Emerging Market Indices of the International Finance Corporation, Indonesian equity market capitalization surged from U.S. $117 million in 1985 to just over U.S. $8 billion at the end of 1990.

There have been numerous dislocations resulting from this rush to liberalize and modernize. Major foreign exchange trading losses at banks with inadequate risk control mechanisms and horrendous settlement problems at the stock exchange were two of the most prominent problems. Yet, the worst of the indigestion appears to be over, and Indonesia's financial and capital market growth is expected to reaccelerate in the near future.

In early 1991, Indonesia's Central Bank and Finance Ministry began pushing through new rules and guidelines to strengthen the country's financial structure. This will both promote a more stable system, and ease foreign participant's anxiety due to the uncertainty about regulatory controls.

The first major area of reform is related to the new Banking Bill. It establishes higher capital adequacy standards for banks, and requires them to demonstrate a minimum of competence before speculating in the foreign exchange markets. This bill will also authorize pension funds to invest in equities and bonds.

The second major upcoming area of reform concerns the equity market. The JSE will be privatized in 1992, and will move to fully computerized settlement. The current Capital Markets Supervisory Agency, or BAPEPAM, which now owns the

JSE, will become simply a market supervisor and a regulator, but will have expanded jurisdiction over new investment vehicles.

The move toward more sophisticated capital-raising vehicles has already begun, with the first equity warrants issued in 1990 and the first convertible Eurobond floated in early 1991. This trend will likely accelerate as Indonesia's market structure becomes more clearly defined in the coming years.

Indonesia has one of the largest and youngest populations in the world, and a rapidly expanding economy. By the middle of this decade, the country's financial markets will — at minimum — reach the stage that Thailand and Malaysia reached in the mid-1980s. The bond, equity, and money markets will be substantially stronger and healthier, and in a position to serve a vital role in Indonesia's economic development. Just as with its Southeast Asian neighbors such as the Philippines and Malaysia, it is inevitable that one day, Indonesian derivative markets will be established in order to make the capital markets more liquid and efficient.

Part 7: China

China, the world's most populous nation, has always sparked dreams of the bountiful "China Market" of a billion customers. The People's Republic's economic reforms have moved in fits and starts since the early 1980s, and its political development has certainly not progressed nearly as far. However, slowly but surely, the basic elements of financial and commodity markets are developing in the Middle Kingdom, and thus, any discussion of the Pacific Rim capital markets would be incomplete if it did not briefly touch upon China.

Since 1988, "grey market" share trading has taken place in Shenzhen, the Special Economic Zone closest to Hong Kong. Shanghai, the site of China's pre-Communist stock market, also began unofficial trading in the late 1980s under the careful guidance of state economists. In December 1990, stock trading in Shanghai became official, and since then, Shanghai has listed eight shares. Beginning in May 1990, the more freewheeling Shenzhen *bourse* has also begun its semi-official trading — under local authorization — of its first five listed companies.

The Shenzhen Securities Exchange officially opened in July 1991, with six shares listed, and as many as 15 companies may be trading by early 1992. There are already over 10 securities firms in Shenzhen, and a few Hong Kong firms are also participating. In fact, Sun Hung Kai Securities of Hong Kong has been instrumental in helping the exchange with numerous technical hurdles.

The future growth of Chinese financial markets depend heavily on local and national government authorities, who have been relatively pragmatic in their development. The Central Bank no longer intends to subsidize the thousands of state enterprises, and hopes to tap the estimated U.S. $130 billion in cash holdings and savings accounts of the nation's citizens. But it cannot access the population's cash horde without forming more structured and efficient capital markets through which its citizens' investment and savings will be channeled into Chinese industrial companies.

The Central Bank is also drafting a major program which will set up a regulatory framework and establish guidelines for foreign portfolio investment. Chinese authorities have also intensively researched futures markets, particularly for agricultural commodities. They worked with the Chicago Board of Trade on feasibility studies for such markets, and also received assistance from the Hong Kong Futures Exchange. In late 1990 and early 1991, provincial cash grain markets opened in several parts of China. The first, The Zhengzhou Grain Wholesale Market, opened in October 1990 featuring wheat trading. Jiangxi and Anhui provinces have followed with rice markets, and Jilin has opened a corn market.

In early 1991, the Communist Party's Central Committee recommended the establishment of grain wholesale and futures markets, giving official support to the provincial undertakings. The already formed cash markets will soon be ready to develop into futures markets, particularly since standardized contract terms and auction price discovery mechanisms have been being introduced.

In addition, a number of Chinese state and province-owned companies are known to be active in the Hong Kong futures market, and the Bank of China and CITIC (China International Trust and Investment Corporation) have also participated in international financial futures markets. The activity level of Chinese entities is expected to increase sharply as 1997 approaches, both within and beyond the Hong Kong futures market.

Despite this impressive growth of market activity, the development of financial futures markets in China is a long way off, probably not until the next century. However, China's higher profile in regional financial futures markets is certain to become a significant factor during this decade.

Part 8: Mongolia

China's neighbor to the north, Mongolia, has taken some of the most dramatic steps toward a free market in recent years. Asia's second oldest communist state has embarked on a sweeping reform process, spearheaded by its prime minister. If all goes according to plan, by the end of 1993 70% of state-owned assets will have been privatized, and Mongolians might pay as much attention to Ulan Batur's stock exchange as they do to the capital's renowned Yak races.

All of Mongolia's 2 million citizens will be entitled to vouchers which will enable them to bid on the shares of state-owned companies. International investors will be allowed to buy up to 100% of Mongolian firms, currency restrictions will be eliminated, and the financial system will be revamped along Western, free market standards.

Financial futures activity is unlikely, but that does not diminish the extent of the changes Asia's second oldest communist state has adapted. If Mongolia can take such dramatic steps as setting up its stock exchange in a former children's entertainment center that still sports a mural of Bugs Bunny, perhaps commodity futures trading should not be ruled out.

Part 9: Vietnam

Although it is one of the poorest countries in the Asian-Pacific region — and with an economy suffering from years of communist mismanagement — Vietnam has a large, young, and (at least in the South) entrepreneurial population. Before the end of the decade, the country could be fully reintegrated into regional trade and investment flows and provide financial opportunities for international investors.

Even before the implementation of needed regulatory and structural changes to the economy, a few bold institutions have launched specialized funds for investment in Vietnam. In mid-1991, the Vietnamese government approved two investment funds. The first, the U.S. $30 million Vietnam Fund, which is managed by Lloyds Bank of Britain and Asia Securities of Taiwan, will invest predominantly in foreign/Vietnamese joint-ventures. The other is a U.S. $100 million fund managed by the Hong Kong subsidiary of Credit Lyonnais Securities. The Credit Lyonnais fund will be structured more like a traditional country fund, with investments in local enterprises. It evisages the proposed Vietnamese stock market as its route for cashing out its investments.

These first tentative steps for foreign investment inflow might encourage other international investors to keep an eye on Vietnam, particularly as a boom in foreign investment and economic growth is expected when the U.S.-led economic embargo is lifted. This could lay the foundation for a Vietnamese capital market.

Conclusion

As illustrated in this chapter, developments within Asian emerging financial markets are occurring at diverse speeds and have different levels of significance for international investors and futures traders. However, if the history of rapid development in the major Pacific Rim financial centers provides any single overarching lesson, it is that once a regional financial community commits itself to reform such as the creation of futures markets, the changes can be dramatic and the growth, spectacular.

Market participants have already witnessed this dynamism in Japan, Australia, Singapore, Hong Kong, and New Zealand and are beginning to see signs of it in the Philippines and Malaysia. International market users will surely witness some of the same dramatic changes in Taiwan and Korea, and eventually, Thailand and

Indonesia. By early in the next century, not only will the economic size of the Pacific Rim far exceed that of either Europe or North America, but the region may also generate more futures and options activity than anywhere else in the world.

28

CONTRACTUAL SAVINGS AND EMERGING SECURITIES MARKETS

Dimitri Vittas
The World Bank
Washington, D.C., United States

Contractual savings institutions, i.e., insurance companies and pension funds, have long been important institutions in several developed countries. However, with some notable exceptions, they have been weak and underdeveloped in most developing countries. To a large extent, this can be explained by the lower level of income of the latter. But to a significant extent, the weakness of contractual savings institutions can also be explained by the adverse impact of repressive regulations and by the existence of pay-as-you-go social security systems that have undermined the potential role that life insurance companies and pension funds can play in different countries.

Contractual savings institutions involve long-term contracts that may span up to 60 years or more. For example, pension schemes may involve 40 years of active participation as contributing workers and 20 years of passive participation as retired beneficiaries. Furthermore, term and endowment life insurance policies normally last for 10 years, often for as long as 30 years, while whole life policies cover the remaining life of insured policyholders.

Because they cover such a long span and are often based on compulsory and/or poorly defined contracts, they raise many complex regulatory issues that parallel, but are more difficult to resolve than, those affecting commercial banks.

*The findings, interpretations, and conclusions expressed in this paper are entirely those of the author and should not be attributed in any manner to the World Bank, to its affiliated organizations, or the members of its Board of Executive Directors or the countries they represent.

These include issues of prudential regulation covering authorization criteria and solvency margins, product and price regulation, and investor protection. Governments have a crucial role to play in establishing a regulatory framework that promotes stability, efficiency, and fairness and ensures that contractual savings institutions fulfill their contracts and deliver the promised benefits to their participants.[1]

The purpose of this chapter is to review briefly the size of contractual savings institutions in selected developed and developing countries and to assess their role in the development of securities markets focusing on five points:

1. The organization of a country's pension system is a major determinant of the structure of the financial system.

2. Contractual savings do not increase the rate of saving but affect the composition of total savings in favor of long-term financial assets.

3. The role of contractual savings institutions in securities markets reflects historical traditions and differences in regulation. Despite their great potential, they are important players in the equity markets of only a few, mostly Anglo-American countries. And they have, thus far, only played a limited part in stimulating the growth of emerging securities markets, even in countries, such as Singapore, Malaysia, Korea, and Chile, where contractual savings institutions have accumulated substantial long-term financial resources.

4. Investment regulations must aim at ensuring the safety and profitability of contractual savings. Encouraging investment prudence and developing effective supervision should be basic objectives of public policy.

5. Contractual savings institutions can have a large impact on securities markets. They have the potential to completely transform the functioning of securities markets, facilitate the privatization process, promote the dispersion of corporate ownership, and enhance corporate efficiency.

Organization of Pension Systems

In general, countries with unfunded pay-as-you-go social pension systems that pay generous benefits have underdeveloped contractual savings institutions, especially company-based pension funds. Germany, Austria, France, Italy, and several other Southern European countries belong to this group.

In contrast, other countries, where social pension systems (funded or unfunded) pay modest pensions, have highly developed occupational pension schemes. These countries are characterized by the accumulation of large financial savings in the form of insurance and pension reserves. Most Anglo-American countries and a few continental European countries (Denmark, the Netherlands, Sweden, and Switzerland) follow this pattern.[2]

In the developing world, the organization of pension systems is also a major distinguishing feature of financial structure. The financial systems of most developing countries are still dominated by commercial banks, but countries with funded pension systems of one form or another, such as Singapore, Malaysia, Egypt, Cyprus, Chile, and Zimbabwe, also have large contractual savings sectors. Other countries, such as Brazil, Indonesia, the Philippines, Jordan, and Turkey have funded pension schemes, though their size in relation to total financial assets is not very large. In contrast, most Latin American and Eastern European countries have pay-as-you-go pension systems that make no or little contribution to the accumulation of financial savings.

Impact on Saving and the Promotion of Long-Term Savings

There is vast and inconclusive literature on the impact of funded and unfunded pension systems on the rate of national saving. Funded systems that are young and lack credibility may involve an increase in overall saving because they generate compulsory savings while consumers are less inclined to adjust their saving behavior with regard to their discretionary income. But as systems mature and gain in credibility, the greater efficiency of saving through contractual savings institutions may lead to changes in consumer behavior that may compensate, and even overcompensate, for the increased availability of future pension incomes.[3] Thus, contractual savings may have a positive impact on the rate of saving in the short run, but this is likely to prove transitory and over the long run their effect on overall saving may even be negative.[4]

Internationally, there is little correlation between pension funding and saving ratios. Singapore and Switzerland, two countries with compulsory participation in funded systems, have very high saving rates, but the United States, the United Kingdom, and Sweden, all countries with large funded systems, have some of the lowest saving rates. Moreover, several countries with underdeveloped contractual savings sectors, such as Italy, Greece, and Portugal, as well as Japan (during the high growth era), Korea and China, have high saving ratios.[5]

While the quantitative impact of contractual savings on aggregate saving is unclear, their qualitative impact on the composition of national savings is beyond dispute: contractual savings cause a shift in favor of long-term financial savings.

Data on the total assets of life insurance companies and pension funds in different countries show that in 1987 contractual savings institutions mobilized resources equal to 133 percent of GDP in Switzerland and 117 percent in the Netherlands. The corresponding ratios were 105 percent in the United Kingdom and 72 percent in the United States. Among developing countries, contractual savings institutions in Singapore and Malaysia controlled resources equal to 78 percent and 48 percent of GDP in the same year. Other developing countries with relatively large contractual savings sectors include Egypt (45 percent), Cyprus (30 percent), Chile (30 percent), and Korea (18 percent). Zimbabwe, Botswana, Jordan, the Philippines, and to a lesser extent, India, Turkey, Indonesia, and Brazil also have significant contractual savings sectors.

The structure of the contractual savings sector differs considerably from country to country. In developed countries with large contractual savings industries, such as Switzerland, the Netherlands, the United Kingdom, and the United States, the predominant type are occupationally based pension funds. In Germany and other European countries as well as Japan, where contractual savings institutions are relatively weak, the predominant type are life insurance companies.

There is also considerable variation in structure among developing countries. In Chile, the dominant role is played by the AFP system based on personal pension plans, in Korea by the life insurance companies, in Egypt, the Philippines, Jordan, and Turkey by the partially funded social security organizations, in Cyprus, Indonesia, and Brazil by company pension funds and in Zimbabwe, Botswana, and India by a combination of provident funds, company-based pension schemes, and life insurance companies.[6]

The creation of funded pension schemes can generate substantial long-term financial savings even in a relatively short period of time. In countries where labor incomes represent 50 percent of national income, a compulsory scheme covering 40 percent of the labor force and imposing a 10 percent contribution rate would accumulate annually funds equal to 2 percent of national income. If the nominal rate of return on fund balances is equal to the nominal rate of growth of GNP, and since in the early years of operation pension benefits would be minimal, these pension schemes would accumulate resources equal to 10 percent of GNP over 5 years and 20 percent over 10 years. After the first 10 years, the pace of accumulation will be affected by the growing volume of benefit payments. On the other hand, expanded coverage and an increase in the share of labor income in total income will tend to accelerate the pace of accumulation.

The experience of Singapore, Malaysia, and, more recently, Chile shows that once a credible and well-run system is put in place, it can accumulate long-term resources at a very fast pace. In Singapore, the resources of the Central Provident Fund rose from 28 percent of GDP in 1976 to 73 percent in 1986, while in Malaysia they grew from 18 percent of GDP in 1980 to 41 percent in 1987 (Vittas and Skully 1991). In Chile, the system of personal pension plans that was introduced in 1981 expanded from a mere 1 percent of GDP in 1981 to 9 percent in 1985 and 26 percent in 1990 (Vittas and Iglesias 1991).

The growth of contractual savings depends on three factors: the coverage of the sector; the level of annual contributions; and the rate of investment returns. In Singapore and Malaysia, the fast growth in the resources of contractual savings institutions was caused by an expansion in coverage, a rise in contribution rates, and the growth in wages. In Singapore, the effective contribution rate amounts to 33 percent and in Malaysia to 18 percent. In Egypt, a country with a funded social security system and a favorable demographic structure, the effective contribution rate is to 22 percent.[7] In Chile, a major factor in the rapid growth of the AFP system was the attainment of very high real rates of return, averaging 13 percent per year in the 1980s, while the contribution rate was only 10 percent (Vittas and Iglesias 1991).

In the United States, and especially in the United Kingdom, contractual savings experienced a large expansion in the 1980s in relation to GDP as a result of the large rise of stock market prices. In the United States, the assets of insurance companies and pension funds grew from 43 percent of GDP in 1970 to 49 percent in 1980 and 67 percent in 1988. In the United Kingdom, they rose from 45 percent in 1970 to 49 percent in 1980 and 120 percent in 1988. The much faster rise in the United Kingdom reflects the greater exposure of contractual savings to the equity market and the stronger performance of life insurance policies.

Role in Securities Markets

The role of contractual savings institutions in the securities markets differs considerably from country to country, reflecting historical traditions and differences in regulation. In the United Kingdom, where fund managers have developed a so-called equity cult since the 1960s, mainly in response to the high rates of inflation, pension funds and life insurance companies accounted in 1988 for 55 percent of corporate equities. In contrast, in the United States they held only 26 percent of corporate equities. However, American long-term institutional investors also held 56 percent of corporate bonds.

The equity cult of U.K. fund managers is also reflected in the composition of their portfolios. Pension funds invested 67 percent of their assets in equities against 51 percent for life insurance companies. In contrast, in the United States, life insurance companies invested less than 10 percent of their assets in equities against over 44 percent for pension funds.

In European countries, contractual savings institutions have a similar pattern to American life insurance companies and place the largest part of their funds in government, corporate, and mortgage bonds and in long-term loans. This is true of insurance companies and pension funds in Switzerland, the Netherlands, and

Germany. It is partly the result of investment regulations and partly the result of a traditional emphasis on conservative investment policies.

A good example of this is provided by the Algemene Burgerlijk Pensioenfonds or ABP, the pension fund for employees of the Dutch public sector. This is one of the largest individual pension funds in the world with over U.S. $80 billion under management. Until recently, ABP was not allowed to invest in overseas assets and its investments in domestic equities and property were limited to 20 percent of assets. However, 90 percent of ABP assets are invested in bonds, loans, and mortgages, with only 5 percent in equities and another 5 percent in property. In 1988, ABP was allowed to invest up to 5 percent of its resources in foreign assets. Its management is seeking an increase in the overall limit on equity and property investments to 30 percent, even though it has a long way to go to reach the current limit of 20 percent.

In Sweden, both the National Pension Insurance Fund and life insurance companies were traditionally required to invest heavily in bonds issued by mortgage credit institutions. In recent years, following the financial deregulation of the mid-1980s, insurance companies have been able to diversify into equities, but the public pension funds have been prevented from investing in equities because of concerns about the volatility of equity prices and about indirect public ownership of industrial companies.

In Singapore and Malaysia, the national provident funds invest over 90 percent of their funds in government securities that earn a slightly positive real rate of return. Despite the enforced captivity of the resources of the Central Provident Fund (CPF), the government of Singapore has refrained from investing all the funds in local development projects but has accumulated a substantial pool of foreign exchange reserves. In 1989, foreign exchange reserves exceeded the total balances of the CPF. The CPF effectively operates as a compulsory national unit trust, investing in foreign assets on behalf of Singaporean households.

In Malaysia and Egypt, the funds of contractual savings institutions have been used for development purposes. In Malaysia, the successful implementation of economic growth policies has ensured a modest real rate of return on the balances of the Employees Provident Fund, but in Egypt the resources of the social security system have been placed with the National Investment Bank, the investments of which have generally suffered from negative returns.

In Chile, the pension funds invest 80 percent of their resources in debt instruments, including state securities that account for 40 percent of total resources. Investments in corporate equities are only 20 percent of total assets, mainly because of the imposition of tight investment restrictions. Equity holdings accounted for 10 percent of total assets in 1989. The large increase since then is due to the relaxation of investment rules in the late 1980s and the boom in stock market prices.

Regulatory Framework and Investment Rules

In countries where contractual savings institutions are underdeveloped and where there are no long-term financial assets in which people can save for retirement purposes, consumers accumulate wealth in real estate, precious metals, and foreign assets that are likely to provide good hedges against inflation. The promotion of contractual savings creates an effective mechanism for channeling such savings through the local financial system to finance an expansion in the supply of productive capital. Efficient contractual savings institutions can help enhance investment productivity, stem, and perhaps even reverse, capital flight, and lower the real rate of interest.

However, the ability of contractual savings institutions to transform the functioning of securities markets and enhance corporate efficiency depends on the orientation and effectiveness of the regulatory framework and especially the regulations that are imposed on their investment portfolios.

The main objective of investment regulations is to ensure that insurance companies and pension funds invest their assets prudently. The basic aim is to prevent undue concentration of investment risks in particular types of securities, industrial sectors, or individual companies. Investment regulations should place maximum limits on permissible holdings and should not make use of minimum requirements that aim to direct investments in particular securities or in favor of particular sectors.

It should be noted that detailed investment rules are not necessary for ensuring the safety of contractual savings. In the United Kingdom, life insurers and pension funds are not subject to detailed investment rules, but are expected to demonstrate that their assets, prudently valued, meet the requirements for technical reserves and solvency margins. This allows for greater freedom of investment and greater flexibility in matching a company's assets with its obligations arising from its particular business mix.

For company-based pension schemes, investment rules are required to ensure that pension reserves are segregated from other funds of the sponsoring company and are invested prudently. The latter implies a limit on the amount of pension reserves that can be invested in the securities and property of the sponsoring employer and the stipulation of diversification requirements similar to those applicable on the technical reserves of insurance companies.

If pension schemes are funded by the creation of book reserves, which are then available for self-financing by the sponsoring company, prudential controls should require that such funds be reinsured with acceptable reinsurers to increase the security of benefits. In Germany, companies have the option to establish insured funds, operate self-administered pension funds, or create book reserves. If they choose the third option, they are required to reinsure their pension liabilities with PSV, a pension insurance company, which takes over the pension liabilities of insolvent firms and is funded by annual assessments on participating employers.

In Chile, the AFP system is subject to draconian investment rules. These have been motivated by the shallowness and lack of credibility of the domestic financial markets. Investment rules aim to limit the exposure of both individual pension funds and the whole of the pension funds sector. They are expressed in different but complementary ways: as a fraction of the securities of each issuing company; as a fraction of the resources of each pension plan; as a fraction of the securities of each issuing company in total company securities; and as a fraction of the resources of each plan in the total of all personal pension plans.[8]

The applied investment rules have caused some distortions in the market. For instance, large pension funds have produced lower returns in recent years because they have been unable to invest the same proportion of their funds in corporate equities with prospects as good as smaller pension funds. For the larger pension funds the binding limit is the fraction of the securities of each issuing company, whereas for smaller funds it is the fraction of their own resources.[9]

For pension fund managers in developed countries, who are generally free to set their own investment guidelines, the application of so many investment limits would appear excessively bureaucratic and inefficient. Limits that are based on the share of an individual pension fund in the total value of all pension funds or in the share of liabilities of an issuer in the total liabilities of all issuers of the same class of instruments may be onerous in practice and difficult both to comply with and to verify. Furthermore, there is a risk that imposing excessively strict investment limits may undermine the concept of private management and may in effect represent a government direction of funds through the back door.

However, in the context of the experience of developing countries, the absence of strong and transparent capital markets, the compulsory nature of the pension system, and the lack of familiarity of pension members with capital market investments, the detailed investment rules appear justified, provided they are revised in a flexible and timely manner to take account of the growing maturity of the system. An approach of gradual liberalization would give pension fund managers the opportunity to develop their skills as professional investment managers and would also allow the capital markets to modernize. Revisions in the investment rules have been effected at regular intervals in Chile. While it was clearly fortunate that AFPs were not allowed to invest in corporate equities during the 1982–1984 financial crisis, they conversely suffered from their restrictions in the late 1980s when stock market returns exceeded other investment alternatives.

A further issue that is difficult to resolve in developing countries regards the authorization of investments in overseas assets. A notable feature of U.K. regulatory practice is that, following the abolition of exchange controls in 1979, institutional investors enjoy complete freedom to invest in foreign assets. Insurance companies and pension funds in most other developed countries, including Canada, Germany, and the Netherlands, are still subject to restrictive regulations on their foreign investments.

For developing countries, allowing institutional investors to invest freely overseas would allow a diversification of country risk but would also institutionalize capital flight. Furthermore, it would deprive the local markets of the beneficial effects of the increased availability of long-term funds.[10] The Chilean experience suggests that institutional investors can be an effective force in stimulating innovation, improving efficiency, and inducing desirable fiscal, legal, and regulatory changes.

Impact on Emerging Securities Markets

A traditional argument against fully funded social security systems and private pension funds has been the concern that in the absence of active securities markets, accumulated funds might be used as captive sources for funding government deficits. Without active and efficient financial markets, private pension funds would be unable to wisely and safely invest their accumulated funds even if they were not used as captive sources of government funding.

This argument was probably valid in the 1960s and 1970s when few developing countries had well-organized securities markets. But in the 1980s the large growth of the so-called emerging securities markets underscores the potential for developing more efficient contractual savings institutions.[11] Moreover, this argument overlooks the dynamic interaction that would evolve between growing pension funds and emerging financial markets and thus underestimates the contribution that contractual savings institutions can make to the development of financial markets.

Nevertheless, it is fair to say that very few, if any, emerging securities markets owe their impressive performance in the 1980s to the presence or impact of contractual savings institutions. In most developing countries where such institutions have accumulated substantial long-term resources, their investments have been mostly channeled towards fixed-interest instruments. Even in Chile, the pension funds have accounted for a small fraction of corporate equities. Of all the markets that are included in the IFC database of emerging securities markets, only those in Brazil, Indonesia, and Zimbabwe have probably benefited from the presence of contractual savings institutions as equity investors.

There can be little doubt that as investment rules are relaxed, contractual savings institutions will be allowed to become important players in the securities markets of a large number of countries. By providing an effective demand for marketable securities and a mechanism for professional fund management, they will encourage the further development of markets and will stimulate financial innovation and efficiency. Institutional investors will exert pressures for better accounting and auditing standards as well as for more meaningful and timely disclosure of information to investors. They will also encourage improved broking and trading arrangements and will help establish more efficient and reliable clearing and settlement facilities. In sum, institutional investors will stimulate the modernization of securities markets.

Contractual savings institutions can also play an important part in facilitating the privatization programs of many countries. In Chile, the pension funds participated successfully in the privatization of state-owned companies. In fact, their equities in privatized companies still represented 95 percent of their total equity portfolios in 1990. Funded pension systems can play a crucial part in the development of the private sector in Eastern European countries.

Contractual savings institutions can also promote a greater dispersion of corporate ownership and contribute to the so-called democratization of capital. However, the use of pension funds as instruments of ownership dispersion may be frustrated by the unwillingness of closely-held companies to suffer a dilution of control. In Chile, the results of investment rules that have allowed greater equity holdings in companies with less-concentrated ownership have been rather poor.

Contractual savings institutions may stimulate greater corporate efficiency by monitoring the performance of the companies in which they invest and exerting some control over the behavior of corporate management. This will depend on their developing the necessary mechanisms for collecting information about corporate performance and the necessary expertise for analyzing the prospects of individual companies and sectors.

Conclusions

Contractual savings institutions are growing in several developing countries. Their potential impact on the development of securities markets is still largely unrealized, although the implications of financial liberalization and the increasing emphasis on private sector development suggest that their role and impact will increase substantially in the future.

Well-regulated contractual savings institutions, essentially pension funds and life insurance companies, are likely to play a crucial part in mobilizing long-term financial resources, developing equity and all types of bond markets (government, corporate, and mortgage bonds), and filling the gap in the supply of term finance that exists in most developing countries. They can play an important part in facilitating the privatization of state-owned companies and in promoting greater dispersion of corporate ownership.

Their success will depend on the existence of a robust and effective regulatory framework that emphasizes stability, efficiency, and fairness and does not use such institutions as tax collectors and captive sources of government funding.

Endnotes

1. Millard Long and Dimitri Vittas. "Financial Regulation—Changing the Rules of the Game," World Bank, CECFP, mimeo, July 1991.

2. It is worth noting that, unlike the traditional distinction of banking systems, the dividing line between countries with developed and countries with underdeveloped contractual savings industries is no longer a simple one between continental European and Anglo-American countries.

3. Henry J. Aaron, Barry P. Bosworth, and Gary Burtless. "Can America Afford to Grow Old? Paying for Social Security." The Brookings Institution, Washington, D.C., 1989.

4. The long-term impact of a transitory increase in the rate of saving may of course be very large, depending on whether the funds are invested wisely and set in train a virtuous circle of high growth followed by high saving.

5. A factor that affects saving behavior seems to be household access to credit facilities. Dimitri Vittas. "Economic and Regulatory Issues of Contractual Savings Institutions," World Bank, CECFP, mimeo, October 1990.

6. See Vittas and Skully (1991) for a discussion of the operating characteristics and merits and demerits of different types of contractual savings institutions. Dimitri Vittas and Michael Skully. "Overview of Contractual Savings Institutions." World Bank, PRE Working Papers, WPS605, March 1991.

7. The effective contribution rate takes account of the payments made by employers and the government. In Egypt, the nominal contribution rate is 26 percent—10 percent by the employee, 15 percent by the employer, and 1 percent by the government. Thus, contributions equal 26 out of a total payroll cost of 116 or slightly over 22 percent.

8. Dimitri Vittas and Augusto Iglesias. "The Rationale and Performance of Personal Pension Plans in Chile." World Bank, CECFP, mimeo, September 1991.

9. Available data show that in 1990 Provida and Santa Maria, the two largest AFPs, achieved real rates of return of 13.3 percent and 14.6 percent respectively against 18.7 percent for Planvital and 18.2 percent for Cuprum (Habitat, 1991, p. 121). A good reference on Chilean AFP's is "Diez Años del Sistema de AFP," Habitat, Santiago, 1991.

10. Available data show U.K. pension funds invest 18 percent of their funds in overseas securities against 16 percent for Japanese contractual savings institutions and less than 5 percent for American pension funds. However, for smaller countries complete freedom may result in much higher proportions of total funds invested in overseas assets.

11. International Finance Corporation (IFC) (1991): *Emerging Stock Markets Factbook.*

CUSTODIAL ISSUES (CLEARING AND SETTLEMENT) OF EQUITIES IN EMERGING MARKETS

Catherine Fry
Operations Manager
Emerging Markets Management
Washington D.C., United States

Settlement procedures in the emerging markets range from the more sophisticated systems of Singapore (which is currently in the process of converting to "scripless" book-entry settlement) to the more inefficient systems of Venezuela (where numerous transfers of documents are required for settlement). The key to minimizing problems and maintaining a good settlement record in these markets is the use of a knowledgeable and efficient global custodian with a good subcustodian network and brokers with good back offices. The investor also plays an important part in the role of liaison between the custodians and brokers. It is also up to the investor to ensure that instructions to all involved parties are clear and complete. Settlements in emerging markets are often more complex than in the more established markets, and an investor in these markets quickly learns that there can never be too much information given, but rather, that too little information may stall or completely halt the settlement process.

The Role of the Global Custodian

The global custodian plays an integral part in the settlement/custody process by providing a subcustodian network, custody and registration, foreign exchange service, corporate action reporting, cash management, income collection, tax reclamation, and portfolio valuation and accounting, as well as performing the basic

Source: Researched by Emerging Markets Management with information from Boston Safe Deposit and Trust Co., Chase Manhattan Bank, N.A., Citibank, N.A., Bankers Trust Company and State Street Bank and Trust Company.

daily settlement duties related to trading. A brief discussion of each area follows. Global custodians may vary greatly in the type of service provided in each of these areas. It is up to the emerging markets investor to confirm that its custodial agent has the capabilities needed in the markets in which the investor will trade.

Subcustodian network.   The emerging markets investor is dependent upon the custodian's subcustodian network, as the global custodian's agent banks are responsible for the movement and custody of all of the investor's international securities. It is important when investing in these markets to have a global custodian who can quickly establish agent bank relationships in new markets being entered by the investor. This timeliness, as well as the quality of the subcustodians, directly reflects on the global custodian. Custodians with the best networks receive on-line reporting from their agent banks and maintain daily communications, thus enabling them to quickly resolve any problems that may arise.

Custody and registration.   As stated above, the global custodian is responsible for custody of the investor's assets, which are generally held locally by its sub custodian agents. Due to the fact that the global custodian has established the local custody accounts, it has the responsibility of ensuring that proper registration of shares is performed. The necessity of registration, as well as the type and time frame required, varies from market to market and the subcustodians are familiar with the practices of their respective markets. The local agents, however, are dependent upon the global custodian for information on beneficial owner residency. Proper registration of an investor's shares is crucial for taxation purposes. Subcustodians are also responsible for ensuring that foreign board registration (where applicable) is performed in a timely manner.

Foreign exchange service.   If foreign exchange service will be needed (the investor may choose to have an agent other than the global custodian perform this function), it is crucial to know that the custodian can perform the service in all the needed markets. Some custodians may not perform foreign exchanges for certain volatile currencies (such as the Argentine peso in the past) which would necessitate settlement in U.S. dollars.

Corporate action reporting.   Custodial agents differ tremendously in the area of corporate actions (proxies, rights issues, splits, bonuses, etc.). U.S. Department of Labor regulations require investment management firms to vote proxies for U.S. pension fund clients, however, the information flow of such documents in the emerging markets is generally poor. Certain custodians are much better than others in obtaining and forwarding proxy voting materials to investment managers. Also, accurate and timely notification of rights issues is important to ensure that the investor may decide upon all such issues, yet this is another area in which custodians provide vastly different levels of information. Custodians with good corporate action departments provide more than just the basic information on rights issues (ex-date, ratio, price, holdings as of ex-date, entitlement) by also noting special information, such as whether rights are tradable or whether the investor may opt to pay for a rights subscription out of an upcoming dividend payment. Entitlement figures are especially useful as some emerging market countries (i.e., Turkey) may round fractional shares up or down on share entitlements. Also useful to investors with large portfolios in these markets are "involuntary corporate action" notices, which are provided regularly by some custodians, but not by all. Involuntaries refer to stock splits, stock bonuses, and stock dividends that occur automatically. Timely notification of such actions allows the investor to update internal records and provides for more accurate reconciliations of portfolios at any given time.

Another crucial piece of information needed on corporate actions regards whether or not new share entitlements will rank "pari passu" with the old shares. Pari passu refers to new shares issued which rank equally with the old (or parent) shares. New shares that do not rank pari passu with the old shares may differ in a number of ways—they may not be entitled to future corporate actions and dividends, they may not have voting rights, or they may be valued at a different (lower) level. In many cases there is a predetermined time frame after which new shares rank pari passu with the old shares, usually at the date of the next dividend payment on the old shares. This distinction between new and old shares must be made in case the investor decides to sell new shares prior to ranking pasi passu, in order to achieve correct valuation and delivery.

Cash Management.   Very few emerging markets offer interest-bearing local currency accounts (and those that do typically offer less than 3% interest), and thus many investors would not wish to keep local currency on hand. Moreover, there is always devaluation risk. Many countries, however, will offer interest on very large local currency accounts, and many custodians are pushing for the countries to allow "omnibus" accounts, combining all investors' local currency in order to meet the requirements. Until such accounts are in place, the investor may place standing instructions with the custodian to bring back all local currency (from sales or other income) to U.S. dollars on a regular basis. The custodian is then responsible for placing the uninvested cash in a short-term, interest-bearing account or other fixed income vehicle.

Income collection.   The custodians rely on their subcustodian banks for collection of income (typically cash dividends) in local markets. Most custodians perform fairly well in providing this service; however, difficulties may arise if proper registration of shares has not been accomplished by the dividend date. (Certain markets, such as Indonesia and Thailand, require foreign registration for dividend entitlement.)

Tax reclamation. Custodians should have a good tax reclamation procedure in place, which includes timely filing of recoverable taxes and tracking of all outstanding claims. This is crucial due to the administrative red tape of some local governments.

Portfolio valuation and accounting. There is tremendous variation among custodians with regard to this area. There are three core requirements for accurate valuations: (1) communications between the global custodian and its network agents must be efficient in order to provide accurate reporting of all trades and corporate actions at any given time; (2) the global custodian must be accurate in the pricing of individual securities (computerized pricing sources used by many banks are not adequate for emerging markets portfolios and a manual review by the custodian is generally needed); and (3) reports must be timely. An investor should review its custodian's reporting to be sure that all report schedules needed may be provided.

Daily settlement duties. Global custodians also differ in the area of routine settlements. It is crucial to have a custodian who specializes in all of the markets in which the investor has holdings. Due to the complex nature of emerging markets, the custodian must have expertise to ensure that settlement occurs on a timely basis. Brokers may make interest claims on late settlement of trades and many of these countries are moving toward stricter regulations concerning "buy-ins." Buy-in procedures vary in the emerging markets (some countries have no such rules) and specify the allowable length of time a trade may fail before the buying broker or the stock exchange steps in and voids the trade. The securities are then purchased on the open market. Such procedures are in place to prevent short selling, and the seller who incurs a buy-in may be charged a penalty. Fines may also be incurred for late payment on the purchase side of transactions in certain markets (Thailand). The competence of the individual subcustodians plays an important part in avoiding such problems. Custodians who excel in this particular area generally utilize subcustodians who do "prematching" of trades prior to settlement date. The global custodian should prescreen all sale transactions to confirm that shares to be sold are in custody at the subcustodian (and not in registration) prior to settlement date. This may be considered a responsibility of the investor, but even the most efficient investor may not be aware of a registration problem in certain markets.

The account representative at the global custodian is the key contact person for the investor and should be knowledgeable in all market practices and capable of problem solving, as problems do arise. The investor is generally not encouraged or allowed to communicate directly with the subcustodians in the global custodian's network, so the account representative is of primary importance for getting information to or from a given market agent.

Computerization.   Most global custodians currently can provide some type of on-line reporting to the investor. This reporting generally allows the investor to view the portfolio when desired; however, many custodians need to do more work in the area of providing reconciled reports on a timely basis for review by the investor.

The Role of Brokers

The selection of brokers used when investing in emerging markets is also vital to efficient settlements. The brokers, whether local or international, are not only relied on by the investor for company and market research, but also must perform, report, and settle trades efficiently. Thus, the broker's back office must be capable of timely and accurate reporting and settlement of all transactions.

Good brokers will also supply an investor with vital information on emerging markets. Corporate action information may come from brokers as well as from custodians. Updates on market particulars affecting trading are also important. In Thailand, for example, all companies have a foreign registration limit, and the investor must know when trading individual companies in this market if their limits have been reached. At that point, the investor cannot purchase local shares and have them registered as foreign, but rather the investor must purchase foreign board shares (which generally trade at a premium). Brokers will keep an investor updated on the latest foreign board limits when trading in Thailand. Also, in Indonesia during 1990, many market practices were changed and information received from brokers regarding these changes was often more timely than that received from global custodians.

Brokers are also a good source for local stock prices, an absolute necessity for an investor in emerging markets. Many computerized pricing sources do not list all the stocks in emerging markets and certain markets listed may lag a day behind due to time differences. Updated pricing information is crucial to reconciliation.

Generally, an investor is charged transaction costs (per trade) at the global custody level and at times at the subcustody level. In order to minimize these costs, the investor may request that a broker "warehouse" (or temporarily hold shares in the broker's account) small trades until a specified minimum size trade is completed. The fewer the trades processed in order to fulfill an order, the smaller the settlement costs for the client.

Institutional investors with multiple portfolios also need brokers to properly allocate shares purchased or sold among the portfolios and report such transactions at an average price, in order to treat all accounts equally.

Other functions performed by the better brokers are prematching of trades (similar to the prematching done by the global custodian) and prescreening of sale transactions. These items are important because many emerging markets are moving toward stricter regulations concerning buy-ins, and brokers themselves may make interest claims on late settling trades. A call from a broker to let the investor know that a custodian does not have instructions in place, prior to settlement date, is always greatly appreciated and can ward off a trade failure. On the sale side, many brokers will confirm with the local subcustodian that shares are available for delivery prior to settlement date.

There are differences among brokers for even the most basic of trade operations, the actual trade confirmations. One would think that the larger, international brokerage houses are always the most efficient and computerized; however, this is not always the case. Even a large brokerage house may process trades manually, and this often means that more errors in calculation are made. At times commissions and/or fees may be miscalculated or left out entirely. It is a time-consuming process for the investor to have to correct a trade and reinstruct a custodian.

By utilizing different brokers in each market, the emerging markets investor will soon learn which have the better back office operations.

Investor Responsibilities

The investor (or investment manager) has various operational responsibilities, the most important being accurate dissemination of information. First of all, trade orders to brokers must be complete. In certain markets, such as Argentina, the investor must specify not only the trade order but also the payment currency (which could be in local currency or U.S. dollars). Brokers must also be given complete account information in order to know where to deliver shares, or in the case of a sale, where shares will be coming from. In certain markets, such as Indonesia, brokers are required to endorse share certificates prior to delivery and must have exact endorsement names of the pertinent accounts. Thus, the investor must also have a complete understanding of market practices.

After the broker has confirmed a trade, the investor is responsible for informing the global custodian. Trades executed should be reported immediately (on trade date whenever possible) to the custodian. This is especially important in those markets with short settlement periods, such as Turkey, Mexico, Korea, and Hong Kong. The trade confirmation to the custodian must contain the number of shares purchased or sold, price per share, commission/fees, trade and settlement dates, foreign exchange instructions, and exact settlement instructions. The security name and description stated on the trade confirmation are vitally important in emerging markets. Unless shares are traded through Euroclear or "DTC," many emerging market securities do not have international security codes, and clear descriptions are needed by the custodian. (DTC—Depository Trust Company—is a central depository for U.S.-listed securities and functions as a computerized clearing and bookkeeping system.) The differences between types of shares can be numerous in these markets (i.e., local versus foreign board; A, B, and C classes; common versus preferred; bearer versus registered; ADRs and ADSs; GDRs and GDSs; etc.). The settlement instructions must also be explicit and state the delivering (or receiving) agent, whether the transaction is DVP, and complete U.S. dollar account information for the broker's account if the trade is settling in U.S. dollars. As stated previously, there can never be too much information given.

When purchasing a "new issue" the investor should inform the custodian that the shares are part of a new issue and state the estimated date of delivery of shares when available, as well as the payment instructions.

The investor is also responsible for checking all trades from brokers to confirm that commission and fee amounts are correct. Also, when settlement is in U.S. dollars, the foreign exchange rate used by the broker should be checked by the investor to be sure it is within an acceptable range.

The investor's role as liaison between custodian and broker varies depending upon the role played by the global custodian account representative. Some custodians refuse to deal directly with the investor's brokers, and thus the investor is contacted regarding all questions and/or problems and must in turn relay them to the brokers. Other custodians will contact the investor's brokers and handle problems independently of the investor. Brokers are generally willing to speak directly with custodians; however, the investor must inform them as to whether or not they are allowed to do so. It is crucial that the investor maintain this role of middleman on a daily basis and keep up-to-date on trade issues. Even at those times when the investor keeps hearing conflicting information (i.e., the broker claims the custodian does not have instructions in place to receive shares, and the custodian claims the broker is not delivering the shares in question), follow-up must be done and questions must be raised in order to resolve problems.

The investor may be required to obtain emerging markets securities prices, not only for internal reconciliation, but also for forwarding to the global custodian. Due to the nature of certain new issues or unlisted country funds the investor may hold in these markets, prices may not be available from computerized pricing systems used by banks. It is the responsibility of the investor to obtain such prices on a regular basis from local market sources.

Certain unlisted securities and country funds in the emerging markets may be held by an entity other than the global custodian or its local agents. At times brokers are allowed to hold an issue for an investor prior to the establishment of a subcustodian in a new market, and specialized country funds may be held by the issuing agents. In such cases, the investor is responsible for seeing that proper registration of any certificates or shares is performed. The investor must also provide the global custodian with all details relating to such issues, including pricing, since the global custodian is not responsible for the custody of these assets.

The investor must be familiar with the registration time frames (which may be very lengthy) in the emerging markets so as to be sure that no sales are processed prior to receipt of shares back from registration.

Common Settlement Practices

For protection of an investor's assets, it is always preferable to settle equity transactions "delivery versus payment" (DVP) or "receipt versus payment" (RVP). In these settlement methods, currency is paid out against actual receipt of shares being purchased, and shares being sold are released against actual receipt of currency. (The term shares here also designates acceptable documents in lieu of shares, where applicable.) These methods may only be used, however, when payment is being made in local currency.

Most banks require a full two days to arrange a foreign exchange transaction, but certain emerging markets have such short settlement periods that, unless a local currency account is kept, settlement cannot be done in local currency, and thus cannot be DVP. With few emerging markets offering foreign investors interest-bearing local currency accounts, settlements in these markets must be done in international currency (generally U.S. dollars) instead of local currency when the settlement time frame is insufficient for a foreign exchange to be completed. Two such markets are Mexico and Turkey.

Special Settlement Issues

In Mexico, settlements are often in U.S. dollars instead of Mexican pesos although delivery is made and shares are held in Mexico. The two-day settlement period in the Mexican market generally is too short for a foreign exchange transaction into Mexican pesos to be done in a timely manner. There are also restrictions on Mexican peso accounts for foreigners, but some local brokers will maintain such accounts for clients. When settlement is in U.S. dollars, instructions to the investor's custodian may state that the custodian is to "receive shares free" (not versus payment) and wire U.S. dollars after receipt of shares. This method of payment may pose problems depending upon the efficiency of the global custodian and its local agent. If a global custodian requires fax or telex confirmation of receipt of shares prior to wiring out the international currency, this confirmation may not be received in time for the international currency to be wired on settlement date and Mexican brokers may make interest claims against custodians making late payments. Another option is to instruct custodians to wire U.S. dollars "free of delivery" on settlement date, with a provision that the custodians must inform the investor if shares are not received on settlement date. Due to the Mexican market's book-entry settlement system and the prematching done by most local custodian banks, the failure rate is very low.

The Turkish market calls for next-day settlement and most global custodians are not able to do a foreign exchange for Turkish lira within one day, thus payment is often made in U.S. dollars. Instructions for purchases in Turkey are like those previously described for Mexico, with payment being made to the Turkish broker's U.S.-dollar account, either "free of delivery" on settlement date or after confirmation of receipt of shares.

For sales in Mexico and Turkey, shares may be released to the local brokers either "free of payment" on settlement date or after payment is made in U.S. dollars from the local broker's U.S.-agent bank.

Another emerging market in which settlement generally occurs in U.S. dollars is the Philippines. Payment must be in U.S. dollars because all foreign exchange transactions must be registered with the Central Bank in order for repatriation to be allowed in the future.

Two other emerging markets with settlement procedures other than DVP are Brazil and Chile.

Until recently, foreign investors were not able to invest directly in Brazil; however, institutional investors were allowed to set up a fund with a local administrator. The foreign investor generally instructs the global custodian to wire U.S. dollars "free" to the Brazilian local administrator's U.S.-dollar account on settlement date. A few days later, the local administrator may report the exact amount of units in the fund that were purchased and the price per unit.

Foreign investors may invest directly in Chile, with Central Bank approval; however, the tax implications make this method prohibitive. Generally, foreign institutional investors will set up a fund with a local administrator. Instructions to global custodians are basically the same as in Brazil. The global custodian is instructed to wire U.S. dollars to the local administrator's U.S.-dollar account on settlement date. The local administrator (or trustee if the fund is set up as a trust) reports the number of units and price per unit purchased within a few days.

Argentina is an emerging market in which the investor may decide whether to settle DVP in local currency or "free" in U.S. dollars. The portfolio manager may make a decision upon placing orders whether it is more advantageous to settle in local currency or U.S. dollars (depending upon the volatility of the local currency at any given time). If payment is made in U.S. dollars for purchases, the investor may instruct the global custodian that U.S.-dollar wire payments are to be sent either "free of delivery" or after confirmation of receipt of shares. For sales with payments being made in U.S. dollars, delivery of shares may be "free of payment" on settlement date or after receipt of U.S. dollars.

New Issues

Another variation to standard settlement procedures arises when an investor in emerging markets invests in a "new issue." Such an issue may be offered in virtually any emerging market, and usually settlement of such requires that payment be made "free of delivery" (at times in U.S. dollars even if the local market practice calls for DVP settlement in local currency), because shares are not available on settlement date. The investor's instructions to the global custodian should be explicit in such cases, with an explanation as to the type of issue, stating that payment must be made "free of delivery," and noting the time frame when shares will become available and the name of the local delivering agent.

Summary

Good communications between the investor, the global custodian, and brokers are vital to trading in emerging markets. All involved need to have a good understanding of local market practices, have efficient procedures in place, and be adept at problem solving. When all three parties fulfill all necessary functions, settlements can run smoothly even in the most difficult of markets.

Local Market Details

Table 29-1 lists information on custody, settlement, registration, fees and taxes for a number of emerging markets. This information is subject to constant changes. Moreover, tax treaties may change applicable withholding taxes. Thus, the reader is cautioned not to rely on this information as a complete guide to doing business but use it only for illustrative purposes.

Table 29-1 Custody, Settlement, Registration, Fees and Taxes in the Emerging Markets

Country	Settlement Period* (Equities)	Settlement Type** (Equities)	Shareholding Form (Equities)	Registration Time-Frame (Equities)	Buy-In Policy	Central Depository	Fees/Taxes for Foreigners***
Argentina	T + 3	Physical or book entry; DVP/RVP or free	Registered	Simultaneous with settlement if book entry; 1 to 2 weeks if physical; shares may not be traded while in registration	No	Yes	Stamp fees; no capital gains tax or withholding tax on dividends; 14.4% on interest
Brazil[1]	T + 2	Book entry (physical for new shares later changed to book entry); DVP/RVP (however, actual physical settlement T + 1 and financial settlement T + 2 at depositories)	Registered	Automatically upon settlement at depositories; 1 to 4 weeks for physical shares; shares may not be traded while in registration	Yes	No (Planned) Both the Sao Paulo and Rio de Janeiro exchanges operate their own clearing depositories	No fees; no capital gains tax; 15% withholding tax on dividends and 15% on interest (both upon repatriation)
Chile[2]	T + 2 (negotiable)	Physical; DVP/RVP	Registered	1 to 2 days; broker initiates; new shares issued for all transactions within 3 weeks; shares may be traded while in registration	No	No (Planned for early 1993)	No fees; 10% withholding tax on distributions abroad of all income (capital gains, interest and dividends) for foreign funds set up under Law 18,657 and 40% for investments set up under Decree 600
China (Shenzhen)	T + 3	Book-entry; DVP/RVP	Registered	Automatically upon settlement	Yes	No (Standard Chartered Bank, Hong Kong Bank and Citibank act as clearing banks and depositories)	Transfer fees and stamp duties; no capital gains tax; 10% withholding tax on dividends and 10% on interest

Table 29-1 **Custody, Settlement, Registration, Fees and Taxes in the Emerging Markets** (*continued*)

Country	Settlement Period* (Equities)	Settlement Type** (Equities)	Shareholding Form (Equities)	Registration Time-Frame (Equities)	Buy-In Policy	Central Depository	Fees/Taxes for Foreigners***
Colombia[3]	T+2 (negotiable to T+5)	Physical; DVP/RVP	Bearer (majority) or registered	15-30 days for registered shares; shares may be traded while in registration	No	No	No fees; no capital gains tax; 19% withholding tax on dividends
Cyprus	T+2 (includes Saturdays)	Physical; DVP/RVP	Registered	Up to 4 weeks; shares may be traded while in registration	No	No	No fees; no capital gains tax or withholding tax on dividends and 10% on interest
Greece	No fixed settlement period; generally Bearer T+2 and Registered T+5 to T+7	Physical; DVP/RVP	Bearer or Registered	5 to 45 days; shares may be traded while in registration	No	No (Currently being established for registered shares.)	Transfer fees; no capital gains tax; 42-50% withholding tax on dividends and 10% on interest
Hong Kong (China plays)	T+2	Physical (book-entry being phased in); DVP/RVP	Registered	3 to 6 weeks; shares may not be traded while in registration	Yes	Yes (Currently being phased in)	Stamp duties and transaction fees; no capital gains tax or withholding tax on dividends or interest
India (Bombay)[4]	T+14 calendar days (generally)	Physical; free	Registered	1 to 4 months; shares may not be traded while in registration	Yes	No	Stamp duties; short term capital gains tax of 65% (under one year) and long term capital gains tax of 10%; 25% withholding tax on dividends and 15% on interest
Indonesia	T+4	Physical; DVP/RVP	Registered	4 to 6 weeks; shares may not be traded while in registration	No (However, fines are charged)	No (Planned)	Transfer fees and VAT; no capital gains tax; 15% withholding tax on dividends and 15% on interest

Table 29-1 Custody, Settlement, Registration, Fees and Taxes in the Emerging Markets (*continued*)

Country	Settlement Period* (Equities)	Settlement Type** (Equities)	Shareholding Form (Equities)	Registration Time-Frame (Equities)	Buy-In Policy	Central Depository	Fees/Taxes for Foreigners***
Jordan[5]	T+3	Physical or book-entry at issuing companies; DVP/RVP	Registered	1 week	No	No	No fees; no capital gains tax or withholding tax on dividends or interest
Korea[6]	T+2 (includes Saturdays)	Phsyical; DVP/RVP	Registered	1 to 2 days; shares may not be traded while in registration	Yes	Yes	No fees; no capital gains tax; 10.75% withholding tax on dividends and 12% on interest
Malaysia	T+5	Physical; DVP/RVP	Registered	3 to 8 weeks; shares may not be traded while in registration	Yes	No (Planned for 1992)	Clearing fees and stamp duties; no capital gains tax; 35% withholding tax on dividends and 20% on interest
Mexico	T+2	Book-entry; DVP/RVP or free	Registered	Simultaneous with settlement	Yes (Not common)	Yes	No fees; no capital gains tax; 0% or 35% withholding tax on dividends; 35% on interest
Pakistan	From 7 to 14 days (every second Monday)	Physical; free	Registered	Up to 45 days; shares may not be traded while in registration	Yes	No	Stamp duties; no capital gains tax; 15% or 16.5% withholding tax on dividends and 30-50% on interest
Peru	T+2	Physical or book-entry; free	Registered	Simultaneous with settlement	Yes	No (CAVAL acts as a central registry for book-entry equities)	No fees; possible 37% capital gains tax (not yet defined for foreign investors); 10% withholding tax on dividends

Table 29-1 Custody, Settlement, Registration, Fees and Taxes in the Emerging Markets (continued)

Country	Settlement Period* (Equities)	Settlement Type** (Equities)	Shareholding Form (Equities)	Registration Time-Frame (Equities)	Buy-In Policy	Central Depository	Fees/Taxes for Foreigners***
Philippines	T+4	Physical; DVP/RVP or free	Registered	4 to 6 weeks; broker initiates registration; new certificates issued for all purchases; shares may be traded while in registration	No	No	Transfer fees and stamp duties; no capital gains tax; 20% withholding tax on dividends and 15% on interest
Portugal	T+4	Physical (a small number are book-entry at the new central depository); DVP/RVP	Registered or bearer	Book-entry shares simultaneous with settlement; registered shares 1 week to 3 months; shares may not be traded while in registration	Yes	Yes (Being phased in)	Transaction fees and stock exchange fees; no capital gains tax on sales of shares held over one year; 25% withholding tax on dividends and 25% on interest
Singapore	T+5	Physical or book-entry; DVP/RVP	Registered	2 to 4 weeks for physical; shares may not be traded while in registration; automatic for book-entry	Yes	Yes (Being phased in)	Clearing fees and stamp duties; no capital gains tax; 30% withholding tax on dividends and 30% on interest
Sri Lanka	T+ up to 2 weeks for physical shares (Physical settlement on 2nd and 4th Fridays; financial settlement on Wednesdays before Fridays); T+5-7 for book-entry	Physical or book-entry; free or DVP/RVP (respectively)	Registered	Up to 2 months for physical shares; broker initiates registration; shares may not be traded while in registration; simultaneous with settlement for book-entry	No (fines imposed on late deliveries)	Yes (Being phased in)	Clearing fees; no capital gains tax; 15% withholding tax on dividends and 33.3% on interest

Country	Settlement Period* (Equities)	Settlement Type** (Equities)	Shareholding Form (Equities)	Registration Time-Frame (Equities)	Buy-In Policy	Central Depository	Fees/Taxes for Foreigners***
Taiwan[7]	T+1	Physical or book-entry; DVP/RVP	Registered	Automatically or 1 day	Yes	Yes	Transaction fees; no capital gains tax; 20% withholding tax on dividends and 20% on interest
Thailand	T+3 (negotiable)	Physical; DVP/RVP	Registered	3 to 5 weeks for listed companies for which the Securities Exchange of Thailand acts as registrar; 4 to 6 weeks for companies which act as their own registrars; shares may not be traded while in registration	Yes	No; however the Securities Exchange of Thailand acts a central clearing house and central depository is scheduled for implementation	Stamp duties; 25% capital gains tax; 10% withholding tax on dividends and 15% on interest
Turkey	T+2	Physical; DVP/RVP or free	Bearer (majority) or registered	4 to 5 weeks (not a common practice); shares may not be traded while in registration	Yes	No	No fees; no capital gains or withholding taxes; 10.5% on interest
Uruguay	T or T+1 (negotiable)	Physical; DVP/RVP	Bearer	Not applicable	No	No	No fees; no capital gains tax or withholding taxes on dividends or interest

Table 29-1 Custody, Settlement, Registration, Fees and Taxes in the Emerging Markets (*continued*)

Country	Settlement Period* (Equities)	Settlement Type** (Equities)	Shareholding Form (Equities)	Registration Time-Frame (Equities)	Buy-In Policy	Central Depository	Fees/Taxes for Foreigners***
Venezuela	No fixed settlement period (negotiable); generally T+4	Physical; DVP/RVP	Registered	2 to 10 days; shares may be traded while in registration	Yes	No	No fees; 30% (maximum) capital gains tax; no withholding tax on dividends or interest

*   T = trade date; number = business days unless otherwise noted

** Physical = actual physical delivery of shares or acceptable documents
    Book-entry = nonphysical settlement (transfers occur between accounts, generally at a central depository or central bank)
    DVP/RVP = delivery vs. payment and receipt vs. payment; free = non-DVP

*** Taxes noted refer to U.S. institutional investors

1 Foreign investors must have a local administrator and a local legal representative
2 Foreign investors must have prior government approval and set up a limited liability company or have a local administrator
3 Foreign investors have approval as well as a local administrator and local legal representative
4 Foreign institutional investors must be registered with the Securities and Exchange Board of India
5 Foreign investors must have government approval prior to investing
6 Foreign investors must have an Investment Registration I.D. number and local standing proxy
7 Restrictions exist for direct investment by foreign investors

Source: Researched by Emerging Markets Management with information from Boston Safe Deposit and Trust Co., Chase Manhattan Bank, N.A., Citibank, N.A. and State Street Bank and Trust Company.

A

WORLD MARKET PERFORMANCE DATA IN LOCAL CURRENCY TERMS
(Priced as of June 28, 1991)

Reprinted with permission from *Closed-End Emerging Country Funds Review* by Michael T. Porter, Smith Barney, Harris, Upham & Co.

Table A-1 Price Performance of Major World Markets (in Local Currency)
(Ranked by Percent Change Since March 31, 1991)

	Price as of 06/30/91	Price as of 03/31/91	Percentage Change since 03/31/91	Price as of 12/31/90	Percentage Change since 12/31/90	Price as of 12/31/89	Percentage Change since 12/31/89	52 week Range High	52 week Range Low	Percent Change Since High	Percent Change Since Low	1980–1991 Range High	1980–1991 Range Low	Percent Change Since High	Percent Change Since Low
Mexico	1,058	803	31.7%	629	68.3%	419	152.6%	1,096	368	-3%	188%	1,096	0.48	-3%	220321%
Taiwan	5,901	5,140	14.8%	4,530	30.3%	9,624	-38.7%	7,664	2,560	-23%	130%	12,495	421	-53%	1301%
South Africa	3,817	3,389	12.6%	3,023	26.3%	2,768	37.9%	3,608	2,640	6%	45%	3,608	457	6%	736%
New Zealand	1,434	1,328	7.9%	1,203	19.2%	1,988	-27.9%	1,911	1,142	-25%	26%	3,969	357	-64%	301%
India	629	589	6.7%	528	19.1%	419	50.0%	763	420	-18%	50%	763	100	-18%	529%
Malaysia	619	583	6.1%	506	22.3%	562	10.0%	635	459	-3%	35%	635	170	-3%	263%
Denmark	367	346	6.1%	315	16.7%	363	1.1%	388	302	-5%	22%	388	58	-5%	533%
Norway	757	717	5.6%	677	11.8%	687	10.2%	915	610	-17%	24%	915	94	-17%	705%
Germany	1,923	1,834	4.9%	1,701	13.0%	2,190	-12.2%	2,403	1,613	-20%	19%	2,414	650	-20%	196%
Sweden	4,063	3,874	4.9%	2,991	35.9%	4,275	-5.0%	4,661	2,778	-13%	46%	4,661	335	-13%	1,113%
Australia	1,506	1,444	4.3%	1,280	17.7%	1,649	-8.7%	1,624	1,205	-7%	25%	2,306	443	-35%	240%
Gold: Bullion	369	356	3.8%	392	-5.6%	401	-7.9%	414	346	-11%	7%	835	285	-56%	30%
Holland	198	196	0.9%	168	17.3%	203	-2.6%	203	162	-3%	22%	211	51	-6%	291%
Italy	586	581	0.9%	517	13.5%	687	-14.7%	764	486	-23%	21%	908	82	-35%	615%
Switzerland	615	610	0.8%	520	18.2%	661	-7.0%	698	487	-12%	26%	734	264	-16%	133%
Singapore	1,490	1,491	-0.1%	1,154	29.1%	1,481	0.6%	1,576	1,080	-5%	38%	1,607	430	-7%	246%
Philippines	1,554	1,560	-0.4%	870	78.6%	1,585	-2.0%	1,735	689	-10%	126%	2,009	102	-23%	1421%
Canada	3,466	3,496	-0.9%	3,257	6.4%	3,970	-12.7%	3,639	3,010	-5%	15%	4,038	1,346	-14%	157%
United States	371	375	-1.1%	330	12.4%	353	5.0%	390	295	-5%	26%	390	98	-5%	279%
UK	2,415	2,457	-1.7%	2,144	12.7%	2,423	-0.3%	2,545	1,990	-5%	21%	2,545	509	-5%	374%
France	471	480	-1.9%	413	14.0%	554	-15.0%	653	395	-28%	19%	565	77	-17%	511%
Hong Kong	3,669	3,746	-2.1%	3,025	21.3%	2,837	29.3%	3,917	2,761	-6%	33%	3,950	676	-7%	443%
Belgium	3,353	3,463	-3.2%	2,974	12.7%	4,003	-16.2%	3,852	2,795	-13%	20%	4,215	704	-20%	376%
Spain	275	284	-3.3%	223	23.1%	297	-7.4%	310	209	-11%	31%	329	39	-16%	605%
Austria	481	502	-4.3%	440	9.3%	493	-2.5%	683	391	-30%	23%	703	99	-32%	386%
Korea	603	652	-7.6%	696	-13.4%	910	-33.8%	814	566	-26%	6%	1,006	93	-40%	547%
Ireland	1,365	1,482	-7.9%	1,208	13.0%	1,766	-22.7%	1,726	1,115	-21%	22%	1,893	1,000	-28%	37%
Japan	23,291	26,207	-11.1%	23,849	-2.3%	38,916	-40.2%	33,193	20,222	-30%	15%	38,916	6,476	-40%	260%
Thailand	765	864	-11.4%	613	24.9%	879	-13.0%	1,144	544	-33%	41%	1,144	102	-33%	650%
Indonesia	346	408	-15.2%	418	-17.1%	400	-13.4%	637	371	-46%	-7%	682	83	-49%	319%

WORLD MARKET PERFORMANCE DATA IN U.S. DOLLAR TERMS
(Priced as of June 28, 1991)

Reprinted with permission from *Closed-End Emerging Country Funds Review* by Michael T. Porter, Smith Barney, Harris, Upham & Co.

Table B-1   Price Performance of Major World Markets (in U.S. Dollar Terms) (Priced as of June 28, 1991. Ranked by Percent Change Since December 31, 1990)

	Percent Change Since 03/31/91	Percent Change Since 12/31/90	Percent Change Since 09/30/90	Percent Change Since 12/31/89	Percent Change Since 12/31/88	52-Week Percent Change Since High	52-Week Percent Change Since Low	1980–1991 Percent Change Since High	1980–1991 Percent Change Since Low
Philippines	-6.1%	65.1%	83.3%	-27.1%	18.7%	-15%	93%	-42%	921%
Hong Kong	5.4%	30.6%	42.2%	35.0%	47.2%	0%	42%	-30%	171%
Singapore	1.7%	27.2%	35.5%	7.6%	58.1%	-4%	36%	-4%	329%
Australia	5.5%	19.8%	2.3%	-10.4%	-6.9%	-8%	25%	-30%	171%
New Zealand	7.6%	18.6%	-7.3%	-29.3%	-27.7%	-26%	24%	-30%	171%
South Africa	12.7%	18.3%	34.6%	29.0%	71.3%	0%	36%	-30%	171%
Sweden	-0.3%	17.9%	13.6%	-7.4%	11.4%	-21%	29%	-30%	171%
Taiwan	4.5%	17.6%	101.0%	-45.0%	7.1%	-15%	109%	-59%	845%
Malaysia	2.8%	15.6%	27.1%	4.4%	64.2%	-8%	27%	-30%	171%
United States	1.3%	15.2%	24.2%	7.6%	36.9%	-3%	29%	-3%	287%
Canada	1.5%	9.3%	12.1%	-9.6%	7.8%	-2%	19%	-11%	194%
Thailand	-22.0%	5.9%	3.8%	-21.8%	70.4%	-41%	21%	-30%	171%
Spain	-11.9%	1.6%	11.1%	-12.4%	-1.8%	-22%	12%	-22%	621%
Denmark	3.3%	0.2%	-1.6%	0.2%	37.8%	-14%	8%	-30%	171%
UK	-3.6%	-0.4%	10.5%	5.8%	27.0%	-11%	11%	-11%	276%
Switzerland	-3.2%	-0.5%	2.9%	-5.1%	8.9%	-19%	7%	-19%	231%
Holland	-4.0%	-2.1%	2.9%	-7.7%	18.0%	-12%	5%	-12%	397%
Japan	-9.1%	-3.8%	11.5%	-38.0%	-29.9%	-25%	15%	-38%	569%
Norway	2.4%	-4.1%	-15.0%	7.6%	54.9%	-25%	8%	-30%	171%
Toronto Golds	6.2%	-4.2%	-14.8%	-25.8%	4.4%	-24%	16%	-30%	171%
Germany	0.9%	-4.6%	4.4%	-14.3%	16.5%	-27%	5%	-27%	319%
France	-7.1%	-5.0%	-2.6%	-18.8%	12.4%	-22%	4%	-30%	171%
Belgium	-8.3%	-5.9%	-3.2%	-22.0%	-7.7%	-22%	3%	-30%	171%
Gold: Bullion	3.5%	-6.0%	-9.0%	-8.2%	-10.3%	-11%	5%	-56%	29%
Ireland	-13.5%	-6.7%	-3.3%	-27.1%	-3.4%	-26%	4%	-30%	171%
Italy	-7.0%	-7.0%	-10.5%	-21.0%	-5.7%	-32%	2%	-32%	322%
Austria	-7.2%	-7.1%	6.5%	-2.3%	121.2%	-35%	8%	-30%	171%
India	-9.9%	-8.4%	-30.8%	7.9%	19.3%	-36%	11%	-30%	171%
Korea	-0.5%	-8.7%	6.2%	-33.9%	-33.6%	-21%	12%	-30%	171%
Indonesia	-17.1%	-22.1%	-32.9%	-23.1%	-3.7%	-50%	3%	-54%	258%

IFC EMERGING MARKETS
PRICE INDICES IN U.S. DOLLAR TERMS
(Priced as of June 28, 1991)

Reprinted with permission from *Closed-End Emerging Country Funds Review* by Michael T. Porter, Smith Barney, Harris, Upham & Co.

Table C-1   IFC Emerging Markets Price Indices (U.S. Dollar Terms)

	Price as of 06/30/91	Price as of 03/31/91	Percent Change Since 03/31/91	Price as of 12/31/90	Percent Change Since 12/31/90	Price as of 12/31/89	Percent Change Since 12/31/89	52 Week Range High	52 Week Range Low	52 Week Percent Change Since High	52 Week Percent Change Since Low	1984–1991 Range High	1984–1991 Range Low	1984–1991 Percent Change Since High	1984–1991 Percent Change Since Low
Latin America	457	461	-0.9%	260.8	75.2%	419.41	8.9%	556	224	-18%	104%	567	40	-19%	1045%
Argentina	95	69	39.2%	41.69	128.9%	128.57	-25.8%	97	40	-2%	140%	290	40	-67%	140%
Brazil	1,360	1,154	17.8%	811.1	67.7%	618.84	119.8%	1,360	623	0%	118%	1,360	97	0%	1305%
Chile	307	290	5.7%	294.58	4.1%	232.56	31.8%	326	264	-6%	16%	326	71	-6%	332%
Colombia	1,132	883	28.2%	724.31	56.3%	576.68	96.3%	1,195	629	-5%	80%	1,195	81	-5%	1294%
Mexico	464	557	-16.7%	491.34	-5.5%	74.93	519.5%	574	150	-19%	210%	574	61	-19%	667%
Venezuela															
Asia															
India	237	241	-1.6%	236	0.6%	203	16.8%	320	211	-26%	13%	320	98	-26%	143%
Indonesia (1)	79	95	-16.3%	97	-18.7%	100	-20.7%	106	79	-25%	0%	149	79	-47%	0%
Korea	289	315	-8.2%	343	-15.7%	467	-38.2%	361	282	-20%	3%	522	83	-45%	249%
Malaysia	151	150	0.8%	132	14.4%	152	-0.6%	164	117	-8%	29%	167	65	-10%	132%
Philippines	1,302	1,378	-5.5%	919	41.7%	1,928	-32.5%	1,464	811	-11%	61%	2,310	100	-44%	1202%
Taiwan, China	775	689	12.6%	640	21.1%	1,300	-40.4%	845	374	-8%	107%	1,767	72	-56%	978%
Thailand	318	402	-20.7%	293	8.7%	404	-21.3%	495	265	-36%	20%	495	83	-36%	282%
Europe/Middle East															
Greece	417	618	-32.6%	531	-21.6%	281	48.1%	919	417	-55%	0%	919	81	-55%	413%
Jordan	95	98	-2.8%	91	4.5%	92	3.1%	102	81	-7%	17%	154	81	-38%	17%
Portugal (2)	423	458	-7.6%	436	-2.9%	654	-35.3%	610	423	-31%	0%	1,908	100	-78%	323%
Turkey (3)	100	146	-31.2%	181	-44.5%	241	-58.4%	427	100	-76%	0%	461	58	-78%	75%
Regional Indices															
IFC Latin America	319	257	24.1%	187	70.8%	231	37.9%	321	172	-1%	85%	321	74	-1%	331%
IFC Asia	283	280	1.1%	267	6.1%	439	-35.6%	305	202	-7%	40%	524	89	-46%	217%

Source: International Finance Corporation. Base date = December 31, 1984 (1) December 1989 = 100 (2) January 1986 = 100 (3) December 1986 = 100

D

CLOSED-END COUNTRY FUNDS
SELECTED DATA
(Priced as of June 28, 1991)

Reprinted with permission from *Closed-End Emerging Country Funds Review* by Michael T. Porter, Smith Barney, Harris, Upham & Co.

Table D-1 Regional and Specialized Closed-End Country Funds

Selected Data Specialized Funds	Listing/Symbol	When Issued	Price as of 06/28/91	NAV as of 06/28/91	Percent Premium/ Discount	Number Shares Outstanding (In Millions)	Total Assets (In Millions)	Market Capitalization (In Millions)	Expense/Avg Net Assets Ratios
ASA Ltd.	NYSE-ASA	1958	$51.63	$46.46	11%	9.6	$446	$496	0.43%
Central Fund of Canada	ASE-CEF	08/05/87	4.13	4.59	-10%	16.8	77	69	NA
Closed-End Bond Funds									
First Australia Prime Inc.	ASE-FAX	04/17/86	10.06	10.32	-2%	86.0	887	865	2.59%
Equity Funds—Regional									
Asia Pacific Fund	NYSE-APB	04/24/87	12.25	13.41	-9%	8.8	118	108	1.85%
Europe Fund	NYSE-EF	04/26/90	10.50	12.16	-14%	8.3	101	88	1.00%
European Warrant Fund	NYSE-EWF	07/17/90	6.75	8.73	-23%	6.0	52	41	2.35%
GT Greater Europe Fund	NYSE-GTF	03/22/90	9.63	11.25	-14%	16.0	180	154	1.05%
Latin America Inv. Fund#	NYSE-LAM	07/27/90	18.25	21.63	-16%	4.0	87	73	3.27%
Pacific Eur. Growth Fund	ASE-PEF	04/20/90	9.25	10.06	-8%	3.4	34	31	1.65%
Scudder New Asia Fund	NYSE-SAF	06/18/87	13.88	15.66	-11%	7.1	111	98	1.84%
Scudder New Europe Fund	NYSE-NEF	02/09/90	8.13	9.97	-19%	16.0	160	130	1.18%
Templeton Emerging Mkt. Fund	NYSE-EMF	02/27/87	17.00	15.80	8%	11.6	183	197	1.86%
Totals:							$2,436	$2,350	1.71% (AVG)

Premium/Discount Analysis Specialized Funds	Prem/Disc as of 06/28/91	Prem/Disc as of Prev. Week	Prem/Disc as of 03/31/91	Prem/Disc as of 12/31/90	Prem/Disc as of 09/30/90	Prem/Disc as of 12/31/89	52-Week High	52-Week Low	52-Week Average Prem/Disc	26-Week Average Prem/Disc
ASA Ltd.	11%	6%	13%	-5%	-15%	-24%	13%	-26%	-7%	4%
Central Fund of Canada	-10%	-8%	-6%	-14%	-3%	4%	6%	-23%	-5%	-7%
Closed-End Bond Funds										
First Australia Prime Inc.	-2%	-2%	-6%	-6%	-12%	-6%	-2%	-16%	-8%	-7%
Equity Funds—Regional										
Asia Pacific Fund	-9%	-8%	-3%	-17%	-13%	12%	5%	-23%	-8%	-5%
Europe Fund	-14%	-14%	-14%	-17%	-19%	NA	6%	-23%	-13%	-13%
European Warrant Fund	-23%	-22%	-25%	-24%	-22%	NA	5%	-27%	-19%	-20%
GT Greater Europe Fund	-14%	-15%	-16%	-18%	-18%	NA	-3%	-21%	-13%	-14%
Latin America Inv. Fund#	-16%	-14%	-16%	-25%	-28%	NA	5%	-28%	-17%	-15%
Pacific Eur. Growth Fund	-8%	-9%	-5%	-14%	-3%	NA	7%	-19%	-7%	-8%
Scudder New Asia Fund	-11%	-7%	-4%	-10%	-18%	-3%	-4%	-26%	-12%	-8%
Scudder New Europe Fund	-19%	-18%	-14%	-21%	-22%	NA	-8%	-24%	-17%	-17%
Templeton Emerging Mkt. Fund	8%	9%	1%	10%	-15%	14%	14%	-19%	2%	6%
Average Premium/Discount	-8.91%	-8.46%	-7.89%	-13.42%	-15.68%	-0.53%				

Table D-2 Regional and Specialized Closed-End Country Funds

Price Performance

	Price as of 06/28/91	% Change Since Prev. Week	Price as of 03/31/91	% Chg Since 03/31/91	Price as of 12/31/90	%Chg Since 12/31/90	Price as of 09/30/90	%Chg Since 09/30/90	Price as of 12/31/89	% CHG Since 12/31/89	52-Week Range High	52-Week Range Low	% Chg From High	% Chg From Low
Specialized Funds														
ASA Ltd.	$51.63	3.0%	$44.00	17.3%	$43.63	18.3%	$50.13	3%	$55.5	-7%	$53	$40	-3%	29%
Central Fund of Canada	4.13	-2.9%	4.06	1.5%	4.06	1.5%	4.94	-16%	5.5	-25%	5	3	-21%	25%
Closed-End Bond Funds														
First Australia Prime Inc.	10.06	1.3%	9.63	4.5%	9.44	6.6%	9.31	8%	8.9	13%	10	9	0%	13%
Equity Funds—Regional														
Asia Pacific Fund	12.25	-1.0%	13.88	-11.7%	10.00	22.5%	10.00	23%	17.8	-31%	15	10	-20%	23%
Europe Fund	10.50	-3.4%	11.25	-6.7%	11.38	-7.7%	10.38	1%	NA	NA	15	10	-30%	1%
European Warrant Fund	6.75	-3.6%	7.63	-11.5%	7.00	-3.6%	7.25	-7%	NA	NA	12	7	-43%	0%
GT Greater Europe Fund	9.63	-1.3%	9.88	-2.5%	9.25	4.1%	9.13	5%	NA	NA	14	9	-33%	7%
Latin America Inv. Fund#	18.25	0.7%	14.50	25.9%	10.75	69.8%	9.25	97%	NA	NA	20	9	-6%	97%
Pacific Eur. Growth Fund	9.25	-1.3%	9.88	-6.3%	8.00	15.6%	8.75	6%	NA	NA	12	8	-23%	19%
Scudder New Asia Fund	13.88	-6.7%	14.75	-5.9%	12.13	14.4%	12.38	12%	15.9	-13%	18	12	-23%	17%
Scudder New Europe Fund	8.13	-3.0%	9.13	-11.0%	8.38	-3.0%	8.13	0%	NA	NA	11	8	-28%	0%
Templeton Emerging Mkt. Fund	17.00	-1.4%	15.38	10.6%	13.13	29.5%	11.75	45%	15.3	11%	18	12	-7%	46%
Average Price Change		-1.7%		0.4%		14.0%		14.7%		-8.5%				

Net Asset Value (NAV) Performance

	NAV as of 06/28/91	% Change Since Prev.Week	NAV as of 03/31/91	% Chg Since 03/31/91	NAV as of 12/31/90	%Chg Since 12/31/90	NAV as of 09/30/90	% Chg Since 09/30/90	NAV as of 12/31/89	% Chg Since 12/31/89	52-Week Range High	52-Week Range Low	% Chg From High	% Chg From Low
Specialized Funds														
ASA Ltd.	$46.46	-1.6%	$39.03	19.0%	$46.15	0.7%	$58.99	-21%	$72.81	-36%	$65	$39	-29%	19%
Central Fund of Canada	4.59	-1.1%	4.34	5.8%	4.75	-3.4%	5.09	-10%	5.30	-13%	5	4	-14%	6%
Closed-End Bond Funds														
First Australia Prime Inc.	10.32	2.1%	10.21	1.1%	10.02	3.0%	10.62	-3%	9.49	9%	11	9	-4%	11%
Equity Funds—Regional														
Asia Pacific Fund	13.41	-0.5%	14.24	-5.8%	12.04	11.4%	11.56	16%	15.78	-15%	17	12	-23%	16%
Europe Fund	12.16	-3.4%	13.08	-7.0%	13.73	-11.4%	12.74	-5%	NA	NA	15	12	-19%	1%
European Warrant Fund	8.73	-2.5%	10.22	-14.6%	9.24	-5.5%	9.30	-6%	NA	NA	11	9	-22%	0%
GT Greater Europe Fund	11.25	-2.1%	11.72	-4.0%	11.26	-0.1%	11.16	1%	NA	NA	15	11	-25%	5%
Latin America Inv. Fund#	21.63	2.4%	17.28	25.2%	14.24	51.9%	12.86	68%	NA	NA	22	13	0%	71%
Pacific Eur. Growth Fund	10.06	-1.9%	10.35	-2.8%	9.33	7.8%	9.01	12%	NA	NA	12	9	-14%	12%
Scudder New Asia Fund	15.66	-2.4%	15.35	2.0%	13.46	16.3%	15.00	4%	16.36	-4%	20	13	-22%	17%
Scudder New Europe Fund	9.97	-2.1%	10.67	-6.6%	10.56	-5.6%	10.40	-4%	NA	NA	13	10	-21%	0%
Templeton Emerging Mkt. Fund	15.80	-0.2%	15.15	4.3%	11.91	32.7%	13.84	14%	13.40	18%	17	11	-9%	38%
Average NAV Change:		-1.1%		1.4%		8.1%		5.5%		-7.0%				

Table D-3   Regional and Specialized Closed-End Country Funds Average Daily Trading Volume— June 1990 Through June 1991 (00's)

Specialized Funds	JUN '91	APR	APR	MAR	FEB	JAN	DEC	NOV	OCT	SEP	AUG	JUL	JUN '90
ASA Ltd.	842	549	477	605	621	826	439	506	729	592	1,476	574	672
Central Fund of Canada	221	112	136	248	278	447	195	125	160	152	415	161	246
Closed-End Bond Funds													
First Australia Prime Inc.	729	1.121	984	747	829	776	709	661	797	596	899	601	500
Regional Funds													
Asia Pacific Fund	116	106	77	125	250	121	139	105	163	99	218	227	156
Europe Fund	118	75	245	137	139	101	68	52	207	62	104	68	177
European Warrant Fund	131	178	162	83	208	118	99	144	113	71	238	495	NA
GT Greater Europe Fund	211	282	175	141	186	189	302	201	141	105	170	101	159
Latin America Inv. Fund#	176	213	198	157	166	103	164	71	122	48	303	631	NA
Pacific Eur. Growth Fund	19	20	22	17	30	27	47	33	32	14	34	18	22
Scudder New Asia Fund	65	60	75	109	252	114	83	68	123	81	208	98	97
Scudder New Europe Fund	289	214	294	231	279	198	261	269	311	246	487	309	390
Templeton Emerging Mkt. Fund	89	94	134	93	132	122	79	140	118	109	311	184	133

Table D-4 Single-Country Closed-End Funds

Selected Data

	Listing/Symbol	When Issued	Price as of 06/28/91	NAV as of 06/28/91	% Discount/Premium	# Shares Outstanding (in millions)	Total Assets (in millions)	Market Capitalization (in millions)	Expenses/Avg Net Assets Ratios
Europe									
Austria Fund#	NYSE-OST	09/21/89	$9.63	$10.68	-10%	8.3	$88	$79	1.75%
Emerging Germany Fund#	NYSE-FRG	03/29/90	7.50	8.59	-13%	14.0	120	105	1.37%
First Iberian Fund	ABE-IBF	04/12/88	8.38	8.61	-3%	6.5	56	55	3.78%
France Growth Fund	NYSE-FRF	05/11/90	7.50	9.58	-22%	11.5	110	86	2.18%
Future Germany Fund	NYSE-FGF	02/27/90	11.75	12.89	-9%	12.6	163	148	1.46%
Germany Fund	NYSE-GER	07/18/86	10.88	10.04	8%	13.1	131	142	1.58%
Growth Fund of Spain	NYSE-GSP	02/14/90	9.25	10.79	-14%	17.4	188	161	1.26%
Irish Investment Fund#	NYSE-IRL	03/30/90	7.13	8.86	-20%	5.0	44	36	1.70%
Italy Fund	NYSE-ITA	02/25/86	10.75	11.36	-5%	6.3	72	68	1.99%
New Germany Fund#	NYSE-GF	01/24/90	9.75	11.45	-15%	28.1	322	274	1.21%
Portugal Fund	NYSE-PGF	11/01/89	9.00	10.22	-12%	5.3	54	48	2.04%
Spain Fund	NYSE-SNF	06/21/88	12.63	11.06	14%	10.0	111	126	2.22%
Swiss Helvetia Fund#	NYSE-SWZ	08/19/87	11.88	12.57	-6%	8.0	101	95	1.77%
Turkish Investment Fund	NYSE-TKF	12/05/89	7.25	7.56	-4%	7.0	53	51	2.00%
UK Fund	NYSE-UKM	08/06/87	8.75	10.10	-13%	4.0	40	35	2.33%
Totals:							$1,654	$1,510	2.16% (AVG)
Asia & Pacific Rim									
First Australia Fund	ASE-IAF	12/12/85	8.38	9.61	-13%	6.0	58	50	2.41%
First Philippine Fund	NYSE-FPF	11/08/89	7.50	10.35	-28%	9.0	93	67	1.87%
India Growth Fund	NYSE-IGF	08/12/88	11.75	14.17	-17%	5.0	71	59	3.42%
Indonesia Fund	NYSE-IF	03/01/90	9.88	9.66	2%	4.6	45	45	2.15%
Jakarta Growth Fund	NYSE-JGF	04/10/90	7.38	7.96	-7%	5.0	40	37	1.83%
Japan OTC Equity Fund	NYSE-JOF	03/14/90	10.50	12.61	-17%	8.5	107	89	1.38%
Korea Fund	NYSE-KF	08/22/84	14.13	10.27	38%	21.6	222	305	1.44%
Malaysia Fund	NYSE-MF	05/08/87	13.38	14.75	-9%	7.3	107	97	1.93%
Singapore Fund	NYSE-SGF	07/24/90	9.88	11.85	-17%	5.1	60	50	2.72%
Taiwan Fund	NYSE-TWN	12/17/86	22.88	22.21	3%	4.2	94	96	2.34%
Thai Capital Fund	NYSE-TC	05/22/90	8.25	9.40	-12%	6.2	58	51	2.43%
Thai Fund	NYSE-TTF	02/17/88	16.50	15.73	5%	10.0	158	165	1.35%
Totals:							$1,112	$1,113	2.11% (AVG)
Latin America									
Brazil Fund	NYSE-BZF	03/31/88	14.63	14.03	4%	12.1	170	177	2.25%
Chile Fund	NYSE-CH	09/27/89	23.38	28.77	-19%	5.4	155	126	2.04%
Emerging Mexico Fund	NYSE-MEF	10/02/90	14.63	17.22	-15%	5.0	86	73	2.36%
Mexico Fund	NYSE-MXF	06/11/81	20.25	23.68	-14%	19.7	467	399	1.45%
Mexico Equity & Inc. Fund	NYSE-MXE	08/14/90	11.75	14.13	-17%	6.3	89	74	1.97%
Totals:							$966	$849	2.01% (AVG)

Table D-5 Single-Country Closed-End Funds

Selected Data

Premium/Discount Analysis	Premium/Disc as of 06/28/91	Premium/Disc as of Prev. Week	Premium/Disc as of 03/31/91	Premium/Disc as of 12/31/90	Premium/Disc as of 09/30/90	Premium/Disc as of 12/31/89	52-Week High	52-Week Low	52-Week Average Prem./Disc.	26-Week Average Prem./Disc.
Europe										
Austria Fund#	-10%	-15%	-10%	-17%	-24%	68%	5%	-30%	-16%	-15%
Emerging Germany Fund#	-13%	-17%	-11%	-19%	-21%	NA	-6%	-23%	-15%	-13%
First Iberian Fund	-3%	0%	-2%	-8%	-19%	27%	15%	-23%	-7%	-3%
France Growth Fund	-22%	-19%	-18%	-21%	-27%	NA	9%	-33%	-16%	-17%
Future Germany Fund	-9%	-13%	-11%	-19%	-20%	NA	-5%	-26%	-13%	-12%
Germany Fund	8%	8%	9%	1%	4%	58%	21%	0%	7%	7%
Growth Fund of Spain	-14%	-13%	-12%	-22%	-28%	NA	-4%	-28%	-16%	13%
Irish Investment Fund#	-20%	-18%	-18%	-26%	-27%	NA	-11%	-33%	-20%	-19%
Italy Fund	-5%	-10%	-6%	-14%	-24%	32%	-2%	-34%	-14%	-11%
New Germany Fund#	-15%	-16%	-13%	-11%	-18%	NA	8%	-21%	-13%	-12%
Portugal Fund	-12%	-9%	-5%	-14%	-26%	23%	8%	-28%	-11%	-11%
Spain Fund	14%	15%	31%	3%	-5%	130%	38%	-8%	11%	19%
Swiss Helvetia Fund#	-6%	-6%	1%	-10%	-10%	16%	3%	-13%	-6%	-5%
Turkish Investment Fund	-4%	-9%	-9%	-18%	-33%	-8%	6%	-36%	-15%	-7%
UK Fund	-13%	-15%	-12%	-17%	-17%	-8%	-8%	-24%	-15%	-14%
Average Premium/Discount:	-8%	-9%	-6%	-14%	-20%	38%				
Asia & Pacific Rim										
First Australia Fund	-13%	-11%	-13%	-14%	-25%	-16%	-3%	-25%	-13%	-10%
First Philippine Fund	-28%	-26%	-16%	-30%	-33%	25%	-13%	-34%	-22%	-20%
India Growth Fund	-17%	-20%	-9%	-23%	-25%	44%	32%	-31%	-10%	-15%
Indonesia Fund	2%	1%	1%	-4%	-21%	NA	17%	-21%	-3%	1%
Jakarta Growth Fund	-7%	-5%	-9%	-23%	-30%	NA	23%	-30%	-9%	-9%
Japan OTC Equity Fund	-17%	-17%	15%	-8%	-17%	NA	34%	-26%	-3%	3%
Korea Fund	38%	37%	36%	11%	11%	85%	64%	10%	33%	31%
Malaysia Fund	-9%	-6%	4%	11%	-1%	36%	17%	-16%	-1%	-2%
Singapore Fund	-17%	-17%	-13%	-20%	-25%	NA	8%	-28%	-16%	-15%
Taiwan Fund	3%	1%	16%	29%	-10%	57%	54%	-10%	24%	20%
Thai Capital Fund	-12%	-5%	0%	-17%	-24%	NA	10%	-24%	-10%	-10%
Thai Fund	5%	9%	10%	18%	14%	50%	26%	-8%	8%	11%
Average Premium/Discount:	-6%	-5%	2%	-8%	-16%	71%				
Latin America										
Brazil Fund	4%	9%	0%	13%	-16%	-32%	21%	-19%	2%	6%
Chile Fund	-19%	-16%	-13%	-10%	-26%	5%	14%	-26%	-11%	-13%
Emerging Mexico Fund	-15%	-16%	-11%	-20%	NA	NA	8%	-20%	-13%	-14%
Mexico Fund	-14%	-15%	-10%	-19%	-15%	-9%	3%	-18%	-9%	-11%
Mexico Equity & Inc. Fund	-17%	-14%	-17%	-13%	-17%	NA	4%	-27%	-14%	-15%
Average Premium/Discount:	-12%	-10%	-10%	-10%	-19%	-12%				

Within the last three years, Smith Barney, Harris Upham & Co. Inc. or one of its affiliates was the manager (comanager) of a public offering of this company.

	06/28/91	Prev.Week	03/31/91	12/31/90	09/30/90	12/31/89
Avg. Prem/Disc Single-Country:	-7.98%	-7.76%	-3.59%	-11.06%	-17.93%	31.86%
Avg. Prem/Disc Rgnl & Spclzd:	-8.91%	-8.46%	-7.89%	-13.42%	-15.68%	-0.53%
Avg. Prem/Disc All Funds:	-8.24%	-7.95%	-4.76%	-11.71%	-17.30%	24.09%

Table D-6   Single-Country Closed-End Funds

	Price as of 06/28/91	% Change Since Previous Week	Price as of 03/31/91	% Change Since 03/31/91	Price as of 12/31/90	% Change since 12/31/90	Price as of 09/30/90	% Change since 09/30/90	Price as of 12/31/89	% Change since 12/31/89	52-Week Range High	52-Week Range Low	% Chg From High	% Chg From Low
Europe														
Austria Fund #	$9.63	0.0%	$10.75	-10.5%	$10.00	-3.8%	$8.63	12%	$20.50	-53%	$16	$9	-38%	12%
Emergency Germany Fund #	8.38	0.0%	7.63	-1.6%	7.63	-1.6%	7.00	7%	NA	NA	11	7	-29%	7%
First Iberian Fund	7.50	-4.3%	9.38	-10.7%	7.75	8.1%	7.13	18%	13.38	-37%	12	7	-29%	22%
France Growth Fund	7.50	-4.8%	8.63	-13.0%	8.13	-7.7%	7.63	-2%	NA	NA	12	7	-36%	3%
Future Germany Fund	11.75	-1.1%	12.00	-2.2%	12.00	-2.2%	10.50	12%	NA	NA	16	11	-28%	12%
Germany Fund	10.88	-4.4%	11.13	-2.2%	11.13	-2.2%	10.63	2%	19.25	-44%	12	11	-33%	2%
Growth Fund of Spain	9.25	-2.6%	10.13	-8.6%	8.00	15.6%	7.00	32%	NA	NA	10	7	-21%	32%
Irish Investment Fund	7.13	-1.7%	8.00	-10.9%	6.75	5.6%	6.75	6%	NA	NA	10	7	-28%	8%
Italy Fund	10.75	2.4%	10.88	-1.1%	9.88	8.9%	10.00	8%	17.00	-37%	15	9	-28%	18%
New Germany Fund #	9.75	-3.7%	10.13	-3.7%	11.38	-14.3%	9.75	0%	NA	NA	15	10	-34%	0%
Portugal Fund	9.00	-2.7%	10.63	-15.3%	9.38	-4.0%	8.63	4%	17.00	-47%	15	9	-38%	4%
Spain Fund	12.63	-2.9%	16.00	-21.1%	10.88	16.1%	10.75	17%	31.75	-60%	18	11	-29%	20%
Swiss Helvetica Fund #	11.88	-2.1%	13.25	-10.4%	11.88	0.0%	11.25	6%	15.13	-21%	15	11	-21%	6%
Turkish Investment Fund	7.25	7.4%	9.50	-23.7%	6.75	7.4%	10.13	-28%	12.00	-40%	13	9	-45%	7%
UK Fund	8.75	-2.8%	10.25	-14.6%	9.00	-2.8%	8.63	1%	10.75	-19%	11	9	-22%	1%
Average Price Change:		-1.5%		-9.7%		1.8%		6.3%		-39.7%				
Asia & Pacific Firm														
First Australia Fund	8.38	-4.3%	8.25	1.5%	7.25	15.5%	7.50	12%	8.75	-4%	9	7	-11%	16%
First Phillipine Fund	7.50	-3.2%	8.63	-13.0%	6.38	17.6%	6.50	15%	13.75	-45%	10	6	-21%	18%
India Growth Fund	11.75	1.1%	13.25	-11.3%	10.75	9.3%	14.25	-18%	19.50	-40%	18	11	-35%	11%
Indonesia Fund	9.88	-3.7%	10.75	-8.1%	10.00	-1.3%	9.63	3%	NA	NA	16	10	-38%	4%
Jakarta Growth Fund	7.38	-4.8%	7.75	-4.8%	6.75	9.3%	6.63	11%	NA	NA	14	7	-46%	11%
Japan OTC Equity Fund	10.50	-2.3%	11.88	-11.6%	8.25	27.3%	7.88	33%	NA	NA	16	8	-34%	38%
Korea Fund	14.13	1.8%	14.75	-4.2%	12.38	14.1%	12.25	15%	34.38	-59%	24	12	-42%	16%
Malaysia Fund	13.38	-4.5%	14.50	-7.8%	11.00	21.6%	11.50	16%	18.75	-29%	18	10	-24%	34%
Singapore Fund	9.88	0.0%	10.00	-7.3%	8.75	12.9%	8.13	22%	NA	NA	12	8	-18%	23%
Taiwan Fund	22.88	1.7%	22.75	0.5%	21.25	7.6%	14.50	58%	35.13	-35%	27	15	-16%	58%
Thai Capital Fund	8.25	-8.3%	10.50	-21.4%	6.75	22.2%	6.38	29%	NA	NA	12	6	-32%	32%
Thai Fund	16.50	-3.6%	19.50	-15.4%	15.38	7.3%	17.63	-6%	32.25	-49%	26	15	-35%	11%
Average Price Change:		-2.5%		-8.1%		13.6%		15.9%		-37.3%				
Latin America														
Brazil Fund	14.63	-4.1%	9.75	50.0%	6.75	116.7%	8.00	83%	9.83	49%	16	7	-7%	121%
Chile Fund	23.38	-0.5%	20.50	14.0%	15.63	49.6%	11.63	101%	15.60	50%	25	11	-7%	105%
Emerging Mexico Fund	14.63	-0.8%	12.25	19.4%	9.00	62.5%	NA	NA	NA	NA	17	9	-13%	67%
Mexico Fund	20.25	-0.6%	16.75	20.9%	12.63	60.4%	11.50	76%	11.38	78%	25	12	-18%	76%
Mexico Equity & Inc. Fund	11.75	-3.1%	10.25	14.6%	9.8	19.0%	9.50	24%	NA	NA	13	8	-10%	40%
Average Price Change:		-1.8%		23.8%		61.6%		70.9%		58.9%				
Avg. Price Change—All Funds		-2.0%		-4.2%		15.7%		18.6%		-25.3%				

Table D-7 Single-Country Closed-End Funds Average Daily Trading Volume (Hundreds)—June 1990 through June 1991

	NAV as of 06/28/91	% Chg Since Prv. Week	NAV As of 03/31/91	% Chg Since 03/31/91	NAV As of 12/31/90	% Chg Since 12/31/90	NAV As of 09/30/90	% Chg Since 09/30/90	NAV As of 12/31/89	% Chg Since 12/31/90	52-Week Range High	52-Week Range Low	% Chg From High	% Chg From Low
Europe														
Austria Fund #	$10.68	-6.1%	$12.00	-11.0%	$12.09	-11.7%	$11.33	-6%	$12.21	-13%	$17	$11	-38%	0%
Emerging Germany Fund #	8.59	-5.3%	8.60	-0.1%	9.40	-8.6%	8.83	-3%	NA	NA	12	9	-26%	0%
First Iberian Fund	8.61	-1.8%	9.54	-9.7%	8.41	2.4%	8.80	-2%	10.57	-19%	12	8	-28%	5%
France Growth Fund	9.58	-1.1%	10.49	-8.7%	10.33	-7.3%	10.40	-8%	NA	NA	12	10	-17%	0%
Future Germany Fund	12.89	-5.2%	12.99	-0.8%	14.12	-8.7%	13.10	-2%	NA	NA	18	13	-28%	0%
Germany Fund	10.04	-5.1%	10.20	-1.6%	11.05	-9.1%	10.26	-2%	12.15	-17%	14	10	-28%	0%
Growth Fund of Spain	10.79	-1.4%	11.51	-6.3%	10.25	5.3%	9.73	11%	NA	NA	13	10	-18%	11%
Irish Invesment Fund #	8.86	-0.3%	9.71	-8.8%	9.11	-2.7%	9.24	-4%	NA	NA	11	9	-21%	4%
Italy Fund	11.36	-3.1%	11.54	-1.6%	11.49	-1.1%	13.24	-14%	12.86	-12%	16	11	-30%	2%
New Germany Fund #	11.45	-4.5%	11.58	-1.1%	12.76	-10.3%	11.87	-4%	NA	NA	16	12	-27%	-1%
Portugal Fund	10.22	0.3%	11.15	-8.3%	10.96	-6.8%	11.59	-12%	13.79	-26%	14	10	-26%	0%
Spain Fund	11.06	-2.2%	12.17	-9.1%	10.57	4.6%	11.34	-2%	13.82	-20%	16	10	-30%	7%
Swiss Helvetica Fund #	12.57	-2.7%	13.13	-4.3%	13.17	-4.6%	12.54	0%	13.05	-4%	16	13	-19%	2%
Turkish Investment Fund	7.56	2.3%	10.47	-27.8%	8.25	-8.4%	15.09	-50%	13.01	-42%	17	7	-56%	2%
UK Fund	10.10	-5.1%	11.67	-13.5%	10.82	-6.7%	10.45	-3%	11.67	-13%	12	10	-19%	0%
Average NAV Change:		-2.8%		-7.5%		-4.9%		-6.7%		-18.3%				
Asia & Pacific Rim														
First Australia Fund	9.61	-1.8%	9.53	0.8%	8.45	13.7%	9.96	-4%	10.41	-8%	10	8	-7%	15%
First Philippines Fund	10.35	-0.8%	10.29	0.6%	9.15	13.1%	9.70	7%	11.03	-6%	11	9	-7%	21%
India Growth Fund	14.17	-2.3%	14.52	-2.4%	13.96	1.5%	18.95	-25%	13.54	-5%	20	13	-30%	13%
Indonesia Fund	9.66	-5.0%	10.64	-9.2%	10.38	-9.2%	12.19	-21%	NA	NA	15	10	-37%	0%
Jakarta Growth Fund	7.96	-2.6%	8.56	-7.0%	8.77	-9.2%	9.51	-16%	NA	NA	11	8	-28%	0%
Japan OTC Equity Fund	12.61	-2.2%	10.32	22.2%	8.93	41.2%	9.53	32%	NA	NA	13	8	-6%	50%
Korea Fund	10.27	1.2%	10.82	-5.1%	11.10	-7.5%	11.00	-7%	18.55	-45%	16	10	-35%	3%
Malaysia Fund	14.75	-0.7%	13.95	5.7%	12.39	19.0%	11.59	27%	13.77	7%	16	12	-5%	27%
Singapore Fund	11.85	-0.1%	11.55	2.6%	10.87	9.0%	10.87	9%	NA	NA	12	11	-3%	9%
Taiwan Fund	22.21	-0.6%	19.64	13.1%	16.51	34.5%	16.11	38%	22.35	-1%	23	14	-4%	58%
Thai Capital Fund	9.40	-0.4%	10.50	-10.5%	8.16	15.2%	8.39	12%	NA	NA	12	8	-19%	21%
Thai Fund	15.73	0.1%	17.77	-11.5%	13.08	20.3%	15.49	2%	18.88	-17%	24	13	-36%	23%
Average NAV Change:		-1.3%		-0.1%		12.0%		4.5%		-9.1%				
Latin America														
Brazil Fund	14.03	0.0%	9.72	44.3%	5.97	135.0%	9.58	46%	18.85	-26%	14	6	0%	135%
Chile Fund	28.77	3.0%	23.60	21.9%	17.44	65.0%	15.77	82%	14.79	95%	29	15	-5%	90%
Emerging Mexico Fund	17.22	-1.5%	13.70	25.7%	11.30	52.4%	NA	NA	NA	NA	18	11	-5%	60%
Mexico Fund	23.68	-1.0%	18.51	27.9%	15.64	51.4%	13.48	76%	12.50	89%	25	13	-3%	76%
Mexico Equity & Inc. Fund	14.13	0.4%	12.37	14.2%	11.29	25.2%	11.42	24%	NA	NA	15	11		26
Average NAV Change:		0.2%		26.8%		65.8%		57.1%		52.8%				
AVG. NAV Change—All Funds:		-1.7%		-0.7%		12.5%		5.9%		-3.7%				

Table D-8 Single-Country Closed-End Funds
Average Daily Trading Volume (Hundreds)—June 1990 through June 1991

Europe	Jun '91	May	Apr	Mar	Feb	Jan	Dec	Nov	Oct	Sep	Aug	Jul	Jun '90
Austria Fund #	151	93	223	122	414	166	184	122	464	149	240	252	188
Emerging Germany Fund #	222	254	502	390	826	296	336	259	419	204	396	242	316
First Iberian Fund	32	34	46	54	151	51	144	81	66	59	99	82	64
France Growth Fund	215	203	345	356	625	508	356	216	399	388	498	314	507
Future Germany Fund	149	226	448	355	485	233	249	191	500	246	528	476	431
Germany Fund	197	246	259	295	601	326	280	209	345	285	511	467	300
Growth Fund of Spain	254	314	572	476	1,056	361	388	285	467	451	521	661	577
Irish Investment Fund #	61	48	63	107	169	81	114	195	297	87	192	101	90
Italy Fund	86	80	110	81	195	93	122	79	151	116	151	158	172
New Germany Fund #	492	473	554	559	845	486	653	500	536	580	764	670	515
Portugal Fund	54	88	140	116	204	74	111	127	50	78	87	84	60
Spain Fund	71	70	119	157	442	110	89	46	63	95	126	97	99
Swiss Helvetica Fund #	79	98	111	146	164	119	94	91	77	69	155	210	144
Turkish Investment Fund	263	62	100	137	285	205	140	86	69	90	352	161	184
UK Fund	56	37	100	87	164	54	59	106	93	44	65	66	115
Asia & Pacific Rim													
First Australia Fund	146	117	69	72	97	64	75	88	107	102	212	151	115
First Philippines Fund	158	136	87	106	211	155	104	65	120	103	147	123	100
India Growth Fund	102	225	36	47	91	39	49	46	62	77	102	76	100
Indonesia Fund	58	79	141	55	113	62	48	58	79	60	100	96	136
Jakarta Growth Fund	73	64	94	53	185	57	84	47	76	95	94	41	155
Japan OTC Equity Fund	164	242	355	278	608	159	122	110	209	165	227	146	299
Korea Fund	318	332	385	388	780	452	392	365	549	386	426	361	469
Malaysia Fund	90	116	99	110	192	135	82	74	193	136	206	176	137
Singapore Fund	104	90	105	146	327	149	122	139	356	128	197	472	NA
Taiwan Fund	85	92	137	85	178	146	178	240	163	136	193	270	263
Thai Capital Fund	95	125	147	146	472	106	70	73	179	80	157	126	351
Thai Fund	133	80	215	123	422	116	141	99	161	150	283	187	219
Latin America													
Brazil Fund	405	612	318	466	338	319	210	133	111	625	625	354	273
Chile Fund	160	132	124	142	73	117	90	75	134	106	106	166	125
Emerging Mexico Fund	351	528	822	469	144	81	75	876	NA	NA	NA	NA	NA
Mexico Fund	767	1,191	898	697	337	371	304	472	436	937	937	1,180	1,165
Mexico Equity & Inc. Fund	205	336	225	146	36	250	162	129	164	NA	NA	NA	NA

E

LATIN AMERICAN COUNTRY
FUNDS FACT SHEETS

Reprinted with permission from *Closed-End Emerging Country Funds Review* by Michael T. Porter, Smith Barney, Harris, Upham & Co.

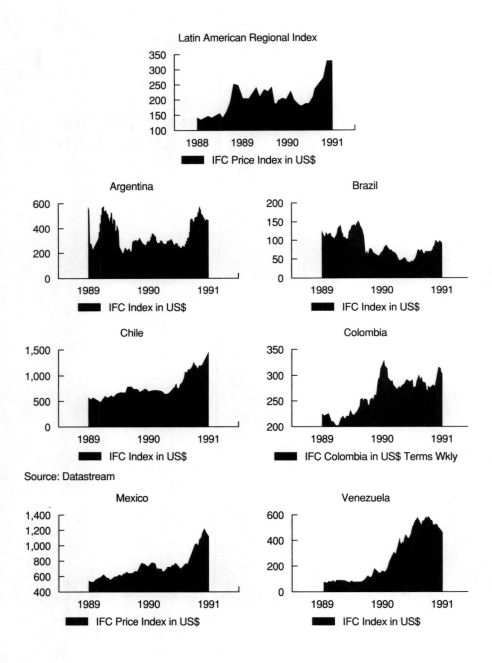

Figure E-2   BRAZIL FUND (BZF)

Listing: NYSE
Launched: April 1988
Offering Price: $12.50
Investment Manager: Scudder, Stevens & Clark
Total Shares: 12,078,395
Total Net Assets: $170 million
Market Capitalization: $177 million

Management Fees: 1.25% of average net assets

Expense Ratio: 2.25%

Recent Dividends: $3.07 paid 1/23/90
$0.12 paid 3/30/90

INVESTMENT OBJECTIVE:

Long-term capital appreciation through investment in securities, primarily equity securities, of Brazilian companies.

Current Disc./Prem.: +4%
52-Week Range: +21% to –19%
Avg. Discount/Premium: +2%
(PRICED AS OF 06/28/91)

SECTOR BREAKDOWN: March 31, 1991:

Industry	% of Assets
Forest Products	15.3
Food and Beverages	13.8
Chemicals	11.3
Mining	10.2
Tobacco	7.6
Petroleum	6.7
Glass	5.4
Electrical Equipment	5.3
Auto Parts	3.5
Textiles and Apparel	3.0
Retailing	3.0
Banking	2.2
Miscellaneous	5.3
CASH & other — Net	7.4
Total	100.0

TOP TEN HOLDINGS: March 31, 1991:

Company	Industry	% of Net Assets
S/A White Martins	Chemicals	7.7
Companhia Souza Cruz Industria e Comercio	Tobacco	7.6
Companhia Suzano de Papel e Celulose	Forest Products	6.9
Petroleo Brasileiro S/A	Petroleum	6.7
Companhia Vale do Rio Doce	Mining	6.3
Aracruz Celulose S.A. "B"	Forest Products	6.3
Sadia Concordia S/A	Food & Beverage	5.5
Companhia Vidraria Santa Marina	Glass	5.4
Companhia Cervejaria Brahma	Food & Beverage	4.8
S.A. de Trindade	Mining	3.7
		61.0

Brazil Fund

Brazil Fund
Premium/Discount to Net Asset Value

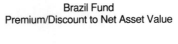

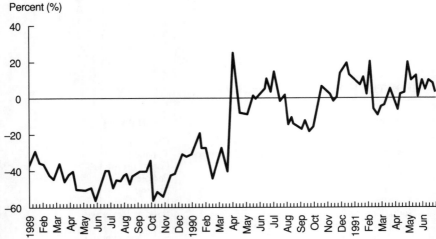

Figure E-3   CHILE FUND (CH)

Listing: NYSE

September 1989
Offering Price: $15.00
Investment Manager: BEA Associates
Total Shares: 5,374,674
Total Net Assets: $155 million
Market Capitalization: $126 million

Management Fees: 1.20% of first $50 million, 1.15% of next $50 million, and 1.10% of excess.

Expense Ratio: 2.04%

Recent Dividends: $1.25 paid 01/23/91
$0.34 paid 01/12/90

INVESTMENT OBJECTIVE:

Total return, consisting of capital appreciation and income, to be achieved by investing primarily in Chilean equity and debt securities.

Current Disc./Prem: –19%
52-Week Range: +14% to –26%
Avg. Discount/Premium: –11%
(PRICED AS OF 06/28/91)

SECTOR BREAKDOWN: December 31, 1990:

Industry	% of Assets
Electric Utilities	22.6
Telecommunications	12.3
Paper & Cellulose	10.7
Forestry	8.8
Investments	6.7
Basic Metals	6.3
Beer, Beverages, Liquor & Tobacco	3.2
Food	2.7
Machinery & Electric	2.5
Fishing	1.7
Mining	1.1
Shipping	1.1
Manufacturing	1.0
Miscellaneous	3.5
CASH & Other — Net	15.9
	100.0

TOP TEN HOLDINGS: December 31, 1990:

Company	Industry	% of Net Assets
Cartones	Paper & Cellulose	10.0
Copec de Chile	Forestry	8.8
Enersis	Electric Utility	8.8
Telefonos de Chile "A" & "B"	Telecommunications	8.4
Endesa de Chile	Electric Utility	5.6
Cap	Basic Metals	5.4
Chilectra	Electric Utility	5.1
Entel	Telecommunications	3.9
Cervezas	Beer, Beverages, Liquors & Tobacco	2.9
Iansa	Food	2.7
		61.6

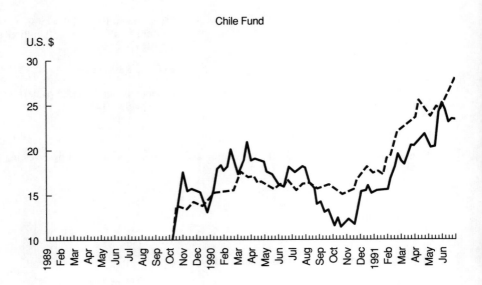

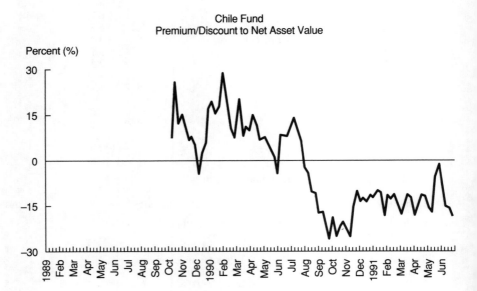

Figure E-4   EMERGING MEXICO FUND (MEF)

Listing: NYSE
average weekly assets.
Launched: October 1990
Offering Price: $12.00
Investment Advisor: Santander Management Inc.
Total Shares: 5,009,000
Total Net Assets: $86 million
Market Capitalization: $73 million

Management & Other Fees: 1.00% of

Expense Ratio: 2.36%

Recent Dividends: $0.312 paid 01/11/91

INVESTMENT OBJECTIVE:

Long-term capital appreciation through investment primarily in equities of Mexican companies.

Current Disc./Prem.: −15%
52-Week Range: +8% to −20%
Avg. Discount/Premium: −13%
(PRICED AS OF 06/28/91)

SECTOR BREAKDOWN: March 31, 1991:

Industry	% of Assets
Construction	16.8
Retail	15.9
Communications	14.0
Food, Beverages, Tobacco	10.5
Industrial Conglomerates	7.8
Other	16.3
CASH & Other — Net	18.7
	100.0

TOP TEN HOLDINGS: March 31, 1991:

Company	Industry
Telefonos de Mexico	Communications
CIFRA	Retail Trade
Grupo Industrial Bimbo	Food, Beverages, Tobacco
Cementos Mexicanos	Construction
Apasco	Construction
Empresa Tolteca de Mexico	Construction
Grupo Condumex	Electrical & Electronic Equipment
Kimberly-Clark de Mexico	Paper
Grupo Carso	Industrial Conglomerate
Vitro	Industrial Conglomerate

Top Ten Holdings As A % of Net Assets: 59.7%

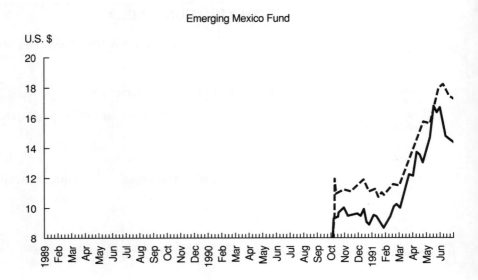

Emerging Mexico Fund

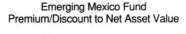

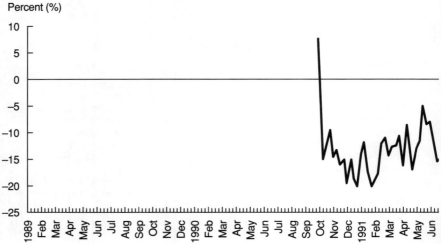

Emerging Mexico Fund
Premium/Discount to Net Asset Value

Figure E-5   LATIN AMERICA INVESTMENT FUND# (LAM)

Listing: NYSE

Launched: July 1990
Offering Price: $15.00
Investment Manager: BEA Associates, Inc.
Sovereign Debt Advisor: Salomon Bros. Asset Mgmt.
Total Shares: 4,007,169

Total Assets: $87 million
Market Capitalization: $73 million

Management and Other Fees: 1.25% of
first $100 million, 1.15% of next $50
million and 1.05% of excess.

Expense Ratio: 3.27%

Recent Dividends: $0.2647 paid
01/04/91.

INVESTMENT OBJECTIVE:

Long-term capital appreciation through investment primarily in Latin American debt and
equity securities. The Fund intends to have at least 65% of its total assets in Brazil, Chile and
Mexico. The Fund's holdings of securities in any other single Latin American country will
be limited to 10% of the Fund's total assets. The Fund is authorized to invest up to 30% of its
assets in Sovereign Debt sponsored by various Latin American countries.

Current Disc./Prem.: –16%
52-Week Range: +5% to –28%
Avg. Discount/Premium:–17%
(PRICED AS OF 06/28/91)

PORTFOLIO COMPOSITION:
December 31, 1990:

	% of Assets
Equities:	
Mexico	29.0
Chile	12.2
Venezuela	10.5
Brazil	3.7
United Kingdom	1.0
Argentina	0.9
Sovereign Debt	18.4
CASH & Other — Net	24.3
Total	100.0

SOVEREIGN DEBT BREAKDOWN:
December 31, 1990:

	% of Assets
Venezuela Conversion Bond, 8.5625%, 04/01/07	5.3
Mexican Fixed Par Bonds 6.25%, 12/31/19	4.0
Costa Rica Bearer Bonds 6.25%, 05/21/10	2.4
Mexican Float.Rate Disc.Bonds 9.53125%, 12/31/19	2.3
Brazil New Money Bond 9.4375%, 10/15/99	1.8
Argentina Bonds 8.40%, 12/28/99	1.0
Argentina Bonex Bond 8.4375%, 06/30/99	1.0
Venezuela New Money Bonds A 8.6875%, 12/18/05	0.4
Venezuela New Money Bonds B 8.5625%, 12/18/05	0.2
	18.4

TOP TEN EQUITY HOLDINGS: December 31, 1990:

	Country—Industry	% of Assets
Telmex Nominative A	Mexico — Telecommunications	5.8
Cifra	Mexico — Retailing	5.7
Sivensa	Venezuela — Metal Products	4.4
Electricad de Caracas	Venezuela — Electric Utilities	3.4
Telefonos de Chile A	Chile — Telecommunications	2.6
Kimberly-Clark Mexicana A	Mexico — Paper	2.2
Soriana A2	Mexico — Retailing	1.9
Entel	Chile — Telecommunications	1.6
Cartones	Chile — Paper & Cellulose	1.6
Copec de Chile	Chile — Forestry	1.5
		30.7

Latin America Investment Fund#

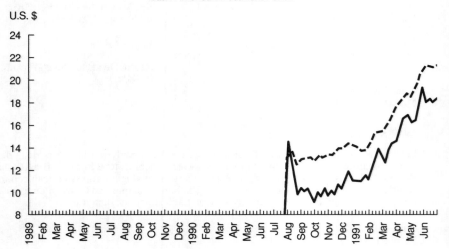

Latin America Investment Fund#
Premium/Discount to Net Asset Value

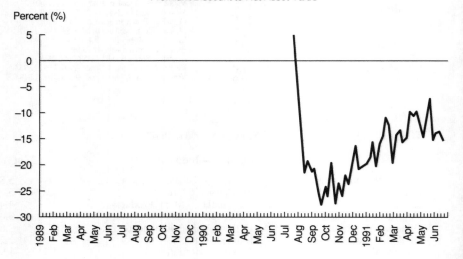

Figure E-6   MEXICO EQUITY AND INCOME FUND (MXE)

Listing: NYSE

Launched: August 1990
Offering Price: $12.00
Local Advisor: Acci Worldwide, S.A.
U.S. Co-Advisor: Advantage Advisors, Inc.
Total Shares: 6,284,479
Total Net Assets: $89 million
Market Capitalization: $74 million

Management & Other Fees: 0.998% of
average monthly assets.

Expense Ratio: 1.97%

Recent Dividends: $0.58 paid 01/07/91

INVESTMENT OBJECTIVE:

High total return from capital appreciation and current income through investment in convertible debt securities issued by Mexican companies and equity and other debt issued by Mexican issuers. The Fund will invest at least 50% in convertible debt securities issued by Mexican companies.

Current Disc./Prem.:−17%
52-Week Range: +4% to −27%
Avg. Discount/Premium: −14%
(PRICED AS OF 06/28/91)

ASSET ALLOCATION: May 10, 1991:

	% of Assets
Mexican Equities	51
Mexican Government Bonds	37
Convertible Bonds	10
Short-Term U.S. Securities	2
Total 100	

TOP EQUITY HOLDINGS: May 10, 1991:

Company	Industry
Telmex	Communications
CIFRA	Retail Trade
Penoles	Mining
Vitro	Development Countries
Kimberly	Paper
Bimbo	Consumer Goods
Cemex	Construction

Mexico Equity & Income Fund

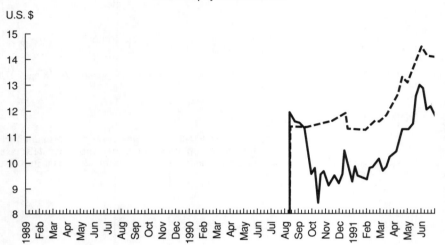

Mexico Equity & Income Fund
Premium/Discount to Net Asset Value

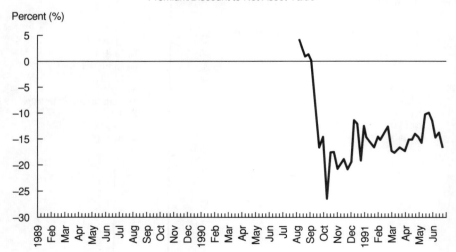

Figure E-7   MEXICO FUND (MXF)

Listing: NYSE

Launched: June 1981
Offering Price: $12.00
Investment Manager: Impulsora de Funda
  Mexico S.A.
Total Shares: 19,718,204
Total Net Assets: $467 million
Market Capitalization: $399 million

Management Fees: 0.85% on first $200
million and 0.70% on excess.

Expense Ratio: 1.45%
Recent Dividends: $0.034 paid01/31/91

$0.0465 paid 11/30/90
$0.02776 paid 08/31/90
$0.039 paid 05/31/90

INVESTMENT OBJECTIVE:

Long-term capital appreciation through investment primarily in equities of Mexican
companies.

Current Disc./Prem.: −14%
52-Week Range: +3% to−18%
Avg. Discount/Premium:−9%
(PRICED AS OF 06/28/91)

SECTOR BREAKDOWN: February 28, 1991:

Industry	% of Assets
Retail Trade	18.7
Development Companies	13.9
Consumer Goods	12.2
Electronics	9.5
Paper	9.0
Construction	8.2
Mining	7.1
Communications	6.3
Banks	6.2
Chemicals & Petrochemicals	4.6
Steel	0.2
CASH — Net	4.1
	100.0

TOP TEN HOLDINGS: February 28, 1991:

Company	Industry	% of Net Assets
CIFRA	Retail Trade	12.5
Kimberly-Clark de Mexico	Paper	8.5
Grupo Industrial Bimbo	Consumer Goods	6.9
Telefonos de Mexico	Communications	6.3
El Puerto de Liverpool	Retail Trade	5.8
Cemex	Construction	4.8
Grupo Industrial Minera Mexico	Mining	4.7
Vitro	Development Company	4.7
Grupo Condumex	Electronics	4.2
Teleindustria Ericsson	Electronics	3.6
		61.9

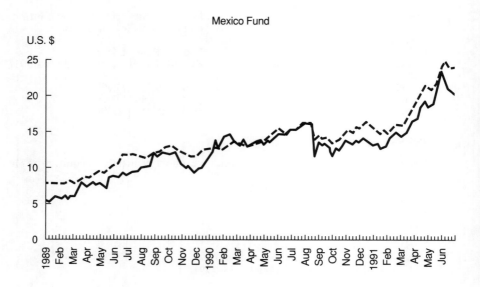

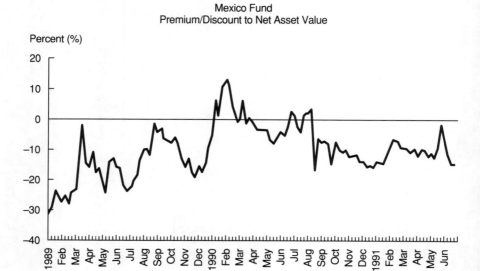

EUROPEAN COUNTRY FUNDS
FACT SHEETS

Reprinted with permission from *Closed-End Emerging Country Funds Review* by Michael T. Porter, Smith Barney, Harris, Upham & Co.

Figure F-1

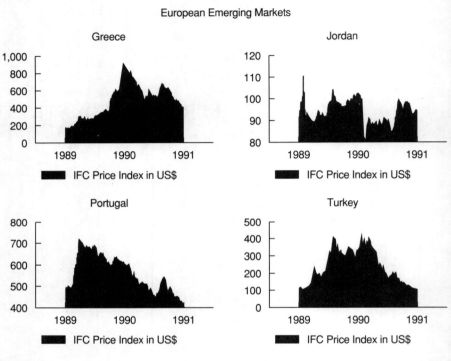

European Emerging Markets

Source: Datastream

Figure F-2   AUSTRIA FUND# (0ST)

Listing: NYSE

Launched: August 1989
Offering Price: $12.00
Investment Manager: Alliance Capital
Total Shares: 8,259,015
Total Net Assets: $88 million
Market Capitalization: $79 million

Management Fees: 1.00% of average net assets for first $50 million, and 0.9% of excess.

Expense Ratio: 1.75%

Recent Dividends: $0.65 paid 01/12/90
$0.20 paid 01/11/91
$0.22 paid 01/11/91

INVESTMENT OBJECTIVE:

Long-term capital appreciation through investment primarily in equity securities of Austrian companies. In addition to at least 65% invested in these equities, the Fund may also invest up to 35% of total assets in Austrian Schilling-denominated fixed income instruments and 20% of total assets in equity or fixed income securities of companies based outside of Austria.

Current Disc./Prem.: -10%
52-Week Range: +5% to -30%
Avg. Discount/Premium: -16%
(PRICED AS OF 06/28/91)

SECTOR BREAKDOWN: April 30, 1991:

Industry	% of Assets
Capital Goods	27.2
Financial Services	24.1
Basic Industries	23.0
Consumer Products & Services	10.3
Utilities	8.7
Multi-Industry	1.5
Unlisted Securities	1.9
CASH .	3.3
	100.0

TOP TEN HOLDINGS: February 28, 1991:

Company	Industry	% of Net Assets
EA Generali	Insurance	11.0
OEMV	Energy	9.0
Verbundgesellschaft	Utility	6.6
Weinerberger Baustoff Industrie	Engineering & Construction	5.9
Papierfabrik Laakirchen	Paper & Forest Products	5.9
Universale-Bau	Engineering & Construction	5.6
Creditanstalt-Bankverein	Banking	4.3
Radex-Heraklith	Mining & Metals	3.6
Oestterr Laenderbank	Banking	3.4
IFE Industrie	Machinery	3.2
Total		58.4

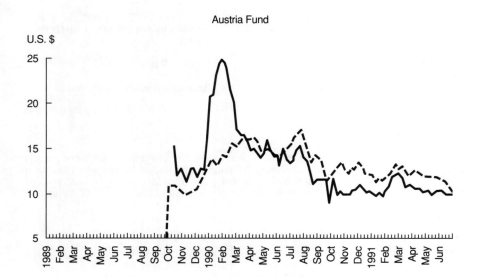

Austria Fund

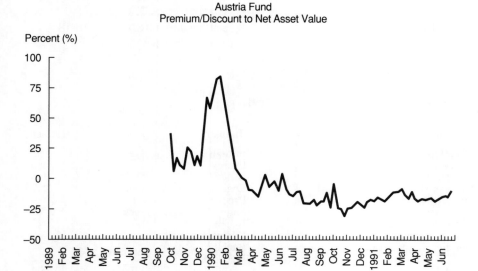

Austria Fund
Premium/Discount to Net Asset Value

Figure F-3   PORTUGAL FUND (PGF)

Listing: NYSE

Launched: November 1989
Offering Price: $15.00
Investment Manager: BEA Associates
Total Shares: 5,297,253
Total Net Assets: $54 million
Market Capitalization: $48 million

Management Fees: 1.20% of first $50
million, 1.15% of next $50 million, and
1.10% of amounts over $100 million.

Expense Ratio: 2.04%

Recent Dividends: $0.84 paid 12/29/89
$0.1158 paid 01/04/91

INVESTMENT OBJECTIVE:

Long-term capital appreciation through investment primarily in equity securities of
Portuguese companies.

Current Disc./Prem.: -12%
52-Week Range: +8% to -28%
Avg. Discount/Premium: -12%
(PRICED AS OF 06/28/91)

SECTOR BREAKDOWN: December 31, 1990:

Industry	% of Assets
Metal Products	9.3
Banks	7.9
Retail Trade	7.3
Construction & Public Works	6.7
Transports & Warehousing	6.3
Non-Metallic Mineral Products	5.5
Financial Institutions	5.5
Telecommunications	5.5
Chemicals & Petroleum Products	5.4
Real Estate Companies & Services	5.3
Wood & Cork	3.1
Other Industries	8.9
Bonds	4.8
CASH — Net	18.6
Total	100.0

TOP TEN HOLDINGS: June 30, 1990:

Company	Industry	% of Net Assets
Continente SA, Modelo Hipermercados	Retail	5.7
Marconi	Telecommunications	5.5
Lusotur Sociedad e Financiera de Turismo	Real Estate & Services	5.3
Jeronimo Martins	Holding Company	4.3
Banco Commercial Portuguese	Bank	4.2
Corporacao Industrial do Notre	Chemicals & Petroleum Products	3.7
Sociedad Financiera Locacao Sofinloc	Financial Institution	3.5
Soares da Costa	Construction & Public Works	3.5
Tertir Terminais de Portugal	Transport & Warehousing	3.3
Corticeira Amorim Sa	Wood & Cork	3.1
		42.1

Portugal Fund

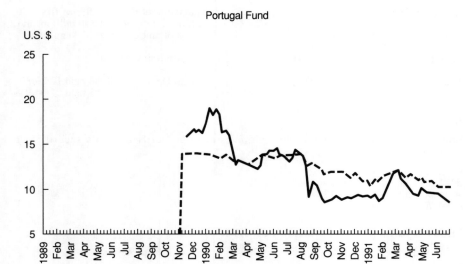

Portugal Fund
Premium/Discount to Net Asset Value

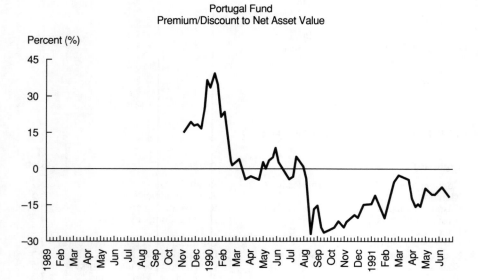

G

ASIAN COUNTRY FUNDS
FACT SHEETS

Reprinted with permission from *Closed-End Emerging Country Funds Review* by Michael T. Porter, Smith Barney, Harris, Upham & Co.

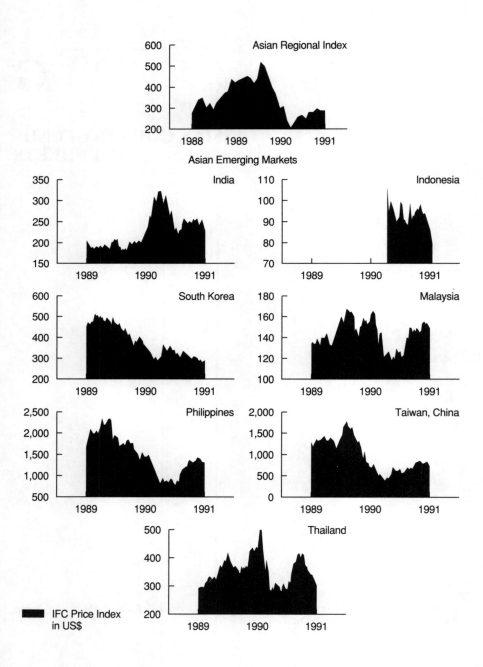

Asian Regional Index

Asian Emerging Markets

India

Indonesia

South Korea

Malaysia

Philippines

Taiwan, China

Thailand

IFC Price Index in US$

Figure G-1   TURKISH INVESTMENT FUND (TKF)

Listing: NYSE

Launched: December 1989
Offering Price: $12.00
Investment Manager: Morgan Stanley
    Asset Management
Total Shares: 7,023,431
Total Net Assets: $53 million
Market Capitalization: $51 million

Management Fees: $0.95% of first $50
million of average weekly assets, 0.75%
in excess of $50 million and 0.55%
over $100 million.
Advisory Fees: 0.20% of first $50 million
of average weekly assets, 0.10% in
excess of $50million and 0.05%
over $100 million.
Expense Ratio: 2.00%
Recent Dividends: $0.03 paid 01/16/90
$0.07 paid 01/16/91

INVESTMENT OBJECTIVE:

Long-term capital appreciation through investment primarily in equity securities of Turkish corporations.

Current Disc./Prem.: –4%
52-Week Range: +6% to –36%
Avg. Discount/Premium: –15%
(PRICED AS OF 06/28/91)

ASSET ALLOCATION: April 30, 1991:

	% of Assets
Electronics	14.5
Food & Beverage	14.0
Iron & Steel	12.7
Cable & Wire	8.7
Cement	6.3
Automotive & Parts	5.8
Financials	5.7
Building Materials	4.4
Chemicals	4.1
Utilities	3.5
Textiles	2.2
Miscellaneous	10.9
Cash & Other	7.2
	100.0

TOP TEN HOLDINGS: April 30, 1991:

Company	Industry	% of Net Assets
Arcelik	Electronics	8.8
Eregli Demir Celik	Iron & Steel	7.1
Izmir Demir Celik	Iron & Steel	5.7
Vestel	Electronics	5.6
Celik Halat	Cement	4.8
Maret	Food & Beverage	4.6
Akbank	Financials	4.5
Otosan	Automotive & Parts	4.5
Petkim	Chemicals	4.1
Guney Biracilik	Food & Beverage	3.0
		52.7

Turkish Investment Fund

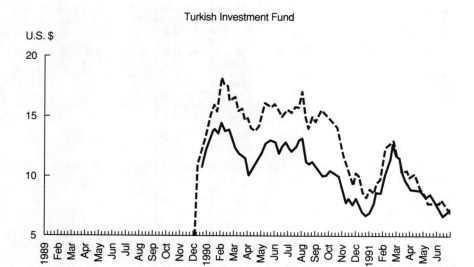

Turkish Investment Fund
Premium/Discount to Net Asset Value

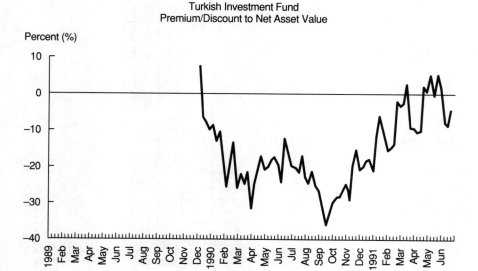

Figure G-3   ASIA PACIFIC FUND (APB)

Listing: NYSE
Launched: April 1987
Offering Price: $10.00
Investment Manager: Baring International
Total Shares: 8,793,120
Total Net Assets: $118 million
Market Capitalization: $108 million

Management Fees: 1.1% of first $50 million, 0.9% of next $50 million, and 0.7% on excess.
Expense Ratio: 1.85%
Recent Dividends: $0.65 paid 06/07/91
$0.615 paid 12/28/90
$0.66 paid 06/29/90
$0.18 paid 01/12/90

INVESTMENT OBJECTIVE:

Long-term capital appreciation through investment primarily in equity securities of companies in the Asia Pacific countries. These countries are Hong Kong, South Korea, Malaysia, the Philippines, Singapore, Taiwan and Thailand.

Current Disc./Prem.: –9%
52-Week Range: +5% to –23%
Avg. Discount/Premium: –8%
(PRICED AS OF 06/28/91)

COUNTRY ALLOCATION: March 31, 1991:

Country	% of Assets
Hong Kong	37.5
Malaysia	16.9
Singapore	21.3
Thailand	19.0
Korea	4.3
Philippines	1.0
	100.0

TOP TEN HOLDINGS: March 31, 1991:

Company	Industry — Country	% of Assets
Siam Cement Co.	Construction — Thailand	6.4
Cheung Kong Holdings	Real Estate — Hong Kong	4.6
Keppel Corp. (Warrants)	Diversified Industries — Singapore	4.2
Hongkong Electric Holdings	Utilities — Hong Kong	4.1
Thai Farmers Bank	Banking — Thailand	3.8
Development Bank of Singapore	Banking — Singapore	3.4
Swire-Pacific	General Trading — Hong Kong	3.3
Dairy Farm Int'l Holdings	Food & Beverage — Hong Kong	3.2
China Light & Power Co.	Utilities — Hong Kong	3.1
Hong Kong Telecommunications	Utilities — Hong Kong	3.1
		39.2

Asia Pacific Fund

U.S. $

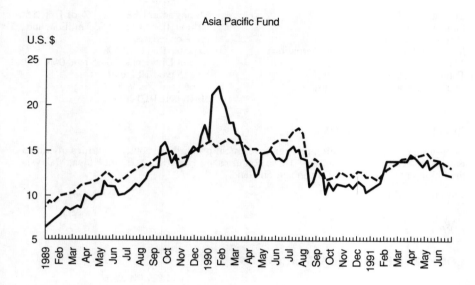

Asia Pacific Fund
Premium/Discount to Net Asset Value

Percent (%)

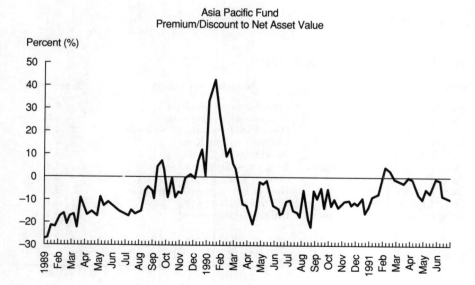

Figure G-4 FIRST PHILIPPINE FUND (FPF)

Listing: NYSE
Launched: November 1989
Offering Price: $12.00
Investment Manager: Clemente Capital
Total Shares: 8,981,293
Total Net Assets: $93 million
Market Capitalization: $67 million

Management Fees: 1.35% of average net assets

Expense Ratio: 1.87%

Recent Dividends: $0.08 paid 01/12/90
$0.59 paid 01/11/91

INVESTMENT OBJECTIVE:

Long-term capital appreciation through investment primarily in equity securities of
Philippines companies.

Current Disc./Prem.: –28%
52-Week Range: -13% to –34%
Avg. Discount/Premium: –22%
(PRICED AS OF 06/28/91)

SECTOR BREAKDOWN: March 31, 1991:

Industry	% of Assets
Telecommunications	15.0
Food & Beverage	9.2
Investment & Finance	8.6
Tires	2.8
Mining	2.6
Light Industry	2.4
Drug & Health Care	2.3
Banking	1.9
Ship Repair	1.5
Miscellaneous	2.1
CASH & Other — Net	51.6
	100.0

TOP TEN HOLDINGS: March 31, 1991:

Company	Industry	% of Net Assets
Philippine Long Distance Telephone	Telecommunications	5.4
Jardine Davies, Inc.	Light Industry	5.3
Sime Darby Tire Philipinas Inc.	Tires	3.6
Metro Drug, Inc. Class A	Drug & Personal Health Care	2.5
Ayala Corporation A	Investment & Finance	2.4
San Miguel - A	Food & Beverage	2.4
Dizon Copper - Silver Mines	Mining	1.4
Keppel Philippines Shipping - A	Ship Repair	0.8
Philex Mining Corp. Class A	Mining	0.8
Philtread Tire & Rubber - A	Tires	0.6
		25.2

First Philippines Fund

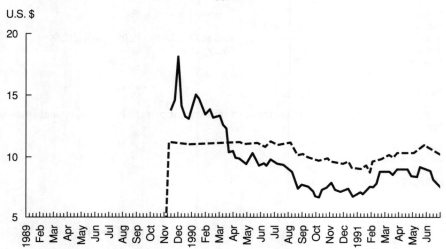

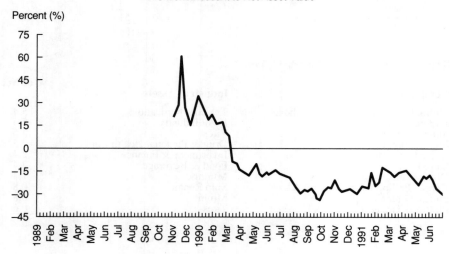

Figure G-5   INDIA GROWTH FUND (IGF)

Listing: NYSE
Launched: August 1988
Offering Price: $12.00
Investment Manager: Unit Trust of India
Total Shares: 5,014,348
Total Net Assets: $71 million
Market Capitalization: $59 million

Management Fees: 0.75% of first $50 million, 0.6% on next $50 million, thereafter 0.46%.

Expense Ratio: 3.42%
Recent Dividends: $1.10 paid 01/26/90
$0.157 paid 01/10/91

INVESTMENT OBJECTIVE:

Long-term capital appreciation through investment primarily in equity securities of Indian companies.

Current Disc./Prem.: –17%
52-Week Range: +32% to –31%
Avg. Discount/Premium: –10%
(PRICED AS OF 06/28/91)

SECTOR BREAKDOWN: December 31, 1990:

Industry	% of Assets
Automobiles & Auto Ancillaries	15.7
Textiles	12.9
Consumer Products	7.9
Tea & Plantation	7.5
Steel & Steel Products	7.4
Aluminum	7.6
Paper	6.9
Fertilizers & Pesticides	6.7
Chemicals & Dyes	4.6
Tires & Tubes	3.3
Petrochemicals	2.4
Other	8.6
CASH & Other — Net	8.4
	100.0

TOP TEN HOLDINGS: December 31, 1990:

Company	Industry	% of Net Assets
Ballarpur Industries	Paper	7.3
GSFC	Fertilizers & Pesticides	6.0
Tata Iron & Steel	Steel & Steel Products	5.2
Tata Tea	Tea & Plantation	4.9
INDALCO	Aluminum	4.8
Colgate Palmolive (India)	Consumer Products	4.6
Grasim Industries	Textiles	4.0
Century Textiles	Textiles	3.6
TELCO	Automobiles & Auto Ancillaries	2.9
Escorts	Automobiles & Auto Ancillaries	2.9
		46.0

India Growth Fund

U.S. $

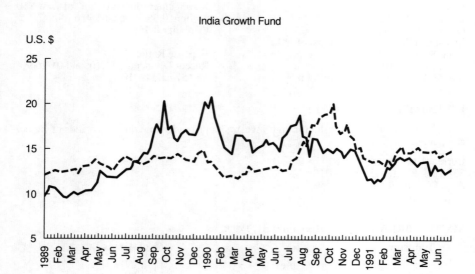

India Growth Fund
Premium/Discount to Net Asset Value

Percent (%)

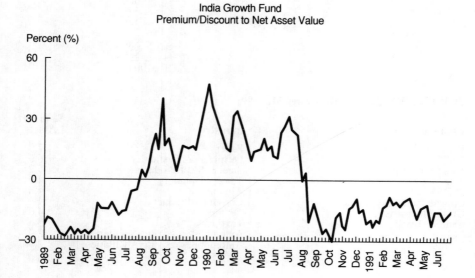

Figure G-6   THE INDONESIA FUND (IF)

Listing: NYSE
Launched: March 1990
Offering Price: $15.00
Investment Manager: BEA Associates
Total Shares: 4,607,169
Total Net Assets: $45 million
Market Capitalization: $45 million

Management Fees: 1.0% of average
monthly assets.

Expense Ratio: 2.15%

Recent Dividends: $0.7236 paid 01/04/91.

INVESTMENT OBJECTIVE:

Long-term capital appreciation by investing primarily in Indonesian securities.

Current Disc./Prem.: +2%
52-Week Range: +17% to –21%
Avg. Discount/Premium: –3%
(PRICED AS OF 06/28/91)

PORTFOLIO COMPOSITION: December 31, 1990:

	% of Assets
Common Stocks	90.4
CASH	19.5
	109.9
Less: Other Assets/Liabilities	9.9
Total	100.0

COUNTRY ALLOCATION: December 31, 1990:

	% of Assets
Indonesia	66.6
Malaysia	13.9
Thailand	8.0
Singapore	1.7
Philippines	0.3
Total	90.4

TOP TEN HOLDINGS: December 31, 1990:

Company	Industry — Country	% of Assets
Astra International	Indonesia — Wholesale Trade	8.6
Pakuwon Jati	Indonesia — Real Estate	5.0
PT United Tractors	Indonesia — Construction & Heavy Equipment	4.4
Proctor & Gamble	Indonesia — Consumer Goods Manufacturing	3.3
Multi Polar	Indonesia — Electronics	2.9
Semen Cibinong	Indonesia — Construction & Heavy Equipment	2.7
Jakarta International Hotel	Indonesia — Hotels	2.7
Siam Cement	Thailand — Construction	2.7
Ficorinvest	Indonesia — Financial Services	2.5
Iki Indah Kabel	Indonesia — Telecommunications	2.5
		37.3

Indonesia Fund

Indonesia Fund
Premium/Discount to Net Asset Value

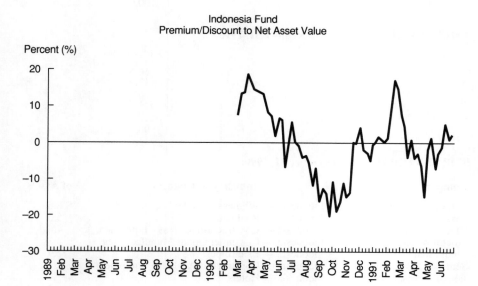

Figure G-7   THE JAKARTA GROWTH FUND (JGF)

Listing: NYSE
Launched: April 1990
Offering Price: $12.00
Inv. Manager: Nomura Capital Management, Inc.
Total Shares: 5,009,000
Total Net Assets: $40 million
Market Capitalization: $37 million

Management and Other Fees: 1.10% of
avg. weekly assets

Expense Ratio: 1.83%
Recent Dividends: $0.14 paid 12/27/90.

INVESTMENT OBJECTIVE:

Long-term capital appreciation through investment primarily in equity securities of
Indonesian companies and non-Indonesian companies that derive a significant proportion of
their revenue from Indonesia.

Current Disc./Prem.: –7%
52-Week Range: +23% to –30%
Avg. Discount/Premium: –9%
(PRICED AS OF 06/28/91)

SECTOR BREAKDOWN: March 31, 1991:

Industry	% of Assets
Consumer Goods/Distribution	13.4
Manufacturing	9.3
Cement	8.9
Finance	7.4
Agriculture	5.5
Textiles	5.5
Food & Beverages	5.2
Conglomerate	4.8
Oil/Gas/Mining	4.1
Property	2.8
Heavy Equipment	2.5
Miscellaneous Industries	8.5
CASH & Other — Net	22.1
	100.0

TOP TEN HOLDINGS: March 31, 1991:

Company	Industry	% of Net Assets
JAPFA Comfeed Indonesia	Agriculture	5.5
Indocement	Cement	5.0
Metrodata Epsindo	Consumer Goods/Distribution	5.0
Astra International	Conglomerate	4.8
Procter & Gamble Indonesia	Consumer Goods/Distribution	4.2
Gadjah Tunggal	Manufacturing	4.1
Petrosea	Oil/Gas/Mining	4.1
Semen Cibinong	Cement	3.9
Indorama Synthetics	Textiles	3.3
United Tractors	Heavy Equipment	2.5
		42.4

Jakarta Growth Fund

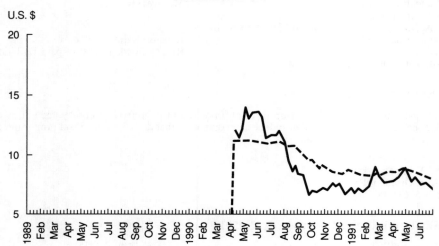

Jakarta Growth Fund
Premium/Discount to Net Asset Value

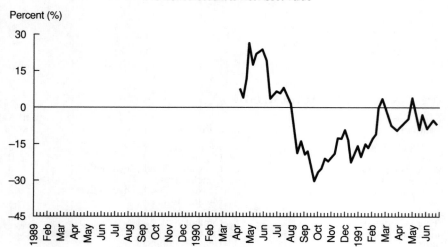

Figure G-8   KOREA FUND (KF)

Listing: NYSE
Launched: August 1984
Offering Price (adj.): $4.00
Investment Manager: Scudder, Stevens & Clark
Total Shares: 21,613,853
Total Net Assets: $222 million
Market Capitalization: $305 million

Management Fees: 1.05% of average
net assets

Expense Ratio: 1.44%
Recent Dividends: $0.75 paid 01/22/91
$1.45 paid 09/25/90
$0.49 paid 01/23/90

INVESTMENT OBJECTIVE:

Long-term capital appreciation through investment primarily in equity securities of South
Korean companies.

Current Disc./Prem.: +38%
52-Week Range: +64% to +10%
Avg. Discount/Premium: +33%
(PRICED AS OF 06/28/91)

SECTOR BREAKDOWN: March 31, 1991:

Industry	% of Assets
Basic Industry	27.5
Technology	15.6
Consumer Cyclical	13.8
Consumer Nondurable	12.6
Financial	12.0
Producer Durables	3.7
Media & Services	3.1
Health	2.8
Energy	2.8
Utilities	1.6
CASH & Other — Net	4.5
Total	100.0

TOP TEN HOLDINGS: March 31, 1991:

Company	Industry	% of Net Assets
Samsung Electronics Co., Ltd.	Consumer Electronics	8.2
Korea Long Term Credit Bank	Financial	5.8
Hyundai Motor Services Co., Ltd.	Automobiles	4.3
Lucky, Ltd.	Basic Industry	3.6
Daelim Industrial Co., Ltd.	Construction	3.6
Samsung Co., Ltd.	Media & Services	3.5
Keum Kang Co., Ltd.	Construction	3.5
Cheil Food & Chemical Co., Ltd.	Consumer Nondurables	3.2
Shinsegae	Department Store Chain	3.1
Dong Bu Steel	Metals	2.6
		41.5

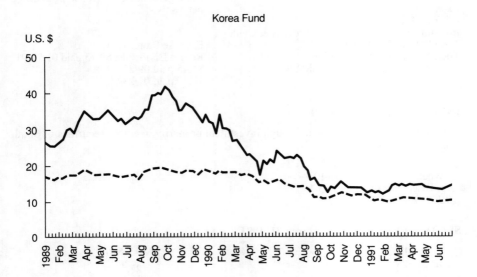

Korea Fund

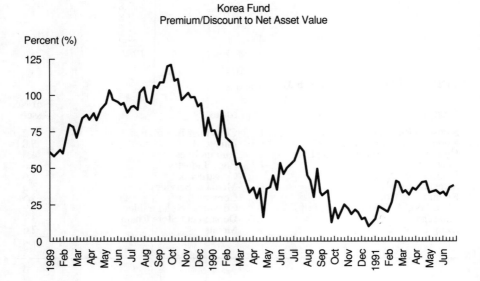

Korea Fund
Premium/Discount to Net Asset Value

Figure G-9   MALAYSIA FUND (MF)

Listing: NYSE

Launched: May 1987

Offering Price: $12.00
Investment Manager: Arab-Malaysian Consultant
Total Shares: 7,259,936
Total Net Assets: $107 million
Market Capitalization: $97 million

Management Fees: 0.84% of average net assets
Sub-Adivsory Fee: 0.22% of average net assets

Expense Ratio: 1.93%
Recent Dividends: $0.11 paid 01/16/90
$0.21 paid 01/15/91

INVESTMENT OBJECTIVE:

Long-term capital appreciation through investment in equity securities of Malaysian companies.

Current Disc./Prem.: -9%
52-Week Range: +17% to -16%
Avg. Discount/Premium: -1%
(PRICED AS OF 06/28/91)

SECTOR BREAKDOWN: March 31, 1991:

Industry	% of Assets
Industrial & Commercial	68.0
Finance Companies	12.5
Property & Development	4.0
Rubbers & Plantations	3.3
Oil Palms	2.3
Tin & Mines	1.8
CASH & Other — Net	8.1
Total	100.0

TOP TEN HOLDINGS: March 31, 1991:

Company	Industry	% of Net Assets
Genting	Industrial & Commercial	5.7
Sime Darby	Industrial & Commercial	5.6
Malaysia International Shippping	Industrial & Commercial	5.6
Malayan Banking	Finance Company	4.6
Kuala Lumpur Kepong	Rubbers & Plantations	3.3
Rothmans of Pall Mall	Industrial & Commercial	3.3
Tan Chong	Industrial & Commercial	3.3
Telekom Malaysia	Industrial & Commercial	3.1
United Engineers Malaysia	Industrial & Commercial	3.0
Perlis Plantations	Industrial & Commercial	2.9
		40.2

Malaysia Fund

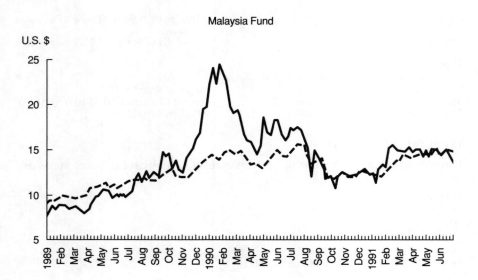

Malaysia Fund
Premium/Discount to Net Asset Value

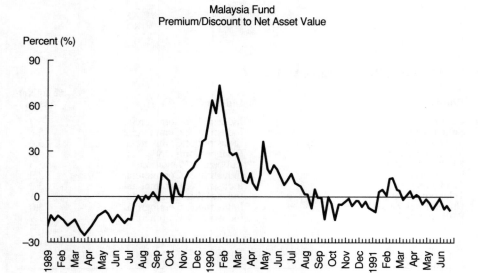

Figure G-10 SCUDDER NEW ASIA FUND (SAF)

Listing: NYSE

Launched: June 1987
Offering Price: $12.00
Investment Manager: Scudder, Stevens & Clark
Total Shares: 7,063,902
Total Net Assets: $111 million
Market Capitalization: $98 million

Management Fees: 1.15% of first $50 million, 1.10% of next $50 million, and 1.00% of excess.

Expense Ratio: 1.84%
Recent Dividends: $0.18 paid 03/30/90
$2.01 paid 01/22/91

INVESTMENT OBJECTIVE:

Long-term capital appreciation through investment primarily in equity securities of Asian companies, including, in particular, equity securities of smaller Japanese companies.

Current Disc./Prem.: –11%
52-Week Range: –4% to –26%
Avg. Discount/Premium: –12%
(PRICED AS OF 06/28/91)

PORTFOLIO BREAKDOWN: March 31, 1991:

	% of Net Assets
Common Stocks	91.9
Repurchase Agreements	4.5
Convertible Bonds	2.7
Limited Partnerships	0.7
Preferred Stocks	0.2
	100.0

COUNTRY BREAKDOWN: March 31, 1991:

Country	% of Portfolio
Japan	39.1
Thailand	12.3
Hong Kong	10.8
Malaysia	9.2
Indonesia	5.5
India	4.6
Korea	4.2
Singapore	3.0
The Philippines	1.0
Other	5.8
Total	95.5

TOP TEN HOLDINGS: March 31, 1991:

Company	Industry — Country	% of Assets
The India Fund	Investment Company — India	4.5
Freeport McMoRan Copper	Mining in Indonesia — United States	1.8
Nintendo Co., Ltd.	Gaming Equipment Manufacturer — Japan	1.7
Keyence Corp.	Specialized Equipment Manufacturer — Japan	1.7
Chiyoda Shoe Shop	Shoe Store Chain — Japan	1.6
American Standard Sanitaryware	Bathroom Fixture Manufacturer — Thailand	1.6
Komori Corp.	Offset Printing Machine Manufacturer — Japan	1.6
MKC, Ltd.	Software Company — Japan	1.6
Matsuo Bridge Co., Ltd.	Bridge Construction — Japan	1.6
Siam Cement Co.	Construction Materials — Thailand	1.6
		19.4

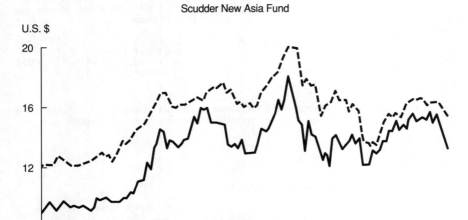

Scudder New Asia Fund

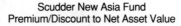

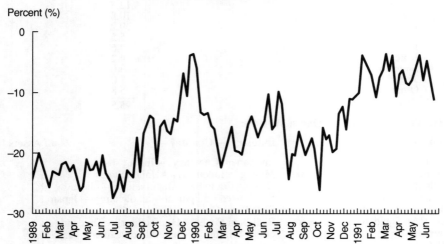

Scudder New Asia Fund
Premium/Discount to Net Asset Value

Figure G-11 THE SINGAPORE FUND (SGF)

Listing: NYSE
Launched: July 1990
Offering Price: $12.00
Inv. Manager: DBS Asset Management Pte. Ltd.
Total Shares: 5,068,502
Total Net Assets: $60 million
Market Capitalization: $50 million

Management and Other Fees: 1.2% of assets up to $50 mil., 1.0% of excess.

Expense Ratio: 2.72%

Recent Dividends: $0.21 paid 12/27/90.

INVESTMENT OBJECTIVE:

Long-term capital appreciation through investment primarily in Singapore equity securities.

Current Disc./Prem.: −17%
52-Week Range: +8% to −28%
Avg. Discount/Premium: −16%
(PRICED AS OF 06/28/91)

SECTOR BREAKDOWN: April 30, 1991:

Industry	% of Assets
Commercial & Industrial	13.5
Shipyards	12.8
Transportation, Marine, Air	9.6
Banks	6.8
Construction Materials	6.5
Property Development	6.3
Communications Media	4.6
Miscellaneous	5.9
Malaysian Equities	5.7
CASH & Other	28.3
	100.0

TOP TEN HOLDINGS: April 30, 1991:

Company	Industry — Country	% of Assets
Singapore Press Holdings	Communications Media — Singapore	4.6
Cycle & Carriage	Commercial & Industrial — Singapore	4.3
Oversea-Chinese Banking Corp.	Banks — Singapore	4.2
Keppel Corporation	Shipyards — Singapore	4.1
Far East Levingston Shipbuilding	Shipyards — Singapore	4.1
Natsteel	Construction Materials — Singapore	3.8
Singapore Aerospace	Commercial & Industrial — Singapore	3.2
Singmarine Industries	Shipyards — Singapore	3.2
Shangri-La Hotel	Hotels — Singapore	2.8
Singapore Petroleum Company	Commercial & Industrial — Singapore	2.8
		37.2

Singapore Fund

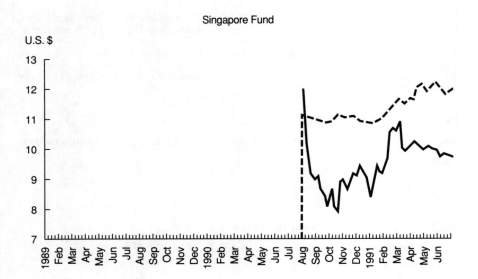

Singapore Fund
Premium/Discount to Net Asset Value

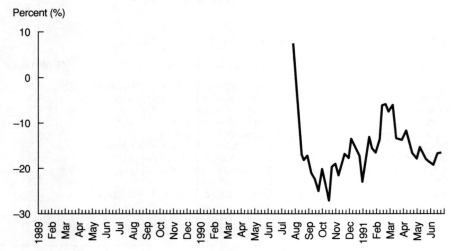

Figure G-12 THE TAIWAN FUND (TWN)

Listing: NYSE
Launched: December 1986
Offering Price: $12.00
Investment Manager: China Securities
 Investment Trust Corp.
Total Shares: 4,214,561
Total Net Assets: $94 million
Market Capitalization: $96 million

Management Fees: 1.50% of average
assets.

Expense Ratio: 2.34%

Recent Dividends: $1.69 paid 06/26/90
$14.75 paid 01/26/90

INVESTMENT OBJECTIVE:

Long-term capital appreciation through investment primarily in equity securities of Taiwan
companies.

Current Disc./Prem.: +3%
52-Week Range: +54% to –10%
Avg. Discount/Premium: +24%
(PRICED AS OF 06/28/91)

SECTOR BREAKDOWN: March 31, 1991:

Industry	% of Assets
Textiles & Apparel	24.8
Plastics	15.0
Electrical & Electronics	6.7
Rubber	5.6
Chemicals	5.5
Industrial Components	5.2
Metals — Steel	5.1
Forest Products & Paper	4.3
Automobiles	3.4
Transportation - Shipping	3.3
Merchandising	2.9
Food & Household Products	2.3
Building Materials/Components	2.2
Financial Services	1.8
CASH & Other Investments — Net	11.9
	100.0

TOP TEN HOLDINGS: March 31, 1991:

Company	Industry	% of Net Assets
Hualan-Taijiran Corp.	Textiles & Apparel	5.6
China General Plastics Corp.	Plastics	5.3
Nan Ya Plastics Corp.	Plastics	4.8
Taiwan Spinning Co.	Textiles & Apparel	4.8
Formosa Plastics Corp.	Plastics	4.3
Long Chen Paper Co.	Forest Products & Paper	4.3
Formosa Taffeta Co.	Textiles & Apparel	4.1
Formosa Chemical & Fiber Co.	Textiles & Apparel	3.5
Lien Hwa Industrial	Chemicals	3.3
China Synthetic Rubber	Rubber	3.3
		43.4

Taiwan Fund

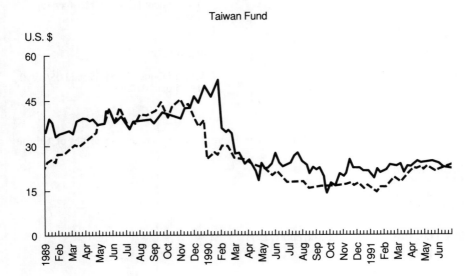

Taiwan Fund
Premium/Discount to Net Asset Value

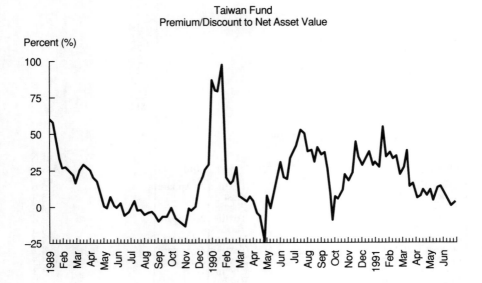

Figure G-13 TEMPLTETON EMERGING MARKETS FUND (EMF)

Listing: NYSE
Launched: February 1987
Offering Price: $10.00
Investment Manager: Templeton, Galbraith
  & Hansberger
Total Shares: 11,598,328
Total Net Assets: $183 million
Market Capitalization: $197 million

Management Fees: 1.25% on average
net assets

Expense Ratio: 1.86%
Recent Dividends: $0.10 paid 12/26/90
$1.78 paid 10/31/90

INVESTMENT OBJECTIVE:

Long-term capital appreciation primarily through investment in equities of emerging markets around the world.

Current Disc./Prem.: +8%
52-Week Range: +14% to –19%
Avg. Discount/Premium: +2%
(PRICED AS OF 06/28/91)

SECTOR BREAKDOWN: February 28, 1991:

Industry	% of Assets
Telecommunications	14.2
Banking & Financial Services	14.1
Multi-Industries	11.5
Food & Household	8.5
Real Estate	8.1
Building Materials & Components/Construction	4.8
Mining & Metals	4.7
Merchandising	4.6
Transportation	4.3
Energy Sources	3.9
Chemicals	2.5
Forest Products & Paper	2.0
Other Industries	8.6
CASH	8.2
Total	100.0

GEOGRAPHIC BREAKDOWN: February 28, 1991:

	% of Assets		% of Assets
Asia:		**Mediterranean:**	
Hong Kong	20.0	Portugal	6.0
Thailand	9.0	Turkey	7.0
Philippines	8.0	Greece	4.0
Singapore	7.0	Jordan	1.0
Malaysia	5.0	Hungary	0.2
	49.0		18.2
Africa:		**Latin America:**	
Nigeria	0.6	Argentina	6.0
Zimbabwe	0.3	Chile	3.0
Swazilan	0.1	Brazil	1.0
	1.0	Mexico	14.0

Figure G-13 continued

TOP TEN HOLDINGS: February 28, 1991:

Company	Industry — Country	% of Assets
Telefonos de Mexico	Telecommunications — Mexico	8.2
Jardine Matheson Holdings	Multi-Industries — Hong Kong	5.1
CIFRA	Merchandising — Mexico	4.3
Dairy Farm International	Food & Household Products — Hong Kong	4.1
Compania Naviera Perez Companc	Energy Sources — Argentina	3.9
Siam Cement	Building Materials & Components — Mexico	3.6
Philippine Long Distance Telephone Co.	Telecommunications — Philippines	2.9
Antofagasta Holdings	Metals & Mining — Chile	2.3
Cheung Kong Holdings	Real Estate — Hong Kong	2.3
Companhia Portuguesa Radio Marconi	Telecommunications — Portugal	2.2
		38.9

Templeton Emerging Markets

U.S. $

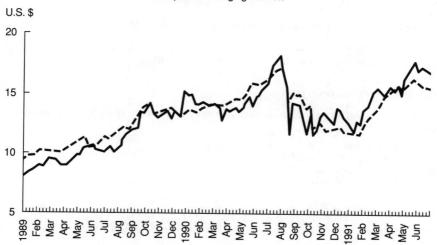

Templeton Emerging Markets
Premium/Discount to Net Asset Value

Percent (%)

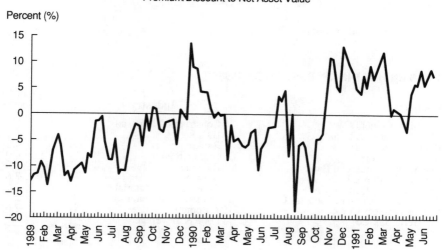

Figure G-14 THAI CAPITAL FUND (TC)

Listing: NYSE
Launched: May 1990
Offering Price: $12.00
Investment Manager: The Mutual Fund Co., Ltd.
Total Shares: 6,158,961
Total Net Assets: $58 million
Market Capitalization: $51 million

Management Fees: 1.20% of avg. assets

Expense Ratio: 2.43%

Recent Dividends: $0.277505 paid 01/30/91.

INVESTMENT OBJECTIVE:

Long-term capital appreciation through investment primarily in equity securities of Thai companies.

Current Disc./Prem.: −12%
52-Week Range: +10% to −24%
Avg. Discount/Premium: −10%
(PRICED AS OF 06/28/91)

SECTOR BREAKDOWN: December 31, 1990:

Industry	% of Assets
Construction Materials	17.3
Banking	16.9
Finance & Securities	7.4
Commercial	6.3
Electrical Equipment	4.5
Food and Beverage	4.4
Insurance	2.9
Automotive	2.0
Hotel	1.8
Services	1.1
Other	9.4
CASH & Other Assets — Net	26.0
	100.0

TOP TEN HOLDINGS: December 31, 1990:

Company	Industry	% of Net Assets
The Siam Cement Co.	Construction Material	8.8
The Thai Farmers Bank	Banking	5.1
Bangkok Bank	Banking	4.3
Saha Union Corp.	Commercial	4.0
The Siam Commercial Bank	Banking	3.9
Bank of Ayudhya, Ltd.	Banking	3.6
The Siam City Cement Co.	Construction Material	2.9
Thai-German Ceramic Industry Co.	Construction Material	2.1
Swedish Motors Corp.	Automotive	2.0
The Serm Suk Co.	Food & Beverage	1.9
		38.5

Thai Capital Fund

U.S. $

Thai Capital Fund
Premium/Discount to Net Asset Value

Percent (%)

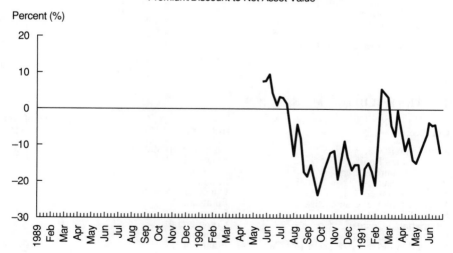

Figure G-15 THAI FUND (TTF)

Listing: NYSE

Launched: February 1988
Offering Price: $12.00
Investment Manager: Mutual Fund Co. Ltd.
Investment Advisor: Morgan Stanley Asset Mgmt.
Total Shares: 10,015,326
Total Net Assets: $158 million
Market Capitalization: $165 million

Management and Other Fees: 1.3% of first $50 million, 0.95% of next $50 million, 0.7% thereafter.

Expense Ratio: 1.35%

Recent Dividends: $2,45 paid 01/16/90
$1.89 paid 01/30/91

INVESTMENT OBJECTIVE:

Long-term capital appreciation through investment primarily in equity securities organized under the laws of the Kingdom of Thailand.

Current Disc./Prem.: +5%
52-Week Range: +26% to -8%
Avg. Discount/Premium: +8%
(PRICED AS OF 06/28/91)

SECTOR BREAKDOWN: March 31, 1991:

Industry	% of Assets
Financial	41.1
Construction Material	25.7
Commercial	9.8
Electrical	2.9
Mining	2.5
Food and Beverage	1.9
Textile and Clothing	1.8
Automotive	1.5
Packaging	1.4
Hotel	1.3
Miscellaneous Industries	4.8
CASH & Other	5.3
	100.0

TOP TEN HOLDINGS: March 31, 1991:

Company	Industry	% of Net Assets
Siam Cement Co.	Construction Material	13.4
Thai Farmers Bank	Financial	6.7
Siam Commercial Bank	FInancial	6.4
Bangkok Bank	Financial	5.1
Siam City Cement Co.	Construction Material	4.2
National Finance & Securities Co.	Financial	3.7
Phatra Thanakit Co.	Financial	3.6
International Cosmetics Co.	Commercial	3.3
Bank of Ayudaya	Financial	3.0
Dhana Siam Finance & Securities Co.	Financial	3.0
		52.4

Thai Fund

U.S. $

Thai Fund
Premium/Discount to Net Asset Value

Percent (%)

H

DIRECTORY OF STOCK EXCHANGES IN EMERGING MARKETS

Source: International Finance Corp.

Argentina
Mercado de Valores de Buenos Aires
25 de Mayo 367
Buenos Aires 1002
    Telephone: (54-1) 313-4522
    Fax: (54-1) 313-4472
    Telex: (390) 17445 MERVA AR
    Trading Hours:
    Mon-Fri 11:30 a.m.-3:00 p.m.

Bangladesh
Dhaka Stock Exchange Ltd.
Stock Exchange Building
9F, Motijheel Commercial Area
Dhaka 1000
    Telephone: (880-2) 239-882/231-935
    Telex: 632150 DSE BJ
    Trading Hours:
    Sat-Thu 11 a.m.-1 p.m.

Barbados
Securities Exchange
6th Floor
Central Bank Building
Church Village
St. Michel
    Telephone: (809) 436-9871/2
    Fax: (809) 429-8942
    Trading Hours:
    Tue & Fri 10 a.m.-12 p.m.
    Office Hours:
    Mon-Fri 8:30 a.m.-4:30 p.m.

Botswana
Stockbrokers Botswana Ltd.
5th Floor, Barclays House
Khama Crescent
Gaborone
Mailing Address:
P.O. Box 41015
    Telephone: (267) 357900
    Fax: (276) 357901
    Trading Hours:
    Mon-Fri 9 a.m.-12 p.m.
    Office Hours:
    Mon-Fri 8 a.m.-4:30 p.m.

Brazil (Rio de Janeiro)
Bolsa de Valores de Rio de Janeiro
Praca XV de Novembro
No. 20, 3rd Floor
Rio de Janeiro 20010
    Telephone: (55-21) 271-1001
    Fax: (55-21) 221-2151
    Telex: 31500
    Trading Hours:
    Mon-Fri 9:30 a.m.-5p.m.
    Office Hours:
    Mon-Fri 8:30 a.m.-6 p.m.

Brazil (Sao Paulo)
Bolsa de Valores de Sao Paulo
Rua Alvares Penteado, 151
Sao Paulo 01012
    Telephone: (55-11) 258-7222
    Fax: (55-11) 36 0871
    Telex: (391) 34088
    Trading Hours:
    Mon-Fri 9:30 a.m.-1 p.m.
    Mon-Fri 2:30-5 p.m. CATS*
    *Computer Assited Trading System
    Office Hours:
    Mon-Fri 9 a.m.-6 p.m.

Chile
Bolsa de Comercio de Santiago
Calle La Bolsa 64
Casilla 123-D
Santiago
    Telephone: (56-2) 698-2001/2002
    Fax: (56-2) 698-2001
    Telex: (352) 340531 BOLCOM
    Trading Hours:
    Mon-Fri 10:30 a.m.-5:30 p.m.
    Office Hours:
    Mon-Fri 10:30 a.m.-4:30 p.m.

China
Shanghai Securities Exchange
15 Huang Pu Road
Shanghai 200080
    Telephone: (86-21)306-3076
    Fax: (86-21)306-3196
    Trading Hours:
    Mon-Fri 9:30-11 a.m./1:30-3 p.m.
    Office Hours:
    Mon-Sat 9 a.m.-5 p.m.

Colombia (Bogotá)
Bolsa de Bogotá
Carrera 8A, No. 13-82, 8
Apartado Aereo 3584
Bogotá
    Telephone: (57-1) 243 65 01
    Fax: (57-1) 281-3170
    Telex: (396) 044807
    Trading Hours:
    Mon-Fri 10:30 a.m.-12 p.m.

Colombia (Medellin)
Bolsa de Medellin S.A.
Carrera 50, No. 50-48, Piso 2
Apartado Aereo 3535
Medellin
    Telephone: (57-4) 2603000
    Fax: (57-4) 2511981
    Telex: (396) 66788
    Trading Hours:
    Mon-Fri 10:30 a.m.-12 p.m./2-3 p.m.

Costa Rica
Costa Rica Stock Exchange
P.0. Box 1736-1000
San Jose
    Telephone: (506) 22 8011
    Fax: (506) 55 0131
    Telex: 2863
    Trading Hours:
    Mon-Fri 10:00 a.m.-11:30 a.m.
    Office Hours:
    Mon-Fri 8:00 a.m.-5:00 p.m.

Côte d'Invoire
Abidjan Stock Exchange
Avenue Marchand-01 Bolte
Abidjan 01
Mailing Address:
Postale 1878
    Telephone: (225) 21-5742
    Fax: (225) 22-1657
    Telex: 2221 Bourse Abidjan
    Trading Hours:
    Tue & Thu opens at 10 a.m.

Cyprus
Cyprus Investment Security Corp.
P.O. Box 597
Nicosia
    Telephone: (357-2) 451535
    Telex: 4449 CISCO CY

Egypt (Alexandria)
Alexandria Stock Exchange
11 Talat Harb Street
Menshia
Alexandria
    Telephone: (20-3) 483-5432

Egypt (Cairo)
Cairo Stock Exchange
4 Sherifien Street
Cairo
    Telephone: (20-1) 392-8526

Greece
Athens Stock Exchange
10 Sophocleous Street
Athens 105 59
    Telephone: (30-1) 3211301
    Fax: (30-1) 3213938
    Telex: (863) 215820 BURS GR
    Trading Hours:
    Mon-Fri 8:30 a.m.-12:30 p.m. (Main market)
    Mon-Fri 12:30-12:50 p.m. (Parallel market)
    Office Hours:
    Mon-Fri 8:30 a.m.-3:30 p.m.

Honduras
Honduras Stock Exchange
P.O. Box 161
San Pedro Sula
    Telephone: (504) 53-4410
    Fax: (504) 53-4480
    Trading Hours:
    Mon-Fri 11:00 a.m.-11:30 a.m.
    Office Hours:
    Mon-Fri 8:00 a.m.-5:00 p.m.

Hungary
Budapest Stock Exchange
Deak Ferenc utca 5.1.151
Budapest 1052
    Trading Hours:
    Tue-Thu 10-11:00 a.m.

India (Bombay)
The Bombay Stock Exchange
Phiroze Jeejeebhoy Towers
Dalal Street
Bombay 400 023
    Telephone: (91-22) 275860/61
    Fax: (91-22) 202-8121
    Telex: (953) 115925 STEX IN
    Trading Hours:
    Mon-Fri 12:00 p.m.-2 p.m.

India (Calcutta)
The Calcutta Stock Exchange Association, Ltd.
7 Lyons Range
Calcutta 700
   Telephone: (91-33) 229366

India (Delhi)
The Delhi Stock Exchange Association, Ltd.
3 and 4/4B Asaf Ali Road
New Delhi 110 002
   Telephone: (91-11) 327-9000
   Fax: (91-11) 326-7112
   Telex: (953) 3165317 DSEAIN
   Trading Hours:
   Mon-Fri 12 p.m.-2:30 p.m.
   Office Hours:
   Mon-Fri 9:30 a.m.-5:30 p.m.
   Sat 9:30 a.m.-4 p.m.

India (Madras)
Madras Stock Exchange
11 Second Line Beach
Madras 600 001
Mailing Address:
P.O. Box 183
   Telephone: (91-44) 514897
   Telex: (953) 418059 MSEX-IN
   Trading Hours:
   Mon-Fri 12 p.m.-2:30 p.m.

Indonesia (Jakarta)
The Jakarta Stock Exchange
Jl Merdeka Selatan 14
Jakarta Pusat 10110
Mailing Address:
P.O. Box 1439
   Telephone: (62-21) 365509
   Fax: (62-21) 350442
   Telex: 45604 BAPEPAM IA
   Trading Hours:
   Mon-Thu 10 a.m.-3 p.m.
   Fri 10 a.m.-12 p.m.

Indonesia (Surabaya)
Surabaya Stock Exchange
J Pemuda No. 29-31
Surabaya
   Trading Hours:
   Mon-Thu 10 a.m.-3 p.m.
   Fri 10 a.m.-12 p.m.

Jamaica
Jamaica Stock Exchange
Bank of Jamaica Tower
Nethersole Place
Kingston
Mailing Address:
P.O. Box 621
   Telephone: (809) 922-0806/7
   Fax: (809) 922-26966
   Telex: 2165/2167
   Trading Hours:
   Tue-Thu 10-11 a.m.

Jordan
Amman Financial Market
P.O. Box 8802
Amman
   Telephone: (962-6) 663170
   Fax: (962-6) 686830
   Telex: (925) 21711
   Trading Hours:
   Sat-Wed 9-9:30 a.m. (Parallel market)
   Sat-Wed 9:45-10 a.m. (Bond market)
   Sat-Wed 10-11:30 a.m. (Regular market)
   Mon-Wed 5-6 p.m. (Regular market)
   Office Hours:
   Sat-Sun 8 a.m.-3:30 p.m.
   Mon-Wed 8 a.m.-7 p.m.
   Thu 8 a.m.-2 p.m.

Kenya
The Nairobi Stock Exchange
P.O. Box 43633
Nairobi
   Telephone: (254-2) 727640
   Fax: (254-2) 729349
   Telex: 25344 BMEW
   Trading Hours:
   Mon-Fri 8 a.m.-5 p.m.

Korea
Korea Stock Exchange
33 Yoido-Dong
Yongdeungpo-ku
Seoul 150-010
   Telephone: (82-2) 780-2271
   Fax: (82-2) 786-0263
   Telex: K 28384 (KOSTEX)
   Trading Hours:
   Mon-Fri 9:40-11:40 a.m./1:20-3:20 p.m.
   Sat 9:40-11:40 a.m.

Kuwait
Kuwait Stock Exchange
Mubarak Al Kabir Street
Safat 13063
Mailing Address:
P.O. Box 22235
    Telephone: (965) 24 23 130/9
    Fax: (965) 2420779/2558832
    Telex: 44105 - 44028
    Trading Hours:
    Sat-Wed 10 a.m.-12:30 p.m./5-7 p.m.

Malaysia
The Kuala Lumpur Stock Exchange
3 & 4th Fl. Exchange Square
Off Jalan Semantan
Damansara Heights
Kuala Lumpur 50490
    Telephone: (60-3) 2546433
    Fax: (60-3) 2557463/2558832
    Telex: KLSE MA (784) 30241
    Trading Hours:
    Mon-Thu 9:30 a.m.-5:30 p.m.
    Fri 9 a.m.-5 p.m.
    Sat 9 a.m.-1 p.m.
    Office Hours:
    Mon-Fri 10 a.m.-12:30 p.m./2:30-4 p.m.

Mauritius
Stock Exchange of Mauritius Ltd.
Rez-de-Chaussee SICOM Bldg.
Sir Celicourt Antelme Street
Port Louis
    Telephone: (230) 088735/36
    Fax: (230) 088676
    Telex: 5291
    Trading Hours:
    Wed 10:30 a.m.-12:30 p.m. (Official market)
    Thu 11 a.m.-12 p.m. (OTC market)
    Office Hours:
    Mon-Fri 9 a.m.-5 p.m.

Mexico
Bolsa Mexicana de Valores, S.A. de C.V.
Paseo de la Reforma, 255
Col. Cuauhtemoc
Mexico D.F. 06500
    Telephone: (52-2) 208-3131
    Fax: (52-2) 208-8972
    Telex: (383) 1762233
    Trading Hours:
    Mon-Fri 10 a.m.-2 p.m. (Money market)/
    10:30 a.m.-1:30 p.m. (Capital market)
    Office Hours:
    Mon-Fri 8:30 a.m.-2:30 p.m./3:30-5:30 p.m.

Morocco
Casablanca Stock Exchange
98, Boulevard Mohammed V
Casablanca 01
    Telephone: (212) 27 93 54/20 03 66
    Fax: (212) 20 03 65
    Telex: 23698 BOURSVAL
    Trading Hours:
    Mon-Fri 11 a.m.-12:30 p.m.
    Office Hours:
    Mon-Fri 8:30 a.m.-12 p.m./2:30 -6:30 p.m.

Nigeria
Nigerian Stock Exchange
Stock Exchange House
2-4 Customs Street
Lagos
Mailing Address:
P.O. Box 2457
    Telephone: (234-1) 660287
    Fax: (234-1) 668724
    Telex: (961) 23567 STEX NG
    Trading Hours:
    Mon-Fri 7:30 a.m.-4:30 p.m.

Pakistan
Karachi Stock Exchange Ltd.
Stock Exchange Building
Stock Exchange Road
Karachi 2
    Telephone: (92-21) 241-9146
    Telex: (952) 2746
    Trading Hours:
    Sat-Wed 10:15 a.m.-2:00 p.m.

Panama
Bolsa de Valores de Panama, S.A.
Calle Elvira Mendez y Calle 52
Edificio Vallarino
Panama
Mailing Address:
Apartado 87-0878
Panama 4
    Telephone: (507) 69-1966
    Fax: (507) 69-2457
    Trading Hours:
    Tue & Thur 9:00 a.m.-10:00 a.m.
    Office Hours:
    Mon-Fri 9:00 a.m.-12:00 noon/2:00 p.m.-5:00 p.m.

Paraguay
Bolsa de Valores y Productos de Asuncion S.A.
Calle Estrella 540
Asuncion

Peru
Lima Stock Exchange
Pasaje Acuna 191
Lima 1
    Telephone: (51-14) 286-280
    Fax: (51-14) 337-650
    Telex: 25856
    Trading Hours:
    Mon-Fri 11:00 a.m.-1:30 p.m.

Philippines (Makati)
Makati Stock Exchange, Inc.
Makati Stock Exchange Building
Ayala Avenue, Makati
Metro Manila
    Telephone: (63-2) 810 1145/1146
    Fax: (63-2) 810 5710/819 1063
    Telex: 45074 MKSE PM
    Trading Hours:
    Mon-Fri 9:30 a.m.-12 p.m.
    Office Hours:
    Mon-Fri 8 a.m.-5 p.m.

Philippines (Manila)
Manila Stock Exchange
Prensa St.
cor Muelle de la Industria
Binondo
Manila
Mailing Address:
P.O. Box 4229
    Telephone: (63-2) 47-11-25/40-88-66
    Fax: (63-2) 471125
    Telex: (722) 40503 MSE PM
    Trading Hours:
    Mon-Fri 9 a.m.-12:15 p.m.
    Office Hours:
    Mon-Fri 8 a.m.-5 p.m.

Portugal (Lisbon)
Lisbon Stock Exchange
Rua dos Fanqueiros, 10
Lisbon 1100
    Telephone: (351-1) 879-416/879-417
    Fax: (351-1) 864-231/877-402
    Telex: (832) 44751 BVLISB P
    Trading Hours:
    Mon-Fri 10 a.m.-4 p.m.
    Office Hours:
    Mon-Fri 9 a.m.-5 p.m.

Portugal (Oporto)
Oporto Stock Exchange
Palacio da Bolsa
Rua Ferreira Borges
4000 Porto
    Telephone: (351-2) 200-2476
    Fax: (351-2) 200-2475
    Telex: 28663
    Trading Hours:
    Mon-Fri 9:30 a.m.-12:30 p.m.

Sri Lanka
The Colombo Securities Exchange
2nd Floor, MacKinnons Bldg.
York Street
Colombo 1
    Telephone: (94-1) 54 65 81/54 52 80
    Fax: (94-1) 44 77 48
    Telex: 21124 MACKINON CE
    Trading Hours:
    Mon-Fri 9:30-11:30 a.m.
    Office Hours:
    Mon-Fri 8:30 a.m.-4:30 p.m.

Taiwan, China
Taiwan Stock Exchange
7-10th Floor, City Building
85 Yen-Ping South Road
Taipei
    Telephone: (886-2) 311 4020
    Fax: (886-2) 311 4004
    Telex: (785) 22914 TSEROC
    Trading Hours:
    Mon-Fri 9 a.m.-12 p.m.
    Sat 9-11 a.m.

Thailand
The Stock Exchange of Thailand
Sinthon Building, 2nd Floor
132 Wireless Road
Bangkok 10500
    Telephone: (66-2) 254-0440/0960
    Fax: (66-2) 254-3040/3069
    Telex: (788) 20126 BEJARATH
    Trading Hours:
    Mon-Fri 9 a.m.-12 p.m.
    Office Hours:
    Mon-Fri 8:30 a.m.-5 p.m.

Trinidad and Tobago
Trinidad & Tobago Stock Exchange
65 Independence Square
Port of Spain
   Telephone: (809) 625-5108/9
   Fax: (809) 623-0089
   Telex: CBTRIN 22532
   Trading Hours:
   Mon-Fri 9:00 a.m.-4:00 p.m.

Tunisia
Tunis Stock Exchange
19 bis, rue Kamel Ataturk
100 Tunis
   Telephone: (216-1) 259-411/259-148
   Fax: (216-1) 347-256
   Telex: 14 931
   Trading Hours:
   Mon-Fri 10-11:30 a.m.
   Office Hours:
   Mon-Fri 8 a.m.-12 p.m./2-6 p.m.

Turkey
Istanbul Menkul Kiymetler Borasi
Rihtimn Cad., No. 245
Gren Han
Karakoy-Istanbul 80030
   Telephone: (90-1) 152 48 00
   Fax: (90-1) 143 72 43
   Telex: (821) 22748 IMKB TR
   Trading Hours:
   Mon-Fri 10 a.m.-12 p.m.
   Office Hours:
   Mon-Fri 8:30 a.m.-5:30 p.m.

Uganda
Kampala Stock Exchange
P.O. Box 8223
Kampala
Expected to start trading in late 1991.

USSR (Leningrad)
Official:
Leningrad Stock Exchange
Plehanova 36, Room 714
191186, Leningrad
   Telephone: (7-812) 312-79-93/312-78-94
   Fax: (7-812) 232-18-86/110-53/71
Unofficial
Skorohodova Street 19, Room 310
197061, Leningrad
   Telephone: (7-812) 238-83-34/232-5500
   Planned Trading Hours:
   Wed 12 noon-2:00 p.m.
   Office Hours:
   Mon-Fri 10:00 a.m.-6:00 p.m.

USSR (Moscow)
Moscow International Stock Exchange
USSR MInistry of Finance
9 Kuibyshev Street
103097, Moscow
    Telephone: 298-91-65
    Fax: 010-7-095/925-08-89
    Telex: 412248 ABAK SU
    Trading operations and procedures still under preparation.

Uruguay
Bolsa de Valores de Montevideo
Misiones 1400
Montevideo
    Telephone: (598-12) 95 49 21
    Fax: (598-12) 96 19 00
    Telex: BOLSA UY 26996
    Trading Hours:
    Mon-Fri 2:00 p.m.-3:00 p.m.

Venezuela
Bolsa de Valores de Caracas
Avda, Urdanela
Banco Central de Venezuela, Piso 19
Caracas
    Telephone: (58-2) 81 51 41
    Fax: (58-2) 838355
    Telex: (395) 26536
    Trading Hours:
    Mon-Fri 11:00 a.m.-12:00 p.m.

Yugoslavia (Belgrade)
Belgrade Stock Exchange
Vladimira Popovica 6
Novi
Belgrade 11070
    Telephone: (38-11) 222 40 49
    Fax: (38-11) 222 43 55
    Telex: 71122 TRZNOVYU
    Trading Hours:
    Tue 10 a.m.-4 p.m.
    Office Hours:
    Mon-Fri 8:30 a.m.-4 p.m.

Yugoslavia (Ljubljana)
Yugoslav Stock Exchange, Inc.
1, Kraigher Square
Ljubljana 61000
　　Telephone: (38-61) 301-959
　　Fax: (38-61) 301-950
　　Telex: (38-61) 31 606
　　Trading Hours:
　　Tue & Thu 11 a.m.-12 p.m.

Zimbabwe Stock Exchange
6th Floor, Southampton Place
Union Avenue
Harare
Mailing Address:
P.O. Box UA 234
　　Telephone: (263-4) 736861
　　Telex: (987) 24196 ZW
　　Trading Hours:
　　Mon-Fri 8 a.m.-4:30 p.m.

INDEX